# Yamaha XV V-Twins
# Service and Repair Manual

## Alan Ahlstrand
## and John H Haynes Member of the Guild of Motoring Writers

(802-352-7AF6)

## Models covered
USA: Yamaha XV535 Virago. 535 cc. 1987 through 1990 and 1993 through 2000
     Yamaha XV535S Virago. 535 cc. 1994 through 1997
     Yamaha XV700 Virago. 699 cc. 1984 through 1987
     Yamaha XV750 Virago. 748 cc. 1981 through 1983 and 1988 through 1997
     Yamaha XV920 Virago. 920 cc. 1982 and 1983
     Yamaha XV920R (chain drive). 920 cc. 1981 and 1982
     Yamaha XV1000 Virago. 981 cc. 1984 and 1985
     Yamaha XV1100 Virago. 1063 cc. 1986 through 1999
     Yamaha XV1100S Virago. 1063 cc. 1997 and 1998
UK:  Yamaha XV535. 535 cc. 1988 through 1997
     Yamaha XV535S. 535 cc. 1994 through 1997
     Yamaha XV535DX. 535 cc. 1998 through 2003
     Yamaha XV750SE Special. 748 cc. 1981 through 1983
     Yamaha XV750 Virago. 748 cc. 1992 through 1996
     Yamaha TR1 (chain drive). 981 cc. 1981 through 1985
     Yamaha XV1000 Virago. 981 cc. 1986 through 1989
     Yamaha XV1100 Virago. 1063 cc. 1989 through 1998

ABCDE
FGHIJ

2

© Haynes Publishing 2006

A book in the Haynes Service and Repair Manual Series

All rights reserved. No part of this book may be reproduced or transmitted in any form or by any means, electronic or mechanical, including photocopying, recording or by any information storage or retrieval system, without permission in writing from the copyright holder.

ISBN 1 84425 062 8

Library of Congress Control Number 2003103518

British Library Cataloguing in Publication Data
A catalogue record for this book is available from the British Library.

Printed in the USA.

**Haynes Publishing**
Sparkford, Yeovil, Somerset BA22 7JJ, England

**Haynes North America, Inc**
861 Lawrence Drive, Newbury Park, California 91320, USA

**Editions Haynes**
4, Rue de l'Abreuvoir
92415 COURBEVOIE CEDEX, France

**Haynes Publishing Nordiska AB**
Box 1504, 751 45 UPPSALA, Sweden

# Contents

## LIVING WITH YOUR YAMAHA XV V-TWIN

### Introduction

### Daily (pre-ride) checks

## MAINTENANCE

### Routine maintenance and servicing

# Contents

## REPAIRS AND OVERHAUL

### Engine, transmission and associated systems

### Chassis components

### Frame and bodywork

### Electrical system

### Wiring diagrams

## REFERENCE

### Index

# Yamaha
## Musical instruments to Motorcycles

### The Yamaha Motor Company

The Yamaha name can be traced back to 1889, when Torakusu Yamaha founded the Yamaha Organ Manufacturing Company. Such was the success of the company, that in 1897 it became Nippon Gakki Limited and manufactured a wide range of reed organs and pianos.

During World War II, Nippon Gakki's manufacturing base was utilised by the Japanese authorities to produce propellers and fuel tanks for their aviation industry. The end of the war brought about a huge public demand for low cost transport and many firms decided to utilise their obsolete aircraft tooling for the production of motorcycles. Nippon Gakki's first motorcycle went on sale in February 1955 and was named the 125 YA-1 Red Dragonfly. This machine was a copy of the German DKW RT125 motorcycle, featuring a single cylinder two-stroke engine with a four-speed gearbox. Due to the outstanding success of this model the motorcycle operation was separated from Nippon Gakki in July 1955 and the Yamaha Motor Company was formed.

The YA-1 also received acclaim by winning two of Japan's biggest road races, the Mt. Fuji Climbing race and the Asama Volcano race. The high level of public demand for the YA-1 led to the development of a whole series of two-stroke singles and twins.

Having made a large impact on their home market, Yamahas were exported to the USA in 1958 and to the UK in 1962. In the UK the signing of an Anglo-Japanese trade agreement during 1962 enabled the sale of Japanese lightweight motorcycles and scooters in Britain. At that time, competition between the many motorcycle producers in Japan had reduced numbers significantly and by the end of the sixties, only the big-four which are familiar with today remained.

Yamaha Europe was founded in 1968 and based in Holland. Although originally set up to market marine products, the Dutch base is now the official European Headquarters and distribution centre. Yamaha motorcycles are built at factories in Holland, Denmark, Norway, Italy, France, Spain and Portugal. Yamahas are imported into the UK by Yamaha Motor UK Ltd, formerly Mitsui Machinery Sales (UK) Ltd. Mitsui and Co. were originally a trading house, handling the shipping, distribution and marketing of Japanese products into western countries. Ultimately Mitsui Machinery Sales was formed to handle Yamaha motorcycles and outboard motors.

Based on the technology derived from its motorcycle operation, Yamaha have produced many other products, such as automobile and lightweight aircraft engines, marine engines and boats, generators, pumps, ATVs, snowmobiles, golf cars, industrial robots, lawnmowers, swimming pools and archery equipment.

The FS1-E - first bike of many sixteen year olds in the UK

### Two-strokes first

Part of Yamaha's success was a whole string of innovations in the two-stroke world. Autolube engine lubrication, pressed steel monocoque frame, electric starting, torque induction, multi-ported engines, reed valves and power valves kept their two-strokes at the forefront of technology.

In the 1960s and 70s the two-stroke engined YAS3 125, YDS1 to YDS7 250 and YR5 350 formed the core of Yamaha's range. By the mid-70s they had been superseded by the RD (Race-Developed) 125, 250, and 350 range of two-stroke twins, featuring improved 7 port engines with reed valve induction. Braking was improved by the use of an hydraulic brake on the front wheel of DX models, instead of the drum arrangement used previously, and cast alloy wheels were available as an option on later RD models. The RD350 was replaced by the RD400 in 1976.

Running parallel with the RD twins was a range of single-cylinder two-strokes. Used in a variety of chassis types, the engine was used in the popular 50 cc FS1-E moped, the V50 to 90 step-thrus, RS100 and 125, YB100 and the DT trail range.

The air-cooled single and twin cylinder RD models were eventually replaced by the LC series in 1980, featuring liquid-cooled engines, radical new styling, spiral pattern cast wheels and cantilever rear suspension (Yamaha's Monoshock). Of all the LC models, the RD350LC, or RD350R as it was later known, has made the most impact in the market. Later models had YPVS (Yamaha Power Valve System) engines, another first for Yamaha - this was essentially a valve located in the exhaust ports which was electronically operated to alter port timing to achieve maximum power output. The RD500LC was the largest two-stroke made by Yamaha and differed from the other LCs by the use of its vee-four cylinder engine.

With the exception of the RD350R, now manufactured in Brazil, the LC range has been discontinued. Two-stroke engined models have given way to environmental pressure, and thus with a few exceptions, such as the TZR125 and TZR250, are used only in scooters and small capacity bikes.

## The Four-strokes

Yamaha concentrated solely on two-stroke models until 1970 when the XS1 was produced, their first four-stroke motorcycle. It was perhaps Yamaha's success with two-strokes that postponed an earlier move into the four-stroke motorcycle market, although their work with Toyota during the

**The distinctive paintwork and trim of the RD models**

1960s had given them a sound base in four-stroke technology.

The XS1 had a 650 cc twin-cylinder SOHC engine and was later to become known as the XS650, appearing also in the popular SE custom form. Yamaha introduced a three cylinder 750 cc engine in 1976, fitted in a sport-tourer frame and called the XS750, TX750 in the USA. The XS750 established

itself well in the sport tourer class and remained in production with very few changes until uprated to 850 cc in 1980.

Other four-strokes followed in 1976, with the introduction of the XS250/360/400 series twins. The XS range was strengthened in 1978 by the four-cylinder XS1100.

The 1980s saw a new family of four-strokes, the XJ550, 650, 750 and 900 Fours. Improvements over the XS range amounted to a slimmer DOHC engine unit due to the relocation of the alternator behind the cylinders, electronic ignition and uprated braking and suspension systems. Models were available mainly in standard trim, although custom-styled Maxims were produced especially for the US market. The XJ650T was the first model from Yamaha to have a turbo-charged engine. Although these early XJ models have now been discontinued, their roots live on in the XJ600S and XJ900S Diversion (Seca II) models.

The FZR prefix encompasses the pure sports Yamaha models. With the exception of the 16-valve FZR400 and FZR600 models, the FZ/FZR750 and FZR1000 used 20-valve engines, two exhaust valves and three inlet valves per cylinder. This concept was called Genesis and gave improved gas flow to the combustion chambers. Other features of the new engine were the use of down-draught carburetors and the engine's inclined angle in the frame, plus the change to liquid-cooling. Lightweight Deltabox design aluminium frames and uprated suspension improved the bikes's handling. The Genesis engine lives on in the YZF750 and 1000 models.

The vee-twin engine has been the mainstay of the XV Virago range. Since 1981 XVs have

**The XS650 led the way for Yamaha's four-stroke range**

Yamaha's XS750 was produced from 1976 to 1982 and then uprated to 850 cc

A new family of four-strokes was released in 1980 with the introduction
of the XJ range

been produced in 535, 700, 750, 920, 1000 and 1100 engine sizes, all using the same basic air-cooled sohc vee-twin engine. Other uses of vee engines have been in the XZ550 of the early 1980s, the XVZ12 Venture and the mighty VMX-12 V-Max.

Anti-lock braking, engine management, catalytic converters and hub center steering are all features found on present-day models, ensuring that Yamaha remain at the forefront of technology.

## The XV Viragos

In 1981 Yamaha unveiled their first V-twin engined models, the 981 cc TR1, the XV750 SE (named Virago in the US) and the XV920R; the XV750 was common to both UK and US markets, whereas the XV920R and TR1 went to US and UK markets respectively. Styling wise, the XV750 Virago was produced in the custom mould with a stepped seat and high handlebars, and the TR1 and XV920R had traditional street bike livery.

Unlike other Japanese manufacturers who had produced vee engines, the design was simple - air-cooling and sohc cylinders. The cylinders were arranged at a 75° angle with both rods off a single crankpin. Each single overhead camshaft was driven by chain, drive coming off the right-hand end of the crankshaft for the front cylinder and off the left-hand end for the rear cylinder. With the carburetors positioned between the two cylinders, the result was a narrow and compact engine. Drive to the rear wheel was by shaft on the XV750 and by enclosed chain on the XV920R and TR1.

Brakes were single or twin disc at the front and drum at the rear. The front forks were air-assisted and the rear Monoshock suspension offered air pressure and damping adjustment.

A year later the XV920 Virago was introduced to the US market. It used the engine of the XV920R but the custom styling and shaft final drive of the smaller XV750 Virago. Unlike the other models in the range, it featured very advanced instrumentation, similar to that used on the XJ750R Seca. The instrument panel incorporated an LCD which provided the rider with information on the sidestand position, brake fluid level, engine oil level, battery electrolyte level, fuel level and also indicated whether the headlight or taillight bulbs had blown. Speedometer and tachometer displays were also electronic. For 1983 however, the XV920 Virago reverted to basic instrumentation. An XV920M Midnight Virago was produced for 1983 and differed from the standard Virago in its use of a black-painted engine, black paintwork and gold trim; a 750 Midnight Virago was also available in the same finish.

The XV750 SE (UK) and XV750 Virago (US) were both discontinued in 1983. The UK market did not see another XV750 until 1992, but in the US it was replaced by the XV700 Virago in 1984, its engine capacity reduction allowing it to slip under the import tariff barrier imposed on big bikes. The 700 Virago had a new frame, conventional twin shock rear suspension and a single-sided exhaust system. Straight-spoke cast wheels replaced the italic pattern wheels of the 750 and a wire

Smallest of the XV range - the 535

spoked-wheel model was available as a cheaper option.

The US XV920 models were replaced by the XV1000 Virago in 1984. Like the XV700, it had a new frame, twin shock rear suspension and a single-sided exhaust system. Gone also were the italic style cast wheels, and instead it used straight-spoked cast wheels. The XV1000 was superseded by the longer-stroke XV1100 for the US market in 1986.

The UK market waited for the big Virago until 1986 when the XV1000 became available. The TR1 had been discontinued the previous year although the Virago could not be seen to be a direct replacement because apart from the engine/transmission unit, it differed in all other respects. Eventually the UK market received the XV1100 Virago in 1989.

With the US import tariff lifted, the XV700 returned to a 748 cc size engine in 1988. In the UK, the XV750 was available from 1992.

The XV models had always been more

popular stateside, that is until the XV535 was introduced. The baby Virago was a best seller in most European countries and was a hit with shorter riders due to its low seat height and easy handling – Yamaha lowered the bike's centre of gravity by locating the main fuel tank beneath the seat and used a dummy tank to house the air filter and electrical components.

The XV535 remained largely unchanged throughout its production with minor modifications to the seat, handlebars and front brake disc and an increase in fuel capacity. A two-piston front brake caliper was fitted from 1995. The XV535S version, introduced in 1994, offered chromed engine covers, a buttoned seat and two-tone paint scheme. This was superseded in the UK by the XV535DX in 1998.

Yamaha's Virago V-twins remained a popular choice with custom riders for over twenty years but inevitably their styling became dated and the range was eventually phased-out in favour of the cruiser-styled XVS Drag Stars.

## Acknowledgements

Our thanks are due to Mitsui Machinery Sales (UK) Ltd for permission to reproduce certain illustrations used in this manual. We would also like to thank NGK Spark Plugs (UK) Ltd for supplying the color spark plug condition photos and the Avon Rubber Company for supplying information on tire fitting.

We would also like to thank Grand Prix Kawasaki/Yamaha, Santa Clara, California, for providing the facilities used for the photographs in the manual; Mark Woodward, service manager, for arranging the facilities and fitting the mechanical work into his shop's busy schedule; and Danny Jewell, service technician, for doing the mechanical work and providing valuable technical information.

Thanks are also due to Paul Branson Motorcycles for supplying the XV535 on the front cover, to Kel Edge for supplying the color transparency of the XV535 on the rear cover, and to Phil Flowers for carrying out the cover photography.

## About this Manual

The aim of this manual is to help you get the best value from your motorcycle. It can do so in several ways. It can help you decide what work must be done, even if you choose to have it done by a dealer; it provides information and procedures for routine maintenance and servicing; and it offers diagnostic and repair procedures to follow when trouble occurs.

We hope you use the manual to tackle the work yourself. For many simpler jobs, doing it yourself may be quicker than arranging an appointment to get the motorcycle into a dealer and making the trips to leave it and pick it up. More importantly, a lot of money can be saved by avoiding the expense the shop must pass on to you to cover its labour and overhead costs. An added benefit is the sense of satisfaction and accomplishment that you feel after doing the job yourself.

References to the left or right side of the motorcycle assume you are sitting on the seat, facing forward.

**We take great pride in the accuracy of information given in this manual, but motorcycle manufacturers make alterations and design changes during the production run of a particular motorcycle of which they do not inform us. No liability can be accepted by the authors or publishers for loss, damage or injury caused by any errors in, or omissions from, the information given.**

## XV535

The XV535 was introduced in 1987 in the US and the following year in the UK.

The engine was an air cooled, 75° V-twin based on the XV750 unit with detail changes in keeping with the reduction in capacity. Carburettor air intake was through an air filter mounted underneath a small dummy fuel tank – the real fuel tank was sited underneath the seat.

Drive was transmitted to the five-speed gearbox via a wet, multi-plate clutch, and to the rear wheel by shaft.

The chassis was a pressed steel backbone frame with tubular swingarm incorporating the drive shaft on the left-hand side. Front suspension was by conventional telescopic forks and rear suspension was by twin, pre-load adjustable shocks.

Braking was by single disc at the front and a drum brake at the rear.

The XV535 was styled from the outset as a chopper-style custom, with twin slash-cut exhaust pipes on the right-hand side, high handlebars and solo rider's seat and pillion pad. The wheels were wire spoked.

Fuel capacity was increased in 1989 when the dummy fuel tank was replaced by a supplementary tank. Minor detail changes included the option of flat handlebars and a slotted front brake disc to reduce brake noise. The starter motor was uprated in 1993, a model with additional chrome, two-tone paint and buttoned seat, the XV535S, was introduced in 1994, and a two-piston front brake caliper was fitted in 1995.

## XV750/XV700

The XV750 was introduced in 1981 as the XV750 Virago in the US and the XV750SE Special in the UK.

The engine was an air cooled, 75° V-twin with one single overhead camshaft per cylinder, each driven by a separate chain from the crankshaft. Twin carburettors were mounted between the cylinders and there were two valves per head. The crankcases were split vertically.

Drive was transmitted to the five-speed gearbox via a wet, multi-plate clutch, and to the rear wheel by shaft.

The chassis was a pressed steel backbone frame. Front suspension was by air-assisted telescopic forks and rear suspension was by triangulated swingarm, incorporating the drive shaft, and five-way adjustable, air-assisted, mono-shock.

Braking was by single disc at the front and a drum brake at the rear.

In 1984 the rear suspension was changed to a swingarm with twin shock absorbers and the bike's overall appearance was revised to reflect the new chopper-style custom image of the Virago marque (see XV1000). Twin front disc brakes were fitted, with both brake calipers of opposed piston design. The 'swirl' pattern cast wheels were replaced by five spoke cast wheels.

Between 1984 and 1987 the engine capacity was reduced to 700 cc to beat US import tariffs and the machine was sold as the XV700.

Further minor detail changes included the fitting of two-piston calipers to the front brakes of UK models from 1994-on.

## XV920/TR1

The XV920R was introduced in the US in 1981. The engine was a larger version of the XV750 motor but with chain drive, denoted by the suffix R, instead of a shaft. The head, cylinder and crankcase castings of the 750 were used, with detail changes, such as larger valves, in keeping with the increase in capacity. The machine was styled along European lines, as opposed to the custom bike look of the XV750, and was sold in the UK with a slightly larger 1000 cc engine as the model TR1.

The shaft drive XV920 Virago was introduced the following year, with the same custom styling as the original XV750. The model was equipped with Yamaha's new CYCOM cycle computer instrumentation and systems monitoring cluster with liquid crystal displays in place of the traditional speedometer and tachometer. A rectangular headlight and adjustable handlebars were fitted.

All XV920 and TR1 models featured triangulated swingarm rear suspension with an air-assisted mono-shock.

## XV1000

The XV1000 was introduced in 1984. The engine was an enlarged version of the original XV920 motor, but the bike's appearance was revised in line with the new chopper-style custom image of the Virago marque. A separate air filter for each carburettor was mounted inside a large chromed cover on each side of the front cylinder head and the fuel tank, footpegs, handlebars, seat and exhaust system were redesigned and repositioned to complement the chopper styling. The mudguards, horns, instruments and numerous engine and rear hub casings were chrome plated and a padded backrest was added for the passenger.

## XV1100

The XV1100 superseded the XV1000 and was introduced to the US market in 1986, then to the UK market in 1989. The increase in engine capacity was achieved by lengthening the piston stroke and the flywheel weight was increased for smoother power delivery. In all other respects the bike was the same as the XV1000.

1994-on UK models were fitted with two-piston calipers in place of the opposed piston calipers on the front disc brakes. A model with custom paint, buttoned seat, headlight visor and chromed covers on the rear shocks, the XV1100S, was available in the US for 1997 and 1998.

# Performance data

Performance data sourced from Motor Cycle News road test features. See the MCN website for up-to-date biking news.

**MCN** www.motorcyclenews.com

**Maximum power**

XV535 model . . . . . . . . . . . . . . . . . . . .45.5 bhp (33.9 kW) @ 7,500 rpm
XV700 model . . . . . . . . . . . . . . . . . . . . . . . . . . . . . . . . . . . .not available
XV750 model . . . . . . . . . . . . . . . . . . . .51.8 bhp (38.6 kW) @ 7,000 rpm
XV920 model . . . . . . . . . . . . . . . . . . . . . . . . . . . . . . . . . . . .not available
TR1 model . . . . . . . . . . . . . . . . . . . . . .56.5 bhp (42.1 kW) @ 6,500 rpm
XV1000 model . . . . . . . . . . . . . . . . . . . . .61 bhp (45.5 kW) @ 6,500 rpm
XV1100 model . . . . . . . . . . . . . . . . . . . .54.1 bhp (40.3 kW) @ 5,500 rpm

**Maximum torque**

XV535 model . . . . . . . . . . . . . . . . . . . .34.7 lbf ft (47 Nm) @ 6,000 rpm
XV700 model . . . . . . . . . . . . . . . . . . . . . . . . . . . . . . . . . . . .not available
XV750 model . . . . . . . . . . . . . . . . . . . .43.5 lbf ft (59 Nm) @ 5,500 rpm
XV920 model . . . . . . . . . . . . . . . . . . . . . . . . . . . . . . . . . . . .not available
TR1 model . . . . . . . . . . . . . . . . . . . . . .53.8 lbf ft (73 Nm) @ 4,000 rpm
XV1000 model . . . . . . . . . . . . . . . . . . . .57.8 lbf ft (78 Nm) @ 5,000 rpm
XV1100 model . . . . . . . . . . . . . . . . . . . .54.2 lb ft (73.5 Nm) @ 3,000 rpm

## Top speed

XV535 model . . . . . . . . . . . . . . . . . . . . . . . . . . . .98 mph (158 km/h)
XV700 model . . . . . . . . . . . . . . . . . . . . . . . . . . .not available
XV750 and XV920 models . . . . . . . . . . . . . . . .108 mph (174 km/h)
TR1 model . . . . . . . . . . . . . . . . . . . . . . . . . . . .118 mph (190 km/h)
XV1000 and XV1100 models . . . . . . . . . . . . . . .119 mph (191 km/h)

## Acceleration

XV535 model
   Time taken to cover a ¼ mile from a standing start . . . . . . .14.8 secs
   Terminal speed after ¼ mile . . . . . . . . . . . . . .86.2 mph (138.6 km/h)
XV700 model
   Time taken to cover a ¼ mile from a standing start . . . . . . .13.2 secs
   Terminal speed after ¼ mile . . . . . . . . . . . . . .100.6 mph (161.8 km/h)
XV750 model
   Time taken to cover a ¼ mile from a standing start . . . . . . .13.7 secs
   Terminal speed after ¼ mile . . . . . . . . . . . . . .95.5 mph (153.6 km/h)
XV920 model
   Time taken to cover a ¼ mile from a standing start . . . . . . .13.8 secs
   Terminal speed after ¼ mile . . . . . . . . . . . . . .99.3 mph (159.7 km/h)
TR1 model
   Time taken to cover a ¼ mile from a standing start . . . . . . .14.3 secs
   Terminal speed after ¼ mile . . . . . . . . . . . . . .96.7 mph (155.5 km/h)
XV1000 model
   Time taken to cover a ¼ mile from a standing start . . . . . . .12.9 secs
   Terminal speed after ¼ mile . . . . . . . . . . . . . .101.1 mph (162.6 km/h)
XV1100 model
   Time taken to cover a ¼ mile from a standing start . . . . . . .12.9 secs
   Terminal speed after ¼ mile . . . . . . . . . . . . . .98.3 mph (158.1 km/h)

## Average fuel consumption

*Miles per Imperial gallon, Miles per litre, Litres per 100 km*
XV535 model . . . . . . . . . . . . . . . . . . . .54.0 mpg, 11.8 mpl, 5.2 l/100 km
   Fuel tank capacity
      1987 and 1988 models . . . . . .8.6 liters (2.3 US gal, 1.9 Imp gal)
      1989-on models . . . . . . . . . . .13.5 liters (3.6 US gal, 3.0 Imp gal)
XV700 model . . . . . . . . . . . . . . . . . . . .35.6 mpg, 7.8 mpl, 7.9 l/100 km
   Fuel tank capacity . . . . . . . . . . .12.5 liters (3.3 US gal, 2.7 Imp gal)
XV750 model . . . . . . . . . . . . . . . . . . . .34.1 mpg, 7.5 mpl, 8.2 l/100 km
   Fuel tank capacity
      1981 through 1983 models . . .12.0 liters (3.1 US gal, 2.6 Imp gal)
      1988-on models . . . . . . . . . . .14.5 liters (3.8 US gal, 3.2 Imp gal)
XV920R chain drive model . . . . . . . .32.9 mpg, 7.2 mpl, 8.5 l/100 km
   Fuel tank capacity . . . . . . . . . . . . .19 liters (5.0 US gal, 4.1 Imp gal)
TR1 model . . . . . . . . . . . . . . . . . . . . .45.7 mpg, 10.0 mpl, 6.1 l/100 km
   Fuel tank capacity . . . . . . . . . . .19.0 liters (5.0 US gal, 4.1 Imp gal)
XV920 shaft drive model . . . . . . . . .38.1 mpg, 8.3 mpl, 7.4 l/100 km
   Fuel tank capacity . . . . . . . . . . .14.5 liters (3.8 US gal, 3.2 Imp gal)
XV1000 model . . . . . . . . . . . . . . . . . .47.0 mpg, 10.3 mpl, 6.0 l/100 km
   Fuel tank capacity . . . . . . . . . . .14.5 liters (3.8 US gal, 3.2 Imp gal)
XV1100 model . . . . . . . . . . . . . . . . . .43.0 mpg, 9.46 mpl, 6.5 l/100 km
   Fuel tank capacity . . . . . . . . . . .16.8 liters (4.4 US gal, 3.6 Imp gal)

## Fuel tank range

XV535 (1987 and 1988 models) . . . . . . . . . . . . . .102.6 miles (165 km)
XV535 (1989-on models) . . . . . . . . . . . . . . . . . . .165.0 miles (265 km)
XV700 model . . . . . . . . . . . . . . . . . . . . . . . . . . .96.1 miles (155 km)
XV750 (1981 through 1983 models) . . . . . . . . . . . .88.6 miles (143 km)
XV750 (1988-on models) . . . . . . . . . . . . . . . . . . .109.1 miles (176 km)
XV920R chain drive model . . . . . . . . . . . . . . . . . .134.8 miles (217 km)
TR1 model . . . . . . . . . . . . . . . . . . . . . . . . . . . . .187.3 miles (301 km)
XV920 shaft drive model . . . . . . . . . . . . . . . . . . .121.9 miles (196 km)
XV1000 model . . . . . . . . . . . . . . . . . . . . . . . . . .150.4 miles (242 km)
XV1100 model . . . . . . . . . . . . . . . . . . . . . . . . . .154.8 miles (249 km)

# Bike spec

## Weights and dimensions

### XV535 models

#### 1987 and 1988 US models

Wheelbase . . . . . . . . . . . . . . . . . . . . . . . . . . .1511 mm (59.5 inches)
Overall length . . . . . . . . . . . . . . . . . . . . . . . . .2210 mm (87.0 inches)
Overall width . . . . . . . . . . . . . . . . . . . . . . . . . .815 mm (32.1 inches)
Overall height . . . . . . . . . . . . . . . . . . . . . . . . .1100 mm (43.3 inches)
Seat height . . . . . . . . . . . . . . . . . . . . . . . . . . .700 mm (27.6 inches)
Ground clearance (minimum) . . . . . . . . . . . . . . .145 mm (5.7 inches)
Weight (with oil and full fuel tank)
   US except California . . . . . . . . . . . . . . . . . . . .185 kg (408 lbs)
   California . . . . . . . . . . . . . . . . . . . . . . . . . . . .186 kg (410 lbs)

#### 1989-on US models

Wheelbase . . . . . . . . . . . . . . . . . . . . . . . . . . .1520 mm (59.8 inches)
Overall length . . . . . . . . . . . . . . . . . . . . . . . . .2225 mm (87.6 inches)
Overall width . . . . . . . . . . . . . . . . . . . . . . . . . .810 mm (31.9 inches)
Overall height . . . . . . . . . . . . . . . . . . . . . . . . .1110 mm (43.7 inches)
Seat height . . . . . . . . . . . . . . . . . . . . . . . . . . .720 mm (28.3 inches)
Ground clearance (minimum) . . . . . . . . . . . . . . .160 mm (6.3 inches)
Weight (with oil and full fuel tank)
   US except California . . . . . . . . . . . . . . . . . . . .195 kg (430 lbs)
   California . . . . . . . . . . . . . . . . . . . . . . . . . . . .196 kg (432 lbs)

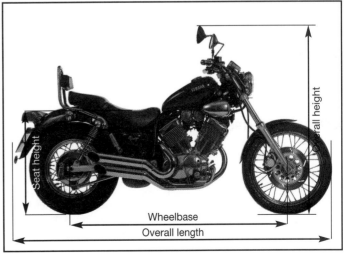

## XV535 models (continued)

### 1988 UK models

Wheelbase . . . . . . . . . . . . . . . . . . . . . . . . . .1520 mm (59.8 inches)
Overall length . . . . . . . . . . . . . . . . . . . . . . . .2225 mm (87.6 inches)
Overall width . . . . . . . . . . . . . . . . . . . . . . . . .810 mm (31.9 inches)
Overall height . . . . . . . . . . . . . . . . . . . . . . . .1100 mm (43.3 inches)
Seat height . . . . . . . . . . . . . . . . . . . . . . . . . .700 mm (27.6 inches)
Ground clearance (minimum) . . . . . . . . . . . . . .160 mm (6.3 inches)
Weight (with oil and full fuel tank) . . . . . . . . . . .188 kg (415 lbs)

### 1989-on UK models

Wheelbase . . . . . . . . . . . . . . . . . . . . . . . . . .1520 mm (59.8 inches)
Overall length . . . . . . . . . . . . . . . . . . . . . . . .2285 mm (90.0 inches)
Overall width
  Flat handlebar . . . . . . . . . . . . . . . . . . . . . . .725 mm (88.6 inches)
  Upright handlebar . . . . . . . . . . . . . . . . . . . .810 mm (31.9 inches)
Overall height
  Flat handlebar . . . . . . . . . . . . . . . . . . . . . . .1070 mm (42.1 inches)
  Upright handlebar . . . . . . . . . . . . . . . . . . . .1110 mm (43.7 inches)
  Seat height . . . . . . . . . . . . . . . . . . . . . . . . .720 mm (28.3 inches)
Ground clearance (minimum) . . . . . . . . . . . . . .160 mm (6.3 inches)
Weight (with oil and full fuel tank) . . . . . . . . . . .195 kg (430 lbs)

### XV700 and XV1000 models

Wheelbase . . . . . . . . . . . . . . . . . . . . . . . . . .1525 mm (60.0 inches)
Overall length . . . . . . . . . . . . . . . . . . . . . . . .2235 mm (88.0 inches)
Overall width . . . . . . . . . . . . . . . . . . . . . . . . .840 mm (33.1 inches)
Overall height . . . . . . . . . . . . . . . . . . . . . . . .1170 mm (46.1 inches)
Seat height . . . . . . . . . . . . . . . . . . . . . . . . . .715 mm (28.1 inches)
Ground clearance (minimum) . . . . . . . . . . . . . .145 mm (5.7 inches)
Weight (with oil and full fuel tank)
  XV700 models (1984 and 1985) . . . . . . . . . . . . . . .225 kg (496 lbs)
  XV700 models (1986 and 1987) . . . . . . . . . . . . . . .229 kg (505 lbs)
  XV1000 models . . . . . . . . . . . . . . . . . . . . . . . . . . .236 kg (520 lbs)

### XV750 models (1981 through 1983)

Wheelbase . . . . . . . . . . . . . . . . . . . . . . . . . .1520 mm (59.8 inches)
Overall length . . . . . . . . . . . . . . . . . . . . . . . .2230 mm (87.8 inches)
Overall width
  US models . . . . . . . . . . . . . . . . . . . . . . . . .805 mm (31.7 inches)
  UK models . . . . . . . . . . . . . . . . . . . . . . . . .840 mm (33.1 inches)
Overall height
  US models . . . . . . . . . . . . . . . . . . . . . . . . .1160 mm (45.7 inches)
  UK models . . . . . . . . . . . . . . . . . . . . . . . . .1210 mm (47.6 inches)
Seat height . . . . . . . . . . . . . . . . . . . . . . . . . .not available
Ground clearance (minimum) . . . . . . . . . . . . . .145 mm (5.7 inches)
Weight (dry)
  US models . . . . . . . . . . . . . . . . . . . . . . . . .225 kg (496 lbs)
  UK models . . . . . . . . . . . . . . . . . . . . . . . . .211 kg (465 lbs)

### XV750 models (1988-on US)

Wheelbase . . . . . . . . . . . . . . . . . . . . . . . . . .1525 mm (60.0 inches)
Overall length . . . . . . . . . . . . . . . . . . . . . . . .2285 mm (90.0 inches)
Overall width . . . . . . . . . . . . . . . . . . . . . . . . .840 mm (33.1 inches)
Overall height . . . . . . . . . . . . . . . . . . . . . . . .1190 mm (46.9 inches)
Seat height . . . . . . . . . . . . . . . . . . . . . . . . . .715 mm (28.1 inches)
Ground clearance (minimum) . . . . . . . . . . . . . .145 mm (5.7 inches)
Weight . . . . . . . . . . . . . . . . . . . . . . . . . . . . .not available

### XV750 models (1992-on UK)

Wheelbase . . . . . . . . . . . . . . . . . . . . . . . . . .1525 mm (60.0 inches)
Overall length . . . . . . . . . . . . . . . . . . . . . . . .2285 mm (90.0 inches)
Overall width . . . . . . . . . . . . . . . . . . . . . . . . .840 mm (33.1 inches)
Overall height . . . . . . . . . . . . . . . . . . . . . . . .1190 mm (46.9 inches)
Seat height . . . . . . . . . . . . . . . . . . . . . . . . . .715 mm (28.1 inches)
Ground clearance (minimum) . . . . . . . . . . . . . .145 mm (5.7 inches)
Weight
  1992 and 1993 models . . . . . . . . . . . . . . . . . . . . .235 kg (518 lbs)
  1994-on models . . . . . . . . . . . . . . . . . . . . . . . . . .236 kg (520 lbs)

### 1982 XV920 (shaft) models

Wheelbase . . . . . . . . . . . . . . . . . . . . . . . . . .1520 mm (59.8 inches)
Overall length . . . . . . . . . . . . . . . . . . . . . . . .2220 mm (87.4 inches)
Overall width . . . . . . . . . . . . . . . . . . . . . . . . .840 mm (33.1 inches)
Overall height . . . . . . . . . . . . . . . . . . . . . . . .1205 mm (47.4 inches)
Seat height . . . . . . . . . . . . . . . . . . . . . . . . . .739 mm (29.1 inches)
Ground clearance (minimum) . . . . . . . . . . . . . .145 mm (5.7 inches)
Weight . . . . . . . . . . . . . . . . . . . . . . . . . . . . .225 kg (496 lbs)

### 1983 XV920 (shaft) models

Wheelbase . . . . . . . . . . . . . . . . . . . . . . . . . .1520 mm (59.8 inches)
Overall length . . . . . . . . . . . . . . . . . . . . . . . .2230 mm (87.8 inches)
Overall width . . . . . . . . . . . . . . . . . . . . . . . . .805 mm (31.7 inches)
Overall height . . . . . . . . . . . . . . . . . . . . . . . .1160 mm (45.7 inches)
Seat height . . . . . . . . . . . . . . . . . . . . . . . . . .739 mm (29.1 inches)
Ground clearance (minimum) . . . . . . . . . . . . . .145 mm (5.7 inches)
Weight . . . . . . . . . . . . . . . . . . . . . . . . . . . . .235 kg (518 lbs)

### XV920R (chain) models

Wheelbase . . . . . . . . . . . . . . . . . . . . . . . . . .1540 mm (60.6 inches)
Overall length . . . . . . . . . . . . . . . . . . . . . . . .2260 mm (89.0 inches)
Overall width . . . . . . . . . . . . . . . . . . . . . . . . .930 mm (36.6 inches)
Overall height . . . . . . . . . . . . . . . . . . . . . . . .1170 mm (46.1 inches)
Seat height . . . . . . . . . . . . . . . . . . . . . . . . . .779 mm (30.7 inches)
Ground clearance (minimum) . . . . . . . . . . . . . .140 mm (5.5 inches)
Weight . . . . . . . . . . . . . . . . . . . . . . . . . . . . .224 kg (493 lbs)

### TR1 model

Wheelbase . . . . . . . . . . . . . . . . . . . . . . . . . .1540 mm (60.6 inches)
Overall length . . . . . . . . . . . . . . . . . . . . . . . .2265 mm (89.2 inches)
Overall width . . . . . . . . . . . . . . . . . . . . . . . . .730 mm (28.7 inches)
Overall height . . . . . . . . . . . . . . . . . . . . . . . .1170 mm (46.1 inches)
Seat height . . . . . . . . . . . . . . . . . . . . . . . . . .Not specified
Ground clearance (minimum) . . . . . . . . . . . . . .140 mm (5.5 inches)
Weight . . . . . . . . . . . . . . . . . . . . . . . . . . . . .220 kg (485 lbs)

### XV1100 models

Wheelbase . . . . . . . . . . . . . . . . . . . . . . . . . .1525 mm (60.0 inches)
Overall length
  US models . . . . . . . . . . . . . . . . . . . . . . . . .2235 mm (88.0 inches)
  UK models . . . . . . . . . . . . . . . . . . . . . . . . .2285 mm (90.0 inches)
Overall width . . . . . . . . . . . . . . . . . . . . . . . . .840 mm (33.1 inches)
Overall height
  1986 and 1987 . . . . . . . . . . . . . . . . . . . . . .1170 mm (46.1 inches)
  1988-on . . . . . . . . . . . . . . . . . . . . . . . . . . .1190 mm (46.9 inches)
Seat height . . . . . . . . . . . . . . . . . . . . . . . . . .715 mm (28.1 inches)
Ground clearance (minimum) . . . . . . . . . . . . . .145 mm (5.7 inches)
Weight (with oil and full fuel tank)
  US models . . . . . . . . . . . . . . . . . . . . . . . . .239 kg (527 lbs)
  UK models
    1986 through 1995 . . . . . . . . . . . . . . . . . . . . .240 kg (528 lbs)
    1996-on . . . . . . . . . . . . . . . . . . . . . . . . . . . . .241 kg (531 lbs)

## Engine – all models

Type ........................................... Air cooled, 75° V-twin
Capacity
  XV535 model ................................... 535 cc
  XV700 model ................................... 699 cc
  XV750 model ................................... 749 cc
  XV920 model ................................... 920 cc
  TR1 and XV1000 models ..................... 981 cc
  XV1100 cc model .............................. 1063 cc
Bore and stroke
  XV535 model ................................... 76.0 x 59.0 mm
  XV700 model ................................... 80.2 x 69.2 mm
  XV750 model ................................... 83.0 x 69.2 mm
  920 cc model ................................... 92.0 x 69.2 mm
  TR1 and XV1000 models ..................... 95.0 x 69.2 mm
  XV1100 model ................................. 95.0 x 75.0 mm
Compression ratio
  XV535 model ................................... 9.0:1
  XV700 model ................................... not available
  XV750 model ................................... 8.7:1
  XV920, TR1, XV1000 and XV1100 models ... 8.3:1
Camshafts ..................................... SOHC, chain driven
Valves ......................................... 2 valves per cylinder
Fuel system
  XV535 models ................................. 2 x 34 mm Mikuni carburettors
  750 cc (1981 through 1983) and all 700 cc models ... 2 x Hitachi carburettors
  750 cc model (1988-on) ...................... 2 x 40 mm Mikuni carburettors
  920 cc and 1000 cc models .................. 2 x 40 mm Hitachi carburettors
  1100 cc model (1986 to 1987) .............. 2 x 40 mm Hitachi carburettors
  1100 cc model (1988-on) .................... 2 x 40 mm Mikuni carburettors
Clutch ......................................... Wet multi-plate, cable operated
Transmission .................................. 5 speed constant mesh
Final drive
  XV920R and TR1 models ..................... Chain
  All other models .............................. Shaft

## Chassis – all models

Type ........................................... Pressed steel, backbone frame
Rake and trail
  XV535 models ................................. 31.5°, 125 mm
  XV700/750 models ............................ 32°, 129 mm
  XV920R and TR1 models ..................... 28.5°, 126 mm
  XV920 (shaft) model .......................... 29.5°, 133 mm
  XV1000 and XV1100 models ................. 32°, 129 mm
Front suspension .............................. Telescopic forks
  Adjustment – 1981 through 1983 XV750/920, all TR1 and
    XV1000 models, 1986 through 1993 XV1100 models ......... Air assisted (damping adjustment on XV920J)
  Adjustment – 1984-on XV700/750, all XV535 models,
    1994-on XV1100 models ................... None
Rear suspension
  1981 through 1983 XV750/920, all TR1 models ... Monoshock with air pressure and damping adjustment
  1984-on XV700/750 models and all XV535 models ... Twin shocks with preload adjustment
  XV1000 and XV1100 models ................. Twin shocks with preload and damping adjustment

Tyre sizes

| | Front | Rear |
|---|---|---|
| XV535 (1987 through 2002) | 3.00S19 4PR | 140/90 15 M/C 70S |
| XV750 (1981 through 1983) and XV920 shaft drive models | 3.50H19 4PR | 130/90 16 67H |
| XV920R and TR1 models | 3.25H19 4PR | 120/90 18 65H |
| 1984-on XV700/750, XV1000 and XV1100 models: | | |
| except 1994-on UK | 100/90 19 57H | 140/90 15 70H |
| 1994-on UK | 100/90 19 57H | 140/90 15 M/C 70H |

Brakes
  Front
    1988 through 1994 XV535 models ......... Single disc with single-piston caliper
    1995 through 2002 XV535 models ......... Single disc with double-piston caliper
    1981 through 1983 XV750 and XV920 models, TR1 model ...... Twin discs with single-piston calipers
    1984-on XV700/750, XV1000 and XV1100 models .......... Twin discs with opposed or double-piston caliper
  Rear
    XV750 (1981 through 1983) ................ 180 mm drum
    All others (1984-on) ....................... 200 mm drum

Professional mechanics are trained in safe working procedures. However enthusiastic you may be about getting on with the job at hand, take the time to ensure that your safety is not put at risk. A moment's lack of attention can result in an accident, as can failure to observe simple precautions.

There will always be new ways of having accidents, and the following is not a comprehensive list of all dangers; it is intended rather to make you aware of the risks and to encourage a safe approach to all work you carry out on your bike.

## Asbestos

● Certain friction, insulating, sealing and other products - such as brake pads, clutch linings, gaskets, etc. - contain asbestos. Extreme care must be taken to avoid inhalation of dust from such products since it is hazardous to health. If in doubt, assume that they do contain asbestos.

## Fire

● Remember at all times that petrol is highly flammable. Never smoke or have any kind of naked flame around, when working on the vehicle. But the risk does not end there - a spark caused by an electrical short-circuit, by two metal surfaces contacting each other, by careless use of tools, or even by static electricity built up in your body under certain conditions, can ignite petrol vapour, which in a confined space is highly explosive. Never use petrol as a cleaning solvent. Use an approved safety solvent.

● Always disconnect the battery earth terminal before working on any part of the fuel or electrical system, and never risk spilling fuel on to a hot engine or exhaust.

● It is recommended that a fire extinguisher of a type suitable for fuel and electrical fires is kept handy in the garage or workplace at all times. Never try to extinguish a fuel or electrical fire with water.

## Fumes

● Certain fumes are highly toxic and can quickly cause unconsciousness and even death if inhaled to any extent. Petrol vapour comes into this category, as do the vapours from certain solvents such as trichloro-ethylene. Any draining or pouring of such volatile fluids should be done in a well ventilated area.

● When using cleaning fluids and solvents, read the instructions carefully. Never use materials from unmarked containers - they may give off poisonous vapours.

● Never run the engine of a motor vehicle in an enclosed space such as a garage. Exhaust fumes contain carbon monoxide which is extremely poisonous; if you need to run the engine, always do so in the open air or at least have the rear of the vehicle outside the workplace.

## The battery

● Never cause a spark, or allow a naked light near the vehicle's battery. It will normally be giving off a certain amount of hydrogen gas, which is highly explosive.

● Always disconnect the battery ground (earth) terminal before working on the fuel or electrical systems (except where noted).

● If possible, loosen the filler plugs or cover when charging the battery from an external source. Do not charge at an excessive rate or the battery may burst.

● Take care when topping up, cleaning or carrying the battery. The acid electrolyte, evenwhen diluted, is very corrosive and should not be allowed to contact the eyes or skin. Always wear rubber gloves and goggles or a face shield. If you ever need to prepare electrolyte yourself, always add the acid slowly to the water; never add the water to the acid.

## Electricity

● When using an electric power tool, inspection light etc., always ensure that the appliance is correctly connected to its plug and that, where necessary, it is properly grounded (earthed). Do not use such appliances in damp conditions and, again, beware of creating a spark or applying excessive heat in the vicinity of fuel or fuel vapour. Also ensure that the appliances meet national safety standards.

● A severe electric shock can result from touching certain parts of the electrical system, such as the spark plug wires (HT leads), when the engine is running or being cranked, particularly if components are damp or the insulation is defective. Where an electronic ignition system is used, the secondary (HT) voltage is much higher and could prove fatal.

# Remember...

✗ **Don't** start the engine without first ascertaining that the transmission is in neutral.

✗ **Don't** suddenly remove the pressure cap from a hot cooling system - cover it with a cloth and release the pressure gradually first, or you may get scalded by escaping coolant.

✗ **Don't** attempt to drain oil until you are sure it has cooled sufficiently to avoid scalding you.

✗ **Don't** grasp any part of the engine or exhaust system without first ascertaining that it is cool enough not to burn you.

✗ **Don't** allow brake fluid or antifreeze to contact the machine's paintwork or plastic components.

✗ **Don't** siphon toxic liquids such as fuel, hydraulic fluid or antifreeze by mouth, or allow them to remain on your skin.

✗ **Don't** inhale dust - it may be injurious to health (see Asbestos heading).

✗ **Don't** allow any spilled oil or grease to remain on the floor - wipe it up right away, before someone slips on it.

✗ **Don't** use ill-fitting spanners or other tools which may slip and cause injury.

✗ **Don't** lift a heavy component which may be beyond your capability - get assistance.

✗ **Don't** rush to finish a job or take unverified short cuts.

✗ **Don't** allow children or animals in or around an unattended vehicle.

✗ **Don't** inflate a tyre above the recommended pressure. Apart from overstressing the carcass, in extreme cases the tyre may blow off forcibly.

✔ **Do** ensure that the machine is supported securely at all times. This is especially important when the machine is blocked up to aid wheel or fork removal.

✔ **Do** take care when attempting to loosen a stubborn nut or bolt. It is generally better to pull on a spanner, rather than push, so that if you slip, you fall away from the machine rather than onto it.

✔ **Do** wear eye protection when using power tools such as drill, sander, bench grinder etc.

✔ **Do** use a barrier cream on your hands prior to undertaking dirty jobs - it will protect your skin from infection as well as making the dirt easier to remove afterwards; but make sure your hands aren't left slippery. Note that long-term contact with used engine oil can be a health hazard.

✔ **Do** keep loose clothing (cuffs, ties etc. and long hair) well out of the way of moving mechanical parts.

✔ **Do** remove rings, wristwatch etc., before working on the vehicle - especially the electrical system.

✔ **Do** keep your work area tidy - it is only too easy to fall over articles left lying around.

✔ **Do** exercise caution when compressing springs for removal or installation. Ensure that the tension is applied and released in a controlled manner, using suitable tools which preclude the possibility of the spring escaping violently.

✔ **Do** ensure that any lifting tackle used has a safe working load rating adequate for the job.

✔ **Do** get someone to check periodically that all is well, when working alone on the vehicle.

✔ **Do** carry out work in a logical sequence and check that everything is correctly assembled and tightened afterwards.

✔ **Do** remember that your vehicle's safety affects that of yourself and others. If in doubt on any point, get professional advice.

● If in spite of following these precautions, you are unfortunate enough to injure yourself, seek medical attention as soon as possible.

## Frame and engine numbers

The frame serial number is stamped into the right side of the frame and printed on a label affixed to the frame. The engine number is stamped into the right upper side of the crankcase. Both of these numbers should be recorded and kept in a safe place so they can be furnished to law enforcement officials in the event of a theft.

The frame serial number, engine serial number and carburetor identification number should also be kept in a handy place (such as with your driver's license) so they are always available when purchasing or ordering parts for your machine.

## Model codes

The procedures in this manual identify the bikes by model year. To determine which model year a given machine is, look for the identification codes in the engine and frame numbers (see table). For further clarification on UK models, refer to the initial frame/ engine number (in parentheses after the code number) for each model year.

## Buying spare parts

Once you have found all the identification numbers, record them for reference when buying parts. Since the manufacturers change specifications, parts and vendors (companies that manufacture various components on the machine), providing the ID numbers is the only way to be reasonably sure that you are buying the correct parts.

Whenever possible, take the worn part to the dealer so direct comparison with the new component can be made. Along the trail from the manufacturer to the parts shelf, there are numerous places that the part can end up with the wrong number or be listed incorrectly.

The two places to purchase new parts for your motorcycle - the accessory store and the franchised dealer - differ in the type of parts they carry. While dealers can obtain virtually every part for your motorcycle, the accessory dealer is usually limited to normal high wear items such as shock absorbers, tune-up parts, various engine gaskets, cables, chains, brake parts, etc. Rarely will an accessory outlet have major suspension components, cylinders, transmission gears, or cases.

Used parts can be obtained for roughly half the price of new ones, but you can't always be sure of what you're getting. Once again, take your worn part to the wrecking yard (breaker) for direct comparison.

Whether buying new, used or rebuilt parts, the best course is to deal directly with someone who specializes in parts for your particular make.

| Year | Code | Year | Code |
|---|---|---|---|
| **XV535 models** | | **XV750 models** | |
| 1987 and 1988 US | 2GV | 1981 through 1983 US | |
| 1989 and 1990 US | 3JC1/3JC2 | XV750 H, J, K | 4X7 |
| 1993 US | 3JC7/3JC8 | XV750 MK | 20X |
| 1994 US | | 1988 US | 3AL/3CM |
| XV535 | 3JCA, 3JCB | 1989 US | 3JL1/3JL2 |
| XV535S | 3JCB, 3JCD | 1990 US | 3JL4/3JL5 |
| 1995 US (49 states) | | 1991 US | 3JL7/3JL8 |
| XV535 | 3JCG | 1992 US | 3JLA/3JLB |
| XV535S | 3JCK | 1993 US | 3JLD/3JLE |
| 1995 US (California) | | 1994 US | 3JLG/3JLH |
| XV535 | 3JCH | 1995 US (49 states) | 3JLK |
| XV535S | 3JCL | 1995 US (California) | 3JLL |
| 1996 US | Not available | 1996 US (49 states) | 3JLN |
| 1997 US (49 states) | | 1996 US (California) | 3JLP |
| XV535 | 3JCV | 1997 US (49 states) | 3JLS |
| XV535S | 3JCY | 1997 US (California) | 3JLT |
| 1997 US (California) | | 1981 – 1983 UK | 5G5 (5G5 - 000101) |
| XV535 | 3JCW | 1992 and 1993 UK | 4FY1 (4FY - 000001) |
| XV535S | 4YN1 | 1994 UK | 4FY4 (4FY - 017101) |
| 1998 US (49 states) | 4YN3 | 1995 UK | 4PW1 (4PW - 000101) |
| 1998 US (California) | 4YN4 | 1996 UK | 4PW3 (4PW - 015101) |
| 1999 US (49 States) | 4YN9 | **XV920 models** | |
| 1999 US (California) | 4YNA | 1981 & 1982 chain drive | 5H1 |
| 2000 US | Not available | 1982 shaft drive | 10L |
| 1988 UK | 3BT1 (2YL - 003101) | 1983 shaft drive | |
| 1989 UK | 3BT2 (2YL - 010101) or | XV920 K | 24M |
| | 3BT5 (2YL - 013101) | XV920 MK | 27Y |
| 1990 UK | 3BTC (2YL - 027101) or | **TR1 models** | |
| | 3BT8 (2YL - 017101) | 1981 UK | 5A8 (5A8 – 000101) |
| 1991 UK | 3BTE (2YL - 031101) or | 1982 – 1985 UK | 19T (5A8 - 120101) |
| | 3BTF (2YL - 033101) | **XV1000 models** | |
| 1992 UK | 3BTK (2YL - 064101) or | 1984 US | 42G/42H |
| | 3BTM (2YL - 073101) | 1985 US | 56V/56W |
| 1993 UK | 3BTR (2YL - 098101) or | 1986 and 1987 UK | 2AE (2AE - 000101) |
| | 3BTT (2YL - 113101) | 1988 and 1989 UK | 3DR1 (2AE - 005101) |
| 1994 UK | | **XV1100 models** | |
| XV535 (flat bars) | 4KU2 (2YL - 145101) or | 1986 and 1987 US | 1TE/1TA |
| | 3BTW (2YL - 136101) | 1988 US | 3CF/3CG |
| XV535 (high bars) | 3BTV (2YL - 125101) or | 1989 US | 3JK1/3JK2 |
| | 3BTY (2YL - 140101) | 1990 US | 3JK4/3JK5 |
| XV535S (flat bars) | 4KU4 (2YL - 168101) | 1991 US | 3JK7/3JK8 |
| XV535S (high bars) | 4KU3 (2YL - 163101) or | 1992 US | 3JKB/3JKC |
| | 4KU7 (2YL - 176101) | 1993 US | 3JKA/3JKE |
| 1995 UK | | 1994 US | 3JKG/3JKH |
| XV535 (flat bars) | 4KUB (2YL - 201101) or | 1995 US (49 states) | 3JKK |
| | 4KU9 (2YL - 206101) | 1995 US (California) | 3JKL |
| XV535 (high bars) | 4KU8 (2YL - 179101) or | 1996 US (49 states) | 3JKR |
| | 4KUA (2YL - 195101) | 1996 US (California) | 3JKN |
| XV535S | 4KUE (2YL - 216101) | 1997 US (49 states) | |
| 1996 UK | | XV1100 | 3JKX |
| XV535 | 4KUK (2YL - 243101) or | XV1100S | 3JKY |
| | 4KUL (2YL - 246101) | 1997 US (California) | |
| XV535 | 4KUH (2YL - 228101) or | XV1100 | 3JKV |
| | 4KUJ (2YL - 239101) | XV1100S | 4NX2 |
| XV535S | 4KUN (2YL - 248101) or | 1998 US (49 states) | |
| | 4KUR (2YL - 265101) | XV1100 | 4XN3 |
| 1997 UK | | XV1100S | 4XN6 |
| XV535 (flat bars) | 4KUY | 1998 US (California) | |
| XV535 (high bars) | 4KUV | XV1100 | 4XN4 |
| XV535S (high bars) | 4YH2 | XV1100S | 4XN7 |
| 1998 UK | 4YH7 | 1999 US (49 states) | 4XNA |
| 1999 UK | 4YH9 | 1999 US (California) | 4XNB |
| 2000 UK | 4YHC | 1989 and 1990 UK | 3LP1 (3LP - 000101) |
| 2001 to 03 UK | 4YHE | 1991 UK | 3LP2 (3LP - 004101) |
| | | 1992 and 1993 UK | 3LP4 (3LP - 010101) |
| **XV700 models** | | 1994 UK | 3LP7 (3LP - 023101) |
| 1984 | 42W/42X | 1995 UK | 3LP9 (3LP - 036101) |
| 1985 | 56E/56F | 1996 UK | 3LPB (3LP - 049101) |
| 1986 and 1987 | 1RM/1RV/1RR/1TU | 1997 UK | 3LPE |
| | | 1998 UK | 3LPG |

**The frame number is stamped in the right side of the frame and is also displayed on a decal**

**The engine number is stamped in the right side of the crankcase**

# 1 Engine/transmission oil level

## Before you start:

✔ Run the engine and allow it to reach normal operating temperature.

*Caution: Do not run the engine in an enclosed space such as a garage or shop.*

✔ Stop the engine and allow the machine to sit undisturbed for about five minutes.

## Bike care:

● If you have to add oil frequently, you should check whether you have any oil leaks. If there is no sign of oil leakage from the joints and gaskets the engine could be burning oil (see *Fault Finding*).

## The correct oil

● Modern, high-revving engines place great demands on their oil. It is very important that the correct oil for your bike is used.
● Always top up with a good quality oil of the specified type and viscosity and do not overfill the engine.

| Oil type | API grade SE or SF (minimum) |
|---|---|
| Oil viscosity - below 15°C (60°F) | SAE 10W30 |
| Oil viscosity - above 5°C (40°F) | SAE 20W40 |

**1** Hold the motorcycle level. With the engine off, check the oil level in the window located at the lower part of the left crankcase cover (XV535 shown).

**2** The oil level should be between the Maximum and Minimum level marks next to the window (XV700-1100 shown).

**3** If the level is below the Minimum mark, remove the oil filler cap from the left side of the crankcase

**4** Add enough oil of the recommended grade and type to bring the level up to the Maximum mark. Do not overfill.

# 2 Brake fluid level

 *Warning: Brake hydraulic fluid can harm your eyes and damage painted surfaces, so use extreme caution when handling and pouring it and cover surrounding surfaces with rag. Do not use fluid that has been standing open for some time, as it absorbs moisture from the air which can cause a dangerous loss of braking effectiveness.*

## Before you start:

✔ Make sure you have the correct hydraulic fluid - DOT 4.
✔ With the motorcycle held level, turn the handlebars until the top of the master cylinder is as level as possible.

## Bike care:

● In order to ensure proper operation of the hydraulic disc brake, the fluid level in the master cylinder reservoir must be properly maintained. If the brake fluid level was low, inspect the brake system for leaks.
● The fluid in the brake master cylinder reservoir will drop slightly as the brake pads wear down.
● Check the operation of the brakes before taking the machine on the road; if there is evidence of air in the system (spongy feel to lever), it must be bled (see Chapter 6).

**1** Look closely at the inspection window in the master cylinder reservoir. Make sure that the fluid level is above the LOWER mark on the reservoir.

**2** If the level is low, the fluid must be replenished. Before removing the master cylinder cover, cover the surrounding area to protect it from brake fluid spills (which will damage the paint) and remove all dust and dirt from the area around the cover.

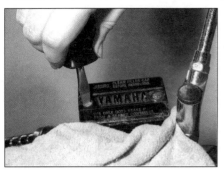

**3** To top up brake fluid, remove the screws and lift off the cover and rubber diaphragm. **Note:** *Do not operate the front brake with the cover removed.*

**4** Add new, clean brake fluid of the recommended type until the level is above the inspection window. Do not mix different brands of brake fluid in the reservoir, as they may not be compatible.

**5** Reinstall the rubber diaphragm and the cover. Tighten the screws evenly, but do not overtighten them.

# 3 Clutch

## Bike care:

● Correct clutch freeplay is necessary to ensure proper clutch operation and reasonable clutch service life. Freeplay normally changes because of cable stretch and clutch wear, so it should be checked and adjusted periodically.

● If the lever is stiff to operate and doesn't return quickly, lubricate the cable (see Chapter 1).

● Too little freeplay might result in the clutch not engaging completely. If there is too much freeplay, the clutch might not release fully.

● If a small amount of cable adjustment is required, use the fine adjuster at the top of the cable. If a large amount of adjustment is required, use the coarse adjuster at the lower end of the cable. If freeplay still can't be adjusted within the Specifications, the cable may be stretched or the clutch may be worn. Refer to Chapter 2 for inspection and repair procedures.

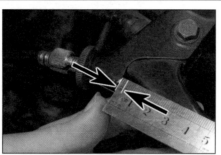

**1** Clutch cable freeplay is checked at the lever on the handlebar. Slowly pull in on the lever until resistance is felt, then note how big the gap is between the lever and its pivot bracket. Compare this distance with the specified value of 2 to 3 mm (0.08 to 0.12 inch).

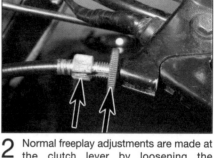

**2** Normal freeplay adjustments are made at the clutch lever by loosening the lockwheel and turning the adjuster until the desired freeplay is obtained. Always retighten the lockwheel once the adjustment is complete.

**3** If freeplay can't be adjusted at the handlebar on XV535 models, check the initial adjustment at the engine. Loosen the locknuts at the clutch cable bracket on the engine. Turn the nuts to achieve the correct freeplay, then tighten them. Make fine adjustments at the handlebar adjuster (see Step 2).

**4** If freeplay can't be adjusted at the handlebar on XV700 through 1100 models, remove the cover from the clutch adjuster on the left side of the engine. Loosen the locknut and turn the adjuster screw clockwise until it seats lightly, then back it out 1/4 turn and tighten the locknut. Make fine adjustments at the handlebar adjuster (see Step 2).

# 4 Suspension, steering and final drive

## Suspension and steering:
● Make sure the steering operates smoothly, without looseness and without binding.
● Check front and rear suspension for smooth operation.

## Drive chain:
● Make sure the drive chain isn't out of adjustment (Chapter 1).

## Shaft drive:
● Check for signs of oil leakage around the final drive housing. If any is evident, check the final drive oil level (Chapter 1).

# 5 Tires

## The correct pressures:
● The tires must be checked when **cold**, not immediately after riding. Note that low tire pressures may cause the tire to slip on the rim or come off. High tire pressures will cause abnormal tread wear and unsafe handling.
● Use an accurate pressure gauge.
● Proper air pressure will increase tire life and provide maximum stability and ride comfort.

## Tire care:
● Check the tires for cuts, tears, nails or other sharp objects and wear. Riding on worn tires is extremely hazardous, as traction and handling are directly affected.
● Check the condition of the tire valve and ensure the dust cap is in place.
● Pick out any stones or nails which may have become embedded in the tire tread. If left, they will eventually penetrate through the casing and cause a puncture.
● If tire damage is apparent, or unexplained loss of pressure is experienced, seek the advice of a tire fitting specialist without delay.

## Tire tread depth:
● At the time of writing UK law requires that tread depth must be at least 1 mm over 3/4 of the tread breadth all the way around the tire, with no bald patches. Many riders, however, consider 2 mm tread depth minimum to be a safer limit.
● Many tires now incorporate wear indicators in the tread. Identify the triangular pointer or TWI mark on the tire sidewall to locate the indicator bar and replace the tire if the tread has worn down to the bar.

| Loading/speed | Front | Rear |
|---|---|---|
| **XV535 - 1987 and 1988 US models** | | |
| Solo riding | 28 psi (1.93 Bars) | 32 psi (2.20 Bars) |
| With passenger or high speed riding | 28 psi (1.93 Bars) | 36 psi (2.48 Bars) |
| **XV535 - 1989 and later US models** | | |
| Solo riding | 29 psi (1.99 Bars) | 33 psi (2.27 Bars) |
| With passenger or high speed riding | 29 psi (1.99 Bars) | 36 psi (2.48 Bars) |
| **XV535 - 1987 through 1995 UK models** | | |
| Solo riding | 28 psi (1.93 Bars) | 32 psi (2.20 Bars) |
| With passenger or high speed riding | 28 psi (1.93 Bars) | 36 psi (2.48 Bars) |
| **XV535 - 1996-on UK models** | | |
| Solo riding | 29 psi (1.99 Bars) | 32 psi (2.20 Bars) |
| With passenger or high speed riding | 29 psi (1.99 Bars) | 36 psi (2.48 Bars) |
| **XV750 - 1981 through 1983,** | | |
| **XV920 - 1983 (shaft drive)** | | |
| Solo riding | 26 psi (1.79 Bars) | 28 psi (1.93 Bars) |
| With passenger | 28 psi (1.93 Bars) | 36 psi (2.48 Bars) |
| High speed riding | 32 psi (2.20 Bars) | 32 psi (2.20 Bars) |
| **XV920 - 1992 (shaft drive)** | | |
| Solo riding | 26 psi (1.79 Bars) | 28 psi (1.93 Bars) |
| With passenger | 28 psi (1.93 Bars) | 40 psi (2.76 Bars) |
| High speed riding | 32 psi (2.20 Bars) | 36 psi (2.48 Bars) |
| **XV920R (chain drive)** | | |
| Solo riding | 26 psi (1.79 Bars) | 28 psi (1.93 Bars) |
| With passenger | 28 psi (1.93 Bars) | 32 psi (2.20 Bars) |
| High speed riding | 28 psi (1.93 Bars) | 32 psi (2.20 Bars) |
| **XV700, 750, 1000 and 1100 - 1984-on** | | |
| Solo riding | 26 psi (1.79 Bars) | 28 psi (1.93 Bars) |
| With passenger | 28 psi (1.93 Bars) | 36 psi (2.48 Bars) |
| Above 353 lbs (160 kg) load | 28 psi (1.93 Bars) | 40 psi (2.76 Bars) |
| High speed riding | 32 psi (2.20 Bars) | 36 psi (2.48 Bars) |
| **TR1 (UK)** | | |
| Solo riding | 26 psi (1.79 Bars) | 28 psi (1.93 Bars) |
| With passenger | 28 psi (1.93 Bars) | 32 psi (2.20 Bars) |
| High speed riding | 28 psi (1.93 Bars) | 32 psi (2.20 Bars) |

**1** Check the tire pressures when the tires are **cold** and keep them properly inflated.

**2** Measure the tread depth at the center of the tire using a tread depth gauge.

**3** Tire tread wear indicator bar and its location marking on the sidewall (arrows).

# 6 Legal and safety checks

## Lighting and signalling:
● Take a minute to check that the headlight, taillight, brake light and turn signals all work correctly.
● Check that the horn sounds when the switch is operated.
● A working speedometer is a statutory requirement in the UK.

## Safety:
● Check that the throttle grip rotates smoothly and snaps shut when released, in all steering positions.
● Check that the engine shuts off when the kill switch is operated.
● Check that sidestand return spring holds the stand securely up when retracted. The same applies to the centerstand (where fitted).

● Following the procedure in your owner's manual, check the operation of the sidestand switch.

## Fuel:
● This may seem obvious, but check that you have enough fuel to complete your journey. If you notice signs of fuel leakage - rectify the cause immediately.
● Ensure you use the correct grade fuel.

# Chapter 1
# Routine maintenance and Servicing

## Contents

## Degrees of difficulty

| Easy, suitable for novice with little experience |  | Fairly easy, suitable for beginner with some experience |  | Fairly difficult, suitable for competent DIY mechanic |  | Difficult, suitable for experienced DIY mechanic |  | Very difficult, suitable for expert DIY or professional |

## XV535 mdoels

### Engine

Spark plugs
  Type (all except 1996-on UK) . . . . . . . . . . . . . . . . . . . . . . . . . . . . . . NGK BP7ES or ND W22EP-U
  Type (1996 and later UK) . . . . . . . . . . . . . . . . . . . . . . . . . . . . . . . . . NGK BPR6ES or ND W20EPR-U
  Gap . . . . . . . . . . . . . . . . . . . . . . . . . . . . . . . . . . . . . . . . . . . . . . . . . . 0.7 to 0.8 mm (0.028 to 0.032 inch)
Valve clearances (COLD engine)
  Intake . . . . . . . . . . . . . . . . . . . . . . . . . . . . . . . . . . . . . . . . . . . . . . . . 0.07 to 0.12 mm (0.003 to 0.005 inch)
  Exhaust . . . . . . . . . . . . . . . . . . . . . . . . . . . . . . . . . . . . . . . . . . . . . . 0.12 to 0.17 mm (0.005 to 0.007 inch)
Engine idle speed . . . . . . . . . . . . . . . . . . . . . . . . . . . . . . . . . . . . . . . 1150 to 1250 rpm
Cylinder compression pressure (at sea level)
  Standard . . . . . . . . . . . . . . . . . . . . . . . . . . . . . . . . . . . . . . . . . . . . . 10.75 Bars (156 psi)
  Maximum . . . . . . . . . . . . . . . . . . . . . . . . . . . . . . . . . . . . . . . . . . . . . 11.78 Bars (171 psi)
  Minimum . . . . . . . . . . . . . . . . . . . . . . . . . . . . . . . . . . . . . . . . . . . . . 9.78 Bars (142 psi)
  Maximum difference between cylinders . . . . . . . . . . . . . . . . . . . . . 0.96 Bars (14 psi)
Carburetor synchronization
  Vacuum at idle speed . . . . . . . . . . . . . . . . . . . . . . . . . . . . . . . . . . . 230 mm Hg (9.06 inch Hg)
  Maximum vacuum difference between cylinders . . . . . . . . . . . . . . . 10 mm Hg (0.39 inch Hg)
Cylinder numbering (from rear to front of bike) . . . . . . . . . . . . . . . . . 1-2

### Tire pressures (cold)

Front
  1987 and 1988 US, 1988 through 1995 UK . . . . . . . . . . . . . . . . . . 1.93 Bars (28 psi)
  1989 and later US, 1996 and later UK . . . . . . . . . . . . . . . . . . . . . . 1.99 Bars (29 psi)
Rear
  Up to 90 kg (198 lbs)
    1987 and 1988 US, all UK models . . . . . . . . . . . . . . . . . . . . . . . 2.2 Bars (32 psi)
    1989 and later US models . . . . . . . . . . . . . . . . . . . . . . . . . . . . . 2.27 Bars (33 psi)
  Above 90 kg (198 lbs) or high speed riding . . . . . . . . . . . . . . . . . . 2.48 bars (36 psi)

### Miscellaneous

Brake pedal position . . . . . . . . . . . . . . . . . . . . . . . . . . . . . . . . . . . . . . 38 mm (1.5 inch) above the top of the footpeg
Shift pedal position . . . . . . . . . . . . . . . . . . . . . . . . . . . . . . . . . . . . . . . 50 to 60 mm (2.0 to 2.4 inches) above the top of the footpeg
Freeplay adjustments
  Throttle grip . . . . . . . . . . . . . . . . . . . . . . . . . . . . . . . . . . . . . . . . . . . 2 to 5 mm (0.08 to 0.20 inch)
  Clutch lever . . . . . . . . . . . . . . . . . . . . . . . . . . . . . . . . . . . . . . . . . . . 2 to 3 mm (0.08 to 0.12 inch)
  Front brake lever . . . . . . . . . . . . . . . . . . . . . . . . . . . . . . . . . . . . . . . 2 to 5 mm (0.08 to 0.20 inch)
  Rear brake pedal . . . . . . . . . . . . . . . . . . . . . . . . . . . . . . . . . . . . . . 20 to 30 mm (0.8 to 1.2 inches)
Battery electrolyte specific gravity . . . . . . . . . . . . . . . . . . . . . . . . . . . 1.280 at 20-degrees C (68-degrees F)
Minimum tire tread depth* . . . . . . . . . . . . . . . . . . . . . . . . . . . . . . . . . 1 mm (0.04 inch)
*In the UK, tread depth must be at least 1 mm over 3/4 of the tread breadth all the way around the tire, with no bald patches.

### Torque specifications

Oil drain plug . . . . . . . . . . . . . . . . . . . . . . . . . . . . . . . . . . . . . . . . . . . 43 Nm (31 ft-lbs)
Oil filter cover bolts . . . . . . . . . . . . . . . . . . . . . . . . . . . . . . . . . . . . . . 10 Nm (7.2 ft-lbs)
Spark plugs . . . . . . . . . . . . . . . . . . . . . . . . . . . . . . . . . . . . . . . . . . . . 12.5 Nm (9 ft-lbs)
Steering head bearing ring nuts
  Initial torque . . . . . . . . . . . . . . . . . . . . . . . . . . . . . . . . . . . . . . . . . . 38 Nm (27 ft-lbs)
  Final torque . . . . . . . . . . . . . . . . . . . . . . . . . . . . . . . . . . . . . . . . . . 10 Nm (7.2 ft-lbs)
Steering stem bolt . . . . . . . . . . . . . . . . . . . . . . . . . . . . . . . . . . . . . . . 54 Nm (39 ft-lbs)
Valve adjuster locknuts . . . . . . . . . . . . . . . . . . . . . . . . . . . . . . . . . . . 14 Nm (10 ft-lbs)
Rocker cover bolts . . . . . . . . . . . . . . . . . . . . . . . . . . . . . . . . . . . . . . 10 Nm (7.2 ft-lbs)
Final drive filler and drain plugs . . . . . . . . . . . . . . . . . . . . . . . . . . . . 23 Nm (17 ft-lbs)

### Recommended lubricants and fluids

Fuel grade . . . . . . . . . . . . . . . . . . . . . . . . . . . . . . . . . . . . . . . . . . . . . Regular unleaded gasoline (petrol)
Engine/transmission oil
  Type . . . . . . . . . . . . . . . . . . . . . . . . . . . . . . . . . . . . . . . . . . . . . . . . API grade SE or SF (minimum)
  Viscosity
    Consistently below 15 degrees C (60 degrees F) . . . . . . . . . . . . . SAE 10W30
    Consistently above 5 degrees C (40 degrees F) . . . . . . . . . . . . . . SAE 20W40
  Capacity
    With filter change . . . . . . . . . . . . . . . . . . . . . . . . . . . . . . . . . . . . 2.8 liters (3.0 US qt, 5.0 Imperial pt)
    Oil change only . . . . . . . . . . . . . . . . . . . . . . . . . . . . . . . . . . . . . 2.6 liters (2.7 US qt, 4.6 Imperial pt)
Brake fluid . . . . . . . . . . . . . . . . . . . . . . . . . . . . . . . . . . . . . . . . . . . . . DOT 4

*OIL FILTER 4X7 13440-90*

Final gear
  Type . . . . . . . . . . . . . . . . . . . . . . . . . . . . . . . . . . . . . . . .  SAE 80 API GL-4 hypoid gear oil
  Capacity . . . . . . . . . . . . . . . . . . . . . . . . . . . . . . . . . . . . .  0.19 liters (0.2 US qt, 0.34 Imp pt)
Wheel bearings . . . . . . . . . . . . . . . . . . . . . . . . . . . . . . . . . .  Medium weight, lithium-based multi-purpose grease
Swingarm pivot bearings . . . . . . . . . . . . . . . . . . . . . . . . . . .  Medium weight, lithium-based multi-purpose grease
Cables and lever pivots . . . . . . . . . . . . . . . . . . . . . . . . . . .  Chain and cable lubricant or 10W30 motor oil
Sidestand/centerstand pivots . . . . . . . . . . . . . . . . . . . . . . .  Chain and cable lubricant or 10W30 motor oil
Brake pedal/shift lever pivots . . . . . . . . . . . . . . . . . . . . . .  Chain and cable lubricant or 10W30 motor oil
Throttle grip . . . . . . . . . . . . . . . . . . . . . . . . . . . . . . . . . . . .  Multi-purpose grease or dry film lubricant

## 1981 through 1983 XV750 through 1000 models and all TR1 models

### Engine

Spark plugs
  Type . . . . . . . . . . . . . . . . . . . . . . . . . . . . . . . . . . . . . . . .  NGK BP7ES or ND W22EP-U
  Gap . . . . . . . . . . . . . . . . . . . . . . . . . . . . . . . . . . . . . . . . .  0.7 to 0.8 mm (0.028 to 0.032 inch)
Valve clearances (COLD engine)
  Intake . . . . . . . . . . . . . . . . . . . . . . . . . . . . . . . . . . . . . . .  0.10 mm (0.004 inch)
  Exhaust . . . . . . . . . . . . . . . . . . . . . . . . . . . . . . . . . . . . . .  0.15 mm (0.006 inch)
Engine idle speed . . . . . . . . . . . . . . . . . . . . . . . . . . . . . . . .  950 to 1050 rpm
Cylinder compression pressure (at sea level)
  XV750 and TR1 . . . . . . . . . . . . . . . . . . . . . . . . . . . . . . . . .  Not specified
  XV920 . . . . . . . . . . . . . . . . . . . . . . . . . . . . . . . . . . . . . . .  9.30 Bars (135 psi) at 300 rpm
Carburetor synchronization
  Vacuum at idle speed . . . . . . . . . . . . . . . . . . . . . . . . . . . .  180 +/- 10 mm Hg (7.09 +/- 0.4 inch Hg)
  Maximum vacuum difference between cylinders . . . . . . . . . . . . . . .  10 mm Hg (0.4 inch Hg)
Cylinder numbering (from rear to front of bike) . . . . . . . . . . . . . . . . . .  1-2

### Tire pressures (cold)

XV750 - 1981 through 1983, XV920 - 1983 (shaft drive)
  Front
    Up to 90 kg (198 lbs) load . . . . . . . . . . . . . . . . . . . . . . . . . . .  1.79 Bars (26 psi)
    90 to 160 kg (198 to 353 lbs) load . . . . . . . . . . . . . . . . . . . .  1.93 Bars (28 psi)
    High speed riding . . . . . . . . . . . . . . . . . . . . . . . . . . . . . . . .  2.20 Bars (32 psi)
  Rear
    Up to 90 kg (198 lbs) . . . . . . . . . . . . . . . . . . . . . . . . . . . . . .  1.93 Bars (28 psi)
    90 to 160 kg (198 to 353 lbs) . . . . . . . . . . . . . . . . . . . . . . . .  2.48 Bars (36 psi)
    High speed riding . . . . . . . . . . . . . . . . . . . . . . . . . . . . . . . .  2.20 Bars (32 psi)
XV920 - 1982 (shaft drive)
  Front
    Up to 90 kg (198 lbs) load . . . . . . . . . . . . . . . . . . . . . . . . . . .  1.79 Bars (26 psi)
    90 to 213 kg (198 to 470 lbs) load . . . . . . . . . . . . . . . . . . . .  1.93 Bars (28 psi)
    High speed riding . . . . . . . . . . . . . . . . . . . . . . . . . . . . . . . .  2.20 Bars (32 psi)
  Rear
    Up to 90 kg (198 lbs) . . . . . . . . . . . . . . . . . . . . . . . . . . . . . .  1.93 Bars (28 psi)
    90 to 213 kg (198 to 470 lbs) . . . . . . . . . . . . . . . . . . . . . . . .  2.76 Bars (40 psi)
    High speed riding . . . . . . . . . . . . . . . . . . . . . . . . . . . . . . . .  2.48 Bars (36 psi)
XV920R (chain drive)
  Front
    Up to 90 kg (198 lbs) load . . . . . . . . . . . . . . . . . . . . . . . . . . .  1.79 Bars (26 psi)
    90 to 213 kg (198 to 470 lbs) load . . . . . . . . . . . . . . . . . . . .  1.93 Bars (28 psi)
    High speed riding . . . . . . . . . . . . . . . . . . . . . . . . . . . . . . . .  1.93 Bars (28 psi)
  Rear
    Up to 90 kg (198 lbs) . . . . . . . . . . . . . . . . . . . . . . . . . . . . . .  1.93 Bars (28 psi)
    90 to 213 kg (198 to 470 lbs) . . . . . . . . . . . . . . . . . . . . . . . .  2.20 Bars (32 psi)
    High speed riding . . . . . . . . . . . . . . . . . . . . . . . . . . . . . . . .  2.20 Bars (32 psi)
TR1 (chain drive) models
  Front
    Up to 90 kg (198 lbs) load . . . . . . . . . . . . . . . . . . . . . . . . . . .  1.79 Bars (26 psi)
    90 to 201 kg (198 to 443 lbs) load . . . . . . . . . . . . . . . . . . . .  1.93 Bars (28 psi)
    High speed riding . . . . . . . . . . . . . . . . . . . . . . . . . . . . . . . .  1.93 Bars (28 psi)
  Rear
    Up to 90 kg (198 lbs) . . . . . . . . . . . . . . . . . . . . . . . . . . . . . .  1.93 Bars (28 psi)
    90 to 201 kg (198 to 443 lbs) . . . . . . . . . . . . . . . . . . . . . . . .  2.20 Bars (32 psi)
    High speed riding . . . . . . . . . . . . . . . . . . . . . . . . . . . . . . . .  2.20 Bars (32 psi)

## 1981 through 1983 XV750 through 1000 models and all TR1 models (continued)

### Miscellaneous

| | |
|---|---|
| Brake pedal position | Not specified |
| Shift pedal position | Not specified |
| Freeplay adjustments | |
| Throttle grip | Not specified |
| Clutch lever | 2 to 3 mm (0.08 to 0.12 inch) |
| Front brake lever | 5 to 8 mm (0.20 to 0.30 inch) |
| Rear brake pedal | 20 to 30 mm (0.8 to 1.2 inches) |
| Battery electrolyte specific gravity | 1.280 at 20-degrees C (68-degrees F) |
| Minimum tire tread depth* | 1 mm (0.04 inch) |

*In the UK, tread depth must be at least 1 mm over 3/4 of the tread breadth all the way around the tire, with no bald patches.*

### Torque specifications

| | |
|---|---|
| Oil drain plug | 43 Nm (31 ft-lbs) |
| Oil filter cover bolts | 10 Nm (7.2 ft-lbs) |
| Spark plugs | 14 Nm (10 ft-lbs) |
| Steering head bearing ring nuts | |
| Initial torque | 25 Nm (18 ft-lbs) |
| Final torque | Back off 1/4 turn |
| Steering stem bolt | |
| XV920 (shaft drive) | 54 Nm (39 ft-lbs) |
| All others | 50 Nm (36 ft-lbs) |
| Valve adjuster locknuts | 27 Nm (19 ft-lbs) |
| Rocker cover bolts | 10 Nm (7.2 ft-lbs) |
| Final drive filler and drain plugs | 23 Nm (17 ft-lbs) |

### Recommended lubricants and fluids

| | |
|---|---|
| Fuel grade | Regular unleaded gasoline (petrol) |
| Engine/transmission oil | |
| Type | API grade SE or SF (minimum) |
| Viscosity | |
| Consistently below 15 degrees C (60 degrees F) | SAE 10W30 |
| Consistently above 5 degrees C (40 degrees F) | SAE 20W40 |
| Capacity | |
| With filter change | 3.1 liters (3.3 US qt, 5.46 Imperial pt) |
| Oil change only | 3.0 liters (3.2 US qt, 5.28 Imperial pt) |
| Brake fluid | DOT 4 |
| Final gear | |
| Type | SAE 80 API GL-4 hypoid gear oil |
| Capacity | 0.20 liters (6.76 US fl oz, 7.04 Imp fl oz) |
| Wheel bearings | Medium weight, lithium-based multi-purpose grease |
| Swingarm pivot bearings | Medium weight, lithium-based multi-purpose grease |
| Cables and lever pivots | Chain and cable lubricant or 10W30 motor oil |
| Sidestand/centerstand pivots | Chain and cable lubricant or 10W30 motor oil |
| Brake pedal/shift lever pivots | Chain and cable lubricant or 10W30 motor oil |
| Throttle grip | Multi-purpose grease or dry film lubricant |

## 1984-on XV700, 750, 1000 and 1100 models (except TR1)

### Engine

| | |
|---|---|
| Spark plugs | |
| Type | |
| 1984 through 1995 US, all UK | NGK BP7ES or ND W22EP-U |
| 1996 US | NGK BPR7ES or ND W22EPR-U |
| Gap | 0.7 to 0.8 mm (0.028 to 0.032 inch) |
| Valve clearances (COLD engine) | |
| Intake | 0.07 to 0.12 mm (0.003 to 0.005 inch) |
| Exhaust | 0.12 to 0.17 mm (0.005 to 0.007 inch) |
| Engine idle speed | 950 to 1050 rpm |

Cylinder compression pressure (at sea level)
 Standard . . . . . . . . . . . . . . . . . . . . . . . . . . . . . . . . . . . . . . . . . . . . . 10.75 Bars (156 psi)
 Maximum . . . . . . . . . . . . . . . . . . . . . . . . . . . . . . . . . . . . . . . . . . . . . 11.78 Bars (171 psi)
 Minimum . . . . . . . . . . . . . . . . . . . . . . . . . . . . . . . . . . . . . . . . . . . . . 8.8 Bars (128 psi)
 Maximum difference between cylinders . . . . . . . . . . . . . . . . . . . . 0.96 Bars (14 psi)
Carburetor synchronization
 Vacuum at idle speed . . . . . . . . . . . . . . . . . . . . . . . . . . . . . . . . . 180 +/- 10 mm Hg (7.09 +/- 0.4 inch Hg)
 Maximum vacuum difference between cylinders . . . . . . . . . . . . . 10 mm Hg (0.4 inch Hg)
Engine idle speed . . . . . . . . . . . . . . . . . . . . . . . . . . . . . . . . . . . . . . . 950 to 1050 rpm
Cylinder numbering (from rear to front of bike) . . . . . . . . . . . . . . . . 1-2

## Tire pressures (cold)
Front
 Up to 90 kg (198 lbs) load . . . . . . . . . . . . . . . . . . . . . . . . . . . . . . 1.79 Bars (26 psi)
 90 kg to maximum load . . . . . . . . . . . . . . . . . . . . . . . . . . . . . . . 1.93 Bars (28 psi)
 High speed riding . . . . . . . . . . . . . . . . . . . . . . . . . . . . . . . . . . . . 2.20 Bars (32 psi)
Rear
 Up to 90 kg (198 lbs) . . . . . . . . . . . . . . . . . . . . . . . . . . . . . . . . . 1.93 Bars (28 psi)
 90 to 160 kg (198 to 353 lbs) . . . . . . . . . . . . . . . . . . . . . . . . . . 2.48 Bars (36 psi)
 160 kg (353 lbs) to maximum load . . . . . . . . . . . . . . . . . . . . . . 2.76 Bars (40 psi)
 High speed riding . . . . . . . . . . . . . . . . . . . . . . . . . . . . . . . . . . . . 2.48 Bars (36 psi)

## Miscellaneous
Brake pedal position . . . . . . . . . . . . . . . . . . . . . . . . . . . . . . . . . . . . . 20 mm (0.8 inch) above bottom of footpeg
Shift pedal position . . . . . . . . . . . . . . . . . . . . . . . . . . . . . . . . . . . . . . Not specified
Freeplay adjustments
 Throttle grip . . . . . . . . . . . . . . . . . . . . . . . . . . . . . . . . . . . . . . . . . Not specified
 Clutch lever . . . . . . . . . . . . . . . . . . . . . . . . . . . . . . . . . . . . . . . . . 2 to 3 mm (0.08 to 0.12 inch)
 Front brake lever . . . . . . . . . . . . . . . . . . . . . . . . . . . . . . . . . . . . . 5 to 8 mm (0.20 to 0.30 inch)
 Rear brake pedal . . . . . . . . . . . . . . . . . . . . . . . . . . . . . . . . . . . . . 20 to 30 mm (0.8 to 1.2 inch)
Battery electrolyte specific gravity . . . . . . . . . . . . . . . . . . . . . . . . . 1.280 at 20-degrees C (68-degrees F)
Minimum tire tread depth* . . . . . . . . . . . . . . . . . . . . . . . . . . . . . . . . 1 mm (0.04 inch)
*In the UK, tread depth must be at least 1 mm over 3/4 of the tread breadth all the way around the tire, with no bald patches.

## Torque specifications
Oil drain plug . . . . . . . . . . . . . . . . . . . . . . . . . . . . . . . . . . . . . . . . . . 43 Nm (31 ft-lbs)
Oil filter cover bolts . . . . . . . . . . . . . . . . . . . . . . . . . . . . . . . . . . . . . 10 Nm (7.2 ft-lbs)
Spark plugs . . . . . . . . . . . . . . . . . . . . . . . . . . . . . . . . . . . . . . . . . . . 20 Nm (14 ft-lbs)
Steering head bearing ring nuts
 Initial torque . . . . . . . . . . . . . . . . . . . . . . . . . . . . . . . . . . . . . . . . 50 Nm (36 ft-lbs)
 Final torque . . . . . . . . . . . . . . . . . . . . . . . . . . . . . . . . . . . . . . . . . 3 Nm (2.2 ft-lbs)
Steering stem nut . . . . . . . . . . . . . . . . . . . . . . . . . . . . . . . . . . . . . . 110 Nm (80 ft-lbs)
Valve adjuster locknuts . . . . . . . . . . . . . . . . . . . . . . . . . . . . . . . . . . 27 Nm (19 ft-lbs)
Rocker cover bolts . . . . . . . . . . . . . . . . . . . . . . . . . . . . . . . . . . . . . . 10 Nm (7.2 ft-lbs)
Final drive filler and drain plugs . . . . . . . . . . . . . . . . . . . . . . . . . . . 23 Nm (17 ft-lbs)

## Recommended lubricants and fluids
Fuel grade . . . . . . . . . . . . . . . . . . . . . . . . . . . . . . . . . . . . . . . . . . . . Regular unleaded gasoline (petrol)
Engine/transmission oil
 Type . . . . . . . . . . . . . . . . . . . . . . . . . . . . . . . . . . . . . . . . . . . . . . . API grade SE or SF (minimum)
 Viscosity
  Consistently below 15 degrees C (60 degrees F) . . . . . . . . . . . . SAE 10W30
  Consistently above 5 degrees C (40 degrees F) . . . . . . . . . . . . SAE 20W40
 Capacity
  With filter change . . . . . . . . . . . . . . . . . . . . . . . . . . . . . . . . . . . 3.1 liters (3.3 US qt, 5.46 Imperial pt)
  Oil change only . . . . . . . . . . . . . . . . . . . . . . . . . . . . . . . . . . . . . 3.0 liters (3.2 US qt, 5.28 Imperial pt)
Brake fluid . . . . . . . . . . . . . . . . . . . . . . . . . . . . . . . . . . . . . . . . . . . . DOT 4
Final gear
 Type . . . . . . . . . . . . . . . . . . . . . . . . . . . . . . . . . . . . . . . . . . . . . . . SAE 80 API GL-4 hypoid gear oil
 Capacity . . . . . . . . . . . . . . . . . . . . . . . . . . . . . . . . . . . . . . . . . . . 0.20 liters (6.76 US fl oz, 7.04 Imp fl oz)
Wheel bearings . . . . . . . . . . . . . . . . . . . . . . . . . . . . . . . . . . . . . . . . Medium weight, lithium-based multi-purpose grease
Swingarm pivot bearings . . . . . . . . . . . . . . . . . . . . . . . . . . . . . . . . Medium weight, lithium-based multi-purpose grease
Cables and lever pivots . . . . . . . . . . . . . . . . . . . . . . . . . . . . . . . . . Chain and cable lubricant or 10W30 motor oil
Sidestand/centerstand pivots . . . . . . . . . . . . . . . . . . . . . . . . . . . . Chain and cable lubricant or 10W30 motor oil
Brake pedal/shift lever pivots . . . . . . . . . . . . . . . . . . . . . . . . . . . . . Chain and cable lubricant or 10W30 motor oil
Throttle grip . . . . . . . . . . . . . . . . . . . . . . . . . . . . . . . . . . . . . . . . . . . Multi-purpose grease or dry film lubricant

**Component locations on right side - XV535 model**

1  Fuel filter
2  Battery
3  Air filter
4  Front brake fluid
   reservoir
5  Throttle cable adjuster
6  Steering head
   bearings
7  Brake pads
8  Engine oil filter
9  Rear brake light switch
10 Rear cylinder spark plug
11 Rear brake adjuster

**Component locations on left side - XV535 model**

1  Clutch cable upper
   adjuster
2  Valves
3  Idle speed and
   synchronizing screw
4  Final drive filler/level plug
5  Final drive drain plug
6  Clutch cable lower
   adjuster
7  Timing plug
8  Engine oil drain plug
9  Engine oil sightglass
10 Engine oil filler cap
11 Front cylinder spark
   plug

1  Battery
2  Steering head bearings
3  Front brake fluid reservoir
4  Throttle cable adjuster
5  Valves
6  Engine oil filter
7  Rear cylinder spark plug
8  Rear brake light switch
9  Rear brake adjuster

1  Clutch cable upper
   adjuster
2  Idle speed and
   synchronizing screws
3  Fuel filter
4  Air filter
5  Drive chain adjuster -
   XV920R and TR1
6  Drive chain inspection
   plug - XV920R and TR1
7  Clutch cable lower
   adjuster
8  Engine oil sightglass
9  Engine oil drain plug
10 Timing cover
11 Engine oil filler
12 Front cylinder spark plug
13 Brake pads
14 Final drive filler/level plug
   - XV750 and 920 Virago
15 Final drive drain plug -
   XV750 and 920 Virago

Component locations on right side - 1981 to 1983 XV750/920 and all TR1 models

Component locations on left side - 1981 to 1983 XV750/920 and all TR1 models

**Component locations on right side - 1984-on XV700, 750, 1000 and 1100 models**

1  Battery
2  Rear cylinder spark plug
3  Idle speed and synchronizing screws
4  Front brake fluid reservoir
5  Throttle cable adjuster
6  Steering head bearings
7  Air filter
8  Brake pads
9  Engine oil filter
10 Rear brake light switch
11 Rear brake adjuster

**Component locations on left side - 1984-on XV700, 750, 1000 and 1100 models**

1  Clutch cable upper adjuster
2  Valves
3  Fuel filter - XV700/750
4  Fuel filter - XV1000/1100
5  Final drive filler/level plug
6  Final drive drain plug
7  Clutch cable lower adjuster
8  Timing cover
9  Engine oil sightglass
10 Engine oil drain plug
11 Engine oil filler cap
12 Front cylinder spark plug

**Note:** *The pre-ride inspection outlined in the owner's manual covers checks and maintenance that should be carried out on a daily basis. It's condensed and included in 'Daily (pre-ride) checks' at the beginning of this manual to remind you of its importance. Always perform the pre-ride inspection at every maintenance interval (in addition to the procedures listed). The intervals listed below are the shortest intervals recommended by the manufacturer for each particular operation during the model years covered in this manual. Your owner's manual may have different intervals for your model.*

## Daily or pre-ride

☐ *See 'Daily (pre-ride) checks' at the beginning of this manual.*

## After the initial 600 miles/1000 km

**Note:** *This check is usually performed by a Yamaha dealer after the first 600 miles (1000 km) from new. Thereafter, maintenance is carried out acccording to the following intervals of the schedule.*

## Every 300 miles/500 km

*Carry out all the items under 'Daily (pre-ride) checks', plus the following*
☐ Check/adjust the drive chain slack (if equipped) (Section 1)

## Every 4000 miles/6000 km or 6 months

*Carry out all the items under the 300 miles (500 km) check, plus the following*
☐ Change the engine oil (Section 2)
☐ Clean the air filter element and replace it if necessary (Section 3)
☐ Adjust the valve clearances (Section 4)
☐ Check cylinder compression (Section 5)
☐ Clean and gap the spark plugs (Section 6)
☐ Lubricate the clutch cable, throttle cable(s) and speedometer cable (Section 7)
☐ Check/adjust throttle cable free play (Section 8)
☐ Check/adjust the idle speed (Section 9)
☐ Check/adjust the carburetor synchronization (Section 10)
☐ Adjust front brake free play (Section 11)
☐ Check/adjust the brake pedal position (Section 11)
☐ Check the brake disc(s) and pads (Section 12)
☐ Check the rear brake shoes for wear (Section 12)
☐ Check the operation of the brake light (Section 13)
☐ Lubricate the clutch and brake lever pivots (Section 7)
☐ Lubricate the shift/brake pedal pivots and the sidestand/centerstand pivots (Section 7)
☐ Check the steering (Section 14)
☐ Check the front forks for proper operation and fluid leaks (Section 15)
☐ Check the tires, wheels and wheel bearings (Section 16)
☐ Check the battery electrolyte level and specific gravity; inspect the breather tube (Section 17)

## Every 4000 miles/6000 km or 6 months (continued)

☐ Check the exhaust system for leaks and check the tightness of the fasteners (Section 18)
☐ Check the cleanliness of the fuel system and the condition of the fuel lines and vacuum hoses (Section 19)
☐ Inspect the crankcase ventilation system (Section 20)
☐ Check the operation of the sidestand switch (Section 21)
☐ Check the security of all fasteners (Section 22)
☐ Check/adjust the shift linkage (Section 23)

## Every 8,000 miles/12,000 km or 12 months

*Carry out all the items under the 4000 miles (6000 km) check, plus the following*
☐ Change the engine oil and oil filter (Section 2)
☐ Replace the spark plugs (Section 6)
☐ Check final gear oil level (if equipped) (Section 24)

## Every 12,000 miles /18,000 km

*Carry out all the items under the 4000 miles (6000 km) check, and the 8000 miles (12,000 km) check, if appropriate, plus the following*
☐ Repack the swingarm bearings (Chapter 5)

## Every 16,000 miles /24,000 km or two years

*Carry out all the items under the 8000 miles (12,000 km) check, and the 12,000 miles (18,000 km) check, if appropriate, plus the following*
☐ Change the final gear oil (if equipped) (Section 24)
☐ Clean and lubricate the steering head bearings (Section 14)

## Every 30,000 miles/50,000 km

☐ Replace the drive chain (if equipped) (Section 1)

## Every two years

☐ Replace the brake master cylinder and caliper seals (Section 25)
☐ Change the brake fluid (Section 26)

## Every four years

☐ Replace the brake hose(s) (Section 27)

**Decals at various locations on the motorcycle include such information as tire pressures . . .**

**. . . special precautions for air-adjustable front forks . . .**

**. . . and drive chain service procedures**

# Introduction

This Chapter covers in detail the checks and procedures necessary for the tune-up and routine maintenance of your motorcycle. Section 1 includes the routine maintenance schedule, which is designed to keep the machine in proper running condition and prevent possible problems. The remaining Sections contain detailed procedures for carrying out the items listed on the maintenance schedule, as well as additional maintenance information designed to increase reliability.

Since routine maintenance plays such an important role in the safe and efficient operation of your motorcycle, it is presented here as a comprehensive check list. For the rider who does all his own maintenance, these lists outline the procedures and checks that should be done on a routine basis.

Maintenance information is printed on labels attached to the motorcycle (see illustrations). If the information on the labels differs from that included here, use the information on the label.

Deciding where to start or plug into the routine maintenance schedule depends on several factors. If you have a motorcycle whose warranty has recently expired, and if it has been maintained according to the warranty standards, you may want to pick up routine maintenance as it coincides with the next mileage or calendar interval. If you have owned the machine for some time but have never performed any maintenance on it, then you may want to start at the nearest interval and include some additional procedures to ensure that nothing important is overlooked. If you have just had a major engine overhaul, then you may want to start the maintenance routine from the beginning. If you have a used machine and have no knowledge of its history or maintenance record, you may desire to combine all the checks into one large service initially and then settle into the maintenance schedule prescribed.

The Sections which outline the inspection and maintenance procedures are written as step-by-step comprehensive guides to the performance of the work. They explain in detail each of the routine inspections and maintenance procedures on the check list. References to additional information in applicable Chapters is also included and should not be overlooked.

Before beginning any maintenance or repair, the machine should be cleaned thoroughly, especially around the oil filter, spark plugs, cylinder head covers, side covers, carburetors, etc. Cleaning will help ensure that dirt does not contaminate the engine and will allow you to detect wear and damage that could otherwise easily go unnoticed.

# Every 300 miles/500 km

### 1 Drive chain and sprockets (chain drive models) - check, adjustment and lubrication

1 The drive chain on models so equipped is completely enclosed in a housing and operates in grease, so periodic lubrication isn't necessary. If the chain appears dry during inspection, refer to Chapter 5 and remove it for inspection.

### Check

2 To check the chain, place the bike on its centerstand and shift the transmission into Neutral. Make sure the ignition switch is off.
3 Pry the cover from the large hole at the lower front of the rear sprocket housing (see illustration).
4 Push up on the bottom run of the chain and measure the slack. Do this every inch or so along the chain until you find the tightest point.

5 Pry the chain up and down and measure its movement, then compare your measurements to the value listed in this Chapter's Specifications. If the bike is equipped with a

**1.3 Look through the viewing hole to measure chain slack**

scale next to the viewing hole (see illustration 1.3), the center pins of the chain should stay between the marks. As wear occurs, the chain will actually stretch, which means adjustment usually involves removing some slack from the chain.
6 The chain should be replaced at the specified mileage interval (see Chapter 5).

### Adjustment

7 If you haven't already done so, rotate the rear wheel until the chain is positioned with the least amount of slack present.
8 Remove the cotter pin from the axle nut and loosen the nut (see illustration).
9 Loosen and back-off the locknuts on the adjuster bolts (see illustration).
10 Turn the axle adjusting nut on both sides of the swingarm until the proper chain tension is obtained (get the adjuster on the chain side close, then set the adjuster on the opposite side). Be sure to turn the adjusting nuts evenly

to keep the rear wheel in alignment. If the adjusting nuts reach the end of their travel, the chain is excessively worn and should be replaced with a new one (see Chapter 5).

**11** When the chain has the correct amount of slack, make sure the marks on the adjusters correspond to the same relative marks on each side of the swingarm. Tighten the axle nut to the torque listed in the Chapter 6 Specifications, then install a new cotter pin and bend it properly. If necessary, turn the nut an additional amount to line up the cotter pin hole with the castellations in the nut - don't loosen the nut to do this.

**12** Tighten the chain adjuster locknuts securely.

1.8 Remove the cotter pin and loosen the nut; the lines in the frame are used for chain adjustment

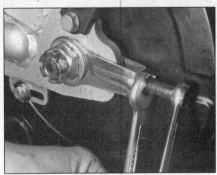

1.9 Loosen and hold the locknut and turn the adjusting bolt to adjust chain slack

# Every 4000 miles/6000 km or 6 months

### 2 Engine oil/filter - change

**1** Consistent routine oil and filter changes are the single most important maintenance procedure you can perform on a motorcycle. The oil not only lubricates the internal parts of the engine, transmission and clutch, but it also acts as a coolant, a cleaner, a sealant, and a protectant. Because of these demands,

**HAYNES HiNT** *Saving a little money on the difference in cost between a good oil and a cheap oil won't pay off if the engine is damaged.*

the oil takes a terrific amount of abuse and should be replaced often with new oil of the recommended grade and type.

**2** Before changing the oil and filter, warm up the engine so the oil will drain easily. Be careful when draining the oil, as the exhaust

pipes, the engine, and the oil itself can cause severe burns.

**3** Support the motorcycle securely over a clean drain pan. Remove the oil filler cap to vent the crankcase and act as a reminder that there is no oil in the engine.

**4** Refer to the appropriate sub-section according to your model.

### XV535 models

**5** Remove the hex-headed oil drain plug, located in the left side of the engine, and allow the old oil to drain fully into the pan **(see illustration)**.

**6** Remove the three Allen bolts from the filter cover and remove the cover **(see illustration)**. Withdraw the oil filter from the engine **(see illustration)**.

**7** Use rags to clean all traces of old oil from the filter housing and cover. Renew the cover O-ring **(see illustration)**.

**8** Install the new filter in the casing with its shoulder facing inwards **(see illustration)**. Check that the cover O-ring is still in place and refit the cover; tighten its bolts to the specified torque setting.

**9** Clean the drain plug threads and install a new sealing washer on the drain plug. Install

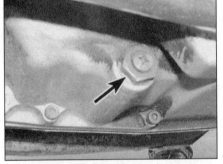

2.5 Oil drain plug location (XV535)

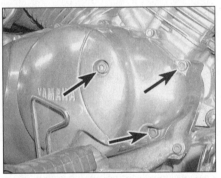

2.6a Remove the three bolts to free the filter cover . . .

2.6b . . . and withdraw the old filter (XV535)

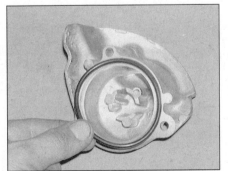

2.7 Renew the cover O-ring (XV535)

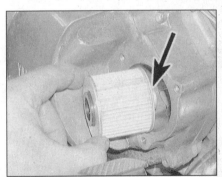

2.8 Install the new filter with its shoulder (arrow) facing inwards (XV535)

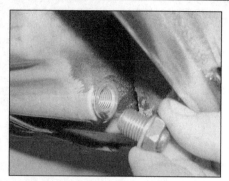

2.9 Install the drain plug using a new sealing washer (XV535)

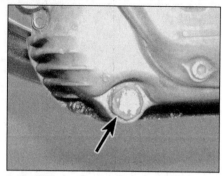

2.11 Oil drain plug location (XV700 to 1100)

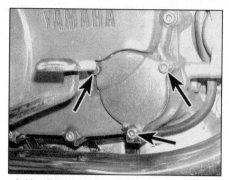

2.12a Remove the three bolts to free the filter cover . . .

2.12b . . . and withdraw the old filter (XV700 to 1100)

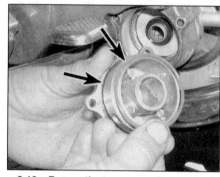

2.13a Renew the two cover O-rings . . .

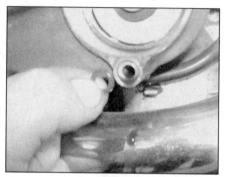

2.13b . . . and the small O-ring set in the casing (XV700 to 1100)

the drain plug and tighten it to the specified torque setting **(see illustration)**.

**10** Fill the crankcase up to the proper level with the correct oil (see *Daily (pre-ride) checks*) and install the filler cap. Run the engine for a few minutes, then recheck the oil level and top up if necessary. Check that there are no leaks from the filter cover or drain plug.

### XV700, 750, 920, 1000 and 1100 models

**11** Remove the oil drain plug, located in the left side of the engine, and allow the old oil to drain fully into the pan **(see illustration)**.

**12** Remove the three Allen bolts from the filter cover and remove the cover **(see illustration)**. Withdraw the oil filter from the engine **(see illustration)**.

**13** Use rags to clean all traces of old oil from the filter housing and cover. Renew the cover O-rings set in the groove and against the shoulder **(see illustration)**, plus the small O-ring set in the casing oil passage **(see illustration)**.

**14** Install the new filter in the casing with its shoulder facing outwards **(see illustration)**. Check that the two cover O-rings are still in position and the small O-ring is located in the oil passage (use a dab of grease around the outside of the O-ring to help it stay in place), then refit the cover. Install the cover bolts, noting the starter motor lead clamp on the lower bolt, and tighten the bolts to the specified torque setting.

**15** Clean the drain plug threads and install a new sealing washer on the drain plug. Install the drain plug and tighten it to the specified torque setting **(see illustration)**.

**16** Fill the crankcase up to the proper level with the correct oil (see Daily (pre-ride) checks) and install the filler cap. Run the engine for a few minutes, then recheck the oil level and top up if necessary. Check that there are no leaks from the filter cover or drain plug.

> **HAYNES HINT** *Check the old oil carefully - if it is very metallic-coloured, then the engine is experiencing wear from running-in (new engine) or insufficient lubrication. If there are flakes or chips of metal in the oil, then something is drastically wrong internally and the engine will have to be disassembled for inspection and repair. If there are pieces of fibre-like material in the oil, the clutch is experiencing excessive wear and should be checked.*

2.14 Install the new filter with its shoulder (arrow) facing outwards (XV700 to 1100)

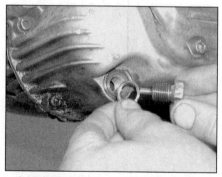

2.15 Install the drain plug using a new sealing washer (XV700 to 1100)

OIL CARE

OIL BANK LINE
**0800 66 33 66**
www.oilbankline.org.uk

*Note: It is antisocial and illegal to dump oil down the drain. To find the location of your local oil recycling bank, call this number free. In the USA, note that any oil supplier must accept used oil for recycling*

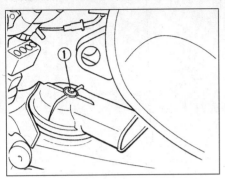

3.2  Remove the screw (1), then lift the housing cover

3.5a  Remove the case cover bolts (arrows) . . .

3.5b  . . . be careful not to lose the spacer tubes and washers

## 3  Air filter element - servicing

### XV535 models

**1**  Remove the top cover (see Chapter 7) or upper fuel tank (see Chapter 3).
**2**  Remove the cover screw and lift off the housing cover (see illustration). Inspect the cover O-ring and replace it if it's damaged or deteriorated.
**3**  Lift out the filter element.

### 1981 through 1983 and all TR1 models

**4**  Remove the left side cover (see Chapter 7).
**5**  Remove the Allen bolts and detach the air filter housing from the motorcycle (see illustrations).
**6**  Lay the housing on a workbench. Remove the screws that hold the halves of the assembly together, then separate them and lift out the element (see illustration).
**7**  Check the filter housing-to-frame seal and the seals inside the filter housing for deterioration or brittleness (see illustrations). Replace the seals as necessary.

### 1984 and later XV700 through 1100 models

**8**  Remove the fuel tank (see Chapter 3).
**9**  Loosen the air duct clamp bolt and remove the mounting bolts, then take the air filter case off the motorcycle (see illustration).
**10**  Remove the air filter case cover (see illustration). Remove the element mounting screw and take the element out (see illustration).

### All models

**11**  Tap the element on a hard surface to shake out dirt. If compressed air is available, use it to clean the element by blowing from the inside out. If the element is extremely dirty or torn, or if dirt can't be blown or tapped out, replace it with a new one.
**12**  Reinstall the filter by reversing the removal procedure. Make sure the element is seated properly in the filter housing before installing the cover.
**13**  Install all components removed for access.

3.6  Separate the housing halves and take the filter element out

3.7a  Check the seal between the filter housing and the frame . . .

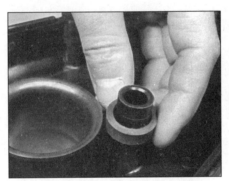

3.7b  . . . and the seals inside the filter housing; replace them if they're deteriorated or brittle

3.9  Loosen the clamp bolt and remove the Allen bolts, then detach the air filter case

3.10a  Remove the cover from the inside of the case

3.10b  Remove the filter element retaining screw, detach the mounting tab and lift out the element

**4.7a Remove the cover bolts (arrows) . . .**

**4.7b . . . and lift the cover off**

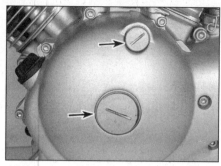

**4.8 Unscrew the timing plug (upper arrow) and the crankcase cover plate (lower arrow)**

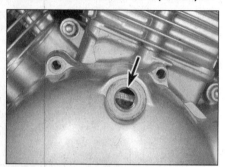

**4.9a The rear cylinder timing mark is the line next to the "T"; align it with the notch (arrow)**

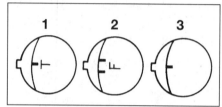

**4.9b XV535 timing marks**

1 Rear cylinder top dead center mark
2 Front cylinder firing range mark
3 Front cylinder top dead center mark

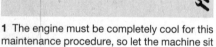

## 4 Valve clearances - check and adjustment

**1** The engine must be completely cool for this maintenance procedure, so let the machine sit overnight before beginning.

**2** Disconnect the cable from the negative terminal of the battery. Remove the spark plugs (see Section 6) so the crankshaft is easier to turn.

**3** Lift or remove the seat (see Chapter 7).

### XV535 models

**4** If you're working on an early model without an upper fuel tank, remove the top cover (see Chapter 7).

**5** If you're working on a later model with an upper fuel tank, remove it (see Chapter 3).

**6** Remove the left and right front side cover (see Chapter 3). Remove the left side cover bracket and the left side cover bracket/electrical component board.

**7** Remove the rocker covers **(see illustrations)**.

**8** Remove the timing plug and the crankcase cover plate from the left side of the engine **(see illustration)**.

**9** Turn the crankshaft clockwise with a socket on the turning bolt (located inside the crankcase cover plate). Watch the edge of the alternator rotor (visible through the timing plug hole) and stop turning when the line next to the T mark is aligned with the notch inside the hole **(see illustrations)**. This places the rear

cylinder at top dead center (TDC) on its compression stroke.

**10** With the engine in this position, both of the valves for the rear cylinder can be checked.

**11** Start with the intake valve clearance. Insert a feeler gauge of the thickness listed in this Chapter's Specifications between the rocker arm and valve stem **(see illustration)**. Pull the feeler gauge out slowly - you should feel a slight drag. If there's no drag, the clearance is too loose. If there's a heavy drag, the clearance is too tight.

**12** To adjust the clearance, loosen the rocker arm locknut with a box wrench (ring spanner) **(see illustration 4.11)**. Turn the adjusting screw with a screwdriver or Allen wrench to change the clearance, then tighten the locknut.

**13** Recheck the clearance with the feeler gauge to make sure it didn't change when you tightened the locknut. Readjust it if necessary.

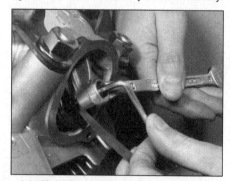

**4.11 Hold the locknut with a box wrench and adjust the valve clearance with an Allen wrench**

**14** Turn the engine clockwise to align the front cylinder's timing mark with the notch in the timing window **(see illustration 4.9b and the accompanying illustration)**. With the timing mark aligned, wiggle the front cylinder's rocker arms. There should be a slight amount of clearance between the rocker arms and valve stems. If the rocker arms are tight, the front piston is on its exhaust stroke, not its compression stroke. Rotate the crankshaft one full turn, line up the timing mark again, then wiggle the rocker arms to be sure the front cylinder is on the compression stroke.

**15** Perform Steps 11 through 13 above on the front cylinder rocker arms to adjust the front cylinder's valve clearances.

**16** Check the O-rings on the rocker covers, timing plug and crankcase cover plate and replace them if they're flattened, broken or have been leaking.

**17** Install the rocker covers and tighten their bolts to the torque listed in this Chapter's Specifications.

**18** Install all components removed for access.

### XV700 through 1100 models

**19** Remove the seat (see Chapter 7) and the fuel tank (see Chapter 3).

**20** If you're working on a 1981 through 1983 model, remove the side covers if they block access to the tappet covers.

**21** If you're working on a 1984 or later model, remove the air filter housing (see Section 3) and the mixture control valve case (see Chapter 3).

**4.14 The single line on the edge of the alternator rotor is the top dead center mark for the front cylinder**

**22** Remove the rocker covers (see illustration).
**23** Remove the alternator cover from the left side of the engine (see illustration).
**24** Turn the crankshaft clockwise with a socket on the turning bolt (located inside the crankcase cover plate). Watch the edge of the alternator rotor (visible through the timing plug hole) and stop turning when the line next to the T mark is aligned with the pointer inside the hole (see illustrations). This places the rear cylinder at top dead center (TDC) on its compression stroke.
**25** Perform Steps 10 through 15 above to adjust the valve clearances on both cylinders.
**26** Check the O-rings on the rocker covers and alternator cover and replace them if they're flattened, broken or have been leaking.
**27** Install the rocker covers and tighten their bolts to the torque listed in this Chapter's Specifications.
**28** Install all components removed for access.

## 5  Cylinder compression - check

**1** Among other things, poor engine performance may be caused by leaking valves, incorrect valve clearances, a leaking head gasket, or worn pistons, rings and/or cylinder walls. A cylinder compression check will help pinpoint these conditions and can also indicate the presence of excessive carbon deposits in the cylinder heads.
**2** The only tools required are a compression gauge and a spark plug wrench. Depending on the outcome of the initial test, a squirt-type oil can may also be needed.
**3** Start the engine and allow it to reach normal operating temperature.
**4** Support the bike securely so it can't be knocked over during this procedure.
**5** Remove the spark plugs (see Section 6, if necessary). Work carefully - don't strip the spark plug hole threads and don't burn your hands.
**6** Disable the ignition by unplugging the primary wires from the coils (see Chapter 4). Be sure to mark the locations of the wires before detaching them.
**7** Install the compression gauge in one of the spark plug holes.
**8** Hold or block the throttle wide open.
**9** Crank the engine over a minimum of four or five revolutions (or until the gauge reading stops increasing) and observe the initial movement of the compression gauge needle as well as the final total gauge reading. Repeat the procedure for the other cylinder and compare the results to the value listed in this Chapter's Specifications.
**10** If the compression in both cylinders built up quickly and evenly to the specified amount, you can assume the engine upper end is in reasonably good mechanical

**4.22  Lift off the rocker cover**

**4.24a  The rear cylinder timing mark is the line next to the "T"; align it with the pointer inside the hole**

condition. Worn or sticking piston rings and worn cylinders will produce very little initial movement of the gauge needle, but compression will tend to build up gradually as the engine spins over. Valve and valve seat leakage, or head gasket leakage, is indicated by low initial compression which does not tend to build up.
**11** To further confirm your findings, add a small amount of engine oil to each cylinder by inserting the nozzle of a squirt-type oil can through the spark plug holes. The oil will tend to seal the piston rings if they are leaking. Repeat the test for the other cylinder.
**12** If the compression increases significantly after the addition of the oil, the piston rings and/or cylinders are definitely worn. If the compression does not increase, the pressure is leaking past the valves or the head gasket. Leakage past the valves may be due to insufficient valve clearances, burned, warped

**6.2  On XV535 models, remove the Allen bolts and lift off the cylinder head side covers**

**4.23  Remove the crankcase outer cover**

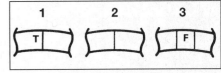

**4.24b  XV700 through 1100 timing marks**

*1  Rear cylinder top dead center mark*
*2  Front cylinder top dead center mark*
*3  Rear cylinder firing range mark*

or cracked valves or valve seats or valves that are hanging up in the guides.
**13** If compression readings are considerably higher than specified, the combustion chambers are probably coated with excessive carbon deposits. It is possible (but not very likely) for carbon deposits to raise the compression enough to compensate for the effects of leakage past rings or valves. Remove the cylinder head and carefully decarbonize the combustion chambers (see Chapter 2).

## 6  Spark plugs - servicing

**1** Make sure your spark plug socket is the correct size before attempting to remove the plugs.
**2** If you're working on an XV535 model, remove the cylinder head side covers (see illustration).
**3** Disconnect the spark plug caps from the spark plugs (see illustrations). If available,

**6.3a  Twist and pull the spark plug caps to detach them from the plugs . . .**

6.3b . . . check the rubber seals for brittleness and the plastic for cracks

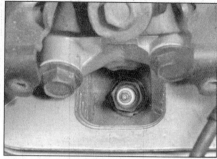

6.3c The plugs are in wells in the cylinder heads; use a socket with a rubber insert to grip the plug

6.7a If the wire gauge doesn't slide between the electrodes with a slight drag, adjustment is required

6.7b To change the gap, bend the side electrode; be careful not to crack the center ceramic insulator

**HAYNES HiNT** *Since the plugs are recessed, slip a short length of hose over the end of the plug to use as a tool to thread it into place. The hose will grip the plug well enough to turn it, but will start to slip if the plug begins to cross-thread in the hole - this will prevent damaged threads and the accompanying repair costs.*

9 Once the plugs are finger tight, the job can be finished with a socket. If a torque wrench is available, tighten the spark plugs to the torque listed in this Chapter's Specifications. If you do not have a torque wrench, tighten the plugs finger tight (until the washers bottom on the cylinder head) then use a wrench to tighten them an additional 1/4 to 1/2 turn. Regardless of the method used, do not over-tighten them.
10 Reconnect the spark plug caps and reinstall the air ducts.

## 7 Lubrication - general

1 Since the controls, cables and various other components of a motorcycle are exposed to the elements, they should be lubricated periodically to ensure safe and trouble-free operation.
2 The footpegs, clutch and brake lever, brake pedal, shift lever and sidestand/centerstand pivots should be lubricated frequently **(see illustrations)**. In order for the lubricant to be applied where it will do the most good, the component should be disassembled. However, if chain and cable lubricant is being used, it can be applied to the pivot joint gaps and will usually work its way into the areas where friction occurs. If motor oil or light grease is being used, apply it sparingly as it may attract dirt (which could cause the controls to bind or wear at an accelerated rate). **Note:** *One of the best lubricants for the control lever pivots is a dry-film lubricant (available from many sources by different names).*
3 To lubricate the throttle and choke cables, disconnect the cable(s) at the lower end, then lubricate the cable with a pressure lube adapter

use compressed air to blow any accumulated debris from around the spark plugs. Remove the plugs **(see illustration)**.
4 Inspect the electrodes for wear. Both the center and side electrodes should have square edges and the side electrode should be of uniform thickness. Look for excessive deposits and evidence of a cracked or chipped insulator around the center electrode. Compare your spark plugs to the color spark plug reading chart at the end of this Manual. Check the threads, the washer and the ceramic insulator body for cracks and other damage.
5 If the electrodes are not excessively worn, and if the deposits can be easily removed with a wire brush, the plugs can be regapped and reused (if no cracks or chips are visible in the insulator). If in doubt concerning the condition

of the plugs, replace them with new ones, as the expense is minimal.
6 Cleaning spark plugs by sandblasting is permitted, provided you clean the plugs with a high flash-point solvent afterwards.
7 Before installing new plugs, make sure they are the correct type and heat range. Check the gap between the electrodes, as they are not preset. For best results, use a wire-type gauge rather than a flat gauge to check the gap **(see illustration)**. If the gap must be adjusted, bend the side electrode only and be very careful not to chip or crack the insulator nose **(see illustration)**. Make sure the washer is in place before installing each plug.
8 Since the cylinder head is made of aluminum, which is soft and easily damaged, thread the plugs into the heads by hand.

7.2a Lubricate the brake pedal pivot . . .

7.2b . . . the footpeg and shift linkage pivots (arrows) - XV1100 shown . . .

7.2c . . . and the brake and clutch lever pivots (brake lever shown; clutch lever similar)

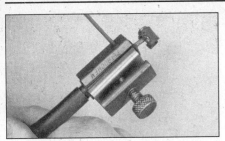

7.3a Lubricating a cable with a pressure lube adapter (make sure the tool seats around the inner cable)

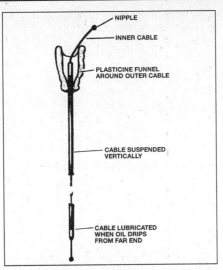

7.3b Oiling a control cable with a funnel

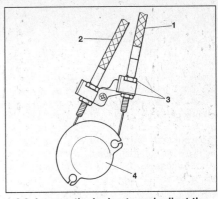

8.9 Loosen the locknuts and adjust the accelerator and decelerator cables

1  Accelerator cable     3  Locknuts
2  Decelerator cable     4  Throttle pulley

(see illustration). If you don't have one, disconnect both ends of the cable and use a funnel (see illustration). See Chapter 3, Part B for the choke cable removal procedure (XV535 models don't have a choke cable). Note: *Yamaha recommends that the throttle twist grip be removed and lubricated whenever the throttle cables are lubricated. Refer to the handlebar switch removal section of Chapter 8.*
4  The speedometer cable should be removed from its housing and lubricated with motor oil or cable lubricant.
5  Refer to Chapter 5 for the swingarm needle bearing and rear suspension linkage lubrication procedures.

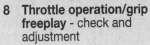

## 8  Throttle operation/grip freeplay - check and adjustment

### Check

1  Make sure the throttle grip rotates easily from fully closed to fully open with the front wheel turned at various angles. The grip should return automatically from fully open to fully closed when released. If the throttle sticks, check the throttle cable(s) for cracks or kinks in the housings. Also, make sure the inner cables are clean and well-lubricated.
2  Check for a small amount of freeplay at the grip and compare the freeplay to the value listed in this Chapter's Specifications. If adjustment is necessary, adjust idle speed first (see Section 9).

### Adjustment

#### Single cable models

3  Loosen the lockwheel at the throttle grip (see illustration 8.12). Turn the adjuster to give a slight amount of freeplay, then tighten the lockwheel.

#### Dual cable models

4  These models use an accelerator cable and a decelerator cable. Initial adjustments are made at the carburetor end of the cable.
5  Remove the seat, and if necessary, the side covers (see Chapter 7).
6  If you're working on an XV535 model, remove the upper fuel tank (see Chapter 3) or the top cover (see Chapter 7).
7  On all except XV535 models, remove the fuel tank (see Chapter 3).

8  Make sure the locknuts at the handlebar throttle cable adjusters are tight (see illustration 8.12).
9  At the carburetors, loosen the cable locknuts (see illustration).
10  Turn the locknuts on the decelerator cable to set freeplay to zero, then tighten the locknuts.
11  Loosen the accelerator cable locknuts, then turn them to bring freeplay at the throttle grip within the range listed in this Chapter's Specifications. Once freeplay is correct, tighten the locknuts.
12  To make fine adjustments, loosen the locknut on the handlebar cable adjuster (see illustration). Turn the adjuster until the desired freeplay is obtained, then retighten the lockwheel.
13  Make sure the throttle grip is in the fully closed position.
14  Make sure the throttle linkage lever contacts the idle adjusting screw when the throttle grip is in the closed throttle position.

⚠ Warning: *Turn the handlebars all the way through their travel with the engine idling. Idle speed should not change. If it does, the cables may be routed incorrectly. Correct this condition before riding the bike.*

8.12 Loosen the lockwheel (A) and turn the adjuster (B) to change freeplay (dual-cable model shown)

## 9  Idle speed - check and adjustment

1  The idle speed should be checked and adjusted before and after the carburetors are synchronized and when it is obviously too high or too low. Before adjusting the idle speed, make sure the valve clearances and spark plug gaps are correct. Also, turn the handlebars back-and-forth and see if the idle speed changes as this is done. If it does, the accelerator cable may not be adjusted correctly, or it may be worn out. This is a dangerous condition that can cause loss of control of the bike. Be sure to correct this problem before proceeding.
2  The engine should be at normal operating temperature, which is usually reached after 10 to 15 minutes of stop and go riding. Support the motorcycle securely and make sure the transmission is in Neutral.
3  Turn the throttle stop screw (see illustration), until the idle speed listed in this Chapter's Specifications is obtained.
4  Snap the throttle open and shut a few times, then recheck the idle speed. If necessary, repeat the adjustment procedure.
5  If a smooth, steady idle can't be achieved, the fuel/air mixture may be incorrect. Refer to Chapter 5 for additional carburetor information.

9.3 The throttle stop screw sets idle speed ('81 - '87 XV700 thru 1100; XV535, '88-on XV750 and 1100 similar)

## 10 Carburetor synchronization - check and adjustment

⚠️ *Warning: Gasoline (petrol) is extremely flammable, so take extra precautions when you work on any part of the fuel system. Don't smoke or allow open flames or bare light bulbs near the work area, and don't work in a garage where a natural gas-type appliance (such as a water heater or clothes dryer) is present. If you spill any fuel on your skin, rinse it off immediately with soap and water. When you perform any kind of work on the fuel system, wear safety glasses and have a class B type fire extinguisher on hand.*

1 Carburetor synchronization is simply the process of adjusting the carburetors so they pass the same amount of fuel/air mixture to each cylinder. This is done by measuring the vacuum produced in each cylinder. Carburetors that are out of synchronization will result in decreased fuel mileage, increased engine temperature, less than ideal throttle response and higher vibration levels.

2 To properly synchronize the carburetors, you will need some sort of vacuum gauge setup, preferably with a gauge for each cylinder, or a mercury manometer, which is a calibrated tube arrangement that utilizes columns of mercury to indicate engine vacuum. You'll also need an auxiliary fuel tank, since the bike's fuel tank must be removed for access to the vacuum fittings and synchronizing screws.

3 A manometer can be purchased from a motorcycle dealer or accessory shop and should have the necessary rubber hoses supplied with it for hooking into the vacuum hose fittings on the carburetors.

4 A vacuum gauge setup can also be purchased from a dealer or fabricated from commonly available hardware and automotive vacuum gauges.

5 The manometer is the more reliable and accurate instrument, and for that reason is preferred over the vacuum gauge setup; however, since the mercury used in the manometer is a liquid, and extremely toxic,

extra precautions must be taken during use and storage of the instrument.

6 Because of the nature of the synchronization procedure and the need for special instruments, most owners leave the task to a dealer service department or a reputable motorcycle repair shop.

### XV535 models

7 Remove the vacuum caps from the intake joint fittings **(see illustration)**. Connect the vacuum gauges or manometer to the fittings.

### 1981 through 1983 models

8 Remove the seat (see Chapter 7). If necessary for access, detach the fuel tank and raise it slightly, leaving the fuel hoses connected (see Chapter 3).

9 Disconnect the smaller hose from the front carburetor's intake joint **(see illustration)**. Remove the rubber cap from the vacuum fitting on the rear carburetor's intake joint, then connect the vacuum gauges or manometer to the hose fitting and vacuum fitting.

### 1984 through 1987 XV700 models

10 Remove the seat (see Chapter 7). Detach the fuel tank at the rear and raise it slightly, leaving the fuel hoses connected.

11 Turn the fuel tap to the PRI position.

12 Disconnect the smaller hose from the front carburetor's intake joint **(see illustration 10.9)**. Remove the rubber cap from the vacuum fitting on the rear carburetor's intake joint, then connect the vacuum gauges or manometer to the hose fitting and vacuum fitting.

### 1984 through 1987 XV1000 and 1100 models

13 Remove the seat (see Chapter 7).

14 Remove the mixture control valve case cover (see Chapter 3). Disconnect the mixture control valve vacuum hose at the T-fitting and connect one of the manometer tubes or vacuum gauges to the fitting.

15 Remove the rubber cap from the vacuum fitting on the rear carburetor's intake joint and connect the other vacuum gauge or manometer tube to it.

### 1988 and later models

16 Remove the seat (see Chapter 7) and the

fuel tank (see Chapter 3). Connect an auxiliary fuel source.

17 If you're working on an 1100 model, remove the left side cover.

18 Disconnect the smaller hose from the front carburetor's intake joint. Remove the rubber cap from the vacuum fitting on the rear carburetor's intake joint, then connect the vacuum gauges or manometer to the hose fitting and vacuum fitting.

### All models

19 Start the engine and let it run until it reaches normal operating temperature.

20 Make sure there are no leaks in the vacuum gauge or manometer setup, as false readings will result.

21 Start the engine and make sure the idle speed is correct. If it isn't, adjust it (see Section 9).

22 The vacuum readings for both of the cylinders should be the same, or at least within the tolerance listed in this Chapter's Specifications. If the vacuum readings vary, adjust as necessary.

23 To perform the adjustment, synchronize the carburetors by turning the synchronizing screw, as needed, until the vacuum is identical or nearly identical for both cylinders **(see illustration 10.9)**. Snap the throttle open and shut 2 or 3 times, then recheck the adjustment and readjust as necessary.

24 When the adjustment is complete, recheck the vacuum readings and idle speed, then stop the engine. Remove the vacuum gauge or manometer and reinstall all parts removed for access.

## 11 Brake lever and pedal position and play - check and adjustment

### Front brakes

1 The front brake lever must have the amount of free play listed in this Chapter's Specifications to prevent brake drag.

2 Operate the lever and check free play. If it's not correct, loosen the adjuster locknut, turn the adjuster to bring free play within the Specifications and tighten the locknut **(see illustration)**.

**10.7 Connect gauges or a manometer (A); get even readings with the screw (B) (XV535; others similar)**

**10.9 Disconnect the smaller hose from the carburetor and connect one of the gauge or manometer tubes**

**11.2 Loosen the locknut and turn the screw to change brake lever freeplay**

**11.4a  Loosen the locknut and turn the bolt to change brake pedal freeplay (this is an XV920) . . .**

**11.4b  . . . and this is an XV1100 (other models similar)**

**12.2  The caliper on chain drive models has a pad inspection window**

### Rear brakes

**3**  The rear brake pedal should be positioned below the top of the footpeg the distance listed in this Chapter's Specifications.

**4**  To adjust the position of the pedal, loosen the locknut on the adjuster, turn the adjuster to set the pedal position and tighten the locknut **(see illustrations)**.

**5**  Check pedal freeplay and compare it to the value listed in this Chapter's Specifications. Adjust if necessary by turning the nut at the rear end of the brake cable or rod.

**6**  If necessary, adjust the brake light switch (see Section 13).

### 12  Brake pads and shoes - wear check

**1**  The front brake pads should be checked at the recommended intervals and replaced with new ones when worn beyond the limit listed in this Chapter's Specifications. Always replace pads in complete sets; if the front brake has two calipers, replace all four pads at the same time.

**2**  To check the front brake pads on chain drive models, flip open the inspection window on the back of the caliper **(see illustration)**. If the pads are worn nearly to the red line, replace them (see Chapter 6).

**3**  On models so equipped, remove the pad cover **(see illustration 2.9a in Chapter 6, Part B)**. Operate the brake lever while you look at the back of the caliper. If the pad wear

indicator is close to the disc **(see illustration)**, the pads are worn excessively and must be replaced with new ones (see Chapter 6).

**4**  On XV535 models, remove the rubber plug from the back of the caliper. Look through the hole and inspect the pads. If the pads are worn near the wear limit listed in the Chapter 6 Specifications, replace them.

**5**  On models without an inspection window or a pad cover, squeeze the front brake lever and look at the edges of the pads. If the pads are worn to near the wear limit listed in the Chapter 6 Specifications, replace them (see Chapter 6).

**6**  To check the rear brake shoes, press the brake pedal firmly while you look at the wear indicator on the brake panel **(see illustration)**. If the indicator pointer is close to the end of its travel, replace the shoes (see Chapter 6).

**7**  If the pads are in good condition, reinstall the covers (if equipped). The words "Uncover for pad service" stamped in the pad covers may be upside down when the cover is installed. This doesn't mean the cover is upside down.

### 13  Brake system - general check

**1**  A routine general check of the brakes will ensure that any problems are discovered and remedied before the rider's safety is jeopardized.

**2**  Check the brake lever and pedal for loose connections, excessive play, bends, and

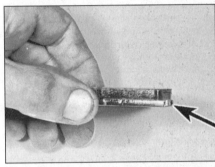

**12.3  If the raised corner (arrow) is close to the disc, the pad is worn and the pads must be replaced**

other damage. Replace any damaged parts with new ones (see Chapter 6).

**3**  Make sure all brake fasteners are tight. Check the brake pads and shoes for wear (see Section 12) and make sure the fluid level in the front brake reservoir is correct (see *'Daily (pre-ride) checks'* at the beginning of this Manual). Look for leaks at the hose connections and check for cracks in the hose(s). If the lever or pedal is spongy, bleed the brakes as described in Chapter 6.

**4**  Make sure the brake light operates when the brake lever is depressed.

**5**  Make sure the brake light is activated just before the rear brake takes effect.

**6**  If adjustment is necessary, hold the switch so it won't rotate and turn the adjusting nut on the switch body **(see illustrations)** until the brake light is activated when required. If the

**12.6  If the pointer is near the end of its travel with the brake pedal depressed, replace the shoes**

**13.6a  Hold the switch so it won't rotate and rotate the nut (arrow) (this is an XV535) . . .**

**13.6b  . . . and this is an XV1100 (700 through 1000 models similar)**

switch doesn't operate the brake lights, check it as described in Chapter 8.

**7** The front brake light switch is not adjustable. If it fails to operate properly, replace it with a new one (see Chapter 8).

### 14 Steering head bearings - check, adjustment and lubrication

**1** The 1987 to 2000 535 models, 1981 to 1983 XV750 and 920 models and all TR1 models use uncaged ball bearings in the steering head. The 2001-on 535 models use caged ball steering head bearings. The 1984-on XV700 to 1100 models use taper roller steering head bearings. All types of bearing can become dented, rough or loose during normal use of the machine. In extreme cases, worn or loose steering head bearings can cause steering wobble which is potentially dangerous.

### Check

**2** To check the bearings, support the motorcycle securely and block the machine so the front wheel is in the air.

**3** Point the wheel straight ahead and slowly move the handlebars from side-to-side. Dents or roughness in the bearing races will be felt and the bars will not move smoothly.

**4** Next, grasp the wheel and try to move it forward and backward. Any looseness in the steering head bearings will be felt as front-to-rear movement of the fork legs. If play is felt in the bearings, adjust the steering head as follows.

### Adjustment

#### XV535 models

**5** Remove the headlight lens (see Chapter 8). Label and disconnect the wiring connectors inside the headlight body. Remove the two bolts that secure the headlight assembly to the lower triple clamp and pull the assembly (together with the turn indicator brackets) down out of the way.

**6** Remove the upper triple clamp bolts, together with the cable guides (see Chapter 5).

**7** Remove the brake master cylinder (see Chapter 6).

**8** Remove the safety clips, nuts and washers that secure the handlebar brackets to the upper triple clamp (see Chapter 5). Lift the handlebar and bracket assembly away from the motorcycle. Separate the indicator light assembly from the handle bracket and lower it out of the way.

**9** Unbolt the speedometer bracket and move the speedometer out of the way (see Chapter 8).

**10** Remove the steering stem nut and the upper triple clamp **(see illustration)**.

**11** Loosen the steering head ring nut all the way **(see illustration)**.

**12** Attach the ring nut wrench to a torque wrench so they form a right angle. Tighten the ring nut to the initial torque listed in this Chapter's Specifications, then loosen it all the way again.

**13** Retighten the ring nut to the final torque listed in this Chapter's Specifications.

**14** Turn the steering from lock to lock and check for binding. If there is any, remove the bearings for inspection (see Chapter 5).

**15** If the steering operates properly, reinstall all parts previously removed. Tighten steering stem nut, triple clamp bolts and handlebar nuts to the torques listed in the Chapter 5 Specifications.

#### 1981 through 1983 XV750 through 1000 models

**16** Loosen the pinch bolt that passes through the rear side of the upper triple clamp.

**17** Beneath the upper triple clamp are two ring nuts **(see illustration)**. Loosen the upper one with a spanner wrench (C-spanner) so the lower nut is free to turn.

**18** Tighten the lower ring nut a little at a time just enough to remove any front-to-rear play in the steering head.

**Caution: Don't overtighten the nut.**

**19** To check the adjustment, place the handlebars in their center position, then move them all the way to right and left. With the front wheel off the ground, the handlebar should move all the way from center to the left or right stop with just a tap. If it takes more effort than this, the bearings are too tight.

#### 1984 and later XV700 through 1100 models

**20** Remove the seat (see Chapter 7) and the fuel tank (see Chapter 3).

**21** Remove the lower screw from the headlight assembly.

**22** Loosen the upper triple clamp bolts (see Chapter 5). This allows the necessary vertical movement of the steering stem in relation to the fork tubes.

**23** Remove the handlebars and upper triple clamp (see Chapter 5).

**24** Remove the lockwasher from the ring nuts.

**25** Use a ring nut wrench (Yamaha tool no. YU-33975/part no. 90890-01430 or equivalent) to remove the upper ring nut.

**26** Carefully tighten the lower ring nut to the initial torque listed in this Chapter's Specifications, then loosen it all the way and retighten to the final torque listed in this Chapter's Specifications.

**27** Turn the steering from lock to lock and check for binding. If there is any, remove the bearings for inspection (see Chapter 7).

**28** If the steering operates properly, install the upper ring nut. Tighten the upper ring nut with fingers so its slots align with those of the lower ring nut (don't allow the lower ring nut to turn). If necessary, use the ring nut wrench to keep the lower ring nut from turning while you tighten the upper ring nut.

**29** Install the lockwasher with its tabs in the ring nut slots.

**30** Recheck the steering head bearings for play as described above. If necessary, repeat the adjustment procedure. Reinstall all parts previously removed. Tighten the steering stem nut and triple clamp bolts to the torques listed in the Chapter 5 Specifications.

### Lubrication

**31** Periodic cleaning and repacking of the steering head bearings is recommended by the manufacturer. Refer to Chapter 5 for steering head bearing lubrication and replacement procedures.

**14.10 Remove the steering stem bolt and lift off the upper triple clamp**

**14.11 Turn the ring nut to adjust steering head bearing play**

**14.17 Loosen the upper ring nut and adjust steering head bearing play with the lower ring nut**

15.3 Check above and below the fork seals (arrow) for signs of oil leakage

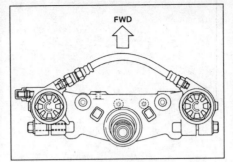

15.13a If there's an air hose between the forks, add air through the air charging valve on the side

15.13b Use an accurate gauge when measuring fork air pressure

## 15 Suspension - servicing

### Check

1 The suspension components must be maintained in top operating condition to ensure rider safety. Loose, worn or damaged suspension parts decrease the vehicle's stability and control.

2 While standing alongside the motorcycle, lock the front brake and push on the handlebars to compress the forks several times. See if they move up-and-down smoothly without binding. If binding is felt, the forks should be disassembled and inspected as described in Chapter 5.

3 Carefully inspect the area around the fork seals for any signs of fork oil leakage (see illustration). If leakage is evident, the seals must be replaced as described in Chapter 5.

4 Check the tightness of all suspension nuts and bolts to be sure none have worked loose.

5 Inspect the shock for fluid leakage and tightness of the mounting nuts. If leakage is found, the shock should be replaced.

6 Support the bike securely so it can't be knocked over during this procedure. Grab the swingarm on each side, just ahead of the axle. Rock the swingarm from side to side - there should be no discernible movement at the rear. If there's a little movement or a slight clicking can be heard, make sure the pivot bolt or shafts are tight. If they're tight but movement is still noticeable, the swingarm will have to be removed and the bearings replaced as described in Chapter 5.

7 Inspect the tightness of the rear suspension nuts and bolts (refer to the Chapter 5 Specifications).

### Adjustments

8 Suspension settings can be adjusted on some models. Note: *The forks must be in good condition with seals that don't leak in order to make accurate adjustments.*

⚠️ Warning: The front fork air pressure, the fork damping settings (if equipped) and the

rear shock absorber settings (twin-shock models) must be even to prevent unstable handling.

9 On 1981 through 1983 XV750 and XV920 models and all TR1 models, front fork air pressure is adjustable. On the XV920J model, front fork damping is also adjustable. The rear suspension unit is adjustable for air pressure and damping.

10 On all XV535 models and 1984-on XV700/750 models, the front forks are not adjustable, but the rear shocks have preload adjustment.

11 On 1984 through 1993 XV1000/1100 models front fork air pressure is adjustable.

On all XV1000/1100 models the rear shocks have preload and damping adjustment.

### 1981 through 1983 XV750/920 and all TR1 models

12 Support the bike securely so it can't be knocked over during this procedure. Raise the front wheel off the ground.

13 On models with separate air charging valves mounted in the tops of the forks, remove the rubber cap from each front fork. If there's an air hose connecting the two forks (see illustration), remove the plastic cap from the air charging valve. Measure fork air pressure with an accurate gauge (see illustrations).

| XV750 SE, H and J models | Front fork | Rear shock absorber | | Loading condition | | | |
|---|---|---|---|---|---|---|---|
| | Air pressure | Air pressure | Damping adjuster | Solo rider | With passenger | With accessory equipments | With accessory equipments and passenger |
| | 0.4 ~ 0.8 kg/cm² (5.7 ~ 11.4 psi) | 1.0 ~ 2.0 kg/cm² (14.2 ~ 28.4 psi) | 1 ~ 3 | O | | | |
| | | 3.0 ~ 4.0 kg/cm² (42.7 ~ 56.9 psi) | 3, 4 | | O | | |
| | | | 4, 5 | | | O | |
| | 0.8 ~ 1.2 kg/cm² (11.4 ~ 17.1 psi) | 4.0 kg/cm² (56.9 psi) | 6 | | | | O |

| XV920 RH, RJ and TR1 models | Front fork | Rear shock absorber | | Loading condition | | | |
|---|---|---|---|---|---|---|---|
| | Air pressure | Air pressure | Damping adjuster | Solo rider | With passenger | With accessory equipments | With accessory equipments and passenger |
| | 0.4 ~ 0.8 kg/cm² (5.7 ~ 11.4 psi) | 1.0 ~ 2.0 kg/cm² (14.2 ~ 28.4 psi) | 1, 2 | O | | | |
| | | 2.0 ~ 3.0 kg/cm² (28.4 ~ 42.7 psi) | 2,3 | | O | | |
| | 0.6 ~ 1.0 kg/cm² (8.5 ~ 14.2 psi) | 3.0 ~ 4.0 kg/cm² (42.7 ~ 56.9 psi) | 4, 5 | | | O | |
| | 0.8 ~ 1.2 kg/cm² (11.4 ~ 17.1 psi) | 4.0 kg/cm² (56.9 psi) | 5, 6 | | | | O |

| XV920 J, K and MK models | Front fork | | Rear shock absorber | | Loading condition | | | |
|---|---|---|---|---|---|---|---|---|
| | Air pressure | Damping adjuster | Air pressure | Damping adjuster | Solo rider | With passenger | With accessory equipments | With accessory equipments and passenger |
| | 39.2 ~ 78.5 kPa (0.4 ~ 0.8 kg/cm², 5.7 ~ 11 psi) | 1 | 98.1 ~ 196 kPa (1.0 ~ 2.0 kg/cm², 14 ~ 28 psi) | 1, 2, 3 | O | | | |
| | | 2 | 196 ~ 294 kPa (2.0 ~ 3.0 kg/cm², 28 ~ 43 psi) | 3, 4 | | O | | |
| | | 3 | 294 ~ 392 kPa (3.0 ~ 4.0 kg/cm², 43 ~ 57 psi) | 4, 5 | | | O | |
| | 78.5 ~ 118 kPa (0.8 ~ 1.2 kg/cm², 11 ~ 17 psi) | 4 | 392 kPa (4.0 kg/cm², 57 psi) | 6 | | | | O |

15.13c Suspension settings (1981 through 1983 XV750/920 and all TR1 models)

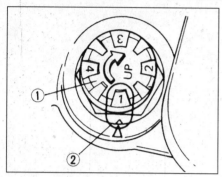

**15.15 XV920J fork damping is adjusted with a knob on top of each fork**

*1 Adjusting knob    2 Index mark*

**15.16a Air pressure and damping for the rear suspension on '81 - '83 models are adjusted with this unit**

**15.16b Take up excessive freeplay with the cable adjusters**

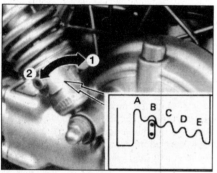

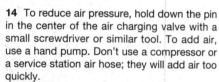

**15.19 Preload adjuster on '84-on XV700/750 models. Turn in direction 2 to increase preload and in direction 1 to reduce it**

**15.20a Preload adjuster on '84-on XV1000 and 1100 models - turn in direction 1 to increase preload and in direction 2 to reduce it**

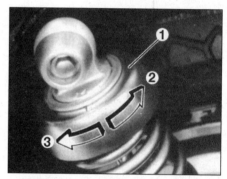

**15.20b Damping adjuster (1) on '84-on XV1000 and 1100 models – turn in direction 2 to reduce damping and in direction 3 to increase it**

**14** To reduce air pressure, hold down the pin in the center of the air charging valve with a small screwdriver or similar tool. To add air, use a hand pump. Don't use a compressor or a service station air hose; they will add air too quickly.

**15** If you're working on an XV920J model, turn the damping adjuster knob on each fork to change the setting **(see illustration)**.

**16** Remove the air valve cap from the rear suspension unit's remote adjuster and check air pressure with an accurate gauge **(see illustration)**. Add or remove air as needed. If

necessary, change the damping setting by turning the adjuster knob. If there's excessive freeplay in the knob, remove the seat and correct it with the cable adjusters **(see illustration)**.

## 1984 and later models

**17** Remove the air valve cap from the side of the fork and check air pressure with an accurate gauge.

**18** To reduce fork air pressure, hold down the pin in the center of the air charging valve with a small screwdriver or similar tool. To add

air, use a hand pump. Don't use a compressor or a service station air hose; they will add air too quickly.

**19** If you're working on an XV535, XV700 or XV750 model, adjust rear suspension by turning the adjuster at the bottom of each shock absorber **(see illustration)**.

**20** If you're working on an XV1000 or 1100, turn the adjuster at the bottom of each shock absorber to set spring preload **(see illustration)**. Turn the adjuster at the top of each shock to adjust damping **(see illustrations)**. **Note:** *Don't leave the damping adjuster between positions or it will automatically adjust to the stiffest setting.*

## 16 Tires/wheels - general check

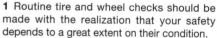

**1** Routine tire and wheel checks should be made with the realization that your safety depends to a great extent on their condition.

**2** Check the tires carefully for cuts, tears, embedded nails or other sharp objects and excessive wear. Operation of the motorcycle with excessively worn tires is extremely hazardous, as traction and handling are directly affected. Measure the tread depth at the center of the tire and replace worn tires with new ones when the tread depth is less than specified.

| | Front fork | Rear shock absorber | | Loading condition | | | |
|---|---|---|---|---|---|---|---|
| | Air pressure | Spring seat | Damping adjuster | Solo rider | With passenger | With accessories, and equipment | With accessories, equipment, and passenger |
| 1 | 39.2 ~ 78.5 kPa (0.4 ~ 0.8 kg/cm², 5.7 ~ 11.4 psi) | 1 ~ 2 | 1 ~ 2 | O | | | |
| 2 | 39.2 ~ 78.5 kPa (0.4 ~ 0.8 kg/cm², 5.7 ~ 11.4 psi) | 3 ~ 5 | 2 ~ 3 | | O | | |
| 3 | 58.8 ~ 98.1 kPa (0.6 ~ 1.0 kg/cm², 8.5 ~ 14.2 psi) | 3 ~ 5 | 3 ~ 4 | | | O | |
| 4 | 78.5 ~ 117.7 kPa (0.8 ~ 1.2 kg/cm², 11.4 ~ 17.1 psi) | 5 | 4 | | | | O |

**15.20c Suspension settings (1984-on XV1000 and XV1100 models)**

16.4 Check tire pressures with an accurate gauge

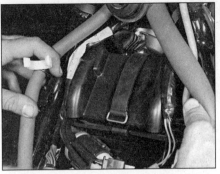

17.4a Unclip the fuel hoses and move them aside . . .

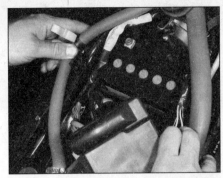

17.4b . . . then remove the securing strap and lift off the battery cover

**3** Repair or replace punctured tires as soon as damage is noted. Do not try to patch a torn tire, as wheel balance and tire reliability may be impaired.

**4** Check the tire pressures when the tires are cold and keep them properly inflated **(see illustration)**. Proper air pressure will increase tire life and provide maximum stability and ride comfort. Keep in mind that low tire pressures may cause the tire to slip on the rim or come off, while high tire pressures will cause abnormal tread wear and unsafe handling.

**5** The cast wheels used on some models are virtually maintenance free, but they should be kept clean and checked periodically for cracks and other damage. Never attempt to repair damaged cast wheels; they must be replaced with new ones.

**6** Where wire spoke wheels are fitted, check them for cracks, flat spots on the rim, bent spokes and other damage. Tap the spokes with a metal screwdriver blade or similar tool and listen to the sound. If the spoke makes a 'clunk' or low-pitched sound it is loose. Spoke tensioning or renewal is a task for a wheel building expert.

**7** Check the valve stem locknuts to make sure they are tight. Also, make sure the valve stem cap is in place and tight. If it is missing, install a new one made of metal or hard plastic.

## 17 Battery electrolyte level/specific gravity - check

*Caution: Be extremely careful when handling or working around the battery. The electrolyte is very caustic and an explosive gas (hydrogen) is given off when the battery is charging. Note: The first Steps describe battery removal. If the electrolyte level is known to be sufficient it won't be necessary to remove the battery.*

**1** This procedure applies to batteries that have removable filler caps, which can be removed to add water to the battery. If the original equipment battery has been replaced by a sealed maintenance-free battery, the electrolyte can't be topped up.

**2** Remove the seat (see Chapter 7).

**3** If necessary for access to remove the battery, remove the side covers (see Chapter 7).

**4** If you're working on an XV535 equipped with an upper fuel tank, detach the fuel hoses from their clips and move them aside. Remove the securing strap and battery cover **(see illustrations)**.

**5** Remove the screws securing the battery cables to the battery terminals (remove the negative cable first, positive cable last) **(see illustration)**. Remove the battery securing strap if you haven't already done so and pull the battery straight up to remove it **(see illustration)**. The electrolyte level will now be visible through the translucent battery case - it should be between the Upper and Lower level marks **(see illustration)**.

**6** If the electrolyte is low, remove the cell

17.5a Pull back the plastic caps (arrows) and undo the terminal screws (negative first, then positive)

17.5c The electrolyte level should be between the marks on the battery case

caps and fill each cell to the upper level mark with distilled water. **Note:** *Some models have a long-life battery equipped with only one filler plug. Do not use tap water (except in an emergency), and do not overfill. The cell holes are quite small, so it may help to use a plastic squeeze bottle with a small spout to add the water. If the level is within the marks on the case, additional water is not necessary.*

**7** Next, check the specific gravity of the electrolyte in each cell with a small hydrometer made especially for motorcycle batteries. These are available from most dealer parts departments or motorcycle accessory stores.

**8** Remove the caps, draw some electrolyte from the first cell into the hydrometer **(see illustration)** and note the specific gravity. Compare the reading to the Specifications

17.5b Lift the battery out

17.8 Check the specific gravity with a hydrometer

listed in this Chapter. **Note:** *Add 0.004 points to the reading for every 10-degrees F above 20-degrees C (68-degrees F) - subtract 0.004 points from the reading for every 10-degrees below 20-degrees C (68-degrees F). Return the electrolyte to the appropriate cell and repeat the check for the remaining cells. When the check is complete, rinse the hydrometer thoroughly with clean water.*

**9** If the specific gravity of the electrolyte in each cell is as specified, the battery is in good condition and is apparently being charged by the machine's charging system.

**10** If the specific gravity is low, the battery is not fully charged. This may be due to corroded battery terminals, a dirty battery case, a malfunctioning charging system, or loose or corroded wiring connections. On the other hand, it may be that the battery is worn out, especially if the machine is old, or that infrequent use of the motorcycle prevents normal charging from taking place.

**11** Be sure to correct any problems and charge the battery if necessary. Refer to Chapter 8 for additional battery maintenance and charging procedures.

**12** On models without a battery cover, secure the battery with the strap **(see illustration 17.5a)**. Install the battery cell caps, tightening them securely. Reconnect the cables to the battery, attaching the positive cable first and the negative cable last. Make sure to install the insulating boot over the terminals.

**13** Install the battery cover (if equipped) and secure it with the strap.

**14** Install all components removed for access. Be very careful not to pinch or otherwise restrict the battery vent tube, as the battery may build up enough internal pressure during normal charging system operation to explode.

**HAYNES HINT** *Battery terminal corrosion can be minimised by applying a layer of petroleum jelly to the terminals after the leads have been connected.*

### 18 Exhaust system - check
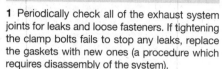

**1** Periodically check all of the exhaust system joints for leaks and loose fasteners. If tightening the clamp bolts fails to stop any leaks, replace the gaskets with new ones (a procedure which requires disassembly of the system).

**2** The exhaust pipe flange nuts at the cylinder heads are especially prone to loosening, which could cause damage to the head. Check them frequently and keep them tight.

### 19 Fuel system - check and filter cleaning or replacement

 **Warning:** *Gasoline (petrol) is extremely flammable, so take extra precautions when you work on any part of the fuel system. Don't smoke or allow open flames or bare light bulbs near the work area, and don't work in a garage where a natural gas-type appliance (such as a water heater or clothes dryer) is present. If you spill any fuel on your skin, rinse it off immediately with soap and water. When you perform any kind of work on the fuel system, wear safety glasses and have a class B type fire extinguisher on hand.*

**1** Check the fuel tank, the tank breather hose, the fuel tap, the lines and the carburetors for leaks and evidence of damage.

**2** If carburetor gaskets are leaking, the carburetors should be disassembled and rebuilt (see Chapter 5).

**3** If the fuel tap is leaking, tightening the screws may help. If leakage persists, the tap should be disassembled and repaired or replaced with a new one.

**4** If the fuel lines are cracked or otherwise deteriorated, replace them with new ones.

### Fuel tap filter cleaning

**5** Remove the fuel tank (see Chapter 3).

**6** Remove the fuel tap screws and detach it from the tank **(see illustration)**.

**7** Clean the filter stack **(see illustration)**. If it's torn or can't be cleaned completely, replace it.

**19.6 The fuel tap is secured to the tank by two screws**

**8** Remove the screws and inspect the fuel tap diaphragm **(see illustration)**. If it's torn, cracked or brittle, replace it.

**9** Reverse Steps 5 through 8 to assemble and install the fuel tap.

### In-line filter replacement

**10** Remove the fuel tank (see Chapter 5).

**11** Disconnect the lines from the filter and remove it from its bracket **(see illustration)**.

**12** Install a new filter and reconnect the lines.

### 20 Crankcase ventilation system - inspection

Inspect the hose that runs from the ventilation fitting on the top of the engine to the air filter case. Make sure it's securely attached. Replace the hose if it's cracked or deteriorated.

### 21 Sidestand switch - check

Inspect the sidestand switch for security, and check for correct operation (Chapter 8A, Section 19).

### 22 Fasteners - check

**1** Since vibration of the machine tends to loosen fasteners, all nuts, bolts, screws, etc. should be periodically checked for proper tightness.

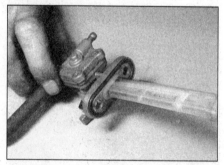

**19.7 Examine and clean the filter stack**

**19.8 Inspect the fuel tap diaphragm**

**19.11 Loosen the clamps and disconnect the hoses from the filter, then remove it from its bracket**

**2** Pay particular attention to the following:
*Spark plugs*
*Engine oil drain plug*
*Oil filter cover bolt and drain plug*
*Gearshift pedal (and linkage, if equipped)*
*Footpegs, sidestand and centerstand (if equipped)*
*Engine mounting bolts*
*Shock absorber or rear suspension unit mounting bolts*
*Front axle (or axle nut) and axle pinch bolt*
*Rear axle nut*
**3** If a torque wrench is available, use it along with the torque specifications at the beginning of this, or other, Chapters.

## 23 Shift linkage -
check and adjustment

**1** Models with a rear set shift linkage can be

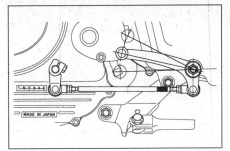

**23.3  The linkage arms should be at right angles to the rod**

adjusted by changing the length of the linkage rod.
**2** If you're working on an XV535 model, measure shift pedal height and compare it to the value listed in this Chapter's Specifications.
**3** Check the alignment of the shift pedal arm and the arm at the other end of the linkage

**23.4  Loosen the locknuts and rotate the rod to change its length**

with the linkage rod. The two arms should be at right angles to the rod (see illustration).
**4** To adjust, loosen the locknuts and turn the linkage rod to change its length, then tighten the locknuts (see illustration).

# Every 8,000 miles/12,000 km or 12 months

## 24 Final drive oil (shaft drive models) - check and change

**1** Final drive oil level should be checked and changed at the specified intervals.

### Check

**2** Support the bike securely in a level position.

⚠ *Warning: The final drive unit may be hot enough to cause burns. Wait until the final drive unit is cool to the touch before checking the level.*

**3** Remove the filler plug from the final drive housing (see illustration).
**4** Look inside the hole and check the oil level. It should be even with the top of the hole (see illustration). If it's low, add oil of the type listed in this Chapter's Specifications with a funnel or hose (see illustration), then reinstall the filler plug and tighten it to the torque listed in this Chapter's Specifications.

**24.4b  Add oil through the filler hole**

### Oil change

**5** Ride the bike to warm the oil so it will drain completely.

⚠ *Warning: Be careful not to touch hot components (including the oil); they may be hot enough to cause burns.*
**6** Remove the filler plug (see illustration 24.3).

**24.3  Remove the filler plug (arrow) to check final drive oil level**

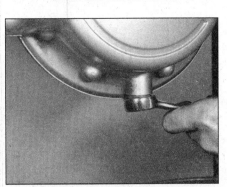

**24.7a  Remove the drain plug . . .**

**7** Remove the drain plug and let the oil drain for 10 to 15 minutes (see illustrations).
**8** Clean the drain plug, reinstall it and tighten it to the torque listed in this Chapter's Specifications.
**9** Fill the final drive unit to the correct level with oil of the type listed in this Chapter's Specifications (see illustrations 24.4a and 24.4b).
**10** Install the filler plug and tighten it to the torque listed in this Chapter's Specifications.

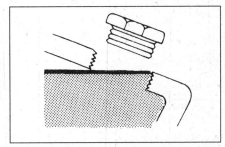

**24.4a  The oil should be even with the top of the filler hole**

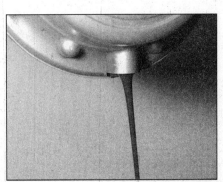

**24.7b  . . . and let the oil drain into a pan, then clean the plug threads and reinstall it**

## Every two years

### 25 Brake master cylinder and caliper seals - replacement

1 Brake system dust seals will deteriote with age and must be replaced with new ones.
2 Refer to Chapter 6A or 6B, Section 3 and 5, as appropriate.

HAYNES HiNT *Old brake fluid is invariably much darker in color than new fluid, making it easier to see when old fluid has been expelled from the system.*

### 26 Brake fluid - renewal

1 Brake system hydraulic fluid will deteriote with age and must be replaced.
2 Refer to Chapter 6A, Section 8.

## Every four years

### 27 Brake hoses - renewal

1 Brake system hoses will deteriote with age and must be replaced with new ones.

2 Refer to Chapter 6A or 6B, Section 7, as appropriate.

# Chapter 2 Part A
# Engine, clutch and transmission (XV535 models)

## Contents

## Degrees of difficulty

| Easy, suitable for novice with little experience |  | Fairly easy, suitable for beginner with some experience |  | Fairly difficult, suitable for competent DIY mechanic |  | Difficult, suitable for experienced DIY mechanic |  | Very difficult, suitable for expert DIY or professional | |
|---|---|---|---|---|---|---|---|---|---|

## Specifications

### General
| | |
|---|---|
| Bore x stroke . . . . . . . . . . . . . . . . . . . . . . . . . . . . . . . . . . . . . . . . . . . | 76 x 59 mm (2.992 x 2.323 inches) |
| Displacement . . . . . . . . . . . . . . . . . . . . . . . . . . . . . . . . . . . . . . . . . . . | 535 cc |
| Compression ratio . . . . . . . . . . . . . . . . . . . . . . . . . . . . . . . . . . . . . . . | 9.0 to 1 |

### Camshafts
| | |
|---|---|
| Lobe height | |
|   Intake (standard) . . . . . . . . . . . . . . . . . . . . . . . . . . . . . . . . . . . . . . | 39.73 mm (1.564 inch) |
|   Intake (limit) . . . . . . . . . . . . . . . . . . . . . . . . . . . . . . . . . . . . . . . . . | 39.63 mm (1.560 inch) |
|   Exhaust (standard) . . . . . . . . . . . . . . . . . . . . . . . . . . . . . . . . . . . . | 39.77 mm (1.566 inch) |
|   Exhaust (limit) . . . . . . . . . . . . . . . . . . . . . . . . . . . . . . . . . . . . . . | 39.67 mm (1.562 inch) |
| Base circle | |
|   Intake (standard) . . . . . . . . . . . . . . . . . . . . . . . . . . . . . . . . . . . . . . | 32.22 mm (1.269 inch) |
|   Intake (limit) . . . . . . . . . . . . . . . . . . . . . . . . . . . . . . . . . . . . . . . . . | 31.22 mm (1.229 inch) |
|   Exhaust (standard) . . . . . . . . . . . . . . . . . . . . . . . . . . . . . . . . . . . . | 32.30 mm (1.272 inch) |
|   Exhaust (limit) . . . . . . . . . . . . . . . . . . . . . . . . . . . . . . . . . . . . . . | 31.30 mm (1.232 inch) |
| Bearing oil clearance . . . . . . . . . . . . . . . . . . . . . . . . . . . . . . . . . . . . | 0.020 to 0.061 mm (0.0008 to 0.0024 inch) |
| Journal diameter . . . . . . . . . . . . . . . . . . . . . . . . . . . . . . . . . . . . . . . | 27.96 to 27.98 mm (1.100 to 1.102 inch) |
| Bearing bore . . . . . . . . . . . . . . . . . . . . . . . . . . . . . . . . . . . . . . . . . . | 28.00 to 28.02 mm (1.102 to 1.103 inch) |
| Camshaft runout limit . . . . . . . . . . . . . . . . . . . . . . . . . . . . . . . . . . . . | 0.03 mm (0.0012 inch) |

## Cylinder head, valves and valve springs

| | |
|---|---|
| Cylinder head warpage limit | 0.03 mm (0.0012 inch) |
| Valve stem bend limit | 0.03 mm (0.0012 inch) |
| Valve head diameter | |
|     Intake | 36.9 to 37.1 mm (1.453 to 1.461 inch) |
|     Exhaust | 31.9 to 32.1 mm (1.256 to 1.264 inch) |
| Valve stem diameter | |
|     Intake | 6.975 to 6.990 mm (0.274 to 0.275 inch) |
|     Exhaust | 6.960 to 6.975 mm (0.273 to 0.274 inch) |
| Valve head edge thickness (intake and exhaust) | |
|     Standard | 1.0 to 1.4 mm (0.04 to 0.06 inch) |
|     Limit | 0.7 mm (0.028 inch) |
| Valve guide inside diameter (intake and exhaust) | |
|     Standard | 7.000 to 7.012 mm (0.275 to 0.276 inch) |
|     Limit | 7.05 mm (0.278 inch) |
| Valve seat width (intake and exhaust) | |
|     Standard | 1.0 to 1.2 mm (0.04 to 0.05 inch) |
|     Limit | 1.4 mm (0.055 inch) |
| Valve face width (intake and exhaust) | 2.3 mm (0.09 inch) |
| Valve inner spring free length (intake and exhaust) | |
|     Standard | 39.9 mm (1.571 inch) |
|     Limit | 37.7 mm (1.48 inch) |
| Valve inner spring installed length (intake and exhaust) | 34.1 mm (1.343 inch) |
| Valve inner spring compressed pressure at installed length | 9.5 to 11.1 kg (21.0 to 24.5 lbs) |
| Valve inner spring bend limit | 1.7 mm (0.067 inch) |
| Valve outer spring free length (intake and exhaust) | |
|     Standard | 43.6 mm (1.717 inch) |
|     Limit | 41.4 mm 1.630 inch) |
| Valve outer spring installed length (intake and exhaust) | 37.1 mm (1.46 inch) |
| Valve outer spring compressed pressure at installed length | 18.7 to 21.9 kg (41.2 to 48.3 lbs) |
| Valve outer spring bend limit | 1.9 mm (0.075 inch) |

## Cylinders

| | |
|---|---|
| Bore diameter | 75.98 to 76.02 mm (2.991 to 2.993 inch) |
| Bore measuring point | 40 mm (1.57 inch) from top of cylinder |
| Taper and out-of-round limit | 0.05 mm (0.002 inch) |

## Pistons

| | |
|---|---|
| Piston diameter | |
|     Standard | 75.92 to 75.97 mm (2.989 to 2.991 inches) |
|     First oversize | 76.50 mm (3.012 inches) |
|     Second oversize | 77.00 mm (3.031 inches) |
| Diameter measuring point | 3.5 mm (0.14 inch) from bottom of skirt |
| Piston-to-cylinder clearance | |
|     Standard | 0.035 to 0.055 mm (0.0014 to 0.0022 inch) |
|     Limit | 0.1 mm (0.004 inch) |
| Ring side clearance | |
|     Top ring | |
|         Standard | 0.03 to 0.07 mm (0.001 to 0.003 inch) |
|         Limit | 0.12 mm (0.005 inch) |
|     Second ring | |
|         Standard | 0.02 to 0.06 mm (0.0008 to 0.0024 inch) |
|         Maximum | 0.12 mm (0.005 inch) |
|     Oil ring | Not specified |
| Ring thickness | |
|     Top ring | 1.2 mm (0.05 inch) |
|     Middle ring | 1.5 mm (0.06 inch) |
|     Oil ring (spacer and rails) | 2.5 mm (0.10 inch) |
| Ring end gap (standard) | |
|     Top and second rings | 0.30 to 0.45 mm (0.012 to 0.018 inch) |
|     Oil ring | 0.2 to 0.8 mm (0.008 to 0.031 inch) |
| Ring end gap (limit) | |
|     Top ring | 0.7 mm (0.028 inch) |
|     Second ring | 0.8 mm (0.031 inch) |
|     Oil ring | Not specified |
| Ring width | |
|     Top ring | 2.9 mm (0.11 inch) |
|     Second ring | 3.2 mm (0.13 inch) |
|     Oil ring | 3.1 mm (0.12 inch) |

## Crankshaft, connecting rods and bearings

| | |
|---|---|
| Main bearing oil clearance | 0.020 to 0.052 mm (0.0008 to 0.0020 inch) |
| Connecting rod side clearance | 0.27 to 0.42 mm (0.011 to 0.017 inch) |
| Connecting rod bearing oil clearance | 0.026 to 0.052 mm (0.001 to 0.002 inch) |
| Crankshaft runout limit (1987 through 1993) | 0.03 mm (0.0012 inch) |
| Crankshaft runout limit (1994-on) | 0.02 mm (0.0008 inch) |

## Oil pump

| | |
|---|---|
| Inner to outer rotor clearance limit | 0.17 mm (0.007 inch) |
| Outer rotor to housing clearance limit | 0.08 mm (0.003 inch) |

## Clutch

| | |
|---|---|
| Friction plate thickness | |
|     Standard | 2.9 to 3.1 mm (0.114 to 0.122 inch) |
|     Minimum | 2.6 mm (0.102 inch) |
| Steel plate thickness | 1.5 to 1.7 mm (0.060 to 0.067 inch) |
| Steel plate warpage limit | 0.2 mm (0.008 inch) |
| Pushrod bend limit | 0.5 mm (0.02 inch) |
| Spring length | |
|     Standard | 39.5 mm (1.56 inch) |
|     Minimum | 38.5 mm (1.52 inch) |

## Transmission

| | |
|---|---|
| Driveshaft and mainshaft runout limit | 0.06 mm (0.0024 inch) |

## Torque specifications

| | |
|---|---|
| Alternator cover bolts | 10 Nm (7.2 ft-lbs) |
| Alternator rotor bolt | see Chapter 8 |
| Cam chain damper stopper bolts | 10 Nm (7.2 ft-lbs) |
| Cam chain tensioner bolts | 12 Nm (8.7 ft-lbs) |
| Cam chain tensioner cap | 20 Nm (14 ft-lbs) |
| Cam sprocket bolt | 55 Nm (40 ft-lbs) |
| Camshaft retainer bolts | 20 Nm (14 ft-lbs) |
| Cam sprocket cover bolts | 10 Nm (7.2 ft-lbs) |
| Camshaft segment (5 mm screw) | 4 Nm (2.9 ft-lbs) |
| Clutch adjuster locknut | 8 Nm (5.8 ft-lbs) |
| Clutch boss nut | 70 Nm (50 ft-lbs) (4) |
| Clutch cover bolts | 10 Nm (7.2 ft-lbs) |
| Clutch pressure plate screws | 8 Nm (5.8 ft-lbs) |
| Clutch push lever screw | 12 Nm (8.7 ft-lbs) |
| Connecting rod nuts | 36 Nm (25 ft-lbs) (2) |
| Crankcase bolts (6 mm) | 10 Nm (7.2 ft-lbs) |
| Crankcase bolts (8 mm) | 24 Nm (17 ft-lbs) |
| Crankcase studs (8 mm) | 13 Nm (9.4 ft-lbs) |
| Crankcase studs (10 mm) | 20 Nm (14 ft-lbs) |
| Cylinder bolt | 10 Nm (7.2 ft-lbs) |
| Cylinder head bolts (8 mm) | 20 Nm (14 ft-lbs) |
| Cylinder head nuts (10 mm) | 35 Nm (25 ft-lbs) |
| Cylinder head flange nuts (8 mm) | 20 Nm (14 ft-lbs) |
| Cylinder head side cover bolts | 10 Nm (7.2 ft-lbs) |
| Driveaxle bearing retainer screws | 25 Nm (18 ft-lbs) (3) |
| Middle drive gear assembly bolts | 25 Nm (18 ft-lbs) |
| Middle drive gear locknut | 120 Nm (85 ft-lbs) (3) |
| Oil passage housing bolts | 10 Nm (7.2 ft-lbs) |
| Oil pump bolts | 7 Nm (5.1 ft-lbs) |
| Primary drive gear nut | 70 Nm (50 ft-lbs) (4) |
| Rocker arm cover bolts | 10 Nm (7.2 ft-lbs) |
| Rocker arm shaft holding bolts | 20 Nm (14 ft-lbs) (1) |
| Shift lever | 22 Nm (16 ft-lbs) (4) |

1  Use new sealing washers.
2  Apply molybdenum disulfide grease to the threads and nut surfaces; follow special tightening procedures in the text.
3  Stake after installation.
4  Use a new lockwasher.

## 1  General information

The engine/transmission unit is an air-cooled V-twin. The valves are operated by overhead camshafts which are chain driven off the crankshaft. The engine/transmission assembly is constructed from aluminum alloy. The crankcase is divided vertically.

The crankcase incorporates a wet sump, pressure-fed lubrication system which uses a gear-driven oil pump and an oil filter mounted in the right-hand side of the crankcase.

Power from the crankshaft is routed to the transmission via the clutch, which is of the coil spring, wet multi-plate type and is gear-driven off the crankshaft. The transmission is a five-speed, constant-mesh unit.

## 2  Operations possible with the engine in the frame

The components and assemblies listed below can be removed without having to remove the engine from the frame. If, however, a number of areas require attention at the same time, removal of the engine is recommended.

*Starter motor*
*Alternator*
*Starter clutch*
*Cam sprockets*
*Clutch and primary drive gear*
*Oil pump*
*External shift linkage*

## 3  Operations requiring engine removal

It is necessary to remove the engine/transmission assembly from the frame to gain access to the following components:

*Cylinder heads, rocker arms and camshafts*
*Cam chains and lower (crankshaft) sprockets*
*Oil pump*

The crankcase halves must be separated to gain access to the following components:

*Crankshaft, connecting rods and bearings*
*Transmission shafts*
*Shift cam and forks*

## 4  Major engine repair - general note

1  It is not always easy to determine when or if an engine should be completely overhauled, as a number of factors must be considered.
2  High mileage is not necessarily an indication that an overhaul is needed, while low mileage, on the other hand, does not preclude the need for an overhaul. Frequency of servicing is probably the single most important consideration. An engine that has regular and frequent oil and filter changes, as well as other required maintenance, will most likely give many miles of reliable service. Conversely, a neglected engine, or one which has not been broken in properly, may require an overhaul very early in its life.
3  Exhaust smoke and excessive oil consumption are both indications that piston rings and/or valve guides are in need of attention. Make sure oil leaks are not responsible before deciding that the rings and guides are bad. Refer to Chapter 1 and perform a cylinder compression check to determine for certain the nature and extent of the work required.
4  If the engine is making obvious knocking or rumbling noises, the connecting rod and/or main bearings are probably at fault.
5  Loss of power, rough running, excessive valve train noise and high fuel consumption rates may also point to the need for an overhaul, especially if they are all present at the same time. If a complete tune-up does not remedy the situation, major mechanical work is the only solution.
6  An engine overhaul generally involves restoring the internal parts to the specifications of a new engine. During an overhaul the piston rings are replaced and the cylinder walls are bored and/or honed. If a rebore is done, then new pistons are also required. The main and connecting rod bearings are generally replaced with new ones and, if necessary, the crankshaft is also replaced. Generally the valves are serviced as well, since they are usually in less than perfect condition at this point. While the engine is being overhauled, other components such as the carburetors and the starter motor can be rebuilt also. The end result should be a like-new engine that will give as many trouble free miles as the original.
7  Before beginning the engine overhaul, read through all of the related procedures to familiarize yourself with the scope and requirements of the job. Overhauling an engine is not all that difficult, but it is time consuming. Plan on the motorcycle being tied up for a minimum of two weeks. Check on the availability of parts and make sure that any necessary special tools, equipment and supplies are obtained in advance.
8  Most work can be done with typical shop hand tools, although a number of precision measuring tools are required for inspecting parts to determine if they must be replaced. Often a dealer service department or motorcycle repair shop will handle the inspection of parts and offer advice concerning reconditioning and replacement.

 **As a general rule, time is the primary cost of an overhaul so it doesn't pay to install worn or substandard parts.**

9  As a final note, to ensure maximum life and minimum trouble from a rebuilt engine, everything must be assembled with care in a spotlessly clean environment.

## 5  Engine - removal and installation

**Note:** *Engine removal and installation should be done with the aid of an assistant to avoid damage or injury that could occur if the engine is dropped. A hydraulic floor jack should be used to support and lower the engine if possible (they can be rented at low cost).*

### Removal

1  Support the bike securely so it can't be knocked over during this procedure. Place a support under the swingarm pivot and be sure the motorcycle is safely braced.
2  Remove the top cover and upper fuel tank (if equipped) (see Chapter 3).
3  Remove the left front side cover and its bracket (see Chapter 7).
4  Remove the right front side cover (see Chapter 7). Unbolt the electrical component board that's mounted beneath the cover, then disconnect the electrical connectors and carburetor hoses and remove the cover mounting plate (see Chapter 7).
5  Drain the engine oil (see Chapter 1).
6  Remove the carburetors (see Chapter 3) and plug the intake openings with clean shop towels.
7  Remove the exhaust system (see Chapter 3).
8  Disconnect the brake light switch wires (see Chapter 8).
9  Unscrew the rear brake adjuster all the way, then remove the spring and brake rod (see Chapter 6).
10  Check for alignment marks on the shift shaft and shift lever (see Section 20). If they aren't visible, make your own marks with a sharp punch. Loosen the pinch bolt and slip the shift lever off the shaft.
11  Remove the shift pedal and left footpeg bracket as an assembly (see Chapter 7).
12  Remove the right footpeg bracket (see Chapter 7).
13  Remove the sidestand (see Chapter 7).
14  Remove the sidestand switch (see Chapter 8).
15  Remove the cylinder head side covers from the front and rear cylinders, then disconnect the spark plug wires (HT leads) (see Spark plugs - servicing in Chapter 1).
16  Disconnect the crankcase ventilation hose from the rear cylinder head **(see illustration)**.
17  Disconnect the clutch cable (see Section 15).
18  Disconnect the ground wire from the right

5.16 Squeeze the hose clamp and pull the breather hose off its fitting

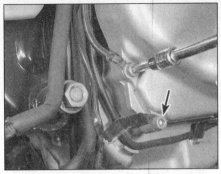

5.18 Remove the bolt and disconnect the ground wire, then loosen the wiring retainer bolts (arrow) and release the harness

5.21 Pull the driveshaft rubber boot away from the middle gear

rear of the engine **(see illustration)**. Loosen the right crankcase cover (clutch cover) Allen bolts and free the starter motor wiring harness from the retainers along the bottom of the crankcase.

**19** Remove the horn (see Chapter 8).

**20** Pull back the ignition coil cover and disconnect the primary (low tension) electrical connectors (see Chapter 4, part A.)

**21** Pull the rubber driveshaft boot away from the engine **(see illustration)**.

**22** Remove the alternator cover. Remove the stator and pick-up coil assembly (see Chapter 8).

**23** Remove the starter motor (see Chapter 8).

**24** Support the engine with a jack and wood block **(see illustration)**. Make sure the support is still in position under the swingarm pivot and that the bike is still securely braced.

**25** Remove the engine mounting bolts at the lower rear of the crankcase, upper rear of the crankcase and at the top of each cylinder **(see illustrations)**.

**26** Disconnect both battery cables from the battery.

 *Warning: Always disconnect the negative cable first and reconnect it last to prevent a battery explosion.*

**27** Make sure no wires or hoses are still attached to the engine assembly.

5.24 Support the engine with a jack and a block of wood

5.25a Remove the lower rear mounting bolt . . .

5.25b . . . and the upper rear mounting bolts . . .

5.25c . . . (there's an upper rear mounting bolt on each side of the engine)

5.25d Unbolt the front cylinder head bracket from the frame

5.25e Unbolt the rear cylinder head mounting brackets from the frame . . .

5.25f . . . (there's one on each side of the engine)

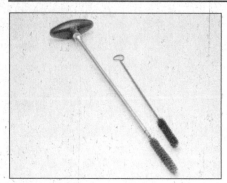

**6.2a A selection of brushes is required for cleaning holes and passages in the engine components**

**6.2b Plastigauge is needed to check the connecting rod oil clearances**

**6.3 An engine stand can be made from short lengths of lumber and lag bolts or nails**

 *Warning: The engine is heavy and may cause injury if it falls. Be sure it's securely supported. Have an assistant help you steady the engine on the jack as you remove it.*

28 Slowly and carefully lower the engine assembly to the floor, then guide it out from under the right side of the bike.

## Installation

29 Installation is the reverse of removal. Note the following points:

a) Don't tighten any of the engine mounting bolts until they all have been installed.

b) Use new gaskets at all exhaust pipe connections.

c) Tighten the engine mounting bolts securely.

d) Adjust the rear brake rod, clutch cable and throttle cable(s) following the procedures in Chapter 1 and Chapter 2.

e) Be sure to refill the engine oil before starting the engine.

## 6 Engine disassembly and reassembly - general information

1 Before disassembling the engine, clean the exterior with a degreaser and rinse it with water.

 *A clean engine will make the job easier and prevent the possibility of getting dirt into the internal areas of the engine.*

2 In addition to the precision measuring tools mentioned earlier, you will need a torque wrench, a valve spring compressor, oil gallery brushes, a piston ring removal and installation tool, a piston ring compressor and a clutch holder tool (which is described in Section 16). Some new, clean engine oil of the correct grade and type, some engine assembly lube (or moly-based grease), a tube of Yamaha Quick Gasket (part no. 11001-05-01) or equivalent, and a tube of RTV (silicone)

sealant will also be required. Although it may not be considered a tool, some Plastigauge should also be obtained to use for checking connecting rod bearing oil clearances **(see illustrations)**.

3 An engine support stand made from short lengths of lumber bolted together will facilitate the disassembly and reassembly procedures **(see illustration)**. The perimeter of the mount should be just big enough to accommodate the crankcase when it's laid on its side for removal of the crankshaft and transmission components. If you have an automotive-type engine stand, an adapter plate can be made from a piece of plate, some angle iron and some nuts and bolts. The adapter plate can be attached to the engine mounting bolt holes.

4 When disassembling the engine, keep "mated" parts together (including gears, cylinders, pistons, etc.) that have been in contact with each other during engine operation. These "mated" parts must be reused or replaced as an assembly.

5 Engine/transmission disassembly should be done in the following general order with reference to the appropriate Sections.

Remove the cylinder heads
Remove the camshafts
Remove the rocker arms
Remove the cylinders

Remove the pistons
Remove the idle gears
Remove the clutch
Remove the oil pump
Remove the external shift mechanism
Remove the middle driven gear
Separate the crankcase halves
Remove the crankshaft and connecting rods
Remove the shift cam/forks
Remove the transmission shafts/gears

6 Reassembly is accomplished by reversing the general disassembly sequence.

## 7 Camshaft chain tensioners - removal and installation

### Removal

*Caution: Once you start to remove the tensioner bolts, you must remove the tensioner all the way and reset it before tightening the bolts. The tensioner extends and locks in place, so if you loosen the bolts partway and then retighten them, the tensioner or cam chain will be damaged.*

1 Remove the tensioner cap bolt and spring while the tensioner is still installed on the engine **(see illustrations)**.

**7.1a Loosen the tensioner cap bolt with a socket or wrench, then unscrew it from the engine (If you're removing both tensioners, it's a good idea to label them F for front and R for rear cylinder) . . .**

**7.1b . . . then withdraw the cap bolt, sealing washer and spring**

7.2a  Remove the tensioner Allen bolts . . .

7.2b  . . . and remove the tensioner and gasket from the engine

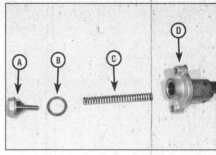

7.3  Tensioner details

a) Cap bolt
b) Sealing washer
c) Spring
d) Tensioner body

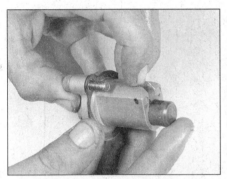

7.4  Lift the latch and compress the tensioner piston into the body

8.3a  Remove four nuts (arrows); the front of the engine is at the bottom of the illustration . . .

8.3b  . . . and two washers (arrows), then lift off the engine mounting bracket . . .

2  Remove the tensioner mounting bolts and take it off the engine (see illustrations).

### Installation

3  Check the sealing washer on the cap bolt for cracks or hardening (see illustration). It's a good idea to replace this washer whenever the tensioner cap is removed.
4  Release the one-way cam on the chain tensioner and compress the tensioner piston into the tensioner body (see illustration).
5  Turn the tensioner so the one-way cam is up and install the tensioner on the cylinder, using a new gasket (see illustration 7.2b).
6  Tighten the mounting bolts to the torque listed in this Chapter's Specifications.
7  Install the tensioner spring, sealing washer

and cap (see illustration 7.1b). Tighten the cap to the torque listed in this Chapter's Specifications.

### 8  Cylinder heads, camshafts and rocker arms - removal, inspection and installation

### Cylinder head removal

1  Remove the engine from the frame (see Section 5).
2  Remove the ignition coil mounting bracket and ignition coils from the rear cylinder (see Chapter 4).
3  Remove the engine mounting bracket, its

washers and nuts from the front cylinder head (see illustrations).
4  Remove the Allen bolts and take off the cam sprocket cover (see illustrations).

**HAYNES HINT**  Stuff clean shop towels into the opening below the cam sprocket so nothing is accidentally dropped into it.

5  Remove the rocker arm covers and their O-rings from the exhaust side and intake side of the cylinder (see illustration).
### Rear cylinder
6  Turn the engine so the rear cylinder is at top dead center on its compression stroke

8.3c  . . . and remove the four washers from beneath the bracket

8.4a  Remove both Allen bolts . . .

8.4b  . . . and take the cam sprocket cover off the cylinder head

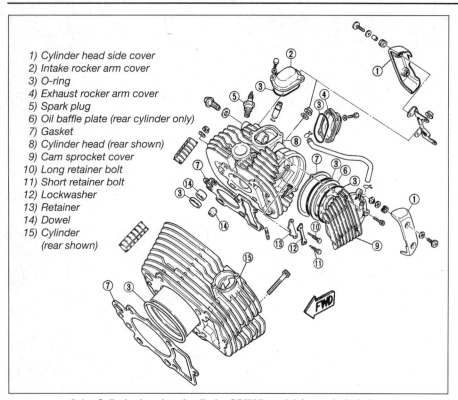

1) Cylinder head side cover
2) Intake rocker arm cover
3) O-ring
4) Exhaust rocker arm cover
5) Spark plug
6) Oil baffle plate (rear cylinder only)
7) Gasket
8) Cylinder head (rear shown)
9) Cam sprocket cover
10) Long retainer bolt
11) Short retainer bolt
12) Lockwasher
13) Retainer
14) Dowel
15) Cylinder
    (rear shown)

8.4c  Cylinder head and cylinder (XV535 models) - exploded view

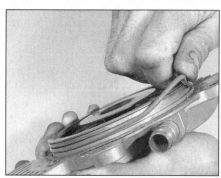

8.4d  Use a pointed tool to remove the O-ring from the cam sprocket cover . . .

8.4e  . . . and on the rear cylinder, remove the oil baffle plate and its O-ring

8.5  Unbolt the rocker arm covers and take them off, together with their O-rings

8.6a  The line next to the T mark on the rotor should be aligned with the notch in the timing window

(see Valve clearance - adjustment in Chapter 1). When the rear cylinder is on its compression stroke, the line on the alternator rotor with a T mark next to it will be aligned with the notch in the timing window (see illustration). Also, the camshaft sprocket mark will be aligned with the mark inside the sprocket housing on the cylinder head (see illustration).

7  Remove the cam chain tensioner for the rear cylinder (see Section 7).

8  Place a piece of wire where you can reach it easily during the next steps.

9  Hold the engine from turning with a socket on the crankshaft turning bolt (see illustration). If the engine is in the frame, you

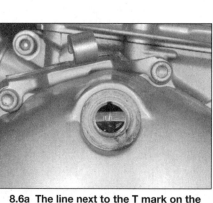

8.6b  The punch mark on the sprocket should align with the arrowhead in the cylinder head (arrows)

8.9  Hold the crankshaft with a socket and loosen the camshaft sprocket

8.11  The oil baffle plate (arrow) is used on the rear cylinder only

8.12 Label the rear sprocket with an "R", then slide it off - be sure the camshaft dowel doesn't fall out

8.13 Once the sprocket is removed, drape the cam chain over the camshaft. Note dowel and pointer (arrows)

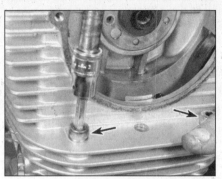

8.14a The cylinder heads are secured by two Allen bolts (arrows) . . .

can also keep it from turning by shifting the transmission into gear and having an assistant hold the rear brake on.

**10** While you hold the engine from turning, loosen the camshaft sprocket bolt **(see illustration 8.9)**.

**11** Unscrew the sprocket bolt and remove the oil baffle plate **(see illustration)**.

**12** Label the sprocket "R" (for rear cylinder) and slide it off the camshaft **(see illustration)**. Make sure the camshaft dowel doesn't fall out of the camshaft.

**HAYNES**
**HINT**

*If the cylinder head is stuck, tap it gently with a rubber or plastic mallet, being careful not to break the cooling fins. Don't pry against the gasket surfaces or they will be gouged.*

**13** Drape the cam chain over the end of the camshaft **(see illustration)**. At this point, the camshaft dowel should be aligned with the pointer cast in the cylinder head.

**14** Loosen the cylinder head nuts and bolts evenly in several stages **(see illustrations)**. Remove the nuts, washer, bolts and engine mounting brackets.

**15** Lift the cylinder head off the studs **(see illustration)**.

**16** Remove the O-ring, dowels and exhaust side chain damper **(see illustrations)**. Tie up the cam chain with wire.

**17** Check the cylinder head gasket and the mating surfaces on the cylinder head and block for leakage, which could indicate

8.14b . . . and five nuts

a) Allen bolts    c) Nut (in spark plug well)
b) Nuts

8.14c Use a socket and extension to remove the nut in the spark plug well . . .

8.14d . . . and pull its washer out with a magnet

8.15 Lift the cylinder head off

8.16a There are three dowels, one with an O-ring (A) and two that fit around studs (B) . . .

8.16b . . . if they're not in the cylinder, they may have remained in the head (arrow)

8.16c Lift out the exhaust side chain damper (arrow)

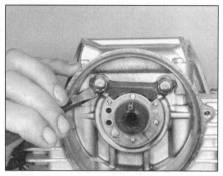

8.22a Flatten the lockwasher tabs with a hammer and chisel (do not strike the cylinder head) . . .

8.22b . . . undo the retainer bolts . . .

8.22c . . . and remove the lockwasher

8.23a Pull the camshaft and bushing out of the head . . .

8.23b . . . and take the bushing off the camshaft

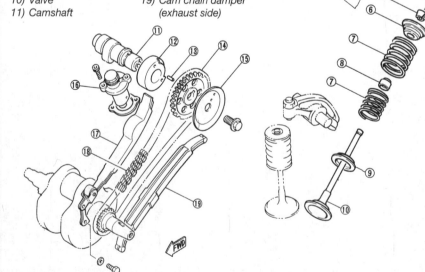

1) Valve adjuster locknut
2) Valve adjuster
3) Rocker arm shaft
4) Rocker arm
5) Valve keepers (collets)
6) Valve spring retainer
7) Valve springs
8) Oil seal
9) Valve spring seat
10) Valve
11) Camshaft
12) Camshaft bushing
13) Camshaft dowel
14) Cam sprocket
15) Oil baffle plate (rear cylinder only)
16) Cam chain tensioner
17) Cam chain damper (intake side)
18) Cam chain
19) Cam chain damper (exhaust side)

8.23c Camshaft, timing chain and valves (XV535 models) - exploded view

warpage. Refer to Section 10 and check the flatness of the cylinder head.

**18** Clean all traces of old gasket material from the cylinder head and block. Be careful not to let any of the gasket material fall into the crankcase, the cylinder bores or the oil passages.

### Front cylinder

**19** Repeat Steps 6 through 18 to remove the front cylinder head, noting that the front camshaft sprocket doesn't have an oil baffle and that the front engine mounting bracket was removed in Step 3.

## *Camshaft removal*

**Note:** *You may need a 10 mm bolt for this procedure.*

**20** If you haven't already done so, remove the rocker arm covers (see illustrations 8.4c and 8.5).

**21** Loosen the rocker arm locknuts and back off the adjusters.

**22** Flatten the tabs on the camshaft bolt lockwasher **(see illustration)**. Remove the bolts, lockwasher and retainer **(see illustrations)**.

**23** Try to pull the camshaft out with fingers **(see illustration)**. If it doesn't come easily, thread a 10 mm bolt into the end of the camshaft and use it as a handle to pull out the camshaft. Once the camshaft is out, remove the bushing **(see illustrations)**.

**8.25a  Remove the rocker arm shaft retaining bolts . . .**

**8.25b  . . . and their sealing washers**

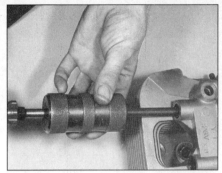

**8.26a  A slide hammer like this one is the easiest way to remove the rocker shafts**

### Rocker arm removal

**24** Remove the camshaft (see Steps 20 through 23).
**25** Remove the rocker arm shaft retaining bolts and sealing washers **(see illustrations)**.
**26** Thread a slide hammer into the end of the rocker shaft **(see illustration)**. Once the rocker shaft clears the rocker arm, take the rocker arm out **(see illustrations)**.

> **TOOL TiP**  *If you don't have a slide hammer, use a long bolt, a large flat washer and a short piece of pipe. Rap the pipe against the washer to pull the rocker shaft out of the rocker arm.*

**27** Remove the remaining rocker shaft and arm, then label them according to cylinder and position (for example, rear intake and rear exhaust) **(see illustration)**.

### Camshaft, chain and cam sprocket inspection

**Note:** *Before replacing camshafts because of damage, check with local machine shops specializing in motorcycle engine work. It may be possible for cam lobes to be welded, reground and hardened, at a cost far lower than that of a new camshaft. If the bearing surfaces in the cylinder head are damaged, it may be possible for them to be bored out to accept bearing inserts. Due to the cost of a new cylinder head it is recommended that all options be explored before condemning it as trash!*

**28** Inspect the cam bearing surfaces of the head. Look for score marks, deep scratches and evidence of spalling (a pitted appearance).
**29** Check the camshaft lobes for heat discoloration (blue appearance), score marks, chipped areas, flat spots and spalling **(see illustration)**. Measure the height of each lobe with a micrometer **(see illustration)** and compare the results to the minimum lobe height listed in this Chapter's Specifications. If damage is noted or wear is excessive, the camshaft must be replaced.
**30** Next, check the camshaft bearing oil clearances. Measure the outer diameter of the camshaft journals and the inner diameter of the bearing surface in the cylinder head and the camshaft bushing **(see illustration)**.

**8.26b  Pull the shaft partway out . . .**

**8.26c  . . . then remove the rocker arm**

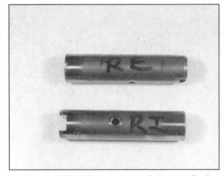

**8.27  Label the shafts according to cylinder (front or rear) and side (intake or exhaust)**

**8.29a  Check the camshaft lobes for wear - this sort of damage will require replacement (or repair)**

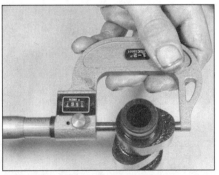

**8.29b  Measure the height of the cam lobes with a micrometer**

**8.30  Compare the camshaft journal diameter with the diameter of the bushing or bearing surface in the cylinder head**

8.32 Check the sprockets for wear and damage

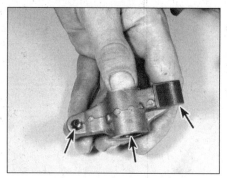

8.34 Check rocker arms for wear (arrows)

8.36 Hold the rocker arm in the installed position and install the shaft, using a bolt as a handle

Subtract the journal diameter from the bearing or bushing bore diameter to obtain the clearance. If it's greater than that listed in this Chapter's Specifications, replace the cylinder head, bushing or camshaft, whichever is worn.

31 Check the visible portion of the cam chain for obvious wear or damage. Except in cases of oil starvation, the chain wears very little. If the chain has stretched excessively, which makes it difficult to maintain proper tension, replace it with a new one (see Section 17).

32 Check the cam sprockets for wear, cracks and other damage, replacing them if necessary (see illustration). If the sprockets are worn, the chain is also worn, and also the sprocket on the crankshaft (which can only be

remedied by replacing the crankshaft). If wear this severe is apparent, the entire engine should be disassembled for inspection.

33 Check the cam chain damper for wear or damage. If it is worn or damaged, the chain may be worn out or improperly adjusted. Refer to Section 17 for cam chain replacement.

### Rocker arm inspection

34 Clean all of the components with solvent and pry them off. Blow through the oil passages in the rocker arms with compressed air, if available. Inspect the rocker arm faces for pits, spalling, score marks and rough spots (see illustration). Check the rocker arm-to-shaft contact areas and the adjusting screws, as well. Look for cracks in each rocker arm. If the faces of the rocker arms are damaged, the rocker arms and the camshafts should be replaced as a set.

35 Measure the diameter of the rocker arm shafts, in the area where the rocker arms ride, and the inside diameter of the rocker arms. Calculate the difference and compare the results with this Chapter's Specifications. If the clearance is beyond the specified limits, replace them as a set.

### Rocker arm installation

36 Coat the rocker shafts and the rocker arm bores with clean engine oil. Thread a bolt into the threads in the end of the exhaust rocker shaft to use as a handle. Position the exhaust

rocker shaft partway into its hole with the threaded end facing out (see illustration). Install the exhaust rocker arm and slide the shaft into the rocker arm. Don't install the holding bolt yet.

37 Repeat Step 36 to install the intake rocker arm.

### Camshaft installation

38 Apply a light coat of engine assembly lube or moly-based grease to the camshaft journals. Position the camshaft bushing on the camshaft.

39 Apply a light coat of engine assembly lube or moly-based grease to the cam lobes.

40 Slide the camshaft into the cylinder head, then install the bushing (see illustrations). Don't let the bushing tilt sideways and jam in its bore. Position the bushing cutout flush with the cylinder head and align the camshaft dowel with the timing mark (see illustration 8.13).

41 Install the retainer (see illustration). Install a new lockwasher and the retainer bolts (the exhaust side bolt is longer than the intake side bolt) (see illustration). Tighten the bolts to the torque listed in this Chapter's Specifications, then bend the lockwasher tabs against the bolt heads.

42 Install new sealing washers on the rocker arm holding bolts (see illustration). Use a screwdriver to position the ends of the rocker shafts so the bolts will align with them (see

8.40a Slide the camshaft into its bearing in the cylinder head . . .

8.40b . . . then install the bushing and align it as shown

8.41a Install the retainer . . .

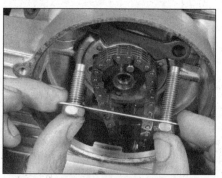

8.41b . . . and the lockwasher and bolts; the long bolt goes on the exhaust side

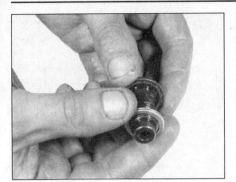

**8.42a Install new sealing washers on the rocker shaft bolts**

**8.42b Use a screwdriver to position the rocker shafts so the bolts will line up with them**

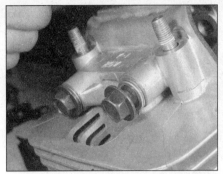

**8.42c Install the bolts with their sealing washers and tighten them to the specified torque**

illustration), then install the bolts with their sealing washers and tighten them to the torque listed in this Chapter's Specifications (see illustration).

## Cylinder head installation
### Rear cylinder head

43 If both cylinder heads have been removed, install the rear cylinder head first.
44 Install the O-ring on the large dowel and install the two smaller dowels, then install the new head gasket on top of the cylinder (see illustrations). Never reuse the old head gasket and don't use any type of gasket sealant.
45 Install the cam chain damper on the exhaust side (if removed) with its UP mark up (see illustration).
46 Position the cylinder head on the studs and guide the cam chain damper through the slot in the cylinder head (see illustration). Be sure the upper end of the cam chain damper fits into the notch in the bottom of the cylinder head (see illustration).
47 Install the cylinder head bolts and nuts together with the engine mounting brackets and cylinder head cover bracket (see illustrations). Four of the shorter nuts go on the rear cylinder head; the longer nuts and the remaining four short nuts go on the front cylinder head. Tighten the bolts and nuts evenly in several stages, in a criss-cross pattern, to the torque listed in this Chapter's Specifications.

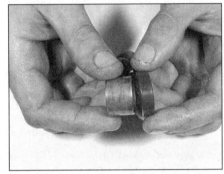

**8.44a Slip the O-ring onto the large dowel . . .**

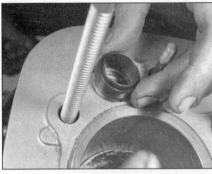

**8.44b . . . and install the large dowel and two small dowels in their bores . . .**

**8.44c . . . and install the head gasket over the studs and dowels**

**8.45 Install the exhaust side cam chain damper in its slot with the UP mark (arrow) up**

**8.46a Move the cam chain and damper aside so they don't obstruct installation of the head**

**8.46b Slip the exhaust side chain damper into its notch (arrow) as the head is lowered into position**

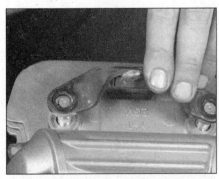

**8.47a Install the engine mounting bracket on the right side of the rear cylinder head . . .**

8.47b ... install the cylinder head cover bracket next and put two of the short nuts onto the studs ...

8.47c ... on the left side, install the mounting bracket (A) and washers (B), then fit two short nuts ...

8.47d ... the installed brackets should look like this

**48** Make sure the camshaft locating dowel is aligned with the mark on the cylinder head (see illustration 8.13).
**49** If you're working on the rear cylinder head, make sure the line on the timing rotor with a T mark next to it aligns with the notch in the timing window (see illustration 8.6a). If it's necessary to turn the crankshaft, hold the timing chain up while you're turning so it doesn't fall off the crankshaft sprocket and become jammed.
**50** Engage the camshaft sprocket with the timing chain so its dowel hole aligns with the dowel (see illustration). Slip the sprocket onto the camshaft over the dowel.
**51** Install the oil baffle plate with its concave

side out, away from the sprocket (see illustration 8.11).
**52** Turn the cam sprocket clockwise far enough to remove all slack in the cam chain, but no farther. Insert a finger in the tensioner hole and push against the chain damper. Make sure the timing marks on the cam sprocket and crankshaft are aligned correctly (see illustrations 8.6a and 8.6b).
**53** With the marks correctly aligned, tighten the cam sprocket bolt to the torque listed in this Chapter's Specifications.
**54** Install the cam chain tensioner (see Section 7).
**55** Adjust the valve clearances (see Chapter 1).

**56** Install the rocker arm covers with new O-rings. Install the intake rocker arm cover with its ridge up (see Valve clearance - adjustment in Chapter 1).
**57** Install the oil baffle and cam sprocket cover, using new O-rings (see illustrations).

### Front cylinder head

**58** Repeat Steps 44 through 46 to install the front cylinder head, noting that the slot in the timing rotor must be aligned with the crankcase pointer when the camshaft dowel is aligned with the cylinder head mark (see illustrations).
**59** Install the washers, cylinder head nuts

8.50 Fit the cam sprocket into the chain so its dowel hole will align with the camshaft dowel

8.57a Install a new O-ring on the cam sprocket cover ...

8.57b ... and one on the oil baffle plate

8.57c Align the hole in the oil baffle plate with the locating pin in the cover (arrows) ...

8.57d ... then press the plate into the cover and install a new gasket

8.58a The line without a T mark next to it must be aligned with the notch in the timing window ...

**8.58b ... and the camshaft dowel must be aligned with the pointer cast in the cylinder head (arrows)**

**8.59a On the left side of the front cylinder head, install the cylinder head cover bracket ...**

**8.59b ... install two washers on the right side ...**

and bolts and engine mounting bracket (see illustrations).

**60** Repeat Steps 48 through 57 to finish installing the cylinder head, noting that there is no oil baffle on the sprocket or in the cam sprocket cover.

**61** Install the ignition coils and their bracket (see Chapter 4).

### Both cylinder heads

**62** Change the engine oil (see Chapter 1).

**63** The remainder of installation is the reverse of the removal steps.

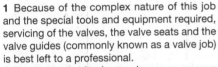

## 9 Valves/valve seats/valve guides - servicing

**1** Because of the complex nature of this job and the special tools and equipment required, servicing of the valves, the valve seats and the valve guides (commonly known as a valve job) is best left to a professional.

**2** The home mechanic can, however, remove and disassemble the head, do the initial cleaning and inspection, then reassemble and deliver the head to a dealer service department or properly equipped motorcycle repair shop for the actual valve servicing. Refer to Section 8 for those procedures.

**3** The dealer service department will remove the valves and springs, recondition or replace

the valves and valve seats, replace the valve guides, check and replace the valve springs, spring retainers and keepers/collets (as necessary), replace the valve seals with new ones and reassemble the valve components.

**4** After the valve job has been performed, the head will be in like-new condition.

 **HAYNES HiNT** *When the head is returned, be sure to clean it again very thoroughly before installation on the engine to remove any metal particles or abrasive grit that may still be present from the valve service operations. Use compressed air, if available, to blow out all the holes and passages.*

## 10 Cylinder head and valves - disassembly, inspection and reassembly

**1** As mentioned in the previous Section, valve servicing and valve guide replacement should be left to a dealer service department or motorcycle repair shop. However, disassembly, cleaning and inspection of the valves and related components can be done (if the necessary special tools are available) by the home mechanic. This way no expense is

incurred if the inspection reveals that service work is not required at this time.

**2** To properly disassemble the valve components without the risk of damaging them, a valve spring compressor is absolutely necessary. This special tool can usually be rented, but if it's not available, have a dealer service department or motorcycle repair shop handle the entire process of disassembly, inspection, service or repair (if required) and reassembly of the valves.

### Disassembly

**3** Remove the camshafts and rocker arms if you haven't already done so (see Section 8). Store the components in such a way that they can be returned to their original locations without getting mixed up.

**4** Before the valves are removed, scrape away any traces of gasket material from the head gasket sealing surface. Work slowly and do not nick or gouge the soft aluminum of the head. Gasket removing solvents, which work very well, are available at most motorcycle shops and auto parts stores.

**5** Carefully scrape all carbon deposits out of the combustion chamber area. A hand held wire brush or a piece of fine emery cloth can be used once the majority of deposits have been scraped away. Do not use a wire brush mounted in a drill motor, or one with extremely stiff bristles, as the head material is

**8.59c ... and install the four long nuts (arrows) on top of the bracket and washers**

*Tighten the cylinder head nuts and bolts at this point*

**8.59d Install four thick washers over the long nuts ...**

**8.59e ... install the mounting bracket, with two thin washers on the left studs; install the remaining thin nuts and tighten to the torque listed in the Specifications**

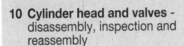

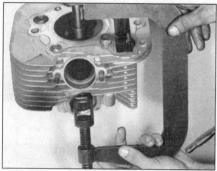

**10.7a Compress the valve springs with a spring compressor . . .**

**10.7b . . . until the keepers/collets are exposed**

**10.7c Remove the keepers/collets with a magnet**

soft and may be eroded away or scratched by the wire brush.

**6** Before proceeding, arrange to label and store the valves along with their related components so they can be kept separate and reinstalled in the same valve guides they are removed from (labeled plastic bags work well for this).

**7** Compress the valve spring on the first valve with a spring compressor, then remove the keepers/collets and the upper spring seat from the valve assembly **(see illustrations)**. Do not compress the springs any more than is absolutely necessary. Carefully release the valve spring compressor and remove the spring and the valve from the head **(see illustration)**. If the valve binds in the guide (won't pull through), push it back into the head and deburr the area

around the keeper/collet groove with a very fine file or whetstone **(see illustration)**.

**8** Repeat the procedure for the remaining valves. Remember to keep the parts for each valve together so they can be reinstalled in the same location.

**9** Once the valves have been removed and labeled, pull off the valve stem seals **(see illustration)** with pliers and discard them (the old seals should never be reused), then remove the lower spring seats.

**10** Next, clean the cylinder head with solvent and dry it thoroughly. Compressed air will speed the drying process and ensure that all holes and recessed areas are clean.

**11** Clean all of the valve springs, keepers/collets, retainers and spring seats with solvent and dry them thoroughly. Do the

parts from one valve at a time so that no mixing of parts between valves occurs.

**12** Scrape off any deposits that may have formed on the valve, then use a motorized wire brush to remove deposits from the valve heads and stems. Again, make sure the valves do not get mixed up.

## Inspection

**13** Inspect the head very carefully for cracks and other damage. If cracks are found, a new head will be required. Check the cam bushing surfaces for wear and evidence of seizure. Check the camshafts and rocker arms for wear as well (see Section 9).

**14** Using a precision straightedge and a feeler gauge, check the head gasket mating surface for warpage **(see illustration)**. Lay the

**10.7d Release the spring pressure and remove the spring retainer . . .**

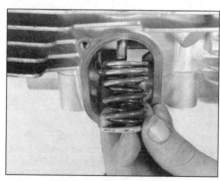

**10.7e . . . and the springs**

**10.7f Pull the valve into the combustion chamber, but don't force it**

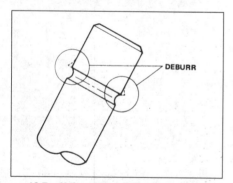

**10.7g If the valve binds in the guide, deburr the area above the keeper groove**

**10.9 Pull the valve stem seal (arrow) off the valve guide**

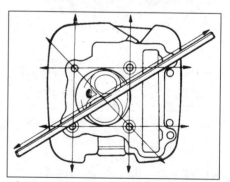

**10.14 Check the cylinder head for warpage with a straightedge and feeler gauge**

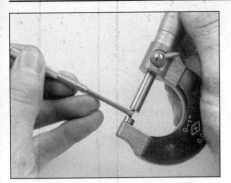

**10.16 Measure the valve guide with a small hole gauge, then measure the hole gauge with a micrometer**

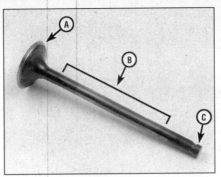

**10.17 Check the valve face (A), stem (B) and keeper/collet groove (C) for signs of wear and damage**

**10.18a Measure the valve stem diameter with a micrometer**

straightedge lengthwise, across the head and diagonally (corner-to-corner), intersecting the head bolt holes, and try to slip a feeler gauge under it, on either side of each combustion chamber. The gauge should be the same thickness as the cylinder head warp limit listed in this Chapter's Specifications. If the feeler gauge can be inserted between the head and the straightedge, the head is warped and must either be machined or, if warpage is excessive, replaced with a new one. Minor surface imperfections can be cleaned up by sanding on a surface plate in a figure-eight pattern with 400 or 600 grit wet or dry sandpaper. Be sure to rotate the head every few strokes to avoid removing material unevenly.

15 Examine the valve seats in each of the combustion chambers. If they are pitted, cracked or burned, the head will require valve service that's beyond the scope of the home mechanic. Measure the valve seat width and compare it to this Chapter's Specifications. If it is not within the specified range, or if it varies around its circumference, valve service work is required.

16 Clean the valve guides to remove any carbon buildup, then measure the inside diameters of the guides (at both ends and the center of the guide) with a small hole gauge and a 0-to-1-inch micrometer **(see illustration)**. Record the measurements for

future reference. These measurements, along with the valve stem diameter measurements, will enable you to compute the valve stem-to-guide clearance. This clearance, when compared to the Specifications, will be one factor that will determine the extent of the valve service work required. The guides are measured at the ends and at the center to determine if they are worn in a bell-mouth pattern (more wear at the ends). If they are, guide replacement is an absolute must.

17 Carefully inspect each valve face for cracks, pits and burned spots. Check the valve stem and the keeper/collet groove area for cracks **(see illustration)**. Rotate the valve and check for any obvious indication that it is bent. Check the end of the stem for pitting and excessive wear and make sure the bevel is the specified width. The presence of any of the above conditions indicates the need for valve servicing.

18 Measure the valve stem diameter **(see illustration)**. By subtracting the stem diameter from the valve guide diameter, the valve stem-to-guide clearance is obtained. If the stem-to-guide clearance is greater than listed in this Chapter's Specifications, the guides and valves will have to be replaced with new ones. Also check the valve stem for bending. Set the valve in a V-block with a dial indicator touching the middle of the stem **(see illustration)**. Rotate the valve and note the

reading on the gauge. If the stem runout exceeds the value listed in this Chapter's Specifications, replace the valve.

19 Check the end of each valve spring for wear and pitting. Measure the free length **(see illustration)** and compare it to this Chapter's Specifications. Any springs that are shorter than specified have sagged and should not be reused. Stand the spring on a flat surface and check it for squareness **(see illustration)**.

20 Check the spring retainers and keepers/collets for obvious wear and cracks. Any questionable parts should not be reused, as extensive damage will occur in the event of failure during engine operation.

21 If the inspection indicates that no service work is required, the valve components can be reinstalled in the head.

### Reassembly

22 Before installing the valves in the head, they should be lapped to ensure a positive seal between the valves and seats. This procedure requires coarse and fine valve lapping compound (available at auto parts stores) and a valve lapping tool. If a lapping tool is not available, a piece of rubber or plastic hose can be slipped over the valve stem (after the valve has been installed in the guide) and used to turn the valve.

23 Apply a small amount of coarse lapping

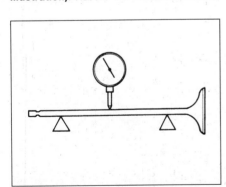

**10.18b Check the valve stem for bends with a V-block (or blocks, as shown here) and a dial indicator**

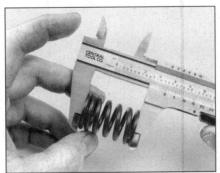

**10.19a Measure the free length of the valve springs**

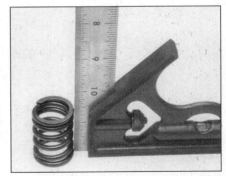

**10.19b Check the valve springs for squareness**

10.23 Apply the lapping compound very sparingly, in small dabs, to the valve face only

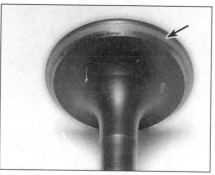

10.24 After lapping, the valve face should have a uniform, unbroken contact pattern (arrow)

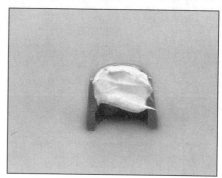

10.28a A small dab of grease will hold the keepers/collets in place on the valve

compound to the valve face **(see illustration)**, then slip the valve into the guide. **Note:** *Make sure the valve is installed in the correct guide and be careful not to get any lapping compound on the valve stem.*

24 Attach the lapping tool (or hose) to the valve and rotate the tool between the palms of your hands. Use a back-and-forth motion rather than a circular motion. Lift the valve off the seat and turn it at regular intervals to distribute the lapping compound properly. Continue the lapping procedure until the valve face and seat contact area is of uniform width and unbroken around the entire circumference of the valve face and seat **(see illustration)**.

10.28b With the keepers/collets secure in their grooves (arrow), release the spring compressor

25 Carefully remove the valve from the guide and wipe off all traces of lapping compound. Use solvent to clean the valve and wipe the seat area thoroughly with a solvent soaked cloth.

26 Repeat the procedure with fine valve lapping compound, then repeat the entire procedure for the remaining valves.

27 Lay the spring seats in place in the cylinder head, then install new valve stem seals on each of the guides **(see illustration 10.9)**. Use an appropriate size deep socket to push the seals into place until they are properly seated. Don't twist or cock them, or they will not seal properly against the valve stems. Also, don't remove them again or they will be damaged.

28 Coat the valve stems with assembly lube or moly-based grease, then install one of them into its guide. Next, install the springs and retainers, compress the springs and install the keepers/collets. **Note:** *Install the springs with the tightly wound coils at the bottom (next to the spring seat).* When compressing the springs with the valve spring compressor, depress them only as far as is absolutely necessary to slip the keepers/collets into place. Apply a small amount of grease to the keepers/collets **(see illustration)** to help hold them in place as the pressure is released from the springs. Make certain that the keepers/collets are securely locked in their retaining grooves **(see illustration)**.

29 Support the cylinder head on blocks so the valves can't contact the workbench top, then very gently tap each of the valve stems with a soft-faced hammer. This will help seat the keepers/collets in their grooves.

**HAYNES HiNT** *Check for proper valve sealing by pouring a small amount of solvent into each of the valve ports. If the solvent leaks past the valve(s) into the combustion chamber area, disassemble the valve(s) and repeat the lapping procedure.*

## 11 Cylinders - removal, inspection and installation

### Removal

1 Following the procedure given in Section 8, remove the cylinder head.

2 Remove the cylinder bolt **(see illustration)**.

3 Lift the cylinder straight up to remove it **(see illustration)**. If it's stuck, tap around its perimeter with a soft-faced hammer, taking care not to break the cooling fins. Don't attempt to pry between the cylinder and the crankcase, as you will ruin the sealing surfaces. As you lift, note the location of the dowel pins and O-ring **(see illustration)**.

11.2 Remove the single Allen bolt that secures the cylinder to the crankcase

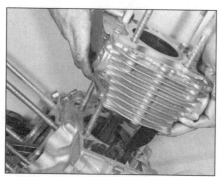

11.3a Lift the cylinder straight up off the studs

11.3b Note the locations of the three dowels (arrows); the large dowel has an O-ring

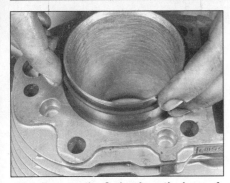

**11.4  Remove the O-ring from the base of the cylinder**

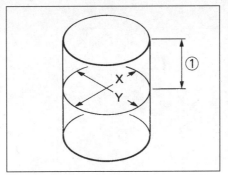

**11.7  Measure the bore at the specified distance from the top of the cylinder (1); measure parallel to the crankshaft centerline, then at right angles to it**

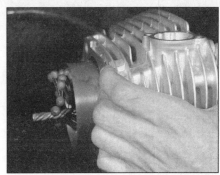

**11.10  Move the hone rapidly up-and-down without stopping**

Be careful not to let these drop into the engine.

4  Stuff clean shop towels around the pistons and remove the gasket **(see illustration)** and all traces of old gasket material from the surfaces of the cylinder, cylinder head and crankcase. Remove the O-ring from the base of the cylinder **(see illustration)**.

### Inspection

5  Don't attempt to separate the liner from the cylinder.

6  Check the cylinder wall carefully for scratches and score marks.

7  Using the appropriate precision measuring tools, check each cylinder's diameter. Measure parallel to the crankshaft axis and across the crankshaft axis, at the depth from the top of the cylinder listed in this Chapter's Specifications **(see illustration)**. Average the two measurements and compare the results to this Chapter's Specifications. If the cylinder walls are tapered, out-of-round, worn beyond the specified limits, or badly scuffed or scored, have them rebored and honed by a dealer service department or a motorcycle repair shop. If a rebore is done, oversize pistons and rings will be required as well.

8  As an alternative, if the precision measuring tools are not available, a dealer service department or motorcycle repair shop will make the measurements and offer advice concerning servicing of the cylinders.

9  If they are in reasonably good condition and

not worn to the outside of the limits, and if the piston-to-cylinder clearances can be maintained properly (see Section 12), then the cylinders do not have to be rebored; honing is all that is necessary.

10  To perform the honing operation you will need the proper size flexible hone with fine stones, or a "bottle brush" type hone, plenty of light oil or honing oil, some shop towels and an electric drill motor. Hold the cylinder block in a vise (cushioned with soft jaws or wood blocks) when performing the honing operation. Mount the hone in the drill motor, compress the stones and slip the hone into the cylinder. Lubricate the cylinder thoroughly, turn on the drill and move the hone up and down in the cylinder at a pace which will produce a fine crosshatch pattern on the cylinder wall with the crosshatch lines intersecting at approximately a 60-degree angle **(see illustration)**. Be sure to use plenty of lubricant and do not take off any more material than is absolutely necessary to produce the desired effect. Do not withdraw the hone from the cylinder while it is running. Instead, shut off the drill and continue moving the hone up and down in the cylinder until it comes to a complete stop, then compress the stones and withdraw the hone. Wipe the oil out of the cylinder and repeat the procedure on the remaining cylinder. Remember, do not remove too much material from the cylinder

wall. If you do not have the tools, or do not desire to perform the honing operation, a dealer service department or motorcycle repair shop will generally do it for a reasonable fee.

11  Next, the cylinders must be thoroughly washed with warm soapy water to remove all traces of the abrasive grit produced during the honing operation. Be sure to run a brush through the bolt holes and flush them with running water. After rinsing, dry the cylinders thoroughly and apply a coat of light, rust-preventative oil to all machined surfaces.

### Installation

12  Lubricate the cylinder bore and piston with plenty of clean engine oil.

13  Install a new O-ring around the base of the cylinder (see illustration 11.4b). Place a new cylinder base gasket on the crankcase **(see illustration)**. Install a new O-ring on the large dowel pin, install it in its bore and make sure the two small dowel pins are in position **(see illustration)**.

14  Attach a piston ring compressor to the piston and compress the piston rings. A large hose clamp can be used instead - just make sure it doesn't scratch the piston, and don't tighten it too much.

15  Install the cylinder block over the pistons and carefully lower it down until the piston crown fits into the cylinder liner **(see illustration)**. While doing this, pull the camshaft chain up, using a hooked tool or a

**11.13a  Place the cylinder base gasket in position**

**11.13b  Make sure the two small dowel pins are in position and install the large dowel pin with its O-ring**

**11.15  If you're very careful, you can install the cylinder over the piston rings without a compressor, but it will make the job easier**

**12.3a The EX mark on top of the piston faces the exhaust (front side of the front cylinder, rear side of the rear cylinder)**

**12.3b Reach into the removal notch with needle-nosed pliers to grasp the circlip**

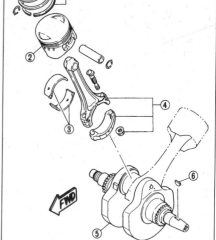

**12.3c Connecting rods and pistons (XV535 models) - exploded view**

1) *Piston rings*
2) *Piston*
3) *Connecting rod bearings*
4) *Connecting rod*
5) *Crankshaft*
6) *Woodruff key (for alternator rotor)*

piece of coat hanger. Also keep an eye on the cam chain guide to make sure it doesn't wedge against the cylinder. Push down on the cylinder, making sure the piston doesn't get cocked sideways, until the bottom of the cylinder liner slides down past the piston rings. A wood or plastic hammer handle can be used to gently tap the cylinder down, but don't use too much force or the piston will be damaged.

**16** Remove the piston ring compressor or hose clamp, being careful not to scratch the piston.

**17** Repeat the procedure to install the remaining cylinder.

**18** The remainder of installation is the reverse of removal.

## 12 Pistons - removal, inspection and installation

**1** The pistons are attached to the connecting rods with piston pins that are a slip fit in the pistons and rods.

**2** Before removing the pistons from the rods, stuff a clean shop towel into each crankcase hole, around the connecting rods. This will prevent the circlips from falling into the crankcase if they are inadvertently dropped.

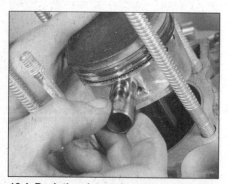

**12.4 Push the piston pin partway out, then grasp it and pull it the rest of the way**

### Removal

**3** Using a sharp scribe, scratch the location of each piston (front or rear cylinder) into its crown (or use a felt pen if the piston is clean enough). Each piston should also have an EX mark on its crown; this mark faces the exhaust side of the cylinder when the piston is installed **(see illustration)**. If not, scribe an arrow into the piston crown before removal. Support the first piston, grasp the circlip with a pointed tool or needle-nose pliers and remove it from the groove **(see illustrations)**.

**4** Push the piston pin out from the opposite end to free the piston from the rod **(see illustration and Tool Tip)**. You may have to deburr the area around the groove to enable the pin to slide out (use a triangular file for this procedure). Repeat the procedure for the other piston.

### Inspection

**5** Before the inspection process can be

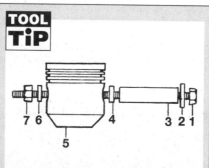

**TOOL TiP**

7 6          4          3 2 1

5

*If the piston pin won't come out, remove the remaining circlip. Fabricate a piston pin removal tool from threaded stock, nuts, washers and a piece of pipe.*
1) *Bolt*            5) *Piston*
2) *Washer*          6) *Washer (B)*
3) *Pipe (A)*        7) *Nut (B)*
4) *Padding (A)*
A *Large enough for piston pin to fit inside*
B *Small enough to fit through piston pin bore*

carried out, the pistons must be cleaned and the old piston rings removed.

**6** Using a piston ring installation tool, carefully remove the rings from the pistons **(see illustration)**. Do not nick or gouge the pistons in the process.

**7** Scrape all traces of carbon from the tops of the pistons. A hand-held wire brush or a piece of fine emery cloth can be used once most of the deposits have been scraped away. Do not, under any circumstances, use a wire brush mounted in a drill motor to remove deposits from the pistons; the piston material is soft and will be eroded away by the wire brush.

**8** Use a piston ring groove cleaning tool to remove any carbon deposits from the ring grooves. Be very careful to remove only the carbon deposits. Do not remove any metal and do not nick or gouge the sides of the ring grooves.

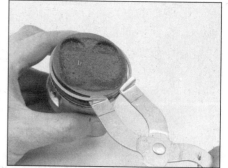

**12.6 Remove the piston rings with a ring removal and installation tool**

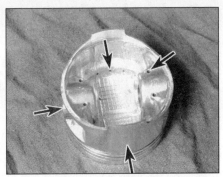

12.11 Check the piston pin bore and the piston skirt for wear; make sure the holes are clear (arrows)

12.13 Measure ring side clearance with a feeler gauge

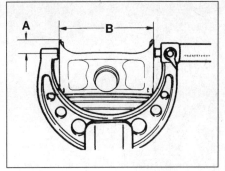

12.14 Measure the piston diameter with a micrometer

*A Specified distance from bottom of piston*
*B Piston diameter*

**TOOL TiP** *If a piston ring groove tool is not available, a piece broken off the old ring will do the job.*

**9** Once the deposits have been removed, clean the pistons with solvent and dry them thoroughly. Make sure the oil return holes below the oil ring grooves are clear.

**10** If the pistons are not damaged or worn excessively and if the cylinders are not rebored, new pistons will not be necessary. Normal piston wear appears as even, vertical wear on the thrust surfaces of the piston and slight looseness of the top ring in its groove. New piston rings, on the other hand, should always be used when an engine is rebuilt.

**11** Carefully inspect each piston for cracks around the skirt, at the pin bosses and at the ring lands **(see illustration)**.

**12** Look for scoring and scuffing on the thrust faces of the skirt, holes in the piston crown and burned areas at the edge of the crown. If the skirt is scored or scuffed, the engine may have been suffering from overheating and/or abnormal combustion, which caused excessively high operating temperatures. The oil pump should be checked thoroughly. A hole in the piston crown, an extreme to be sure, is an indication that abnormal combustion (pre-ignition) was occurring. Burned areas at the edge of the piston crown are usually evidence of spark

knock (detonation). If any of the above problems exist, the causes must be corrected or the damage will occur again.

**13** Measure the piston ring-to-groove clearance by laying a new piston ring in the ring groove and slipping a feeler gauge in beside it **(see illustration)**. Check the clearance at three or four locations around the groove. Be sure to use the correct ring for each groove; they are different. If the clearance is greater than specified, new pistons will have to be used when the engine is reassembled.

**14** Check the piston-to-bore clearance by measuring the bore (see Section 13) and the piston diameter. Make sure that the pistons and cylinders are correctly matched. Measure the piston across the skirt on the thrust faces at a 90-degree angle to the piston pin, at the distance from the bottom of the skirt listed in this Chapter's Specifications **(see illustration)**. Subtract the piston diameter from the bore diameter to obtain the clearance. If it is greater than specified, the cylinders will have to be rebored and new oversized pistons and rings installed. If the appropriate precision measuring tools are not available, the piston-to-cylinder clearances can be obtained, though not quite as accurately, using feeler gauge stock. Feeler gauge stock comes in 12-inch lengths and various thicknesses and is generally available at auto parts stores. To check the clearance,

select a feeler gauge of the same thickness as the piston clearance listed in this Chapter's Specifications and slip it into the cylinder along with the appropriate piston. The cylinder should be upside down and the piston must be positioned exactly as it normally would be. Place the feeler gauge between the piston and cylinder on one of the thrust faces (90-degrees to the piston pin bore). The piston should slip through the cylinder (with the feeler gauge in place) with moderate pressure. If it falls through, or slides through easily, the clearance is excessive and a new piston will be required. If the piston binds at the lower end of the cylinder and is loose toward the top, the cylinder is tapered, and if tight spots are encountered as the feeler gauge is placed at different points around the cylinder, the cylinder is out-of-round. Repeat the procedure for the remaining pistons and cylinders. Be sure to have the cylinders and pistons checked by a dealer service department or a motorcycle repair shop to confirm your findings before purchasing new parts.

**15** Apply clean engine oil to the pin, insert it into the piston and check for freeplay by rocking the pin back-and-forth **(see illustration)**. If the pin is loose, new pistons and pins must be installed.

**16** Refer to Section 13 and install the rings on the pistons.

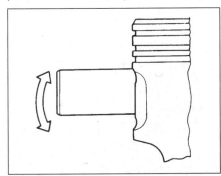

12.15 Slip the pin into the piston and try to wiggle it; if it's loose, replace the piston and pin

12.17a Slip the circlip into its bore with its gap away from the removal notch in the piston . . .

12.17b . . . and push the circlip all the way into its groove; make sure it's securely seated

13.3 Measure ring end gap with a feeler gauge

13.5 If the end gap is too small, clamp a file in a vise and file the ring ends (from the outside in only) to enlarge the gap slightly

13.9a Install the oil ring expander first

## Installation

**17** Install the pistons in their original locations with the EX marks toward the exhaust sides. Lubricate the pins and the rod bores with clean engine oil. Install new circlips in the grooves in the inner sides of the pistons (don't reuse the old circlips). Push the pins into position from the opposite side and install new circlips. Compress the circlips only enough for them to fit in the piston. Make sure the clips are properly seated in the grooves **(see illustrations)**.

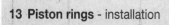 

## 13 Piston rings - installation

**1** Before installing the new piston rings, the ring end gaps must be checked.
**2** Lay out the pistons and the new ring sets so the rings will be matched with the same piston and cylinder during the end gap measurement procedure and engine assembly.
**3** Insert the top (No. 1) ring into the bottom of the first cylinder and square it up with the cylinder walls by pushing it in with the top of the piston **(see illustration)**. The ring should be about one inch above the bottom edge of the cylinder. To measure the end gap, slip a feeler gauge between the ends of the ring and compare the measurement to this Chapter's Specifications.

**4** If the gap is larger or smaller than specified, double check to make sure that you have the correct rings before proceeding.
**5** If the gap is too small, it must be enlarged or the ring ends may come in contact with each other during engine operation, which can cause serious damage. The end gap can be increased by filing the ring ends very carefully with a fine file **(see illustration)**. When performing this operation, file only from the outside in.
**6** Excess end gap is not critical unless it is greater than 0.040 in. (1 mm). Again, double check to make sure you have the correct rings for your engine.
**7** Repeat the procedure for each ring that will be installed in the first cylinder and for each ring in the remaining cylinder. Remember to keep the rings, pistons and cylinders matched up.
**8** Once the ring end gaps have been checked/corrected, the rings can be installed on the pistons.
**9** The oil control ring (lowest on the piston) is installed first. It is composed of three separate components. Slip the expander into the groove, then install the upper side rail **(see illustrations)**. Do not use a piston ring installation tool on the oil ring side rails as they may be damaged. Instead, place one end of the side rail into the groove between the spacer expander and the ring land. Hold it firmly in place and slide a finger around the

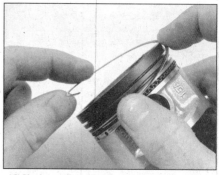

13.9b Installing an oil ring side rail - don't use a ring installation tool to do this

piston while pushing the rail into the groove. Next, install the lower side rail in the same manner.
**10** After the three oil ring components have been installed, check to make sure that both the upper and lower side rails can be turned smoothly in the ring groove.
**11** Install the second (middle) ring next **(see illustration)**. Do not mix the top and middle rings. They can be identified by their profiles **(see illustration)**, as well as the fact that the top ring is thinner than the middle ring.
**12** To avoid breaking the ring, use a piston ring installation tool and make sure that the identification mark is facing up **(see illustration)**. Fit the ring into the middle groove on the piston. Do not expand the ring

13.11a Install the middle ring with its identification mark up

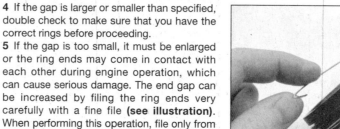

TOP RING

SECOND RING

13.11b The top and middle rings can be identified by their profiles

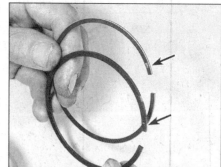

13.12 The top and middle rings have identifying marks (arrows); these must be up when installed

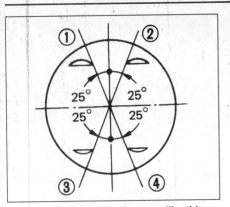

**13.15 Arrange the ring gaps like this**

1) *Top compression ring*
2) *Oil ring lower rail*
3) *Oil ring upper rail*
4) *Second compression ring*

**14.2 Pull off the shaft and no. 1 idler gear**

**14.3a Pull out the Woodruff key . . .**

**14.3b . . . take the no. 2 idler gear off the crankshaft . . .**

**14.3c . . . and locate the washer (it may have stuck to the back of the no. 2 idler gear)**

any more than is necessary to slide it into place.
**13** Finally, install the top ring in the same manner. Make sure the identifying mark is facing up.
**14** Repeat the procedure for the remaining piston and rings. Be very careful not to confuse the top and second rings.
**15** Once the rings have been properly installed, stagger the end gaps, including those of the oil ring side rails **(see illustration)**.

## 14 Idler gears - removal, inspection and installation

**1** Remove the alternator rotor and starter clutch (see Chapter 8).
**2** Remove the no. 1 idler gear and its shaft **(see illustration)**.
**3** Remove the Woodruff key from the crankshaft and pull off the no. 2 idler gear **(see illustrations)**. The washer behind the gear will fall as it's removed, so be careful not to lose it **(see illustration)**.
**4** Check the gears for cracks, chips, or

damaged teeth. Replace them as a set if problems are found.
**5** Installation is the reverse of the removal steps. Make sure the Woodruff key is in its slot **(see illustration 14.3a)**.

## 15 Clutch cable - replacement

**1** Pull out the cotter pin and remove the clevis pin from the lower end of the clutch cable **(see illustration)**. Loosen the locknuts and detach the cable from the bracket on the engine.
**2** Loosen the cable locknut and adjuster at

the handlebar **(see illustration)**. Disconnect the cable from the clutch lever **(see illustration)**.
**3** Installation is the reverse of the removal steps. Adjust the clutch free-play (see *'Daily (pre-ride) checks'* at the beginning of this Manual).

## 16 Clutch and primary gears - removal, inspection and installation

### *Removal*

**1** Drain the engine oil and remove the oil filter (see Chapter 1).

**15.1 Remove the cotter pin, disconnect the cable from the release lever and loosen the locknuts**

**15.2a Loosen the adjuster, align its slot with the cable and pull the cable out of the adjuster . . .**

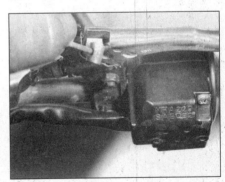

**15.2b . . . then pivot the cable out of the lever slot and lower its end out of the lever**

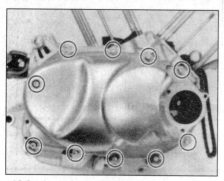

**16.2a  Loosen the bolts 1/4 turn at a time in a criss-cross pattern; note that some secure wiring**

**16.2b  Separate the clutch cover from the crankcase . . .**

**16.2c  . . . if it's difficult to remove, use the pry points at the front . . .**

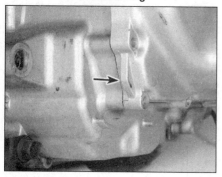

**16.2d  . . . and at the rear**

**16.3  Remove the snap-ring (arrow) and take off the oil pump driven gear**

**16.4a  Loosen the clutch spring bolts evenly**

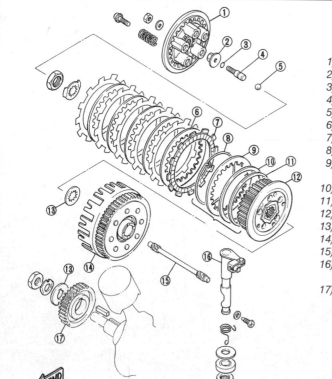

1) Pressure plate
2) Push plate
3) O-ring
4) Short pushrod
5) Steel ball
6) Metal plates
7) Friction plates
8) Wire circlip
9) Clutch damper plate
10) Seat spring
11) Seat plate
12) Clutch boss
13) Retaining plate
14) Clutch housing
15) Long pushrod
16) Push lever assembly
17) Primary drive gear

**16.4b  Clutch (XV535 models) exploded view**

**2** Loosen the right-hand crankcase cover bolts in a criss-cross pattern, 1/4 turn at a time **(see illustration)**. Once they're all loose, remove the bolts and take the cover off **(see illustration)**. If it's stuck, pry gently at the two pry points **(see illustrations)**. Don't pry anywhere else or the gasket surface may be damaged.

**3** Remove the snap-ring and take off the oil pump driven gear **(see illustration)**.

**4** Loosen the pressure plate screws evenly in a criss-cross pattern, then remove the screws and springs **(see illustrations)**.

**5** Remove the pressure plate, then take off the friction plates and metal plates as a set **(see illustrations)**.

**6** Remove the steel ball and the long pushrod **(see illustration)**.

**7** Bend back the lockwasher on the clutch boss

**16.5a  Take off the pressure plate . . .**

16.5b . . . together with the push piece (A) and short pushrod (B)

16.5c The friction plates and metal plates can be removed as a set

16.6a Pull out the steel ball with a magnet . . .

16.6b . . . then pull out the long pushrod

16.7a Bend back the lockwasher

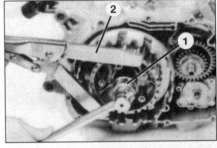

16.7b You'll need a tool to keep the clutch hub from turning; this is the Yamaha special tool . . .

1) Clutch boss nut     2) Holding tool

nut (see illustration). Loosen the nut, using a special holding tool (Yamaha tool no. YM-91402, part no. 90890-04086 or equivalent) to prevent the clutch housing from turning (see illustration). An alternative to this tool can be fabricated from some steel strap, bent at the ends and bolted together in the middle (see illustration). Once the nut is loose, remove it (see illustration).

8 Remove the lockwasher and discard it (see illustration). Use a new one during installation.

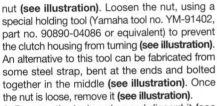

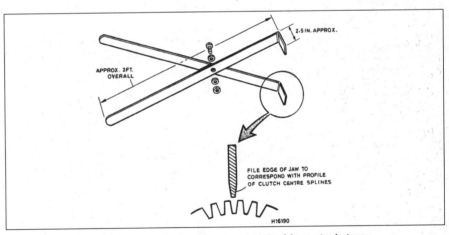

16.7c . . . or you can make your own tool from steel strap

You can make a clutch holding tool by drilling through a steel plate and friction plate and bolting them together. Slip the bolted plates into their normal installed position to lock the clutch housing and clutch boss together. To keep the engine from turning, wedge a rag between the teeth of the primary drive gear and the driven gear on the clutch housing.

**TOOL TiP**

16.7d Remove the nut . . .

16.8 . . . and the lockwasher

16.9a  Pull the clutch boss off . . .

16.9b  . . . and remove the holding plate

16.10a  Bend back the lockwasher (arrow) . . .

16.10b  . . . then wedge a rag between the gears to keep them from turning and loosen the nut

16.11a  Remove the lockwasher . . .

**9** Remove the clutch boss and holding plate **(see illustrations)**.

**10** Bend back the lockwasher from the nut that secures the primary drive gear **(see illustration)**. Wedge a rag between the driven gear and drive gear teeth to keep the gears from turning, then loosen the nut **(see illustration)**. Once the nut is loose, slide the clutch housing/driven gear off and remove the nut.

**11** Remove the lockwasher, retaining plate and oil pump drive gear **(see illustrations)**.

**12** Remove the primary drive gear and Woodruff key **(see illustrations)**.

### Inspection

**13** If the clutch has been chattering (juddering), remove the wire ring and the steel

16.11b  . . . the retaining plate . . .

16.11c  . . . the oil pump drive gear . . .

16.12a  . . . the primary drive gear . . .

16.12b  . . . and the Woodruff key (arrow)

16.13a  Pull one end of the wire circlip out of its hole in the clutch boss . . .

16.13b  . . . and work the circlip out of its groove

**16.13c  Pull off the clutch damper plate . . .**

**16.13d  . . . the seat spring . . .**

**16.13e  . . . and the seat plate**

plate, seat spring and seat plate that make up the clutch damper **(see illustrations)**. These parts need not be removed if the clutch hasn't been chattering.

**14** Examine the splines on both the inside and the outside of the clutch boss. If any wear is evident, replace the clutch boss with a new one.

**15** Measure the free length of the clutch springs **(see illustration)**. Replace the springs as a set if any one of them is not within the values listed in this Chapter's Specifications.

**16** If the lining material of the friction plates smells burnt or if it's glazed, new parts are required. If the metal clutch plates are scored or discolored, they must be replaced with new ones. Measure the thickness of each friction plate **(see illustration)** and compare the results to this Chapter's Specifications. Replace the friction plates as a set if any are near the wear limit.

**17** Lay the metal plates, one at a time, on a perfectly flat surface (such as a piece of plate glass) and check for warpage by trying to slip a gauge between the flat surface and the plate **(see illustration)**. The feeler gauge should be the same thickness as the warpage limit listed in this Chapter's Specifications. Do this at several places around the plate's circumference. If the feeler gauge can be slipped under the plate, it is warped and should be replaced with a new one.

**18** Check the tabs on the friction plates for

excessive wear and mushroomed edges. They can be cleaned up with a file if the deformation is not severe.

**19** Check the edges of the slots in the clutch housing for indentations made by the friction plate tabs. If the indentations are deep they can prevent clutch release, so the housing should be replaced with a new one. If the indentations can be removed easily with a file, the life of the housing can be prolonged to an extent.

**20** Check the teeth on the primary drive gear and driven gear for wear or damage and replace them if defects are found. The driven gear is replaced together with the clutch housing.

**21** Check the pressure plate and push plate for wear and damage. Replace any worn or damaged parts.

**22** Check the pushrods and the steel ball for wear or damage and replace them if defects are visible. Install a new O-ring on the short pushrod **(see illustration 16.5b)**.

**23** Check the bearing surface in the center of the clutch housing and replace the clutch housing if it's worn or damaged.

**24** Clean all traces of old gasket material from the clutch cover and its mating surface on the crankcase.

### Installation

**25** Install the primary drive gear Woodruff key, then install the primary drive gear, oil

pump drive gear and retaining plate **(see illustrations 16.11b, 16.11c, 16.12a and 16.12b)**.

**26** Install a new lockwasher on the retaining plate. Make sure the lockwasher tabs fit into the notches in the retaining plate, then install the nut.

**27** Coat the clutch housing bearing surface with clean engine oil, then slip the clutch housing onto the crankshaft **(see illustration 16.10a)**.

**28** Wedge a rag between the primary drive gear and the driven gear on the clutch housing so they can't turn, then tighten the nut to the torque listed in this Chapter's Specifications. Bend the lockwasher against the nut to hold it **(see illustration)**.

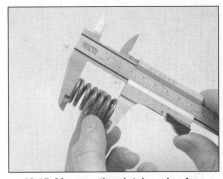

**16.15  Measure the clutch spring free length**

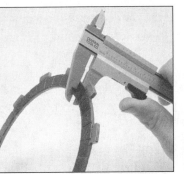

**16.16  Measure the thickness of the friction plates**

**16.17  Check the metal plates for warpage**

**16.28  With the nut tightened to the specified torque, bend the lockwasher against one of the flats**

**16.29 Install the oil pump driven gear and secure it with a new snap-ring**

**16.30 Install the clutch boss lockwasher**

**16.31 Once the nut is tightened to the specified torque, bend the lockwasher against the nut**

**29** Install the oil pump driven gear and secure it with the snap-ring **(see illustration)**.

**30** Install the clutch holding plate, then the clutch boss **(see illustrations 16.9b and 16.9a)**. Install a new lockwasher **(see illustration)**. Install the nut with its recessed side toward the clutch boss and tighten it slightly **(see illustration 16.7e)**.

**31** Hold the clutch boss and housing from turning with one of the methods described in Step 7. Tighten the clutch boss nut to the torque listed in this Chapter's Specifications, then bend the lockwasher against the nut to secure it **(see illustration)**.

**32** If you removed the clutch damper, reverse

Step 13 to install it. The OUTSIDE mark on the seat spring faces out (away from the engine). Make sure the wire ring is securely seated in its groove in the clutch boss.

**33** Coat the pushrods and steel ball with multipurpose grease. Install the long pushrod and ball in the engine and the short pushrod in the pressure plate **(see illustrations 16.6b, 16.6a and 16.5b)**.

**34** Coat one of the friction plates with engine oil and install it in the clutch housing so its double notch aligns with the embossed marks on the clutch housing **(see illustration)**. If there aren't any visible marks on the clutch housing, align the double notches on all of the friction plates with each other. Engage the

tabs on the friction plate with the slots in the clutch housing.

**35** Coat a metal plate with engine oil and install it on top of the friction plate with its rounded side in. Continue to install alternate friction and metal plates, coated with engine oil (a friction plate is the last one installed). Align the double notch on each remaining friction plate with the clutch housing marks (if equipped) or with the double notches on the previously installed friction plates. **Note:** *If any of the friction plates fit tightly in the clutch housing, remove all of the friction and metal plates, then reinstall them so the single notches are aligned with the clutch housing marks (see illustration).*

**36** Install the pressure plate, springs and screws. Tighten the screws evenly in a criss-cross pattern to the torque listed in this Chapter's Specifications.

**37** Loosen the locknut on the clutch mechanism freeplay adjuster **(see illustration)**. Push the lever by hand toward the front of the engine as far as it will go, then note the positions of the lever mark and the match mark on the crankcase **(see illustration)**. If they aren't aligned, turn the adjuster in or out until they are, then tighten the locknut.

**38** Remove the snap-ring and pry the seal out of the clutch cover **(see illustrations)**. Tap in a new seal with a socket the same diameter as the seal, then install a new snap-ring. Make

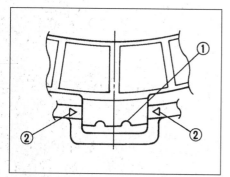

**16.34 Align the double notches in the friction plates (1) with the marks on the clutch housing (2) . . .**

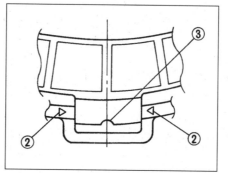

**16.35 . . . if tight friction plates impede clutch movement, align the single notches (3) with the marks (2)**

**16.37a Loosen the adjuster locknut (arrow)**

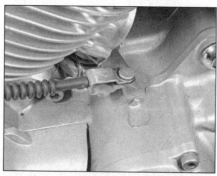

**16.37b Align the clutch lever mark with the mark on the crankcase**

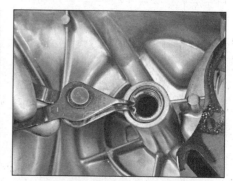

**16.38a Remove the snap-ring . . .**

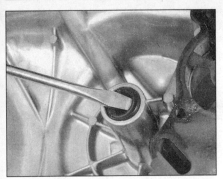

16.38b . . . and pry out the seal

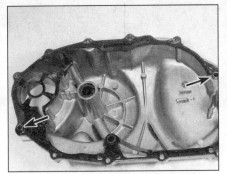

16.38c Make sure the dowels are in position (arrows) and install the gasket

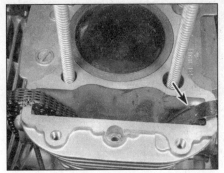

17.2a Lift out the exhaust side chain damper (arrow) . . .

sure the clutch cover dowels are in position and install a new gasket **(see illustration)**.
**39** Install the clutch cover over the dowels, then install and finger-tighten the bolts. Four of the bolts retain wiring harness clamps.
**40** Tighten the bolts in stages, using a criss-cross pattern, to the torque listed in this Chapter's Specifications.
**41** Install a new oil filter (see Chapter 1).
**42** Fill the crankcase with the recommended type and amount of engine oil (see Chapter 1).
**43** The remainder of installation is the reverse of the removal steps.

### 17 Cam chains and dampers - removal, inspection and installation

#### Removal

**1** Remove the cylinder head (see Section 8).
**Rear cylinder**
**2** Lift the exhaust side chain damper out of its slot **(see illustrations)**.
**3** Remove the alternator and starter clutch (see Chapter 8).
**4** Remove the idler gears (see Section 14).
**5** Unbolt the intake side cam chain damper and lift it out **(see illustration 17.2b)** and the accompanying illustration).

**6** Slip the cam chain off the crankshaft sprocket and remove it.
**Front cylinder**
**7** Remove the clutch and primary gears (see Section 16).
**8** Lift the intake side chain damper out of its slot.
**9** Unbolt the exhaust side cam chain damper and lift it out **(see illustration)**.
**10** Slip the cam chain off the crankshaft sprocket and remove it **(see illustration)**.

#### Inspection

**11** Check the chain for binding and obvious

damage. If these conditions are visible, or if the chain appears to be stretched, replace it.
**12** Check the dampers for deep grooves, cracking and other obvious damage and replace them if necessary **(see illustration)**.
**13** Check the sprocket teeth for wear or damage. Replace the cam sprockets if undesirable conditions are found. The entire crankshaft must be replaced if the crankshaft sprockets are worn or damaged.

#### Installation

**14** Installation is the reverse of the removal steps. Be sure to align the timing marks on the crankshaft sprocket and cam sprocket as described in Section 8.

17.2b . . . the bottom end fits into a slot in the crankcase

a) Chain damper slot
b) Intake side chain damper bolts

17.5 Take the intake side chain guide off the crankcase

17.9 Remove the exhaust side chain damper bolts (arrows) and lift the chain damper out

17.10 Slip the chain off the sprocket and remove it

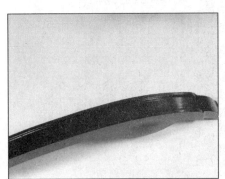

17.12 Check the friction surface of each damper for wear or scoring

18.2a Remove the oil pump mounting bolts . . .

18.2b . . . and take the pump off . . .

18.3 . . . then remove the dowel with O-ring and separate O-ring (arrow)

18.5a The cover screw (arrow) may be tight enough to require an impact driver

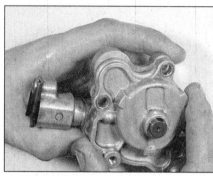

18.5b Lift off the cover . . .

## 18 Oil pump - removal, inspection and installation

**Note:** *The oil pump can be removed with the engine in the frame.*

### Removal

1 Remove the oil pump driven gear and the clutch (see Section 16).
2 Remove the oil pump mounting bolts and remove the pump **(see illustrations)**.
3 Remove the oil pump dowel and O-rings **(see illustration)**.

### Disassembly, inspection and reassembly

4 Wash the oil pump in solvent, then dry it off.
5 Remove the pump housing screw (use an impact driver if it's tight) **(see illustration)**. Lift off the housing **(see illustration)**.
6 Lift off the rotors **(see illustrations)**.
7 Check the pump body and rotors for scoring and wear. If any damage or uneven or excessive wear is evident, replace the pump (individual parts aren't available). If you are rebuilding the engine, it's a good idea to install a new oil pump.
8 Measure the clearance between the inner and outer rotors and between the outer rotor and housing **(see illustrations)**. Replace the pump if the clearance is excessive.

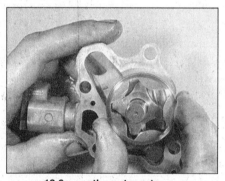

18.6a . . . the outer rotor . . .

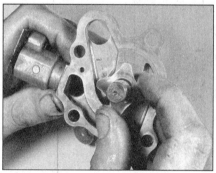

18.6b . . . and the inner rotor

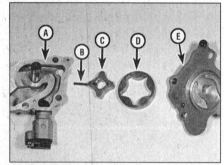

18.6c Pump body and rotors
A) Pump body
B) Drive pin
C) Inner rotor
D) Outer rotor
E) Cover

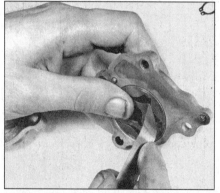

18.8a Measure the tip clearance between the inner and outer rotors

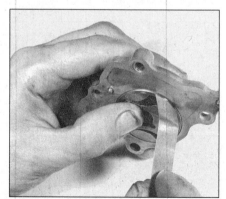

18.8b . . . and the clearance between the outer rotor and housing

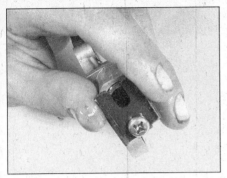

18.9a Remove the screw (use an impact driver if it's tight) . . .

18.9b . . . take off the cover . . .

18.9c . . . dump out the spring . . .

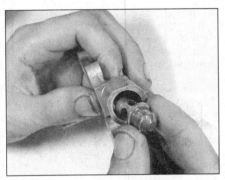

18.9d . . . and the relief valve

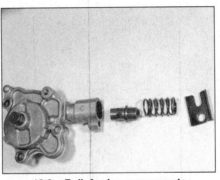

18.9e Relief valve components

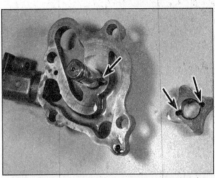

18.10 Be sure the drive pin aligns with the slot in the inner rotor (arrows)

9  Remove the screw and retaining plate, then take out the spring and relief valve (see illustrations). Check the valve for scoring or other damage and check the spring for weakness. Replace the oil pump if any of the relief valve parts are in doubtful condition.

10  If the pump is good, reverse the disassembly steps to reassemble it. Make sure the pin is centered in the rotor shaft so it will align with the slot in the inner rotor (see illustration).

## Installation

11  Before installing the pump, prime it by pouring oil into it while turning the shaft by hand - this will ensure that it begins to pump oil quickly.

*Caution: Also pour oil into the crankcase oil passages to prevent engine damage on start-up.*

12  Installation is the reverse of removal, with the following additions:

a)  *Be sure the dowel and O-rings are in position (see illustration).*

b)  *Tighten the pump mounting bolts to the torque listed in this Chapter's Specifications.*

## 19 Oil strainer - removal, inspection and installation

1  Drain the engine oil (see Chapter 1) and unbolt the oil passage housing from the engine (see illustration).

2  Take the oil passage housing off. If the strainer comes out with the housing, pull them apart (see illustration). If it stays in the engine, pull it out (see illustration).

18.12 Be sure the dowel pin and O-rings (arrows) are fitted; pour engine oil into the passages before installing the oil pump

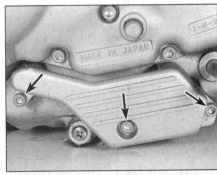

19.1 Remove the Allen bolts (arrows) and take off the oil passage housing

19.2a Pull the strainer out of the housing . . .

19.2b . . . or out of the engine

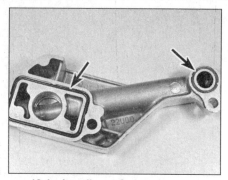

19.4a Install new O-rings in the oil passage housing (arrows)

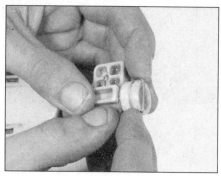

19.4b . . . and on the strainer

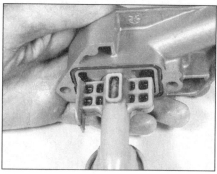

19.5 Push the strainer into the oil passage housing until it seats securely

20.2 There should be a punch mark next to the shift lever slot (arrows); if not, make your own

20.8a Remove the circlip (arrow) . . .

3 Check all parts for visible wear or damage. If the strainer is so clogged it can't be cleaned, replace it.
4 Remove the O-rings and install new ones (see illustrations).
5 Push the strainer into the oil passage housing (see illustration).
6 Installation is the reverse of the removal steps. Make sure the end of the strainer engages its tab in the far side of the crankcase. Tighten the oil passage housing bolts to the torque listed in this Chapter's Specifications. Fill the engine oil.

## 20 External shift mechanism - removal, inspection and installation

### Shift lever and pedal

1 Support the bike securely so it can't be knocked over during this procedure.
2 Look for a punch mark on the end of the lever shaft (see illustration). This should align with the groove in the lever. If you can't find it, make your own punch mark so the lever can be realigned correctly during installation.
3 Remove the lever pinch bolt (see illustration 20.2). Pull the lever off the shaft, together with the linkage rod.
4 If it's necessary to separate the shift pedal from the footpeg assembly, remove the assembly as described in Chapter 7.
5 Installation is the reverse of removal. Adjust the linkage as needed with the nuts on the linkage shaft (see Chapter 1).

### Shift mechanism removal

6 Disconnect the shift lever from the shaft (Steps 1 through 3).
7 Remove the clutch housing/primary driven gear (see Section 16). Remove the alternator cover (see Chapter 8).
8 Remove the circlip and washer from the shift shaft (see illustrations).
9 Pull on the stopper lever to disengage it from the shift cam and unhook the torsion spring from its post (see illustrations). Slide the shift shaft and stopper lever out of the crankcase (see illustration). Keep track of the washer on the shift shaft so it isn't lost.

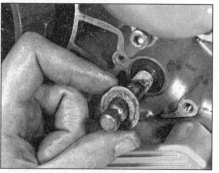

20.8b . . . and the washer

20.9a Pull the stopper lever in the direction shown by the arrow . . .

20.9b . . . and unhook the torsion spring (arrow) from its post

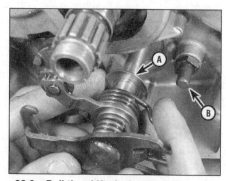

20.9c Pull the shift shaft out, taking care not to lose the washer (A); check guide bar (B) for looseness

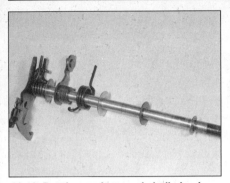

20.10 Put the washers and circlip back on the shaft so they won't be lost

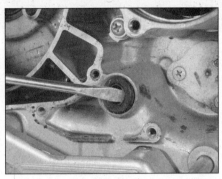

20.15a Pry the shift shaft seal out of the crankcase . . .

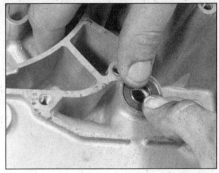

20.15b . . . press a new seal in with fingers or a socket the same diameter as the seal

**10** Reassemble the components on the shaft to keep them in order **(see illustration)**.

### Shift mechanism inspection

**11** Inspect the shift shaft guide bar **(see illustration 20.9c)**. If it's worn or damaged, replace it. If it's loose, bend back its lockwasher, unscrew it, reinstall it with a new lockwasher and tighten it securely. Bend the new lockwasher against the nut to secure it.
**12** Check the shift shaft for bends and damage to the splines. If the shaft is bent, you can attempt to straighten it, but if the splines are damaged it will have to be replaced. Inspect the pawls and springs on the shift shaft and replace the shaft if they're worn or damaged.
**13** Check the condition of the stopper lever and spring. Replace the stopper lever if it's worn where it contacts the shift cam. Replace the spring if it's distorted.
**14** Inspect the pins on the end of the shift cam. If they're worn or damaged, you'll have to disassemble the crankcase to replace the shift cam.
**15** Inspect the shift shaft seal and replace it if it's worn or damaged **(see illustrations)**. It's a good idea to replace the seal whenever the shift shaft is removed.

### Installation

**16** Remove the circlip and smaller washer from the shift shaft. Be sure the larger washer

is on the shift shaft, then install the shift shaft and stopper lever in the crankcase. Engage the stopper lever with the shift cam and position the torsion spring against its post **(see illustration)**.
**17** Install the plain washer and circlip on the other end of the shift shaft **(see illustrations 20.8b and 20.8a)**.
**18** The remainder of installation is the reverse of the removal steps.
**19** Adjust the shift pedal position (see Chapter 1).
**20** Check the engine oil level and add some, if necessary (see Chapter 1).

### 21 Middle driven gear - removal, inspection and installation

### Removal

**1** Remove the engine from the frame (see Section 5).
**2** Unbolt the middle gear case from the engine **(see illustrations)**.
**3** Remove four bolts that secure the bearing housing to the case **(see illustration)**. Remove the bearing housing and any shims, writing down the number and location of the shims for use during installation **(see illustrations)**.

20.16 The external shift linkage should look like this when it's installed

21.2a Remove the Allen bolts (arrows) . . .

21.2b . . . and take the middle driven gear case off

21.3a Remove four bolts . . .

21.3b . . . pull the middle driven gear back from the crankcase . . .

21.3c ... pull out the shims and write down their locations ...

21.3d ... then pull the assembly out of the engine

21.4 Remove the O-ring from the housing with a pointed tool

21.9 Inspect the ball bearing in the engine; have it replaced if it's worn or damaged

21.10 Install a new O-ring on the middle driven gear case

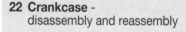

## 22 Crankcase - disassembly and reassembly

1 To examine and repair or replace the crankshaft, middle driveshaft, connecting rods, bearings, or transmission components, the crankcase must be split into two parts.

### Disassembly

2 Remove the cylinder heads, cylinders, pistons and cam chains (see Sections 8, 11, 12 and 17).
3 Remove the alternator (Chapter 8) and pick-up coil (Chapter 4).
4 Remove the clutch and primary gears, oil pump and idler gears (see Sections 16, 18 and 14).
5 Remove the external shift linkage (see Section 20).
6 Remove the middle driven gear (see Section 21).
7 Remove the oil strainer (see Section 19).
8 The shift cam must be positioned so it doesn't hang up on the crankcase when separating the halves (see illustration). Rotate it to the correct position if necessary.
9 Remove the crankcase bolts in the reverse of the tightening sequence (start with the highest-numbered bolt and work to the lowest) (see illustrations). Note that one bolt secures the engine protector bracket (see illustration).

4 Remove the O-ring from the bearing housing (see illustration).

### Inspection

5 Check the universal joint and ball bearing on the middle driven shaft for looseness or stiff movement.
6 Check the shaft splines and the teeth of the middle driven gear for wear or damage.
7 Check the damper spring for looseness or obvious damage such as breakage.
8 If any of the above conditions exist, have the middle driven gear disassembled and repaired by a Yamaha dealer or other qualified motorcycle repair shop.
9 Spin the middle driven gear bearing in the crankcase with fingers and check for looseness, excessive noise or rough movement (see illustration). If these conditions are found, have the bearing replaced by a Yamaha dealer or other qualified motorcycle repair shop.

### Installation

10 Installation is the reverse of the removal steps, with the following additions:
a) If the middle driven gear was disassembled, have gear lash adjusted by a Yamaha dealer or other qualified motorcycle repair shop. If not, reinstall the shims in their original positions.
b) Use new O-rings on the bearing housing and middle driven gear case (see illustration).

22.8 Position the shift cam so it aligns with the notches in the crankcase

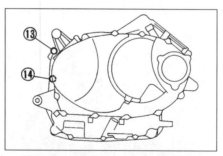

22.9a Loosen the crankcase bolts in sequence, starting with the highest number bolts (in the right side of the crankcase) ...

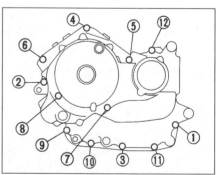

22.9b ... and working to the lowest (in the left side of the crankcase)

22.9c  The engine protector bracket is bolted to the front of the crankcase

22.10a  Lift the right crankcase half off the left half . . .

22.10b  . . . prying gently at the pry points if necessary . . .

**10** Carefully separate the crankcase halves **(see illustration)**. As you lift, pry gently and evenly at the pry points around the crankcase seam **(see illustrations)**. Tap alternately on the transmission shafts, front engine mounting boss and shift cam. If the halves won't separate easily, make sure all fasteners have been removed. Don't pry against the crankcase mating surfaces or they'll leak.

**11** Look for the O-ring and dowels **(see illustrations)**. If they're not in one of the crankcase halves, locate them.

**12** Remove the oil baffle plate (where fitted) from the right-hand crankcase half if the crankcases are being replaced. Otherwise it can be left in place **(see illustration)**.

**13** Refer to Sections 24 through 28 for information on the internal components of the crankcase.

### Reassembly

**14** Make sure the crankshaft and transmission shafts are correctly positioned in the upper crankcase half (see Sections 25 and 28).

**15** Remove all traces of sealant from the crankcase mating surfaces. Be careful not to let any fall into the case as this is done. Check to make sure the large dowel (with a new O-ring) and the two small dowels are in place **(see illustrations)**.

**16** Pour some engine oil over the transmission gears, the crankshaft main

22.10c  . . . (these are spaced around the crankcase) . . .

22.10d  . . . insert a screwdriver in each pry point and apply gentle pressure

22.11a  Remove the small dowels (there's one at each end of the crankcase) . . .

22.11b  . . . and the large dowel with its O-ring

22.12  The oil baffle plate can be left in position unless the crankcase half is to be replaced

22.15a  Install a new O-ring . . .

22.15b  . . . the large dowel and the two small dowels

bearings and the shift cam. Also pour oil into the exposed internal oil passages. Don't get any oil on the crankcase mating surfaces.

17 Apply a thin, even bead of Yamaha Bond or Quick Gasket sealant (part no. ACC-11001-05-01) or equivalent to the crankcase mating surfaces.

*Caution: Don't apply an excessive amount of sealant.*

18 Check the position of the shift cam. Make sure it's turned so it won't obstruct assembly of the cases (see illustration 22.8).

19 Carefully assemble the crankcase halves over the dowels.

*Caution: The crankcase halves should fit together completely without being forced. If they're slightly apart, DO NOT force them together by tightening the crankcase bolts.*

20 Install the crankcase bolts in their holes (see illustrations 22.9a and 22.9b). Bolts 1 through 12 have steel washers.

21 Tighten the bolts in numerical order, starting with the lowest-numbered bolt and working to the highest. Tighten all bolts to the torque listed in this Chapter's Specifications.

**Note:** *There are different torque settings for the 8mm bolts and the 6mm bolts.*

22 Turn the mainshaft and the transmission driveshaft to make sure they turn freely. Also make sure the crankshaft turns freely. Rotate the shift cam by hand to make sure the transmission shifts into the different gear positions.

23 The remainder of assembly is the reverse of disassembly.

24 Be sure to refill the engine oil (see Chapter 1).

## 23 Crankcase components - inspection and servicing

1 After the crankcases have been separated and the crankshaft, shift cam and forks and transmission components removed, the crankcases should be cleaned thoroughly with new solvent and dried with compressed air.

2 Remove any oil passage plugs that haven't already been removed. All oil passages should be blown out with compressed air.

3 All traces of old gasket sealant should be removed from the mating surfaces. Minor damage to the surfaces can be cleaned up with a fine sharpening stone or grindstone. Check both crankcase halves very carefully for cracks and other damage.

*Caution: Be very careful not to nick or gouge the crankcase mating surfaces or leaks will result.*

4 If any damage is found that can't be repaired, replace the crankcase halves as a set.

## 24 Main and connecting rod bearings - general note

1 Even though main and connecting rod bearings are generally replaced with new ones during the engine overhaul, the old bearings should be retained for close examination as they may reveal valuable information about the condition of the engine.

2 Bearing failure occurs mainly because of lack of lubrication, the presence of dirt or other foreign particles, overloading the engine and/or corrosion. Regardless of the cause of bearing failure, it must be corrected before the engine is reassembled to prevent it from happening again.

3 When examining the bearings, remove the rod bearings from the connecting rods and caps and lay them out on a clean surface in the same general position as their location on the crankshaft journals. This will enable you to match any noted bearing problems with the corresponding side of the crankshaft journal. The main bearings are pressed into the crankcase halves and are only removed if they need to be replaced.

4 Dirt and other foreign particles get into the engine in a variety of ways. It may be left in the engine during assembly or it may pass through filters or breathers. It may get into the oil and from there into the bearings. Metal chips from machining operations and normal engine wear are often present. Abrasives are sometimes left in engine components after reconditioning operations such as cylinder honing, especially when parts are not thoroughly cleaned using the proper cleaning methods. Whatever the source, these foreign objects often end up imbedded in the soft bearing material and are easily recognized. Large particles will not imbed in the bearing and will score or gouge the bearing and journal. The best prevention for this cause of bearing failure is to clean all parts thoroughly and keep everything spotlessly clean during engine reassembly. Frequent and regular oil and filter changes are also recommended.

5 Lack of lubrication or lubrication breakdown has a number of interrelated causes. Excessive heat (which thins the oil), overloading (which squeezes the oil from the bearing face) and oil leakage or throw off (from excessive bearing clearances, worn oil pump or high engine speeds) all contribute to lubrication breakdown. Blocked oil passages will also starve a bearing and destroy it. When lack of lubrication is the cause of bearing failure, the bearing material is wiped or extruded from the steel backing of the bearing. Temperatures may increase to the point where the steel backing and the journal turn blue from overheating.

6 Riding habits can have a definite effect on bearing life. Full throttle low speed operation, or lugging the engine, puts very high loads on bearings, which tend to squeeze out the oil film.

These loads cause the bearings to flex, which produces fine cracks in the bearing face (fatigue failure). Eventually the bearing material will loosen in pieces and tear away from the steel backing. Short trip driving leads to corrosion of bearings, as insufficient engine heat is produced to drive off the condensed water and corrosive gases produced. These products collect in the engine oil, forming acid and sludge. As the oil is carried to the engine bearings, the acid attacks and corrodes the bearing material.

7 Incorrect bearing installation during engine assembly will lead to bearing failure as well. Tight fitting bearings which leave insufficient bearing oil clearances result in oil starvation. Dirt or foreign particles trapped behind a bearing insert result in high spots on the bearing which lead to failure.

8 To avoid bearing problems, clean all parts thoroughly before reassembly, double check all bearing clearance measurements and lubricate the new bearings with engine assembly lube or moly-based grease during installation.

## 25 Crankshaft and main bearings - removal, inspection, main bearing selection and installation

### *Crankshaft removal*

1 Separate the crankcase halves (see Section 22).

2 Lift the crankshaft out, together with the connecting rods, and set them on a clean surface (see illustration).

### *Inspection*

3 If you haven't already done so, mark and remove the connecting rods from the crankshaft (see Section 26).

4 Clean the crankshaft with solvent, using a rifle-cleaning brush to scrub out the oil passages. If available, blow the crank dry with compressed air. Check the main and connecting rod journals for uneven wear, scoring and pits. Rub a copper coin across the journal several times - if a journal picks up copper from the coin, it's too rough. Replace the crankshaft.

5 Check the camshaft chain sprockets on the

**25.2 Lift the crankshaft and connecting rods out of the crankcase**

**25.6  Place the crankshaft in V-blocks or a holding fixture and check for runout with a dial indicator**

**25.7a  Measure journal diameter with a micrometer**

**25.7b  Measure main bearing diameter with a hole gauge . . .**

**25.7c  . . . then measure the gauge diameter with a micrometer**

**25.10  Press the main bearing out; apply pressure from the side opposite the locating tab**

**25.11a  This special Yamaha tool is used to press in the main bearings . . .**

crankshaft for chipped teeth and other wear. If any undesirable conditions are found, replace the crankshaft. Check the chains as described in Section 17. Check the rest of the crankshaft for cracks and other damage. It should be magnafluxed to reveal hidden cracks - a dealer service department or motorcycle machine shop will handle the procedure.

**6** Set the crankshaft on V-blocks and check the runout with a dial indicator touching the alternator and clutch mounting surfaces **(see illustration)**. Compare your findings with this Chapter's Specifications. If the runout exceeds the limit, replace the crank.

### Main bearing selection

**Note:** *This procedure requires precision*

*measuring equipment, a press and a special Yamaha tool. If you don't have the necessary equipment, have the procedure done by a dealer service department or motorcycle repair shop.*

**7** Measure the diameter of the main bearing journals with a micrometer **(see illustration)**. Measure the inside diameter of the main bearings with a hole gauge and micrometer **(see illustrations)**. The difference between the two measurements is bearing clearance.

**8** The clearance should be within the range listed in this Chapter's Specifications.

**9** If clearance is greater than the service limit listed in this Chapter's Specifications and new

bearings don't solve the problem, replace the crankshaft.

**10** If the clearance is greater than the service limit listed in this Chapter's Specifications but journal diameter is within specifications, press the main bearings out of their bores **(see illustration)**.

**11** Measure the diameter of the bearing bores in the crankcase halves with a micrometer. If they're greater than the maximum listed in this Chapter's Specifications, replace the crankcase halves as a set. If they're within the specified limits, refer to this Chapter's Specifications for the bearing color code and install new bearings **(see illustrations)** (the color is painted on the edge of the bearing).

**25.11b  . . . the bearing fits over the support . . .**

**25.11c  . . . and the plate fits on top of the support with its flat aligned with the bearing locating tab; a handle is threaded into the support to contact the press ram**

**25.11d  Align the locating tab with the notch and press the bearing into its bore**

**25.14 Coat the bearing with assembly lube or moly-based grease**

**25.15a Guide the crankshaft into the main bearing . . .**

**25.15b . . . and position the connecting rods so they're aligned with the cylinders**

**12** If any crank journal is out-of-round or tapered or the bearing clearance is beyond the limit listed in this Chapter's Specifications with new bearings, replace the crankshaft.

### Installation

**13** Install the connecting rods on the crankshaft at this point if they were removed (see Section 26).
**14** Lubricate the bearings with engine assembly lube or moly-based grease **(see illustration)**.
**15** Carefully lower the crankshaft into place **(see illustration)**. Align the connecting rods with the cylinders **(see illustration)**.
**16** Assemble the case halves (see Section 22) and check to make sure the crankshaft and the transmission shafts turn freely.

---

**26 Connecting rods and bearings** - removal, inspection, bearing selection and installation

### Removal

**1** Before removing the connecting rods from the crankshaft, insert a feeler gauge between the crankshaft and the big end of each connecting rod and between the two connecting rods and measure the side clearance **(see illustration)**. If the clearance on any rod is greater than that listed in this Chapter's Specifications, that rod will have to be replaced with a new one.
**2** Using a center punch or felt pen, mark the position of each rod and cap, relative to its

position on the crankshaft (left or right) **(see illustration)**.
**3** Unscrew the bearing cap nuts, separate the cap from the rod, then detach the rod from the crankshaft **(see illustrations)**. If the cap is stuck, tap on the ends of the rod bolts with a soft-faced hammer to free them.
**4** Roll the bearing inserts sideways to separate them from the rods and caps. Keep them in order so they can be reinstalled in their original locations. Wash the parts in solvent and dry them with compressed air, if available.

### Inspection

**5** Check the connecting rods for cracks and other obvious damage. Lubricate the piston pin for each rod, install it in the proper rod and check for play **(see illustration)**. If it wobbles, replace the connecting rod and/or the pin.
**6** Examine the connecting rod bearing inserts. If they are scored, badly scuffed or appear to have been seized, new bearings must be installed. Always replace the bearings in the connecting rods as a set. If they are badly damaged, check the corresponding crankshaft journal. Evidence of extreme heat, such as discoloration, indicates that lubrication failure has occurred. Be sure to thoroughly check the oil pump and pressure relief valves as well as all oil holes and passages before reassembling the engine.
**7** Have the rods checked for twist and bending at a dealer service department or other motorcycle repair shop.

**26.1 Measure big end play between the two rods and between the rods and crankshaft**

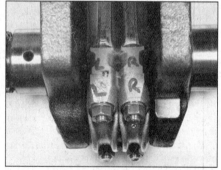

**26.2 Label the rods and caps according to their position on the crankshaft (left or right)**

**26.3a Undo the connecting rod nuts . . .**

**26.3b . . . and take off the caps**

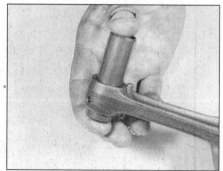

**26.5 Slip the piston pin into the rod and rock it back-and-forth to check for looseness**

26.11 Lay a strip of Plastigauge on the journal, parallel to the crankshaft centerline

26.13 Place the Plastigauge scale next to the flattened Plastigauge to measure the bearing clearance

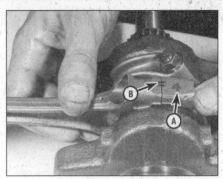

26.18a The number on the connecting rod (A) is used for bearing selection; use the letter (B) to align the cap and rod

## Connecting rod bearing selection

**8** If the bearings and journals appear to be in good condition, check the oil clearances as follows:

**9** Start with the rod for one cylinder. Wipe the bearing inserts and the connecting rod and cap clean, using a lint-free cloth.

**10** Install the bearing inserts in the connecting rod and cap. Make sure the tab on the bearing engages with the notch in the rod or cap.

**11** Wipe off the connecting rod journal with a lint-free cloth. Lay a strip of Plastigauge across the top of the journal, parallel with the journal axis **(see illustration)**.

**12** Position the connecting rod on the journal, then install the rod cap and nuts. Tighten the nuts to the torque listed in this Chapter's Specifications, but don't allow the connecting rod to rotate at all.

**13** Unscrew the nuts and remove the connecting rod and cap from the journal, being very careful not to disturb the Plastigauge. Compare the width of the crushed Plastigauge to the scale printed in the Plastigauge envelope to determine the bearing oil clearance **(see illustration)**.

**14** If the clearance is within the range listed in this Chapter's Specifications and the bearings are in perfect condition, they can be reused. If the clearance is greater than the wear limit, replace the bearing inserts with new inserts that have the same color code, then check the clearance once again. Always replace all of the inserts at the same time.

**15** The clearance should be within the range listed in this Chapter's Specifications.

**16** If the clearance is greater than the maximum clearance listed in this Chapter's Specifications, measure the diameter of the connecting rod journal with a micrometer. Yamaha doesn't provide diameter or wear limit specifications, but by measuring the diameter at a number of points around the journal's circumference, you'll be able to determine whether or not the journal is out-of-round. Take the measurement at each end of the journal to determine if the journal is tapered.

**17** If any journal is tapered or out-of-round or bearing clearance is beyond the maximum listed in this Chapter's Specifications (with new bearings), replace the crankshaft.

**18** Each connecting rod has a 3 or 4 stamped on it in ink **(see illustration)**. Subtract this number from the connecting rod journal number on the crankshaft to get a bearing number **(see illustration)**. For example, the number on the connecting rod shown in the accompanying illustration is 4. The corresponding number for that connecting rod's journal, stamped into the crankshaft, is 2. Subtracting 2 from 4 produces 2, which is the bearing number for that journal. According to the accompanying chart, bearing no. 2 is color-coded black **(see illustration)**. The color codes are painted on the edges of the bearings **(see illustration)**.

**19** Repeat the bearing selection procedure for the remaining connecting rods.

## Installation

**20** Wipe off the bearing inserts, connecting rods and caps. Install the inserts into the rods and caps, using your hands only, making sure the tabs on the inserts engage with the notches in the rods and caps **(see illustration)**. When all the inserts are installed, lubricate them with engine assembly lube or moly-based grease **(see illustration)**. Don't get any lubricant on the mating surfaces of the rod or cap.

**21** Assemble each connecting rod to its proper journal, referring to the previously

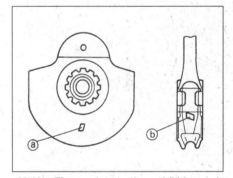

26.18b The number on the rod (b) is used with the number on the crankshaft (a) to select rod bearings

| BEARING COLOR CODE | |
|---|---|
| No. 1 | Blue |
| No. 2 | Black |
| No. 3 | Brown |
| No. 4 | Green |

26.18c Calculate the bearing number by subtracting the crankshaft number from the connecting rod number, then use the bearing number to select a color code

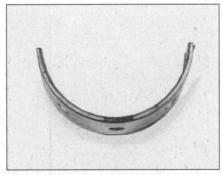

26.18d The color code is painted on the side of the bearing

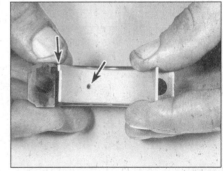

26.20a Be sure the tab fits in the notch and the oil hole in the bearing aligns with the oil hole in the connecting rod (arrows)

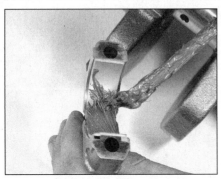

**26.20b Coat the bearings with assembly lube or moly-based grease**

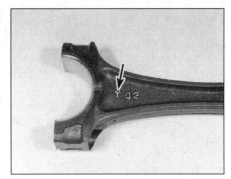

**26.21a The Y mark on the connecting rod (arrow) faces the outside of the engine**

**26.21b If the halves of the letter on the rod and cap don't fit together, the wrong cap is on the rod (or the cap is on backwards)**

applied cylinder numbers. Make sure the Y mark on the rod is toward the outside of the

**26.22 Tighten to the specified torque in stages (see text)**

engine **(see illustration)**. Also, the letter present at the rod/cap seam on one side of the connecting rod should fit together perfectly when the rod and cap are assembled **(see illustration)**. If it doesn't, the wrong cap is on the rod. Fix this problem before assembling the engine any further.

22 When you're sure the rods are positioned correctly, lubricate the threads of the rod bolts and the surfaces of the nuts with molybdenum disulfide grease and tighten the nuts to the torque listed in this Chapter's Specifications **(see illustration)**. **Note:** *Snug both nuts evenly, then tighten them to the specified torque in a continuous motion. If you must stop tightening between 32 and 36 Nm (22 and 25 ft-lbs), loosen the nuts to a torque less than 32 Nm (22 ft-lbs), then retighten them to the*

specified torque in one continuous motion.
23 Turn the rods on the crankshaft. If either of them feels tight, tap on the bottom of the connecting rod caps with a hammer - this should relieve stress and free them up. If it doesn't, recheck the bearing clearance.
24 As a final step, recheck the connecting rod side clearances (see Step 1). If the clearances aren't correct, find out why before proceeding with engine assembly.

## 27 Shift cam and forks - removal, inspection and installation

### Removal

1 Remove the engine and separate the crankcase halves (see Sections 5 and 22).
2 Pull the guide bars out and disengage the shift forks from the gear grooves **(see illustrations)**.
3 As soon as they're removed, reassemble the guide bars and forks so they can be reinstalled in their correct positions **(see illustration)**.
4 Pull the shift cam out of the case **(see illustration)**.

### Inspection

5 Check the edges of the grooves in the shift cam for signs of excessive wear. Check the pin on each shift cam for wear and damage **(see illustration)**. If undesirable conditions are found, replace the shift cam.
6 Check the shift forks for distortion and

**27.2a Lift the guide bars out . . .**

**27.2b . . . and disengage the forks from the gear grooves**

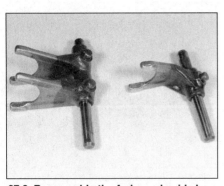

**27.3 Reassemble the forks and guide bars so they don't get mixed up**

**27.4 Pull the shift cam out of its bore in the crankcase**

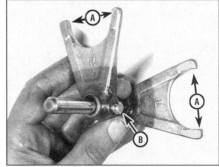

**27.5 Check for wear at the fork tips (A) and guide pins (B)**

27.8a  Oil the end of the shift cam and slip it into its bore in the crankcase

27.8b  Position the shift fork marked L in the left-hand gear groove with its letter facing the right side of the engine . . .

27.8c  . . . place the shift fork marked R in the groove next to the fork marked L . . .

wear, especially at the fork tips **(see illustration 27.5)**. If they are discolored or severely worn they are probably bent. If damage or wear is evident, check the shift fork groove in the corresponding gear as well. Inspect the guide pins and the shaft bore for excessive wear and distortion and replace any defective parts with new ones.

**7**  Check the shift fork guide bars for evidence of wear, galling and other damage **(see illustration 27.5)**. Make sure the shift forks

move smoothly on the bar. If the bar is worn or bent, replace it with a new one.

### Installation

**8**  Installation is the reverse of removal, noting the following points:

a)  *Lubricate all parts with engine oil before installing them.*

b)  *Use the numbers and letters on the forks to position them correctly. The forks are numbered from one to three, starting from*

*the left side of the engine. The numbers face the left side of the engine when the forks are installed. The letters L, C and R (left, center and right) also indicate fork position (see illustrations). The letters face the right side of the engine when installed.*

c)  *Engage the follower pin on each shift fork with the shift cam as you pass the guide bar through the fork. Position the shift cam and forks in the neutral position (see illustrations).*

27.8d  . . . install the longer guide bar through the two forks . . .

27.8e  . . . (the assembled forks should look like this)

27.8f  Install the shift fork marked C in its groove with the letter facing the right side of the engine . . .

27.8g  . . . and install the shorter guide bar through the fork . . .

27.8h  . . . (the assembled fork and guide bar should look like this)

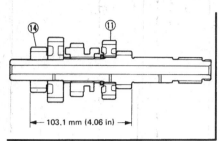

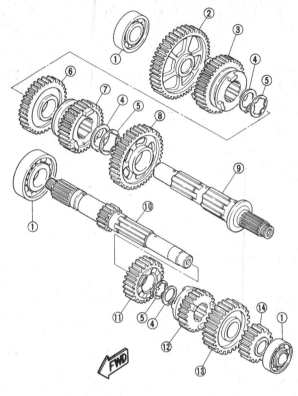

1) Bearing
2) First wheel gear
3) Fourth wheel gear
4) Snap-ring
5) Thrust washer
6) Third wheel gear
7) Fifth wheel gear
8) Second wheel gear
9) Driveaxle
10) Main axle
11) Fourth pinion gear
12) Third pinion gear
13) Fifth pinion gear
14) Second pinion gear

28.3a Transmission gears and shafts (XV535 models)

28.3b Remove first wheel gear

28.4 Take the fourth wheel gear off the driveaxle

### 28 Transmission shafts - removal, disassembly, inspection, reassembly and installation

#### Removal and disassembly

**Driveaxle and middle drive gear**

**1** Remove the engine and separate the crankcase halves (see Sections 5 and 22).
**2** Remove the shift drum and forks (see Section 27).
**3** Remove the first wheel gear **(see illustrations)**.

28.5a Remove the snap-ring . . .

28.5b . . . and the thrust washer

28.6 Remove the third wheel gear and main axle assembly together

28.7 Remove the fifth wheel gear

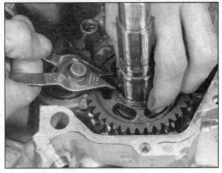

28.8a Remove the snap-ring . . .

28.8b . . . and the thrust washer

**HAYNES HINT** *Place the gears on a rod in order as they are removed so they can be reassembled in the same order and facing in the same direction.*

4 Remove the fourth wheel gear (see illustration).
5 Remove the snap-ring and thrust washer (see illustrations).
6 Remove the third wheel gear and main axle assembly together (see illustration).
7 Remove the fifth wheel gear (see illustration).
8 Remove the snap-ring and thrust washer (see illustrations).
9 Remove the second wheel gear (see illustration).
10 The driveaxle and middle drive gear can be left in the crankcase unless they or their ball bearing need to be replaced. If any of these parts are worn or damaged, bend back the staked portion of the middle drive gear locknut (see illustration). Secure the driveaxle in a soft-jawed vise, then remove the locknut and lift the driveaxle out of the bearing (see illustrations).
11 If the bearing needs to be replaced, undo its four retaining screws with a no. 30 Torx bit and remove the two retainers (see illustrations).
*Caution: The screws are staked in place. Don't use anything other than the correct*

28.9 Remove the second wheel gear

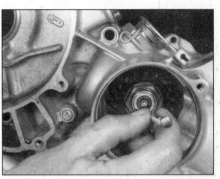

28.10a Bend back the staked portion of the locknut with a hammer and punch or small chisel

28.10b Place the driveaxle in a vise with padded jaws to prevent damage to the splines . . .

28.10c . . . remove the locknut . . .

28.10d . . . and lift the driveaxle out of the crankcase

28.11a If the bearing has to be replaced, remove a short retainer screw (A) and the longer screws (B) . . .

28.11b . . . be sure to use the proper Torx bit to prevent rounding out the screw heads

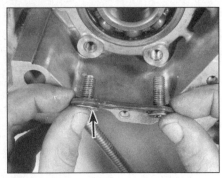

28.11c Remove the screws and retainers, noting the location of the short screw (arrow)

28.12a Lift the bearing out of its bore (if it's tight, tap it out from the other side) . . .

28.12b . . . and lift out the shims; keep these with the bearing so they can be reinstalled

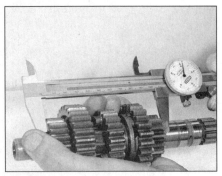

28.13 Measure the length of the gearset on the main axle assembly and compare to the Specifications

28.14a Press the main axle out of second pinion gear until it's loose . . .

bit to loosen them or they'll be rounded out. Note that one of the screws is shorter than the other three (see illustration). Be sure to reinstall it in the correct location or the clutch release mechanism will be obstructed.

12 Lift the bearing out of its bore, then remove the shims (see illustrations). Keep the shims with the bearing so the correct number can be reinstalled.

### Main axle

Note: Disassembly and reassembly of the main axle require a hydraulic press.

13 Before disassembly, measure the length of the gearset on the main axle (see illustration). The length is determined by how far the gears are pressed onto the shaft. Compare it to the value in illustration 28.3a.

14 Place the main axle in a press with a bearing splitter behind second pinion gear (see illustration). Press the main axle out of second pinion gear. Once the gear is loose, take it off the shaft (see illustration).

15 Take fifth pinion gear off the shaft (see illustration), then take off third pinion gear (see illustration).

16 Remove the snap-ring and thrust washer, then take off fourth pinion gear (see illustrations).

### Inspection

17 Wash all of the components in clean solvent and dry them off. Rotate the ball

28.14b . . . then remove the gear from the shaft

28.15a Take off fifth pinion gear . . .

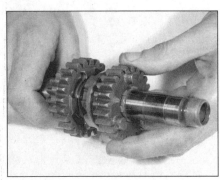

28.15b . . . and third pinion gear

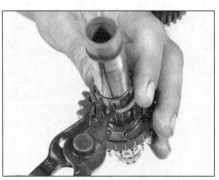

28.16a Remove the snap-ring . . .

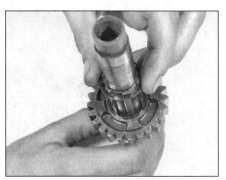

28.16b . . . the thrust washer . . .

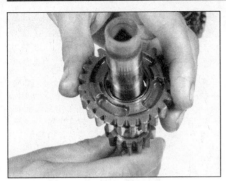

28.16c . . . and fourth pinion gear

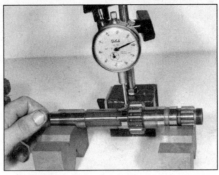

28.21 Check the shafts for runout with V-blocks and a dial indicator

28.22a Stake the bearing retainer screws . . .

bearing on the shaft, feeling for tightness, rough spots and excessive looseness and listening for noises. If any of these conditions are found, replace the bearing with a press.

**18** Check the ball bearing that was removed from the other end of the shaft and replace it if it has any of the conditions described in Step 6. The bearing should also be replaced if oil has been leaking from its seal.

**19** Check the gear teeth for cracking and other obvious damage. Check the gear bushings and the surface in the inner diameter of each gear for scoring or heat discoloration. If the gear or bushing is damaged, replace it.

**20** Inspect the dogs and the dog holes in the gears for excessive wear. Replace the paired gears as a set if necessary.

**21** Place the shafts in V-blocks and check runout with a dial indicator **(see illustration)**. Replace the shaft if runout exceeds the value listed in this Chapter's Specifications.

### Assembly and installation

**22** If the middle gear and driveaxle were removed, reverse the removal steps to install them. Be sure the short screw goes in the correct hole **(see illustration 28.11a)**. Stake the screws **(see illustration)**. Install a new locknut, tighten it to the torque listed in this Chapter's Specifications and stake it **(see illustration)**.

**23** Reverse Steps 15 and 16 to assemble the main axle **(see illustration)**. Press second pinion gear onto the shaft **(see illustration 28.23a and the accompanying illustration)**.

**24** Install the second wheel gear, thrust washer, snap-ring and fifth wheel gear on the driveaxle **(see illustrations)**.

**25** Install the third wheel gear and main axle together **(see illustration)**.

**26** Reverse Steps 3 through 5 to complete assembly. The assembled gears should be in the neutral position **(see illustrations)**.

**27** The remainder of installation is the reverse of the removal steps.

28.22b . . . and the middle drive gear locknut

28.23a The assembled main axle should look like this

28.23b Press second pinion gear onto the shaft until the gearset is the specified length

28.24a Install second wheel gear . . .

28.24b . . . the thrust washer . . .

28.24c . . . the snap-ring . . .

28.24d . . . and fifth wheel gear

28.25 Install third wheel gear on the main axle at the same time you install the driveaxle in its bearing

28.26a When the gears are in neutral, the gear dogs (arrows) are not engaged with the slots in the gears next to them and the gears can be turned independently of each other (driveaxle shown)

28.26b The assembled gears and shafts should look like this

## 29 Initial start-up after overhaul

1 Make sure the engine oil level is correct, then remove the spark plugs from the engine. Place the engine kill switch in the Off position and unplug the primary (low tension) wires from the coils.
2 Turn on the key switch and crank the engine over with the starter several times to build up oil pressure. Reinstall the spark plugs, connect the wires and turn the switch to On.

3 Make sure there is fuel in the tank, then turn the fuel tap to the On position and operate the choke.
4 Start the engine and allow it to run at a moderately fast idle until it reaches operating temperature.
5 Check carefully for oil leaks and make sure the transmission and controls, especially the brakes, function properly before road testing the machine. Refer to Section 30 for the recommended break-in procedure.
6 Upon completion of the road test, and after the engine has cooled down completely, recheck the valve clearances (see Chapter 1).

## 30 Recommended break-in procedure

1 Any rebuilt engine needs time to break-in, even if parts have been installed in their original locations. For this reason, treat the machine gently for the first few miles to make sure oil has circulated throughout the engine and any new parts installed have started to seat.
2 Even greater care is necessary if the engine has been rebored or a new crankshaft has been installed. In the case of a rebore, the engine will have to be broken in as if the machine were new. This means greater use of the transmission and a restraining hand on the throttle until at least 500 miles have been covered. There's no point in keeping to any set speed limit - the main idea is to keep from lugging the engine and to gradually increase performance until the 500 mile mark is reached. These recommendations can be lessened to an extent when only a new crankshaft is installed. Experience is the best guide, since it's easy to tell when an engine is running freely. The following recommendations, which Yamaha provides for new motorcycles, can be used as a guide:
a) 0 to 90 miles (0 to 150 km): Keep engine speed below 3,000 rpm. Turn off the engine after each hour of operation and let it cool for 5 to 10 minutes. Vary the engine speed and don't use full throttle.
b) 90 to 300 miles (150 to 500 km): Don't run the engine for long periods above 4,000 rpm. Rev the engine freely through the gears, but don't use full throttle.
c) 300 to 600 miles (500 to 1000 km): Don't use full throttle for prolonged periods and don't cruise at speeds above 5,000 rpm.
d) At 600 miles (1,000 km): Change the engine oil and filter. Full throttle can be used after this point.
3 If a lubrication failure is suspected, stop the engine immediately and try to find the cause. If an engine is run without oil, even for a short period of time, severe damage will occur.

# Chapter 2 Part B
# Engine, clutch and
# transmission (XV700-1100 models)

## Contents

## Degrees of difficulty

| Easy, suitable for novice with little experience |  | Fairly easy, suitable for beginner with some experience | | Fairly difficult, suitable for competent DIY mechanic |  | Difficult, suitable for experienced DIY mechanic | | Very difficult, suitable for expert DIY or professional | |

## Specifications

### XV700 and XV750 models

#### General

Bore x stroke
   XV700 . . . . . . . . . . . . . . . . . . . . . . . . . . . . . . . . . . . . . . . . . . . 80.2 x 69.2 mm (3.16 x 2.72 inches)
   XV750 . . . . . . . . . . . . . . . . . . . . . . . . . . . . . . . . . . . . . . . . . . . 83.0 x 69.2 mm (3.268 x 2.72 inches)
Displacement
   XV700 . . . . . . . . . . . . . . . . . . . . . . . . . . . . . . . . . . . . . . . . . . . 699 cc
   XV750 . . . . . . . . . . . . . . . . . . . . . . . . . . . . . . . . . . . . . . . . . . . 748 cc
Compression ratio
   1981 though 1983 . . . . . . . . . . . . . . . . . . . . . . . . . . . . . . . . . . . 8.7 to 1
   1984-on . . . . . . . . . . . . . . . . . . . . . . . . . . . . . . . . . . . . . . . . . . 9.0 to 1

## Camshafts

Lobe height
  Intake . . . . . . . . . . . . . . . . . . . . . . . . . . . . . . . . . . . . . . . . . . . . . . . . 39.17 mm (1.5421 inch)
  Exhaust . . . . . . . . . . . . . . . . . . . . . . . . . . . . . . . . . . . . . . . . . . . . . . . 39.20 mm (1.5433 inch)
Base circle
  1981 through 1983
    Intake . . . . . . . . . . . . . . . . . . . . . . . . . . . . . . . . . . . . . . . . . . . . . . 32.00 mm (1.2598 inch)
    Exhaust . . . . . . . . . . . . . . . . . . . . . . . . . . . . . . . . . . . . . . . . . . . . . 32.00 mm (1.2598 inch)
  1984-on
    Intake . . . . . . . . . . . . . . . . . . . . . . . . . . . . . . . . . . . . . . . . . . . . . . 32.23 mm (1.2689 inch)
    Exhaust . . . . . . . . . . . . . . . . . . . . . . . . . . . . . . . . . . . . . . . . . . . . . 32.36 mm (1.2701 inch)
Bearing oil clearance . . . . . . . . . . . . . . . . . . . . . . . . . . . . . . . . . . . . . 0.020 to 0.061 mm (0.0008 to 0.0024 inch)
Journal diameter (1981 through 1983)
  Rear cylinder . . . . . . . . . . . . . . . . . . . . . . . . . . . . . . . . . . . . . . . . . . . 24.976 to 24.980 mm (0.9830 to 0.9835 inch)
  Front cylinder . . . . . . . . . . . . . . . . . . . . . . . . . . . . . . . . . . . . . . . . . 23.976 to 23.9809 mm (0.9435 to 0.9440 inch)
Journal diameter (1984-on) . . . . . . . . . . . . . . . . . . . . . . . . . . . . . . . . 24.96 to 24.98 mm (0.9827 to 0.9835 inch)
Bearing bore (1981 through 1983)
  Rear cylinder . . . . . . . . . . . . . . . . . . . . . . . . . . . . . . . . . . . . . . . . . . . 25.000 to 25.021 mm (0.9843 to 0.9851 inch)
  Front cylinder . . . . . . . . . . . . . . . . . . . . . . . . . . . . . . . . . . . . . . . . . 24.000 to 24.021 mm (0.9448 to 0.9456 inch)
Bearing bore (1984-on) . . . . . . . . . . . . . . . . . . . . . . . . . . . . . . . . . . . 25.00 to 25.021 mm (0.9843 to 0.9851 inch)
Camshaft runout limit . . . . . . . . . . . . . . . . . . . . . . . . . . . . . . . . . . . . . 0.03 mm (0.0012 inch)
Rocker arm inside diameter . . . . . . . . . . . . . . . . . . . . . . . . . . . . . . . . 14.000 to 14.018 mm (0.5511 to 0.5518 inch)
Rocker arm shaft diameter . . . . . . . . . . . . . . . . . . . . . . . . . . . . . . . . 13.975 to 13.990 mm (0.5501 to 0.5507 inch)
Rocker arm to shaft clearance . . . . . . . . . . . . . . . . . . . . . . . . . . . . . . 0.010 to 0.043 mm (0.0004 to 0.0017 inch)

## Cylinders

Bore diameter (XV700)
  Standard . . . . . . . . . . . . . . . . . . . . . . . . . . . . . . . . . . . . . . . . . . . . . . . 80.2 mm (3.157 inches)
  Limit . . . . . . . . . . . . . . . . . . . . . . . . . . . . . . . . . . . . . . . . . . . . . . . . . . . 80.3 mm (3.161 inches)
Bore diameter (XV750)
  Standard . . . . . . . . . . . . . . . . . . . . . . . . . . . . . . . . . . . . . . . . . . . . . . . 83.0 mm (3.267 inches)
  Limit . . . . . . . . . . . . . . . . . . . . . . . . . . . . . . . . . . . . . . . . . . . . . . . . . . . 83.1 mm (3.272 inches)
Bore measuring point
  Through 1987 . . . . . . . . . . . . . . . . . . . . . . . . . . . . . . . . . . . . . . . . . . Top, center and bottom of cylinder
  1988-on . . . . . . . . . . . . . . . . . . . . . . . . . . . . . . . . . . . . . . . . . . . . . . . 35 mm (1.38 inch) from top of bore
Taper and out-of-round limit . . . . . . . . . . . . . . . . . . . . . . . . . . . . . . . 0.05 mm (0.002 inch)

## Pistons

Piston diameter (XV700)
  Standard . . . . . . . . . . . . . . . . . . . . . . . . . . . . . . . . . . . . . . . . . . . . . . . 80.135 to 80.185 mm (3.155 to 3.157 inches)
  First oversize . . . . . . . . . . . . . . . . . . . . . . . . . . . . . . . . . . . . . . . . . . . 80.50 mm (3.17 inches)
  Second oversize . . . . . . . . . . . . . . . . . . . . . . . . . . . . . . . . . . . . . . . . 81.00 mm (3.19 inches)
Piston diameter (XV750)
  Standard . . . . . . . . . . . . . . . . . . . . . . . . . . . . . . . . . . . . . . . . . . . . . . . 82.95 to 82.97 mm (3.266 to 3.267 inches)
  First oversize . . . . . . . . . . . . . . . . . . . . . . . . . . . . . . . . . . . . . . . . . . . 83.50 mm (3.278 inches)
  Second oversize . . . . . . . . . . . . . . . . . . . . . . . . . . . . . . . . . . . . . . . . 84.00 mm (3.307 inches)
Diameter measuring point . . . . . . . . . . . . . . . . . . . . . . . . . . . . . . . . . 9.5 mm (0.37 inch) from bottom of skirt
Piston-to-cylinder clearance . . . . . . . . . . . . . . . . . . . . . . . . . . . . . . . 0.040 to 0.060 mm (0.0014 to 0.0022 inch)
Ring side clearance (1981 through 1983)
  Top and second rings . . . . . . . . . . . . . . . . . . . . . . . . . . . . . . . . . . . . 0.04 to 0.08 mm (0.0016 to 0.0031 inch)
  Oil ring . . . . . . . . . . . . . . . . . . . . . . . . . . . . . . . . . . . . . . . . . . . . . . . . Not specified
Ring side clearance (1984-on)
  Top ring . . . . . . . . . . . . . . . . . . . . . . . . . . . . . . . . . . . . . . . . . . . . . . . 0.04 to 0.08 mm (0.0016 to 0.0031 inch)
  Second ring . . . . . . . . . . . . . . . . . . . . . . . . . . . . . . . . . . . . . . . . . . . . 0.03 to 0.07 mm (0.0012 to 0.0028 inch)
  Oil ring . . . . . . . . . . . . . . . . . . . . . . . . . . . . . . . . . . . . . . . . . . . . . . . . Zero to 0.04 mm (zero to 0.0016 inch)
Ring thickness (1981 through 1983) . . . . . . . . . . . . . . . . . . . . . . . . . Not specified
Ring thickness (1984-on)
  Top and second rings . . . . . . . . . . . . . . . . . . . . . . . . . . . . . . . . . . . . 1.2 mm (0.05 inch)
  Oil ring (spacer and rails) . . . . . . . . . . . . . . . . . . . . . . . . . . . . . . . . . 2.5 mm (0.10 inch)
Ring end gap (1981 through 1983)
  Top and second rings . . . . . . . . . . . . . . . . . . . . . . . . . . . . . . . . . . . . 0.3 to 0.5 mm (0.0118 to 0.0197 inch)
  Oil ring . . . . . . . . . . . . . . . . . . . . . . . . . . . . . . . . . . . . . . . . . . . . . . . . 0.3 to 0.9 mm (0.0118 to 0.0351 inch)
Ring end gap (1984-on)
  Top and second rings . . . . . . . . . . . . . . . . . . . . . . . . . . . . . . . . . . . . 0.20 to 0.40 mm (0.008 to 0.016 inch)
  Oil ring . . . . . . . . . . . . . . . . . . . . . . . . . . . . . . . . . . . . . . . . . . . . . . . . 0.2 to 0.7 mm (0.0078 to 0.0276 inch)
Ring width (1981 through 1983) . . . . . . . . . . . . . . . . . . . . . . . . . . . . Not specified
Ring width (1984-on)
  Top ring . . . . . . . . . . . . . . . . . . . . . . . . . . . . . . . . . . . . . . . . . . . . . . . 3.2 mm (0.126 inch)
  Second ring . . . . . . . . . . . . . . . . . . . . . . . . . . . . . . . . . . . . . . . . . . . . 3.6 mm (0.142 inch)
  Oil ring . . . . . . . . . . . . . . . . . . . . . . . . . . . . . . . . . . . . . . . . . . . . . . . . 2.8 mm (0.110 inch)

## Cylinder head, valves and valve springs

| | |
|---|---|
| Cylinder head warpage limit | 0.03 mm (0.0012 inch) |
| Valve stem bend limit | 0.03 mm (0.0012 inch) |
| Valve head diameter | |
|     Intake | 43.0 to 43.02 mm (1.690 to 1.698 inch) |
|     Exhaust | 37.0 to 37.2 mm (1.460 to 1.468 inch) |
| Valve stem diameter | |
|     Intake | 7.975 to 7.990 mm (0.311 to 0.314 inch) |
|     Exhaust | 7.960 to 7.975 mm (0.3134 to 0.3140 inch) |
| Valve head edge thickness limit | 1.3 +/- 0.2 mm (0.051 +/- 0.008 inch) |
| Valve guide inside diameter | 8.000 to 8.012 mm (0.3150 to 0.3155 inch) |
| Valve seat width limit | 1.3 +/- 0.1 mm (0.051 +/- 0.004 inch) |
| Valve face width | 2.1 mm (0.083 inch) |
| Valve inner spring free length | 45.3 mm (1.783 inch) |
| Valve inner spring installed length | 38.0 mm (1.496 inch) |
| Valve inner spring bend limit | 2.0 mm (0.0787 inch) |
| Valve outer spring free length | 44.6 mm (1.756 inch) |
| Valve outer spring installed length | 40.0 mm (1.575 inch) |
| Valve outer spring bend limit | 2.0 mm (0.0787 inch) |

## Crankshaft, connecting rods and bearings

| | |
|---|---|
| Connecting rod side clearance | 0.370 to 0.474 mm (0.0146 to 0.0187 inch) |
| Connecting rod bearing oil clearance | 0.030 to 0.054 mm (0.0012 to 0.0021 inch) |
| Crankshaft runout limit | 0.02 mm (0.0008 inch) |

## Oil pump (1981 through 1983)

| | |
|---|---|
| Inner to outer rotor clearance | 0.03 to 0.09 mm (0.0012 to 0.0035 inch) |
| Crankshaft rotor thickness | 6 mm (0.236 inch) |
| Transmission rotor thickness | 4 mm (0.157 inch) |

## Oil pump (1984-on)

| | |
|---|---|
| Inner to outer rotor clearance | 0.03 to 0.09 mm (0.0012 to 0.0035 inch) |
| Outer rotor to housing clearance | 0.03 to 0.08 mm (0.0012 to 0.0031 inch) |
| Rotor to straightedge clearance | 0.03 to 0.09 mm (0.0012 to 0.0035 inch) |

## Clutch

| | |
|---|---|
| Friction plate thickness | |
|     Standard | 2.9 to 3.1 mm (0.116 to 0.124 inch) |
|     Minimum | 2.8 mm (0.11 inch) |
| Steel plate thickness | 1.5 to 1.7 mm (0.059 to 0.067 inch) |
| Steel plate warpage limit | 0.1 mm (0.004 inch) |
| Pushrod bend limit | 0.5 mm (0.02 inch) |
| Spring length | |
|     Standard | 41.2 mm (1.622 inch) |
|     Minimum | 40.2 mm (1.582 inch) |

## Transmission

| | |
|---|---|
| Driveaxle and mainshaft runout limit | 0.08 mm (0.0031 inch) |

## Torque specifications

| | |
|---|---|
| Alternator cover bolts | 10 Nm (7.2 ft-lbs) |
| Alternator cover screws | 7 Nm (5.1 ft-lbs) |
| Alternator rotor nut | See Chapter 8 |
| Cam chain damper bolt | 8 Nm (5.8 ft-lbs) |
| Cam chain damper bolt locknut | 12 Nm ((8.7 ft-lbs) |
| Cam chain tensioner bolts | 10 Nm (7.2 ft-lbs) |
| Cam sprocket bolt | 55 Nm (40 ft-lbs) |
| Cam sprocket cover bolts | 10 Nm (7.2 ft-lbs) |
| Camshaft retainer bolts | 20 Nm (14 ft-lbs) |
| Clutch push screw locknut | 12 Nm (8.7 ft-lbs) |
| Clutch boss nut | 70 Nm (50 ft-lbs) (4) |
| Clutch cover bolts | 10 Nm (7.2 ft-lbs) |
| Clutch pressure plate screws | 8 Nm (5.8 ft-lbs) |
| Connecting rod nuts | 48 Nm (35 ft-lbs) (2) |
| Crankcase bolts (6 mm) | 10 Nm (7.2 ft-lbs) |
| Crankcase bolts (10 mm) | 39 Nm (28 ft-lbs) |
| Cylinder bolts | 10 Nm (7.2 ft-lbs) |
| Cylinder nuts (12 mm) | |
|     First stage | 50 Nm (36 ft-lbs) (3) |
|     Second stage | 64 Nm (46 ft-lbs) |

## Torque specifications (XV700 and XV750 models) (continued)

| | |
|---|---|
| Cylinder head bolts (8 mm) | 20 Nm (14 ft-lbs) |
| Cylinder head nuts (10 mm) | 40 Nm (29 ft-lbs) |
| Intermediate gear stopper plate bolts | 10 Nm (7.2 ft-lbs) |
| Oil line union bolts | 20 Nm (14 ft-lbs) (1) |
| Oil pump bolts | 10 Nm (7.2 ft-lbs) |
| Oil pump chain cover bolts | 10 Nm (7.2 ft-lbs) |
| Oil pump sprocket bolts | 12 Nm (8.7 ft-lbs) |
| Primary drive gear nut | 110 Nm (80 ft-lbs) (4) |
| Rocker arm cover bolts | 10 Nm (7.2 ft-lbs) |
| Rocker arm shaft holding bolts | 38 Nm (27 ft-lbs) (1) |
| Shift fork guide bar stopper screws | 7 Nm (5.1 ft-lbs) (5) |
| Shift pedal pinch bolt | 10 Nm (7.2 ft-lbs) |

1  Use new sealing washers.
2  Apply molybdenum disulfide grease to the threads and nut surfaces; follow special tightening procedure in the text.
3  Apply engine oil to the threads.
4  Use a new lockwasher.
5  Apply Loctite Stud 'n' Bearing Mount or equivalent to the threads.

# XV920 models
## General

| | |
|---|---|
| Bore x stroke | 92.0 x 69.2 mm (3.622 x 2.72 inches) |
| Displacement | 920 cc |
| Compression ratio | 8.3 to 1 |

## Camshafts and rocker arms

| | |
|---|---|
| Lobe height | |
|   Intake | 39.17 mm (1.5421 inch) |
|   Exhaust | 39.20 mm (1.5433 inch) |
| Base circle (intake and exhaust) | 32.00 mm (1.2598 inch) |
| Bearing oil clearance | 0.020 to 0.054 mm (0.0008 to 0.0021 inch) |
| Journal diameter | |
|   RH and RJ models | |
|     Rear cylinder | 23.967 to 23.980 mm (0.9435 to 0.9440 inch) |
|     Front cylinder | 24.967 to 24.980 mm (0.9830 to 0.9835 inch) |
|   J, K, MK models (both cylinders) | 24.96 to 24.98 mm (0.9827 to 0.9835 inch) |
| Bearing bore | |
|   RH and RJ models | |
|     Rear cylinder | 24.000 to 24.021 mm (0.9448 to 0.9456 inch) |
|     Front cylinder | 25.000 to 25.021 mm (0.9843 to 0.9851 inch) |
|   J, K, MK models | 25.00 to 25.021 mm (0.9843 to 0.9851 inch) |
| Camshaft runout limit | 0.03 mm (0.0012 inch) |
| Rocker arm inside diameter | 14.000 to 14.018 mm (0.5511 to 0.5518 inch) |
| Rocker arm shaft diameter | 13.975 to 13.990 mm (0.5501 to 0.5507 inch) |
| Rocker arm to shaft clearance | 0.010 to 0.043 mm (0.0004 to 0.0017 inch) |

## Cylinder head, valves and valve springs

| | |
|---|---|
| Cylinder head warpage limit | 0.03 mm (0.0012 inch) |
| Valve stem bend limit | 0.03 mm (0.0012 inch) |
| Valve head diameter | |
|   RH and RJ models | |
|     Intake | 43.0 to 43.02 mm (1.690 to 1.698 inch) |
|     Exhaust | 37.0 to 37.2 mm (1.460 to 1.468 inch) |
|   J, K, MK models | |
|     Intake | 47.0 to 47.2 mm (1.850 to 1.858 inch) |
|     Exhaust | 39.0 to 39.2 mm (1.540 to 1.548 inch) |
| Valve stem diameter | |
|   Intake | 7.975 to 7.990 mm (0.311 to 0.314 inch) |
|   Exhaust | 7.960 to 7.975 mm (0.3134 to 0.3140 inch) |
| Valve head edge thickness limit | 1.3 +/- 0.2 mm (0.051 +/- 0.008 inch) |
| Valve guide inside diameter | 8.000 to 8.012 mm (0.3150 to 0.3155 inch) |
| Valve seat width limit | 1.3 +/- 0.1 mm (0.051 +/- 0.004 inch) |
| Valve face width | 2.1 mm (0.083 inch) |
| Valve inner spring free length | 45.3 mm (1.783 inch) |
| Valve inner spring installed length | 38.0 mm (1.496 inch) |
| Valve inner spring bend limit | 2.0 mm (0.0787 inch) |
| Valve outer spring free length | 44.6 mm (1.756 inch) |
| Valve outer spring installed length | 40.0 mm (1.575 inch) |
| Valve outer spring bend limit | 2.0 mm (0.0787 inch) |

## Cylinders

Bore diameter
  Standard ..................................................... 92.0 mm (3.622 inches)
  Limit ........................................................ Not specified
Bore measuring point ......................................... Top, center and bottom of cylinder
Taper and out-of-round limit ................................. 0.05 mm (0.002 inch)

## Pistons

Piston diameter
  Standard ..................................................... 92.0 mm (3.622 inches)
  First oversize ............................................... 93.25 mm (3.67 inches)
  Second oversize .............................................. 93.50 mm (3.68 inches)
Diameter measuring point ..................................... 14.6 mm (0.575 inch) from bottom of skirt
Piston-to-cylinder clearance ................................. 0.045 to 0.065 mm (0.0018 to 0.0026 inch)
Ring side clearance (J, K, MK models)
  Top ring ..................................................... 0.04 to 0.08 mm (0.0016 to 0.0031 inch)
  Second ring .................................................. 0.03 to 0.07 mm (0.0012 to 0.0028 inch)
  Oil ring ..................................................... Zero
Ring thickness (J, K, MK models)
  Top ring ..................................................... 1.5 mm (0.06 inch)
  Second ring .................................................. 2.0 mm (0.08 inch)
  Oil ring (spacer and rails) .................................. 4.0 mm (0.16 inch)
Ring end gap (J, K, MK models)
  Top and second rings ......................................... 0.20 to 0.40 mm (0.008 to 0.016 inch)
  Oil ring ..................................................... 0.3 to 0.6 mm (0.0012 to 0.0024 inch)
Ring width (J, K, MK models)
  Top ring ..................................................... 3.8 mm (0.15 inch)
  Second ring .................................................. 4.0 mm (0.16 inch)
  Oil ring ..................................................... 3.9 mm (0.15 inch)

## Crankshaft, connecting rods and bearings

Connecting rod side clearance ................................ 0.370 to 0.474 mm (0.0146 to 0.0187 inch)
Connecting rod bearing oil clearance ......................... 0.030 to 0.054 mm (0.0012 to 0.0021 inch)
Crankshaft runout limit ...................................... 0.02 mm (0.0008 inch)

## Oil pump

Inner to outer rotor clearance ............................... 0.03 to 0.09 mm (0.0012 to 0.0035 inch)
Crankshaft rotor thickness ................................... 6 mm (0.236 inch)
Transmission rotor thickness ................................. 4 mm (0.157 inch)

## Clutch

Friction plate thickness
  Standard ..................................................... 2.9 to 3.1 mm (0.116 to 0.124 inch)
  Minimum ...................................................... 2.8 mm (0.11 inch)
Steel plate thickness ........................................ 1.5 to 1.7 mm (0.059 to 0.067 inch)
Steel plate warpage limit .................................... 0.1 mm (0.004 inch)
Pushrod bend limit ........................................... 0.5 mm (0.02 inch)
Spring length
  Standard ..................................................... 41.2 mm (1.622 inch)
  Minimum ...................................................... 40.2 mm (1.582 inch)

## Transmission

Driveaxle and mainshaft runout limit ......................... 0.08 mm (0.0031 inch)

## Torque specifications

Alternator cover bolts ....................................... 10 Nm (7.2 ft-lbs)
Alternator cover screws ...................................... 7 Nm (5.1 ft-lbs)
Alternator rotor nut ......................................... See Chapter 8
Cam chain damper bolt ........................................ 8 Nm (5.8 ft-lbs)
Cam chain damper bolt locknut ................................ 12 Nm ((8.7 ft-lbs)
Cam chain tensioner bolts .................................... 10 Nm (7.2 ft-lbs)
Cam sprocket bolt ............................................ 55 Nm (40 ft-lbs)
Cam sprocket cover bolts ..................................... 10 Nm (7.2 ft-lbs)
Camshaft retainer bolts ...................................... 20 Nm (14 ft-lbs)
Clutch push screw locknut .................................... 12 Nm (8.7 ft-lbs)
Clutch boss nut .............................................. 70 Nm (50 ft-lbs) (4)
Clutch cover bolts ........................................... 10 Nm (7.2 ft-lbs)
Clutch pressure plate screws ................................. 8 Nm (5.8 ft-lbs)
Connecting rod nuts .......................................... 48 Nm (35 ft-lbs) (2)
Crankcase bolts (6 mm) ....................................... 10 Nm (7.2 ft-lbs)
Crankcase bolts (10 mm) ...................................... 39 Nm (28 ft-lbs)

## Torque specifications (XV920 models) (continued)

| | |
|---|---|
| Cylinder bolts | 10 Nm (7.2 ft-lbs) |
| Cylinder head 12 mm nuts | |
|   First stage | 50 Nm (36 ft-lbs) (3) |
|   Second stage | 64 Nm (46 ft-lbs) |
| Cylinder head bolts (8 mm) | 20 Nm (14 ft-lbs) |
| Cylinder head nuts (10 mm) | 40 Nm (29 ft-lbs) |
| Intermediate gear stopper plate bolts | 10 Nm (7.2 ft-lbs) |
| Oil line union bolts | 20 Nm (14 ft-lbs) (1) |
| Oil pump bolts | 10 Nm (7.2 ft-lbs) |
| Oil pump chain cover bolts | 10 Nm (7.2 ft-lbs) |
| Oil pump sprocket bolts | 12 Nm (8.7 ft-lbs) |
| Primary drive gear nut | 110 Nm (80 ft-lbs) (4) |
| Rocker arm cover bolts | 10 Nm (7.2 ft-lbs) |
| Rocker arm shaft holding bolts | 38 Nm (27 ft-lbs) (1) |
| Shift fork guide bar stopper screws | 7 Nm (5.1 ft-lbs) (5) |
| Shift pedal pinch bolt | 10 Nm (7.2 ft-lbs) |

1 Use new sealing washers.
2 Apply molybdenum disulfide grease to the threads and nut surfaces; follow special tightening procedure in the text.
3 Apply engine oil to the threads.
4 Use a new lockwasher.
5 Apply Loctite Stud 'n' Bearing Mount or equivalent to the threads.

# XV1000 models

## General

| | |
|---|---|
| Bore x stroke | 95.0 x 69.2 mm (3.74 x 2.72 inches) |
| Displacement | 981 cc |
| Compression ratio | 8.3 to 1 |

## Camshafts

| | |
|---|---|
| Lobe height | |
|   Intake | 39.17 mm (1.5421 inch) |
|   Exhaust | 39.20 mm (1.5433 inch) |
| Base circle | |
|   Intake | 32.17 mm (1.2665 inch) |
|   Exhaust | 32.27 mm (1.2705 inch) |
| Bearing oil clearance | 0.020 to 0.061 mm (0.0008 to 0.0024 inch) |
| Journal diameter | 24.96 to 24.98 mm (0.9827 to 0.9835 inch) |
| Bearing bore | 25.00 to 25.021 mm (0.9843 to 0.9851 inch) |
| Camshaft runout limit | 0.03 mm (0.0012 inch) |
| Rocker arm inside diameter | 14.000 to 14.018 mm (0.5511 to 0.5518 inch) |
| Rocker arm shaft diameter | 13.975 to 13.990 mm (0.5501 to 0.5507 inch) |
| Rocker arm to shaft clearance | 0.010 to 0.043 mm (0.0004 to 0.0017 inch) |

## Cylinder head, valves and valve springs

| | |
|---|---|
| Cylinder head warpage limit | 0.03 mm (0.0012 inch) |
| Valve stem bend limit | 0.03 mm (0.0012 inch) |
| Valve head diameter | |
|   Intake | 47.0 to 47.02 mm (1.850 to 1.858 inch) |
|   Exhaust | 39.0 to 39.2 mm (1.540 to 1.562 inch) |
| Valve stem diameter | |
|   Intake | 7.975 to 7.990 mm (0.311 to 0.314 inch) |
|   Exhaust | 7.960 to 7.975 mm (0.3134 to 0.3140 inch) |
| Valve head edge thickness limit | 1.3 +/- 0.2 mm (0.051 +/- 0.008 inch) |
| Valve guide inside diameter | 8.000 to 8.012 mm (0.3150 to 0.3155 inch) |
| Valve seat width limit | 1.3 +/- 0.1 mm (0.051 +/- 0.004 inch) |
| Valve face width | 2.1 mm (0.083 inch) |
| Valve inner spring free length | 45.3 mm (1.783 inch) |
| Valve inner spring installed length | 38.0 mm (1.496 inch) |
| Valve inner spring bend limit | 2.0 mm (0.0787 inch) |
| Valve outer spring free length | 44.6 mm (1.756 inch) |
| Valve outer spring installed length | 40.0 mm (1.575 inch) |
| Valve outer spring bend limit | 2.0 mm (0.0787 inch) |

## Cylinders

| | |
|---|---|
| Bore diameter | |
|   Standard | 95.0 mm (3.740 inches) |
|   Limit | 95.1 mm (3.744 inches) |
| Bore measuring point | Top, center and bottom of cylinder |
| Taper and out-of-round limit | 0.05 mm (0.002 inch) |

## Pistons

Piston diameter
    Standard . . . . . . . . . . . . . . . . . . . . . . . . . . . . . . . . . . . . . . . . . . 94.945 to 94.965 mm (3.738 to 3.739 inches)
    First oversize . . . . . . . . . . . . . . . . . . . . . . . . . . . . . . . . . . . . . 95.50 mm (3.76 inches)
    Second oversize . . . . . . . . . . . . . . . . . . . . . . . . . . . . . . . . . . 96.00 mm (3.78 inches)
Diameter measuring point . . . . . . . . . . . . . . . . . . . . . . . . . . . . 14.6 mm (0.575 inch) from bottom of skirt
Piston-to-cylinder clearance . . . . . . . . . . . . . . . . . . . . . . . . . . 0.045 to 0.065 mm (0.0018 to 0.0026 inch)
Ring side clearance
    Top ring . . . . . . . . . . . . . . . . . . . . . . . . . . . . . . . . . . . . . . . . . . . . 0.04 to 0.08 mm (0.0016 to 0.0031 inch)
    Second ring . . . . . . . . . . . . . . . . . . . . . . . . . . . . . . . . . . . . . . . 0.03 to 0.07 mm (0.0012 to 0.0028 inch)
    Oil ring . . . . . . . . . . . . . . . . . . . . . . . . . . . . . . . . . . . . . . . . . . . . Zero
Ring thickness
    Top and second rings . . . . . . . . . . . . . . . . . . . . . . . . . . . . . . 1.5 mm (0.06 inch)
    Oil ring (spacer and rails) . . . . . . . . . . . . . . . . . . . . . . . . . . 3.8 mm (0.15 inch)
Ring end gap
    Top and second rings . . . . . . . . . . . . . . . . . . . . . . . . . . . . . . 0.30 to 0.50 mm (0.012 to 0.020 inch)
    Oil ring . . . . . . . . . . . . . . . . . . . . . . . . . . . . . . . . . . . . . . . . . . . . 0.3 to 0.9 mm (0.012 to 0.035 inch)
Ring width
    Top ring . . . . . . . . . . . . . . . . . . . . . . . . . . . . . . . . . . . . . . . . . . . . 3.8 mm (0.15 inch)
    Second ring . . . . . . . . . . . . . . . . . . . . . . . . . . . . . . . . . . . . . . . 4.0 mm (0.16 inch)
    Oil ring . . . . . . . . . . . . . . . . . . . . . . . . . . . . . . . . . . . . . . . . . . . . 3.9 mm (0.153 inch)

## Crankshaft, connecting rods and bearings

Connecting rod side clearance . . . . . . . . . . . . . . . . . . . . . . . . 0.370 to 0.474 mm (0.0146 to 0.0187 inch)
Connecting rod bearing oil clearance . . . . . . . . . . . . . . . . . . . 0.030 to 0.054 mm (0.0012 to 0.0021 inch)
Crankshaft runout limit . . . . . . . . . . . . . . . . . . . . . . . . . . . . . . . 0.02 mm (0.0008 inch)

## Oil pump

Inner to outer rotor clearance . . . . . . . . . . . . . . . . . . . . . . . . . 0.03 to 0.09 mm (0.0012 to 0.0035 inch)
Outer rotor to housing clearance . . . . . . . . . . . . . . . . . . . . . . 0.03 to 0.08 mm (0.0012 to 0.0031 inch)
Rotor to straightedge clearance . . . . . . . . . . . . . . . . . . . . . . . 0.03 to 0.09 mm (0.0012 to 0.0035 inch)

## Clutch

Friction plate thickness
    Standard . . . . . . . . . . . . . . . . . . . . . . . . . . . . . . . . . . . . . . . . . . 2.9 to 3.1 mm (0.116 to 0.124 inch)
    Minimum . . . . . . . . . . . . . . . . . . . . . . . . . . . . . . . . . . . . . . . . . . . 2.8 mm (0.11 inch)
Steel plate thickness . . . . . . . . . . . . . . . . . . . . . . . . . . . . . . . . . 1.5 to 1.7 mm (0.059 to 0.067 inch)
Steel plate warpage limit . . . . . . . . . . . . . . . . . . . . . . . . . . . . . 0.1 mm (0.004 inch)
Pushrod bend limit . . . . . . . . . . . . . . . . . . . . . . . . . . . . . . . . . . . 0.5 mm (0.02 inch)
Spring length
    Standard . . . . . . . . . . . . . . . . . . . . . . . . . . . . . . . . . . . . . . . . . . 41.2 mm (1.622 inch)
    Minimum . . . . . . . . . . . . . . . . . . . . . . . . . . . . . . . . . . . . . . . . . . . 40.2 mm (1.582 inch)

## Transmission

Driveaxle and mainshaft runout limit . . . . . . . . . . . . . . . . . . . . 0.08 mm (0.0031 inch)

## Torque specifications

Alternator cover bolts . . . . . . . . . . . . . . . . . . . . . . . . . . . . . . . . . 10 Nm (7.2 ft-lbs)
Alternator cover screws . . . . . . . . . . . . . . . . . . . . . . . . . . . . . . . 7 Nm (5.1 ft-lbs)
Alternator rotor nut . . . . . . . . . . . . . . . . . . . . . . . . . . . . . . . . . . . See Chapter 8
Cam chain damper bolt . . . . . . . . . . . . . . . . . . . . . . . . . . . . . . . 8 Nm (5.8 ft-lbs)
Cam chain damper bolt locknut . . . . . . . . . . . . . . . . . . . . . . . . 12 Nm ((8.7 ft-lbs)
Cam chain tensioner bolts . . . . . . . . . . . . . . . . . . . . . . . . . . . . 10 Nm (7.2 ft-lbs)
Cam sprocket bolt . . . . . . . . . . . . . . . . . . . . . . . . . . . . . . . . . . . 55 Nm (40 ft-lbs)
Cam sprocket cover bolts . . . . . . . . . . . . . . . . . . . . . . . . . . . . . 10 Nm (7.2 ft-lbs)
Camshaft bushing bolts . . . . . . . . . . . . . . . . . . . . . . . . . . . . . . 20 Nm (14 ft-lbs)
Clutch push screw locknut . . . . . . . . . . . . . . . . . . . . . . . . . . . . 12 Nm (8.7 ft-lbs)
Clutch boss nut . . . . . . . . . . . . . . . . . . . . . . . . . . . . . . . . . . . . . 70 Nm (50 ft-lbs) (4)
Clutch cover bolts . . . . . . . . . . . . . . . . . . . . . . . . . . . . . . . . . . . 10 Nm (7.2 ft-lbs)
Clutch pressure plate screws . . . . . . . . . . . . . . . . . . . . . . . . . 8 Nm (5.8 ft-lbs)
Connecting rod nuts . . . . . . . . . . . . . . . . . . . . . . . . . . . . . . . . . 48 Nm (35 ft-lbs) (2)
Crankcase bolts (6 mm) . . . . . . . . . . . . . . . . . . . . . . . . . . . . . . 10 Nm (7.2 ft-lbs)
Crankcase bolts (10 mm) . . . . . . . . . . . . . . . . . . . . . . . . . . . . . 39 Nm (28 ft-lbs)
Cylinder bolts . . . . . . . . . . . . . . . . . . . . . . . . . . . . . . . . . . . . . . . 10 Nm (7.2 ft-lbs)
Cylinder head bolts (8 mm) . . . . . . . . . . . . . . . . . . . . . . . . . . . 20 Nm (14 ft-lbs)
Cylinder head nuts (10 mm) . . . . . . . . . . . . . . . . . . . . . . . . . . . 35 Nm (25 ft-lbs)
Cylinder head nuts (12 mm) . . . . . . . . . . . . . . . . . . . . . . . . . . . 50 Nm (36 ft-lbs)
Intermediate gear stopper plate bolts . . . . . . . . . . . . . . . . . . 10 Nm (7.2 ft-lbs)
Oil line union bolts . . . . . . . . . . . . . . . . . . . . . . . . . . . . . . . . . . . 20 Nm (14 ft-lbs) (1)
Oil pump bolts . . . . . . . . . . . . . . . . . . . . . . . . . . . . . . . . . . . . . . . 10 Nm (7.2 ft-lbs)
Oil pump chain cover bolts . . . . . . . . . . . . . . . . . . . . . . . . . . . . 10 Nm (7.2 ft-lbs)

## Torque specifications (XV1000 models) (continued)

Oil pump sprocket bolts . . . . . . . . . . . . . . . . . . . . . . . . . . . . . . . . . . . . . . 12 Nm (8.7 ft-lbs)
Primary drive gear nut . . . . . . . . . . . . . . . . . . . . . . . . . . . . . . . . . . . . . . . . . 110 Nm (80 ft-lbs) (4)
Rocker arm cover bolts . . . . . . . . . . . . . . . . . . . . . . . . . . . . . . . . . . . . . . . 10 Nm (7.2 ft-lbs)
Rocker arm shaft holding bolts . . . . . . . . . . . . . . . . . . . . . . . . . . . . . . . . 38 Nm (27 ft-lbs) (1)
Shift fork guide bar stopper screws . . . . . . . . . . . . . . . . . . . . . . . . . . . 7 Nm (5.1 ft-lbs) (5)
Shift pedal pinch bolt . . . . . . . . . . . . . . . . . . . . . . . . . . . . . . . . . . . . . . . . 10 Nm (7.2 ft-lbs)

1  Use new sealing washers.
2  Apply molybdenum disulfide grease to the threads and nut surfaces; follow special tightening procedure in the text.
3  Apply engine oil to the threads.
4  Use a new lockwasher.
5  Apply Loctite Stud 'n' Bearing Mount or equivalent to the threads.

# XV1100 models

## General

Bore x stroke . . . . . . . . . . . . . . . . . . . . . . . . . . . . . . . . . . . . . . . . . . . . . . . . . 95.0 x 75.0 mm (3.74 x 2.95 inches)
Displacement . . . . . . . . . . . . . . . . . . . . . . . . . . . . . . . . . . . . . . . . . . . . . . . . . 1063cc
Compression ratio . . . . . . . . . . . . . . . . . . . . . . . . . . . . . . . . . . . . . . . . . . . 8.3 to 1

## Camshafts

Lobe height
  Intake . . . . . . . . . . . . . . . . . . . . . . . . . . . . . . . . . . . . . . . . . . . . . . . . . . . . 39.17 mm (1.5421 inch)
  Exhaust . . . . . . . . . . . . . . . . . . . . . . . . . . . . . . . . . . . . . . . . . . . . . . . . . . 39.20 mm (1.5433 inch)
Base circle
  Intake . . . . . . . . . . . . . . . . . . . . . . . . . . . . . . . . . . . . . . . . . . . . . . . . . . . . 32.17 mm (1.2665 inch)
  Exhaust . . . . . . . . . . . . . . . . . . . . . . . . . . . . . . . . . . . . . . . . . . . . . . . . . . 32.27 mm (1.2705 inch)
Bearing oil clearance . . . . . . . . . . . . . . . . . . . . . . . . . . . . . . . . . . . . . . . . 0.020 to 0.061 mm (0.0008 to 0.0024 inch)
Journal diameter . . . . . . . . . . . . . . . . . . . . . . . . . . . . . . . . . . . . . . . . . . . . 24.96 to 24.98 mm (0.9827 to 0.9835 inch)
Bearing bore . . . . . . . . . . . . . . . . . . . . . . . . . . . . . . . . . . . . . . . . . . . . . . . . 25.00 to 25.021 mm (0.9843 to 0.9851 inch)
Camshaft runout limit . . . . . . . . . . . . . . . . . . . . . . . . . . . . . . . . . . . . . . . 0.03 mm (0.0012 inch)
Rocker arm inside diameter . . . . . . . . . . . . . . . . . . . . . . . . . . . . . . . . . . 14.000 to 14.018 mm (0.5511 to 0.5518 inch)
Rocker arm shaft diameter . . . . . . . . . . . . . . . . . . . . . . . . . . . . . . . . . . . 13.975 to 13.990 mm (0.5501 to 0.5507 inch)
Rocker arm to shaft clearance . . . . . . . . . . . . . . . . . . . . . . . . . . . . . . . 0.009 to 0.033 mm (0.00035 to 0.00130 inch)

## Cylinders

Bore diameter
  Standard . . . . . . . . . . . . . . . . . . . . . . . . . . . . . . . . . . . . . . . . . . . . . . . . . 95.000 to 95.005 mm (3.7402 to 3.7403 inches)
  Limit . . . . . . . . . . . . . . . . . . . . . . . . . . . . . . . . . . . . . . . . . . . . . . . . . . . . . 95.1 mm (3.744 inches)
Bore measuring point
  Through 1987 . . . . . . . . . . . . . . . . . . . . . . . . . . . . . . . . . . . . . . . . . . . . Top, center and bottom of cylinder
  1988-on . . . . . . . . . . . . . . . . . . . . . . . . . . . . . . . . . . . . . . . . . . . . . . . . . . 35 mm (1.38 inch) from top of cylinder
Taper and out-of-round limit . . . . . . . . . . . . . . . . . . . . . . . . . . . . . . . . . 0.05 mm (0.002 inch)

## Pistons

Piston diameter
  Standard . . . . . . . . . . . . . . . . . . . . . . . . . . . . . . . . . . . . . . . . . . . . . . . . . 94.93 to 94.98 mm (3.737 to 3.739 inches)
  First oversize . . . . . . . . . . . . . . . . . . . . . . . . . . . . . . . . . . . . . . . . . . . . . 95.50 mm (3.76 inches)
  Second oversize . . . . . . . . . . . . . . . . . . . . . . . . . . . . . . . . . . . . . . . . . . 96.00 mm (3.78 inches)
Diameter measuring point
  Through 1987 . . . . . . . . . . . . . . . . . . . . . . . . . . . . . . . . . . . . . . . . . . . . 14.6 mm (0.575 inch) from bottom of skirt
  1988-on . . . . . . . . . . . . . . . . . . . . . . . . . . . . . . . . . . . . . . . . . . . . . . . . . . 3 mm (0.12 inch) from bottom of piston skirt
Piston-to-cylinder clearance . . . . . . . . . . . . . . . . . . . . . . . . . . . . . . . . . 0.045 to 0.065 mm (0.0018 to 0.0026 inch)
Ring side clearance
  Top ring . . . . . . . . . . . . . . . . . . . . . . . . . . . . . . . . . . . . . . . . . . . . . . . . . . 0.04 to 0.08 mm (0.0016 to 0.0031 inch)
  Second ring . . . . . . . . . . . . . . . . . . . . . . . . . . . . . . . . . . . . . . . . . . . . . . 0.03 to 0.07 mm (0.0012 to 0.0028 inch)
  Oil ring . . . . . . . . . . . . . . . . . . . . . . . . . . . . . . . . . . . . . . . . . . . . . . . . . . . Not specified
Ring thickness
  Top ring . . . . . . . . . . . . . . . . . . . . . . . . . . . . . . . . . . . . . . . . . . . . . . . . . . 1.5 mm (0.06 inch)
  Second ring . . . . . . . . . . . . . . . . . . . . . . . . . . . . . . . . . . . . . . . . . . . . . . 1.2 mm (0.0472 inch)
  Oil ring (spacer and rails) . . . . . . . . . . . . . . . . . . . . . . . . . . . . . . . . . 2.5 mm (0.0984 inch)
Ring end gap
  Top ring . . . . . . . . . . . . . . . . . . . . . . . . . . . . . . . . . . . . . . . . . . . . . . . . . . 0.3 to 0.5 mm (0.012 to 0.020 inch)
  Second ring . . . . . . . . . . . . . . . . . . . . . . . . . . . . . . . . . . . . . . . . . . . . . . 0.3 to 0.45 mm (0.012 to 0.018 inch)
  Oil ring . . . . . . . . . . . . . . . . . . . . . . . . . . . . . . . . . . . . . . . . . . . . . . . . . . . 0.2 to 0.7 mm (0.008 to 0.0276 inch)
Ring width
  Top and second rings . . . . . . . . . . . . . . . . . . . . . . . . . . . . . . . . . . . . . 3.8 mm (0.15 inch)
  Oil ring . . . . . . . . . . . . . . . . . . . . . . . . . . . . . . . . . . . . . . . . . . . . . . . . . . . 3.4 mm (0.13 inch)

## Cylinder head, valves and valve springs
Cylinder head warpage limit .................................... 0.03 mm (0.0012 inch)
Valve stem bend limit ........................................... 0.03 mm (0.0012 inch)
Valve head diameter
    Intake ....................................................... 47.0 to 47.02 mm (1.850 to 1.858 inch)
    Exhaust ..................................................... 39.0 to 39.2 mm (1.540 to 1.562 inch)
Valve stem diameter
    Intake ....................................................... 7.975 to 7.990 mm (0.311 to 0.314 inch)
    Exhaust ..................................................... 7.960 to 7.975 mm (0.3134 to 0.3140 inch)
Valve head edge thickness limit ............................... 1.3 +/- 0.2 mm (0.051 +/- 0.008 inch)
Valve guide inside diameter .................................... 8.000 to 8.012 mm (0.3150 to 0.3155 inch)
Valve seat width limit .......................................... 1.3 +/- 0.1 mm (0.051 +/- 0.004 inch)
Valve face width ............................................... 2.1 mm (0.083 inch)
Valve inner spring free length ................................. 43.39 mm (1.708 inch)
Valve inner spring installed length ............................ 38.0 mm (1.496 inch)
Valve inner spring bend limit .................................. 1.9 mm (0.0748 inch)
Valve outer spring free length ................................. 45.33 mm (1.785 inch)
Valve outer spring installed length ............................ 40.0 mm (1.575 inch)
Valve outer spring bend limit .................................. 1.9 mm (0.0748 inch)

## Crankshaft, connecting rods and bearings
Connecting rod side clearance ................................. 0.370 to 0.474 mm (0.0146 to 0.0187 inch)
Connecting rod bearing oil clearance .......................... 0.030 to 0.054 mm (0.0012 to 0.0021 inch)
Crankshaft runout limit ........................................ 0.02 mm (0.0008 inch)

## Oil pump
Inner to outer rotor clearance ................................. 0.03 to 0.09 mm (0.0012 to 0.0035 inch)
Outer rotor to housing clearance .............................. 0.03 to 0.08 mm (0.0012 to 0.0031 inch)
Rotor to straightedge clearance ............................... 0.03 to 0.09 mm (0.0012 to 0.0035 inch)

## Clutch
Friction plate thickness
    Standard ..................................................... 2.9 to 3.1 mm (0.116 to 0.124 inch)
    Minimum ..................................................... 2.8 mm (0.11 inch)
Steel plate thickness .......................................... 1.9 to 2.1 mm (0.075 to 0.083 inch)
Steel plate warpage limit ...................................... 0.1 mm (0.004 inch)
Pushrod bend limit ............................................ 0.5 mm (0.02 inch)
Diaphragm spring height
    Standard ..................................................... 7.2 mm (0.283 inch)
    Minimum ..................................................... 6.5 mm (0.256 inch)
    Warpage limit ................................................ 0.1 mm (0.004 inch)

## Transmission
Driveaxle and mainshaft runout limit .......................... 0.08 mm (0.0031 inch)

## Torque specifications
Alternator cover bolts ......................................... 10 Nm (7.2 ft-lbs)
Alternator cover screws ....................................... 7 Nm (5.1 ft-lbs)
Alternator rotor nut ........................................... See Chapter 8
Cam chain damper bolt ........................................ 8 Nm (5.8 ft-lbs)
Cam chain damper bolt locknut ................................ 12 Nm (8.7 ft-lbs)
Cam chain tensioner bolts ..................................... 10 Nm (7.2 ft-lbs)
Cam sprocket bolt ............................................ 55 Nm (40 ft-lbs)
Cam sprocket cover bolts ..................................... 10 Nm (7.2 ft-lbs)
Camshaft retainer bolts ....................................... 20 Nm (14 ft-lbs)
Clutch push screw locknut .................................... 12 Nm (8.7 ft-lbs)
Clutch boss nut .............................................. 70 Nm (50 ft-lbs) (4)
Clutch cover bolts ........................................... 10 Nm (7.2 ft-lbs)
Clutch pressure plate screws ................................. 8 Nm (5.8 ft-lbs)
Clutch diaphragm spring bolts ................................ 10 Nm (7.2 ft-lbs)
Connecting rod nuts .......................................... 48 Nm (35 ft-lbs) (2)
Crankcase bolts (6 mm) ...................................... 10 Nm (7.2 ft-lbs)
Crankcase bolts (10 mm) ..................................... 39 Nm (28 ft-lbs)
Cylinder bolts ............................................... 10 Nm (7.2 ft-lbs)
Cylinder head bolts (8 mm) ................................... 20 Nm (14 ft-lbs)
Cylinder head nuts (10 mm) ................................... 35 Nm (25 ft-lbs)
Cylinder head nuts (12 mm) ................................... 50 Nm (36 ft-lbs)
Intermediate gear stopper plate bolts ......................... 10 Nm (7.2 ft-lbs)
Oil line union bolts ........................................... 20 Nm (14 ft-lbs) (1)
Oil pump bolts ............................................... 10 Nm (7.2 ft-lbs)
Oil pump chain cover bolts .................................... 10 Nm (7.2 ft-lbs)

## Torque specifications (XV1100 models) (continued)

Oil pump sprocket bolts . . . . . . . . . . . . . . . . . . . . . . . . . . . . . . . . 12 Nm (8.7 ft-lbs)
Primary drive gear nut . . . . . . . . . . . . . . . . . . . . . . . . . . . . . . . . . 110 Nm (80 ft-lbs) (4)
Rocker arm cover bolts . . . . . . . . . . . . . . . . . . . . . . . . . . . . . . . . . 10 Nm (7.2 ft-lbs)
Rocker arm shaft holding bolts . . . . . . . . . . . . . . . . . . . . . . . . . . 38 Nm (27 ft-lbs) (1)
Shift fork guide bar stopper screws . . . . . . . . . . . . . . . . . . . . . . 7 Nm (5.1 ft-lbs) (5)
Shift pedal pinch bolt . . . . . . . . . . . . . . . . . . . . . . . . . . . . . . . . . 10 Nm (7.2 ft-lbs)

*1 Use new sealing washers.*
*2 Apply molybdenum disulfide grease to the threads and nut surfaces; follow special tightening procedure in the text.*
*3 Apply engine oil to the threads.*
*4 Use a new lockwasher.*
*5 Apply Loctite Stud 'n' Bearing Mount or equivalent to the threads.*

## 1 General information

**Note:** *Some of the procedures in this Chapter are listed as applying to 1981 through 1983 models. If you're working on a 1984 or 1985 TR1 model, use the 1981 through 1983 procedures.*

The engine/transmission unit is an air-cooled V-twin. The valves are operated by overhead camshafts which are chain driven off the crankshaft. The engine/transmission assembly is constructed from aluminum alloy. The crankcase is divided vertically.

The crankcase incorporates a wet sump, pressure-fed lubrication system which uses a chain-driven oil pump and an oil filter mounted in the right-hand side.

Power from the crankshaft is routed to the transmission via the clutch, which is of the wet multi-plate type and is gear-driven off the crankshaft. The transmission is a five-speed, constant-mesh unit.

## 2 Operations possible with the engine in the frame

The components and assemblies listed below can be removed without having to remove the engine from the frame. If, however, a number of areas require attention at the same time, removal of the engine is recommended.

*Starter motor*
*Alternator*
*Oil pump*
*Starter clutch*
*Cam sprockets*
*Clutch and primary drive gear*
*External shift linkage*

## 3 Operations requiring engine removal

It is necessary to remove the engine/transmission assembly from the frame to gain access to the following components:
*Cylinder heads, rocker arms and camshafts*
*Cylinders and pistons*
*Cam chains and intermediate gears*

The crankcase halves must be separated to gain access to the following components:
*Crankshaft, connecting rods and bearings*
*Transmission shafts*
*Shift cam and forks*
*Oil pressure relief valve*

## 4 Major engine repair - general note

1 It is not always easy to determine when or if an engine should be completely overhauled, as a number of factors must be considered.
2 High mileage is not necessarily an indication that an overhaul is needed, while low mileage, on the other hand, does not preclude the need for an overhaul. Frequency of servicing is probably the single most important consideration. An engine that has regular and frequent oil and filter changes, as well as other required maintenance, will most likely give many miles of reliable service. Conversely, a neglected engine, or one which has not been broken in properly, may require an overhaul very early in its life.
3 Exhaust smoke and excessive oil consumption are both indications that piston rings and/or valve guides are in need of attention. Make sure oil leaks are not responsible for deciding that the rings and guides are bad. Refer to Chapter 1 and perform a cylinder compression check to determine for certain the nature and extent of the work required.
4 If the engine is making obvious knocking or rumbling noises, the connecting rod and/or main bearings are probably at fault.
5 Loss of power, rough running, excessive valve train noise and high fuel consumption rates may also point to the need for an overhaul, especially if they are all present at the same time. If a complete tune-up does not remedy the situation, major mechanical work is the only solution.
6 An engine overhaul generally involves restoring the internal parts to the specifications of a new engine. During an overhaul the piston rings are replaced and the cylinder walls are bored and/or honed. If a rebore is done, then new pistons are also required. The main and connecting rod bearings are generally replaced with new ones

and, if necessary, the crankshaft is also replaced. Generally the valves are serviced as well, since they are usually in less than perfect condition at this point. While the engine is being overhauled, other components such as the carburetors and the starter motor can be rebuilt also. The end result should be a like-new engine that will give as many trouble free miles as the original.
7 Before beginning the engine overhaul, read through all of the related procedures to familiarize yourself with the scope and requirements of the job. Overhauling an engine is not all that difficult, but it is time consuming. Plan on the motorcycle being tied up for a minimum of two weeks. Check on the availability of parts and make sure that any necessary special tools, equipment and supplies are obtained in advance.
8 Most work can be done with typical shop hand tools, although a number of precision measuring tools are required for inspecting parts to determine if they must be replaced. Often a dealer service department or motorcycle repair shop will handle the inspection of parts and offer advice concerning reconditioning and replacement.

 **HAYNES HINT** *As a general rule, time is the primary cost of an overhaul so it doesn't pay to install worn or substandard parts.*

9 As a final note, to ensure maximum life and minimum trouble from a rebuilt engine, everything must be assembled with care in a spotlessly clean environment.

## 5 Engine - removal and installation

 **Warning: Engine removal and installation should be done with the aid of an assistant to avoid damage or injury that could occur if the engine is dropped. A hydraulic floor jack should be used to support and lower the engine if possible (they can be rented at low cost).**

### Removal

1 Support the bike securely so it can't be knocked over during this procedure. Place a

5.9 Squeeze the clip, slide it down the hose and disconnect the hose from the fitting

5.20a Unbolt the front cylinder mounting bracket from the frame

5.20b Remove the rear cylinder bracket-to-frame bolts (arrow); there's one on each side of the bike

support under the swingarm pivot and be sure the motorcycle is safely braced.

**2** Remove the seat and side covers (see Chapter 7). Disconnect the battery cables from the battery (see Chapter 1).

 *Warning: Always disconnect the negative cable first and reconnect it last to prevent a battery explosion.*

**3** Remove the fuel tank and air cleaner housing (see Chapter 3).

**4** If you're working on a 1981 through 1983 model, remove the battery (see Chapter 1).

**5** Drain the engine oil (see Chapter 1).

**6** Remove the exhaust system (see Chapter 3). If you're working on a 1981 through 1983 model, remove the battery box together with the right muffler/silencer bracket.

**7** Remove the brake light switch (see Chapter 8). Remove the brake pedal and the rear footpeg brackets (see Chapter 7). If you're working on a 1981 through 1983 model, remove the front footpegs and brackets as well.

**8** Disconnect the mixture control valve hoses (see Chapter 3). If you're working on a 1984 or later model, remove the mixture control valve case.

**9** Disconnect the crankcase ventilation hose from the rear cylinder head **(see illustration)**.

**10** Disconnect the throttle and choke cables from the carburetors (see Chapter 3). Disconnect the fuel lines and plug or cap them to prevent fuel leaks. If you're working on an XV1100, disconnect the vacuum sensor hose.

**11** Remove the ignition coil cover and disconnect the primary (low tension) coil wires (see Chapter 4). If you're working on an XV1100, disconnect the vacuum sensor hose and electrical connector.

**12** Disconnect the clutch cable from the engine (see Section 16).

**13** Remove the sidestand (see Chapter 7).

**14** Disconnect the spark plug wires (HT leads) (see Spark plugs - servicing in Chapter 1).

**15** Disconnect the ground/earth wire from the engine.

**16** If you're working on a 1981 through 1983

model, disconnect the cable from the starter relay to the starter motor at the relay (see Chapter 8).

**17** Disconnect the wires for the alternator, sidestand switch, oil level switch (if equipped), neutral switch and starter motor.

**18** If you're working on a shaft drive model, pull the rubber driveshaft boot away from the engine. If you're working on a chain drive model, remove the engine sprocket (see Chapter 5).

**19** Support the engine with a jack and wood block. Make sure the support is still in position under the swingarm pivot and that the bike is still securely braced.

**20** Remove the engine mounting bolts at the top of each cylinder **(see illustrations)**. If you're working on a 1981 through 1983 model, remove the mounting stud at the rear of the engine **(see illustration)**. If you're working on a 1984 or later model, remove the mounting bolts at the upper rear and lower rear of the engine.

**21** Make sure no wires or hoses are still attached to the engine assembly.

 *Warning: The engine is heavy and may cause injury if it falls. Be sure it's securely supported. Have an assistant help you steady the engine on the jack as you remove it.*

**22** Slowly and carefully lower the engine assembly to the floor, disengaging the

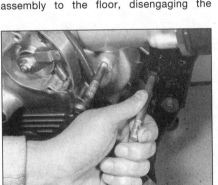

5.20c Remove the mounting stud at the rear on 1981 through 1983 models

driveshaft (if equipped) as you do so. Guide the engine out from under the right side of the bike.

### Installation

**23** Installation is the reverse of removal. Note the following points:

a) If you're working on a shaft drive model, engage the driveshaft with the swingarm as the engine is moved into position. Some models have a viewing port in the swingarm, covered by a plug **(see illustration)**.

b) Don't tighten any of the engine mounting fasteners until they all have been installed.

c) Use new gaskets at all exhaust pipe connections.

d) Tighten the engine mounting bolts (and stud, if equipped) securely.

e) Adjust the rear brake rod, clutch cable and throttle cable(s) following the procedures in Chapter 1 and Chapter 3.

f) Be sure to refill the engine oil before starting the engine.

## 6 Engine disassembly and reassembly -
general information

**1** Before disassembling the engine, clean the exterior with a degreaser and rinse it with water.

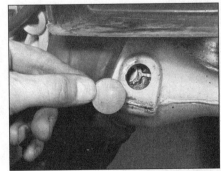

5.23 Look through the viewing port to align the driveshaft with the middle driven gear

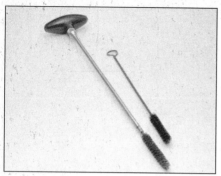

6.2a  A selection of brushes is required for cleaning holes and passages in the engine components

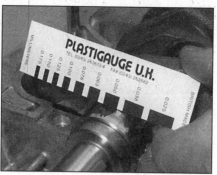

6.2b  Plastigauge is needed to check the connecting rod oil clearances

6.3  An engine stand can be made from short lengths of 2 x 4 lumber and lag bolts or nails

**HAYNES HiNT** *A clean engine will make the job easier and prevent the possibility of getting dirt into the internal areas of the engine.*

**2** In addition to the precision measuring tools mentioned earlier, you will need a torque wrench, a valve spring compressor, oil gallery brushes, a piston ring removal and installation tool, a piston ring compressor and a clutch holder tool (which is described in Section 17). Some new, clean engine oil of the correct grade and type, some engine assembly lube (or moly-based grease), a tube of Yamaha Quick Gasket (part no. 11001-05-01) or equivalent, and a tube of RTV (silicone) sealant will also be required. Although it may not be considered a tool, some Plastigauge should also be obtained to use for checking connecting rod bearing oil clearances **(see illustrations)**.

**3** An engine support stand made from short lengths of lumber bolted together will facilitate the disassembly and reassembly procedures **(see illustration)**. The perimeter of the mount should be just big enough to accommodate the crankcase when it's laid on its side for removal of the crankshaft and transmission components. If you have an automotive-type engine stand, an adapter plate can be made from a piece of plate, some angle iron and some nuts and bolts. The adapter plate can be attached to the engine mounting bolt holes.

**4** When disassembling the engine, keep "mated" parts together (including gears, cylinders, pistons, etc.) that have been in contact with each other during engine operation. These "mated" parts must be reused or replaced as an assembly.

**5** Engine/transmission disassembly should be done in the following general order with reference to the appropriate Sections.

Remove the cylinder heads
Remove the camshafts
Remove the rocker arms
Remove the cylinders
Remove the pistons
Remove the clutch and primary gear

Remove the alternator rotor and starter clutch (see Chapter 8)
Remove the oil pump
Remove the external shift mechanism
Remove the cam chains and intermediate gears
Separate the crankcase halves
Remove the crankshaft and connecting rods
Remove the shift cam/forks
Remove the transmission shafts/gears
Remove the oil pressure relief valve

**6** Reassembly is accomplished by reversing the general disassembly sequence.

**7  Camshaft chain tensioners - removal and installation**

### Removal

*Caution: Once you start to remove the tensioner bolts, you must remove the tensioner all the way and reset it before tightening the bolts. The tensioner extends and locks in place, so if you loosen the bolts partway and then retighten them, the tensioner or cam chain will be damaged.*

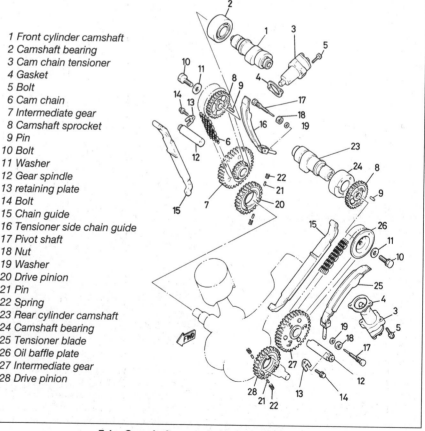

1 Front cylinder camshaft
2 Camshaft bearing
3 Cam chain tensioner
4 Gasket
5 Bolt
6 Cam chain
7 Intermediate gear
8 Camshaft sprocket
9 Pin
10 Bolt
11 Washer
12 Gear spindle
13 retaining plate
14 Bolt
15 Chain guide
16 Tensioner side chain guide
17 Pivot shaft
18 Nut
19 Washer
20 Drive pinion
21 Pin
22 Spring
23 Rear cylinder camshaft
24 Camshaft bearing
25 Tensioner blade
26 Oil baffle plate
27 Intermediate gear
28 Drive pinion

7.1a  Camshaft, cam chains and tensioners

**7.1b If the engine has Type A tensioners, remove the Allen bolts (arrows) and take the tensioner out**

**7.2a If the engine has Type B tensioners, unscrew the tensioner from the body and take it out**

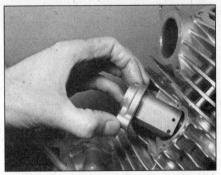

**7.2b Remove the Allen bolts and take the tensioner body out of the cylinder**

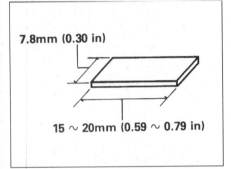

**7.3 Cam chain tensioner keeper dimensions**

7.8mm (0.30 in)

15 ~ 20mm (0.59 ~ 0.79 in)

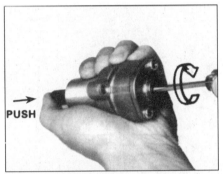

PUSH

**7.5 Turn the screwdriver clockwise while pushing the tensioner piston into the body**

1 If you're working on a model with Type A tensioners, remove the Allen bolts and take the tensioner off **(see illustrations)**.

2 If you're working on a model with hex-head (Type B) tensioners, remove the tensioner cap bolt and spring while the tensioner is still installed on the engine **(see illustration)**. Remove the tensioner body Allen bolts and take it off the engine **(see illustration)**.

## Installation

### Type A tensioners

3 Fabricate a keeper tool from steel 1 mm (0.039 inch) thick **(see illustration)**.
4 Pry the rubber plug out of the tensioner.
5 Insert a small screwdriver and turn it clockwise while pushing the tensioner piston into the tensioner **(see illustration)**. When the piston is all the way in, hold it there, remove the screwdriver and install the keeper tool to hold the tensioner in position.
6 Install the tensioner on the engine, using a new gasket. Tighten the mounting bolts to the torque listed in this Chapter's Specifications. Remove the keeper tool and install the rubber plug.

### Type B tensioners

7 Install the tensioner body on the cylinder, using a new gasket, and tighten its mounting bolts to the torque listed in this Chapter's Specifications.
8 Check the sealing washer on the cap bolt for cracks or hardening. It's a good idea to

replace this washer whenever the tensioner cap is removed.
9 Release the one-way cam on the chain tensioner and compress the tensioner piston into the tensioner body (see Part A of this Chapter). Install the tensioner on the cylinder, using a new gasket.
10 Install the tensioner spring, sealing washer and cap. Tighten the cap to the torque listed in this Chapter's Specifications.

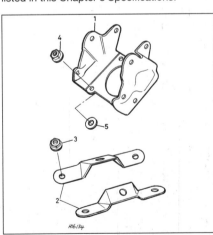

**8.3 engine mounting brackets**

1  *Front cylinder mounting bracket*
2  *Rear cylinder mounting bracket*
3  *Flange nuts (short)*
4  *Flange nuts (long)*
5  *Washers*

## 8  Cylinder heads, camshafts and rocker arms - removal, inspection and installation

### Cylinder head removal

1 Remove the engine from the frame (see Section 5).
2 Remove the ignition coil mounting bracket and ignition coils from the front cylinder (see Chapter 4). Remove the carburetors, intake joints and air induction pipes (if equipped) (see Chapter 3).
3 Remove the engine mounting bracket, its washers and nuts from the front cylinder head **(see illustration)**.
4 Remove the Allen bolts and take off the cam sprocket cover **(see illustrations)**.

> **HAYNES HiNT** *Stuff clean shop towels into the opening below the cam sprocket so nothing is accidentally dropped into it.*

5 Remove the rocker arm covers and their O-rings from the exhaust side and intake side of the cylinder **(see illustration)**.

### Rear cylinder

6 Turn the engine so the rear cylinder is at top dead center on its compression stroke (see *Valve clearance - adjustment* in Chapter 1).

**8.4a Remove the cam sprocket cover; use a new O-ring on installation**

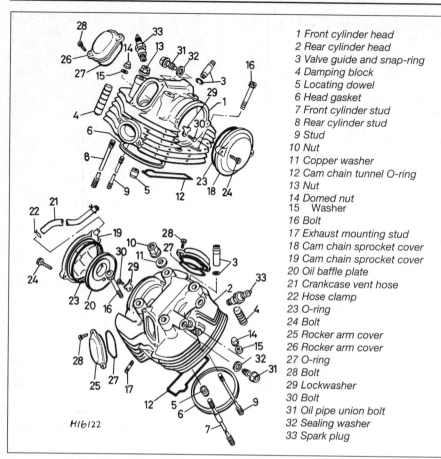

1 Front cylinder head
2 Rear cylinder head
3 Valve guide and snap-ring
4 Damping block
5 Locating dowel
6 Head gasket
7 Front cylinder stud
8 Rear cylinder stud
9 Stud
10 Nut
11 Copper washer
12 Cam chain tunnel O-ring
13 Nut
14 Domed nut
15 Washer
16 Bolt
17 Exhaust mounting stud
18 Cam chain sprocket cover
19 Cam chain sprocket cover
20 Oil baffle plate
21 Crankcase vent hose
22 Hose clamp
23 O-ring
24 Bolt
25 Rocker arm cover
26 Rocker arm cover
27 O-ring
28 Bolt
29 Lockwasher
30 Bolt
31 Oil pipe union bolt
32 Sealing washer
33 Spark plug

H16122

**8.4b  Cylinder heads (1981 through 1983 models) - exploded view**

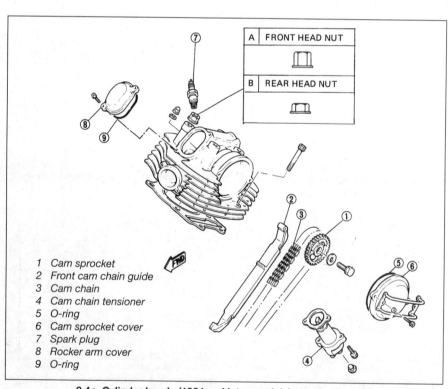

| A | FRONT HEAD NUT |
| B | REAR HEAD NUT |

1 Cam sprocket
2 Front cam chain guide
3 Cam chain
4 Cam chain tensioner
5 O-ring
6 Cam sprocket cover
7 Spark plug
8 Rocker arm cover
9 O-ring

**8.4c  Cylinder heads (1984 and later models) - exploded view**

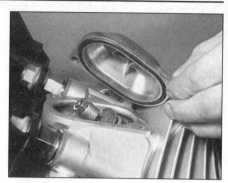

**8.5  Remove the rocker arm cover; use a new O-ring on installation**

When the rear cylinder is on its compression stroke, the line on the alternator rotor with a T mark next to it will be aligned with the notch in the timing window **(see illustration)**. Also, the camshaft sprocket mark will be aligned with the mark inside the sprocket housing on the cylinder head **(see illustration)**.

**7** Remove the cam chain tensioner for the rear cylinder (see Section 7).

**8** Place a piece of mechanic's wire where you can reach it easily during the next steps.

**9** Hold the engine from turning with a socket on the alternator rotor bolt. If the engine is in the frame, you can also keep it from turning by shifting the transmission into gear and having an assistant hold the rear brake on.

**10** While you hold the engine from turning, loosen and unscrew the camshaft sprocket bolt.

**11** Slide the sprocket off the camshaft, making sure the camshaft dowel doesn't fall out of the camshaft.

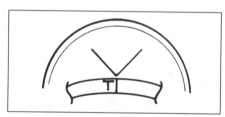

**8.6a  Align the line next to the T mark with the pointer**

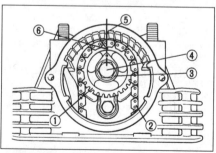

**8.6b  Align the cast pointer in the cylinder head with the sprocket timing mark**

1 Cam sprocket
2 Cam chain
3 Washer
4 Sprocket bolt
5 Cast pointer
6 Sprocket timing mark

8.13  Drape the cam chain over the cylinder head to keep it on the sprocket; tie it up if necessary

8.14a  Remove the oil pipe union bolt at the cylinder head . . .

8.14b  . . . and at the crankcase; use new sealing washers on installation

**12** Disengage the sprocket from the chain. Label the sprocket "R" (for rear cylinder) and set it aside.
**13** Drape the cam chain over the cylinder head **(see illustration)**. At this point, the camshaft dowel should be aligned with the pointer cast in the cylinder head.
**14** Remove the external oil line **(see illustrations)**.
**15** Loosen the cylinder head nuts and bolts evenly in several stages **(see illustrations)**. Remove the nuts, washers, bolts and engine mounting brackets.
**16** Hold the cam chain and lift the cylinder head off the studs **(see illustration)**.

8.15a  Four of the rear cylinder head nuts also secure the engine mounting brackets

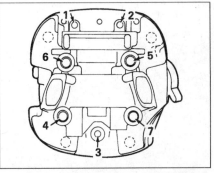

8.15b  Cylinder head nut LOOSENING sequence

*If the cylinder head is stuck, tap it gently with a rubber or plastic mallet, being careful not to break the cooling fins. Don't pry against the gasket surfaces or they will be gouged.*

**17** Remove the dowels and front side chain damper **(see illustration)**. Support the cam chain so it doesn't drop down off the lower sprocket.
**18** Check the cylinder head gasket (and the separate O-ring around the cam chain tunnel on 1981 through 1983 models) and the mating surfaces on the cylinder head and cylinder for leakage, which could indicate warpage. Refer to Section 10

and check the flatness of the cylinder head.
**19** Clean all traces of old gasket material from the cylinder head and the top of the cylinder. Be careful not to let any of the gasket material fall into the crankcase, the cylinder bore or the oil passages.

**Front cylinder**

**20** Repeat Steps 6 through 19 to remove the front cylinder head, noting that the front camshaft sprocket has an oil baffle. The hole in the baffle should be aligned with the cast pointer when the rear cylinder is at TDC on its compression stroke **(see illustration)**.

**Camshaft removal**

**21** If you haven't already done so, remove

the rocker arm covers (see illustrations 8.4b, 8.4c and 8.5).
**22** Loosen the rocker arm locknuts and back off the adjusters.
**23** Remove the bolt and camshaft retainer plate **(see illustration)**.
**24** Remove the camshaft **(see illustration)**.

**Rocker arm removal**

**25** Remove the camshaft (see Steps 21 through 24).
**26** Remove the rocker arm shaft retaining bolt and sealing washer.
**27** Thread a slide hammer into the end of the rocker shaft. Once the rocker shaft clears the

8.16  Support the cam chain while you lift the head off the studs

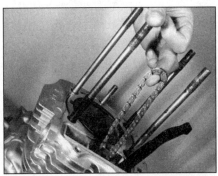

8.17  Keep the cam chain supported and lift the front side chain damper out

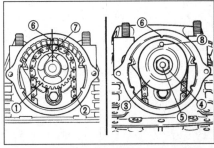

8.20  Align the cast pointer in the cylinder head with the sprocket timing mark and the oil baffle hole

1  Cam sprocket
2  Cam chain
3  Oil baffle
4  Washer
5  Sprocket bolt
6  Cast pointer
7  Sprocket timing mark
8  Oil baffle hole

8.23 With the camshaft dowel aligned with the cast pointer in the cylinder head, unbolt the retainer

8.24 Slowly remove the camshaft from the head; be careful not to nick or gouge the bearing surfaces

8.27 When the rocker shaft is partway out, remove the rocker arm

rocker arm, take the rocker arm out (see illustration).

**TOOL TiP**

If you don't have a slide hammer, use a long bolt and a pair of Vise Grips. Thread the bolt into the rocker arm, grip it with the Vise Grips, then tap against the Vise Grips with a hammer to pull the rocker shaft out.

28 Remove the remaining rocker shaft and arm, then label them according to cylinder and position (for example, rear intake and rear exhaust).

### Camshaft, chain and cam sprocket inspection

29 This is the same as for XV535 models. Refer to Part A of this Chapter for procedures and to this Chapter's Specifications.

### Rocker arm and shaft inspection

30 This is the same as for XV535 models. Refer to Part A of this Chapter for procedures and to this Chapter's Specifications.

### Camshaft installation

31 Apply a light coat of engine assembly lube or moly-based grease to the camshaft journals. Position the camshaft bushing on the camshaft.
32 Apply a light coat of engine assembly lube or moly-based grease to the cam lobes.
33 Slide the camshaft into the cylinder head, then install the bushing (see illustrations 8.24 and 8.23). Don't let the bushing tilt sideways and jam in its bore. Align the bushing cutout with the retainer bolt hole and align the camshaft dowel with the timing mark (see illustration 8.23).
34 Install the retainer (see illustration 8.23). Tighten the bolt to the torque listed in this Chapter's Specifications.

### Rocker arm and shaft installation

35 Coat the rocker shafts and the rocker arm bores with clean engine oil. Thread a bolt into the threads in the end of the exhaust rocker shaft to use as a handle. Position the exhaust rocker shaft partway into its hole with the threaded end facing out (see illustration). Install the exhaust rocker arm and slide the shaft into the rocker arm.

Repeat this procedure to install the intake rocker arm.
36 Install the retaining bolt with a new sealing washer in the left hole (as you face the cylinder head). The right hole is for the oil line union bolt.

### Cylinder head installation

#### Rear cylinder head

37 If both cylinder heads have been removed, install the rear cylinder head first.
38 Install the dowels and the new head gasket on top of the cylinder (see illustrations 8.4b and 8.4c). If you're working on a 1981 through 1983 model, install the O-ring in the groove around the cam chain tunnel (see illustration). Never reuse the old head gasket and don't use any type of gasket sealant.
39 Install the front side cam chain damper (if removed).
40 Position the cylinder head on the studs and guide the cam chain damper through the cam chain tunnel (see illustration 8.16).
41 Install the cylinder head bolts and nuts together with the engine mounting brackets (see illustration 8.15a). Four of the shorter nuts go on the rear cylinder head; the longer nuts and the remaining four short nuts go on the front cylinder head. Tighten the bolts and nuts evenly in several stages, in the specified sequence, to the torque listed in this Chapter's Specifications (see illustration).

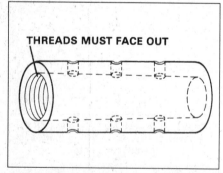

**THREADS MUST FACE OUT**

8.35 Ensure the threads face out when the shaft is installed, or there will be no way to remove the shaft

8.38 Early models have an O-ring (separate from the head gasket) around the cam chain tunnel

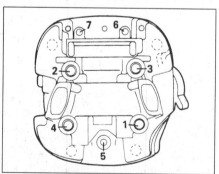

8.41 Cylinder head nut and bolt TIGHTENING sequence

**8.44 Align the dimple in the sprocket with the cast pointer in the cylinder head**

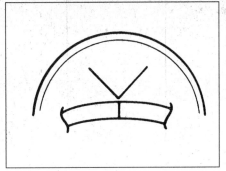

**8.51 Crankshaft timing mark for front cylinder**

**8.52a The longer nuts go on the front cylinder head . . .**

42 Make sure the camshaft locating dowel is aligned with the mark on the cylinder head **(see illustration 8.23)**.

43 Make sure the line on the timing rotor with a T mark next to it aligns with the notch in the timing window **(see illustration 8.6a)**. If it's necessary to turn the crankshaft, hold the timing chain up while you're turning so it doesn't fall off the crankshaft sprocket and become jammed.

44 Engage the camshaft sprocket with the timing chain so its dowel hole aligns with the dowel. Slip the sprocket onto the camshaft over the dowel. The dimple in the sprocket should be aligned with the pointer on the cylinder head **(see illustration)**.

45 Turn the cam sprocket clockwise far enough to remove all slack in the front run of the cam chain, but no farther. Insert a finger in the tensioner hole and push against the chain damper. Make sure the timing marks on the cam sprocket and crankshaft are aligned correctly **(see illustrations 8.6a and 8.6b)**.

46 With the marks correctly aligned, install the washer and cam sprocket bolt and tighten to the torque listed in this Chapter's Specifications.

47 Install the cam chain tensioner (see Section 7).

48 Adjust the valve clearances (see Chapter 1).

49 Install the rocker arm covers with new O-rings.

50 Install the cam sprocket cover, using a new O-ring.

### Front cylinder head

51 Repeat Steps 38 through 40 to install the front cylinder head, noting that the slot in the timing rotor must be aligned with the crankcase pointer when the camshaft dowel is aligned with the cylinder head mark **(see illustration)**.

52 Install the washers, cylinder head nuts and bolts and engine mounting bracket **(see illustrations)**.

53 Repeat Steps 42 through 51 to finish installing the cylinder head, noting that there is an oil baffle on the sprocket **(see illustration)**.

54 Install the ignition coils and their bracket (see Chapter 4).

### Both cylinder heads

55 Change the engine oil (see Chapter 1).

56 The remainder of installation is the reverse of the removal steps.

---

## 9 Valves/valve seats/valve guides - servicing

1 Because of the complex nature of this job and the special tools and equipment required, servicing of the valves, the valve seats and the

valve guides (commonly known as a valve job) is best left to a professional.

2 The home mechanic can, however, remove and disassemble the head, do the initial cleaning and inspection, then reassemble and deliver the head to a dealer service department or properly equipped motorcycle repair shop for the actual valve servicing. Refer to Section 8 for those procedures.

3 The dealer service department will remove the valves and springs, recondition or replace the valves and valve seats, replace the valve guides, check and replace the valve springs, spring retainers and keepers/collets (as necessary), replace the valve seals with new ones and reassemble the valve components.

4 After the valve job has been performed, the head will be in like-new condition.

> **HAYNES HINT** *When the head is returned, be sure to clean it again very thoroughly before installation on the engine to remove any metal particles or abrasive grit that may still be present from the valve service operations. Use compressed air, if available, to blow out all the holes and passages.*

## 10 Cylinder head and valves - disassembly, inspection and reassembly

These procedures are the same as for XV535 models. Refer to Part A of this Chapter for procedures and Part B for specifications.

## 11 Cylinders - removal, inspection and installation

### Removal

1 Following the procedure given in Section 8, remove the cylinder head.

**8.52b . . . and the front engine mounting bracket fits on the studs**

**8.53 Install the oil baffle next to the front cylinder's cam sprocket, facing in the direction shown**

11.2 Remove the three Allen bolts to detach the cylinder from the crankcase

11.3 Support the timing chain and pull the cylinder off the studs

**2** Remove the cylinder bolts **(see illustration)**.
**3** Lift the cylinder straight up to remove it, supporting the cam chain as you do so **(see illustration)**. If it's stuck, tap around its perimeter with a soft-faced hammer, taking care not to break the cooling fins. Don't attempt to pry between the cylinder and the crankcase, as you will ruin the sealing surfaces. As you lift, note the location of the

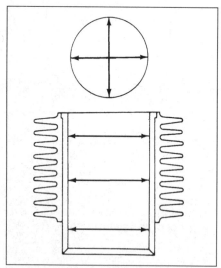

11.7 On '81 - '87 models, measure the diameter at the top, center and bottom; on 1988-on models, measure at the specified distance from the top

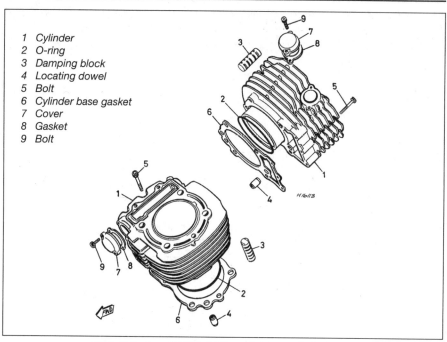

1 Cylinder
2 O-ring
3 Damping block
4 Locating dowel
5 Bolt
6 Cylinder base gasket
7 Cover
8 Gasket
9 Bolt

11.4 Cylinders (XV700-1100 models) - exploded view

dowel pins and O-ring. Be careful not to let these drop into the engine.
**4** Stuff clean shop towels around the pistons and remove the gasket and all traces of old gasket material from the surfaces of the cylinder, cylinder head and crankcase. Remove the O-ring from the base of the cylinder **(see illustration)**. **Note:** *Don't remove the rubber sleeves from the cylinder studs.*

### Inspection

**5** Don't attempt to separate the liner from the cylinder.
**6** Check the cylinder wall carefully for scratches and score marks.
**7** Using the appropriate precision measuring tools, check each cylinder's diameter. Measure parallel to the crankshaft axis and across the crankshaft axis, at the depth from the top of the cylinder listed in this Chapter's Specifications **(see illustration)**. Average the two measurements and compare the results to this Chapter's Specifications. If the cylinder walls are tapered, out-of-round, worn beyond the specified limits, or badly scuffed or scored, have them rebored and honed by a dealer service department or a motorcycle repair shop. If a rebore is done, oversize pistons and rings will be required as well.
**8** As an alternative, if the precision measuring tools are not available, a dealer service department or motorcycle repair shop will make the measurements and offer advice concerning servicing of the cylinders.
**9** If they are in reasonably good condition and not worn to the outside of the limits, and if the piston-to-cylinder clearances can be maintained properly (see Section 12), then the

cylinders do not have to be rebored; honing is all that is necessary.
**10** For honing, refer to Chapter 2, Part A.

### Installation

**11** Lubricate the cylinder bore and piston with plenty of clean engine oil.
**12** Install a new O-ring around the base of the cylinder **(see illustration 11.4)**. Place a new cylinder base gasket on the crankcase. Install a new O-ring on the large dowel pin, install it in its bore and make sure the two small dowel pins are in position.
**13** Attach a piston ring compressor to the piston and compress the piston rings. A large hose clamp can be used instead - just make sure it doesn't scratch the piston, and don't tighten it too much. **Note:** *If you're experienced and very careful, you can install the cylinder without using a ring compressor, but the compressor will make the job easier and reduce the chance of breaking a ring.*
**14** Install the cylinder block over the pistons and carefully lower it down until the piston crown fits into the cylinder liner **(see illustration 11.3)**. While doing this, pull the camshaft chain up, using a hooked tool or a piece of coat hanger if necessary. Also keep an eye on the cam chain guide to make sure it doesn't wedge against the cylinder. Push down on the cylinder, making sure the piston doesn't get cocked sideways, until the bottom of the cylinder liner slides down past the piston rings. A wood or plastic hammer handle can be used to gently tap the cylinder down, but don't use too much force or the piston will be damaged.
**15** Remove the ring compressor or hose clamp, being careful not to scratch the piston.

**16** Repeat the procedure to install the remaining cylinder.

**17** The remainder of installation is the reverse of removal.

## 12 Pistons - removal, inspection and installation

Removal, inspection and installation procedures for the pistons are the same as for XV535 models. Refer to Part A of this Chapter for procedures and this Chapter's Specifications.

## 13 Piston rings - installation

Piston ring installation procedures are the same as for XV535 models. Refer to Part A of this Chapter for procedures and to this Chapter's Specifications.

## 14 Cam chains and intermediate gears - removal, inspection and installation

### Removal

**1** Remove the engine (see Section 5).

**2** Remove the cylinder head(s) and cylinder(s) (see Sections 8 and 11).

**3** If you're working on the front cylinder, remove the retaining bolt and lift out the rear cam chain damper **(see illustration)**.

**4** Remove the bolt and stopper plate **(see illustration)**. Pull out the spindle, then remove the intermediate gear and timing chain **(see illustration)**. Label the parts (F for front cylinder or R for rear cylinder).

**5** If you're working on the rear cylinder, remove the retaining bolt and lift out the rear cam chain damper.

### Inspection

**6** Thoroughly clean all parts in solvent and blow them dry with compressed air.

**7** Check the cam chain(s) for obvious wear and damage and replace it if these conditions are found. Note how far the cam chain tensioner has extended; if it's near the end of its travel, the cam chain is stretched and should be replaced. **Note:** *If the chain is replaced, the intermediate gear and its drive gear on the crankshaft should also be replaced. Replacing only one of the components will cause rapid wear of the other two.*

**8** Check the intermediate gear(s) for worn or damaged teeth and replace them if these conditions are found. The two plates that make up the gear should move separately

**14.3 Remove the bolt and locknut and lift the cam chain damper out**

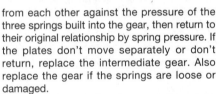

**14.4b ... then pull out the spindle and remove the intermediate gear**

from each other against the pressure of the three springs built into the gear, then return to their original relationship by spring pressure. If the plates don't move separately or don't return, replace the intermediate gear. Also replace the gear if the springs are loose or damaged.

**9** Check the chain dampers for deep grooves or separation from the steel backing and replace them if these conditions are found.

### Installation

**10** If the intermediate gears weren't marked for location during removal, identify the front and rear cylinder intermediate gears by the location of the spring stoppers **(see illustration)**.

**14.11 Tighten the chain guide bolt, then tighten the locknut to secure the bolt (front cylinder shown)**

**14.4a Remove the bolt and pull out the retaining plate ...**

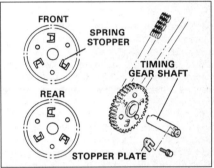

**14.10 The locations of the intermediate gears can be determined by looking at the spring stoppers**

### Rear cylinder

**11** Install the rear cam chain damper. Tighten its bolt to the torque listed in this Chapter's Specifications, then tighten the locknut against the crankcase to secure the bolt **(see illustration)**.

**12 Note:** *This procedure assumes the alternator rotor is installed on the engine. If it isn't, ignore the steps which don't apply.* Align the sighting hole in the alternator rotor with the centerlines of the crankshaft and the intermediate gear spindle hole **(see illustration)**.

**13** Place the cam chain on the sprocket teeth of the intermediate gear. Position the intermediate gear in light contact with its drive gear on the crankshaft **(see illustration)**.

**14.12 Align the rotor sighting hole with the centerlines of the crankshaft and gear spindle hole**

14.13 With the cam chain on the sprocket teeth of the gear, lower the gear into position

14.15a Pry the plates of the gear into alignment with a punch inserted through the alignment holes

14.15b The alignment mark on the gear must be aligned with the crankshaft keyway

14 There's an alignment hole in each of the plates that make up the intermediate gear. The holes are used to align the gear teeth on each plate with each other when the intermediate gear is installed. The holes are slightly offset from each other when the intermediate gear is not installed.

15 Insert a center punch through the offset holes in the two plates. Use a prying motion to align the holes (which will align the gear teeth on the two plates) (see illustration). Hold the plates in the aligned position and mesh the intermediate gear with the crankshaft drive gear so the timing marks on the gears are aligned (see illustration).

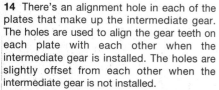

14.16 With the rotor installed, look through the hole (arrow) to be sure the alignment mark is correct

*Caution: If you're installing a new gear that came with an alignment pin installed in the holes, don't forget to remove the pin after installing the gear. The pin will fall out when the engine is run and may cause severe damage.*

16 Install the spindle in the intermediate gear and secure it with the stopper plate and bolt (see illustration). Look through the sighting hole in the alternator rotor to be sure the intermediate gear and timing gear holes are correctly aligned.

17 Make sure the cam chain is still engaged with the sprocket on the intermediate gear and support it so it won't fall off (tie it to part of the engine with wire).

### Front cylinder

18 Place the cam chain on the sprocket teeth of the intermediate gear. Position the intermediate gear in light contact with its drive gear on the crankshaft.

19 Align the teeth on the front cylinder's intermediate gear as described in Steps 13 and 14 above, then engage the gear with its drive pinion so the timing marks are aligned (see illustration).

20 Install the spindle and secure it with the retaining plate and bolt (see illustration).

21 Make sure the cam chain is still engaged with the sprocket on the intermediate gear, then install the front cylinder's rear cam chain

damper (see illustrations 14.3 and 14.11). Tighten the bolt and locknut to the torque listed in this Chapter's Specifications.

### All models

22 The remainder of installation is the reverse of the removal steps.

---

### 15 Oil pump and pick-up - removal, inspection and installation

### Removal

1 Remove the alternator rotor and starter clutch (see Chapter 8).

2 Unbolt the oil pump chain cover and take it off (see illustration).

3 Unbolt the oil pump driven sprocket and separate it from the pump (see illustration). Lift the chain off the crankshaft sprocket.

4 Unbolt the oil pump and pull it away from the engine, taking care not to damage the strainer screen on the pick-up (see illustrations). Remove the pump dowel and two O-rings.

### Disassembly, inspection and reassembly

5 Wash the oil pump in solvent, then dry it off.

14.19 The alignment mark on the front cylinder's gear must align with the mark on the drive gear

14.20 Install the stopper plate and tighten the bolt to the specified torque

15.2 Remove the oil pump chain cover

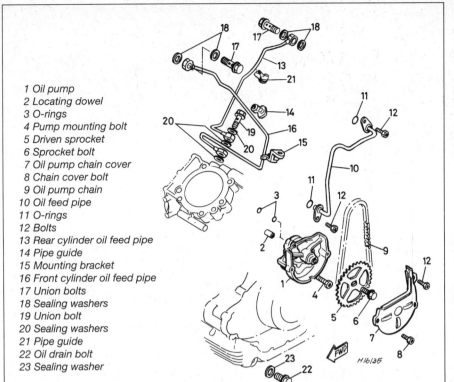

1 Oil pump
2 Locating dowel
3 O-rings
4 Pump mounting bolt
5 Driven sprocket
6 Sprocket bolt
7 Oil pump chain cover
8 Chain cover bolt
9 Oil pump chain
10 Oil feed pipe
11 O-rings
12 Bolts
13 Rear cylinder oil feed pipe
14 Pipe guide
15 Mounting bracket
16 Front cylinder oil feed pipe
17 Union bolts
18 Sealing washers
19 Union bolt
20 Sealing washers
21 Pipe guide
22 Oil drain bolt
23 Sealing washer

15.3 Oil pump and delivery pipes (XV700-1100 models) - exploded view

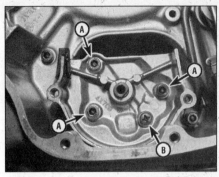

15.4a Remove the Allen bolts (A) to detach the pump; the screw (B) holds the pump together

15.4b Pull the pump out of the engine, taking care not to damage the strainer screen

6 Separate the strainer screen from the pickup (see illustration). Remove three screws and detach the pick-up from the pump (see illustration).
7 Remove the screw that holds the pump housings together. Lift off the housings and both sets of rotors (see illustrations).
8 Check the pump body and rotors for scoring and wear. If any damage or uneven or excessive wear is evident, replace the pump (individual parts aren't available). If you are rebuilding the engine, it's a good idea to install a new oil pump.
9 Measure the clearance between the inner and outer rotors and between the outer rotor

15.6a Separate the strainer screen from the pick-up

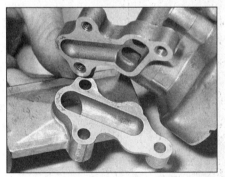

15.6b Remove three Phillips screws and detach the pick-up from the pump

15.7a Lift off the rotor housing . . .

15.7b . . . the outer rotor . . .

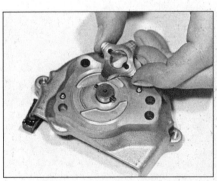

15.7c . . . and the inner rotor

**15.7d Lift off the remaining rotor housing and oil pump shaft . . .**

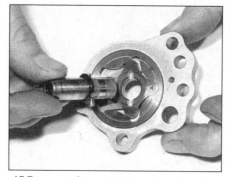

**15.7e . . . and separate the shaft from the rotors**

**15.7f Note the marks on the rotors; they must face in the same direction when the pump is assembled**

and housing **(see illustrations)**. Replace the pump if the clearance is excessive.

**10** Lay a straightedge across the pump body and measure the side clearance between the rotors and straightedge with a feeler gauge (see illustration 15.9b). Replace the pump if the clearance is excessive.

**11** If the pump is good, reverse the disassembly steps to reassemble it. Make sure the pins are centered in the rotor shaft so they will align with the slots in the inner rotors.

**12** Inspect the oil pump drive chain and sprockets. Replace all three components as a set if any one of them is worn or damaged.

**13** To replace the oil pump drive sprocket, remove it from the crankshaft with a puller

**15.9a Measure oil pump clearances with a feeler gauge**

**(see illustration). Note:** *Removal will damage the sprocket. It must be replaced with a new one if it's removed from the crankshaft.* Position the new sprocket on the crankshaft

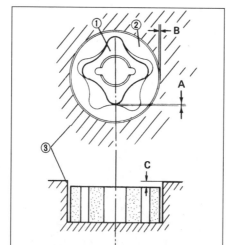

**15.9b Oil pump measurement points**

1  Inner rotor
2  Outer rotor
3  Pump housing
A  Inner to outer rotor clearance
B  Outer rotor to housing clearance
C  Side clearance

with the teeth toward the crankcase **(see illustration)**, then drive it all the way on with a hammer and a piece of pipe **(see illustration)**.

### Installation

**14** Before installing the pump, prime it by pouring oil into it while turning the shaft by hand - this will ensure that it begins to pump oil quickly.

*Caution: Also pour oil into the crankcase oil passages to prevent engine damage on start-up.*

**15** Be sure the oil feed pipe, dowel and O-rings are in position **(see illustration)**.

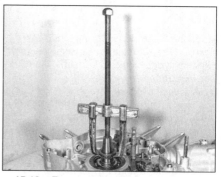

**15.13a Remove the oil pump sprocket from the crankshaft with a puller**

*The sprocket must be replaced with a new one whenever it's removed*

**15.13b Place the new sprocket on the crankshaft with its teeth toward the crankcase . . .**

**15.13c . . . and drive the sprocket all the way on with a hammer and piece of pipe**

**15.15 Make sure the dowel and both O-rings are in position**

**15.17 Install the chain on the drive sprocket, engage the driven sprocket and bolt it to the oil pump**

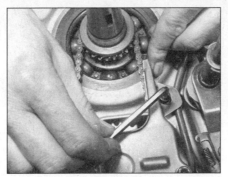

**15.18 Push the arm of the chain cover against the chain to tension it and tighten the cover bolts**

**16.1 Remove the Allen bolts (arrows) and take the cover off the release mechanism**

**16** Position the pump on the engine and tighten its mounting bolts to the torque listed in this Chapter's Specifications.

**17** Slip the chain over the crankshaft sprocket. Engage the chain with the oil pump driven sprocket, then install the sprocket on the pump **(see illustration)**. Install the sprocket bolt and tighten it to the torque listed in this Chapter's Specifications.

**18** Install the chain cover loosely. Push it against the chain to tension it, then tighten the cover bolts to the torque listed in this Chapter's Specifications **(see illustration)**.

**19** The remainder of installation is the reverse of the removal steps.

---

**16 Clutch cable replacement and release mechanism - removal and installation**

### Clutch cable replacement

**1** Remove the cover from the release mechanism on the left side of the engine **(see illustration)**.

**2** Loosen the cable locknut and adjuster at the handlebar **(see illustration)**. Disconnect the cable from the clutch lever.

**3** Bend back the metal tang and disconnect the lower end of the clutch cable from the release lever **(see illustration)**.

**4** Attach a piece of string (somewhat longer

than the clutch cable) to one end of the cable. Free the cable from any retainers and remove it from the motorcycle, pulling the string with it. The string will remain in position and act as a guide to route the cable correctly during installation.

**5** Installation is the reverse of the removal steps. If you're installing a new cable, attach the string to it and pull the cable into position with the string so it's routed correctly.

**6** Adjust the clutch free-play (see *'Daily (pre-ride) checks'* at the beginning of this Manual).

### Release mechanism removal and installation

**7** Disconnect the clutch cable at the engine (see above).

**16.2 Loosen the cable adjuster, then slide the cable out of the slot and free it from the lever**

**8** Remove the alternator cover (see Chapter 8).

**9** Remove the nut and detach the clutch operating lever from the push screw **(see illustration)**.

**10** Remove the push screw, ball retainer and thrust housing from the alternator cover **(see illustrations)**.

**11** Pry the release mechanism oil seal out of the alternator cover **(see illustration)**. Install a new one. It should go in with thumb pressure, but if necessary, tap it in with a hammer and a socket the same diameter as the seal.

**12** Installation is the reverse of the removal steps.

**13** Adjust clutch free-play (see *'Daily (pre-ride) checks'* at the beginning of this Manual).

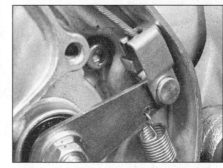

**16.3 Bend back the metal tang on the lever bracket and slip the end of the cable out of the bracket**

**16.9 Unhook the spring and remove the nut from the operating lever**

**16.10a Lift out the push screw . . .**

**16.10b . . . and the thrust housing; the locating pin on the thrust housing fits into a hole in the cover**

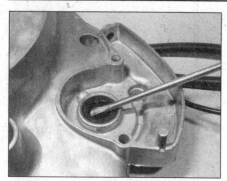

16.11 Pry out the old oil seal and install a new one

17.3 Remove the clutch cover; note the locations of the dowels

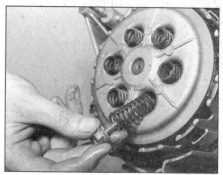

17.4a Remove the pressure plate screws, washers and springs . . .

17.4b . . . then take off the pressure plate

## 17 Clutch and primary gears -
removal, inspection and installation

### Removal

1 Drain the engine oil and remove the oil filter (see Chapter 1).

2 Remove the footpeg and brake pedal, then loosen the right-hand crankcase cover bolts in a criss-cross pattern, 1/4 turn at a time.

3 Once the bolts are all loose, remove the bolts and take the cover off (see illustration). If it's struck, pry gently at the pry points around the cover. Don't pry anywhere else or the gasket surface may be damaged.

4 If you're working on a coil spring clutch, loosen the pressure plate screws evenly in a criss-cross pattern, then remove the screws and springs and take off the pressure plate (see illustrations).

5 If you're working on a diaphragm spring clutch, remove the bolts, plate washer, clutch spring, spring seat and pressure plate (see illustration 17.4c).

6 Remove the thrust washer and thrust bearing (see illustration).

7 Remove the push piece and pushrod (see illustrations).

17.6 Remove the thrust washer and thrust bearing

17.7a Remove the push piece . . .

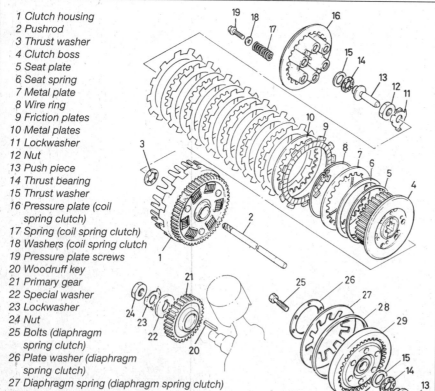

1 Clutch housing
2 Pushrod
3 Thrust washer
4 Clutch boss
5 Seat plate
6 Seat spring
7 Metal plate
8 Wire ring
9 Friction plates
10 Metal plates
11 Lockwasher
12 Nut
13 Push piece
14 Thrust bearing
15 Thrust washer
16 Pressure plate (coil spring clutch)
17 Spring (coil spring clutch)
18 Washers (coil spring clutch)
19 Pressure plate screws
20 Woodruff key
21 Primary gear
22 Special washer
23 Lockwasher
24 Nut
25 Bolts (diaphragm spring clutch)
26 Plate washer (diaphragm spring clutch)
27 Diaphragm spring (diaphragm spring clutch)
28 Spring seat (diaphragm spring clutch)
29 Pressure plate (diaphragm spring clutch)

17.4c Clutch (XV700-1100 models) - exploded view

17.7b . . . and the pushrod

17.8  Remove the clutch plates

17.9a  Bend the lockwasher tab away from the nut

**8** Remove the clutch plates (a friction plate comes off first, followed by a steel plate, then alternating friction and steel plates) **(see illustration)**.
**9** Bend back the lockwasher on the clutch boss nut **(see illustration)**. Loosen the nut, using a special holding tool (Yamaha tool no. YM-91402, part no. 90890-04086 or equivalent) to prevent the clutch housing from turning **(see illustrations)**. An alternative to these tool can be fabricated from some steel strap, bent at the ends and bolted together in the middle (see Part A of this Chapter). You can also make a holding tool by drilling through a steel plate and friction plate and bolting them together (see Part A of this Chapter). Slip the bolted plates into their normal installed position

to lock the clutch housing and clutch boss together. To keep the engine from turning, wedge a rag between the teeth of the primary drive gear and the driven gear on the clutch housing. Once the nut is loose, remove it.
**10** Remove the lockwasher and discard it. Use a new one during installation.
**11** Remove the clutch boss and thrust washer **(see illustrations)**.
**12** Bend back the lockwasher from the nut that secures the primary drive gear. Wedge a rag between the driven gear and drive gear teeth to keep the gears from turning, then loosen the nut. Once the nut is loose, slide the clutch housing/driven gear off and remove the nut, lockwasher and special washer **(see illustrations)**.

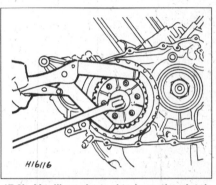

17.9b  You'll need a tool to keep the clutch from turning; this is one type of Yamaha special tool . . .

17.9c . . . this is another type

17.9d  Hold the clutch housing so it won't turn and loosen the nut

17.11a  Remove the clutch boss . . .

17.11b . . . and the thrust washer

17.12a  With the primary gear nut loose, slide off the clutch boss, then remove the primary gear nut . . .

17.12b . . . the lockwasher and the special washer

**17.13 Take the primary drive gear and Woodruff key off the crankshaft**

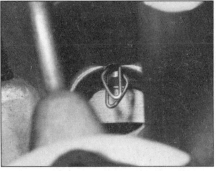

**17.14 Push the ends of the wire ring through the hole in the clutch boss**

**17.15 Inspect the clutch boss splines**

**13** Remove the primary drive gear and Woodruff key **(see illustration)**.

### Inspection

**14** If the clutch has been chattering (juddering), remove the wire ring **(see illustration)**. Remove the steel plate, seat spring and seat plate that make up the clutch damper **(see illustration 17.4c)**. These parts need not be removed if the clutch hasn't been chattering.

**15** Examine the splines on both the inside and the outside of the clutch boss **(see illustration)**. If any wear is evident, replace the clutch boss with a new one.

**16** If you're working on a coil spring clutch, measure the free length of the clutch springs **(see illustration)**. Replace the springs as a

set if any one of them is not within the values listed in this Chapter's Specifications.

**17** If you're working on a diaphragm spring clutch, measure the free height and warpage of the diaphragm spring **(see illustrations)**. Replace the spring if it's sagged or warped.

**18** If the lining material of the friction plates smells burnt or if it's glazed, new parts are required. If the metal clutch plates are scored or discolored, they must be replaced with new ones. Measure the thickness of each friction plate **(see illustration)** and compare the results to this Chapter's Specifications. Replace the friction plates as a set if any are near the wear limit.

**19** Lay the metal plates, one at a time, on a perfectly flat surface (such as a piece of plate glass) and check for warpage by trying to slip

a gauge between the flat surface and the plate **(see illustration)**. The feeler gauge should be the same thickness as the warpage limit listed in this Chapter's Specifications. Do this at several places around the plate's circumference. If the feeler gauge can be slipped under the plate, it is warped and should be replaced with a new one.

**20** Check the tabs on the friction plates for excessive wear and mushroomed edges. They can be cleaned up with a file if the deformation is not severe.

**21** Check the edges of the slots in the clutch housing for indentations made by the friction plate tabs **(see illustration)**. If the indentations are deep they can prevent clutch release, so the housing should be replaced with a new one. If the indentations can be

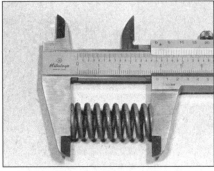

**17.16 Measure the free length of the clutch springs (coil spring models)**

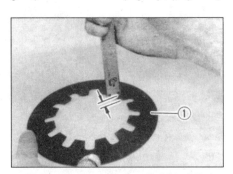

**17.17a Measure the free height of the diaphragm spring with a vernier caliper . . .**
*1 Diaphragm spring*

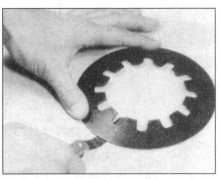

**17.17b . . . and check it for warpage with a feeler gauge**

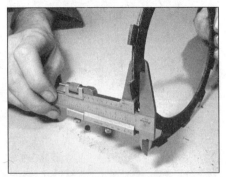

**17.18 Check the amount of wear on each clutch friction plate**

**17.19 Check the metal plates for warpage with a feeler gauge**

**17.21 Check the slots in the clutch housing for uneven wear**

**17.22 Check the driven gear teeth for wear or damage**

**17.23 Check the pressure plate for wear and damage (coil spring pressure plate shown)**

**17.24 Check the push piece, thrust bearing and washer for wear and damage**

removed easily with a file, the life of the housing can be prolonged to an extent.

22 Check the teeth on the primary drive gear and driven gear for wear or damage and replace them if defects are found. The driven gear is replaced together with the clutch housing **(see illustration)**. Check the bearing surface in the center of the clutch housing and replace the clutch housing if it's worn or damaged.

23 Check the pressure plate for wear and damage **(see illustration)**. Replace any worn or damaged parts.

24 Check the push piece, thrust bearing and washer for wear or damage **(see illustration)**. Check the pushrod, especially at the ends. Replace any parts that show wear or damage.

25 Clean all traces of old gasket material from the clutch cover and its mating surface on the crankcase.

## Installation

26 Install the primary drive gear Woodruff key, then install the primary drive gear **(see illustration 17.13)**.

27 Install the special washer and a new lockwasher on the primary drive gear. Make sure the lockwasher tabs fit into the notches in the special washer **(see illustration 17.12b)**, then install the nut.

28 Coat the clutch housing bearing surface with clean engine oil, then slip the clutch housing onto the crankshaft **(see illustration 17.12a)**.

29 Wedge a rag between the primary drive gear and the driven gear on the clutch housing so they can't turn, then tighten the primary drive gear nut to the torque listed in this Chapter's Specifications. Bend the lockwasher against the nut.

30 Install the thrust washer, then the clutch boss **(see illustrations 17.11b and 17.11a)**. Install a new lockwasher. Install the nut with its recessed side toward the clutch boss and tighten it slightly **(see illustration 17.9a)**.

31 Hold the clutch boss and housing from turning with one of the methods described in Step 9. Tighten the clutch boss nut to the torque listed in this Chapter's Specifications, then bend the lockwasher against the nut to secure it.

32 If you removed the clutch damper, reverse Step 14 to install it. If there's an OUTSIDE mark on the seat spring, face it out (away from the engine). Make sure the wire ring is securely seated in its groove in the clutch boss.

33 Coat one of the friction plates with engine oil and install it in the clutch housing. Engage the tabs on the friction plate with the slots in the clutch housing.

34 Coat a metal plate with engine oil and install it on top of the friction plate with its rounded side in. Continue to install alternate friction and metal plates, coated with engine oil (a friction plate is the last one installed).

35 Coat the pushrod with multi-purpose grease and install it in the engine **(see illustration 17.7b)**.

36 If you're working on a coil spring clutch, install the pressure plate, springs and screws. Tighten the screws evenly in a criss-cross pattern to the torque listed in this Chapter's Specifications.

37 If you're working on a diaphragm spring clutch, install the pressure plate, spring seat, spring and plate washer **(see illustration 17.4c)**. Install the plate washer bolts and tighten them evenly, in a criss-cross pattern, to the torque listed in this Chapter's Specifications.

38 Install the clutch cover over the dowels and a new gasket, then install and finger-tighten the bolts. Some of the bolts along the bottom retain wiring harness clamps **(see illustration)**.

39 Tighten the bolts in stages, using a criss-cross pattern, to the torque listed in this Chapter's Specifications.

40 Install a new oil filter and fill the crankcase with the recommended type and amount of engine oil (see Chapter 1).

41 The remainder of installation is the reverse of the removal steps.

## 18 External shift mechanism - removal, inspection and installation

### Shift lever and pedal

1 Support the bike securely so it can't be knocked over during this procedure.

2 Look for a punch mark on the end of the lever shaft. This should align with the groove in the lever or pedal. If you can't find it, make your own punch mark so the lever or pedal can be realigned correctly during installation.

3 Remove the lever or pedal pinch bolt **(see illustration)**. Pull the lever or pedal off the shaft, together with the linkage rod.

4 Installation is the reverse of removal. Adjust the linkage (if equipped) as needed with the nuts on the linkage shaft (see Chapter 1).

### Shift mechanism removal

5 Disconnect the shift lever from the shaft (Steps 1 through 3).

6 Remove the alternator cover (see Chapter 8).

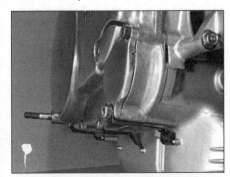

**17.38 Several of the bottom clutch cover bolts secure wiring harness clips**

**18.3 Loosen the pinch bolt and detach the shift lever from the shift shaft (rearset shift linkage shown)**

**18.7a Pull the lever in the direction shown (arrow) until it clears the shift cam, then slide out the shift mechanism**

**18.7b Remove the C-clip at each end of the shaft and slide the parts off for inspection**

7 Pull the lever on the shift mechanism away from the shift cam, then slide the shift mechanism out of the crankcase (see illustrations).

## Shift mechanism inspection

8 Inspect the shift shaft guide bar in the crankcase. If it's worn or damaged, replace it. If it's loose, bend back its lockwasher, unscrew it, reinstall it with a new lockwasher and tighten it securely. Bend the new lockwasher against the nut to secure it.
9 Remove the C-clips from each end of the shift shaft, then separate the components from the shaft (see illustration).
10 Check the shift shaft for bends and damage to the splines. If the shaft is bent, you can attempt to straighten it, but if the splines are

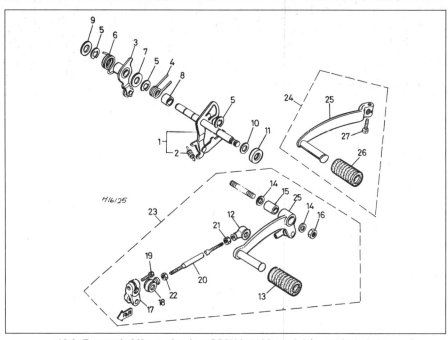

**18.9 External shift mechanism (XV700-1100 models) - exploded view**

1 Shift arm and shaft
2 Return spring
3 Stopper lever
4 Shaft return spring
5 C-clip
6 Stopper lever spring
7 Washer
8 Bushing (if equipped)
9 Washer
10 Washer
11 Oil seal
12 Rear boot
13 Pedal pad
14 Thrust washer
15 Bushing
16 Nut
17 Linkage end piece
18 Front boot
19 Pinch bolt
20 Linkage rod
21 Rear adjusting nut
22 Front adjusting nut
23 Shift pedal and linkage - rearset type
24 Shift pedal - direct type
25 Shift pedal
26 Pedal pad
27 Pinch bolt

damaged it will have to be replaced. Inspect the pawls and springs on the shift shaft and replace the shaft if they're worn or damaged.
11 Check the condition of the stopper lever and spring (see illustration). Replace the stopper lever if it's worn where it contacts the shift cam. Replace the spring if it's distorted.
12 Inspect the pins on the end of the shift cam. If they're worn or damaged, you'll have to disassemble the crankcase to replace them.
13 Pry the shift pedal oil seal out of the alternator cover (see illustration). Install a new seal so its open side will face into the

engine when the cover is installed. You should be able to push the new seal in with thumbs, but if it won't go, tap it in with a hammer and a socket the same diameter as the seal.
14 Reassemble the shift mechanism components on the shaft.

## Installation

15 Be sure the washers are on the shift shaft, then install the shift shaft in the crankcase. Engage the stopper lever with the shift cam and position the torsion spring against its post (see illustration).

**18.11 Check the stopper arm roller and spring for wear and damage**

**18.13 Pry the oil seal out of the cover and tap a new one in**

**18.15 The legs of the shaft return spring should be on either side of the shift shaft guide bar**

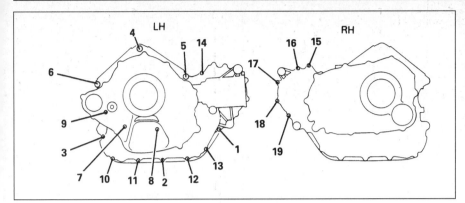

20.8 Crankcase bolt TIGHTENING sequence

20.9 With all fasteners removed, lift the right crankcase half off the left crankcase half

**16** The remainder of installation is the reverse of the removal steps.
**17** Adjust the shift pedal position (see Chapter 1).
**18** Check the engine oil level and add some, if necessary (see Chapter 1).

## 19 Middle gears and shafts (shaft drive models)

The middle driveshaft and middle driven shaft on these models are mounted in the left crankcase casting. Access to the shafts is gained by splitting the crankcase. Removal of the shafts for inspection is a complicated procedure which requires a number of special tools. For this reason, removal and disassembly of the shafts should be done by a Yamaha dealer or other qualified repair shop.

You can probably save considerable money on labor charges by removing the engine and doing most of the engine disassembly yourself. However, be sure to check with the shop first to find out how much disassembly to do. Some shops may not be willing to work on a partially disassembled engine.

## 20 Crankcase - disassembly and reassembly

**1** To examine and repair or replace the crankshaft, middle drive and driven shafts, connecting rods, bearings, or transmission components, the crankcase must be split into two parts.

### Disassembly

**2** Remove the cylinder heads, cylinders, pistons and cam chains (see Sections 8, 11, 12 and 14).
**3** Remove the alternator, starter motor and starter drive (see Chapter 8).
**4** Remove the oil level switch and neutral switch (see Chapter 8).
**5** Remove the oil pump and oil feed line (see Section 15).
**6** Remove the clutch and primary gear (see Section 17).
**7** Remove the external shift linkage (see Section 18).
**8** Remove the crankcase bolts in the reverse of the tightening sequence (start with the highest-numbered bolt and work to the lowest) (see illustration).
**9** Carefully lift the right crankcase half away

from the left crankcase half (see illustration). As you lift, pry gently and evenly at the pry points around the crankcase seam. Tap alternately on the transmission shafts. If the halves won't separate easily, make sure all fasteners have been removed. Don't pry against the crankcase mating surfaces or they'll leak.
**10** Look for the O-rings and dowels (see illustrations). If they're not in one of the crankcase halves, locate them.
**11** Refer to Sections 21 through 25 for information on the internal components of the crankcase.

### Reassembly

**12** Make sure the crankshaft and transmission shafts are correctly positioned in the left crankcase half (see Sections 23 and 26). Make sure the shift cam is correctly aligned with the neutral switch (see Section 26).
**13** Remove all traces of sealant from the crankcase mating surfaces. Be careful not to let any fall into the case as this is done. Check to make sure the dowels are in place in the right crankcase half (see illustration 20.10c and 20.10d). Also make sure the orange and black O-rings are in place in their grooves (see illustrations 20.10a and 20.10b).
**14** Pour some engine oil over the

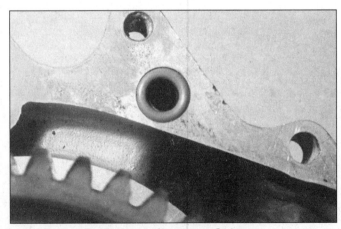

20.10a Locate the orange O-ring . . .

20.10b . . . and the black O-ring

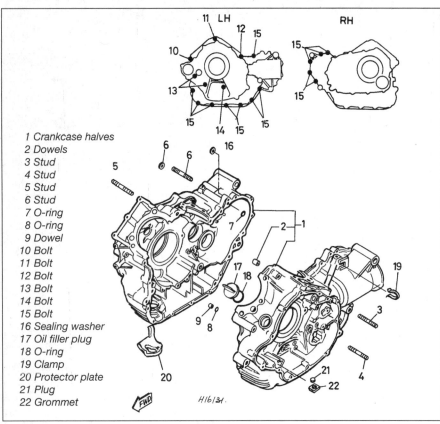

1 Crankcase halves
2 Dowels
3 Stud
4 Stud
5 Stud
6 Stud
7 O-ring
8 O-ring
9 Dowel
10 Bolt
11 Bolt
12 Bolt
13 Bolt
14 Bolt
15 Bolt
16 Sealing washer
17 Oil filler plug
18 O-ring
19 Clamp
20 Protector plate
21 Plug
22 Grommet

**20.10c Crankcase halves - shaft drive models**

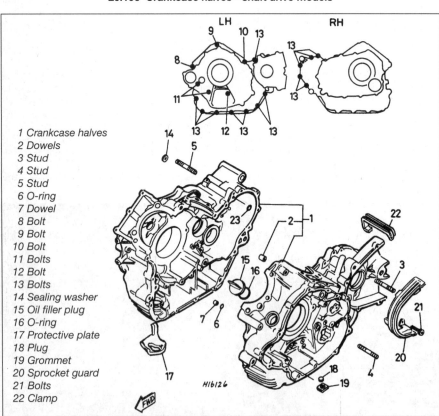

1 Crankcase halves
2 Dowels
3 Stud
4 Stud
5 Stud
6 O-ring
7 Dowel
8 Bolt
9 Bolt
10 Bolt
11 Bolts
12 Bolt
13 Bolts
14 Sealing washer
15 Oil filler plug
16 O-ring
17 Protective plate
18 Plug
19 Grommet
20 Sprocket guard
21 Bolts
22 Clamp

**20.10d Crankcase halves - chain drive models**

transmission gears, the crankshaft main bearings and the shift cam. Also pour oil into the exposed internal oil passages. Don't get any oil on the crankcase mating surfaces.

15 Apply a thin, even bead of Yamaha Bond or Quick Gasket sealant (part no. ACC-11001-05-01) or equivalent to the crankcase mating surfaces.

*Caution: Don't apply an excessive amount of sealant.*

16 Carefully assemble the crankcase halves over the dowels.

*Caution: The crankcase halves should fit together completely without being forced. If they're slightly apart, DO NOT force them together by tightening the crankcase bolts.*

17 Install the crankcase bolts in their holes **(see illustration 20.8).**

18 Tighten the bolts in numerical order, starting with the lowest-numbered bolt and working to the highest. Tighten all bolts to the torque listed in this Chapter's Specifications. **Note:** *There are different torque settings for the 10mm bolts and the 6mm bolts.*

19 Turn the mainshaft and the transmission driveshaft to make sure they turn freely. Also make sure the crankshaft turns freely. Rotate the shift cam by hand to make sure the transmission shifts into the different gear positions.

20 The remainder of assembly is the reverse of disassembly.

21 Be sure to refill the engine oil (see Chapter 1).

## 21 Crankcase components - inspection and servicing

1 After the crankcases have been separated and the crankshaft, shift cam and forks and transmission components removed, the crankcases should be cleaned thoroughly with new solvent and dried with compressed air.

2 Remove any oil passage plugs that haven't already been removed. All oil passages should be blown out with compressed air.

3 All traces of old gasket sealant should be removed from the mating surfaces. Minor damage to the surfaces can be cleaned up with a fine sharpening stone or grindstone. *Caution: Be very careful not to nick or gouge the crankcase mating surfaces or leaks will result. Check both crankcase halves very carefully for cracks and other damage. If any damage is found that can't be repaired, replace the crankcase halves as a set.*

4 Spin the bearings in the crankcase halves **(see illustration)** with fingers and check for looseness, roughness or excessive noise. Replace the bearings if these conditions are found. Remove the bearings with fingers, or if necessary, with a slide hammer **(see illustrations).**

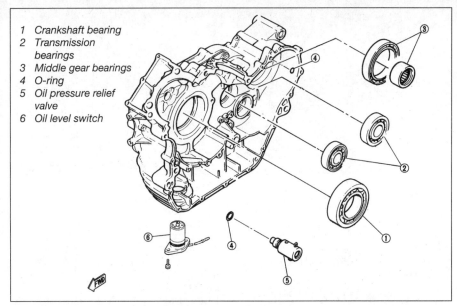

1  Crankshaft bearing
2  Transmission bearings
3  Middle gear bearings
4  O-ring
5  Oil pressure relief valve
6  Oil level switch

21.4a  Right crankcase half components

21.4b  Use a slide hammer to remove the bearings if they don't lift out easily . . .

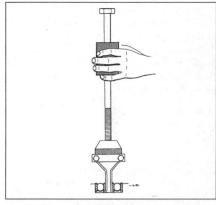

21.4c  . . . the slide hammer's puller attachment fits behind the bearing like this

**5** Remove the oil seal from behind the transmission mainshaft bearing in the left side of the crankcase (see illustration). Make sure the oil passages behind the seal is clear and the bearing bore is clean (see illustration), then tap in a new oil seal.
**6** Set the new bearings in their bores, then tap them into position with a bearing driver or a socket that bears against the bearing outer race (see illustrations). Note: Special equipment is required for access to the middle gear bearings.

**22 Oil pressure relief valve -** removal, inspection and installation

**1** Disassemble the crankcase (see Section 20).
**2** Work the oil pressure relief valve out of the crankcase (it's held in by an O-ring) (see illustration 21.4a).

**3** Push the plunger into the relief valve and check for free movement (see illustration). If the valve sticks, perform Steps 4 and 5 to disassemble and inspect it.
**4** Straighten the cotter pin and pull it out (see illustration). Remove the spring retainer, spring and plunger.

21.5a  Pry the oil seal out of the bearing bore . . .

21.5b  . . . make sure the oil passage is clear and tap in a new seal

21.6a  Push the bearing straight into its housing . . .

21.6b  . . . then drive it all the way in with a bearing driver or socket that bears against the outer race

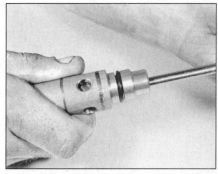

22.3  Push in on the relief valve plunger to make sure it moves freely

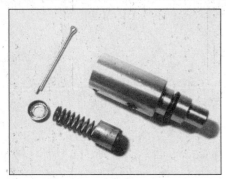

**22.4 Check the relief valve parts for wear or damage**

**22.6 Coat the new O-ring with engine oil and work the relief valve back into its bore**

**23.3a Use a puller like this one to push the crankshaft out of the bearing**

5 Check all parts for wear and damage. Clean the parts thoroughly, reassemble the valve and recheck its movement. If the valve still sticks, replace it.
*Caution: If you reuse the relief valve, install a new cotter pin before installing the relief valve in the engine.*
6 Install a new O-ring on the valve **(see illustration)**. Coat the O-ring with engine oil and work the valve back into its bore in the crankcase.

## 23 Crankshaft and main bearings - removal, inspection and installation

**Note:** *The crankshaft is a tight interference fit in its ball bearing in the left crankcase half. Special tools are required for removal and installation. Substitutes for the Yamaha factory tools are described and illustrated in this Section, but even these may be difficult to*

obtain. *If you don't have the proper tools or substitutes, don't try to drive the crankshaft out or back in. Take the left crankcase half to a Yamaha dealer or other qualified shop for crankshaft removal and installation.*

### Crankshaft removal

1 Separate the crankcase halves (see Section 20).
2 Remove the oil pump drive sprocket from the crankshaft (see Section 15).
3 Attach a puller to the crankshaft and push it out of the main bearing **(see illustrations)**.
*Caution: Support the crankshaft as it's removed so it doesn't fall.*

### Inspection

4 If you haven't already done so, mark and remove the connecting rods from the crankshaft (see Section 25).
5 Clean the crankshaft with solvent, using a rifle-cleaning brush to scrub out the oil passages. Make sure the oil passage plugs

are tight **(see illustration)**. Check the crankshaft for cracks and other damage. It should be magnafluxed to reveal hidden cracks - a dealer service department or motorcycle machine shop will handle the procedure.
6 If available, blow the crank dry with compressed air. Check the main and connecting rod journals for uneven wear, scoring and pits. Rub a copper coin across the journal several times - if a journal picks up copper from the coin, it's too rough. Replace the crankshaft.
7 Set the crankshaft on V-blocks and check the runout with a dial indicator touching the alternator and primary drive gear mounting surfaces **(see illustration)**. Compare your findings with this Chapter's Specifications. If

**23.5 Make sure the oil passage plugs are tight**

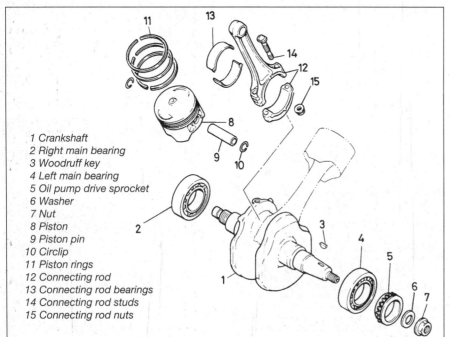

1 Crankshaft
2 Right main bearing
3 Woodruff key
4 Left main bearing
5 Oil pump drive sprocket
6 Washer
7 Nut
8 Piston
9 Piston pin
10 Circlip
11 Piston rings
12 Connecting rod
13 Connecting rod bearings
14 Connecting rod studs
15 Connecting rod nuts

**23.3b Crankshaft details**

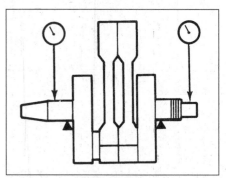

**23.7 Check crankshaft runout with a pair of dial indicators**

the runout exceeds the limit, replace the crankshaft.

### Main bearing inspection and replacement

**8** The crankshaft rides in ball bearings which are pressed into steel sleeves in the aluminum case halves **(see illustration)**.
**9** Spin the bearings with fingers and check for looseness, roughness or excessive noise. If the condition of the bearings is doubtful or definitely bad, have them pressed out and new ones pressed in by a Yamaha dealer or other qualified repair shop.

### Installation

**10** Install the connecting rods on the crankshaft at this point if they were removed (see Section 25).
**11** To pull the crankshaft into the ball bearing in the left crankcase half, you'll need a puller that can be attached to the threaded end of the crankshaft with a sleeve nut. This can be fabricated **(see illustration)**, but the puller must apply force to the inner race of the ball bearing. A puller that's braced against the outer race of the ball bearing will transfer the installation force to the balls and retainers, damaging the bearing. The same thing will happen if the crankshaft is driven into the bearing with a hammer.
**12** Carefully lower the crankshaft into the bearing until it stops **(see illustration)**. Make sure the crankshaft isn't cocked sideways in the bearing.
**13** Thread a sleeve nut onto the end of the crankshaft **(see illustration)**. Install a thick-walled metal tube over the end of the crankshaft to act as a spacer. The tube must be large enough to fit over the crankshaft, but small enough that it rests on the inner race of the ball bearing.
**14** Attach a puller to the sleeve nut with its plate resting on the metal tube **(see illustration)**.
**15** Tighten the puller bolt to pull the crankshaft into its bearing.
**16** Remove the puller and align the connecting rods with the cylinders.
**17** Assemble the case halves (see Sec-

**23.8 The crankshaft bearings are mounted in steel sleeves**

tion 20) and check to make sure the crankshaft and the transmission shafts turn freely.

## 24 Connecting rod bearings - general note

**1** Even though connecting rod bearings are generally replaced with new ones during the engine overhaul, the old bearings should be retained for close examination as they may reveal valuable information about the condition of the engine.
**2** Bearing failure occurs mainly because of lack of lubrication, the presence of dirt or other foreign particles, overloading the engine and/or corrosion. Regardless of the cause of bearing failure, it must be corrected before the engine is reassembled to prevent it from happening again.
**3** When examining the bearings, remove the rod bearings from the connecting rods and caps and lay them out on a clean surface in the same general position as their location on the crankshaft journals. This will enable you to match any noted bearing problems with the corresponding side of the crankshaft journal.
**4** Dirt and other foreign particles get into the engine in a variety of ways. It may be left in the engine during assembly or it may pass through filters or breathers. It may get into the

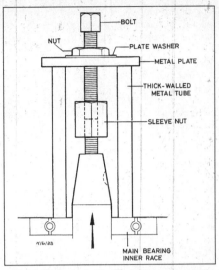

**23.11 Set up a puller like this one to pull the crankshaft into the left main bearing**

oil and from there into the bearings. Metal chips from machining operations and normal engine wear are often present. Abrasives are sometimes left in engine components after reconditioning operations such as cylinder honing, especially when parts are not thoroughly cleaned using the proper cleaning methods. Whatever the source, these foreign objects often end up imbedded in the soft bearing material and are easily recognized. Large particles will not imbed in the bearing and will score or gouge the bearing and journal. The best prevention for this cause of bearing failure is to clean all parts thoroughly and keep everything spotlessly clean during engine reassembly. Frequent and regular oil and filter changes are also recommended.
**5** Lack of lubrication or lubrication breakdown has a number of interrelated causes. Excessive heat (which thins the oil), overloading (which squeezes the oil from the bearing face) and oil leakage or throw off (from excessive bearing clearances, worn oil pump or high engine speeds) all contribute to lubrication breakdown. Blocked oil passages will also starve a bearing and destroy it. When

**23.12 Push the crankshaft into the bearing as far as it will go (don't let it tilt sideways and jam)**

**23.13 Thread a sleeve nut onto the end of the crankshaft**

**23.14 Place a tube over the crankshaft, position the plate on top, and thread the puller bolt into the sleeve nut**

lack of lubrication is the cause of bearing failure, the bearing material is wiped or extruded from the steel backing of the bearing. Temperatures may increase to the point where the steel backing and the journal turn blue from overheating.

**6** Riding habits can have a definite effect on bearing life. Full throttle low speed operation, or lugging (laboring) the engine, puts very high loads on bearings, which tend to squeeze out the oil film. These loads cause the bearings to flex, which produces fine cracks in the bearing face (fatigue failure). Eventually the bearing material will loosen in pieces and tear away from the steel backing. Short trip driving leads to corrosion of bearings, as insufficient engine heat is produced to drive off the condensed water and corrosive gases produced. These products collect in the engine oil, forming acid and sludge. As the oil is carried to the engine bearings, the acid attacks and corrodes the bearing material.

**7** Incorrect bearing installation during engine assembly will lead to bearing failure as well. Tight fitting bearings which leave insufficient bearing oil clearances result in oil starvation. Dirt or foreign particles trapped behind a bearing insert result in high spots on the bearing which lead to failure.

**8** To avoid bearing problems, clean all parts thoroughly before reassembly, double check

**25.3 Remove the nuts and separate the cap from the connecting rod**

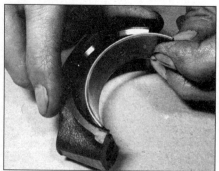

**25.10 Make sure the tab aligns with the notch**

*When installing the bearing upper half, make sure the oil holes in the bearing and connecting rod are aligned*

all bearing clearance measurements and lubricate the new bearings with engine assembly lube or moly-based grease during installation.

## 25 Connecting rods and bearings - removal, inspection, bearing selection and installation

### Removal

**1** Before removing the connecting rods from the crankshaft, insert a feeler gauge between the crankshaft and the big end of each connecting rod and between the two connecting rods and measure the side clearance **(see illustration 26.1 in Part A of this Chapter)**. If the clearance on any rod is greater than that listed in this Chapter's Specifications, that rod will have to be replaced with a new one.

**2** Using a center punch or felt pen, mark the position of each rod and cap, relative to its position on the crankshaft (left or right) **(see illustration 26.2 in Part A of this Chapter)**. **Note:** *The rear cylinder connecting rod may have one or two oil holes in the upper side of the big end (the front cylinder connecting rod on all models has one oil hole). Look at the rear cylinder connecting rod before removing the rods and determine whether it has one or two oil holes.*

**3** Unscrew the bearing cap nuts, separate the cap from the rod, then detach the rod from the crankshaft **(see illustration 23.3b and the accompanying illustration)**. If the cap is stuck, tap on the ends of the rod bolts with a soft-faced hammer to free them.

**4** Roll the bearing inserts sideways to separate them from the rods and caps. Keep them in order so they can be reinstalled in their original locations. Wash the parts in solvent and dry them with compressed air, if available.

### Inspection

**5** Check the connecting rods for cracks and other obvious damage. Lubricate the piston pin for each rod, install it in the proper rod and

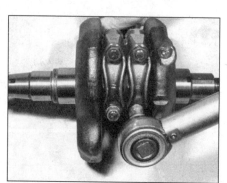

**25.12 Tighten the cap nuts to the specified torque in one continuous motion**

check for play **(see illustration 26.5 in Part A of this Chapter)**. If it wobbles, replace the connecting rod and/or the pin.

**6** Examine the connecting rod bearing inserts. If they are scored, badly scuffed or appear to have been seized, new bearings must be installed. Always replace the bearings in the connecting rods as a set. If they are badly damaged, check the corresponding crankshaft journal. Evidence of extreme heat, such as discoloration, indicates that lubrication failure has occurred. Be sure to thoroughly check the oil pump and pressure relief valves as well as all oil holes and passages before reassembling the engine.

**7** Have the rods checked for twist and bending at a dealer service department or other motorcycle repair shop.

### Connecting rod bearing selection

**8** If the bearings and journals appear to be in good condition, check the oil clearances as follows:

**9** Start with the rod for one cylinder. Wipe the bearing inserts and the connecting rod and cap clean, using a lint-free cloth.

**10** Install the bearing inserts in the connecting rod and cap **(see illustration)**. Make sure the tab on the bearing engages with the notch in the rod or cap.

**11** Wipe off the connecting rod journal with a lint-free cloth. Lay a strip of Plastigauge across the top of the journal, parallel with the journal axis **(see illustration 26.11 in Part A of this Chapter)**.

**12** Position the connecting rod on the journal, then install the rod cap and nuts. Tighten the nuts to the torque listed in this Chapter's Specifications **(see illustration)**, but don't allow the connecting rod to rotate at all.

**13** Unscrew the nuts and remove the connecting rod and cap from the journal, being very careful not to disturb the Plastigauge. Compare the width of the crushed Plastigauge to the scale printed in the Plastigauge envelope to determine the bearing oil clearance **(see illustration)**.

**25.13 Place the Plastigauge scale next to the flattened Plastigauge to measure the bearing clearance**

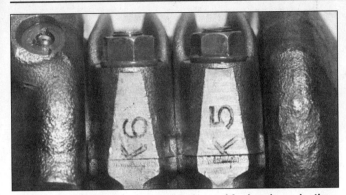

25.18a The connecting rod number is used for bearing selection; use the letter to align the rod and cap

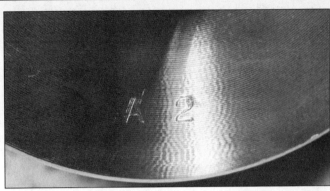

25.18b The letter on the crankshaft is used together with the connecting rod number to select bearings

14 If the clearance is within the range listed in this Chapter's Specifications and the bearings are in perfect condition, they can be reused. If the clearance is greater than the wear limit, replace the bearing inserts with new inserts that have the same color code, then check the clearance once again. Always replace all of the inserts at the same time.

15 The clearance should now be within the range listed in this Chapter's Specifications.

16 If the clearance is greater than the maximum clearance listed in this Chapter's Specifications, measure the diameter of the connecting rod journal with a micrometer. Yamaha doesn't provide diameter or wear limit specifications, but by measuring the diameter at a number of points around the journal's circumference, you'll be able to determine whether or not the journal is out-of-round. Take the measurement at each end of the journal to determine if the journal is tapered.

17 If any journal is tapered or out-of-round or bearing clearance is beyond the maximum listed in this Chapter's Specifications (with new bearings), replace the crankshaft.

18 Each connecting rod has a number stamped on it in ink (see illustration). Subtract this number from the connecting rod journal number on the crankshaft to get a bearing number (see illustration). For example, the number on the right connecting rod shown in the accompanying illustration is 5. The corresponding number for that connecting rod's journal, stamped into the crankshaft, is 2. Subtracting 2 from 5 produces 3, which is the bearing number for that journal. According to

the accompanying chart, bearing no. 3 is color-coded brown (see illustration). The color codes are painted on the edges of the bearings (see illustration).

19 Repeat the bearing selection procedure for the remaining connecting rods.

### Installation

20 Wipe off the bearing inserts, connecting rods and caps. Install the inserts into the rods and caps, using your hands only, making sure the tabs on the inserts engage with the notches in the rods and caps (see illustration 25.10). When all the inserts are installed, lubricate them with engine assembly lube or moly-based grease. Don't get any lubricant on the mating surfaces of the rod or cap.

21 Assemble each connecting rod to its proper journal, referring to the previously applied cylinder numbers. Make sure the Y mark on each rod is toward the tapered end of the crankshaft. The letter present at the rod/cap seam on one side of the connecting rod should fit together perfectly when the rod and cap are assembled (see illustration 25.18a). If it doesn't, the wrong cap is on the rod. Fix this problem before assembling the engine any further.

22 When you're sure the rods are positioned correctly, lubricate the threads of the rod bolts and the surfaces of the nuts with molybdenum disulfide grease and tighten the nuts to the torque listed in this Chapter's Specifications

(see illustration 25.12). Note: *Snug both nuts evenly, then tighten them to the specified torque in a continuous motion. If you must stop tightening between 32 and 36 Nm (22 and 25 ft-lbs), loosen the nuts to a torque less than 32 Nm (22 ft-lbs), then retighten them to the specified torque in one continuous motion.*

23 Turn the rods on the crankshaft. If either of them feels tight, tap on the bottom of the connecting rod caps with a hammer - this should relieve stress and free them up. If it doesn't, recheck the bearing clearance.

24 As a final step, recheck the connecting rod side clearances (see Step 1). If the clearances aren't correct, find out why before proceeding with engine assembly.

### 26 Transmission - removal, disassembly, inspection, reassembly and installation

### Removal

1 Remove the engine and separate the crankcase halves (see Sections 5 and 20).

2 If you're working on a shaft drive model, lift the middle driven gear pinion off the middle drive gear shaft (see illustration).

3 If you're working on a chain drive model, remove the drive sprocket's shock absorber

| BEARING COLOR CODE | |
|---|---|
| No. 1 | Blue |
| No. 2 | Black |
| No. 3 | Brown |
| No. 4 | Green |
| No. 5 | Yellow |

25.18c Subtract the crankshaft number from the connecting rod number, and use the bearing number to select a color code

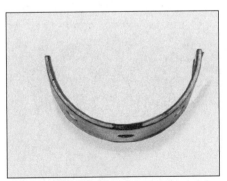

25.18d The color codes, painted on the sides of the bearings, identify bearing thickness

26.2 Lift the middle driven gear pinion off the middle gear driveshaft (shaft drive models)

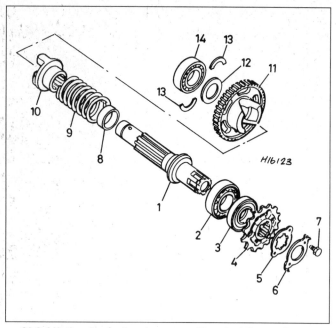

**26.3 Lift the shock absorber assembly out of the crankcase (chain drive models)**

| | |
|---|---|
| 1 Shock absorber shaft | 6 Tab washer |
| 2 Bearing | 7 Bolts |
| 3 Oil seal | 8 Collar |
| 4 Engine sprocket | 9 Spring |
| 5 Splined lockwasher | 10 Spring end plate |

| | |
|---|---|
| 11 Middle driven gear pinion | |
| 12 Thrust washer | |
| 13 Spring retaining collars | |
| 14 Bearing | |

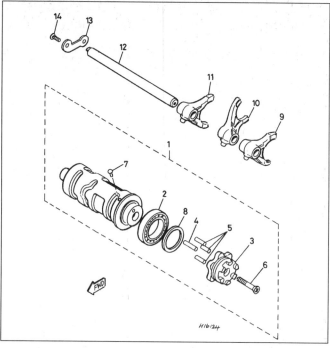

**26.4 Shift cam and forks (XV700-1100 models) - exploded view**

| | |
|---|---|
| 1 Shift cam assembly | 5 Shift pins |
| 2 Shift cam bearing | 6 Screw |
| 3 Cam plate | 7 Neutral pin |
| 4 Shift pin | 8 Washer |
| | 9 Left shift fork |

| | |
|---|---|
| 10 Center shift fork | |
| 11 Right shift fork | |
| 12 Shift fork guide bar | |
| 13 Stopper plate | |
| 14 Screws | |

**26.6 Lift the transmission shafts out of the crankcase together**

**26.7 Lift the shift cam out of the crankcase**

assembly from the crankcase **(see illustration)**.

**4** Pull the shift fork guide bar out of the forks and crankcase **(see illustration)**.

**5** Remove the two uppermost shift forks from the gear grooves.

**6** Lift the transmission shafts out of the crankcase together **(see illustration)**.

**7** Lift the shift cam out of the crankcase **(see illustration)**.

**8** Reassemble the shift forks on the guide bar so you don't forget how they go **(see illustration 26.4)**.

**26.9a Remove the snap-ring and thrust washer . . .**

**26.9b . . . slide the fifth pinion gear off the mainshaft . . .**

**26.9c . . . and slide second-third pinion gear off the shaft**

26.9d  Remove the snap-ring . . .

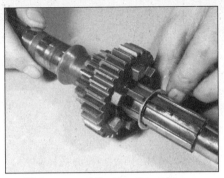

26.9e  . . . and the thrust washer . . .

26.9f  . . . and slide off fourth pinion gear

26.9g  First pinion gear is integral with the mainshaft

## Transmission disassembly

### Mainshaft

**9**  To disassemble the mainshaft, refer to the accompanying illustrations **(see illustrations)**.

 *Place the gears on a rod in order as they are removed so they can be reassembled in the same order and facing in the same direction.*

### Driveaxle

**10**  To disassemble the driveaxle, refer to the **accompanying illustrations**. Slide each gear onto a rod, such a wooden dowel or plastic pipe, as soon as it's removed from the shaft.

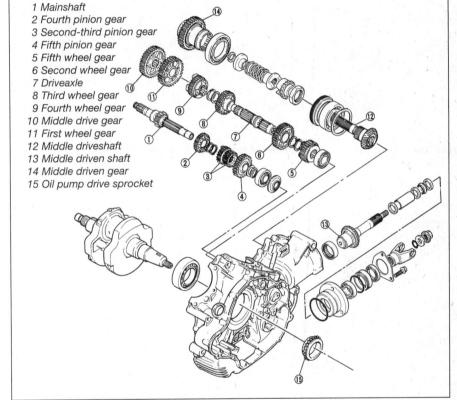

1  Mainshaft
2  Fourth pinion gear
3  Second-third pinion gear
4  Fifth pinion gear
5  Fifth wheel gear
6  Second wheel gear
7  Driveaxle
8  Third wheel gear
9  Fourth wheel gear
10  Middle drive gear
11  First wheel gear
12  Middle driveshaft
13  Middle driven shaft
14  Middle driven gear
15  Oil pump drive sprocket

26.9h  Transmission shafts (XV700-1100 models) - exploded view

26.10a  Slide the fifth wheel gear off the driveaxle

26.10b  Remove the snap-ring . . .

26.10c . . . and the thrust washer . . .

26.10d . . . and slide second wheel gear off

26.10e At the other end of the driveaxle, slide off the middle drive gear . . .

26.10f . . . the first wheel gear . . .

26.10g . . . and the fourth wheel gear

26.10h Remove the snap-ring . . .

## Inspection

11 Wash all of the components in clean solvent and dry them off. Rotate the ball bearings in the left side of the transmission case, feeling for tightness, rough spots and excessive looseness and listening for noises. If any of these conditions are found, replace the bearing with a blind hole puller (see illustrations 21.4b and 21.4c). Check the oil seal behind the mainshaft bearing; it's a good idea to replace it as a precaution (see Section 21).

12 Check the gear teeth for cracking and other obvious damage. Check the gear bushings and the surface in the inner diameter of each gear for scoring or heat discoloration (see illustration). If the gear or bushing is damaged, replace it.

13 Inspect the dogs and the dog holes in the gears for excessive wear. Replace the paired gears as a set if necessary.

14 Place the shaft in V-blocks and check runout with a dial indicator. Replace the shaft if runout exceeds the value listed in this Chapter's Specifications.

15 If you're working on a shaft drive model, inspect the middle drive gear (see illustration). Replace the gear if the teeth or splines are worn or damaged. Replace the bearing if it's loose, rough or noisy.

16 Check the edges of the grooves in the shift cam for signs of excessive wear. Check

26.10i . . . and the thrust washer . . .

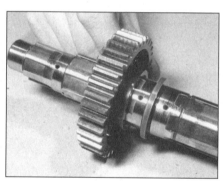

26.10j . . . and the third wheel gear . . .

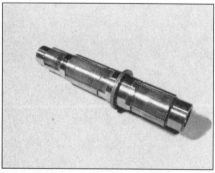

26.10k . . . from the driveaxle

26.12 Check the gear bushings (if equipped) for wear or damage

26.15 Check the teeth, splines and bearing on the middle drive gear

**26.19 The stopper plate can be left in position unless it's loose or the crankcases are to be replaced**

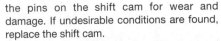

*If you remove it, use Loctite Stud 'n' Bearing Mount or equivalent on the screw threads*

**26.20 Remove the cam plate if necessary to remove the shift cam bearing**

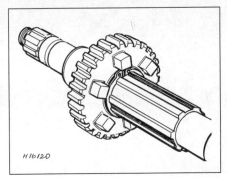

**26.21 Install the snap-rings with their ends in the correct position**

the pins on the shift cam for wear and damage. If undesirable conditions are found, replace the shift cam.

17 Check the shift forks for distortion and wear, especially at the fork tips **(see illustration 27.5 in Part A of this Chapter)**. If they are discolored or severely worn they are probably bent. If damage or wear is evident, check the shift fork groove in the corresponding gear as well. Inspect the guide pins and the shaft bore for excessive wear and distortion and replace any defective parts with new ones.

18 Check the shift fork guide bar for evidence of wear, galling and other damage. Make sure the shift forks move smoothly on the bar. If the bar is worn or bent, replace it with a new one.

19 Check the stopper plate in the crankcase for looseness **(see illustration)**. If the plate is loose, remove its screws and apply thread locking compound (Loctite Stud 'n' Bearing Mount or equivalent) to the threads. Reinstall the screws and tighten them to the torque listed in this Chapter's Specifications.

20 Check the bearing on the shift cam for looseness, noise or rough movement. If its condition is in doubt, remove the cam plate to replace the bearing **(see illustration)**. **Note:** *The cam plate screw may be very tight. Use an impact driver to remove it. It's a good idea to*

make sure there's a replacement screw in stock at your local Yamaha dealer before removing the old screw.

### Assembly and installation

21 Assemble the transmission shafts by reversing the disassembly steps. Install the snap-rings with the sharp edges toward the gears they're retaining, and their rounded edges away from the gears. Coat all parts with clean engine oil during assembly. Position the ends of the snap-rings correctly **(see illustration)**.

22 Install the shift cam in the crankcase **(see illustration 26.7)**. Install the neutral switch (see Chapter 8) and engage the shift cam with it **(see illustration)**.

23 Mesh the gears on both transmission shafts and position the shift fork on the fifth

pinion gear. Use the numbers on the forks to position them correctly. The forks are numbered from one to three, starting from the left side of the engine.

24 Install the transmission shafts and fifth pinion gear shift fork as an assembly **(see illustration 26.6)**.

25 Engage the shift fork pin with the shift cam **(see illustration)**.

26 Install the remaining two shift forks in their gear grooves and engage their pins with the shift cam **(see illustration)**.

27 Slide the shift fork guide bar through the forks **(see illustration)**. Turn the guide bar so its flat is aligned with the middle drive gear teeth **(see illustration)**.

28 The remainder of installation is the reverse of the removal steps.

**26.22 Install the neutral switch, then turn the shift cam to align with it**

**26.25 Engage the pin on the fifth pinion gear shift fork with the groove in the shift cam**

**26.26 Install the remaining two shift forks and engage their pins with the shift cam grooves**

**26.27a Slide the guide bar through the forks . . .**

**26.27b . . . and align its flat with the teeth of the middle drive gear**

## 27 Initial start-up after overhaul

1 Make sure the engine oil level is correct, then remove the spark plugs from the engine. Place the engine kill switch in the Off position and unplug the primary (low tension) wires from the coils.

2 Turn on the key switch and crank the engine over with the starter several times to build up oil pressure. Reinstall the spark plugs, connect the wires and turn the switch to On.

3 Make sure there is fuel in the tank, then turn the fuel tap to the On position and operate the choke.

4 Start the engine and allow it to run at a moderately fast idle until it reaches operating temperature.

5 Check carefully for oil leaks and make sure the transmission and controls, especially the brakes, function properly before road testing the machine. Refer to Section 28 for the recommended break-in procedure.

6 Upon completion of the road test, and after the engine has cooled down completely, recheck the valve clearances (see Chapter 1).

## 28 Recommended break-in procedure

1 Any rebuilt engine needs time to break-in, even if parts have been installed in their original locations. For this reason, treat the machine gently for the first few miles to make sure oil has circulated throughout the engine and any new parts installed have started to seat.

2 Even greater care is necessary if the engine has been rebored or a new crankshaft has been installed. In the case of a rebore, the engine will have to be broken in as if the machine were new. This means greater use of the transmission and a restraining hand on the throttle until at least 500 miles (800 km) have been covered. There's no point in keeping to any set speed limit - the main idea is to keep from lugging the engine and to gradually increase performance until the 500 mile (800 km) mark is reached. These recommendations can be lessened to an extent when only a new crankshaft is installed. Experience is the best guide, since it's easy to tell when an engine is running freely. The following recommendations, which Yamaha provides for new motorcycles, can be used as a guide:

a) *0 to 90 miles (0 to 150 km): Keep engine speed below 3,000 rpm. Turn off the engine after each hour of operation and let it cool for 5 to 10 minutes. Vary the engine speed and don't use full throttle.*

b) *90 to 300 miles (150 to 500 km): Don't run the engine for long periods above 4,000 rpm. Rev the engine freely through the gears, but don't use full throttle.*

c) *300 to 600 miles (500 to 1000 km): Don't use full throttle for prolonged periods and don't cruise at speeds above 5,000 rpm.*

d) *At 600 miles (1,000 km): Change the engine oil and filter. Full throttle can be used after this point.*

3 If a lubrication failure is suspected, stop the engine immediately and try to find the cause. If an engine is run without oil, even for a short period of time, severe damage will occur.

# Chapter 3 Part A
# Fuel and exhaust systems (XV535 models)

## Contents

## Degrees of difficulty

**Easy,** suitable for novice with little experience  | **Fairly easy,** suitable for beginner with some experience  | **Fairly difficult,** suitable for competent DIY mechanic  | **Difficult,** suitable for experienced DIY mechanic 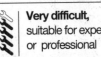 | **Very difficult,** suitable for expert DIY or professional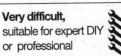

## Specifications

### Carburetor

| | |
|---|---|
| Type ................................... | Mikuni BDS34 (two) |
| Jet sizes | |
|   Main jet | |
|     1987 and 1988 .......................... | 135 |
|     1989 through 1993 | |
|       Front cylinder ........................ | 137.5 |
|       Rear cylinder ........................ | 135 |
|     1994-on US | |
|       Front cylinder ........................ | 137.5 |
|       Rear cylinder ........................ | 135 |
|     1994 and 1995 UK, 1994 and later Canada ................ | 135 |
|     1996 and later UK ....................... | 107.5 |
|   Main air jet ............................. | 140 |
|   Jet needle/clip position | |
|     1987 and 1988 US and Canada | |
|       Front cylinder ........................ | 5DZ7-1 |
|       Rear cylinder ........................ | 5DZ8-1 |
|     1990 through 1993 US and Canada | |
|       Front cylinder ........................ | 5DZ17-1 |
|       Rear cylinder ........................ | 5DZ18-1 |
|     1994-on US | |
|       Front cylinder ........................ | 5DZ17-1 |
|       Rear cylinder ........................ | 5DZ18-1 |
|     1994-on Canada | |
|       Front cylinder ........................ | 5DZ9-3 |
|       Rear cylinder ........................ | 5DZ10-3 |
|     1988 through 1995 UK | |
|       Front cylinder ........................ | 5DZ10-3 |
|       Rear cylinder ........................ | 5DZ9-3 |
|     1996 and later UK | |
|       Front cylinder ........................ | 5DZ13-3 |
|       Rear cylinder ........................ | 5DZ14-4 |

Jet sizes (continued)

| | |
|---|---|
| Main nozzle | Y-O |
| Pilot air jet no. 1 | |
|   1987 and 1988 US | 60 |
|   All others | 70 |
| Pilot air jet no. 2 | |
|   1987 and 1988 US | 160 |
|   All others | 170 |
| Pilot jet | |
|   1987 and 1988 US | 32.5 |
|   All others | 35 |
| Pilot screw | |
|   1987 and 1988 US | Preset (not specified) |
|   1990 through 1993 US and Canada | 2-1/2 turns out |
|   1994 and later US, 1995 Canada, 1996 and later UK | 2-1/2 turns out |
|   1995 and later Canada | Not specified |
|   1988 through 1995 UK | 2 turns out |
| Valve seat size | 1.5 |
| Starter jet | |
|   Except 1994 US | 40 |
|   1994 US | 35 |
| Fuel level | 13.5 to 14.5 mm (0.53 to 0.57 inch) |

## Fuel tank

| | |
|---|---|
| Fuel grade | Regular unleaded gasoline (petrol) |
| Capacity | |
|   1987 and 1988 models | 8.6 liters (2.3 US gal, 1.9 Imp gal), including reserve of 2.5 liters (0.7 US gal, 0.5 Imp gal) |
|   1989-on models | 13.5 liters (3.6 US gal, 3.0 Imp gal), including reserve of 2.5 liters (0.7 US gal, 0.5 Imp gal) |

## Tightening torques

| | |
|---|---|
| Carburetor joint bolts | 12 Nm (8.7 ft-lbs) |
| Exhaust pipe-to-cylinder head nuts | 20 Nm (14 ft-lbs) |
| Exhaust pipe rear joint bolt | 10 Nm (7.2 ft-lbs) |
| Muffler/silencer chamber bolt and nut | 20 Nm (14 ft-lbs) |

## 1 General information

The fuel system consists of the fuel tank, the fuel tap and filter, the carburetors and the connecting lines, hoses and control cables and an electric fuel pump.

The carburetors used on these motorcycles are two Mikunis with butterfly-type throttle valves. For cold starting, an enrichment circuit is actuated by a choke lever mounted on the left side of the bike.

The exhaust system routes exhaust gases into a muffler/silencer chamber under the bike and then into twin exhaust pipes on the right side.

Many of the fuel system service procedures are considered routine maintenance items and for that reason are included in Chapter 1.

## 2 Fuel tank - removal and installation

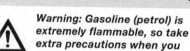

**Warning: Gasoline (petrol) is extremely flammable, so take extra precautions when you work on any part of the fuel system. Don't smoke or allow open flames or bare light bulbs near the work area, and don't work in a garage where a natural gas-type appliance (such as a water heater or clothes dryer) is present. If you spill any fuel on your skin, rinse it off immediately with soap and water. When you perform any kind of work on the fuel system, wear safety glasses and have a fire extinguisher suitable for class B fires (flammable liquids) on hand.**

1 All models have a main fuel tank mounted beneath the seat. Later models also have an upper fuel tank mounted forward of the seat on top of the upper frame section in the traditional position (on early models, what looks like a fuel tank is actually a cover).

2 Support the bike securely so it can't be knocked over during this procedure.

3 Remove the seat (see Chapter 7).

### Upper fuel tank

4 Free the fuel hoses from the clips on top of the battery cover, remove the cover and disconnect the negative cable from the battery (see illustrations).

5 Remove the upper tank mounting bolts and washers (see illustrations). Remove the metal collars from inside the left and right rubber dampers, then remove all three dampers.

6 Hold a pan under the fittings to catch

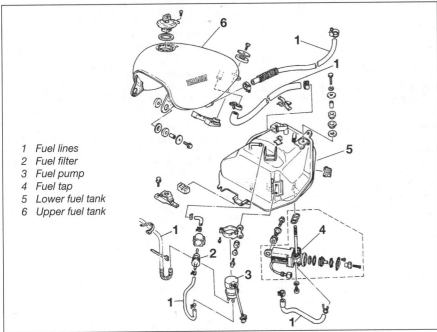

A  Clips
B  Hose clamps
C  Tank mounting bolts
D  Battery positive cable (always disconnect the negative cable first)

2.4a  Release the fuel hoses from the clips on top of the battery cover

1  Fuel lines
2  Fuel filter
3  Fuel pump
4  Fuel tap
5  Lower fuel tank
6  Upper fuel tank

2.4b  Fuel tanks and lines (models with upper fuel tank)

drained fuel, lift the upper tank and disconnect the fuel hoses (see illustrations). Lift the tank off the bike.

 **Warning: Pour the drained fuel into a safe fuel storage container. Don't leave it in the drain pan.**

### Main fuel tank

**7** If you're working on a bike with an upper fuel tank, remove it. Disconnect the upper tank hoses from their fittings on the main tank (see illustrations 2.4a and 2.4b).
**8** Remove the left side cover (see Chapter 7).
**9** If you're working on a bike without an upper fuel tank, remove the fuel filler cap.
**10** Remove the left passenger footpeg bracket (see illustration).

2.5a  Remove the upper tank mounting bolt at the rear . . .

2.5b  . . . and one on each side

2.6a  Lift the tank and disconnect the hoses from the fittings (arrows) . . .

2.6b  . . . there's a fuel hose on each side

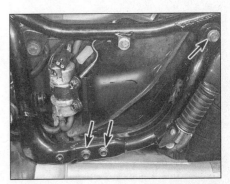

2.10  Remove the mounting bolts (arrows) and take off the footpeg bracket

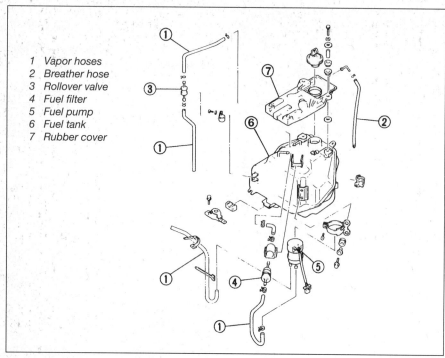

1  Vapor hoses
2  Breather hose
3  Rollover valve
4  Fuel filter
5  Fuel pump
6  Fuel tank
7  Rubber cover

2.11  Fuel tank and lines (models without upper fuel tank)

11  Remove the fuel filter (see Chapter 1 and the accompanying illustration).
12  Disconnect the fuel pump electrical connector and the line that runs from the pump to the carburetors (see Section 12). If you plan to remove the fuel pump, this is a good time to do it; if not, it can be left attached to the tank.
13  If you're working on a bike without an upper fuel tank, remove the rubber cover from the top of the main tank (see illustration).
14  Remove the tank mounting bolts and disengage the rubber dampers from the brackets (see illustrations).
15  Check to make sure all hoses and wires have been disconnected, then remove the tank through the left side of the frame.

### All models

16  Before installing the tank, check the condition of the hoses
and rubber mounting dampers - if they're

hardened, cracked, or show any other signs of deterioration, replace them.
17  When replacing the tank, reverse the above procedure. Make sure the tank seats properly and does not pinch any control cables or wires.

## 3  Fuel tank - cleaning and repair

1  All repairs to the fuel tank should be carried out by a professional who has experience in this critical and potentially dangerous work. Even after cleaning and flushing of the fuel system, explosive fumes can remain and ignite during repair of the tank.
2  If the fuel tank is removed from the vehicle, it should not be placed in an area where sparks or open flames could ignite the fumes coming out of the tank. Be especially careful

inside garages where a natural gas-type appliance is located, because the pilot light could cause an explosion.

## 4  Idle fuel/air mixture adjustment - general information

1  Due to the increased emphasis on controlling motorcycle exhaust emissions, certain governmental regulations have been formulated which directly affect the carburetion of this machine. In order to comply with the regulations, the carburetors on some models have a metal sealing plug pressed into the hole over the pilot screw (which controls the idle fuel/air mixture) on each carburetor, so they can't be tampered with. These should only be removed in the event of a complete carburetor overhaul, and even then the screws should be returned to their original settings. The pilot screws on other models are accessible, but the use of an exhaust gas analyzer is the only accurate way to adjust the idle fuel/air mixture and be sure the machine doesn't exceed the emissions regulations.
2  If the engine runs extremely rough or blows black smoke at idle or continually stalls, and if a carburetor overhaul does not cure the problem, take the motorcycle to a Yamaha dealer service department or other repair shop equipped with an exhaust gas analyzer. They will be able to properly adjust the idle fuel/air mixture to achieve a smooth idle and restore low speed performance.

## 5  Carburetor overhaul - general information

1  Poor engine performance, hesitation, hard starting, stalling, flooding and backfiring are all signs that major carburetor maintenance may be required.
2  Keep in mind that many so-called carburetor problems are really not carburetor problems at all, but mechanical problems within the engine or ignition system

2.13  Work the drain fitting (arrow) free of the rubber cover and lift the cover out

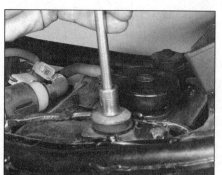

2.14a  Remove the mounting bolts . . .

2.14b  . . . and detach the rubber dampers from the brackets

6.6  Free the hose from the retaining clips

6.8  If this wiring harness obstructs removal, detach it from its clip (arrow) and move it out of the way

6.9  Loosen the clamp and pull the fuel line off the fitting

malfunctions. Try to establish for certain that the carburetors are in need of maintenance before beginning a major overhaul.

**3** Check the fuel filter, the fuel lines, the fuel tank breather hose(s), the rollover valve (models with evaporative emission control), the intake manifold hose clamps, the vacuum hoses, the air filter element, the cylinder compression, the spark plugs, the carburetor synchronization and the fuel pump before assuming that a carburetor overhaul is required.

**4** Most carburetor problems are caused by dirt particles, varnish and other deposits which build up in and block the fuel and air passages. Also, in time, gaskets and O-rings shrink or deteriorate and cause fuel and air leaks which lead to poor performance.

**5** When the carburetor is overhauled, it is generally disassembled completely and the parts are cleaned thoroughly with a carburetor cleaning solvent and dried with filtered, unlubricated compressed air. The fuel and air passages are also blown through with compressed air to force out any dirt that may have been loosened but not removed by the solvent. Once the cleaning process is complete, the carburetor is reassembled using new gaskets, O-rings and, generally, a new inlet needle valve and seat.

**6** Before disassembling the carburetors, make sure you have a carburetor rebuild kit (which will include all necessary O-rings and

other parts), some carburetor cleaner, a supply of rags, some means of blowing out the carburetor passages and a clean place to work. It is recommended that only one carburetor be overhauled at a time to avoid mixing up parts.

**7** Don't separate the carburetors from each other unless one of the joints between them is leaking. The carburetors can be overhauled completely without being separated, and reconnecting them properly can be difficult.

## 6  Carburetors and intake joints - removal and installation

> **Warning: Gasoline (petrol) is extremely flammable, so take extra precautions when you work on any part of the fuel system. Don't smoke or allow open flames or bare light bulbs near the work area, and don't work in a garage where a natural gas-type appliance (such as a water heater or clothes dryer) is present. If you spill any fuel on your skin, rinse it off immediately with soap and water. When you perform any kind of work on the fuel system, wear safety glasses and have an extinguisher suitable for class B fires (flammable liquids) on hand.**

### Removal

**1** Remove the seat (see Chapter 7).

**2** If you're working on a model with an upper fuel tank, remove it (see Section 2).

**3** If you're working on a model without an upper fuel tank, remove the top cover (see Chapter 7).

**4** Remove the left front side cover and its bracket (see Chapter 7).

**5** Remove the right front side cover and the electrical component board beneath it (see Chapter 7).

**6** Work the hose on the right side free of the clips **(see illustration)**.

**7** Disconnect the throttle cable from the pulley (see Section 9).

**8** The wiring harness on the right side may interfere with removal **(see illustration)**. If it does, free it from its clip and move it aside. On 1991 and later UK models, disconnect the carburetor heater unit valve from each carburetor.

**9** Disconnect the fuel inlet line from the carburetor fitting **(see illustration)**.

**10** Loosen the clamp screws and disconnect the air cleaner joints from the carburetors **(see illustrations)**. Push the joints up off the carburetors with a screwdriver (they'll fold into the air cleaner cavity in the frame).

**11** Loosen the screws on the carburetor joints **(see illustration)**. Work the carburetors free of the joints and lift them out **(see**

6.10a  Loosen the clamping band screws on the air cleaner joints . . .

6.10b  . . . insert a screwdriver between the joint and carburetor (arrow) and push the joint up

6.11a  Loosen the clamping bands (upper arrows); alternatively unbolt the intake joints (lower arrows)

6.11b Work the carburetors free of the intake joints (if they're still bolted to the engine) . . .

6.11c . . . and remove the carburetors from the left side of the bike

6.13a Remove the Allen bolts (arrows) . . .

illustrations). **Note:** *You can also unbolt the joints from the cylinder heads and remove the carburetor assembly and joints together.*

**12** After the carburetors have been removed, stuff clean rags into the joints or intake ports to prevent the entry of dirt or other objects.

**13** Inspect the carburetor joints **(see illustration)**. If they're cracked or brittle, replace them. The O-rings should be replaced whenever the joints are removed **(see illustration)**.

## Installation

**14** Engage the carburetor assembly with the intake joints. Lightly lubricate the ends of the throttle cables (or cable) with multi-purpose grease and attach them to the throttle pulley. Make sure the accelerator cable (and decelerator cable if equipped) are in their proper positions.

**15** Pull the air cleaner joints down from the air cleaner cavity and fit them over the carburetors.

**16** Make sure the carburetor is seated securely in the intake joints and the air cleaner joints are fitted securely over the carburetors, then tighten the clamping band screws.

**17** Adjust the throttle grip freeplay (see Chapter 1).

**18** The remainder of installation is the reverse of the removal steps.

**19** Check and, if necessary, adjust the idle speed and carburetor synchronization (see Chapter 1).

6.13b . . . and take the intake joints off; replace the O-rings (arrow)

---

**7  Carburetors** - disassembly, inspection, cleaning and reassembly

⚠ **Warning:** *Gasoline (petrol) is extremely flammable, so take extra precautions when you work on any part of the fuel system. Don't smoke or allow open flames or bare light bulbs near the work area, and don't work in a garage where a natural gas-type appliance (such as a water*

heater or clothes dryer) is present. If you spill any fuel on your skin, rinse it off immediately with soap and water. When you perform any kind of work on the fuel system, wear safety glasses and have a fire extinguisher suitable for class B type fires (flammable liquids) on hand.

## Disassembly

**1** Remove the carburetors from the machine as described in Section 6. Set the assembly on a clean working surface. **Note:** *Work on one carburetor at a time to avoid getting parts mixed up* **(see illustration)**. Most disassembly

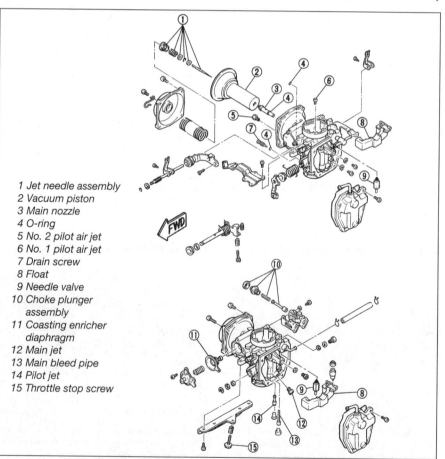

1 Jet needle assembly
2 Vacuum piston
3 Main nozzle
4 O-ring
5 No. 2 pilot air jet
6 No. 1 pilot air jet
7 Drain screw
8 Float
9 Needle valve
10 Choke plunger assembly
11 Coasting enricher diaphragm
12 Main jet
13 Main bleed pipe
14 Pilot jet
15 Throttle stop screw

FWD

7.1 Carburetors (XV535 models) - exploded view

7.2a  Remove the float chamber cover screws and take off the cover . . .

7.2b  . . . remove the other float chamber cover . . .

7.2c  . . . disconnect the fuel and vent lines and set them aside

and cleaning procedures can be accomplished without separating the carburetors. If they must be separated, a surface plate will be needed to join them.

**2** Remove the float chamber cover screws **(see illustration)**. Take off both float chamber covers, the fuel lines and the vent lines **(see illustrations)**.

**3** Slide the float off its pivot pin and lift out the needle valve **(see illustrations)**.

**4** Unscrew the main jet, the jet block retaining screws and the main nozzle holder, then lift the jet block out **(see illustrations)**.

**5** Remove the two rubber plugs from the end

7.3a  Pull out the float . . .

7.3b  . . . and lift out the needle valve

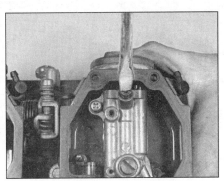

7.4a  Unscrew the main jet . . .

7.4b  . . . and the main nozzle holder . . .

7.4c  . . . remove the O-ring with a pointed tool . . .

7.4d  . . . remove the jet block screws . . .

7.4e  . . . then lift out the jet block and remove its gasket

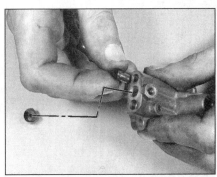

7.5a  Pull the two rubber plugs out of their passages . . .

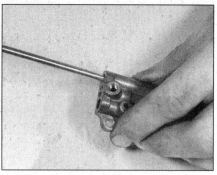

7.5b ... unscrew the pilot jet ...

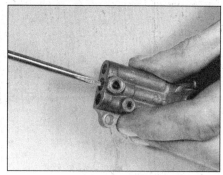

7.5c ... and the main bleed pipe

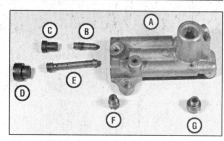

7.5d  Jet block components

A  Jet block      E  Main bleed pipe
B  Pilot jet      F  Main jet
C  Rubber plug    G  Main nozzle holder
D  Rubber plug

7.6a  Remove the screws and lift off the coasting enricher valve cover ...

7.6b ... then lift out the spring and diaphragm

of the jet block, then unscrew the pilot jet and main bleed pipe **(see illustrations)**.

**6** Remove the front carburetor's coasting enricher valve cover, spring and diaphragm **(see illustrations)**.

**7** Remove the vacuum chamber cover screws **(see illustrations)**. One of the screws requires a Torx bit (Yamaha US tool no. YU-05258/UK part no. 90890-05349).

**8** Lift off the vacuum chamber cover and remove the spring **(see illustration)**. Separate the vacuum piston diaphragm from the carburetor body, using care not to tear it, then remove the O-ring from the passage with a pointed tool **(see illustrations)**.

7.7a  Note the locations of the hose clips and remove the cover screws ...

7.7b ... one of the screws requires a Torx bit

7.8a  Lift off the cover ...

7.8b ... and remove the spring

7.8c  Carefully separate the diaphragm from the carburetor body without tearing it ...

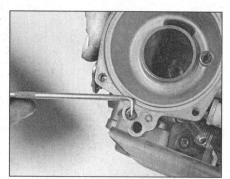

7.8d ... and remove the O-ring

7.9a Remove the O-ring from the main nozzle . . .

7.9b . . . then push the main nozzle into the throttle bore (arrow) and remove it

7.10a Unscrew the no. 2 pilot air jet from the vacuum chamber . . .

**9** Push the main nozzle into the throttle bore, then remove the nozzle and its O-ring **(see illustrations)**.

**10** Unscrew the pilot air jets from the vacuum chamber (no. 2) and from the throttle bore (no. 1) **(see illustrations)**.

**11** Loosen the two screws that secure the choke link **(see illustration)**. Remove the pivot screw, retaining clip and washer and take off the choke lever **(see illustrations)**.

**12** Remove the clip, retainer, spring and choke link **(see illustrations)**.

**13** Remove the washer and choke link bushing from each carburetor **(see illustrations)**.

7.10b . . . and the no. 1 pilot air jet from the throttle bore (arrow)

7.11a Loosen the choke link securing screws (there's one for each carburetor) . . .

7.11b . . . remove the choke lever pivot screw . . .

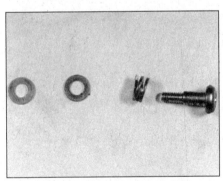

7.11c . . . its spring and washers

7.11d Remove the clip and washers . . .

7.11e . . . and take off the choke lever

7.12a Remove the clip from the end of the choke link with a pointed tool . . .

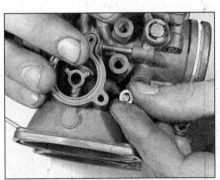

7.12b . . . remove the spring retainer . . .

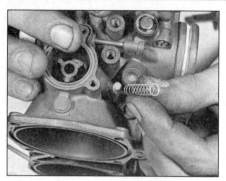

7.12c . . . the spring . . .

7.12d . . . and pull out the choke link

7.13a Pry the washer and bushing loose with a pointed tool . . .

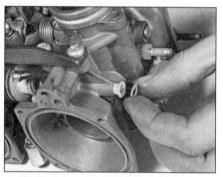

7.13b . . . and remove them from the choke shaft passage

7.15a Detach the upper stay plate . . .

**14** This completes disassembly necessary to clean and inspect the jets and passages. One of the choke plunger assemblies and one of the coasting enrichers are located between the carburetors. To remove and inspect these, the carburetors must be separated as described in the following steps.

**15** Remove two of the screws from the upper stay plate and two from the lower stay plate **(see illustrations)**. Note how the synchronizing screw fits in the linkage, then pull the carburetors apart **(see illustrations)**.

**16** Remove the choke plunger and housing from the carburetor **(see illustrations)**.

7.15b . . . and the lower stay plate . . .

7.15c . . . note carefully how the synchronizing screw fits in the linkage . . .

7.15d . . . and pull the carburetors apart

7.16a Unscrew the choke plunger . . .

7.16b . . . and take it out of the housing

7.16c Remove the housing mounting screws . . .

**7.16d . . . and take the housing and gasket off the carburetor body**

**7.17  Remove two screws and take the throttle pulley assembly off**

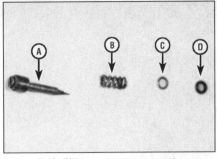

**7.19  Pilot screw components**

A  Pilot screw          C  Washer
B  Spring               D  O-ring

**17** Remove the throttle pulley assembly **(see illustration)**.
**18** Remove the remaining coasting enricher **(see illustrations 7.6a and 7.6b)**.
**19** The pilot (idle mixture) screw is located in a passage in the carburetor body. On US models, this screw is hidden behind a plug which will have to be removed if the screw is to be taken out. To do this, drill a hole in the plug, being careful not to drill into the screw, then pry the plug out or remove it with a small slide hammer. On all models, turn the pilot screw in, counting the number of turns until it bottoms lightly. Record that number for use when installing the screw. Now remove the pilot screw along with its spring, washer and O-ring **(see illustration)**.

### Inspection

**20** Remove the O-ring from each float chamber cover **(see illustration)**.
**21** Check the operation of the choke plunger. If it doesn't move smoothly, replace it, along with the return spring. Inspect the needle on the end of the choke plunger and replace it if it's worn.
**22** Check the tapered portion of the pilot screw for wear or damage. Replace the pilot screw if necessary.
**23** Check the carburetor body, float chamber cover and vacuum chamber cover for cracks, distorted sealing surfaces and other damage. If any defects are found, replace the faulty component, although replacement of the

entire carburetor will probably be necessary (check with your parts supplier for the availability of separate components).
**24** Check the diaphragm for splits, holes and general deterioration. Holding it up to a light will help to reveal problems of this nature.
**25** Insert the vacuum piston in the carburetor body and see that it moves up-and-down smoothly. Check the surface of the piston for wear. If it's worn excessively or doesn't move smoothly in the bore, replace the carburetor.
**26** Remove the screw that secures the jet needle in the vacuum piston **(see illustration)**. Remove the jet needle, spring, washer, clip and O-ring **(see illustrations)**. Check the jet needle for straightness by rolling it on a flat

surface (such as a piece of glass). Replace it if it's bent or if the tip is worn.
**27** Operate the throttle shaft to make sure the throttle butterfly valve opens and closes smoothly. If it doesn't, replace the carburetor.
**28** Check the coasting enricher diaphragm for tears or brittleness **(see illustration)**. Replace them if their condition is in doubt.
**29** Check the floats for damage. This will usually be apparent by the presence of fuel inside one of the floats. If the floats are damaged, they must be replaced. Check the float needle valve seating face; if a pronounced groove has formed on the taper, replace the needle valve. Also, check that the tip on the opposite end of the needle valve moves freely against spring pressure.

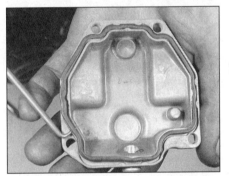

**7.20  Remove the O-ring from each float chamber cover with a pointed tool**

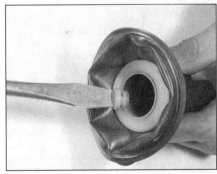

**7.26a  Remove the screw from inside the vacuum piston . . .**

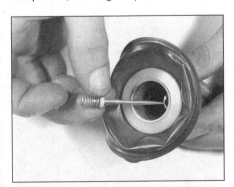

**7.26b  . . . and lift out the jet needle . . .**

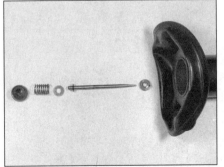

**7.26c  . . . together with the spring, washer, clip and O-ring**

**7.28  Check the coasting enricher solenoid diaphragms for cracks or brittleness**

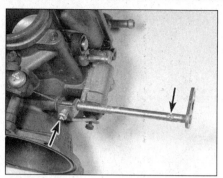

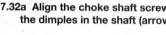

7.32a Align the choke shaft screws with the dimples in the shaft (arrows)

7.32b Align the protrusion in the diaphragm with the notch in the carburetor body (arrow)

7.32c Align the tab on the coasting enricher diaphragm with the notch in the carburetor body (arrow)

## Cleaning

*Caution: Use only a petroleum based solvent for carburetor cleaning. Don't use caustic cleaners.*

**30** Submerge the metal components in the solvent for approximately thirty minutes (or longer, if the directions recommend it).

**31** After the carburetor has soaked long enough for the cleaner to loosen and dissolve most of the varnish and other deposits, use a brush to remove the stubborn deposits. Rinse it again, then dry it with compressed air. Blow out all of the fuel and air passages in the main body.

*Caution: Never clean the jets or passages with a piece of wire or a drill bit, as they will be enlarged, causing the fuel and air metering rates to be upset.*

## Reassembly

*Caution: When installing the jets, be careful not to over-tighten them - they're made of soft material and can strip or shear easily.*

**Note:** *When reassembling the carburetors, be sure to use the new O-rings, gaskets and other parts supplied in the rebuild kit.*

**32** Assembly is the reverse of the disassembly steps, with the following additions.

a) *When connecting the carburetors to each other, lay them on a surface plate while tightening the stay plate screws to ensure proper alignment.*

b) *When installing the choke plunger, align its screws with the dimples in the shaft* **(see illustration)**.

c) *Align the slot in the main nozzle with the projection inside the jet block.*

d) *Align the projection on the jet needle washer with the hole in the vacuum piston.*

e) *Align the protrusion on the vacuum piston diaphragm with the notch in the carburetor body* **(see illustration)**.

f) *Align the tab on the coasting enricher diaphragm with the slot in the carburetor body* **(see illustration)**.

g) *Install the carburetors (see Section 6) and check the fuel level (see Section 8).*

## 8  Carburetors -
### fuel level adjustment

⚠️ *Warning: Gasoline (petrol) is extremely flammable, so take extra precautions when you work on any part of the fuel system. Don't smoke or allow open flames or bare light bulbs near the work area, and don't work in a garage where a natural gas-type appliance (such as a water heater or clothes dryer) is present. If you spill any fuel on your skin, rinse it off immediately with soap and water. When you perform any kind of work on the fuel*

system, wear safety glasses and have a fire extinguisher suitable for class B type fires (flammable liquids) on hand.

**1** Support the bike securely so it can't be knocked over during this procedure.

**2** Place a floor jack under the bike and position it so the carburetors are vertical.

**3** Attach Yamaha service tool YM-01312-A (part no. 90890-01312) to the drain fitting on the bottom of one of the carburetor float chambers (both will be checked) **(see illustration)**. This is a clear plastic tube graduated in millimeters. An alternative is to use a length of clear plastic tubing and an accurate ruler. Hold the graduated tube (or the free end of the clear plastic tube) vertically against the float chamber cover.

**4** Unscrew the drain screw at the bottom of the float chamber a couple of turns **(see illustration)**, then start the engine and let it idle - fuel will flow into the tube. Wait for the fuel level to stabilize, then note how far the fuel level is below the line on the float chamber cover.

**5** Measure the distance between the indicator line and the top of the fuel level in the tube or gauge. This distance is the fuel level - write it down on a piece of paper, tighten the drain screw, then move on to the other carburetor and check it the same way.

**6** Compare your fuel level readings to the value listed in this Chapter's Specifications. If the fuel level in either carburetor is not correct, remove the float chamber cover and bend the tang up or down as necessary **(see illustration)**, then

8.3 Connect the tool to one of the drain fittings (arrows)

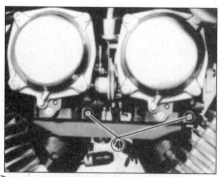

8.4 Loosen the float chamber drain screw (4)

8.6 Bend the float tang to change fuel level

9.1  Loosen the throttle cable adjuster locknuts and loosen the adjusters (arrows)

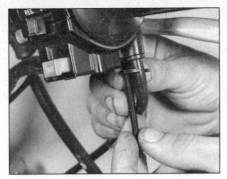

9.2  Remove the screw that secures the throttle cables to the housing

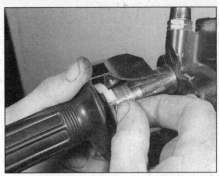

9.3a  Slip the cable out of its groove . . .

9.3b  . . . and disengage the end from the pulley

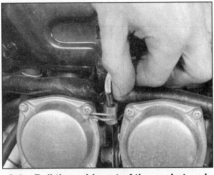

9.4a  Pull the cable out of the socket and slip the cable sideways through the slot to disengage it . . .

9.4b  . . . then slide the end of the cable sideways out of the pulley

recheck the fuel level. **Note:** *It isn't necessary to remove the carburetors from the motorcycle since the float chamber screws are accessible from the left side, but be sure the fuel valves turned off and the float chambers drained of fuel before doing so.*

## 9  Throttle cables and grip - removal, installation and adjustment

### Removal

**1** Loosen the throttle cable(s) with the adjusters **(see illustration)**.
**2** Remove the throttle cable securing screw at the handlebar **(see illustration)**.
**3** Remove the handlebar switch mounting screws. Separate the halves of the handlebar switch and detach the throttle cable(s) from the throttle grip pulley **(see illustrations)**.
**4** Detach the throttle cables from the throttle pulley at the carburetors **(see illustrations)**. Remove the cables, noting how they are routed.
**5** Slide the throttle grip off the handlebar.

### Installation

**6** Clean the handlebar and apply a light coat of multi-purpose grease.
**7** Route the cable(s) into place, following the same route as noted n removal - the cables should pass behind the upper part of the right

fork leg. Make sure they don't interfere with any other components and aren't kinked or bent sharply.
**8** Lubricate the ends of the accelerator cable (and decelerator cable if equipped) with multi-purpose grease and connect them to the throttle pulleys at the carburetors and at the throttle grip.

### Adjustment

**9** Follow the procedure outlined in Chapter 1, Throttle operation/grip freeplay - check and adjustment, to adjust the cables.

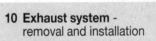

10.2a  Exhaust system (XV535 models) - exploded view

1  *Exhaust pipe gaskets*
2  *Exhaust pipe-to-rear joint gasket*
3  *Joint pipe (rear cylinder)*
4  *Exhaust pipe assembly*

**10** Turn the handlebars back and forth to make sure the cables don't cause the steering to bind. With the engine idling, turn the handlebars back and forth and make sure idle speed doesn't change. If it does, find and fix the cause before riding the motorcycle.

## 10  Exhaust system - removal and installation

### Removal

**1** Support the bike securely so it can't be knocked over during this procedure.
**2** Remove the nuts that secure the front exhaust pipe to the cylinder head **(see illustrations)**.

10.2b  Detach the front exhaust pipe flange from the cylinder head

10.3a Remove the Allen bolts and disconnect the rear exhaust pipe from the joint . . .

10.3b . . . and remove the nuts that secure the rear joint to the cylinder head

10.4 Unbolt the bracket at the right passenger footpeg

**3** Remove the Allen bolts and detach the rear exhaust pipe from the joint pipe at the cylinder head **(see illustration)**. Remove the nuts and detach the joint pipe from the head **(see illustration)**.
**4** Unbolt the muffler/silencer bracket at the right passenger footpeg **(see illustration)**.
**5** Support the muffler/silencer chamber with a jack and unbolt it from the frame **(see illustration)**. Lower the exhaust system away from the bike and take it out.
**6** Installation is the reverse of removal, with the following additions:
a) *Use new gaskets at the cylinder head (see illustration).*
b) *Tighten all fasteners to the torque settings listed in this Chapter's Specifications.*

10.5 With the exhaust system supported, unbolt the muffler/silencer chamber

10.6 Use new gaskets for installation

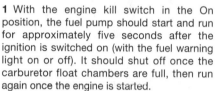

## 11 Fuel pump - circuit check and fuel pump test

**1** With the engine kill switch in the On position, the fuel pump should start and run for approximately five seconds after the ignition is switched on (with the fuel warning light on or off). It should shut off once the carburetor float chambers are full, then run again once the engine is started.
**2** The fuel pump circuit consists of the pump, the pump relay, the igniter unit (which controls the fuel pump as well as ignition timing), the engine kill switch, the ignition switch, the main and ignition fuses, the battery and related wiring.
**3** Lift the seat and prop it up.
**4** Check the battery condition and charge (see Chapter 1 and Chapter 8).
**5** Check the main and ignition fuses, the ignition switch and the engine kill switch (see Chapter 8). Replace them if they're defective, then try the fuel pump again.

### Pump won't run, fuel warning light off

**6** If the pump won't run while the engine is running, or if it won't run for five seconds with the ignition switch On, the kill switch in Run and the fuel warning light off, check battery

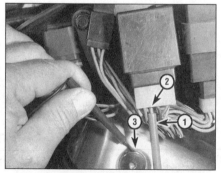

11.6 Connect the voltmeter positive (1) to the red/white wire terminal (2) and the negative to ground/earth (3)

voltage to the pump. Disconnect the electrical connector at the relay and connect a 0-20 volt DC voltmeter between the red/white wire terminal in the harness and a good grounding/earthing point (bare metal on the engine) **(see illustration)**.
**7** Turn the ignition switch to On and the engine kill switch to Run, then push the Start switch. The voltmeter should indicate at least 12 volts.
**8** If the reading is less than 12 volts, check the wiring in the fuel pump circuit for breaks or bad connections. Be sure to check the battery terminal connections and the battery ground/earth cable connection to the motorcycle.
**9** If the reading is at least 12 volts, the wiring is good. Check the fuel reserve switch (see Chapter 8).
a) *If the reserve switch is bad, replace it.*
b) *If the pump won't run with the engine running, go to Step 10. If the pump won't run for five seconds with the ignition switch On and the kill switch in Run, go to Step 11.*
**10** Disconnect the electrical connector from the fuel pump relay **(see illustration)**. Connect a short length of wire between the blue/black wire terminal and the red/white wire terminal in the harness side of the relay connector. With the ignition switch On and the kill switch in Run, push the Start and Reserve switches. The fuel pump should run.

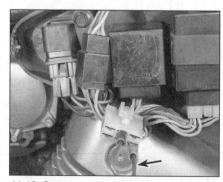

11.10 Connect a short jumper wire (arrow) between the red/white and blue/black wire terminals

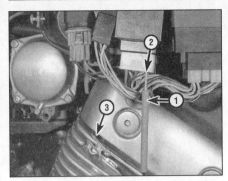

**11.11 Connect the voltmeter positive (1) to the blue/black wire terminal (2) and the negative to ground/earth (3)**

a) *If the fuel pump won't run, test it (see below).*
b) *If the fuel pump now runs, check the wiring and connections in the fuel pump circuit. If they're good, the fuel pump relay is probably defective. Replace it.*

**11** Reconnect the connector to the fuel pump relay. Insert the voltmeter positive probe into the back of the blue/black wire connector and connect the voltmeter negative lead to ground/earth (bare metal on the motorcycle) **(see illustration)**. With the ignition switch On and the kill switch in Run, push the Start and Reserve switches. The voltmeter should indicate at least 11 volts.

a) *If voltage is less than 11 volts, the fuel pump relay is probably defective. Replace it.*
b) *If voltage is 11 volts or more, check the wiring and connections in the fuel pump circuit. If they're good, the fuel pump is probably defective. Test it (see below).*

### Pump won't run, fuel warning light on

**12** If the pump won't run for five seconds with the ignition switch On, the kill switch in Run and the fuel warning light on, check the fuel reserve switch (see Chapter 8).

a) *If the fuel reserve switch is bad, replace it.*
b) *If the switch is good, go to Step 13.*

**13** Disconnect the electrical connector from the fuel pump relay **(see illustration)**. Connect the positive lead of a 0-20 volt

**12.2 Disconnect the wiring connector and remove the fuel pump relay**

voltmeter to the red-green wire in the harness side of the connector and the negative voltmeter lead to a good grounding/earthing point (bare metal on the engine). With the ignition switch On and the engine kill switch in Run, push the start switch.

a) *If it's less than 12 volts, check the wiring and connections in the fuel pump circuit.*
b) *If it's 12 volts or more, perform Step 11 above.*

### Pump won't shut off after 30 seconds

**14** Disconnect the fuel sender electrical connector **(see illustration)**. Connect the terminals in the harness side of the sender connector to each other with a short length of wire.

**15** With the sender harness terminals connected to each other, connect the positive lead of a 0-20 volt voltmeter to the back side of the blue/black wire terminal in the fuel pump relay connector **(see illustration 11.11)**. Connect the voltmeter negative lead to a good grounding/earthing point (bare metal on the engine).

**16** With the ignition switch On and the kill switch in Run, push the Start switch and note the voltmeter reading.

a) *If the reading is zero after about 30 seconds, the fuel sender is probably defective. Test it as described in Chapter 8.*

**12.5 Loosen clamps (A), disconnect (B), remove bolts (C) and take the pump out; loosen screw (D) to remove the pump bracket**

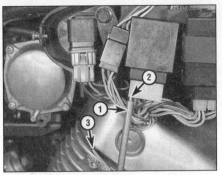

**11.13 Connect the voltmeter positive (1) to the red/green wire terminal (2) and the negative to ground/earth (3)**

**11.14 Connect the terminals in the harness side of the fuel sender to each other**

b) *If the reading is more than zero after about 30 seconds, check the wiring and connections in the fuel pump circuit. If they're good, the fuel pump relay is probably defective. Replace it.*

### Fuel pump test

**17** Disconnect the wiring connector from the fuel pump. Connect the pump directly to the battery with two lengths of wire (positive to blue/black; negative to black). If the pump doesn't run, replace it.

## 12 Fuel pump and relay - replacement

### Fuel pump relay replacement

**1** Remove the right front side cover (see Chapter 7).
**2** Disconnect the wiring connector from the relay **(see illustration)**.
**3** Remove the relay from its mounting bracket, install a new one and reconnect the wiring connector.

### Fuel pump replacement

**4** Remove the left rear side cover (see Chapter 7).
**5** Loosen the fuel line clamps and push the ends of the fuel lines off the pump fittings **(see illustration)**.
**6** Disconnect the pump electrical connector. Remove the mounting bolts and take the pump out **(see illustration 12.5).**
**7** Loosen the clamp screw and slide the pump out of its bracket.
**8** Installation is the reverse of the removal steps.

## 13 Air induction system (1990-on US models) - inspection and component replacement

**1** The air induction system uses exhaust gas pulses to suck fresh air into the exhaust ports, where it mixes with hot combustion gases. The additional oxygen provided by the fresh

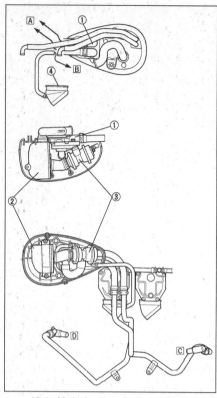

**13.1 Air induction system details**

| | |
|---|---|
| *1 Reed valve* | *A To cylinders* |
| *2 Air cleaner* | *B To air cut valve* |
| *3 Air cut valve* | *C To no. 1 cylinder* |
| *4 Rear cylinder* | *D To no. 2 cylinder* |
| *carburetor joint* | |

air allows combustion to continue for a longer time, reducing unburned hydrocarbons in the exhaust **(see illustration)**. Reed valves allow the flow of air into the ports and prevent exhaust gas from flowing into the system. The air cut valve shuts off the flow of air into the system during deceleration to prevent backfiring.

**2** Check the hoses for loose connections, damage and deterioration. Tighten or replace loose or damaged hoses.

**3** To replace system components, remove the left side cover (see Chapter 7). Disconnect the air hoses and the metal tubes **(see illustrations)**, remove the mounting screws and take the assembly off the motorcycle **(see illustrations)**.

**4** Installation is the reverse of the removal steps.

**13.3a  Pipe connections at the cylinder heads are secured by screw-type hose clamps**

## 14 Evaporation control system (California models)

**1** The evaporation control system used on California models prevents fuel vapor from escaping into the atmosphere. When the engine isn't running, the vapor is stored in a canister, then routed into the combustion chambers for burning when the engine starts **(see Illustration)**.

**2** The hoses should be checked periodically for loose connections, damage and deterioration. Tighten or replace the hoses as needed.

**3** To remove the canister, disconnect the hoses and remove the mounting bolts. To install it, bolt the canister to the motorcycle and reconnect the hoses.

### Rollover valve

**4** The rollover valve allows passage of vapors to the canister when it's in its normal upright

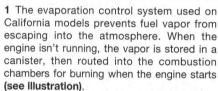

**13.3c  Hose-to-pipe connections are secured by spring-type clamps**

**13.3b  The pipes are attached to the right side of the engine with two Allen bolts**

position. The valve is designed to block the flow of vapors if the motorcycle is rolled over.

**5** To test the valve, disconnect its hoses and remove the mounting screw **(see illustration 14.1)**. It should be possible to blow air through the valve when it's upright, but not when it's turned upside down. If the valve doesn't perform as described, replace.

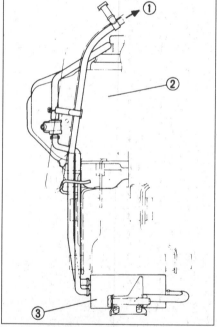

**14.1 Evaporation control system details (California models)**

*1 To carburetor    2 Fuel tank    3 Canister*

# Chapter 3  Part B
# Fuel and exhaust systems (XV700-1100 models)

## Contents

## Degrees of difficulty

| | | | | |
|---|---|---|---|---|
| **Easy,** suitable for novice with little experience  | **Fairly easy,** suitable for beginner with some experience  | **Fairly difficult,** suitable for competent DIY mechanic 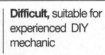 | **Difficult,** suitable for experienced DIY mechanic | **Very difficult,** suitable for expert DIY or professional |

## Specifications

### XV700 models

**Fuel tank**

Fuel grade ........................................... Regular unleaded gasoline (petrol)
Capacity
  Total .............................................. 12.5 liters (3.3 US gal, 2.7 Imperial gal)
  Reserve .......................................... 2.5 liters (0.6 US gal, 0.5 Imperial gal)

**Carburetors**

Type ................................................ Hitachi HSC40 (two)
Main jet
  Rear cylinder .................................... 128
  Front cylinder ................................... 132
Main air jet ......................................... 50
Jet needle .......................................... Y-32
Needle jet .......................................... 3.2
Pilot air jet ......................................... 190
Pilot jet ............................................. 42
Pilot screw ......................................... Preset (turns out not specified)
Valve seat size ..................................... 2.0
Starter jet .......................................... 40
Fuel level .......................................... 0 +/- 1.0 mm (0 +/- 0.039 inch)

**Tightening torques**

Carburetor joint bolts ............................... 10 Nm (7.2 ft-lbs)
Exhaust pipe-to-cylinder head nuts .................. 20 Nm (14 ft-lbs)

### XV750 models (1981 through 1983)

**Fuel tank**

Fuel grade ........................................... Regular unleaded gasoline (petrol)
Capacity
  Total .............................................. 12 liters (3.17 US gal, 2.64 Imperial gal)
  Reserve .......................................... 2.6 liters (0.67 US gal, 0.57 Imperial gal)

## XV750 models (1981 through 1983) (continued)

### Carburetors
Type ........................................................ Hitachi HSC40 (two)
Main jet ..................................................... 122
Main air jet ................................................. 50
Jet needle (US models)
    Rear cylinder ......................................... Y-23
    Front cylinder ........................................ Y-22
Jet needle (UK models)
    Rear cylinder ......................................... Y-21
    Front cylinder ........................................ Y-20
Needle jet .................................................. Not specified
Pilot air jet
    US ................................................... 185
    UK ................................................... 180
Pilot jet .................................................... 41
Pilot screw ................................................. Preset (turns out not specified)
Valve seat size ............................................. 2.0
Starter jet ................................................. 40
Fuel level
    Rear cylinder ......................................... 1.0 +/- 1.0 mm (0.039 +/- 0.039 inch)
    Front cylinder ........................................ 2.0 +/- 1.0 mm (0.078 +/- 0.039 inch)

### Tightening torques
Carburetor joint bolts ...................................... 10 Nm (7.2 ft-lbs)
Exhaust pipe-to-cylinder head nuts .......................... 20 Nm (14 ft-lbs)

## XV750 models (1988-on)

### Fuel tank
Fuel grade .................................................. Regular unleaded gasoline (petrol)
Capacity
    Total ................................................ 14.5 liters (3.8 US gal, 3.2 Imperial gal)
    Reserve .............................................. 2.5 liters (0.65 US gal, 0.5 Imperial gal)

### Carburetors
Type ........................................................ Mikuni BST40 (two)
Main jet ..................................................... 122.5
Main air jet ................................................. 80
Jet needle .................................................. 5DL12
Needle jet .................................................. Y-4
Pilot air jet ................................................ 60
Pilot jet .................................................... 40
Pilot screw ................................................. Preset (turns out not specified)
Valve seat size ............................................. 2.3
Starter jet ................................................. 35
Fuel level .................................................. 1.5 to 2.5 mm (0.6 to 1.0 inch)

### Tightening torques
Carburetor joint bolts ...................................... 10 Nm (7.2 ft-lbs)
Exhaust pipe-to-cylinder head nuts .......................... 20 Nm (14 ft-lbs)

## XV920 shaft drive models

### Fuel tank
Fuel grade .................................................. Regular unleaded gasoline (petrol)
Capacity
    Total ................................................ 14.5 liters (3.83 US gal, 3.19 Imperial gal)
    Reserve .............................................. 2.0 liters (0.53 US gal, 0.44 Imperial gal)

### Carburetors
Type ........................................................ Hitachi HSC40 (two)
Main jet
    Rear cylinder ......................................... 126
    Front cylinder ........................................ 128
Main air jet ................................................. 50
Jet needle
    Rear cylinder ......................................... Y-25
    Front cylinder ........................................ Y-24
Needle jet .................................................. Not specified
Pilot air jet
    US ................................................... 185
    UK ................................................... 180

| | |
|---|---|
| Pilot jet | 41 |
| Pilot screw | Preset (turns out not specified) |
| Valve seat size | 2.0 |
| Starter jet | 40 |
| Fuel level | |
|    Rear cylinder | 1.0 +/- 1.0 mm (0.039 +/- 0.039 inch) |
|    Front cylinder | 2.0 +/- 1.0 mm (0.078 +/- 0.039 inch) |

**Tightening torques**

| | |
|---|---|
| Carburetor joint bolts | 10 Nm (7.2 ft-lbs) |
| Exhaust pipe-to-cylinder head nuts | 20 Nm (14 ft-lbs) |

## XV920 chain drive models

**Fuel tank**

| | |
|---|---|
| Fuel grade | Regular unleaded gasoline (petrol) |
| Capacity | |
|    Total | 19 liters (5.02 US gal, 4.18 Imperial gal) |
|    Reserve | 3.2 liters (0.84 US gal, 0.70 Imperial gal) |

**Carburetors**

| | |
|---|---|
| Type | Hitachi HSC40 (two) |
| Main jet | |
|    Rear cylinder | 126 |
|    Front cylinder | 124 |
| Main air jet | 50 |
| Jet needle | |
|    Rear cylinder | Y-22 |
|    Front cylinder | Y-22 |
| Needle jet | Not specified |
| Pilot air jet | 18 |
| Pilot jet | 41 |
| Pilot screw | Preset (turns out not specified) |
| Valve seat size | 2.0 |
| Starter jet | 40 |
| Fuel level | |
|    Rear cylinder | 1.0 +/- 1.0 mm (0.039 +/- 0.039 inch) |
|    Front cylinder | 2.0 +/- 1.0 mm (0.078 +/- 0.039 inch) |

**Tightening torques**

| | |
|---|---|
| Carburetor joint bolts | 10 Nm (7.2 ft-lbs) |
| Exhaust pipe-to-cylinder head nuts | 20 Nm (14 ft-lbs) |

## XV1000 shaft drive models

**Fuel tank**

| | |
|---|---|
| Fuel grade | Regular unleaded gasoline (petrol) |
| Capacity | |
|    Total | 14.5 liters (3.8 US gal, 3.2 Imperial gal) |
|    Reserve | 3.0 liters (0.79 US gal, 0.66 Imperial gal) |

**Carburetors**

| | |
|---|---|
| Type | Hitachi HSC40 (two) |
| Main jet | |
|    Rear cylinder | 124 |
|    Front cylinder | 132 |
| Main air jet | 50 |
| Jet needle | |
|    Rear cylinder | Y-34 |
|    Front cylinder | Y-33 |
| Needle jet | 3.2 |
| Pilot air jet | 190 |
| Pilot jet | 40 |
| Pilot screw | Preset (turns out not specified) |
| Valve seat size | 2.0 |
| Starter jet | 40 |
| Fuel level | 0 +/- 1.0 mm (0 +/- 0.039 inch) |

**Tightening torques**

| | |
|---|---|
| Carburetor joint bolts | 10 Nm (7.2 ft-lbs) |
| Exhaust pipe-to-cylinder head nuts | 20 Nm (14 ft-lbs) |

## XV1000 chain drive models (TR1)

**Fuel tank**

| | |
|---|---|
| Fuel grade | Regular unleaded gasoline (petrol) |
| Capacity | |
|    Total | 19 liters (5.02 US gal, 4.18 Imperial gal) |
|    Reserve | 3.8 liters (1.0 US gal, 0.84 Imperial gal) |

**Carburetors**

| | |
|---|---|
| Type | Hitachi HSC40 (two) |
| Main jet | |
|    Rear cylinder | 126 |
|    Front cylinder | 124 |
| Main air jet | 50 |
| Jet needle | |
|    Rear cylinder | Y-21 |
|    Front cylinder | Y-20 |
| Needle jet | Not specified |
| Pilot air jet | 175 |
| Pilot jet | 43 |
| Pilot screw | Preset (turns out not specified) |
| Valve seat size | 2.0 |
| Starter jet | 40 |
| Fuel level | |
|    Rear cylinder | 1.0 +/- 1.0 mm (0.039 +/- 0.039 inch) |
|    Front cylinder | 2.0 +/- 1.0 mm (0.078 +/- 0.039 inch) |

**Tightening torques**

| | |
|---|---|
| Carburetor joint bolts | 10 Nm (7.2 ft-lbs) |
| Exhaust pipe-to-cylinder head nuts | 20 Nm (14 ft-lbs) |

## XV1100 models (1986 and 1987)

**Fuel tank**

| | |
|---|---|
| Fuel grade | Regular unleaded gasoline (petrol) |
| Capacity | |
|    Total | 16.8 liters (4.43 US gal, 3.69 Imperial gal) |
|    Reserve | 3.0 liters (0.79 US gal, 0.66 Imperial gal) |

**Carburetors**

| | |
|---|---|
| Type | Hitachi HSC40 (two) |
| Main jet | |
|    Rear cylinder | 122 |
|    Front cylinder | 128 |
| Main air jet | 50 |
| Jet needle | Y-33 |
| Needle jet | 3.2 |
| Pilot air jet | 100 |
| Pilot jet | 40 |
| Pilot screw | Preset (turns out not specified) |
| Valve seat size | 1.4 |
| Starter jet | 40 |
| Fuel level | 0 +/- 1.0 mm (0 +/- 0.039 inch) |

**Tightening torques**

| | |
|---|---|
| Carburetor joint bolts | 10 Nm (7.2 ft-lbs) |
| Exhaust pipe-to-cylinder head nuts | 20 Nm (14 ft-lbs) |

## XV1100 models (1988-on)

**Fuel tank**

| | |
|---|---|
| Fuel grade | Regular unleaded gasoline (petrol) |
| Capacity | |
|    Total | 16.8 liters (4.43 US gal, 3.69 Imperial gal) |
|    Reserve | 3.0 liters (0.79 US gal, 0.66 Imperial gal) |

**Carburetors**

| | |
|---|---|
| Type | Mikuni BST40 (two) |
| Main jet (all except 1996 UK) | |
|    Rear cylinder | 122.5 |
|    Front cylinder | 125 |
| Main jet (1996 UK, front and rear) | 122.5 |

| | |
|---|---|
| Main air jet | 80 |
| Jet needle | 5DL8 |
| Needle jet (except 1996 UK) | Y-4 |
| Needle jet (1996 UK) | Y-3 |
| Pilot air jet | |
| No. 1 | 60 |
| No. 2 | 140 |
| Pilot jet | 40 |
| Pilot screw (except 1996 UK) | Turns out not specified |
| Pilot screw (1996 UK) | |
| Front cylinder | 2-1/4 turns out |
| Rear cylinder | 3 turns out |
| Valve seat size | 1.5 |
| Starter jet | 35 |
| Fuel level | 1.5 to 2.5 mm (0.6 to 1.0 inch) |

**Tightening torques**

| | |
|---|---|
| Carburetor joint bolts | 10 Nm (7.2 ft-lbs) |
| Exhaust pipe-to-cylinder head nuts | 20 Nm (14 ft-lbs) |

## 1  General information

The fuel system consists of the fuel tank, the fuel tap and filter, the carburetors and the connecting lines, hoses and control cables. XV1000 and XV1100 models use an electric fuel pump.

The carburetors used on these motorcycles are two Hitachis (early models) or Mikunis (later models) with butterfly-type throttle valves. For cold starting, an enrichment circuit is actuated by a choke lever mounted on the left side of the bike.

The exhaust system routes exhaust gases into a pair of mufflers (silencers) which are mounted on either side of the bike or both on the right side, depending on model.

Many of the fuel system service procedures are considered routine maintenance items and for that reason are included in Chapter 1.

## 2  Fuel tank - removal and installation

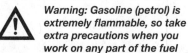

⚠ **Warning: Gasoline (petrol) is extremely flammable, so take extra precautions when you work on any part of the fuel system. Don't smoke or allow open flames or bare light bulbs near the work area, and don't work in a garage where a natural gas-type appliance (such as a water heater or clothes dryer) is present. If you spill any fuel on your skin, rinse it off immediately with soap and water. When you perform any kind of work on the fuel system, wear safety glasses and have a fire extinguisher suitable for class B fires (flammable liquids) on hand.**

1  Support the bike securely so it can't be knocked over during this procedure.
2  Remove the seat (see Chapter 7).
3  Detach the rear end of the tank from the motorcycle. If you're working on an early model, remove the clip **(see illustration)**. If you're working on a later model, remove the bolt.
4  Pull the tank backward to separate it from its mounting dampers. Label and disconnect the hoses and wires and remove the tank from the motorcycle.
5  Before installing the tank, check the condition of the hoses and rubber mounting dampers - if they're hardened, cracked, or show any other signs of deterioration, replace them.
6  To install the tank, reverse the above procedure. Make sure the tank seats properly and does not pinch any control cables or wires.

## 3  Fuel tank - cleaning and repair

1  All repairs to the fuel tank should be carried out by a professional who has experience in

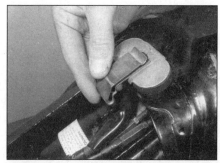

**2.3  On early models, remove the clip to detach the tank; on later models, remove the mounting bolt**

this critical and potentially dangerous work. Even after cleaning and flushing of the fuel system, explosive fumes can remain and ignite during repair of the tank.
2  If the fuel tank is removed from the vehicle, it should not be placed in an area where sparks or open flames could ignite the fumes coming out of the tank. Be especially careful inside garages where a natural gas-type appliance is located, because the pilot light could cause an explosion.

## 4  Idle fuel/air mixture adjustment - general information

1  Due to the increased emphasis on controlling motorcycle exhaust emissions, certain governmental regulations have been formulated which directly affect the carburetion of this machine. In order to comply with the regulations, the carburetors on some models have a metal sealing plug pressed into the hole over the pilot screw (which controls the idle fuel/air mixture) on each carburetor, so they can't be tampered with. These should only be removed in the event of a complete carburetor overhaul, and even then the screws should be returned to their original settings. The pilot screws on other models are accessible, but the use of an exhaust gas analyzer is the only accurate way to adjust the idle fuel/air mixture and be sure the machine doesn't exceed the emissions regulations.
2  If the engine runs extremely rough or blows black smoke at idle or continually stalls, and if a carburetor overhaul does not cure the problem, take the motorcycle to a Yamaha dealer service department or other repair shop equipped with an exhaust gas analyzer. They will be able to properly adjust the idle fuel/air mixture to achieve a smooth idle and restore low speed performance.

## 5  Carburetor overhaul - general information

**1** Poor engine performance, hesitation, hard starting, stalling, flooding and backfiring are all signs that major carburetor maintenance may be required.

**2** Keep in mind that many so-called carburetor problems are really not carburetor problems at all, but mechanical problems within the engine or ignition system malfunctions. Try to establish for certain that the carburetors are in need of maintenance before beginning a major overhaul.

**3** Check the fuel filter, the fuel lines, the fuel tank breather hose(s), the rollover valve (if equipped), the intake manifold hose clamps, the vacuum hoses, the air filter element, the cylinder compression, the spark plugs, the carburetor synchronization and the fuel pump before assuming that a carburetor overhaul is required.

**4** Most carburetor problems are caused by dirt particles, varnish and other deposits which build up in and block the fuel and air passages. Also, in time, gaskets and O-rings shrink or deteriorate and cause fuel and air leaks which lead to poor performance.

**5** When the carburetor is overhauled, it is generally disassembled completely and the parts are cleaned thoroughly with a carburetor cleaning solvent and dried with filtered, unlubricated compressed air. The fuel and air passages are also blown through with compressed air to force out any dirt that may have been loosened but not removed by the solvent. Once the cleaning process is complete, the carburetor is reassembled using new gaskets, O-rings and, generally, a new inlet needle valve and seat.

**6** Before disassembling the carburetors, make sure you have a carburetor rebuild kit (which will include all necessary O-rings and other parts), some carburetor cleaner, a supply of rags, some means of blowing out the carburetor passages and a clean place to work. It is recommended that only one carburetor be overhauled at a time to avoid mixing up parts.

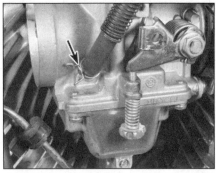

**6.3  Squeeze the clip (arrowed) and slide it down the fuel line, then pry the fuel line off the fitting**

**7** Don't separate the carburetors from each other unless one of the joints between them is leaking. The carburetors can be overhauled completely without being separated, and reconnecting them properly can be difficult.

## 6  Carburetors and intake joints - removal and installation

⚠️ **Warning: Gasoline (petrol) is extremely flammable, so take extra precautions when you work on any part of the fuel system. Don't smoke or allow open flames or bare light bulbs near the work area, and don't work in a garage where a natural gas-type appliance (such as a water heater or clothes dryer) is present. If you spill any fuel on your skin, rinse it off immediately with soap and water. When you perform any kind of work on the fuel system, wear safety glasses and have an extinguisher suitable for class B fires (flammable liquids) on hand.**

### Removal

**1** Lift or remove the seat as necessary (see Chapter 7) and remove the fuel tank (see Section 2). If you're working on a 1984 or later model, remove the mixture control valve case (see Chapter 7).

**2** Disconnect the throttle and choke cables (see Section 9).

**6.4  Loosen the air hose screws (A) and the choke cable screw (B), then disconnect the choke cable (C)**

**3** Disconnect the fuel inlet lines from the carburetor fittings **(see illustration)**. Label and disconnect all hoses, vacuum lines and wires.

**4** Loosen the clamp screws and disconnect the air cleaner hoses from the carburetors **(see illustration)**. Detach the hoses from the air cleaner and carburetors and remove them from the motorcycle.

**5** Loosen the clamp screws on the carburetor intake joints. Twist the carburetors clockwise to free them from the joints and lift them out **(see illustrations)**.

**6** After the carburetors have been removed, stuff clean rags into the joints or intake ports to prevent the entry of dirt or other objects.

**7** Inspect the air cleaner hoses and carburetor intake joints. If they're cracked or brittle, replace them **(see illustration)**.

### Installation

**8** Installation is the reverse of the removal steps, with the following additions:
a) Lightly lubricate the ends of the throttle cable(s) and the choke cable with multi-purpose grease and attach them to the throttle pulley and choke lever. Make sure the accelerator cable (and decelerator cable if equipped) are in their proper positions.
b) Make sure the carburetor is seated securely in the intake joints and the air cleaner hoses are fitted securely over the carburetors, then tighten the clamping band screws.

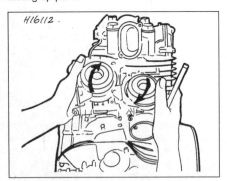

**6.5a  Loosen the intake joint clamp screws and twist the carburetors clockwise . . .**

**6.5b  . . . to free them from the intake joints**

**6.7  Label and disconnect any vacuum hoses attached to the intake joints**

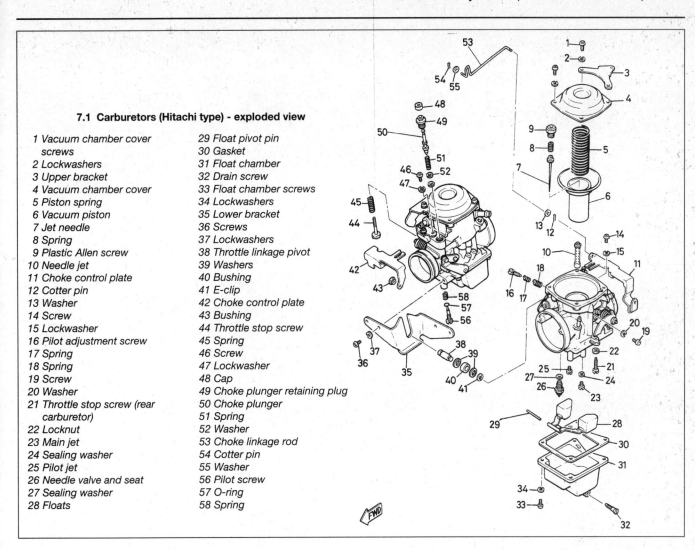

**7.1 Carburetors (Hitachi type) - exploded view**

1 Vacuum chamber cover screws
2 Lockwashers
3 Upper bracket
4 Vacuum chamber cover
5 Piston spring
6 Vacuum piston
7 Jet needle
8 Spring
9 Plastic Allen screw
10 Needle jet
11 Choke control plate
12 Cotter pin
13 Washer
14 Screw
15 Lockwasher
16 Pilot adjustment screw
17 Spring
18 Spring
19 Screw
20 Washer
21 Throttle stop screw (rear carburetor)
22 Locknut
23 Main jet
24 Sealing washer
25 Pilot jet
26 Needle valve and seat
27 Sealing washer
28 Floats

29 Float pivot pin
30 Gasket
31 Float chamber
32 Drain screw
33 Float chamber screws
34 Lockwashers
35 Lower bracket
36 Screws
37 Lockwashers
38 Throttle linkage pivot
39 Washers
40 Bushing
41 E-clip
42 Choke control plate
43 Bushing
44 Throttle stop screw
45 Spring
46 Screw
47 Lockwasher
48 Cap
49 Choke plunger retaining plug
50 Choke plunger
51 Spring
52 Washer
53 Choke linkage rod
54 Cotter pin
55 Washer
56 Pilot screw
57 O-ring
58 Spring

c) Adjust the throttle grip freeplay (see Chapter 1).
d) Check and, if necessary, adjust the idle speed and carburetor synchronization (see Chapter 1).

**7 Carburetors** - disassembly, inspection, cleaning and reassembly

⚠ **Warning: Gasoline (petrol) is extremely flammable, so take extra precautions when you work on any part of the fuel system. Don't smoke or allow open flames or bare light bulbs near the work area, and don't work in a garage where a natural gas-type appliance (such as a water heater or clothes dryer) is present. If you spill any fuel on your skin, rinse it off immediately with soap and water. When you perform any kind of work on the fuel system, wear safety glasses and have a fire extinguisher suitable for class B type fires (flammable liquids) on hand.**

### Hitachi carburetors

#### Disassembly

**1** Remove the carburetors from the machine as described in Section 6. Set the assembly on a clean working surface. **Note:** *Work on one carburetor at a time to avoid getting parts mixed up* **(see illustration)**. *Most disassembly and cleaning procedures can be* accomplished without separating the carburetors.
**2** Remove the screws and detach the top bracket from the carburetor assembly.
**3** Remove the cotter pin and washer and disconnect the choke linkage rod from the left carburetor **(see illustration)**.
**4** Remove the screws and detach the bottom bracket **(see illustration)**.
**5** Carefully note how the carburetors fit

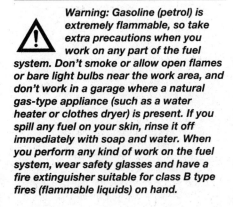

**7.3 Remove the cotter pin and washer and disconnect the choke linkage rod**

**7.4 Remove the screws and detach the bottom bracket**

7.5a  Note carefully how the carburetors fit together . . .

7.5b  . . . then pull them apart

7.6  Remove the E-clip and separate the linkage assembly

7.7  Remove the screws and lift off the vacuum chamber cover, spring and gasket

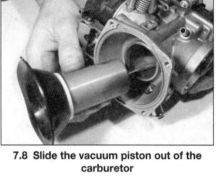

7.8  Slide the vacuum piston out of the carburetor

together, then pull them apart (see illustrations).

6 Detach the E-clip from the center pivot of the throttle linkage and separate the two halves of the linkage assembly (see illustration).

7 Remove the vacuum chamber cover screws. Take off the cover and gasket and remove the piston spring (see illustration).

8 Taking care not to tear the diaphragm, lift the piston and jet needle out of the carburetor (see illustration).

9 Detach the choke control plate and slip it out of its groove in the choke plunger (see illustration).

10 Unscrew the choke plunger from the carburetor (see illustration).

11 Remove the float chamber cover screws and lift off the cover and gasket (see illustration).

12 Slide the float off its pivot pin and lift out the float together with the needle valve (see illustrations).

13 Unscrew the needle valve seat and remove it, together with the sealing washer and filter cap (see illustration).

14 Make sure the screwdriver is an exact fit in the slot of the pilot jet, then unscrew it (see illustration). Unscrew the main jet and remove its sealing washer (see illustration).

15 Turn the carburetor over and tap it on your hand so the needle jet slides down out of the carburetor body (see illustration). Remove the needle jet through the throttle bore.

7.9  Slip the choke control plate fingers out of the groove in the choke plunger

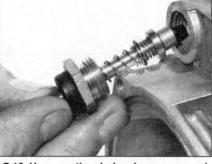

7.10  Unscrew the choke plunger cap and take the plunger out of the carburetor body

7.11  Remove the float chamber cover and gasket

7.12a  Push the float pivot pin partway out with a thin punch, then pull it clear . . .

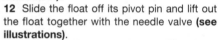

7.12b  . . . and lift out the floats together with the needle valve

**7.13 Unscrew the needle valve seat and remove it together with its sealing washer**

**7.14a Unscrew the pilot jet . . .**

**7.14b . . . and the main jet and sealing washer**

**16** The pilot (idle mixture) screw is located in a passage in the carburetor body. On US models, this screw is hidden behind a plug which will have to be removed if the screw is to be taken out. To do this, drill a hole in the plug, being careful not to drill into the screw, then pry the plug out or remove it with a small slide hammer. On all models, turn the pilot screw in, counting the number of turns until it bottoms lightly. Record that number for use when installing the screw. Now remove the pilot screw along with its spring, washer and O-ring **(see illustration 7.1)**.

**Inspection**

**17** Remove the plastic Allen screw from inside the piston, then remove the jet needle and spring **(see illustration)**. Separate the screw and spring from the jet needle **(see**

**illustration)**. Check the jet needle for straightness by rolling it on a flat surface (such as a piece of glass). Replace it if it's bent or if the tip is worn. Check the jet needle and the needle jet **(see illustration)** for wear where they contact each other and replace them if they're worn. Make sure the small holes in the needle jet are clear.

**18** Check the operation of the choke plunger **(see illustration)**. If it doesn't move smoothly, replace it, along with the return spring. Inspect the needle on the end of the choke plunger and replace it if it's worn.

**19** Check the tapered portion of the pilot screw for wear or damage. Replace the pilot screw if necessary.

**20** Check the carburetor body, float chamber cover and vacuum chamber cover for cracks,

distorted sealing surfaces and other damage. If any defects are found, replace the faulty component, although replacement of the entire carburetor will probably be necessary (check with your parts supplier for the availability of separate components).

**21** Check the diaphragm for splits, holes and general deterioration. Holding it up to a light will help to reveal problems of this nature.

**22** Insert the vacuum piston in the carburetor body and see that it moves up-and-down smoothly. Check the surface of the piston for wear. If it's worn excessively or doesn't move smoothly in the bore, replace the carburetor.

**23** Operate the throttle shaft to make sure the throttle butterfly valve opens and closes smoothly **(see illustration)**. If it doesn't, replace the carburetor.

**7.15 Tap the carburetor in your hand to shake the needle jet free of its bore**

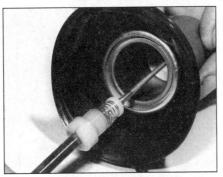

**7.17a Remove the plastic Allen screw, the spring and jet needle . . .**

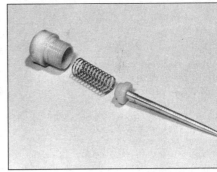

**7.17b . . . then separate the components**

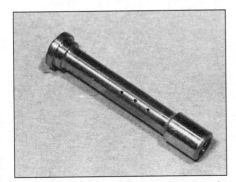

**7.17c Check the needle jet for wear and clogged holes**

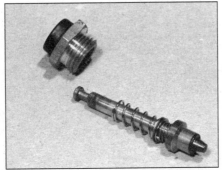

**7.18 Check the choke plunger for sticky operation and a worn needle**

**7.23 Check the throttle valve shaft and carburetor body for wear**

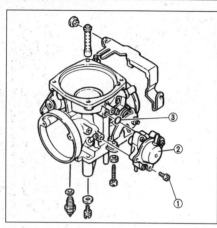

**7.24  Remove the screws (1), the coasting enricher (2) and the O-ring (3)**

24 If you're working on a 1986 or 1987 XV1100, remove the coasting enricher diaphragm and check it for tears or brittleness **(see illustration)**. Replace it if its condition is in doubt.

25 Check the floats for damage. This will usually be apparent by the presence of fuel inside one of the floats. If the floats are damaged, they must be replaced.

26 Check the needle valve for wear or damage **(see illustration)**. If there's a pronounced groove around the tip of the valve, replace it.

27 Check the needle valve seat for wear or damage **(see illustration)**. Check the filter cap for clogging and clean or replace it as necessary. The sealing washer should be replaced whenever the needle valve seat is removed.

## Cleaning

*Caution: Use only a petroleum based solvent for carburetor cleaning. Don't use caustic cleaners.*

28 Submerge the metal components in the solvent for approximately thirty minutes (or longer, if the directions recommend it).

29 After the carburetor has soaked long enough for the cleaner to loosen and dissolve most of the varnish and other deposits, use a brush to remove the stubborn deposits. Rinse it again, then dry it with compressed air. Blow

**7.30  Position the diaphragm tab in the notch**

out all of the fuel and air passages in the main body.

*Caution: Never clean the jets or passages with a piece of wire or a drill bit, as they will be enlarged, causing the fuel and air metering rates to be upset.*

## Reassembly

*Caution: When installing the jets, be careful not to over-tighten them - they're made of soft material and can strip or shear easily.*

**Note:** When reassembling the carburetors, be sure to use the new O-rings, gaskets and other parts supplied in the rebuild kit.

30 Assembly is the reverse of the disassembly steps, with the following additions.

**7.26  Check the needle valve for wear at the tip**

**7.27  Check the needle valve seat for wear and the filter for clogging or tears; fit a new sealing washer**

a) Be sure the needle jet is pushed all the way into its bore. When you install the vacuum piston, be sure the jet needle fits into the needle jet.

b) Align the protrusion on the vacuum piston and diaphragm with the notch in the carburetor body **(see illustration)**.

c) Install the carburetors (see Section 6) and check the fuel level (see Section 8).

## *Mikuni carburetors*

### Disassembly

31 Remove the carburetors from the machine as described in Section 6. Set the assembly on a clean working surface. **Note:** *Work on one carburetor at a time to avoid getting parts mixed up* **(see illustration)**. *The throttle*

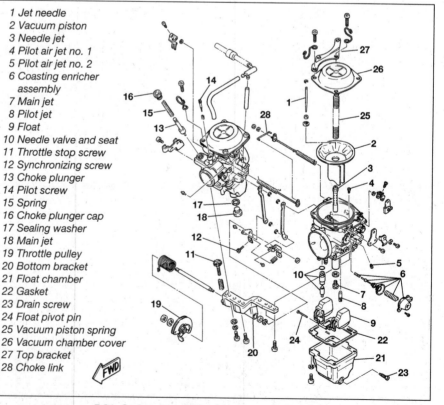

1 Jet needle
2 Vacuum piston
3 Needle jet
4 Pilot air jet no. 1
5 Pilot air jet no. 2
6 Coasting enricher assembly
7 Main jet
8 Pilot jet
9 Float
10 Needle valve and seat
11 Throttle stop screw
12 Synchronizing screw
13 Choke plunger
14 Pilot screw
15 Spring
16 Choke plunger cap
17 Sealing washer
18 Main jet
19 Throttle pulley
20 Bottom bracket
21 Float chamber
22 Gasket
23 Drain screw
24 Float pivot pin
25 Vacuum piston spring
26 Vacuum chamber cover
27 Top bracket
28 Choke link

**7.31  Carburetors (Mikuni type) - exploded view**

*valves, vacuum pistons and choke plungers can be removed and inspected without separating the carburetors.*

**32** Remove the screws and detach the top bracket.

**33** Disconnect the choke link that fits between the choke shafts.

**34** Carefully note how they're assembled, then remove the synchronizing screw and spring. Remove the nut and lockwasher from their locations on the throttle shaft next to the synchronizing screw and spring.

**35** Remove its mounting screws and detach the throttle shaft assembly. Carefully note how they fit together, then detach the throttle levers and collar and separate the carburetors.

**36** Working on one carburetor, remove the lever and washer at the end of the choke shaft, then remove the choke shaft and spring from the carburetor.

**37** Remove the choke plunger nut, then remove the spring and choke plunger from the carburetor.

**38** Remove the vacuum chamber cover screws. Carefully lift off the cover, taking care not to tear the diaphragm.

**39** Remove the spring and the diaphragm, together with the vacuum piston.

**40** Unscrew pilot air jet no. 1 from its bore underneath the diaphragm.

**41** Remove the screws and detach the coasting enricher valve from the carburetor. Remove the large spring, diaphragm, holder, pushrod and small spring from the coasting enricher housing.

**42** Unscrew pilot air jet no. 2 from its bore in the coasting enricher housing.

**43** Remove the float chamber cover screws, then detach the cover and gasket.

**44** Push out the float pivot pin with a small-diameter punch (2 mm) and remove the floats.

**45** Remove the screw and take out the needle valve seat.

**46** Unscrew and remove the pilot jet and the main jet together with its washer. Remove the needle jet.

### Inspection

**47** Remove the spring seat from inside the piston, then remove the clip, ring and jet needle. Check the jet needle for straightness by rolling it on a flat surface (such as a piece of glass). Replace it if it's bent or if the tip is worn. Check the jet needle and the needle jet for wear where they contact each other and replace them if they're worn. Make sure the small holes in the needle jet are clear.

**48** Check the operation of the choke plunger. If it doesn't move smoothly, replace it, along with the return spring. Inspect the needle on the end of the choke plunger and replace it if it's worn.

**49** Check the carburetor body, float chamber cover and vacuum chamber cover for cracks, distorted sealing surfaces and other damage. If any defects are found, replace the faulty component, although replacement of the

entire carburetor will probably be necessary (check with your parts supplier for the availability of separate components).

**50** Check the diaphragm for splits, holes and general deterioration. Holding it up to a light will help to reveal problems of this nature.

**51** Insert the vacuum piston in the carburetor body and see that it moves up-and-down smoothly. Check the surface of the piston for wear. If it's worn excessively or doesn't move smoothly in the bore, replace the carburetor.

**52** Operate the throttle shaft to make sure the throttle butterfly valve opens and closes smoothly. If it doesn't, replace the carburetor.

**53** Check the coasting enricher diaphragm for tears or brittleness. Replace it if its condition is in doubt.

**54** Check the floats for damage. This will usually be apparent by the presence of fuel inside one of the floats. If the floats are damaged, they must be replaced.

**55** Check the needle valve for wear or damage **(see illustration 7.26)**. If there's a pronounced groove around the tip of the valve, replace it.

**56** Check the needle valve seat for wear or damage. Check the filter cap for clogging and clean or replace it as necessary. The sealing washer should be replaced whenever the needle valve seat is removed.

### Cleaning

**57** Perform Steps 28 and 29 above to clean the carburetor components.

### Reassembly

*Caution: When installing the jets, be careful not to over-tighten them - they're made of soft material and can strip or shear easily.*

**Note:** When reassembling the carburetors, be sure to use the new O-rings, gaskets and other parts supplied in the rebuild kit.

**58** Assembly is the reverse of the disassembly steps, with the following additions.

a) *Be sure the needle jet is pushed all the way into its bore. When you install the vacuum piston, be sure the jet needle fits into the needle jet.*

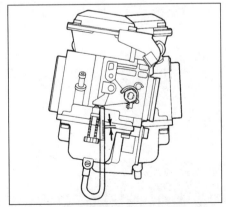

**8.3 A gauge like this or a clear tube and ruler can be used to measure fuel level**

b) *Align the protrusion on the vacuum piston and diaphragm with the notch in the carburetor body.*

c) *Install the carburetors (see Section 6) and check the fuel level (see Section 8).*

## 8 Carburetors - fuel level adjustment

> *Warning: Gasoline (petrol) is extremely flammable, so take extra precautions when you work on any part of the fuel system. Don't smoke or allow open flames or bare light bulbs near the work area, and don't work in a garage where a natural gas-type appliance (such as a water heater or clothes dryer) is present. If you spill any fuel on your skin, rinse it off immediately with soap and water. When you perform any kind of work on the fuel system, wear safety glasses and have a fire extinguisher suitable for class B type fires (flammable liquids) on hand.*

**1** Support the bike securely in an upright position so it can't be knocked over during this procedure.

**2** Remove components as necessary for access to the float chamber drain screws.

**3** Attach Yamaha service tool no. YM-01312 (UK part no. 90890-01312) to the drain fitting on the bottom of one of the carburetor float chambers (both will be checked) **(see illustration)**. This is a clear plastic tube graduated in millimeters. An alternative is to use a length of clear plastic tubing and an accurate ruler. Hold the graduated tube (or the free end of the clear plastic tube) vertically against the float chamber cover.

**4** Unscrew the drain screw at the bottom of the float chamber a couple of turns, then start the engine and let it idle - fuel will flow into the tube. Wait for the fuel level to stabilize, then note how far the fuel level is below the line on the float chamber cover.

**5** Measure the distance between the indicator line and the top of the fuel level in the tube or gauge. This distance is the fuel level - write it down on a piece of paper, tighten the drain screw, then move on to the other carburetor and check it the same way.

**6** Compare your fuel level readings to the value listed in this Chapter's Specifications. If the fuel level in either carburetor is not correct, remove the float chamber cover and bend the tang up or down as necessary, then recheck the fuel level.

## 9 Throttle cables and grip - removal, installation and adjustment

### Removal

**1** Loosen the throttle cable(s) with the adjusters and remove the throttle cable

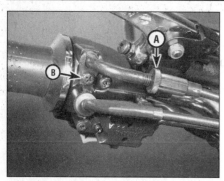

9.1 Loosen the locknut (A) and turn the adjuster to create slack; remove the cable securing screw (B)

9.3a Pull the cable housing out of the bracket and slip the cable through the slot (arrow) . . .

9.3b . . . then align the cable with the slot in the throttle pulley fitting and slip the cable end out

securing screw at the handlebar **(see illustration)**.

2 Remove the handlebar switch mounting screws. Separate the halves of the handlebar switch and detach the throttle cable(s) from the throttle grip pulley (see Chapter 8).

3 Detach the throttle cables from the throttle pulley at the carburetors **(see illustrations)**. Remove the cables, noting how they are routed.

4 Slide the throttle grip off the handlebar.

## Installation

5 Clean the handlebar and apply a light coat of multi-purpose grease.

10.1 Loosen the screw and detach the cable housing from the bracket

6 Route the cable(s) into place, following the same route noted on removal. Make sure they don't interfere with any other components and aren't kinked or bent sharply.

7 Lubricate the ends of the accelerator cable (and decelerator cable if equipped) with multi-purpose grease and connect them to the throttle pulleys at the carburetors and at the throttle grip.

## Adjustment

8 Follow the procedure outlined in Chapter 1, Throttle operation/grip freeplay - check and adjustment, to adjust the cables.

9 Turn the handlebars back and forth to make sure the cables don't cause the steering to bind. With the engine idling, turn the handlebars back and forth and make sure idle speed doesn't change. If it does, find and fix the cause before riding the motorcycle.

## 10 Choke cable - removal and installation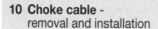

1 Remove the choke cable bracket at the carburetors **(see illustration)**. Align the cable with the slot in the lever and remove it from the lever.

2 Remove the choke lever securing screw at the handlebar **(see illustration)**. Remove the lever and disconnect the choke cable from the pulley.

3 Installation is the reverse of the removal steps.

## 11 Exhaust system - removal and installation

## Removal

1 Support the bike securely so it can't be knocked over during this procedure.

2 Remove the nuts that secure the front exhaust pipe to the cylinder head **(see illustration)**.

3 Support the exhaust system so it can't fall and remove the mounting fasteners **(see illustrations)**. Lower the exhaust system away from the bike and take it out.

## Installation

4 Installation is the reverse of removal, with the following additions:
a) *Use new gaskets at the cylinder head.*
b) *Tighten all fasteners to the torque settings listed in this Chapter's Specifications.*

10.2 Remove the screw (arrow) and detach the choke lever

11.2 Remove the nuts that secure the flange plate to the cylinder head

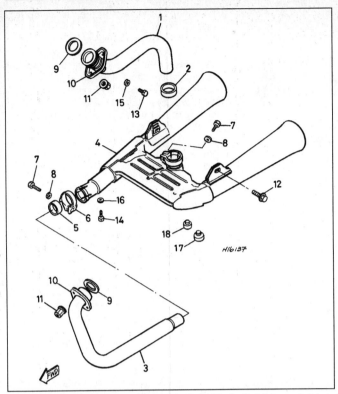

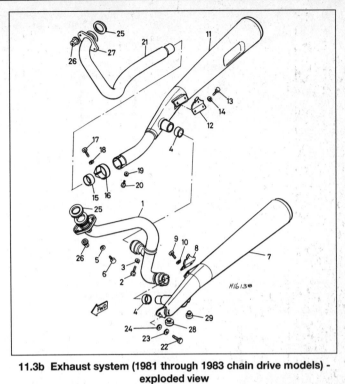

**11.3a  Exhaust system (1981 through 1983 shaft drive models) - exploded view**

| | | |
|---|---|---|
| 1 Rear cylinder pipe | 7 Bolt | 13 Bolt |
| 2 Gasket | 8 Washer | 14 Bolt |
| 3 Front cylinder pipe | 9 Sealing ring | 15 Washer |
| 4 Muffler/silencer pipe | 10 Flange plate | 16 Washer |
| 5 Gasket | 11 Nut | 17 Rubber damper |
| 6 Clamp | 12 Bolt | 18 Rubber damper |

**11.3b  Exhaust system (1981 through 1983 chain drive models) - exploded view**

| | | |
|---|---|---|
| 1 Rear cylinder pipe | 11 Right muffler/silencer | 20 Bolt |
| 2 Bolt | 12 Mounting bracket | 21 Front cylinder pipe |
| 3 Washer | 13 Bolt | 22 Bolt |
| 4 Gasket | 14 Lockwasher | 23 Lockwasher |
| 5 Washer | 15 Gasket | 24 Washer |
| 6 Bolt | 16 Clamp | 25 Sealing ring |
| 7 Left muffler/silencer | 17 Bolt | 26 Nut |
| 8 Mounting bracket | 18 Washer | 27 Flange plate |
| 9 Bolt | 19 Washer | 28 Rubber damper |
| 10 Lockwasher | | 29 Rubber damper |

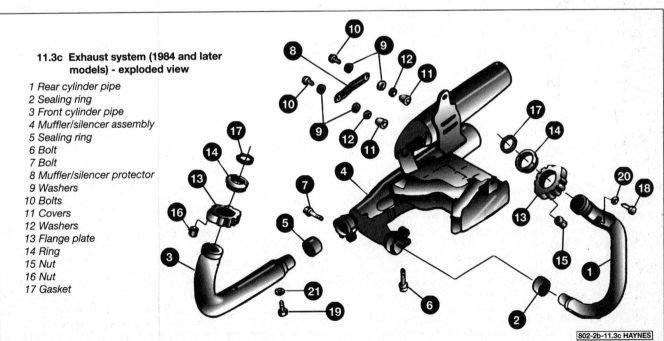

**11.3c  Exhaust system (1984 and later models) - exploded view**

1 Rear cylinder pipe
2 Sealing ring
3 Front cylinder pipe
4 Muffler/silencer assembly
5 Sealing ring
6 Bolt
7 Bolt
8 Muffler/silencer protector
9 Washers
10 Bolts
11 Covers
12 Washers
13 Flange plate
14 Ring
15 Nut
16 Nut
17 Gasket

802-2b-11.3c HAYNES

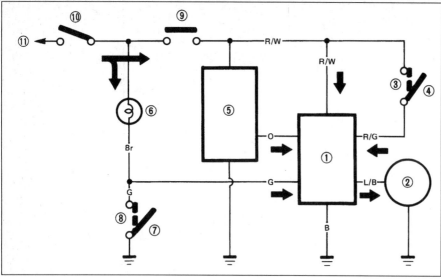

**12.2 Fuel pump circuit**

1 Fuel pump controller
2 Fuel pump
3 Fuel reserve switch (Res
    position)
4 Fuel reserve switch (On
    position)
5 Igniter unit
6 Fuel warning light
7 Fuel sender (Full position)
8 Fuel sender (Empty
    position)
9 Engine kill switch
10 Ignition (main key) switch
11 To main fuse and battery

## 12 Fuel pump - circuit check and fuel pump test

1 With the engine kill switch in the On position, the fuel pump should start and run for approximately five seconds after the ignition is switched on (with the fuel warning light on or off). It should shut off once the carburetor float chambers are full, then run again once the engine is started.

2 The fuel pump circuit consists of the pump, the pump controller, the igniter unit (which controls the fuel pump as well as ignition timing), the engine kill switch, the ignition switch, the main and ignition fuses, the battery and related wiring **(see illustration)**.

3 Lift or remove the seat.

4 Check the battery condition and charge (see Chapter 1 and Chapter 8).

5 Check the main and ignition fuses, the ignition switch and the engine kill switch (see Chapter 8). Replace them if they're defective, then try the fuel pump again.

### Pump won't run after engine is started

6 If the pump won't run while the engine is running, check battery voltage to the pump. Disconnect the fuel pump electrical connector and connect a 20-volt DC voltmeter between the blue/black wire terminal in the harness and a good grounding/earthing point (bare metal on the engine).

7 Turn the ignition switch to On and the engine kill switch to Run, then push the Start switch. The voltmeter should indicate more than 11 volts. If the reading is more than

11 volts, test the fuel pump (see Step 24 below).

8 If the reading is less than 11 volts, test the output voltage of the igniter's orange lead. To do this, check the spark output of the rear cylinder (see Chapter 4). If the spark will jump the specified gap, you can assume that the igniter output voltage is within specifications. Go to Step 10 below.

9 If the spark won't jump the specified gap, measure the igniter input voltage at the red wire **(see illustration 12.2)**.

a) *If it's at least 12 volts, the igniter may be defective. Check the ignition system as described in Chapter 4.*

b) *If there's no voltage at the red wire, check the engine kill switch, ignition main key switch and the main fuse. Check the wiring in the fuel pump circuit for breaks or bad connections. Be sure to check the battery terminal connections and the battery ground/earth cable connection to the motorcycle.*

10 Make sure the fuel pump controller ground/earth wire is clean and tight. If it is, test the fuel pump controller (see Step 24 below).

### Fuel pump doesn't run for five seconds when ignition is switched on

11 With the fuel reserve switch set to Res and the kill switch in the On position, switch on the ignition. If the fuel level in the carburetors is low, the pump should run for five seconds. If it doesn't, perform the following steps.

12 Place the ignition switch, kill switch and fuel reserve switch in the On position, but don't start the engine.

13 Check for voltage at the fuel pump (see Step 6 above).

a) *If it's more than 11 volts, go to Step 14.*

b) *If it's less than 11 volts, go to Step 17.*

14 Turn the fuel reserve switch to the Res position and recheck voltage.

a) *If it's still more than 11 volts, test the fuel pump (see Step 24 below).*

b) *If it's less than 11 volts, go to Step 15.*

15 Connect a 0-20 volt voltmeter between the red/green wire at the fuel pump controller and a good ground/earth connection (bare metal on the motorcycle).

a) *If there's no voltage, test the reserve switch (see Chapter 8).*

b) *If the reading is 12 volts, go to Step 16.*

16 Make sure the fuel pump controller ground/earth wire (black) is clean and tightly connected. If this doesn't solve the problem, test the fuel pump controller (see Step 25 below).

17 If voltage at the fuel pump was less than 11 volts in Step 14, Connect the positive lead of a 0-20 volt voltmeter to the pump controller red/white wire and the negative lead to ground/earth.

a) *If there's no voltage, check the ignition switch, kill switch, main fuse and battery (see Chapter 8).*

b) *If the reading is 12 volts, make sure the fuel pump controller ground/earth wire (black) is clean and tightly connected. If this doesn't solve the problem, test the fuel pump controller (see Step 25 below).*

### Fuel pump doesn't stop with warning light on

18 The fuel pump should stop running within 30 seconds if the fuel warning light comes on with the engine running. If it doesn't, perform Steps 19 through 23 below.

19 Disconnect the fuel pump electrical connector and connect a 20-volt DC voltmeter between the blue/black wire terminal in the harness and a good grounding/earthing point (bare metal on the engine) **(see illustration 12.2)**.

20 Locate the green wire in the fuel sender connector.

21 Start the engine. Disconnect the green wire and note the reading on the voltmeter 30 seconds later.

a) *If there's no voltage, check the fuel pump circuit wiring for breaks or bad connections. Repair as necessary.*

b) *If there's more than 11 volts, go to Step 22.*

22 Test the fuel sender (see below).

a) *If the resistance is not within the range listed in this Chapter's Specifications, replace the sender.*

b) *If the sender is good, go to Step 23.*

23 Make sure the fuel pump controller ground/earth wire is clean and tightly connected. Repair as necessary. If this doesn't solve the problem, test the fuel pump controller (see below).

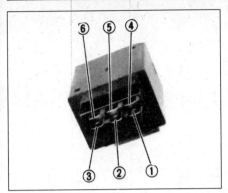

12.27a Fuel pump controller terminals

## Fuel pump test

24 Disconnect the wiring connector from the fuel pump. Connect the pump directly to the battery with two lengths of wire (positive to blue/black; negative to black). If the pump doesn't run, replace it.

13.1 The fuel pump is located under this cover

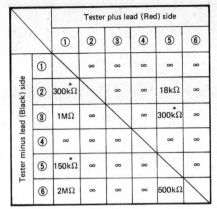

| Tester plus lead (Red) side | | | | | | |
|---|---|---|---|---|---|---|
| | ① | ② | ③ | ④ | ⑤ | ⑥ |
| ① | | ∞ | ∞ | ∞ | ∞ | ∞ |
| ② | 300kΩ* | | ∞ | ∞ | 18kΩ | ∞ |
| ③ | 1MΩ | ∞ | | ∞ | 300kΩ* | ∞ |
| ④ | ∞ | ∞ | ∞ | | ∞ | ∞ |
| ⑤ | 150kΩ* | ∞ | ∞ | ∞ | | ∞ |
| ⑥ | 2MΩ | ∞ | ∞ | ∞ | 500kΩ | |

*(leftmost column label, rotated: Tester minus lead (Black) side)*

12.27b Connect an ohmmeter between terminal pairs and note the readings

*Wait a few seconds after connecting the ohmmeter to take this reading.*

## Fuel pump controller test

25 Remove the seat (see Chapter 7).
26 Unplug the fuel pump controller and remove it.
27 Connect an ohmmeter between the controller terminals in turn and measure the resistance (see illustrations). If the resistance is not as specified, replace the controller.

## Fuel sender test

28 Remove the fuel tank (see Section 2).
29 Remove the screws and detach the sender from the tank.
30 Connect an ohmmeter to the terminals of the sender harness. Raise the float to a height of 42 mm (XV700) or 22 mm (XV1000/1100) from the base and note the meter reading. It should be 0.9 to 1.3 K-ohms if the sender is functioning correctly.

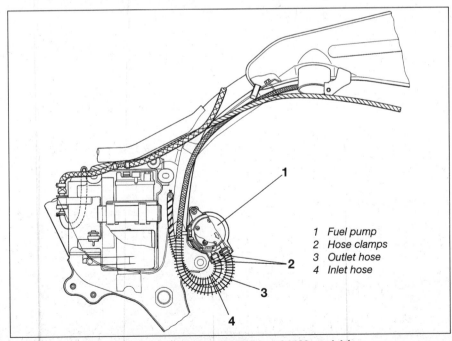

1 Fuel pump
2 Hose clamps
3 Outlet hose
4 Inlet hose

13.2 Fuel pump hoses (XV1000 and 1100 models)

## 13 Fuel pump - replacement

1 Remove the cover from the fuel pump (see illustration).
2 Loosen the fuel line clamps and push the ends of the fuel lines off the pump fittings (see illustration).
3 Disconnect the pump electrical connector. Remove the mounting bolts and take the pump out.
4 Installation is the reverse of the removal steps.

## 14 Mixture control valve (all 1981 through 1983 models and TR1; 1984 and 1985 XV700)

### Testing

1 If you're working on a 1981 through 1983 model, unclip the plastic cowl for access to the mixture control valve (see illustration).
2 If you're working on a 1984 or 1985 XV700, remove the case cover (on the left side of the motorcycle between the cylinders).
3 Start the engine and let it idle. Hold a strip of paper next to the inlet side of the valve.
4 Raise engine speed to 5,000 rpm. The paper should be pulled toward the valve by air flow. If it isn't, check the vacuum hoses to the valve (see illustrations). If they're in good condition and properly connected, replace the valve.

14.1 Remove the plastic cowl for access to the mixture control valve

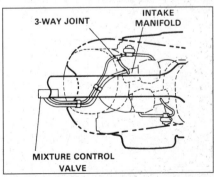

14.4a Mixture control valve hose routing (1981 through 1983 models)

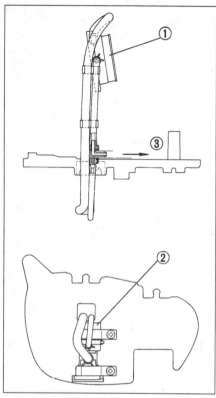

14.4b  Mixture control valve hose routing
(1984 through 1987 XV700 models)

1  Carburetor intake joint
2  Mixture control valve
3  To fuel tap

## Replacement

**5** Detach the valve from its clip **(see illustration)**. Label and disconnect the hoses.
**6** Attach the hoses to the valve and secure it in its clip.

14.5  Unclip the mixture control valve and
disconnect its hoses

## 15  Air induction system (XV1000, XV1100 and 1988 and later XV750)

**1** The air induction system uses exhaust gas pulses to suck fresh air into the exhaust ports, where it mixes with hot combustion gases. The additional oxygen provided by the fresh air allows combustion to continue for a longer time, reducing unburned hydrocarbons in the exhaust. Reed valves allow the flow of air into the ports and prevent exhaust gas from flowing into the system. The air cut valve shuts off the flow of air into the system during deceleration to prevent backfiring. The system uses a mixture control valve similar to that described in Section 14.
**2** Check the hoses for loose connections, damage and deterioration **(see illustrations)**. Tighten or replace loose or damaged hoses.
**3** To replace system components, remove the left side cover. Disconnect the hoses, remove the mounting screws and take the assembly off the motorcycle.
**4** To test the mixture control valve, refer to Section 14.

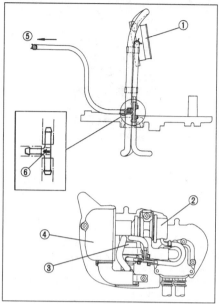

15.2a  Air induction system hose routing
(1984 and 1985 XV1000 models)

1  Carburetor intake joint
2  Air cutoff valve
3  Mixture control valve
4  Air filter case
5  To pressure sensor
6  Arrow mark (toward pressure sensor)

**5** To inspect the reed valve, remove the Allen bolts and disassemble the reed valve case. Measure the height of the reed valves from the base. If it's not as listed in this Chapter's Specifications, replace the reed valve. Replace the reed valve assembly gasket if it's brittle, cracked or torn.
**6** Installation is the reverse of the removal steps.

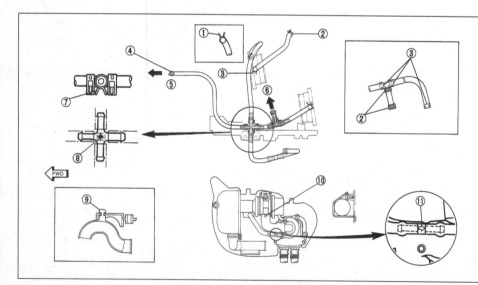

1  Face clamp ends downward
2  Face clamp ends outward
3  Face clamp ends inward
4  Face clamp ends toward front of motorcycle
5  To pressure sensor
6  To coasting enricher (1986 and 1987 models)
7  Face clamp ends downward
8  Face arrow mark toward pressure sensor
9  Place hose bend projection in square hole
10 Face white paint mark toward air cutoff valve
11 Face arrow mark toward air cut valve

15.2b  Air induction system hose routing (1986 and later XV1100 models)

1 Face clamp ends inward
2 To fuel tap
3 Face clamp ends downward
4 Place hose bend projection in square hole
5 Face white paint mark toward air cut valve
6 Face arrow mark toward air cut valve

15.2c  Air induction system hose routing (1988 and later XV750 models)

## 16 Evaporation control system (California models) - inspection and canister replacement

1 The evaporation control system used on California models prevents fuel vapor from escaping into the atmosphere. When the engine isn't running, the vapor is stored in a canister, then routed into the combustion chambers for burning when the engine starts (see illustration).
2 The hoses should be checked periodically for loose connections, damage and deterioration. Tighten or replace the hoses as needed.
3 To remove the canister, disconnect the hoses and remove the mounting bolts. To install it, bolt the canister to the motorcycle and reconnect the hoses.

## 17 Throttle position sensor (1996 UK 1100)

### Adjustment

1 Locate the throttle position sensor on the carburetor. It can be identified by its wire colors: blue, black/blue and yellow.
2 To adjust sensor idle position, connect an ohmmeter between the blue and black-blue wire terminals in the sensor side of the connector. Set the ohmmeter at R x 1000. Move the throttle linkage to full throttle position and note the reading.
3 Multiply the reading obtained in Step 2 by 0.13 and 0.15 to obtain the correct range for resistance of the throttle position sensor at idle. For example, if the reading was 5500 ohms, multiply that number by 0.13, then by 0.15. The results, 715 and 825, are the lower and upper limits of the throttle position sensor's idle reading.
4 Set the ohmmeter at R x 100 and connect it between the yellow and black/blue terminals in the sensor side of the connector. With the throttle at idle, the ohmmeter reading should be within the range established in Step 3.
5 If the ohmmeter reading is not within the specified range, loosen the throttle position sensor screws and rotate it to change its position (the ohmmeter reading will change at the same time). Once the reading is within the correct range, tighten the screws. Disconnect the ohmmeter and reconnect the electrical connector to the sensor.

### Testing and replacement

6 To test the sensor off the motorcycle, disconnect its electrical connector. Remove the mounting screws and take the sensor off the bike.
7 Connect an ohmmeter between the blue and black/blue terminals in the sensor electrical connector. It should indicate 4000 - 6000 ohms; replace the sensor if it doesn't.
8 Connect the ohmmeter between the yellow and black/blue terminals in the connector. Turn the sensor slowly and note the reading; it should start at zero and rise to 4000 - 6000 ohms. If not, replace the sensor.

16.1  Evaporation control system (California models)

1 Battery case
2 Canister
3 Rollover valve

A Install rollover valve in the correct direction

B Insert canister tube into battery case slot

**Notes**

# Chapter 4 Part A
## Ignition system (XV535 models)

## Contents

General information .................................... 1
Igniter - check, removal and installation ..................... 5
Ignition coils - check, removal and installation ............... 3
Ignition system - check ................................... 2
Pick-up coil - check, removal and installation ............... 4
Spark plugs - replacement ..................... See Chapter 1

## Degrees of difficulty

| Easy, suitable for novice with little experience  | Fairly easy, suitable for beginner with some experience  | Fairly difficult, suitable for competent DIY mechanic | Difficult, suitable for experienced DIY mechanic | Very difficult, suitable for expert DIY or professional 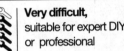 |
|---|---|---|---|---|

## Specifications

### General
Spark plug cap resistance (UK models) ......................... 10,000 ohms at 20-degrees C (68-degrees F)
Spark plug arcing distance .................................... 6 mm (1/4 inch)
Pick-up coil resistance
  1987 through 1993 ......................................... 140 to 170 ohms at 20-degrees C (68-degrees F)
  1994-on .................................................. 182 to 222 ohms at 20-degrees C (68-degrees F)
Ignition timing ............................................. Not adjustable

### Ignition coil
1987 through 1993 US models
  Primary resistance .......................................... 3.8 to 4.6 ohms at 20-degrees C (68-degrees F)
  Secondary resistance ....................................... 10,600 to 15,800 ohms at 20-degrees C (68-degrees F)
1994-on US models
  Primary resistance .......................................... 3.6 to 4.8 ohms at 20-degrees C (68-degrees F)
  Secondary resistance ....................................... 11,200 to 15,200 ohms at 20-degrees C (68-degrees F)
1988 UK models
  Primary resistance .......................................... 3.8 to 4.6 ohms at 20-degrees C (68-degrees F)
  Secondary resistance ....................................... 10,600 to 15,800 ohms at 20-degrees C (68-degrees F)
1989 through 1993 UK models
  Primary resistance .......................................... 3.8 to 4.6 ohms at 20-degrees C (68-degrees F)
  Secondary resistance ....................................... 12,000 to 14,500 ohms at 20-degrees C (68-degrees F)
1994-on UK models
  Primary resistance .......................................... 3.8 to 4.6 ohms at 20-degrees C (68-degrees F)
  Secondary resistance ....................................... 10,100 to 15,800 ohms at 20-degrees C (68-degrees F)

### 1 General information

This motorcycle is equipped with a battery operated, fully transistorized, breakerless ignition system. The system consists of the following components:
*Pick-up coil*
*Igniter unit*
*Battery and fuse*
*Ignition coils*
*Spark plugs*
*Ignition (main), engine kill (stop), sidestand and neutral switches*
*Primary and secondary (HT) circuit wiring*

The transistorized ignition system functions on the same principle as a breaker point DC ignition system with the pick-up coil and igniter performing the tasks previously associated with the breaker points and mechanical advance system. As a result, adjustment and maintenance of ignition components is eliminated (with the exception of spark plug replacement). Models through 1993 use two pick-up coils; 1994 and later models use a single pick-up coil.

Because of their nature, the individual ignition system components can be checked but not repaired. If ignition system troubles occur, and the faulty component can be isolated, the only cure for the problem is to replace the part with a new one. Keep in mind that most electrical parts, once purchased, can't be returned. To avoid unnecessary expense, make very sure the faulty component has been positively identified before buying a replacement part.

## 2 Ignition system - check

⚠️ **Warning: Because of the very high voltage generated by the ignition system, extreme care should be taken when these checks are performed.**

1 If the ignition system is the suspected cause of poor engine performance or failure to start, a number of checks can be made to isolate the problem.

2 Make sure the engine kill switch is in the Run position.

### Engine will not start

3 Disconnect one of the spark plug wires, connect the wire to a spare spark plug and lay the plug on the engine with the threads contacting the engine. If necessary, hold the spark plug with an insulated tool. Crank the engine over and make sure a well-defined, blue spark occurs between the spark plug electrodes.

⚠️ **Warning: Don't remove one of the spark plugs from the engine to perform this check - atomized fuel being pumped out of the open spark plug hole could ignite, causing severe injury!**

4 If no spark occurs, the following checks should be made:

5 Unscrew a spark plug cap from a plug wire and lay the plug wire on the cylinder head. Crank the engine over and check for spark again. If a strong blue spark occurs between the end of the wire and the engine, the plug cap or plug is faulty. If not, go to the next steps.

6 Make sure all electrical connectors are clean and tight. Check all wires for shorts, opens and correct installation.

7 Check the battery voltage with a voltmeter and - on models equipped with batteries having removable filler caps - check the specific gravity with a hydrometer (see Chap-

ter 1). If the voltage is less than 12-volts or if the specific gravity is low, recharge the battery.

8 Check the ignition fuse and the fuse connections. If the fuse is blown, replace it with a new one; if the connections are loose or corroded, clean or repair them.

9 Refer to Chapter 8 and check the ignition switch, engine kill switch, neutral switch and sidestand switch.

10 Refer to Section 3 and check the ignition coil primary and secondary resistance.

11 Refer to Section 4 and check the pick-up coil resistance.

12 If the preceding checks produce positive results but there is still no spark at the plug, remove the igniter and have it checked by a Yamaha dealer service department or other repair shop equipped with the special tester required.

### Engine starts but misfires

13 If the engine starts but misfires, make the following checks before deciding that the ignition system is at fault.

14 The ignition system must be able to produce a spark across a six millimeter (1/4-inch) gap (minimum). A simple test fixture **(see Tool Tip)** can be constructed to make sure the minimum spark gap can be jumped. Make sure the fixture electrodes are positioned six millimeters apart.

15 Connect one of the spark plug wires to the protruding test fixture electrode, then attach the fixture's alligator clip to a good engine ground/earth.

16 Crank the engine over (it may start and run on the remaining cylinder) and see if well-defined, blue sparks occur between the test fixture electrodes. If the minimum spark gap test is positive, the ignition coil for that cylinder is functioning properly. Repeat the check on the spark plug wire that is connected to the other coil. If the spark will not jump the gap during either test, or if it is weak (orange colored), refer to steps 5 through 11 of this Section and perform the component checks described.

## 3 Ignition coils - check, removal and installation

### Check

1 In order to determine conclusively that the ignition coils are defective, they should be tested by an authorized Yamaha dealer service department which is equipped with the special electrical tester required for this check.

2 However, the coils can be checked visually (for cracks and other damage) and the primary and secondary coil resistances can be measured with an ohmmeter. If the coils are undamaged, and if the resistances are as specified, they are probably capable of proper operation.

3 To check the coils for physical damage, they must be removed (see Step 9). To check the resistances, simply remove the ignition coil cover from the forward side of the front cylinder's mounting bracket, unplug the primary circuit electrical connectors from the coil(s) and remove the spark plug wire from the plug that is connected to the coil being checked. Mark the locations of all wires before disconnecting them.

4 To check the coil primary resistance, attach one ohmmeter lead to one of the primary terminals and the other ohmmeter lead to the other primary terminal **(see illustration)**.

5 Place the ohmmeter selector switch in the Rx1 position and compare the measured resistance to the value listed in this Chapter's Specifications.

6 If the coil primary resistance is as specified, check the coil secondary resistance by disconnecting either meter lead from the primary terminal connector and attaching it to the spark plug wire (HT) terminal **(see illustration)**.

7 Place the ohmmeter selector switch in the Rx1000 position and compare the measured resistance to the values listed in this Chapter's Specifications.

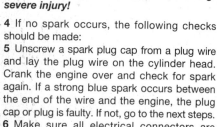

**TOOL TiP**

*A simple spark gap testing fixture can be made from a block of wood, a large alligator clip, two nails, a screw and a piece of wire*

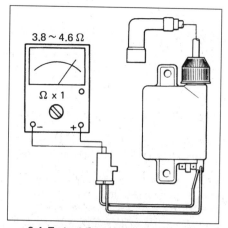

3.4 **To test the primary resistance, connect the ohmmeter leads between the coil primary terminals**

3.8 ~ 4.6 Ω
Ω × 1

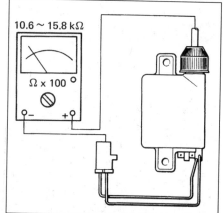

3.6 **Test the secondary resistance with the ohmmeter between the plug wire and a primary terminal**

10.6 ~ 15.8 kΩ
Ω × 100

**3.9  Disconnect the coil primary connectors**

**3.10  Unbolt the coil bracket and remove it together with the coils**

**4.1a  The pick-up coil connector on '87 - '93 models is on the underside of the igniter at the rear (arrow)**

**8** If the resistances are not as specified, the coil is probably defective and should be replaced with a new one.

### Removal and installation

**9** To remove the coils, refer to Chapter 4 and remove the upper fuel tank (later models) or Chapter 7 to remove the top cover (early models), then disconnect the spark plug wires from the plugs. After labeling them with tape to aid in reinstallation, unplug the coil primary circuit electrical connectors **(see illustration)**.
**10** Unbolt the coil bracket and remove it from the frame **(see illustration)**. Remove the coil mounting bolts and take the coil(s) off the bracket.
**11** Installation is the reverse of removal. Make sure the primary circuit electrical connectors are attached to the proper terminals; use their wire colors for identification (see the *Wiring diagrams* at the end of the book).

### 4  Pick-up coil - check, removal and installation

### Check

**1** Remove the right front side cover (see

Chapter 7). On 1987 through 1993 models, locate the four-pin pick-up coil wiring connector at the igniter **(see illustration)**. On 1994 and later models, follow the gray and black wires from the igniter to the two-pin connector in the wiring harness **(see illustration)**. Disconnect the connector. **Note:** *On 1987 through 1993 models, it may be easier to remove the igniter for access to the connector (see Section 5).*
**2** Make the test on the pick-up coil side of the connector. Probe the terminals in the connector with an ohmmeter and compare the resistance reading with the value listed in this Chapter's Specifications. On 1987 through 1993 models two tests are required: brown to green and red to blue.
**3** If the pick-up coil(s) fail the above test, it must be replaced.

### Removal

**4** Remove the alternator cover from the left side of the engine (see Chapter 8).
**5** Unscrew the mounting screws and remove the pick-up coil(s) **(see illustration)**.

### Installation

**6** Installation is the reverse of the removal steps.

### 5  Igniter - check, removal and installation

### Check

**1** The igniter is checked by process of elimination (when all other possible causes have been checked and eliminated, the igniter is at fault). Because the igniter is expensive and can't be returned once purchased, consider having a Yamaha dealer test the ignition system before you buy a new igniter.

### Removal and installation

**2** Remove the right front side cover and the bracket inside it (see Chapter 7).
**3** Slide the electrical component board off its mounting posts to detach it from the bracket. Turn the component board around so the igniter mounting screws are visible. Unplug the electrical connector, remove the mounting screws and take the igniter out **(see illustration)**.
**4** Installation is the reverse of the removal steps.

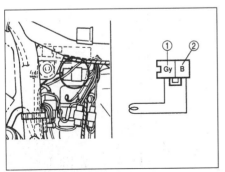

**4.1b  The pick-up coil connector on 1994-on models is in the harness; it is identified by its wire colors**

*1 Gray          2 Black*

**4.5  Pick-up coil mounting screws (arrows) - two-coil type shown**

**5.3  Unplug the connectors and remove the screws (arrows) to detach the igniter from the board**

**Notes**

# Chapter 4  Part B
## Ignition system (XV700-1100 models)

## Contents

## Degrees of difficulty

| Easy, suitable for novice with little experience | | Fairly easy, suitable for beginner with some experience | | Fairly difficult, suitable for competent DIY mechanic | | Difficult, suitable for experienced DIY mechanic | | Very difficult, suitable for expert DIY or professional | |
|---|---|---|---|---|---|---|---|---|---|

## Specifications

### General

Spark plug cap resistance
  All except TR1 models . . . . . . . . . . . . . . . . . . . . . . . . . . . . . . .   5000 ohms at 20-degrees C (68-degrees F)
  TR1 models . . . . . . . . . . . . . . . . . . . . . . . . . . . . . . . . . . . . . . . .   7000 ohms at 20-degrees C (68-degrees F)
Spark plug arcing distance . . . . . . . . . . . . . . . . . . . . . . . . . . . . . .   6 mm (1/4 inch)
Pick-up coil resistance
  Dual pick-up coils . . . . . . . . . . . . . . . . . . . . . . . . . . . . . . . . . . .   124 to 186 ohms at 20-degrees C (68-degrees F)
  Single pick-up coil . . . . . . . . . . . . . . . . . . . . . . . . . . . . . . . . . .   182 to 222 ohms at 20-degrees C (68-degrees F)
Pressure sensor output voltage . . . . . . . . . . . . . . . . . . . . . . . . . .   3.00 +/- 0.05 volts
Ignition timing . . . . . . . . . . . . . . . . . . . . . . . . . . . . . . . . . . . . . . .   Not adjustable

### Ignition coil

1981 through 1983 models
  Primary resistance . . . . . . . . . . . . . . . . . . . . . . . . . . . . . . . . . .   2.7 ohms +/- 15% at 20-degrees C (68-degrees F)
  Secondary resistance . . . . . . . . . . . . . . . . . . . . . . . . . . . . . . . .   8500 ohms +/- 15% at 20-degrees C (68-degrees F)
1984-on models
  Primary resistance . . . . . . . . . . . . . . . . . . . . . . . . . . . . . . . . . .   3.57 to 4.83 ohms at 20-degrees C (68-degrees F)
  Secondary resistance . . . . . . . . . . . . . . . . . . . . . . . . . . . . . . . .   11,220 to 15,180 ohms at 20-degrees C (68-degrees F)

## 1  General information

These motorcycles are equipped with a battery operated, fully transistorized, breakerless ignition system. The system consists of the following components:
  *Pick-up coil(s)*
  *Igniter unit*
  *Battery and fuse*
  *Ignition coils*

  *Spark plugs*
  *Ignition (main), engine kill (stop), sidestand and neutral switches*
  *Primary and secondary (HT) circuit wiring*

The transistorized ignition system functions on the same principle as a breaker point DC ignition system with the pick-up coil or coils and igniter performing the tasks previously associated with the breaker points and mechanical advance system. As a result, adjustment and maintenance of ignition components is eliminated (with the exception of spark plug replacement). Models through

1990 use two pick-up coils; 1991 and later models use a single pick-up coil.

Because of their nature, the individual ignition system components can be checked but not repaired. If ignition system troubles occur, and the faulty component can be isolated, the only cure for the problem is to replace the part with a new one. Keep in mind that most electrical parts, once purchased, can't be returned. To avoid unnecessary expense, make very sure the faulty component has been positively identified before buying a replacement part.

## 2 Ignition system - check

**Warning: Because of the very high voltage generated by the ignition system, extreme care should be taken when these checks are performed.**

**1** If the ignition system is the suspected cause of poor engine performance or failure to start, a number of checks can be made to isolate the problem.

**2** Make sure the engine kill switch is in the Run position.

### Engine will not start

**3** Disconnect one of the spark plug wires, connect the wire to a spare spark plug and lay the plug on the engine with the threads contacting the engine. If necessary, hold the spark plug with an insulated tool. Crank the engine over and make sure a well-defined, blue spark occurs between the spark plug electrodes.

**Warning: Don't remove one of the spark plugs from the engine to perform this check - atomized fuel being pumped out of the open spark plug hole could ignite, causing severe injury!**

**4** If no spark occurs, the following checks should be made:

**5** Unscrew a spark plug cap from a plug wire and lay the plug wire on the cylinder head. Crank the engine over and check for spark again. If a strong blue spark occurs between the end of the wire and the engine, the plug cap or plug is faulty. If not, go to the next steps.

**6** Make sure all electrical connectors are clean and tight. Check all wires for shorts, opens and correct installation.

**7** Check the battery voltage with a voltmeter and - on models equipped with batteries having removable filler caps - check the specific gravity with a hydrometer (see Chapter 1). If the voltage is less than 12-volts or if the specific gravity is low, recharge the battery.

**8** Check the ignition fuse and the fuse connections. If the fuse is blown, replace it with a new one; if the connections are loose or corroded, clean or repair them.

**9** Refer to Chapter 8 and check the ignition switch, engine kill switch, neutral switch and sidestand switch.

**10** Refer to Section 3 and check the ignition coil primary and secondary resistance.

**11** Refer to Section 4 and check the pick-up coil resistance.

**12** If the preceding checks produce positive results but there is still no spark at the plug, remove the igniter and have it checked by a Yamaha dealer service department or other repair shop equipped with the special tester required.

### Engine starts but misfires

**13** If the engine starts but misfires, make the following checks before deciding that the ignition system is at fault.

**14** The ignition system must be able to produce a spark across a six millimeter (1/4-inch) gap (minimum). A simple test fixture **(see illustration 2.14 in Part A of this Chapter)** can be constructed to make sure the minimum spark gap can be jumped. Make sure the fixture electrodes are positioned six millimeters apart.

**15** Connect one of the spark plug wires to the protruding test fixture electrode, then attach the fixture's alligator clip to a good engine ground/earth.

**16** Crank the engine over (it may start and run on the remaining cylinder) and see if well-defined, blue sparks occur between the test fixture electrodes. If the minimum spark gap test is positive, the ignition coil for that cylinder is functioning properly. Repeat the check on the spark plug wire that is connected to the other coil. If the spark will not jump the gap during either test, or if it is weak (orange colored), refer to steps 5 through 11 of this Section and perform the component checks described.

## 3 Ignition coils - check, removal and installation

### Check

**1** In order to determine conclusively that the ignition coils are defective, they should be tested by an authorized Yamaha dealer service department which is equipped with the special electrical tester required for this check.

**2** However, the coils can be checked visually (for cracks and other damage) and the primary and secondary coil resistances can be measured with an ohmmeter. If the coils are undamaged, and if the resistances are as specified, they are probably capable of proper operation.

**3** To check the coils for physical damage, they must be removed (see Step 9). To check the resistances, simply remove the ignition coil cover from the forward side of the front cylinder's mounting bracket, unplug the primary circuit electrical connectors from the coil(s) and remove the spark plug wire from the plug that is connected to the coil being checked. Mark the locations of all wires before disconnecting them.

**4** To check the coil primary resistance, attach one ohmmeter lead to one of the primary terminals and the other ohmmeter lead to the other primary terminal **(see illustration)**.

**5** Place the ohmmeter selector switch in the Rx1 position and compare the measured resistance to the value listed in this Chapter's Specifications.

**6** If the coil primary resistance is as specified, check the coil secondary resistance by disconnecting either meter lead from the primary terminal connector and attaching it to the spark plug wire (HT) terminal **(see illustration)**.

**7** Place the ohmmeter selector switch in the Rx1000 position and compare the measured resistance to the values listed in this Chapter's Specifications.

**8** If the resistances are not as specified, the coil is probably defective and should be replaced with a new one.

### Removal and installation

**9** If you're working on an XV1000 or XV1100 model, remove the pressure sensor from the ignition coil cover located on top of the front cylinder's engine mounting bracket.

**10** Remove the ignition coil cover, then disconnect the spark plug wires from the plugs. Label the primary circuit electrical connectors with tape to aid in reinstallation, then disconnect them.

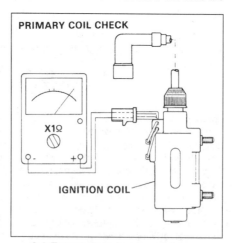

**3.4 To test the primary resistance, connect the ohmmeter between the primary terminals**

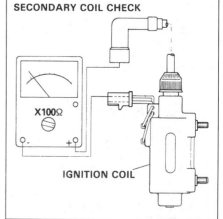

**3.6 Test the secondary resistance with the ohmmeter between the plug wire and a primary terminal**

**3.11 Disconnect the coil connectors and remove the fasteners to separate them from the bracket**

**5.3 The igniter is under the fuel tank on '81 - '83 models (shown), or forward of the rear fender**

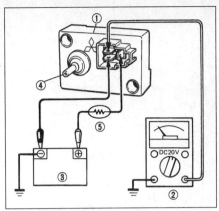

**6.2 Pressure sensor test connections**

*1  Pressure sensor*   *4  Pressure hose fitting*
*2  Voltmeter*        *5  180-ohm resistor*
*3  Battery*

11 Unbolt the coils from the engine mounting bracket and remove them **(see illustration)**.
12 Installation is the reverse of removal. Make sure the primary circuit electrical connectors are attached to the proper terminals; use their wire colors for identification (see the Wiring diagrams at the end of the book).

---

### 4  Pick-up coils - check, removal and installation

#### Check

1 If you're working on a 1981 through 1983 model, remove the fuel tank (see Chapter 3).
2 If you're working on a 1984 or later model, remove the seat, the left side cover and the luggage box (see Chapter 7).
3 On 1981 through 1990 models, locate the four-pin pick-up coil wiring connector at the igniter **(see illustration 5.3)**. On 1991 and later models, follow the gray and black wires from the igniter to the two-pin connector in the wiring harness. Disconnect the connector.
4 Make the test on the pick-up coil side of the connector. Probe the terminals in the connector with an ohmmeter and compare the resistance reading with the value listed in this Chapter's Specifications. On 1981 through 1990 models two tests are required:

brown to green (rear cylinder) and red to blue (front cylinder).
5 If the pick-up coil(s) fail the above test, it must be replaced.

#### Removal

6 Remove the alternator cover from the left side of the engine (see Chapter 8).
7 Unscrew the mounting screws and remove the pick-up coil(s) (see Chapter 8).

#### Installation

8 Installation is the reverse of the removal steps.

---

### 5  Igniter - check, removal and installation

#### Check

1 The igniter is checked by process of elimination (when all other possible causes have been checked and eliminated, the igniter is at fault). Because the igniter is expensive and can't be returned once purchased, consider having a Yamaha dealer test the ignition system before you buy a new igniter.

#### Removal and installation

1 If you're working on a 1981 through 1983 model, remove the fuel tank (see Chapter 3).

2 If you're working on a 1984 or later model, remove the seat, the left side cover and the luggage box (see Chapter 7).
3 Unplug the electrical connector, remove the mounting screws and take the igniter out **(see illustration)**.
4 Installation is the reverse of the removal steps.

---

### 6  Pressure sensor (1984 and later XV1000 and XV1100 models) - testing, removal and installation

1 Remove the pressure sensor mounting screws. Disconnect the electrical connector and pressure hose and remove the pressure sensor from the ignition coil cover.
2 Connect a 12-volt battery and 180-ohm resistor to the pressure sensor **(see illustration)**. Connect a 0-20 volt voltmeter between the pressure sensor and ground. Compare the output voltage to the value listed in this Chapter's Specifications. If it's incorrect, replace the pressure sensor.
3 Installation is the reverse of the removal steps.

**Notes**

# Chapter 5 Part A Steering, suspension and final drive (XV535 models)

## Contents

## Degrees of difficulty

| | | | | |
|---|---|---|---|---|
| **Easy,** suitable for novice with little experience  | **Fairly easy,** suitable for beginner with some experience  | **Fairly difficult,** suitable for competent DIY mechanic  | **Difficult,** suitable for experienced DIY mechanic | **Very difficult,** suitable for expert DIY or professional 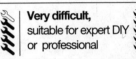 |

## Specifications

### Front suspension

Fork spring length
  1987 and 1988 US models
    Standard ........................................... 531.6 mm (20.9 inches)
    Minimum ........................................... 526.6 mm (20.7 inches)
  1990-on US models and all UK models
    Standard ........................................... 546.6 mm (21.5 inches)
    Minimum ........................................... 541.6 mm (21.3 inches)
Fork oil capacity ........................................ 228 cc (7.71 US fl oz, 8.03 lmp fl oz)
Fork oil type .......................................... SAE 10W fork oil
Fork oil level .......................................... 176 mm (6.93 inches) below top of inner fork tube*
*With spring removed and fork fully compressed.

### Rear suspension

Rear spring free length
  1987 and 1988 US models
    Standard ........................................... 266 mm (10.5 inches)
    Minimum ........................................... 261 mm (10.3 inches)
  1990-on US models and all UK models
    Standard ........................................... 237.5 mm (9.35 inches)
    Minimum ........................................... 232.2 mm (9.15 inches)
Rear spring installed length ............................. 229 mm (9.01 inches)
Swingarm endplay and side play limits .................... 1 mm (0.04 inch)

### Torque specifications

Front forks
  Damper rod bolt ...................................... 23 Nm (17 ft-lbs)**
  Upper triple clamp pinch bolts .......................... 20 Nm (14 ft-lbs)
  Lower triple clamp pinch bolts .......................... 38 Nm (27 ft-lbs)
Handlebars and steering stem
  Handlebar bracket-to-upper triple clamp nuts
    All US, UK with 8 mm nuts ........................... 20 Nm (14 ft-lbs)
    UK with 10 mm or 12 mm nuts ....................... 32 Nm (22 ft-lbs)
  Handlebar to bracket clamp bolts ........................ 20 Nm (14 ft-lbs)
  Steering stem bolt .................................... 54 Nm (39 ft-lbs)
  Steering head bearing ring nut .......................... see Chapter 1
Rear shock absorber upper bolts .......................... 20 Nm (14 ft-lbs)
Rear shock absorber lower bolts/nuts ...................... 30 Nm (22 ft-lbs)
Swingarm pivot shaft .................................... 75 Nm (54 ft-lbs)
Final drive unit to swingarm nuts .......................... 42 Nm (30 ft-lbs)
**Apply non-permanent thread locking agent to the bolt threads.

2.2a  On early models, pry off the rubber cover . . .

2.2b  . . . later models use a pair of plugs

2.2c  Remove the bolts to detach the brackets; the arrow cast in each bracket must face forward

2.5  Pull out the clip (arrow) and remove the nut and washers to detach the bracket from the triple clamp

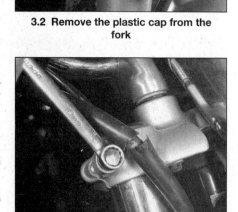

3.2  Remove the plastic cap from the fork

## 1  General information

The front forks are of the conventional coil spring, hydraulically-damped telescopic type.

The rear suspension consists of twin shock absorbers with coil springs and a swingarm.

Final drive is of the shaft type.

## 2  Handlebar - removal and installation

1  The handlebar is a one-piece unit that's secured to the upper triple clamp by a pair of brackets.

2  To remove the handlebar from its brackets, pry out the rubber plug(s) and remove the bolts that secure the top half of each bracket (see illustrations). Lift the handlebar out.

3  If the handlebar must be removed for access to other components, such as the forks or the steering head, it's not necessary to disconnect the cables, wires or hoses, but it is a good idea to support the assembly with a piece of wire or rope, to avoid unnecessary strain on the cables, wires and the brake hose.

4  If the handlebar is to be removed completely, refer to Chapter 2 for clutch cable removal procedures, Chapter 6 for the brake master cylinder removal procedures, Chap-

ter 3 for the throttle grip removal procedure and Chapter 8 for the switch removal procedure.

5  To remove a bracket from the upper triple clamp, pull out the safety clip and remove the nut and washers (see illustration), then lift the bracket out.

6  Check the handlebar and brackets for cracks and distortion and replace them if any undesirable conditions are found. If the brackets were removed, check their rubber mounts for brittleness or deterioration.

7  Installation is the reverse of the removal steps. Tighten the nuts and bolts to the torques listed in this Chapter's Specifications.

## 3  Fork oil change

1  Support the bike securely so it can't be knocked over during this procedure. The front wheel must be raised off the ground using a jack and wood support under the crankcase, or axle stands.

2  Remove the plastic fork caps (see illustration).

3  Loosen the upper triple clamp pinch bolts (see illustration).

4  Press down the spring seat with a suitable tool (such as a large Phillips screwdriver). Remove the stopper ring, then slowly release the spring pressure and lift out the spring seat and spring (see illustrations).

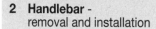

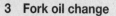

3.3  Loosen the upper triple clamp bolts

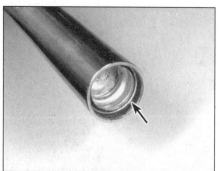

3.4a  Press the spring seat down against the spring pressure and pry out the stopper ring (arrow) . . .

3.4b  . . . then remove the spring seat with its O-ring and the spring

**3.5 Remove the fork drain screw (arrow)**

**3.8 Pour the specified amount of oil into the top of the fork**

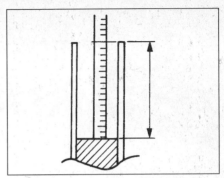

**3.9 Measure fork oil level with the fork fully compressed and the spring removed**

**5** Place a drain pan under the fork leg and remove the drain screw **(see illustration)**.

 *Warning: Do not allow the fork oil to contact the tire, brake disc or pads. If it does, wash off the tire, clean the disc with brake system cleaner and replace the pads with new ones before riding the motorcycle.*

**6** After most of the oil has drained, slowly compress and release the forks to pump out the remaining oil. An assistant will most likely be required to do this.

**7** Check the drain screw gasket and spring seat O-ring for damage and replace them if necessary. Clean the threads of the drain screw with solvent and let it dry, then install the screw and gasket, tightening it securely.

**8** Pour the type and amount of fork oil, listed in this Chapter's Specifications, into the fork tube through the opening at the top **(see illustration)**.

**9** Remove the jack from under the engine and slowly pump the forks a few times to purge the air. Measure the level of the oil in the fork with the fork fully compressed and without the spring in position **(see illustration)**. Compare it to the value listed in this Chapter's Specifications. Add or remove oil as necessary.

**10** Coat the O-ring on the spring seat with a thin layer of multi-purpose grease. Install the spring (with its closer-wound coils at the top), spring seat and stopper ring **(see illustrations 3.4b and 3.4a)**.

**11** Install the fork cap.

**12** The remainder of installation is the reverse of the removal steps. Tighten all fasteners to the torque listed in this Chapter's Specifications.

---

### 4 Forks - removal and installation

#### Removal

**1** Support the bike securely so it can't be knocked over during this procedure.

**2** Place a jack under the engine and raise it slightly to lift the front tire off the ground.

**3** Remove the brake caliper and front wheel (see Chapter 6).

**4** Remove the front fender (see Chapter 7).

**5** Remove any wiring harness clamps or straps from the fork tubes.

**6** If the fork will be disassembled after removal, read through the disassembly procedure (see Section 5), paying special attention to the damper rod bolt removal steps. If you don't have the necessary special tool or a substitute for it, you can remove the damper rod bolt before the fork is disassembled, while the spring tension will keep the damper rod from spinning inside the fork tube.

**7** Loosen the upper and lower triple clamp bolts **(see illustrations)**, then slide the fork tubes down and remove the forks from the motorcycle.

**HAYNES HiNT** *If the fork legs are seized, spray the area with penetrating oil and allow time for it to soak in before trying again.*

#### Installation

**8** Slide each fork leg into the lower triple clamp.

**9** Slide the fork legs up, installing the tops of the tubes into the upper triple clamp. Position the top of the fork tube so that it is level with the top surface of the upper triple clamp.

**10** The remainder of installation is the reverse of the removal procedure. Tighten all fasteners to the torques listed in this Chapter's Specifications and the Chapter 6 Specifications.

**11** Pump the front brake lever several times to bring the pads into contact with the disc.

---

### 5 Forks - disassembly, inspection and reassembly

#### Disassembly

**1** Remove the forks following the procedure in Section 4. Work on one fork leg at a time to avoid mixing up the parts.

**2** Remove the fork cap, stopper ring, spring seat and spring (see Section 3, Step 4).

**3** Invert the fork assembly over a container and allow the oil to drain out **(see illustration)**.

**4.7a Loosen the upper triple clamp bolts . . .**

**4.7b . . . and the lower triple clamp bolts**

**5.3 Pour the fork oil into a container**

**5.4a Pry the dust seal out of the outer fork tube**

**4** Pry the dust seal from the outer tube **(see illustrations)**.

**5** Pry the retaining ring from its groove in the outer tube **(see illustration)**. Slide the dust seal and retaining ring off the inner fork tube.

**6** Prevent the damper rod from turning using a holding handle (Yamaha tool no. YM-01326, part no. 90890-01326) and adapter (Yamaha tool no. YM-01300-01, part no. 90890-01294) **(see illustration)** passed down through the fork inner tube to engage the damper rod head. Unscrew the Allen bolt at the bottom of the outer tube and remove the copper washer **(see illustrations)**. **Note:** *If you don't have access to these tools, a piece of hardwood dowel can be used instead. Cut a taper on the end of the dowel to fit into the damper rod head. Another alternative is to loosen*

1 Fork cap
2 Stopper ring
3 Spring seat
4 O-ring
5 Fork spring
6 Teflon ring
7 Rebound spring
8 Damper rod
9 Oil lock piece
10 Inner fork tube
11 Outer tube bushing
12 Dust cover
13 Retaining clip
14 Oil seal
15 Outer fork tube
16 Drain screw

**5.4b Front fork (XV535 models) - exploded view**

*the damper rod bolt before removing the fork cap; the pressure of the fork spring will keep the damper rod from turning.*

**7** Pull out the damper rod and the rebound spring **(see illustration)**. Don't remove the Teflon ring from the damper rod unless a new one will be installed.

**8** Hold the outer tube and yank the inner tube away from it, repeatedly (like a slide hammer), until the seal and outer tube guide bushing pop loose **(see illustration)**.

**9** Remove the oil seal and slide bushing from the inner tube, and the oil lock piece from the outer tube.

**5.5 Pry out the retaining ring**

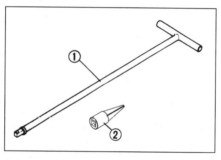

**5.6a This Yamaha tool is used to keep the damper rod from turning**
*1 Handle   2 Adapter*

**5.6b Loosen the damper rod bolt with an Allen wrench . . .**

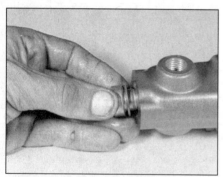

**5.6c . . . and remove the bolt and its copper washer - use a new copper washer during reassembly**

**5.7 Remove the damper rod and spring - don't separate the Teflon ring from the damper rod**

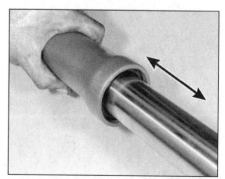

**5.8 To separate the tubes, yank them apart several times - the slide hammer effect will pull them apart**

5.14 Fit the oil lock piece onto the exposed end of the damper rod

5.17 A section of pipe can be used as a slide hammer (tape the ends of the pipe so it doesn't scratch the fork tube)

5.18 Use the same tool to drive the oil seal into position

## Inspection

**10** Clean all parts in solvent and blow them dry with compressed air, if available. Check the inner and outer fork tubes, the guide bushing and the damper rod for score marks, scratches, flaking of the chrome and excessive or abnormal wear. Look for dents in the tubes and replace them if any are found. Check the fork seal seat for nicks, gouges and scratches. If damage is evident, leaks will occur around the seal-to-outer tube junction. Replace worn or defective parts with new ones.

**11** Have the inner fork tube checked for runout at a dealer service department or other repair shop.

 **Warning: If it is bent, it should not be straightened; replace it with a new one.**

**12** Measure the overall length of the long (fork) spring and check it for cracks and other damage. Compare the length to the minimum length listed in this Chapter's Specifications. If it's defective or sagged, replace both fork springs with new ones. Never replace only one spring.

## Reassembly

**13** Install the rebound spring on the damper rod. Install the damper rod in the inner fork tube, then let it slide slowly down until it protrudes from the bottom of the inner fork tube.

**14** Install the oil lock piece over the end of the damper rod that protrudes from the fork tube **(see illustration)**.
**15** Install the inner fork tube in the outer fork tube.
**16** Apply non-permanent thread locking agent to the damper rod bolt, then install the bolt with its copper washer and tighten it to the torque listed in this Chapter's Specifications **(see illustration 5.6b)**. Hold the damper rod from turning with the tool used in Step 6. **Note:** *If you didn't use the tool, tighten the damper rod bolt after the fork spring and cap bolt are installed.*
**17** Slide the outer tube guide bushing down the inner tube. Using a special bushing driver (Yamaha tool no. YM-01367 and YM-8010, part nos. 90890-01367 and 90890-01370 or equivalent), drive the bushing into place until it's fully seated. If you don't have access to one of these tools, it is highly recommended that you take the assembly to a Yamaha dealer service department or other motorcycle repair shop to have this done. It is possible, however, to drive the bushing into place using a section of pipe and an old guide bushing **(see illustration)**. Wrap tape around the ends of the pipe to prevent it from scratching the fork tube.
**18** Lubricate the lips and the outer diameter of the oil seal with the recommended fork oil (see Chapter 1) and slide it down the inner tube, with the numbered side of the seal

facing up. Drive the seal into place with the same tools used to drive in the slide bushing **(see illustration)**. If you don't have access to these, it is recommended that you take the assembly to a Yamaha dealer service department or other motorcycle repair shop to have the seal driven in. If you are very careful, the seal can be driven in with a hammer and a drift punch. Work around the circumference of the seal, tapping gently on the outer edge of the seal until it's seated. Be careful - if you distort the seal, you'll have to disassemble the fork again and end up taking it to a dealer anyway!
**19** Install the retaining ring, making sure the ring is completely seated in its groove **(see illustration)**.
**20** Install the dust seal, making sure it seats completely **(see illustration)**. The same tool used to drive in the oil seal can be used for the dust seal.
**21** Install the drain screw and a new gasket, if it was removed.
**22** Add the recommended type and amount of fork oil (see Section 3).
**23** Install the fork spring, with the closer-wound coils at the top.
**24** Refer to Section 4 and install the spring seat, stopper ring and fork cap.
**25** Install the fork by following the procedure outlined in Section 4. If you won't be installing the fork right away, store it in an upright position.

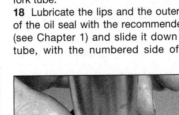

## 6 Steering head bearings - replacement

### Removal

**1** If the steering head bearing check/adjustment (see Chapter 1) does not remedy excessive play or roughness in the steering head bearings, the entire front end must be disassembled and the bearings and races replaced with new ones.

**2** Refer to Section 4 and remove the front forks.

5.19 Install the retaining ring and make sure it fits securely in its groove

5.20 Slide the dust seal down the fork tube and tap it into position

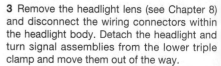

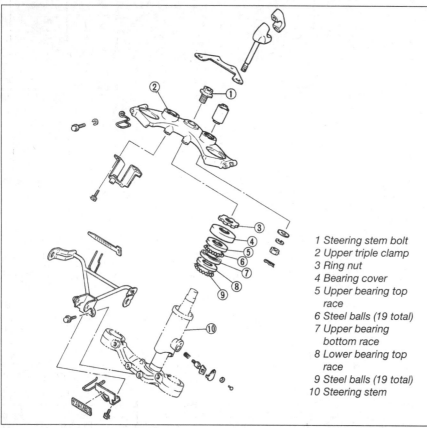

1 Steering stem bolt
2 Upper triple clamp
3 Ring nut
4 Bearing cover
5 Upper bearing top race
6 Steel balls (19 total)
7 Upper bearing bottom race
8 Lower bearing top race
9 Steel balls (19 total)
10 Steering stem

6.5a  Steering head and bearings (XV535 models) - exploded view

**3** Remove the headlight lens (see Chapter 8) and disconnect the wiring connectors within the headlight body. Detach the headlight and turn signal assemblies from the lower triple clamp and move them out of the way.
**4** Remove the safety clips, nuts and washers that secure the handlebar brackets to the triple clamp. Lift the handlebar and brackets up and support the handlebar to prevent strain on the cables and hoses.
**5** Unbolt the cable retainers and the brake hose retainer from the triple clamp **(see illustrations)**. Detach the speedometer housing and bracket from the triple clamp and position them out of the way.
**6** Remove the steering stem bolt and lift the upper triple clamp off the steering head **(see illustrations)**.
**7** Remove the ring nut with a special wrench such as Yamaha tool YU-33975 (part no. 90890-01403) **(see illustration)**. Remove the bearing cover, upper race and 19 steel balls **(see illustrations)**. On later models (2001-on) remove the caged ball bearing.
**8** Lower the steering stem partway out of the steering head and remove the 19 steel balls from the lower bearing **(see illustration)**. On later models (2001-on) remove the caged ball bearing.

### Inspection

**9** Check the bearings for wear. Look for cracks, dents, and pits in the races and flat spots, pitting or galling on the bearing balls. Replace any defective parts with new ones. If a new bearing is required, replace both

6.5b  The brake hose retainer bolt is accessible from underneath the triple clamp

6.6a  Undo the steering stem bolt with a box wrench (ring spanner) . . .

6.6b  . . . and lift it off . . .

6.6c  . . . and lift off the upper triple clamp

6.7a  Loosen the ring nut with a ring nut wrench (C-spanner)

6.7b  Take the ring nut off the steering stem

**6.7c Lift off the bearing cover and the upper bearing top race (arrow)**

**6.7d Remove the 19 steel balls**

**6.8 Lower the steering stem and lower bearing balls out of the steering head**

bearings, their races and both dust seals as a set.

**10** To remove the bearing races, drive them out of the steering head with a hammer and long rod or punch **(see illustrations)**. A slide hammer with the proper internal-jaw puller will also work.

**11** Since the races are an interference fit in the frame, installation will be easier if the new races are left overnight in a refrigerator. This will cause them to contract and slip into place in the frame with very little effort. When installing the races, tap them gently into place with a hammer and punch or a large socket **(see illustrations)**. Do not strike the bearing surface or the race will be damaged.

**12** Inspect the steering stem/lower triple clamp for cracks and other damage. Do not attempt to repair any steering components. Replace them with new parts if defects are found.

**13** Tap the seal and lower bearing race off the steering stem with a hammer and punch **(see illustration)**. The seal will be ruined during this process, so don't remove it unless you plan to install a new one.

**14** Install a new seal with its concave side down, then install the lower bearing bottom race **(see illustrations)**.

### Installation

**15** Pack the lower bearing bottom race with high-quality bearing grease (preferably a

**6.10a Insert a long punch or rod from below to tap out the upper bearing bottom race . . .**

**6.10b . . . and from above to tap out the lower bearing top race**

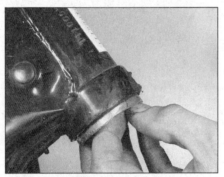

**6.11a Position the lower bearing top race in the steering head . . .**

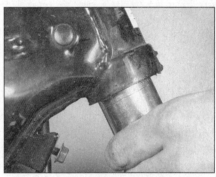

**6.11b . . . and tap it into position with a socket just smaller in diameter than the race**

**6.11c Tap the upper bearing bottom race into position with the same tools . . .**

**6.11d . . . the race should look like this when installed**

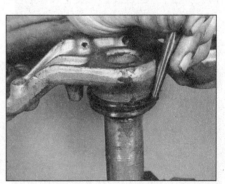

**6.13 Tap the seal and lower bearing bottom race off the steering stem**

6.14a Install a new seal with its concave side down . . .

6.14b . . . the seal should look like this when installed

6.14c Install the lower bearing bottom race with its groove up

moly-based grease). Stick 19 steel balls to the grease around the race, then add more grease (see illustrations). On 2001-on models install the caged balls. Note: *A small hand-operated grease gun will make this job easier.*

16 Pack the upper bearing and install the steel balls (or caged balls – 2001-on models) in the same way as for the lower bearing (see illustration).

17 Slip the steering stem into the steering head, taking care not to dislodge any of the bearing balls (see illustration).

18 Install the top race on top of the upper bearing balls, then install the bearing cover and the ring nut (see illustrations).

19 Refer to Chapter 1 and adjust the bearings.

20 The remainder of installation is the reverse of the removal steps.

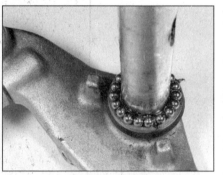

6.15a Pack the race with grease and install 19 steel balls . . .

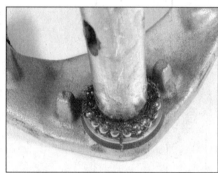

6.15b . . . then pack more grease on top of the balls

6.16a Apply a layer of grease to the upper bearing bottom race . . .

6.16b . . . stick 19 steel balls to the grease . . .

6.16c . . . then add more grease

6.17 Slip the steering stem into the steering head, taking care not to dislodge the steel balls

6.18a Install the upper bearing top race with its flat side up

6.18b Install the bearing cover over the race

6.18c  Install the ring nut and adjust the bearings

7.2  Remove the shock cover fasteners (arrows); one of the fasteners may also secure the backrest

7.3a  Remove the upper mounting bolt

## 7  Rear shock absorbers - removal, inspection and installation

### Removal

**1** Support the bike securely so it can't be knocked over during this procedure. Place a jack beneath the frame to lift the rear tire off the ground and support the swingarm so it can't drop.
**2** Remove the cover from the top end of the shock absorber (see illustration). On models so equipped, remove the backrest (see Chapter 7).
**3** Unbolt the top end of the shock from the frame (see illustrations).

**4** Remove the bolt that secures the lower end of the right shock or the nut that secures the lower end of the left shock (see illustration). Rotate the top end of the shock toward the rear of the bike and take it off.

### Inspection

**5** Check the shock for obvious physical damage and the coil spring for looseness or signs of fatigue; replace both shock absorbers as a pair if these conditions are found. Except for mounting bushings, replacement parts are not available.
**6** Check the shock for signs of oil or gas leaks and replace it if you find any. Yamaha specifies releasing the nitrogen gas pressure before throwing away the shock absorber.

⚠ **Warning:** *Wear eye protection while drilling to prevent injury from flying metal chips. To release the gas pressure, drill a hole through the cylinder wall at a point 10 mm (0.4 inch) from the top of the nitrogen reservoir (see illustration). The hole should be 2 to 3 mm (0.08 to 0.12 inch) in diameter.*
**7** Inspect the pivot hardware at the top and bottom of the shock and replace any worn or damaged parts.

### Installation

**8** Coat the pivot points with a thin layer of multi-purpose lithium-based grease. Install the shock with the tightly wound spring coils

7.4  The bottom of the left shock absorber is secured by a nut

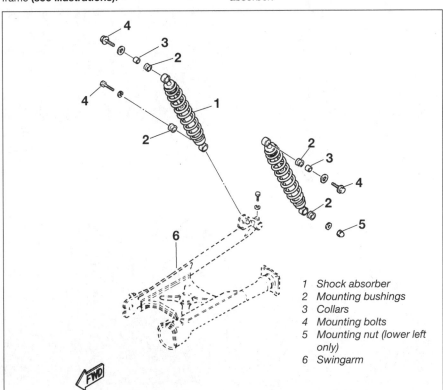

1  Shock absorber
2  Mounting bushings
3  Collars
4  Mounting bolts
5  Mounting nut (lower left only)
6  Swingarm

7.3b  Rear shock absorber details (XV535 models)

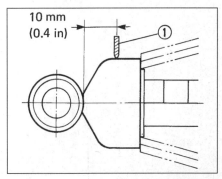

7.6  A hole must be drilled in the nitrogen reservoir before throwing the shock absorber away

down. Tighten the top bolts, then the bottom right bolt, then the bottom left nut to the torques listed in this Chapter's Specifications.

## 8  Swingarm bearings - check

1 Refer to Chapter 6 and remove the rear wheel, then refer to Section 7 and remove the rear shock absorbers.
2 Grasp the rear of the swingarm with one hand and place your other hand at the junction of the swingarm and the frame. Try to move the rear of the swingarm from side-to-side. Any wear (play) in the bearings should be felt as movement between the swingarm and the frame at the front. The swingarm will actually be felt to move forward and backward at the front (not from side-to-side). If any play is noted, the bearings should be replaced with new ones (see Section 11).
3 Next, move the swingarm up and down through its full travel. It should move freely, without any binding or rough spots. If it does not move freely, refer to Section 10 for servicing procedures.

9.5a  Remove the nuts and lockwashers . . .

9.5b  . . . and take the final drive unit off the swingarm

## 9  Driveshaft and final drive - removal, inspection and installation

### Removal

1 Support the bike securely so it can't be knocked over during this procedure.
2 Remove the exhaust system (see Chapter 3).
3 Remove the rear wheel (see Chapter 6).

4 Remove the rear shock absorbers (see Section 7).
5 Remove the nuts and lockwashers and detach the final gear assembly from the swingarm (see illustrations).
6 Remove the spring from the end of the driveshaft (see illustration).
7 Slide the driveshaft out of the swingarm (see illustration).
8 Slide the boot and coupling gear off the driveshaft (see illustrations).
9 Slide the forward boot up the driveshaft slightly, remove the snap-ring and slide the forward boot off (see illustration).

### Inspection

10 Thoroughly clean the driveshaft and

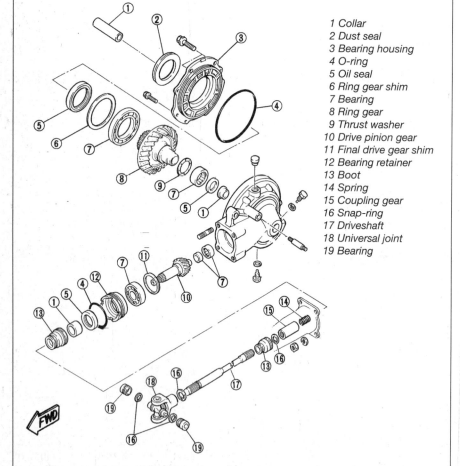

1 Collar
2 Dust seal
3 Bearing housing
4 O-ring
5 Oil seal
6 Ring gear shim
7 Bearing
8 Ring gear
9 Thrust washer
10 Drive pinion gear
11 Final drive gear shim
12 Bearing retainer
13 Boot
14 Spring
15 Coupling gear
16 Snap-ring
17 Driveshaft
18 Universal joint
19 Bearing

9.5c  Driveshaft and final drive unit (XV535 models) - exploded view

9.6  Take out the spring

9.7  Pull the driveshaft backward and take it out of the swingarm

**9.8a  Slide the boot off the coupling gear**

**9.8b  Slide the coupling gear off the shaft**

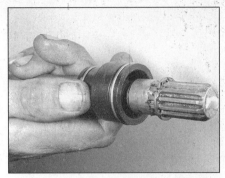

**9.9  Remove the snap-ring, then slide the forward boot off**

related parts with solvent. Wipe the final gear assembly clean with a rag moistened in solvent.

**11** Check all parts for obvious wear or damage and replace any worn or damaged parts.

**12** The final drive unit requires special tools to measure and adjust gear backlash. The procedure is complicated and should be done by a dealer service department or other qualified shop. Rotate the pinion shaft (the one that mates with the driveshaft) by hand. The ring gear splines (the part that mates with the rear wheel) should rotate smoothly. If rotation feels rough or jerky or if it's noisy, have the final drive unit disassembled and inspected.

### Installation

**13** Installation is the reverse of the removal steps, with the following additions:

a)  *Lubricate the driveshaft splines with multi-purpose lithium-based grease.*

b)  *Apply silicone sealant to the mating surfaces of the swingarm and final drive unit.*

c)  *Make sure the spring is in place in the end of the driveshaft* **(see illustration)**.

d)  *Use new lockwashers and tighten the final drive-to-swingarm nuts to the torque listed in this Chapter's Specifications.*

**9.13  Be sure the spring is in position before installing the final drive unit**

e)  *Check the oil level in the final drive unit and top up as needed (see Chapter 1).*

## 10 Swingarm -
### removal and installation

**1** Support the bike securely so it can't be knocked over during this procedure.

**2** Remove the exhaust system (see Chapter 3).

**3** Remove the rear wheel and disconnect the rear brake pedal and rod, noting that the cable must be detached from

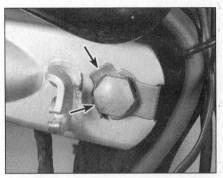

**10.6a  Bend back the lockwasher tabs (arrows) . . .**

its slot in the swingarm (see Chapter 6).

**4** Remove the rear shock absorbers (see Section 7).

**5** Remove the right rear side cover (see Chapter 7).

**6** Bend back the tabs on the lockwasher that secures the swingarm pivot shaft head **(see illustration)**. Unscrew the swingarm pivot shaft and take it out **(see illustration)**.

**7** Remove the final gear assembly and driveshaft (see Section 9).

**8** Pull the swingarm off the motorcycle **(see illustrations)**.

**9** Installation is the reverse of the removal steps, with the following additions:

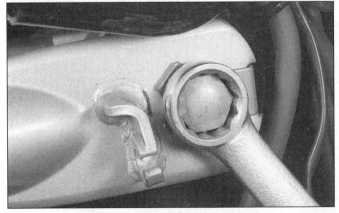

**10.6b  . . . and remove the pivot shaft**

**10.8a  Pull the swingarm back to remove it**

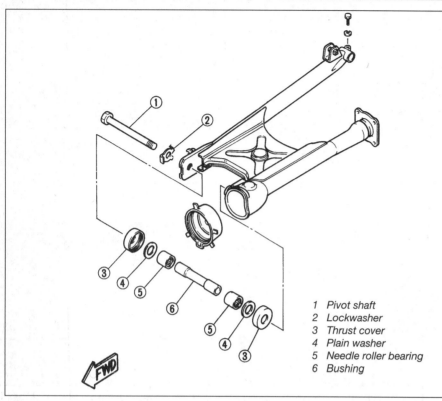

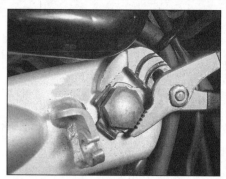

**10.9 Bend the lockwasher tabs against the head of the pivot shaft**

**10.8b Swingarm (XV535 models) - exploded view**

1 Pivot shaft
2 Lockwasher
3 Thrust cover
4 Plain washer
5 Needle roller bearing
6 Bushing

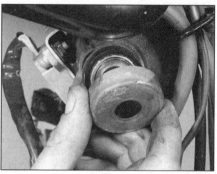

**11.2 Pry the thrust cover loose and pull it off**

a) Apply multi-purpose lithium grease to the driveshaft splines.

b) Install the swingarm without the driveshaft, then install the driveshaft as described in Section 9.

c) Use a new lockwasher and be sure its tab engages the slot in the swingarm. Tighten the pivot shaft to the torque listed in this Chapter's Specifications, then bend the lockwasher against the flats on the shaft head **(see illustration)**.

## 11 Swingarm bearings -
### inspection and replacement

1 Remove the swingarm (see Section 10).
2 Pry off the thrust cover and remove the plain washer from each side of the frame **(see illustration)**.

3 Slide the bushing out **(see illustration)**.
4 Inspect the bearings **(see illustration)**. If they're dry, lubricate them with lithium base waterproof wheel bearing

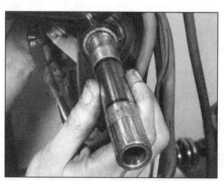

**11.3 Pull out the bushing**

grease. If they're worn or damaged, take the motorcycle to a Yamaha dealer or motorcycle repair shop for bearing replacement.

**11.4 The bearings may require a blind hole puller for removal**

# Chapter 5 Part B
## Steering, suspension and final drive (XV700-1100 models)

## Contents

## Degrees of difficulty

| Easy, suitable for novice with little experience |  | Fairly easy, suitable for beginner with some experience |  | Fairly difficult, suitable for competent DIY mechanic |  | Difficult, suitable for experienced DIY mechanic | | Very difficult, suitable for expert DIY or professional |  |

## Specifications

### Front suspension
Fork spring length
  1981 through 1983 XV750 ............................... 635 mm (25.0 inches)
  XV920 J, K and MK ...................................... 624.7 mm (24.6 inches)
  XV920 RH, RJ and TR1 .................................. 577.5 mm (22.7 inches)
  1984 and 1985 models (except TR1) .................... 508 mm (20.0 inches)
  1986-on models ........................................ 513 mm (20.2 inches)
Fork oil capacity (US)
  1981 through 1983 XV750 ............................... 278 cc (9.40 US fl oz, 9.78 Imp fl oz)
  XV920 J ............................................... 303 cc (10.24 US fl oz, 10.66 Imp fl oz)
  XV920 K and MK ........................................ 290 cc (9.80 US fl oz, 10.20 Imp fl oz)
  XV920 RH and RJ ....................................... 264 cc (8.92 US fl oz, 9.30 Imp fl oz)
  1984 and 1985 XV700 .................................. 389 cc (13.1 US fl oz, 13.7 Imp fl oz)
  1986-on XV700 and 750 ................................ 396 cc (13.4 US fl oz, 13.9 Imp fl oz)
  XV1000 and 1100 ...................................... 372 cc (12.6 US fl oz, 13.1 Imp fl oz)
Fork oil type ............................................ SAE 10W fork oil
Fork oil level (US)
  1981 through 1983 models ............................. Not specified
  XV700, XV750, XV1000 ................................. 155 mm (6.1 inches) below top of inner fork tube*
  XV1100 ............................................... 179 mm (7.0 inches) below top of inner fork tube*
Fork oil capacity (UK)
  1981 through 1983 XV750 ............................... 278 cc (9.40 US fl oz, 9.78 Imp fl oz)
  TR1 .................................................. 264 cc (8.92 US fl oz, 9.30 Imp fl oz)
  1986-on XV750, 1000 and 1100 ......................... 396 cc (13.4 US fl oz, 13.9 Imp fl oz)
Fork oil level (UK)
  1981 through 1983 XV750 and TR1 ...................... Not specified
  1992-on XV750, 1994 XV1100 ........................... 155 mm (6.1 inches) below top of inner fork tube*
  1986 through 1993 XV1000 and 1100 .................... 179 mm (7.0 inches) below top of inner fork tube*
*With spring removed and fork fully compressed.
**Note:** *The fork oil capacity can be increased on UK 1992-on XV750 and 1989-on XV1100 models from 396 cc to 409 cc if a clicking sound is heard from the forks when travelling over uneven road surfaces or under hard braking. If the increased capacity is used, the oil level will be 137 mm.*

## Rear suspension

Rear spring free length
    1981 through 1983 XV750 . . . . . . . . . . . . . . . . . . . . . . . . . . . . . . 167 mm (6.57 inches)
    XV920 J, K, MK . . . . . . . . . . . . . . . . . . . . . . . . . . . . . . . . . . . . . . 168.5 mm (6.63 inches)
    XV920 RH, RJ and TR1 . . . . . . . . . . . . . . . . . . . . . . . . . . . . . . . . 172 mm (6.77 inches)
    1984 and 1985 models (except TR1) . . . . . . . . . . . . . . . . . . . . 223 mm (8.78 inches)
    1986-on XV700 and XV750 . . . . . . . . . . . . . . . . . . . . . . . . . . . . . 224.5 mm (8.83 inches)
    1986-on XV1100 . . . . . . . . . . . . . . . . . . . . . . . . . . . . . . . . . . . . . . 216.5 mm (8.5 inches)
Rear spring sag limit . . . . . . . . . . . . . . . . . . . . . . . . . . . . . . . . . . . . 5 mm (0.20 inch)
Swingarm end play and side play limits . . . . . . . . . . . . . . . . . . . . . 1 mm (0.04 inch)

## Torque specifications

**1981 through 1983 models**
Front forks
    Damper rod bolt . . . . . . . . . . . . . . . . . . . . . . . . . . . . . . . . . . . . . . . 20 Nm (14 ft-lbs)**
    Triple clamp pinch bolts . . . . . . . . . . . . . . . . . . . . . . . . . . . . . . . . 20 Nm (14 ft-lbs)
Handlebars and steering stem
    Handlebar bracket to upper triple clamp nuts (XV920J only) . . . . . . . 23 Nm (17 ft-lbs)
    Handlebar pinch bolts (XV920J only)
        Inner sections . . . . . . . . . . . . . . . . . . . . . . . . . . . . . . . . . . . . . . 30 Nm (22 ft-lbs)
        Outer sections . . . . . . . . . . . . . . . . . . . . . . . . . . . . . . . . . . . . . . 13 Nm (9 ft-lbs)
    Steering stem bolt
        XV920 J, K, MK . . . . . . . . . . . . . . . . . . . . . . . . . . . . . . . . . . . . . 50 Nm (36 ft-lbs)
        All others . . . . . . . . . . . . . . . . . . . . . . . . . . . . . . . . . . . . . . . . . . 54 Nm (39 ft-lbs)
    Steering head bearing ring nut . . . . . . . . . . . . . . . . . . . . . . . . . . see Chapter 1
Rear suspension unit pivot bolt . . . . . . . . . . . . . . . . . . . . . . . . . . . 45 Nm (32.5 ft-lbs)
Swingarm pivot bolt . . . . . . . . . . . . . . . . . . . . . . . . . . . . . . . . . . . . . 78 Nm (56 ft-lbs)
Final drive unit to swingarm nuts . . . . . . . . . . . . . . . . . . . . . . . . . . 43 Nm (31 ft-lbs)

**1984-on models**
Front forks
    Damper rod bolt . . . . . . . . . . . . . . . . . . . . . . . . . . . . . . . . . . . . . . . 23 Nm (17 ft-lbs)**
    Upper triple clamp pinch bolts . . . . . . . . . . . . . . . . . . . . . . . . . . . 20 Nm (14 ft-lbs)
    Lower triple clamp pinch bolts . . . . . . . . . . . . . . . . . . . . . . . . . . . 23 Nm (17 ft-lbs)
    Cap bolt . . . . . . . . . . . . . . . . . . . . . . . . . . . . . . . . . . . . . . . . . . . . . . 23 Nm (17 ft-lbs)
Handlebars and steering stem
    Handlebar bracket to upper triple clamp nuts
        All except 1988-on XV750 . . . . . . . . . . . . . . . . . . . . . . . . . . . . not specified
        1988-on XV750 . . . . . . . . . . . . . . . . . . . . . . . . . . . . . . . . . . . . . 59 Nm (43 ft-lbs)
    Handlebar pinch bolts . . . . . . . . . . . . . . . . . . . . . . . . . . . . . . . . . . 20 Nm (14 ft-lbs)
    Steering stem nut . . . . . . . . . . . . . . . . . . . . . . . . . . . . . . . . . . . . . 110 Nm (80 ft-lbs)
    Steering head bearing ring nut . . . . . . . . . . . . . . . . . . . . . . . . . . see Chapter 1
Rear shock absorber upper bolts . . . . . . . . . . . . . . . . . . . . . . . . . . 20 Nm (14 ft-lbs)
Rear shock absorber lower bolts/nuts . . . . . . . . . . . . . . . . . . . . . . 30 Nm (22 ft-lbs)
Swingarm pivot shafts
    Left pivot shaft . . . . . . . . . . . . . . . . . . . . . . . . . . . . . . . . . . . . . . . . 100 Nm (72 ft-lbs)
    Right pivot shaft
        All except 1988-on XV750 . . . . . . . . . . . . . . . . . . . . . . . . . . . . 5.5 Nm (4 ft-lbs)
        1988-on XV750 . . . . . . . . . . . . . . . . . . . . . . . . . . . . . . . . . . . . . 6 Nm (4.3 ft-lbs)
    Right pivot shaft nut . . . . . . . . . . . . . . . . . . . . . . . . . . . . . . . . . . . 100 Nm (72 ft-lbs)
Final drive unit to swingarm nuts
    All except 1988-on XV750 . . . . . . . . . . . . . . . . . . . . . . . . . . . . . . 43 Nm (32 ft-lbs)
    1988-on XV750 . . . . . . . . . . . . . . . . . . . . . . . . . . . . . . . . . . . . . . . 42 Nm (30 ft-lbs)
**Apply non-permanent thread locking agent to the bolt threads.*

---

## 1  General information

The front forks are of the conventional coil spring, hydraulically-damped telescopic type. Fork air pressure is adjustable on 1981 through 1983 XV750/920 models, all TR1 and XV1000 models, and 1986 through 1993 XV1100 models.

The rear suspension on 1981 through 1983 models consists of a single shock absorber with concentric coil spring and a swingarm. Suspension damping and shock absorber air pressure are adjustable.

The rear suspension on 1984 and later models consists of twin shock absorbers with concentric coil springs and a swingarm.

Chain final drive is used on XV920 RH, RJ and RK models, as well as on 1981 through 1985 XV1000 (TR1) models sold in the UK. All other motorcycles covered in this Chapter use shaft final drive.

**2.2a Pry up the bolt cover, then remove the handlebar cover bolt and cover**

**2.2b Remove the trim caps from the handlebar bracket Allen bolts**

## 2 Handlebar(s) - removal and installation

### All models except XV920J

**1** The handlebar is a one-piece unit that's secured to the upper triple clamp by a pair of brackets.

**2** To remove the handlebar from its brackets, remove the trim cover (if equipped) and remove the bolts that secure the top half of each bracket **(see illustrations)**. Lift the handlebar out.

**3** If the handlebar must be removed for access to other components, such as the forks or the steering head, it's not necessary to disconnect the cables, wires or hoses, but it is a good idea to support the assembly with a piece of wire or rope, to avoid unnecessary strain on the cables, wires and the brake hose.

**4** If the handlebar is to be removed completely, refer to Chapter 2 for clutch cable removal procedures, Chapter 6 for the brake master cylinder removal procedures, Chapter 3 for the throttle grip removal procedure and Chapter 8 for the switch removal procedure.

**5** To remove a bracket from the upper triple clamp, pull out the safety clip and remove the nut, lockwasher and washer, then lift the bracket out.

1 Upper triple clamp
2 Top bolt
3 Steering stem pinch bolt
4 Fork pinch bolt
5 Washer
6 Nut
7 Washer
8 Lockwasher
9 Nut
10 Safety clip
11 Bearing locknut
12 Bearing cover
13 Upper bearing top race
14 Upper bearing balls
15 Upper bearing bottom race
16 Lower bearing top race
17 Lower bearing balls
18 Lower bearing bottom race
19 Dust seal
20 Steering stem/lower triple clamp
21 Bolt
22 Washer
23 Handlebar bracket (lower half)
24 Handlebar bracket (upper half)
25 Bolt
26 Plug (chain drive models only)
27 Handlebar cover
28 Washer
29 Screw or bolt
30 Trim cover
31 Bearing ring nut
32 Cable guide

**2.2c Steering head and handlebar brackets (1981 through 1983 models except XV920J) - exploded view**

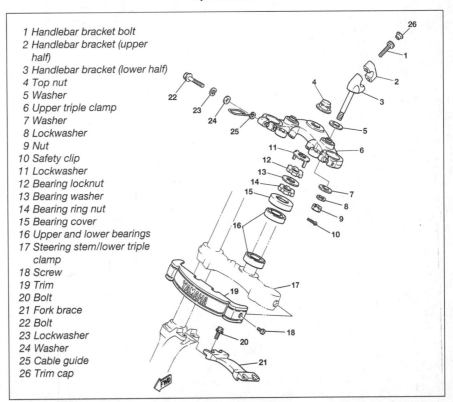

1 Handlebar bracket bolt
2 Handlebar bracket (upper half)
3 Handlebar bracket (lower half)
4 Top nut
5 Washer
6 Upper triple clamp
7 Washer
8 Lockwasher
9 Nut
10 Safety clip
11 Lockwasher
12 Bearing locknut
13 Bearing washer
14 Bearing ring nut
15 Bearing cover
16 Upper and lower bearings
17 Steering stem/lower triple clamp
18 Screw
19 Trim
20 Bolt
21 Fork brace
22 Bolt
23 Lockwasher
24 Washer
25 Cable guide
26 Trim cap

**2.2d Steering head and handlebar brackets (1984 and later models) - exploded view**

**2.7a  The arrow mark on each handlebar bracket must point to the front of the motorcycle**

**2.7b  Align the handlebar dot with the the bracket gap; the gaps at the front and back must be even**

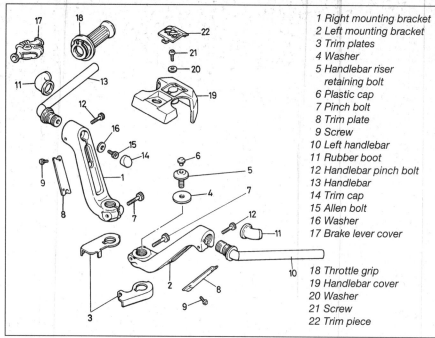

1 Right mounting bracket
2 Left mounting bracket
3 Trim plates
4 Washer
5 Handlebar riser retaining bolt
6 Plastic cap
7 Pinch bolt
8 Trim plate
9 Screw
10 Left handlebar
11 Rubber boot
12 Handlebar pinch bolt
13 Handlebar
14 Trim cap
15 Allen bolt
16 Washer
17 Brake lever cover
18 Throttle grip
19 Handlebar cover
20 Washer
21 Screw
22 Trim piece

**2.8  Handlebars (XV920J) - exploded view**

**6** Check the handlebar and brackets for cracks and distortion and replace them if any undesirable conditions are found. If the brackets were removed, check their rubber mounts for brittleness or deterioration.

**7** Installation is the reverse of the removal steps, with the following additions:
a)  Make sure the arrow cast in the top half of each bracket points forward (**see illustration**).
b)  Align the dot on the handlebar with the gap in the bracket (**see illustration**). Tighten the nuts and bolts to the torques listed in this Chapter's Specifications and be sure the gaps at the front and rear of each bracket are even.

### XV920J models

**8** Pry the trim piece out of the handlebar cover, then remove the screw, the washer and the cover (**see illustration**).

**9** Pry the plastic caps out of the handlebar riser retaining bolts, then remove the retaining bolts and washers and loosen the pinch bolts.

**10** Lift the handlebars off the mounting bracket (**see illustration**).

**11** If the handlebar must be removed for access to other components, such as the forks or the steering head, it's not necessary to disconnect the cables, wires or hoses, but it is a good idea to support the assembly with a piece of wire or rope, to avoid unnecessary strain on the cables, wires and the brake hose.

**12** If the handlebar is to be removed completely, refer to Chapter 2 for clutch cable removal procedures, Chapter 6 for the brake master cylinder removal procedures, Chapter 3 for the throttle grip removal procedure and Chapter 8 for the switch removal procedure.

**13** To remove the brackets from the upper triple clamp, pull out the safety clips and remove the nuts, lockwashers and washers (**see illustration 2.10**), then lift the bracket out.

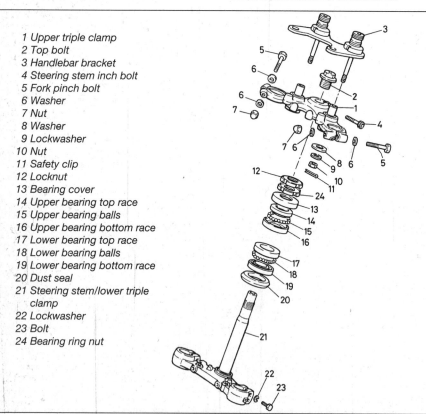

1 Upper triple clamp
2 Top bolt
3 Handlebar bracket
4 Steering stem inch bolt
5 Fork pinch bolt
6 Washer
7 Nut
8 Washer
9 Lockwasher
10 Nut
11 Safety clip
12 Locknut
13 Bearing cover
14 Upper bearing top race
15 Upper bearing balls
16 Upper bearing bottom race
17 Lower bearing top race
18 Lower bearing balls
19 Lower bearing bottom race
20 Dust seal
21 Steering stem/lower triple clamp
22 Lockwasher
23 Bolt
24 Bearing ring nut

**2.10  Steering head and handlebar bracket (XV920J) - exploded view**

14 Check the handlebar and bracket for cracks and distortion and replace them if any undesirable conditions are found.

15 Installation is the reverse of the removal steps, with the following additions:
a) *Adjust the handlebar position (see Section 3).*
b) *Tighten the nuts and bolts to the torques listed in this Chapter's Specifications.*

### 3 Handlebar adjustment (XV920J models)

1 There are two handlebar adjustments: the risers can be rotated on the bracket to one of three positions, and the handlebars themselves can be raised or lowered to one of three positions.

2 To adjust the risers, refer to Section 2 and detach the handlebars from their bracket. Place the risers in one of the three adjustment positions, then refer to Section 2 and install the risers.

3 To adjust the handlebars, remove the trim caps from the tops of the risers **(see illustration 2.8)**. Loosen the Allen bolts that secure the handlebars in the risers and loosen the pinch bolts. Pull the handlebars out of the risers far enough to rotate them to one of the three adjustment positions, then push the handlebars all the way back in.

4 Tighten the Allen bolts to the torque listed in this Chapter's Specifications and install the trim caps.

⚠️ *Warning: Don't adjust the risers or the handlebars to any position other than the three positions provided; this could cause loss of steering control.*

### 4 Steering head bearings (1981 through 1983 models) - replacement

1 Ball bearings are used in the steering head of 1981 through 1983 XV750 and 920 models and in all TR1 models. If the steering head bearing check/adjustment (see Chapter 1) does not remedy excessive play or roughness in the steering head bearings, the entire front end must be disassembled and the bearings and races replaced with new ones.

### Removal (all models except XV920J)

2 Remove the front wheel (see Chapter 6).
3 Refer to Section 7 and remove the front forks.
4 Disconnect the negative cable from the battery to prevent an accidental short circuit while disconnecting electrical wiring.
5 Cover the fuel tank with a blanket to prevent damage.
6 Remove the handlebar and place it back out of the way. It shouldn't be necessary to disconnect the cables or brake hose, but if necessary, remove tie wraps to allow slack in the cables. Also, make sure the master cylinder stays upright to prevent fluid leakage.

7 Remove the headlight lens (see Chapter 8) and disconnect the wiring connectors within the headlight body.

### XV750 models

8 Remove the single screw that controls vertical adjustment of the headlight.
9 Unscrew the speedometer cable from the speedometer and remove two Allen bolts that secure the instrument bracket. Pull the headlight assembly and instrument cluster forward, away from the upper triple clamp.
10 Remove the fuse holder cover and detach the fuse holder from the lower triple clamp.
11 Remove the left horn (see Chapter 8), then detach the brake hose from its retaining clip on the horn mounting bracket.
12 Disconnect the wires from the right horn, then detach the horn mounting bracket from the lower triple clamp.

### XV920 and XV1000 (TR1) models

13 Unbolt the headlight brackets from the lower triple clamp **(see illustration)**. Remove the nut that attaches the top of each headlight bracket to the instrument cluster studs at the upper triple clamp **(see illustration)**.
14 Disconnect the speedometer cable and electrical connectors from the instrument cluster, then lift the cluster clear of the triple clamp and pull the headlight assembly forward out of the way.
15 Remove the fuse holder and the horn, then unbolt the brake hose joint from the lower triple clamp without disconnecting any hydraulic lines.

### All models

16 Check the steering stem and lower triple clamp to make sure nothing is still attaching them to the motorcycle.
17 The bearing balls may fall out and be lost during the next steps. It's a good idea to place a blanket on the floor to prevent them from bouncing and rolling. Try to catch the balls with a magnet as the steering stem is lowered. This will be easier if an assistant is available.

18 Loosen the steering stem pinch bolt and remove the top bolt **(see illustration 2.2c)**. Lift the upper triple clamp away from the steering stem.
19 Remove the steering stem locknut with a spanner wrench (C-spanner).
20 Remove the bearing ring nut with the spanner wrench (C-spanner). Remove the upper bearing top race and collect the 19 bearing balls with a magnet.
21 Slowly lower the lower triple clamp away from the steering head until the lower bearing balls are exposed. Try to catch them with the magnet (there are 19).
22 Lower the steering stem out of the steering head.

### Removal (XV920J)

23 Remove the front wheel (see Chapter 6).
24 Refer to Section 7 and remove the front forks.
25 Disconnect the negative cable from the battery to prevent an accidental short circuit while disconnecting electrical wiring.
26 Cover the fuel tank with a blanket to prevent damage.
27 Detach the handlebar risers from the bracket on the upper triple clamp and lace them back out of the way (see Section 3). It shouldn't be necessary to disconnect the cables or brake hose, but if necessary, remove tie wraps to allow slack in the cables. Also, make sure the master cylinder stays upright to prevent fluid leakage.
28 Remove the headlight lens (see Chapter 8) and disconnect the wiring connectors within the headlight body.
29 Remove the plastic trim piece from the lower triple clamp, then unbolt the headlight bracket from the lower triple clamp.
30 Remove the instrument cluster (see Chapter 8).
31 Remove the top bolt and the upper triple clamp **(see illustration 2.10)**. Move the headlight assembly out of the way.
32 Remove the fuse holder, horns and brake hose joint from the lower triple clamp.
33 Perform Steps 16 through 22 above to remove the steering stem and bearings from the steering head.

**4.13a Unbolt the headlight brackets from the lower triple clamp . . .**

**4.13b . . . and remove the nuts that secure the brackets and instrument cluster to the upper clamp**

## Inspection

**34** This is the same as for XV535 models. Refer to Part A of this Chapter.

## Installation

**35** Installation of the bearings and steering stem in the steering head is the same as for XV535 models. Refer to Part A of this Chapter.
**36** Refer to Chapter 1 and adjust the bearings.
**37** The remainder of installation is the reverse of the removal steps.

---

### 5  Steering head bearings (1984 and later models) - replacement

**1** Tapered roller bearings are used in the steering head of 1984 and later models. If the steering head bearing check/adjustment (see Chapter 1) does not remedy excessive play or roughness in the steering head bearings, the entire front end must be disassembled and the bearings and races replaced with new ones.

## Removal

**2** Remove the front wheel (see Chapter 6).
**3** Refer to Section 7 and remove the front forks.
**4** Disconnect the negative cable from the battery to prevent an accidental short circuit while disconnecting electrical wiring.
**5** Cover the fuel tank with a blanket to prevent damage.
**6** Remove the handlebar and place it back out of the way. It shouldn't be necessary to disconnect the cables or brake hose, but if necessary, remove tie wraps to allow slack in the cables. Also, make sure the master cylinder stays upright to prevent fluid leakage.
**7** Remove the headlight lens (see Chapter 8) and disconnect the wiring connectors within the headlight body. Remove the headlight assembly mounting bolts, one inside the headlight body and two that attach the headlight body and brake hose joint to the lower triple clamp. Move the headlight assembly out of the way.
**8** Disconnect the instrument cluster electrical connectors.

**5.10a Remove the washer and the lower ring nut**

**5.10b Remove the bearing cover**

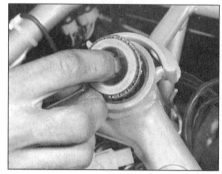

**5.11a Lift the upper bearing out of the steering head . . .**

**5.11b . . . and lower the steering stem out of the steering head**

**9** Remove the steering stem nut and lift off the upper triple clamp, together with the instrument cluster **(see illustration 2.2d)**.
**10** Remove the lockwasher, bearing locknut and second washer from the steering stem. Remove the lower ring nut and bearing cover **(see illustrations)**.
**11** Remove the upper bearing **(see illustration)**, then lower the steering stem and lower triple clamp assembly out of the steering head **(see illustration)**. If it's stuck, tap gently on top of the steering stem with a plastic mallet or a hammer and a wood block.

## Inspection and installation

**12** Clean all the parts with solvent and dry them thoroughly, using compressed air, if available. If you do use compressed air, don't

let the bearings spin as they're dried - it could ruin them. Wipe the old grease out of the frame steering head and bearing races.
**13** Examine the races in the steering head for cracks, dents and pits. If even the slightest amount of wear or damage is evident, the races should be replaced with new ones.
**14** To remove the upper race, drive it out of the steering head from below with a hammer and punch **(see illustration)**. A slide hammer with the proper internal-jaw puller will also work.
**15** The lower race can be removed in the same way as the upper race if there's enough room for the punch to bear against the race. If there isn't, use a puller tool which can hook the race and be locked into position **(see illustrations)**. Tap against the tool with a

**5.14 Drive out the upper race from below with a punch**

**5.15a The lower race may not leave room for a punch to be placed against it . . .**

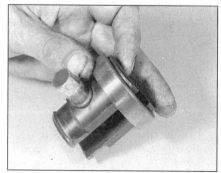

**5.15b . . . so, insert a tool like this one into the race and expand it so it grips the race securely . . .**

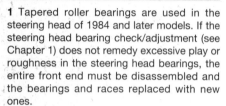

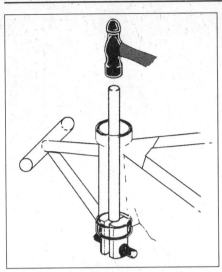

**5.15c . . . then drive out the tool and race together with a hammer and punch**

hammer and punch to drive the race and tool out of the steering head **(see illustration)**.
**16** Since the races are an interference fit in the frame, installation will be easier if the new races are left overnight in a refrigerator. This will cause them to contract and slip into place in the frame with very little effort. When installing the races, tap them gently into place with a hammer and punch or a large socket. Do not strike the bearing surface or the race will be damaged.
**17** Check the bearings for wear. Look for cracks, dents, pits in or flat spots on the bearing rollers. Replace any defective parts with new ones. If a new bearing is required, replace both of them as a set.
**18** Don't remove the lower bearing unless it, or the grease seal beneath it, must be replaced **(see illustration)**. Remove the bearing from the steering stem with a bearing splitter and puller setup. These can be rented. Tap the lower bearing on with a hammer and piece of pipe the same diameter as the bearing inner race. Don't tap against the rollers or roller cage or the bearing will be ruined. As an alternative, take the steering stem to a Yamaha dealer or motorcycle repair

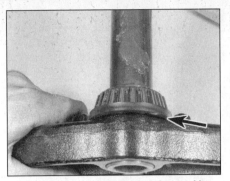

**5.18 Remove the lower bearing and its grease seal (arrow) if they need to be replaced**

shop and have the old bearing pressed off and a new one pressed on.
**19** Inspect the steering stem/lower triple clamp for cracks and other damage. Don't attempt to repair any steering components. Replace them with new parts if defects are found.
**20** Pack the bearings with high-quality grease (preferably a moly-based grease) **(see illustration)**. Coat the outer races with grease also.
**21** Insert the steering stem/lower triple clamp into the steering head. Install the upper bearing and lower ring nut. Refer to Chapter 1 and adjust the bearings.
**22** The remainder of installation is the reverse of the removal steps.

# 6  Fork oil change

**1** Support the bike securely so it can't be knocked over during this procedure. Place it on the centerstand (if equipped). The front wheel must be raised off the ground using a jack and wood support under the crankcase, or with axle stands.
**2** On all except XV920J models, remove the plastic fork caps **(see illustration)**.
**3** On all except XV700 models, press on the

**5.20 Work the grease completely into the rollers**

air valve with a small screwdriver or similar tool to release the fork air pressure.
**4** If you're working on an XV920 K or MK, the easiest way to make an opening for the new fork oil is to unscrew the air valve core with a core removal tool **(see illustration)**. As an alternative, unscrew the air valve itself.
**5** If you're working on a 1981 through 1983 XV750, a chain drive XV920 or a TR1, press down the spring seat with a socket that will fit over the air valve. Use an extension on the socket so you can grip it **(see illustration)**. Remove the stopper ring, then slowly release the spring pressure and lift out the spring seat and spring **(see illustration)**.

**6.2 Remove the plastic cap from the fork**

**6.4 Unscrewing the air valve core on models with separate air valves will provide a way to add fork oil**

**6.5a Push the fork cap down against spring pressure with a socket big enough to fit over the air valve**

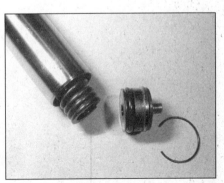

**6.5b Remove the retainer, then remove the fork cap and spring**

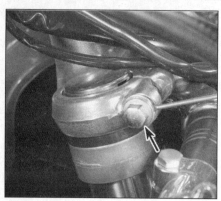

6.6 Loosen the upper triple clamp bolts (arrow); 1994 1100 model shown

6.9 Remove the drain screw from the bottom of the fork leg

6.12 Add the specified amount of fork oil

6 Loosen the upper triple clamp pinch bolts **(see illustration)**.
7 If you're working on an XV920J, unscrew the fork cap.
8 On all other models, unscrew the fork cap with an Allen bolt bit. **Note:** *If you don't have an Allen bolt bit of the correct size, use a bolt with a head size that fits into the fork cap. Turn the bolt with locking pliers.*
9 Place a drain pan under the fork leg and remove the drain screw **(see illustration)**.

⚠ *Warning: Do not allow the fork oil to contact the tire, brake disc or pads. If it does, wash off the tire, clean the disc with brake system cleaner and replace the pads with new ones before riding the motorcycle.*

10 After most of the oil has drained, slowly compress and release the forks to pump out the remaining oil. An assistant will most likely be required to do this.
11 Check the drain screw gasket and spring seat O-ring (if equipped) for damage and replace them if necessary. Clean the threads of the drain screw with solvent and let it dry, then install the screw and gasket, tightening it securely.

12 Pour the type and amount of fork oil, listed in this Chapter's Specifications, into the fork tube through the opening at the top **(see illustration)**.
13 Remove the jack from under the engine and slowly pump the forks a few times to purge the air.
14 If fork oil level is specified for the bike you're working on, measure the level of the oil in the fork with the fork fully compressed and without the spring in position **(see illustration)**. Compare it to the value listed in this Chapter's Specifications. Add or remove oil as necessary, then install the spring.
15 If you're working on a 1981 through 1983 XV750, coat the O-ring on the spring seat with a thin layer of multi-purpose grease. Install the spring seat and stopper ring **(see illustrations 3.4a and 3.4b in Part A of this Chapter)**.
16 If you're working on an XV920J, install the cap bolt assembly **(see illustration)**.

*Caution: The cap bolt should sit as shown in the illustration before you try to screw it in. If it sits higher, the damping adjusting rod is out of position. Turn the cap bolt so*

*the bottom end of the damping adjusting rod engages the semicircular hole in the top of the damper rod inside the fork. Forcing the cap bolt in when it sits too high will ruin the damping adjuster.*

17 On all other models, install the fork cap and tighten it to the torque listed in this Chapter's Specifications.
18 The remainder of installation is the reverse of the removal steps. Tighten all fasteners to the torque listed in this Chapter's Specifications.
19 On models with air valves, adjust fork air pressure (see Chapter 1).

## 7 Forks -
### removal and installation

### Removal

1 Support the bike securely so it can't be knocked over during this procedure. Place it on the centerstand (if equipped).
2 Place a jack under the engine and raise it slightly to lift the front tire off the ground.

6.14 Pour in the specified amount of oil - on later models, measure the level and adjust it as needed

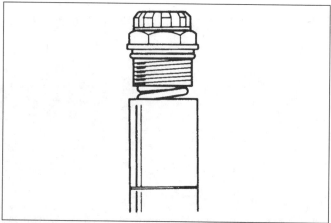

6.16 The fork cap should sit like this - if not, reposition the end of the damping adjusting rod

**7.7a Remove the trim screw (A); remove the trim caps (B), then loosen the lower triple clamp bolts**

3 Remove the brake caliper and front wheel (see Chapter 6).
4 Remove the front fender (see Chapter 7).
5 Remove any wiring harness clamps or straps from the fork tubes.
6 If the fork will be disassembled after removal, read through the disassembly procedure (see Section 8), paying special attention to the damper rod bolt removal steps. If you don't have the necessary special tool or a substitute for it, you can remove the damper rod bolt before the fork is disassembled, while the spring tension will keep the damper rod from spinning inside the fork tube. This is also a good time to loosen the fork top bolt (if equipped), as it will eliminate the need to clamp the fork tube in a vise after it's removed.
7 Loosen the upper triple clamp bolts (see illustration 6.5b). Remove the trim cover and loosen the lower triple clamp bolts (see illustrations), then slide the fork tubes down and remove the forks from the motorcycle.

**HAYNES HiNT** *If the fork legs are seized, spray the area with penetrating oil and allow time for it to soak in before trying again.*

### Installation

8 Slide each fork leg into the lower triple clamp.
9 Slide the fork legs up, installing the tops of the tubes into the upper triple clamp. Position the top of the fork tube so that it is level with the top surface of the upper triple clamp.
10 The remainder of installation is the reverse of the removal procedure. Tighten all fasteners to the torques listed in this Chapter's Specifications and the Chapter 6 Specifications.
11 Pump the front brake lever several times to bring the pads into contact with the disc.

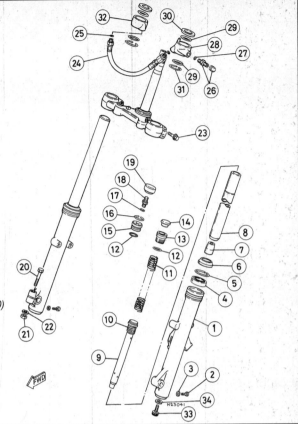

1 Outer fork tube
2 Drain screw
3 Gasket
4 Oil seal
5 Retainer
6 Dust seal
7 Damper rod seat
8 Inner fork tube
9 Damper rod
10 Rebound spring
11 Fork spring
12 O-ring (XV920)
13 Top bolt (XV920)
14 Plastic cap (XV920)
15 Fork cap (XV750)
16 Retainer (XV750)
17 O-ring (XV750)
18 Air valve (XV750)
19 Cap (XV750)
20 Bolt
21 Nut
22 Lockwasher
23 Bolt
24 Air charging hose (XV920)
25 O-ring (XV920)
26 Air valve (XV920)
27 O-ring (XV920)
28 Left air hose union
29 O-ring (XV920)
30 Seal (XV920)
31 Retainer (XV920)
32 Right air hose union

**7.7b Front forks (XV750 and XV920 K and MK models) - exploded view**

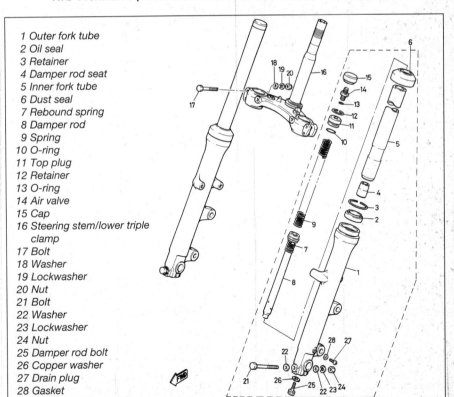

1 Outer fork tube
2 Oil seal
3 Retainer
4 Damper rod seat
5 Inner fork tube
6 Dust seal
7 Rebound spring
8 Damper rod
9 Spring
10 O-ring
11 Top plug
12 Retainer
13 O-ring
14 Air valve
15 Cap
16 Steering stem/lower triple clamp
17 Bolt
18 Washer
19 Lockwasher
20 Nut
21 Bolt
22 Washer
23 Lockwasher
24 Nut
25 Damper rod bolt
26 Copper washer
27 Drain plug
28 Gasket

**7.7c Front forks (chain drive XV920 and XV1000/TR1 models) - exploded view**

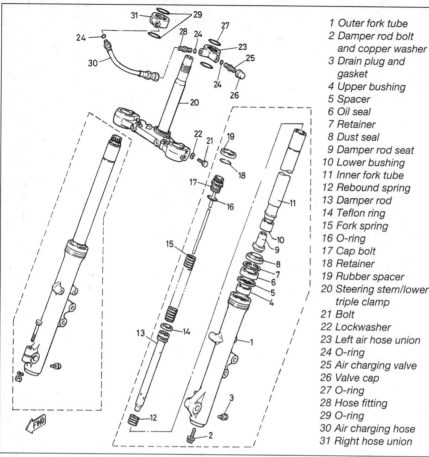

1 Outer fork tube
2 Damper rod bolt and copper washer
3 Drain plug and gasket
4 Upper bushing
5 Spacer
6 Oil seal
7 Retainer
8 Dust seal
9 Damper rod seat
10 Lower bushing
11 Inner fork tube
12 Rebound spring
13 Damper rod
14 Teflon ring
15 Fork spring
16 O-ring
17 Cap bolt
18 Retainer
19 Rubber spacer
20 Steering stem/lower triple clamp
21 Bolt
22 Lockwasher
23 Left air hose union
24 O-ring
25 Air charging valve
26 Valve cap
27 O-ring
28 Hose fitting
29 O-ring
30 Air charging hose
31 Right hose union

**7.7d  Front forks (XV920J) - exploded view**

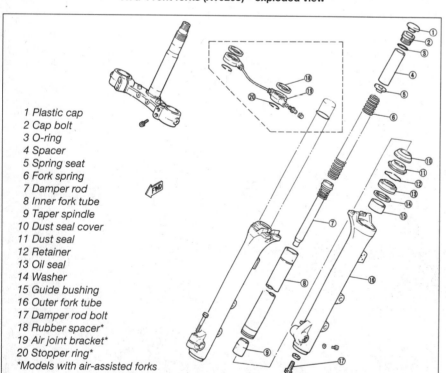

1 Plastic cap
2 Cap bolt
3 O-ring
4 Spacer
5 Spring seat
6 Fork spring
7 Damper rod
8 Inner fork tube
9 Taper spindle
10 Dust seal cover
11 Dust seal
12 Retainer
13 Oil seal
14 Washer
15 Guide bushing
16 Outer fork tube
17 Damper rod bolt
18 Rubber spacer*
19 Air joint bracket*
20 Stopper ring*
*Models with air-assisted forks

**7.7e  Front forks (1984 and later models) - exploded view**

## 8  Forks - disassembly, inspection and reassembly

### Disassembly

**Note:** *The following procedures apply to 1981 through 1983 XV750 models, XV920 K, MK, RH and RJ models and the 1982 through 1985 XV1000 (TR1). The forks used on XV920J models, as well as on all 1984 and later models except the TRI, require a press, special tools and procedures for disassembly, including heating the outer fork tube with a torch. Fork overhaul on these models should be done by a Yamaha dealer service department or other qualified repair shop.*

**1** Remove the forks following the procedure in Section 6. Work on one fork leg at a time to avoid mixing up the parts.
**2** On all except XV920K and MK models, remove the fork cap, stopper ring, spring seat and spring **(see illustrations 6.5a, 6.5b and the accompanying illustration)**.
**3** If you're working on an XV920K or MK, unscrew the top bolt with an Allen bolt bit.
**Note:** *If you don't have an Allen bolt bit of the correct size, use a bolt with a head size that fits into the top bolt. Turn the bolt with locking pliers.*
**4** Invert the fork assembly over a container and allow the oil to drain out.
**5** Prevent the damper rod from turning using a holding handle (Yamaha tool no. YM-01326,

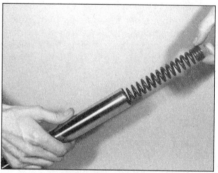

**8.2  Remove the fork spring**

**8.5a Prevent the damper rod from turning with a tool like this; it fits into the top end of the damper rod**

**8.5b Remove the damper rod bolt and its copper washer**

**8.6a Pull the upper fork tube out of the lower tube**

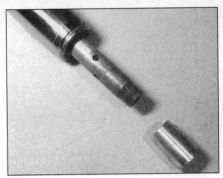

**8.6b Take the damper rod seat off the damper rod**

part no. 90890-01326) and adapter (Yamaha tool no. YM-01300-01, part no. 90890-01294) **(see illustration)** passed down through the fork inner tube to engage the damper rod head. Unscrew the Allen bolt at the bottom of the outer tube and remove the copper washer **(see illustration)**. **Note:** *If you don't have access to these tools, a piece of hardwood dowel can be used instead. Cut a taper on the end of the dowel to fit into the damper rod head. Another alternative is to loosen the damper rod bolt before removing the fork cap; the pressure of the fork spring will keep the damper rod from turning.*

6 Pull the inner fork tube out of the fork leg and separate the damper rod seat from the damper rod **(see illustrations)**.
7 Pull out the damper rod and the rebound spring **(see illustration)**. Don't remove the Teflon ring from the damper rod unless a new one will be installed.
8 Carefully pry the oil seal from the fork leg **(see illustration)**.

### Inspection

9 Clean all parts in solvent and blow them dry with compressed air, if available. Check the inner and outer fork tubes, the damper rod and its seat for score marks, scratches, flaking of the chrome and excessive or abnormal wear **(see illustrations)**. This type of fork doesn't use bushings; the inner fork tube rubs directly against the inner surface of

the fork leg. If the inner tube fits loosely in the outer tube, the outer tube is probably worn; if so, replace it. Look for dents in the tubes and replace them if any are found. Check the fork seal seat for nicks, gouges and scratches. If damage is evident, leaks will occur around the seal-to-outer tube junction. Replace worn or defective parts with new ones.
10 Have the inner fork tube checked for runout at a dealer service department or other repair shop.

⚠️ **Warning: If it is bent, it should not be straightened; replace it with a new one.**

11 Measure the overall length of the long spring and check it for cracks and other damage. Compare the length to the minimum length listed in this Chapter's Specifications. If it's defective or sagged, replace both fork springs with new ones. Never replace only one spring.

### Reassembly

12 Install the rebound spring on the damper rod. Install the damper rod in the inner fork tube, then let it slide slowly down until it protrudes from the bottom of the inner fork tube.
13 Install the damper rod seat over the end of the damper rod that protrudes from the fork tube **(see illustration 8.6b)**.
14 Install the inner fork tube in the outer fork tube.

15 Apply non-permanent thread locking agent to the damper rod bolt, then install the bolt with its copper washer and tighten it to the torque listed in this Chapter's Specifications. Hold the damper rod from turning with the tool used in Step 5. **Note:** *If you didn't use the tool, tighten the damper rod bolt after the fork spring and cap bolt are installed.*
16 Lubricate the lips and the outer diameter of the oil seal with the recommended fork oil (see Chapter 1) and slide it down the inner tube, with the closed side of the seal facing up. Drive the seal into place with the same tools used to drive in the slide bushing **(see illustration 5.18 in Part A of this Chapter)**. If you don't have access to these, it is

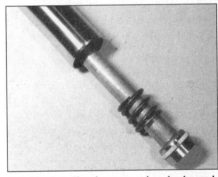

**8.7 Remove the damper rod and rebound spring from the inner fork tube**

**8.8 Pry the oil seal out of the lower fork tube**

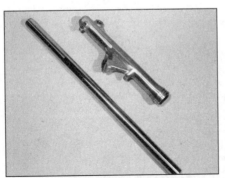

**8.9a Inspect the inner and outer fork tubes; they must be replaced if worn or damaged**

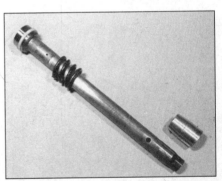

**8.9b Check the damper rod, its seat and the rebound spring for wear or damage**

**9.1a The remote adjuster handle should turn freely**

recommended that you take the assembly to a Yamaha dealer service department or other motorcycle repair shop to have the seal driven in. If you are very careful, the seal can be driven in with a hammer and a drift punch. Work around the circumference of the seal, tapping gently on the outer edge of the seal until it's seated. Be careful - if you distort the seal, you'll have to disassemble the fork again and end up taking it to a dealer anyway!

**17** Install the dust seal, making sure it seats completely. The same tool used to drive in the oil seal can be used for the dust seal.

**18** Install the drain screw and a new gasket, if it was removed.

**19** Add the recommended type and amount of fork oil (see Section 3).

**20** Install the fork spring, with the closer-wound coils at the top.

**21** Refer to Section 6 and install the spring seat, stopper ring and fork cap or cap bolt.

**22** Install the fork by following the procedure outlined in Section 7. If you won't be installing the fork right away, store it in an upright position.

### 9  Rear suspension unit (1981 through 1983 models and TR1) - inspection, removal and installation

#### Removal

**1** Lift or remove the seat. Check for loose

1 Shock absorber
2 Upper bushing
3 Lower bushing
4 Sleeves
5 Upper spring seat
6 Spring
7 Lower spring seat
8 Seating ring
9 Retaining ring
10 Attachment pin
11 Pivot bolt
12 O-ring
13 Air hose
14 Control cables
15 O-rings
16 Remove adjuster unit upper half
17 Seal
18 O-ring
19 Allen bolt
20 Remote adjuster unit lower half
21 Remote adjuster handle
22 Screw
23 Screw
24 Nut
25 O-ring
26 Air charging valve
27 Cap
28 Cotter pin

**9.1b Rear suspension unit (1981 through 1983 models) - exploded view**

mountings and for visible wear or damage. Look for oil leaks. Turn the remote adjuster handle and make sure it rotates freely **(see illustrations)**. If the suspension unit is to be removed, press down on the air valve core with a small screwdriver or similar tool and release the air pressure.

**2** Remove the fuel tank (see Chapter 3) and the rear wheel (see Chapter 6).

**3** On the right side of the bike, remove the rubber cover to expose the end of the attachment pin that secures the suspension unit to the swingarm **(see illustration)**. Remove the cotter pin from the attachment pin **(see illustration)**.

**4** Tap the attachment pin out with a soft

metal drift and hammer **(see illustration)**. **Note:** *If the attachment pin won't come out easily, soak it with penetrating oil and allow time for the oil to work. If necessary, support the other side of the swingarm with a wood block while tapping the attachment pin out.*

**5** Remove the two Allen bolts that secure the remote adjuster to the frame. Don't disconnect the cables or the air hose from the adjuster; free them from any clips and place them alongside the suspension unit so they won't be in the way during removal.

**6** At the top of the suspension unit, remove the pivot bolt that attaches it to the frame **(see illustration)**.

**9.3a Remove the rubber cover . . .**

**9.3b . . . and remove the cotter pin**

**9.4 Tap the attachment pin out**

9.6  Remove the pivot bolt

9.7  Guide the suspension unit out of the frame

9.10  The adjuster ring should turn freely

**7** Lift the suspension unit and remove it rearward **(see illustration)**.

## Inspection

**8** If the remote adjuster won't turn freely, remove its center screw and the three small screws and take it apart for cleaning. **Note:** *If the screws won't turn easily, don't try to force them or the heads may be stripped out. Apply plenty of penetrating oil and give it time to work. Once the assembly is apart, inspect its O-ring (it's a good idea to replace it as a matter of course). Pack the housing with multi-purpose lithium based grease, then assemble the adjuster.*

**9** Check the cables for damage such as kinked or dented housings and replace them if they're damaged. If the cables move stiffly, lubricate them (see Chapter 1). If this doesn't help. replace them.

**10** Check the suspension unit for obvious wear or damage that may have been missed while it was on the bike. If it's leaking air or oil, replace it. The adjuster ring should turn freely **(see illustration)**; if it's stiff, apply penetrating oil and work it back and forth until it loosens up.

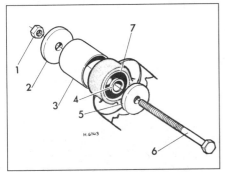

9.12b  Fabricated bushing removal tool

*1   High-strength nut*
*2   Thick washer*
*3   Metal tube (large enough for the bushing to fit inside)*
*4   Bushing sleeve*
*5   Thick washer*
*6   High-strength bolt*
*7   Bushing*

⚠ *Warning: The suspension unit contains compressed nitrogen gas and requires special disposal procedures for safety. Refer to Part A of this Chapter for the safe disposal method.*

**11** Check for air leaks by applying soapy water to the air hose connections, then adding a small amount of air through the charging valve with a hand pump. If bubbles appear, there's a leak. The most likely cause is a failed O-ring. If the hose or charging valve leak, replace them.

**12** Inspect the mounting bushings at the end of the suspension unit **(see illustration)**. If they're deteriorated or if the rubber has separated from the metal, replace them. A puller tool can be fabricated from a bolt, nut, washers and a piece of tubing **(see illustration)**. It may be more practical to have the bushings pressed out and new ones pressed in by a dealer service department. **Caution: Don't try to hammer the bushings out. This will place side loads on the suspension unit and damage it.**

**13** To remove the spring from the suspension unit, compress it with a coil spring compressor designed for suspension springs. These can be rented from tool rental centers.

⚠ *Warning: The spring is powerful. Don't try to compress it with makeshift tools or it may slip and cause injury. With the*

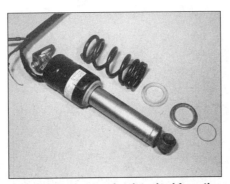

9.13  The spring can be detached from the suspension unit

spring compressed, remove the retaining clip, seating ring and lower spring seat **(see illustration)**.

**14** Measure the free length of the spring and compare it to the value listed in this Chapter's Specifications. If it's sagged, replace it. Check the seating ring, spring seat and retaining ring for wear or damage and replace them as necessary. Make sure the retaining ring groove in the suspension unit is free of burrs.

**15** Install the spring on the suspension unit so its closely wound coils will be downward when the unit is installed on the bike. Compress the spring with the special tool, then install the seating ring and spring seat. Install the retaining ring and make sure it's securely seated in its groove **(see illustration)**. Release the spring tension and remove the compressor.

9.12a  Check the bushings and the metal sleeves for wear and damage

9.15  Secure the spring seat with the retaining clip, making sure the clip seats securely in its groove

**9.17 Make sure the cables and hose are clear of the suspension unit and secure them in their clips**

## Installation

16 Guide the suspension unit into position. Coat the shaft of the pivot bolt with a thin layer of multi-purpose grease (but keep the grease off the bolt threads), then install the bolt and tighten it to the torque listed in this Chapter's Specifications.

17 Place the remote adjuster near its installed position. Route the cables and air hose so they're clear of the suspension unit and install them in the clips **(see illustration)**. Make sure the cable sheath is in position.

18 Coat the attachment pin with anti-seize compound and install it in the frame and suspension unit. Install a new cotter pin and bend the ends.

**10.2a The right shock is secured by bolts (arrows); the left is secured by a bolt (top) and a nut (bottom)**

19 The remainder of installation is the reverse of the removal steps.

## 10 Rear shock absorbers (1984 and later models) - removal, inspection and installation

### Removal

1 Support the bike securely so it can't be knocked over during this procedure. Place a jack beneath the frame to lift the rear tire off the ground and support the swingarm so it can't drop.

2 Unbolt the top end of the shock from the frame **(see illustrations)**.

3 Remove the bolt that secures the lower end of the right shock or the nut that secures the lower end of the left shock. Rotate the top end of the shock toward the rear of the bike and take it off.

### Inspection

4 Check the shock for obvious physical damage and the coil spring for looseness or signs of fatigue; replace both shock absorbers as a pair if these conditions are found. Except for mounting bushings, replacement parts are not available.

5 Check the shock for signs of oil or gas leaks and replace it if you find any.

6 Inspect the pivot hardware at the top and bottom of the shock and replace any worn or damaged parts.

### Installation

7 Coat the pivot points with a thin layer of multi-purpose lithium-based grease. Install the shock with the tightly wound spring coils downward. Tighten the top bolts, then the bottom right bolt, then the bottom left nut to the torques listed in this Chapter's Specifications.

## 11 Swingarm bearings - check

1 Refer to Chapter 6 and remove the rear wheel, then refer to Section 9 to detach the lower end of the suspension unit or Section 10 to remove the rear shock absorbers.

2 Grasp the rear of the swingarm with one hand and place your other hand at the junction of the swingarm and the frame. Try to move the rear of the swingarm from side-to-side. Any wear (play) in the bearings should be felt as movement between the swingarm and the frame at the front. The swingarm will actually be felt to move forward and backward at the front (not from side-to-side). If any play is noted, the bearings should be replaced with new ones (see Section 12).

3 Next, move the swingarm up and down through its full travel. It should move freely, without any binding or rough spots. If it does not move freely, refer to Sections 14 and 15 for servicing procedures.

## 12 Driveshaft and final drive (shaft drive models) - removal, inspection and installation

### Removal

1 Support the bike securely so it can't be knocked over during this procedure.

2 Remove the exhaust system (see Chapter 3).

3 Remove the rear wheel (see Chapter 6).

1 Shock absorbers
2 Swingarm
3 Bearing
4 Grease seal
5 Collar
6 Lockwasher
7 Left pivot shaft
8 Pivot cover
9 Right pivot shaft
10 Nut
11 Rubber boot

**10.2b Rear suspension (1984 and later models) - exploded view**

**12.7a  Pull the final drive assembly and driveshaft clear of the swingarm**

**4** If you're working on a 1981 through 1983 model, remove the attachment pin to separate the lower end of the suspension unit from the swingarm (see Section 9).

**5** If you're working on a 1984 or later model, remove the left rear shock absorber (see Section 10).

**6** Remove the nuts and lockwashers that secure the final drive unit to the swingarm. If you're working on a 1981 through 1983 model, remove the single bolt and nut as well.

**7** Pull the final gear assembly away from the swingarm, together with the driveshaft **(see illustrations)**.

## Inspection

**8** Wipe the final gear assembly clean with a rag moistened in solvent.

**9** Check all parts for obvious wear or damage and replace any worn or damaged parts.

**10** Check the driveshaft splines for step wear. Make sure the snap-ring at the rear end of the driveshaft is securely seated in its groove **(see illustrations)**.

**11** The final drive unit requires special tools to measure and adjust gear backlash. The procedure is complicated and should be done by a dealer service department or other qualified shop. Rotate the driveshaft by hand. The ring gear splines (the part that mates with the rear wheel) should rotate smoothly. If rotation feels rough or jerky or if it's noisy, have the final drive unit disassembled and inspected.

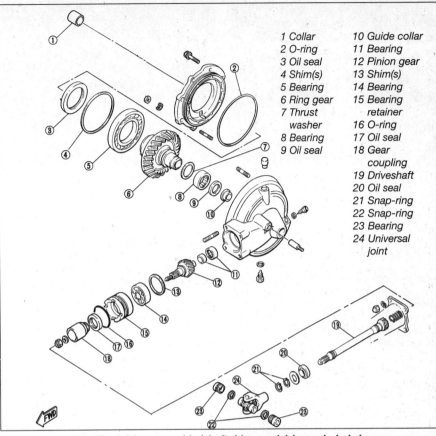

| | |
|---|---|
| 1 Collar | 10 Guide collar |
| 2 O-ring | 11 Bearing |
| 3 Oil seal | 12 Pinion gear |
| 4 Shim(s) | 13 Shim(s) |
| 5 Bearing | 14 Bearing |
| 6 Ring gear | 15 Bearing |
| 7 Thrust | retainer |
| washer | 16 O-ring |
| 8 Bearing | 17 Oil seal |
| 9 Oil seal | 18 Gear |
| | coupling |
| | 19 Driveshaft |
| | 20 Oil seal |
| | 21 Snap-ring |
| | 22 Snap-ring |
| | 23 Bearing |
| | 24 Universal |
| | joint |

**12.7b  Final drive assembly (shaft drive models) - exploded view**

## Installation

**12** Installation is the reverse of the removal steps, with the following additions:

a) Lubricate the driveshaft splines with multi-purpose lithium-based grease.

b) Apply silicone sealant to the mating surfaces of the swingarm and final drive unit.

c) Use new lockwashers and tighten the final drive-to-swingarm nuts to the torque listed in this Chapter's Specifications.

d) Check the oil level in the final drive unit and top up as needed (see Chapter 1).

## 13 Drive chain, sprockets and coupling bearing - removal, inspection and installation

**Note:** Removal of the drive chain requires that it be separated with a chain breaker. If you don't have this tool, it may be less expensive to have the work done by a dealer service department than to buy it.

### Removal

**1** Remove the rear wheel (see Chapter 6).

**2** Remove the shift pedal pinch bolt.

**3** Loosen the clamp that secures the left muffler/silencer to the front exhaust pipe.

**12.10a  Check the driveshaft splines for step wear**

**12.10b  Make sure the snap-ring is securely located in its groove**

**13.3  Remove the left footpeg bracket, together with the muffler/silencer**

**13.4 Loosen the screws on the chain case clamps**

**13.5a Loosen the cover bolts with an Allen wrench . . .**

**13.5b . . . evenly, in a criss-cross pattern**

Remove the nut and bolt that secure the left front footpeg bracket to the motorcycle, then remove the bracket together with the left muffler/silencer **(see illustration)**.

4 Loosen the clamp screws and slide the upper and lower chain cases backward away from the engine sprocket housing **(see illustration)**.

5 Remove the Allen bolts and detach the sprocket housing from the engine **(see illustrations)**.

*Caution: The housing may be stuck to the engine with sealant. If it's difficult to remove, make sure all fasteners have been removed. Don't pry against gasket surfaces or they will be gouged. Tap gently around the edge of the cover to free it.*

6 At this point, it's necessary to disconnect the chain. For access, loosen the clamp and detach the lower chain case from the rear sprocket housing. Turn the rear sprocket until

you locate the soft link, then use the chain breaker tool to separate it.

7 Lift the chain off the front sprocket and turn the rear sprocket while pulling the chain out of the cases.

8 Loosen the clamp and detach the upper chain case from the rear sprocket housing. Unbolt the chain cases from the swingarm and remove them **(see illustration)**.

9 Remove two bolts, lockwashers and plain washers and detach the rear sprocket housing from the motorcycle **(see illustration)**.

10 Remove five Allen bolts and detach the sprocket retaining ring from the rear sprocket housing.

*Caution: If the retaining ring is stuck in the sprocket housing, pry it gently and evenly to free it. Don't let it tilt sideways while prying or it may crack.*

11 Once the retaining ring is free, remove its O-ring.

### Inspection

12 Check the sprockets for wear or damage **(see illustration)**. Refer to Steps 18 and 19 below and replace the sprockets if wear or damage can be seen. **Note:** *The chain and both sprockets should be replaced as a set, even if only one component is visibly defective. Installing a new chain on worn sprockets or a worn chain on new sprockets will accelerate wear of the new components.*

13 Check the sprocket retaining ring oil seal for wear and replace it as necessary.

14 Clean all parts thoroughly with solvent. Be

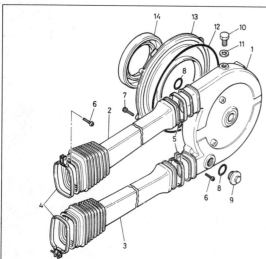

1  *Rear sprocket housing*
2  *Upper chain case*
3  *Lower chain case*
4  *Front chain case clamps*
5  *Rear chain case clamps*
6  *Clamp screws*
7  *Sprocket housing cover bolts*
8  *O-ring*
9  *Access plug*
10 *Filler plug*
11 *Sealing washer*
12 *O-ring*
13 *Sprocket retaining ring*
14 *Grease seal*

**13.5c Final drive housing (chain drive models) - exploded view**

**13.8 These two bolts secure the chain cases to the swingarm**

**13.9 Remove the bolts, lockwashers and washers (arrows) to detach the sprocket housing**

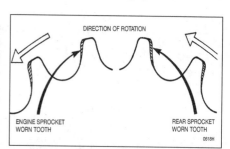

**13.12 Check the sprockets in the areas indicated to see if they are worn excessively**

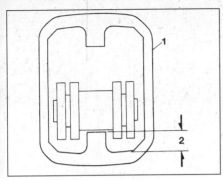

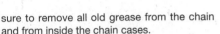

**13.16 Chain case internal rib measurement**

*1 Chain case    2 Rib height*

**13.18 The engine sprocket is secured by two bolts and a lockwasher**

**13.35 Coat the mating surface of the engine sprocket housing with silicone sealant**

sure to remove all old grease from the chain and from inside the chain cases.

**15** Place the chain on a clean flat surface and stretch it out straight. Squeeze the chain links together, keeping the chain in a straight line. Measure the length of the chain. Secure one end of the chain to the flat surface, then pull it out straight and measure its length again. If the difference between the two measurements is more than one-quarter inch per foot of chain length, replace the chain. **Note:** *Do not use an O-ring chain. The O-rings will be damaged by being pulled through the grease in the chain cases and sprocket housings.*

**16** Check the chain cases for cracks or brittleness and replace as necessary. Measure the height of the internal ribs and compare it to the value listed in this Chapter's Specifications **(see illustration)**. If the ribs are worn, replace the chain cases.

**17** Check the sprocket housings for cracks or other damage and replace as necessary. Make sure the breather on the engine sprocket housing is clear of obstructions.

### Sprocket replacement

**18** To replace the engine sprocket, flatten the tabs on the lockwashers and remove the sprocket bolts **(see illustration)**. Slide the sprocket off and install the new one. Install a new lockwasher, tighten the bolts to the torque listed in this Chapter's Specifications, then bend the lockwasher tabs against the bolts.

**19** To replace the rear sprocket, loosen the lockwasher tabs **(see illustration 6.5c in Chapter 6, Part B)**. Remove the nuts and lockwashers and lift off the sprocket. Install the new sprocket and new lockwashers. Tighten the sprocket evenly, in a criss-cross pattern to the torque listed in this Chapter's Specifications, then bend the lockwasher tabs against the nuts.

### Coupling bearing replacement

**20** Remove the bearing snap-ring from the coupling **(see illustration 6.5c in Chapter 6, Part B)**.

**21** Pry out the grease seal and remove the spacer.

**22** Lift out the bearing. If it won't come easily, tap it out from the wheel side of the coupling toward the sprocket side.

**23** Pack a new bearing with grease and tap it in from the sprocket side. Use a bearing driver or a socket that bears against the bearing outer race.

**24** Install the spacer and tap in a new grease seal with its open side toward the bearing.

**25** Install the snap-ring.

### Installation

**26** To keep the chain from falling on the ground and picking up small bits of dirt as it's installed, place clean rags, newspaper or cardboard on the ground under the chain run.

**27** Apply a light coat of the grease specified for the chain (see Chapter 1) to the O-ring on the sprocket retaining ring.

**28** Assemble the rear sprocket and retainer to the rear sprocket housing. Be careful not to push the large O-ring out of position when installing the retainer in the housing.

**29** Thread the chain into the top opening in the housing onto the sprocket. Turn the sprocket and work the chain around and out the bottom opening.

**30** Slip the upper and lower chain cases over the chain, then tie the ends of the chain together with wire.

**31** Slide the upper chain case onto the rear sprocket housing and tighten its clamp. Don't slide the lower chain case on yet; leave a gap between the lower chain case and the rear sprocket housing.

**32** Turn the rear sprocket so the ends of the chain are in the gap between the lower chain case and the rear sprocket. This will provide access to reconnect the chain permanently.

**33** Install the chain cases and rear sprocket housing on the bike, engaging the chain with the engine sprocket, and tighten their mounting bolts loosely.

**34** Install the soft link and connect the chain with a chain installation tool. Slide the lower chain case onto the rear sprocket housing and tighten its clamp.

**35** Clean all sealant from the mating surfaces of the engine sprocket cover and the engine. Coat the cover surface with silicone sealant **(see illustration)**, then install it on the engine. Tighten the bolts evenly, in a criss-cross pattern.

**36** The remainder of installation is the reverse of the removal steps.

**37** Adjust the chain tension (see Chapter 1) before you tighten the chain case and rear sprocket housing bolts.

**38** Add the specified grease to the rear sprocket housing filler hole (see Chapter 1).

**39** Test ride the motorcycle and check for leaks.

---

## 14 Swingarm - removal, inspection and installation

### Removal

**1** Support the bike securely so it can't be knocked over during this procedure.

**2** Remove the exhaust system (see Chapter 3).

**3** Remove the rear wheel (see Chapter 6).

**4** Remove the rear suspension unit or shock absorbers (see Section 9 or Section 10).

**5** If you're working on a shaft drive model, remove the final drive assembly (see Section 12).

**6** If you're working on a chain drive model, the final drive assembly (chain cases and rear sprocket housing) can be removed together with the swingarm or removed from the motorcycle first. If you're removing the swingarm to inspect or replace the bearings, remove the engine sprocket cover and detach the engine sprocket from the engine, but leave the rest of the final drive assembly (chain cases and rear sprocket housing) attached to the swingarm (see Section 13).

### 1981 through 1983 models and TR1

**7** If you're working on a shaft drive model, bend back the lockwasher tabs that secure

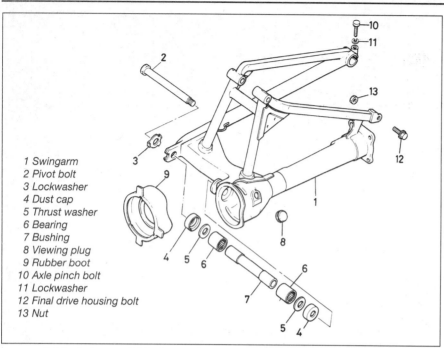

1 Swingarm
2 Pivot bolt
3 Lockwasher
4 Dust cap
5 Thrust washer
6 Bearing
7 Bushing
8 Viewing plug
9 Rubber boot
10 Axle pinch bolt
11 Lockwasher
12 Final drive housing bolt
13 Nut

14.7a  Swingarm (1981 through 1983 shaft drive models) - exploded view

14.7b  The pivot bolt head on 1981 through 1983 shaft drive models is secured by a lockwasher

14.7c  Detach the rubber boot from the engine

the head of the swingarm pivot bolt **(see illustration)**. Support the swingarm and remove the pivot bolt **(see illustration)**. Separate the rubber boot from the engine

14.7d  Pull the swingarm rearward so its ends clear the frame mounting bracket

14.8a  The pivot bolt on chain drive models is secured by a nut and plain washer

**(see illustration)** and remove the swingarm from the motorcycle **(see illustration)**.
8  If you're working on a chain drive model, remove the nut and plain washer from the swingarm pivot bolt **(see illustrations)**. Support the swingarm and remove the pivot bolt, then remove the swingarm from the motorcycle.

### 1984 and later models

9  Pry off the pivot cover on each side of the swingarm **(see illustration 10.2b)**.
10  Support the swingarm. On the left side,

flatten the lockwasher tabs and unscrew the pivot shaft. On the right side, remove the nut and the pivot shaft.
11  Detach the swingarm boot from the engine and remove the swingarm.

### *Inspection*

12  Check the swingarm for obvious damage,

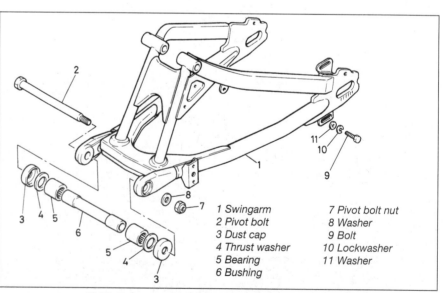

1 Swingarm
2 Pivot bolt
3 Dust cap
4 Thrust washer
5 Bearing
6 Bushing
7 Pivot bolt nut
8 Washer
9 Bolt
10 Lockwasher
11 Washer

14.8b  Swingarm (chain drive models) - exploded view

**14.12 Check the swingarm for cracks and bending**

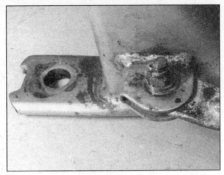

**14.13 If the pivot bolt holes are worn to an oval shape, replace the swingarm**

**14.14 Check the rubber boot for hardness or cracks**

such as cracks or bending and replace it as necessary **(see illustration)**.

13 Check the swingarm mounting holes for ovaling **(see illustration)**.

14 Check the rubber boot for cracks or deterioration and replace it as necessary **(see illustration)**.

15 Refer to Section 15 and inspect the swingarm bearings. If you're working on a 1981 through 1983 model, calculate the swingarm side clearance.

## Installation

16 Installation is the reverse of the removal steps, with the following additions:

a) *Use a new lockwasher and be sure its tab engages the slot in the swingarm.*

b) *Tighten the pivot bolt, nut or shafts to the torque listed in this Chapter's Specifications* **(see illustration)**. *On 1984 and later models, tighten the right side, then the left side. On all shaft drive models, bend the lockwasher against the flats on the shaft head or nut* **(see illustration 10.2b or 14.7b)**.

c) *If you're working on a 1981 through 1983 shaft drive model, remove the viewing plug from the left side of the swingarm so you can see the end of the driveshaft when aligning it with the engine.*

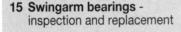

**15 Swingarm bearings -** inspection and replacement

1 Remove the swingarm (see Section 10).

### *1981 through 1983 models and TR1*

2 Pry off the thrust cover and remove the plain washer from each side of the frame **(see illustration)**.

3 Slide the bushing out **(see illustration)**.

4 Inspect the bearings **(see illustration)**. If they're dry, lubricate them with lithium base waterproof wheel bearing grease. If they're worn or damaged, it's best to take the motorcycle to a Yamaha dealer or motorcycle repair shop for bearing replacement. The bearings can be tapped out with a long rod inserted from the opposite side of the bike, but they'll be ruined in the process. The new bearings will also be ruined when they're tapped in unless you have a drift that fits precisely inside the bearings and also has a shoulder that will apply pressure to the circumference of the bearing.

5 Check the dust caps, thrust washers and seals for wear or damage and replace them as necessary **(see illustration)**.

6 Calculate the swingarm side clearance. Measure the length of the bushing and the

**14.16 Tighten the pivot bolt, then bend the lockwasher tabs against the bolt head**

**15.2 Pry the dust caps off the frame**

**15.3 Pull out the bushing**

**15.4 Clean the needle roller bearings and check them or wear and damage**

**15.5 Check the dust cap, thrust washer and seal for wear and damage**

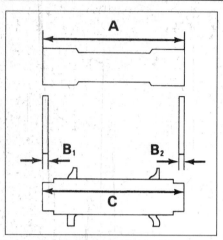

**15.6 Swingarm side clearance measurement (1981 through 1983 models)**

A    Bushing length
B1   Thrust washer thickness
B2   Thrust washer thickness
C    Frame mounting point length

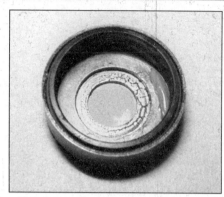

**15.7 Grease the inside of each dust cap**

frame crossmember **(see illustration)**. Measure the thickness of the two thrust washers. Add the thickness of both thrust washers to the frame crossmember length, then subtract this total from the length of the bushing to obtain the side clearance; that is, side clearance = A - (B1 + B2 + C). Compare the measurement to the value listed in this Chapter's Specifications. If the measured clearance is excessive, replace the thrust washers or bushing, whichever is most worn.

**7** Lubricate the insides of the dust caps with multi-purpose lithium grease **(see illustration)**.

## 1984 and later models

**8** Remove the bearing collars, then pry the grease seals out **(see illustration 10.2b)**. Rotate the bearings with a finger and check them for roughness or looseness. If the bearings need to be replaced, remove them with a blind hole puller and slide hammer.

**9** Pack the new bearings with waterproof wheel bearing grease, then tap them into position with a bearing driver or socket that bears against the bearing outer race. **Note:** *If you don't have the necessary puller and slide hammer, it may be less expensive to have a dealer service department replace the bearings than to rent the tools.*

# Chapter 6 Part A
# Brakes, wheels and tires (XV535 models)

## Contents

## Degrees of difficulty

| Easy, suitable for novice with little experience 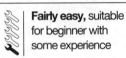 | Fairly easy, suitable for beginner with some experience  | Fairly difficult, suitable for competent DIY mechanic 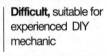 | Difficult, suitable for experienced DIY mechanic 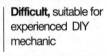 | Very difficult, suitable for expert DIY or professional 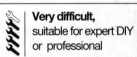 |
|---|---|---|---|---|

## Specifications

### Brakes

| | |
|---|---|
| Brake fluid type ..................................... | See Chapter 1 |
| Front brake disc thickness | |
|   Standard ........................................ | 5.0 mm (0.20 inch) |
|   Minimum* ....................................... | 4.5 mm (0.18 inch) |
| Disc runout limit ................................... | 0.15 mm (0.006 inch) |
| Front brake pad thickness (new) ...................... | 6.2 mm (0.26 inch) |
| Wear limit ........................................ | 0.8 mm (0.03 inch) |
| Rear brake drum inside diameter | |
|   Standard ........................................ | 200 mm (7.87 inches) |
|   Maximum ........................................ | 201 mm (7.91 inches) |
| Rear brake shoe lining thickness | |
|   Standard ........................................ | 4 mm (0.16 inch) |
|   Minimum ........................................ | 2 mm (0.08 inch) |

*Refer to marks stamped into the disc (they supersede information printed here)*

### Wheels and tires

| | |
|---|---|
| Wheel runout | |
|   Radial (up-and-down) ............................. | 2.0 mm (0.08 inch) |
|   Axial (side-to-side) .............................. | 2.0 mm (0.08 inch) |
| Tire pressures ..................................... | See Chapter 1 |
| Tire sizes | |
|   Front ........................................... | 3.00S-19 4PR |
|   Rear ............................................ | 140/90-15M/C 70S |

### Torque specifications

| | |
|---|---|
| Caliper lower mounting bolt (to bracket) | |
|   1987 to 1994 models .............................. | 18 Nm (13 ft-lbs) |
|   1995-on models ................................. | 22 Nm (16 ft-lbs) |
| Caliper bracket bolts (to fork leg) ...................... | 35 Nm (25 ft-lbs) |
| Front axle ........................................ | 58 Nm (42 ft-lbs) |
| Front axle pinch bolt ............................... | 20 Nm (14 ft-lbs) |
| Brake disc mounting bolts | |
|   1987 to 1994 models .............................. | 20 Nm (14 ft-lbs)* |
|   1995-on models ................................. | 23 Nm (17 ft-lbs)* |
| Union (banjo fitting) bolts ............................ | 26 Nm (19 ft-lbs) |
| Master cylinder mounting bolts ....................... | 9 Nm (6.5 ft-lbs) |
| Rear axle nut | |
|   1987 and 1988 models ............................ | 105 Nm (75 ft-lbs) |
|   1989-on models ................................. | 107 Nm (77 ft-lbs) |

## Torque specifications (continued)

Rear axle pinch bolt . . . . . . . . . . . . . . . . . . . . . . . . . . . . . . . . . . . . . . . . . . .  16 Nm (11 ft-lbs)
Rear wheel clutch hub bolts
   1987 and 1988 models . . . . . . . . . . . . . . . . . . . . . . . . . . . . . . . . .  69 Nm (50 ft-lbs)
   1989-on models . . . . . . . . . . . . . . . . . . . . . . . . . . . . . . . . . . . . . . .  62 Nm (45 ft-lbs)
Brake rod nuts . . . . . . . . . . . . . . . . . . . . . . . . . . . . . . . . . . . . . . . . . . . . . . .  20 Nm (14 ft-lbs)**
*Use new lockwashers.*
**Use new cotter pins.*

## 1  General information

The models covered in this Chapter are equipped with a hydraulic disc brake at the front. 1987 to 1994 models are fitted with a single piston brake caliper, 1995-on models are fitted with a two-piston caliper. All models have a mechanical drum brake at the rear.

All XV535 models are equipped with wire spoke wheels and tubed tires.

*Caution: Disc brake components rarely require disassembly. Do not disassemble components unless absolutely necessary. If any hydraulic brake line connection in the system is loosened, the entire system should be disassembled, drained, cleaned and then properly filled and bled upon reassembly. Do not use solvents on internal brake components. Solvents will cause*

seals to swell and distort. Use only clean brake fluid, brake cleaner or alcohol for cleaning. Use care when working with brake fluid as it can injure your eyes and it will damage painted surfaces and plastic parts.*

## 2  Brake pads - replacement

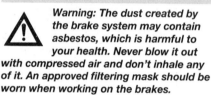

⚠️ **Warning: The dust created by the brake system may contain asbestos, which is harmful to your health. Never blow it out with compressed air and don't inhale any of it. An approved filtering mask should be worn when working on the brakes.**

1  Support the bike securely so it can't be knocked over during this procedure.
2  Remove the caliper lower mounting bolt **(see illustration)**. Rotate the caliper up to expose the pads **(see illustration)**.

**2.2a  Remove the lower mounting bolt from the caliper . . .**

**2.2b  . . . and pivot the caliper up to expose the pads**

3  Remove the pads and pad springs **(see illustration)**. Note that on 1995-on models fitted with a two-piston caliper, an additional pad spring is fitted to the rear edge of the brake pads **(see illustration 2.11 in part B of this Chapter)**. Measure the amount of friction material left on the pads and replace them as a pair if worn, fouled with oil or damaged in any way.
4  Check the condition of the brake discs (see Section 4). If they are in need of machining or replacement, follow the procedure in that Section to remove them.
5  Remove the cover and diaphragm from the master cylinder reservoir and siphon out some fluid. Push the pistons into the caliper as far as possible, while checking the master cylinder reservoir to make sure it doesn't overflow. If you can't depress the pistons with thumb pressure, try using a C-clamp (G-clamp). If the piston sticks, remove the caliper and overhaul it as described in Section 3.

⚠️ **Warning: Step 6 is necessary to ensure that the pads move freely in the calipers.**

6  Because a large amount of salt is used on roads in the UK, special lubrication of the pads and calipers is required. Before installing the pads on UK models, apply a thin film of Duckhams Copper 10 or equivalent to the following areas **(see illustrations)**:
a)  To the edges of the metal backing on the brake pads
b)  To the areas of the caliper where the pads rub
c)  To the threads of the caliper mounting bolts.

**2.3a  Remove the pads; the rounded edge of each pad (arrow) faces the rear of the motorcycle**

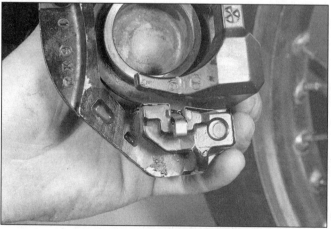

**2.3b  Remove the pad springs**

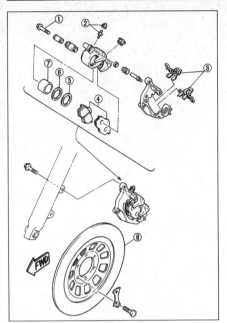

**2.3c  Front brake caliper (XV535 models) - exploded view**

1  Caliper mounting bolt
2  Bleed valve and cap
3  Pad springs
4  Pads
5  Dust seal
6  Piston seal
7  Piston
8  Brake disc

Apply a thin film of Shin-Etsu G-40M or equivalent silicone grease to the following:
d)  Exposed areas of the caliper pistons
e)  The areas of the pad backing plates that contact the pistons.
**Caution: Don't use too much Copper 10. Make sure no Copper 10 contacts the brake discs or the pad friction surfaces.**
7  Install the pads and springs in the caliper. The rounded edge of the pad faces the rear of the motorcycle **(see illustration 2.3a)**.
8  Refill the master cylinder reservoir (see Chapter 1) and install the diaphragm and cover.
9  Operate the brake lever several times to bring the pads into contact with the disc. Check the operation of the brakes carefully before riding the motorcycle.

### 3  Brake caliper - removal, overhaul and installation

**Warning: If a caliper indicates the need for an overhaul (usually due to leaking fluid or sticky operation), all old brake fluid should be flushed from the system. Also, the dust created by the brake system may contain asbestos, which is harmful to your health. Never blow it out with compressed air and don't inhale any of it. An approved**

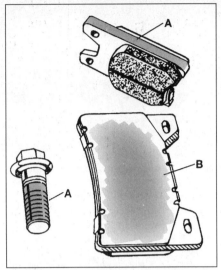

**2.6a  Special lubricants are required anywhere salt is used on the roads to prevent corrosion**

A  Apply Duckhams Copper 10 or equivalent to the shaded areas
B  Apply Shin-Etsu G-40M or equivalent silicone grease to the shaded areas

*filtering mask should be worn when working on the brakes. Do not, under any circumstances, use petroleum-based solvents to clean brake parts. Use brake cleaner or denatured alcohol only!*

### Removal

1  Support the bike securely so it can't be knocked over during this procedure.
2  Disconnect the brake hose from the caliper. Remove the brake hose banjo fitting bolt and separate the hose from the caliper **(see illustrations)**. Discard the sealing washers. Place the end of the hose in a container and operate the brake lever to pump out the fluid. Once this is done, wrap a clean shop rag tightly around the hose fitting to soak up any drips and prevent contamination.
3  Unscrew the caliper mounting bolts and

**3.2a  Unscrew the banjo bolt; there's a sealing washer on each side of the fitting**

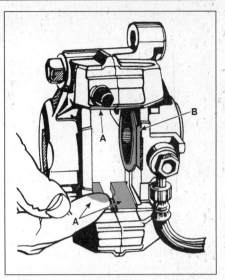

**2.6b  Apply lubricant to the pad friction areas and to the exposed portion of the caliper pistons**

A  Duckhams Copper 10
B  Shin-Etsu G-40M or equivalent silicone grease

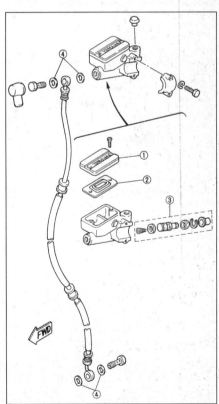

**3.2b  Master cylinder and brake line (XV535 models) - exploded view**

1  Reservoir cover
2  Diaphragm
3  Piston assembly and spring
4  Sealing washers

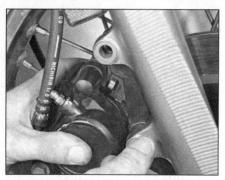

**3.3 Remove the mounting bolts and separate the caliper from the fork leg**

**3.5a Blow air into the fluid inlet to push the piston out; keep your fingers out of the way to prevent injury**

**3.5b Remove the piston from the bore**

separate the caliper from the front fork **(see illustration)**.

## Overhaul

**4** Clean the exterior of the caliper with denatured alcohol or brake system cleaner.

**5** Place a few rags between the piston and the caliper frame to act as a cushion, then use compressed air, directed into the fluid inlet, to remove the piston **(see illustration 2.3c and the accompanying illustrations)**. Note that 1995-on models are fitted with a two-piston caliper; mark each piston and the caliper body to ensure that the pistons can be matched to their original bores on reassembly – the pistons are of different sizes. Use only enough air pressure to ease the piston(s) out. If a piston is blown out, even with the cushion in place, it may be damaged.

⚠️ **Warning: Never place your fingers in front of the piston in an attempt to catch or protect it when applying compressed air, as serious injury could occur.**

**6** If compressed air isn't available, reconnect the caliper to the brake hose and pump the brake lever until the piston is free.

**7** Using a wood or plastic tool, remove the dust seal **(see illustration)**. Metal tools may damage the bore.

**8** Using a wood or plastic tool, remove the piston seal from the groove in the caliper bore **(see illustration)**.

**9** Clean the piston and the bore with denatured alcohol, clean brake fluid or brake system cleaner and blow dry them with filtered,

unlubricated compressed air. Inspect the surfaces of the piston for nicks and burrs and loss of plating. Check the caliper bore, too. If surface defects are present, the caliper must be replaced. If the caliper is in bad shape, the master cylinder should also be checked.

**10** Lubricate the piston seal with clean brake fluid and install it in its groove in the caliper bore. Make sure it isn't twisted and seats completely. Note that on 1995-on models fitted with a two-piston caliper, the seals are of different sizes corresponding with the different sizes of caliper bore. Take care to ensure that the correct size seals are fitted to the correct bores.

**11** Lubricate the dust seal with clean brake fluid and install it in its groove, making sure it seats correctly.

**12** Lubricate the piston with clean brake fluid and install it into the caliper bore. Using your thumbs, push the piston all the way in, making sure it doesn't get cocked in the bore.

**13** The caliper body should be able to slide in relation to its mounting bracket. If it's seized or stiff in operation, remove the caliper-to-bracket lower bolt and slide the body off the bracket's slider pin. Inspect the slider pin and lower bolt for wear and coat them with high-temperature disc brake grease. If the dust boots are split or cracked, replace them with new ones.

## Installation

**14** Install the caliper, tightening the mounting bolts to the torque listed in this Chapter's Specifications.

**15** Connect the brake hose to the caliper, using new sealing washers on each side of the fitting. The neck of the hose union should fit between the two cast lugs on the caliper body. Tighten the banjo fitting bolt to the torque listed in this Chapter's Specifications.

**16** Fill the master cylinder with the recommended brake fluid (see Chapter 1) and bleed the system (see Section 8). Check for leaks.

**17** Check the operation of the brakes carefully before riding the motorcycle.

| | |
|---|---|
| **4** | **Brake disc** - inspection, removal and installation |

## Inspection

**1** Support the bike securely so it can't be knocked over during this procedure.

**2** Visually inspect the surface of the disc for score marks and other damage. Light scratches are normal after use and won't affect brake operation, but deep grooves and heavy score marks will reduce braking efficiency and accelerate pad wear. If the disc is badly grooved it must be machined or replaced.

**3** To check disc runout, mount a dial indicator to the fork leg with the plunger on the indicator touching the surface of the disc about 1/2-inch from the outer edge **(see illustration)**. Slowly turn the wheel and watch the indicator needle, comparing your reading

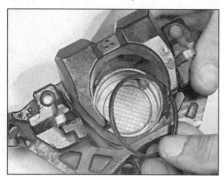

**3.7 Remove the dust seal with fingers or a wood or plastic tool**

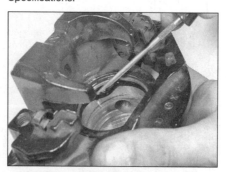

**3.8 Remove the piston seal from its groove (a toothpick can be used as a removal tool)**

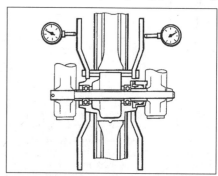

**4.3 Position a dial indicator against the disc and spin the wheel to measure runout**

with the limit listed in this Chapter's Specifications or stamped on the disc itself. If the runout is greater than allowed, check the hub bearings for play (see Chapter 1). If the bearings are worn, replace them and repeat this check. If the disc runout is still excessive, it will have to be replaced.

**4** The disc must not be machined or allowed to wear down to a thickness less than the minimum allowable thickness, listed in this Chapter's Specifications. The thickness of the disc can be checked with a micrometer. If the thickness of the disc is less than the minimum allowable, it must be replaced.

### Removal

**5** Remove the wheel (see Section 11 for front wheel removal or Section 12 for rear wheel removal).

*Caution: Don't lay the wheel down and allow it to rest on the disc - the disc could become warped. Set the wheel on wood blocks so the disc doesn't support the weight of the wheel.*

**6** Mark the relationship of the disc to the wheel, so it can be installed in the same position. Bend back the lockwasher tabs and remove the bolts that retain the disc to the wheel **(see illustration 2.3c)**. Loosen the bolts a little at a time, in a criss-cross pattern, to avoid distorting the disc. Once all the bolts are loose, take the disc off.

**7** Take note of any paper shims that may be present where the disc mates to the wheel. If there are any, mark their position and be sure to include them when installing the disc.

### Installation

**8** Position the disc on the wheel, aligning the previously applied match marks (if you're reinstalling the original disc). Make sure the arrow (stamped on the disc) marking the direction of rotation is pointing in the proper direction.

**9** Apply a non-hardening thread locking compound to the threads of the bolts. Install the bolts with new lockwashers, tightening them a little at a time, in a criss-cross pattern, until the torque listed in this Chapter's Specifications is reached. Clean off all grease

**5.5 Unscrew the banjo bolt (arrow); there's a sealing washer on each side of the fitting**

from the brake disc using acetone or brake system cleaner.

**10** Install the wheel.

**11** Operate the brake lever several times to bring the pads into contact with the disc. Check the operation of the brakes carefully before riding the motorcycle.

---

### 5   Front brake master cylinder - removal, overhaul and installation

**1** If the master cylinder is leaking fluid, or if the lever does not produce a firm feel when the brake is applied, and bleeding the brakes does not help, master cylinder overhaul is recommended.

**2** Before disassembling the master cylinder, read through the entire procedure and make sure that you have the correct rebuild kit. Also, you will need some new, clean brake fluid of the recommended type, some clean rags and internal snap-ring pliers. **Note:** *To prevent damage to the paint from spilled brake fluid, always cover the top cover or upper fuel tank when working on the master cylinder.*

*Caution: Disassembly, overhaul and reassembly of the brake master cylinder must be done in a spotlessly clean work area to avoid contamination and possible failure of the brake hydraulic system components.*

**5.6 Remove the mounting bolts (arrows); note the UP mark, which must be upright**

### Removal

**3** Loosen but do not remove the screws holding the reservoir cover in place **(see illustration 3.2b)**.

**4** Disconnect the electrical connectors from the brake light switch (see Chapter 8).

**5** Pull back the rubber boot (if equipped), loosen the banjo fitting bolt **(see illustration)** and separate the brake hose from the master cylinder. Wrap the end of the hose in a clean rag and suspend the hose in an upright position or bend it down carefully and place the open end in a clean container. The objective is to prevent excessive loss of brake fluid, fluid spills and system contamination.

**6** Remove the master cylinder mounting bolts **(see illustration)** and separate the master cylinder from the handlebar.

*Caution: Do not tip the master cylinder upside down or brake fluid will run out.*

### Overhaul

**7** Remove the locknut and unscrew the brake lever pivot bolt **(see illustrations)**. Remove the lever and its return spring **(see illustration)**.

**8** Detach the top cover and the rubber diaphragm, then drain the brake fluid into a suitable container. Remove the splash plate from the bottom of the reservoir (if equipped), then wipe any remaining fluid out of the reservoir with a clean rag.

**5.7a  Remove the locknut from the lever pivot bolt . . .**

**5.7b  . . . and unscrew the bolt**

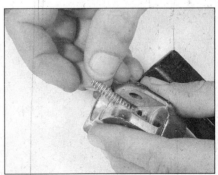

**5.7c  Remove the lever spring**

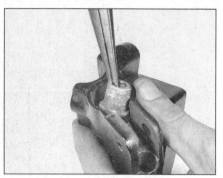

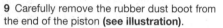
**5.9 Remove the rubber boot**

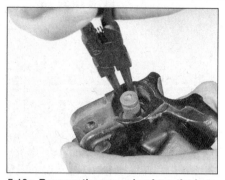
**5.10a Remove the snap-ring from the bore**

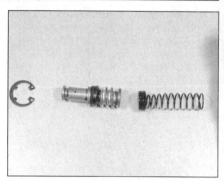
**5.10b Piston component details**

**9** Carefully remove the rubber dust boot from the end of the piston **(see illustration)**.
**10** Using snap-ring pliers, remove the snap-ring **(see illustration)** and slide out the piston assembly and the spring **(see illustration)**. Lay the parts out in the proper order to prevent confusion during reassembly.
**11** Clean all of the parts with brake system cleaner (available at motorcycle dealerships and auto parts stores), isopropyl alcohol or clean brake fluid. *Caution: Do not, under any circumstances, use a petroleum-based solvent to clean brake parts. If compressed air is available, use it to dry the parts thoroughly (make sure it's filtered and unlubricated). Check the master cylinder bore for corrosion, scratches, nicks and score marks. If damage is evident, the master cylinder*

*must be replaced with a new one. If the master cylinder is in poor condition, then the calipers should be checked as well.*
**12** The dust seal, piston assembly and spring are included in the rebuild kit. Use all of the new parts, regardless of the apparent condition of the old ones.
**13** Before reassembling the master cylinder, soak the piston and the rubber cup seals in clean brake fluid for ten or fifteen minutes. Lubricate the master cylinder bore with clean brake fluid, then carefully insert the piston and related parts in the reverse order of disassembly. Make sure the lips on the cup seals do not turn inside out when they are slipped into the bore.
**14** Depress the piston, then install the snap-ring (make sure the snap-ring is properly seated in the groove). Install the rubber dust

boot (make sure the lip is seated properly in the piston groove).

### Installation

**15** Attach the master cylinder to the handlebar, making sure the UP mark is upright, and tighten the bolts to the torque listed in this Chapter's Specifications.
**16** Connect the brake hose to the master cylinder, using new sealing washers. Tighten the banjo fitting bolt to the torque listed in this Chapter's Specifications. Fill the master cylinder with the recommended brake fluid (see Chapter 1), then refer to Section 8 and bleed the air from the system.

**6   Rear drum brakes** - removal, overhaul and installation

### Shoe removal

**1** Before you start, inspect the rear brake wear indicator (see Chapter 1).
**2** Disconnect the rear brake rod **(see illustrations)**. Disconnect the brake cable from the lever (see Step 13). Remove the rear wheel (see Section 12).
**3** Lift the brake panel out of the wheel **(see illustration)**.
**4** Fold the shoes toward each other to release the spring tension **(see illustration)**. Remove the shoes and springs from the brake panel **(see illustration)**.

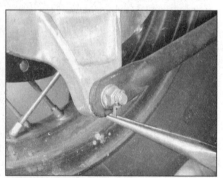
**6.2a Remove the cotter pin and nut and detach the brake rod from the brake panel . . .**

**6.2b . . . and from the swingarm**

**6.3 Remove the brake panel from the wheel**

**6.4a Fold the shoes in a V to release spring tension, then remove them from the panel**

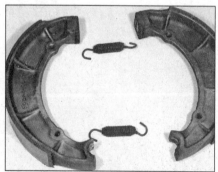
**6.4b Rear brake shoes and springs**

1 Short spacer
2 Washer
3 Rear brake lever
4 Brake wear indicator
5 Brake panel
6 Brake cam
7 Brake shoes
8 Rear wheel bearing
9 Collar
10 Long spacer
11 Brake rod
12 Hub dust seal
13 Clutch hub

6.8b Check the brake cam and pivot post
(arrows) for wear or damage

6.8a Rear wheel and brake (XV535 models) - exploded view

### Shoe inspection

5 Check the linings for wear, damage and signs of contamination from road dirt and water. If the linings are visibly defective, replace them.
6 Measure the thickness of the lining material (just the lining material, not the metal backing) and compare with the value listed in this Chapter's Specifications. Replace the shoes if the lining material is worn to less than the minimum.
7 Check the ends of the shoes where they contact the brake cam and pivot post. Replace the shoes if there's visible wear.
8 Check the brake cam and pivot post for wear and damage. If necessary, make match marks on the cam and cam lever, then remove the pinch bolt, lever, wear indicator pointer, seal and cam (see illustrations).
9 Check the brake drum (inside the wheel) for wear or damage. Measure the diameter at several points with a brake drum micrometer (or have this done by a Yamaha dealer). If the measurements are uneven (indicating the brake drum is out of round) or if there are scratches deep enough to snag a fingernail, have the drum turned (skimmed) by a dealer to correct the surface. If the drum has to be turned (skimmed) beyond the wear limit to remove the defects, replace it.
10 Check the brake cam for looseness in the brake panel hole. If it feels loose, replace the brake cam or panel, whichever is worn.

### Shoe installation

11 Apply high-temperature brake grease to the ends of the springs, the cam and the pivot post.
12 Hook the springs to the shoes. Position the shoes in a V on the panel, then fold them down into position (see illustration 6.4a). Make sure the ends of the shoes fit correctly against the cam and on the pivot post (see illustration).

### Rear brake cable and return spring removal and installation

13 Push the brake lever forward and unscrew the adjuster nut (see illustration).
14 Pull the cable forward, then slide it out of the slot to free it from the swingarm bracket (see illustration).
15 Slide the cable out of the forward bracket

6.12 The assembled brake panel should look like this

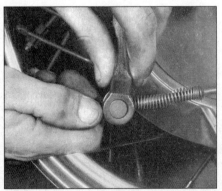

6.13 Unscrew the adjusting nut from the rear end of the brake cable

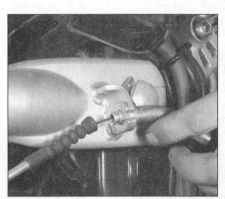

6.14 Pull the cable forward, then slide it through the slot in the swingarm bracket

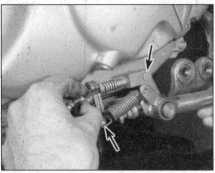

**6.15 Slide the cable through the slot in the bracket, then remove the cotter pin and clevis pin (upper arrow) to free it; unhook the spring from its post (lower arrow), then from the pedal arm**

**8.5 Place a box wrench (ring spanner) over the bleed valve, then connect a length of clear tubing**

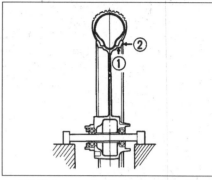

**9.2 Measure wheel runout with a dial indicator, if one is available**

1  Radial (up-and-down) runout
2  Axial (side-to-side) runout

**(see illustration)**. Remove the cotter pin and clevis pin and detach the cable from the pedal arm.

**16** To remove the pedal spring, unhook it from its post, then from the pedal arm.

**17** Installation is the reverse of the removal steps. Adjust the rear brake (see Chapter 1).

## 7  Brake hose -
### inspection and replacement

### Inspection

**1** Once a week, or if the motorcycle is used less frequently, before every ride, check the condition of the brake hose.

**2** Twist and flex the rubber hoses **(see illustration 3.2b)** while looking for cracks, bulges and seeping fluid. Check extra carefully around the areas where the hoses connect with the banjo fittings, as these are common areas for hose failure.

**3** Inspect the metal banjo fittings connected to brake hoses. If the fittings are rusted, scratched or cracked, replace them.

### Replacement

**4** The brake hose has a banjo fitting on each end of the hose. Cover the surrounding area with plenty of rags and unscrew the union bolt on either end of the hose. Detach the hose from any clips that may be present **(see illustration 3.2b)** and remove the hose.

**5** Position the new hose, making sure it isn't twisted or otherwise strained, between the two components. Install the union bolts, using new sealing washers on both sides of the fittings, and tighten them to the torque listed in this Chapter's Specifications.

**6** Flush the old brake fluid from the system, refill the system with the recommended fluid (see Chapter 1) and bleed the air from the system (see Section 8). Check the operation of the front brake carefully before riding the motorcycle.

## 8  Brake system bleeding

**1** Bleeding the brake is simply the process of removing all the air bubbles from the brake fluid reservoirs, the lines and the brake calipers. Bleeding is necessary whenever a brake system hydraulic connection is loosened, when a component or hose is replaced, or when the master cylinder or caliper is overhauled. Leaks in the system may also allow air to enter, but leaking brake fluid will reveal their presence and warn you of the need for repair.

**2** To bleed the brakes, you will need some new, clean brake fluid of the recommended type (see Chapter 1), a length of clear vinyl or plastic tubing, a small container partially filled with clean brake fluid, some rags and a wrench to fit the brake caliper bleeder valves.

**3** Cover the top cover or upper fuel tank and other painted components to prevent damage in the event that brake fluid is spilled.

**4** Remove the reservoir cap or cover and slowly pump the brake lever a few times, until no air bubbles can be seen floating up from the holes at the bottom of the reservoir. Doing this bleeds the air from the master cylinder end of the line. Reinstall the reservoir cap or cover.

**5** Slip a box wrench (ring spanner) over the caliper bleed valve **(see illustration)**. Attach one end of the clear vinyl or plastic tubing to the bleed valve and submerge the other end in the brake fluid in the container.

**6** Remove the reservoir cover and check the fluid level. Do not allow the fluid level to drop below the lower mark during the bleeding process.

**7** Carefully pump the brake lever three or four times and hold it while opening the caliper bleeder valve. When the valve is opened, brake fluid will flow out of the caliper into the clear tubing and the lever will move toward the handlebar.

**8** Retighten the bleed valve, then release the brake lever gradually. Repeat the process until no air bubbles are visible in the brake fluid leaving the caliper and the lever is firm when applied. **Note:** *Remember to add fluid to the reservoir as the level drops. Use only new, clean brake fluid of the recommended type. Never re-use the fluid lost during bleeding.*

**9** Replace the reservoir cover, wipe up any spilled brake fluid and check the entire system for leaks.

> **HAYNES HINT**
> *If bleeding is difficult, it may be necessary to let the brake fluid in the system stabilize for a few hours (it may be aerated). Repeat the bleeding procedure when the tiny bubbles in the system have settled out.*

## 9  Wheels -
### inspection and repair

**1** Clean the wheels thoroughly to remove mud and dirt that may interfere with the inspection procedure or mask defects. Make a general check of the wheels and tires as described in Chapter 1.

**2** Support the bike securely so it can't be knocked over during this procedure. Place a jack beneath the engine to raise the front wheel off the ground, or beneath the frame to raise the rear wheel off the ground. Attach a dial indicator to the fork slider or the swingarm and position the stem against the side of the rim. Spin the wheel slowly and check the side-to-side (axial) runout of the rim, then compare your readings with the value listed in this Chapter's Specifications **(see illustration)**. In order to accurately check radial runout with the dial indicator, the wheel would have to be removed from the machine and the tire removed from the wheel. With the axle clamped in a vise, the wheel can be rotated to check the runout.

**3** An easier, though slightly less accurate, method is to attach a stiff wire pointer to the fork or the swingarm and position the end a fraction of an inch from the wheel (where the wheel and tire join). If the wheel is true, the distance from the pointer to the rim will be constant as the wheel is rotated. Repeat the procedure to check the runout of the rear wheel. **Note:** *If wheel runout is excessive, refer to the appropriate Section in this Chapter and check the wheel bearings very carefully before replacing the wheel or paying to have it trued.*

**4** If damage is evident, or if runout in either direction is excessive, the wheel will have to be trued or, if damage is severe, replaced with a new one.

**11.3a Loosen the axle pinch bolt . . .**

**11.3b . . . and unscrew the axle**

## 10 Wheels - alignment check

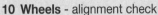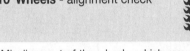

**1** Misalignment of the wheels, which may be due to a cocked rear wheel or a bent frame or triple clamps, can cause strange and possibly serious handling problems. If the frame or triple clamps are at fault, repair by a frame specialist or replacement with new parts are the only alternatives.

**2** To check the alignment you will need an assistant, a length of string or a perfectly straight piece of wood and a ruler graduated in 1/64 inch increments. A plumb bob or other suitable weight will also be required.

**3** Support the motorcycle in a level position, then measure the width of both tires at their widest points. Subtract the smaller measurement from the larger measurement, then divide the difference by two. The result is the amount of offset that should exist between the front and rear tires on both sides.

**4** If a string is used, have your assistant hold one end of it about half way between the floor and the rear axle, touching the rear sidewall of the tire.

**5** Run the other end of the string forward and pull it tight so that it is roughly parallel to the floor. Slowly bring the string into contact with the front sidewall of the rear tire, then turn the front wheel until it is parallel with the string. Measure the distance from the front tire sidewall to the string.

**6** Repeat the procedure on the other side of the motorcycle. The distance from the front tire sidewall to the string should be equal on both sides.

**7** As was previously pointed out, a perfectly straight length of wood may be substituted for the string. The procedure is the same.

**8** If the distance between the string and tire is greater on one side, or if the rear wheel appears to be cocked, refer to Chapter 5, Swingarm bearings - check, and make sure the swingarm is tight.

**9** If the front-to-back alignment is correct, the wheels still may be out of alignment vertically.

**10** Using the plumb bob, or other suitable weight, and a length of string, check the rear wheel to make sure it is vertical. To do this, hold the string against the tire upper sidewall and allow the weight to settle just off the floor. When the string touches both the upper and lower tire sidewalls and is perfectly straight, the wheel is vertical.

**11** Once the rear wheel is vertical, check the front wheel in the same manner. If both wheels are not perfectly vertical, the frame and/or major suspension components are bent.

## 11 Front wheel - removal and installation

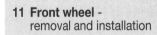

### Removal

**1** Support the bike securely so it can't be knocked over during this procedure. Raise the front wheel off the ground by placing a floor jack, with a wood block on the jack head, under the engine.

**2** Disconnect the speedometer cable from the drive unit (see Chapter 8).

**3** Loosen the axle pinch bolt and unscrew the axle **(see illustrations)**.

**4** Support the wheel, then pull out the axle **(see illustration)** and carefully lower the wheel away from the forks.

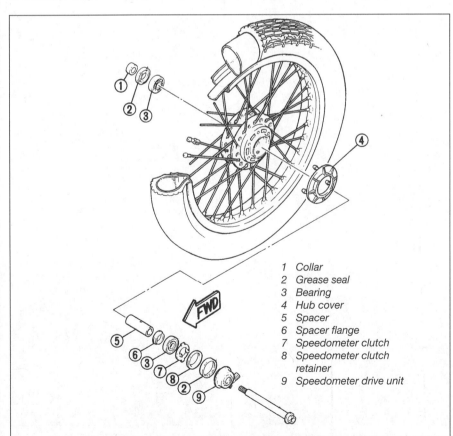

1  Collar
2  Grease seal
3  Bearing
4  Hub cover
5  Spacer
6  Spacer flange
7  Speedometer clutch
8  Speedometer clutch retainer
9  Speedometer drive unit

**11.4 Front wheel details (XV535 models)**

**11.5a Remove the collar from the right side . . .**

**11.5b . . . and the speedometer drive unit from the left side**

**11.8 Be sure the speedometer drive unit notches align with the speedometer clutch lugs (arrows)**

**5** Remove the collar from the right side and the speedometer drive unit from the left side **(see illustrations)**. Set the wheel aside. *Caution: Don't lay the wheel down and allow it to rest on the brake disc - the disc could become warped. Set the wheel on wood blocks so the disc doesn't support the weight of the wheel. Note: Don't operate the front brake lever with the wheel removed.*

### Inspection

**6** Roll the axle on a flat surface such as a piece of plate glass. If it's bent at all, replace it. If the axle is corroded, remove the corrosion with fine emery cloth.
**7** Check the condition of the wheel bearings (see Section 13).

### Installation

**8** Installation is the reverse of removal. Apply a thin coat of grease to the seal lip, then slide the axle into the hub. Slide the wheel into place. Make sure the lugs in the speedometer drive clutch line up with the notches in the speedometer drive unit **(see illustration)**. Make sure the protrusion on the inner side of the left fork fits into the notch in the speedometer drive unit.
**9** Slip the axle into place, then tighten the axle to the torque listed in this Chapter's Specifications. Tighten the axle pinch bolt to the torque listed in this Chapter's Specifications.
**10** Apply the front brake, pump the forks up and down several times and check for binding and proper brake operation.

### 12 Rear wheel - removal and installation

### Removal

**1** Support the bike securely so it can't be knocked over during this procedure.
**2** Detach the rear brake rod from the brake panel and the cable from the brake lever (see Section 6).
**3** Remove the cotter pin from the axle nut, then remove the nut and washer **(see illustrations)**.
**4** Loosen the axle pinch bolt **(see illustration)**.
**5** Support the wheel, slide the axle out and

**12.3a Straighten the cotter pin and pull it out . . .**

**12.3b . . . unscrew the axle nut . . .**

**12.3c . . . and remove the washer**

**12.4 Loosen the axle pinch bolt**

**12.5a Pull the axle out . . .**

**12.5b . . . remove the washer . . .**

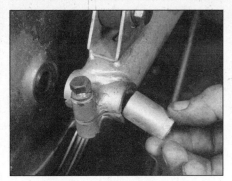

**12.5c  . . . and the short spacer**

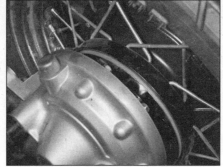

**12.5d  Separate the wheel from the final drive . . .**

**12.5e  . . . and remove the long spacer**

remove the washer and short spacer **(see illustrations)**. Pull the wheel to the right and remove it from the final drive assembly, then remove the long spacer **(see illustration 6.8b and the accompanying illustrations).**

**6**  Before installing the wheel, check the axle for straightness by rolling it on a flat surface such as a piece of plate glass (if the axle is corroded, first remove the corrosion with fine emery cloth). If the axle is bent at all, replace it.

**7**  Check the condition of the wheel bearings (see Section 13).

### Installation

**8**  Installation is the reverse of the removal steps, with the following additions:

a)  *Apply a light coat of multi-purpose lithium-based grease to the lips of the oil seals and to the splines on the final drive and wheel hub.*

b)  *Be sure the long spacer is in place before installing the wheel (see illustration).*

c)  *Tighten the axle nut to the torque listed in this Chapter's Specifications. Install a new cotter pin, tightening the axle nut an additional amount, if necessary, to align the hole in the axle with the castellations on the nut.*

d)  *Tighten the axle pinch bolt to the torque listed in this Chapter's Specifications.*

**9**  Adjust the bear brake (see Chapter 1) and check its operation carefully before riding the motorcycle.

## 13  Wheel bearings - inspection and maintenance

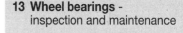

**1**  Support the bike securely so it can't be knocked over during this procedure and remove the wheel. See Section 11 (front wheel) or 12 (rear wheel).

**2**  Set the wheel on blocks so as not to allow the weight of the wheel to rest on the brake disc or hub.

### Front wheel bearings

**3**  From the right side of the wheel, lift out the collar (if you haven't already done so - **see illustrations 11.4 and 11.5a**), then pry out the grease seal **(see illustration)**.

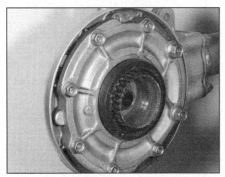

**12.8  Be sure the long spacer is in place before installing the wheel**

**13.3  Pry out the grease seal on the brake disc side of the wheel**

**13.4a  Pry the grease seal loose . . .**

**13.4b  . . . and lift it out**

**13.4c  Lift out the speedometer clutch retainer . . .**

**13.4d  . . . and the speedometer clutch**

**13.5 Drive out the opposite bearing with a long rod**

**13.6 Lift out the spacer**

**13.7 Drive out the remaining bearing**

**4** From the left side of the wheel, lift out the speedometer drive unit (if you haven't already done so - **see illustration 11.5b**), then pry out the grease seal **(see illustration)**. Lift out the speedometer clutch retainer and speedometer clutch **(see illustrations)**.

**5** Using a metal rod (preferably a brass drift punch) inserted through the center of the hub bearing, tap evenly around the inner race of the opposite bearing to drive it from the hub **(see illustration)**.

**6** Turn the wheel over and remove the bearing spacer **(see illustration)**.

**7** Turn the wheel back over and remove the remaining bearing using the same technique **(see illustration)**.

**8** Clean the bearings with a high flash-point solvent (one which won't leave any residue) and blow them dry with compressed air (don't let the bearing spin as you dry them). Apply a few drops of oil to the bearing. Hold the outer race of the bearing and rotate the inner race - if the bearing doesn't turn smoothly, has rough spots or is noisy, replace it with a new one.

**9** If the bearing checks out okay and will be re-used, wash it in solvent once again and dry it, then pack the bearing with high-quality bearing grease.

**10** Thoroughly clean the hub area of the wheel. Install the bearing into the recess in the hub, with the marked or sealed side facing out. Using a bearing driver or a socket large enough to contact the outer race of the bearing, drive it in **(see illustration)** until it's completely seated **(see illustration)**. Install a new grease seal on top of the bearings with its closed side out **(see illustration)**. It should be possible to push the seal in with even finger pressure, but if necessary use a seal driver, large socket or a flat piece of wood to drive the seal into place.

**11** Turn the wheel over and install the bearing spacer and bearing, driving the bearing into place as described in Step 10 **(see illustrations)**.

**12** Install the speedometer clutch and retainer on the left side of the wheel, then install the grease seal **(see illustrations)**.

**13** Install the speedometer drive unit, making sure the lugs in the speedometer clutch align with the notches in the gear **(see illustration 11.8)**.

**14** Clean off all grease from the brake disc using acetone or brake system cleaner.

**13.10a Drive in the bearing with a socket or bearing driver that contacts the outer race**

**13.10b The installed bearing should look like this**

**13.10c Install the grease seal with its closed side out**

**13.11a Install the spacer**

**13.11b Drive in the remaining bearing**

**13.12a Install the speedometer clutch . . .**

13.12b . . . and its retainer

13.12c  Install the remaining grease seal

13.16a  The dust seal is secured by four screws and the clutch hub by five bolts

**15** Make sure the collar is in place **(see illustration 11.5a)** and install the wheel.

### Rear wheel bearings

**16** If necessary for inspection, the dust seal and clutch hub can be detached from the wheel **(see illustration 6.8b and the accompanying illustrations)**. The rear wheel bearings can be removed and installed with these parts in place.

**17** Rear wheel bearing removal, inspection and installation are generally the same as for front wheel bearings (see Steps 5 through 11 above and the accompanying illustrations). On installation, be sure to install the spacer and its collar between the bearings. Apply non-permanent thread locking agent to the threads of the clutch hub bolts and tighten them to the torque listed in this Chapter's Specifications.

13.16b  Drive out the bearings with a long rod

13.16c  Lift out the spacer and collar (be sure to reinstall both during assembly)

13.16d  Drive the clutch hub side bearing into position with a bearing driver or socket on the outer race

13.16e  Make sure the spacer and collar are in place, then drive in the bearing on the opposite side

13.16f  Spin the bearings with a finger to make sure they turn easily

## 14 Tubed tires -
### general information

### General information

**1** The wheels fitted to all 535 models are designed to take tubed tires fitted with and inner tube. Do not fit tubeless tires to these wheel rims.

**2** Refer to *Daily (pre-ride) checks* at the beginning of this manual, and to the scheduled checks in Chapter 1 for tire and wheel maintenance.

### Fitting new tires

**3** When selecting new tires, refer to the tire information label on the motorcycle and the tire options listed in the owners manual. Ensure that front and rear tire types are compatible, the correct size and correct speed rating; if necessary seek advice from a Yamaha dealer or tire fitting specialist **(see illustration)**.

**4** It is recommended that tires are fitted by a motorcycle tire specialist rather than attempted in the home workshop. The specialist will also be able to balance the wheels after tire fitting.

**5** If a puncture occurs, replace the inner tube with a new one rather than attempting a repair. Make sure that the object which caused the puncture is removed from the tire.

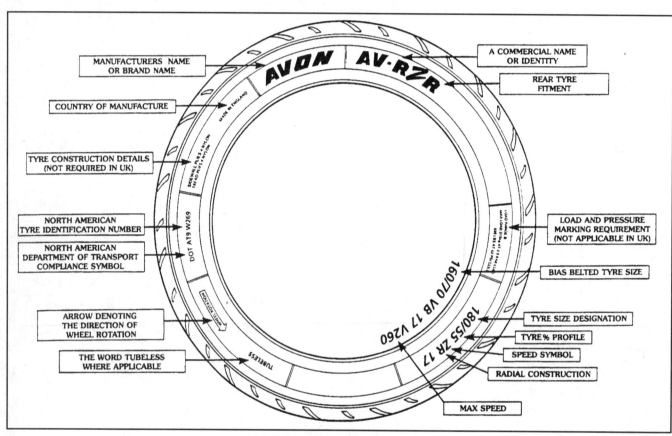

**14.4 Common tyre sidewall markings**

# Chapter 6 Part B
## Brakes, wheels and tires (XV700-1100 models)

## Contents

## Degrees of difficulty

| | | |
|---|---|---|
| **Easy,** suitable for novice with little experience  | **Fairly easy,** suitable for beginner with some experience  | **Fairly difficult,** suitable for competent DIY mechanic  |

| | |
|---|---|
| **Difficult,** suitable for experienced DIY mechanic  | **Very difficult,** suitable for expert DIY or professional |

## Specifications

### Brakes

| | |
|---|---|
| Brake fluid type ......................................... | See Chapter 1 |
| Front brake disc thickness | |
| 1981 through 1983 XV750 | |
|   Standard ...................................... | 7 mm (0.28 inch) |
|   Minimum* ..................................... | 6.5 mm (0.256 inch) |
| 1983 XV920 ........................................ | Not specified |
| All others | |
|   Standard ...................................... | 5.0 mm (0.20 inch) |
|   Minimum* ..................................... | 4.5 mm (0.18 inch) |
| Disc runout limit ....................................... | 0.15 mm (0.006 inch) |
| Front brake pad thickness | |
| 1981 through 1983 XV750 | |
|   New ........................................... | 5.7 mm (0.224 inch) |
|   Wear limit .................................... | 1.2 mm (0.047 inch) |
| 1983 XV920 ........................................ | Not specified |
| 1981 and 1982 XV920R | |
|   New ........................................... | 11.0 mm (0.433 inch) |
|   Wear limit .................................... | 6.0 mm (0.236 inch) |
| XV1000 chain drive (TR1) | |
|   New ........................................... | 6.5 mm (0.256 inch) |
|   Wear limit .................................... | 1.5 mm (0.059 inch) |
| 1984-on (except 1994-on UK) | |
|   New ........................................... | 5.5 mm (0.217 inch) |
|   Wear limit .................................... | 0.5 mm (0.020 inch) |
| 1994-on UK | |
|   New ........................................... | 6.1 mm (0.24 inch) |
|   Wear limit .................................... | 0.8 mm (0.03 inch) |
| Rear brake drum inside diameter | |
| 1981 through 1983 XV750 | |
|   Standard ...................................... | 180 mm (7.087 inch) |
|   Maximum ...................................... | Not specified |
| All others | |
|   Standard ...................................... | 200 mm (7.87 inches) |
|   Maximum ...................................... | 201 mm (7.91 inches) |
| Rear brake shoe lining thickness | |
|   Standard ...................................... | 4 mm (0.16 inch) |
|   Minimum ...................................... | 2 mm (0.08 inch) |

*Refer to marks stamped into the disc (they supersede information printed here)

## Wheels and tires

Wheel runout
  Radial (up-and-down) . . . . . . . . . . . . . . . . . . . . . . . . . . . . . . . . . . 2.0 mm (0.08 inch)
  Axial (side-to-side) . . . . . . . . . . . . . . . . . . . . . . . . . . . . . . . . . . . . 2.0 mm (0.08 inch)
Tire pressures . . . . . . . . . . . . . . . . . . . . . . . . . . . . . . . . . . . . . . . . . See Chapter 1
Tire sizes
  1981 through 1983 XV750 and XV920 shaft drive models
    Front . . . . . . . . . . . . . . . . . . . . . . . . . . . . . . . . . . . . . . . . . . . . . 3.50H 19 4PR
    Rear . . . . . . . . . . . . . . . . . . . . . . . . . . . . . . . . . . . . . . . . . . . . . 130/90 16 67H
  XV920 and XV1000 (TR1) chain drive models
    Front . . . . . . . . . . . . . . . . . . . . . . . . . . . . . . . . . . . . . . . . . . . . . 3.25H19 4PR
    Rear . . . . . . . . . . . . . . . . . . . . . . . . . . . . . . . . . . . . . . . . . . . . . 120/90 18 65H
  1984 and later models
    Front . . . . . . . . . . . . . . . . . . . . . . . . . . . . . . . . . . . . . . . . . . . . . 100/90 19 57H
    Rear (except 1994-on UK) . . . . . . . . . . . . . . . . . . . . . . . . . . . . 140/90 15 70H
    Rear (1994-on UK) . . . . . . . . . . . . . . . . . . . . . . . . . . . . . . . . . 140/90 15 M/C 70H

## Torque specifications

### 1981 through 1983 models

Front axle nut
  XV750 . . . . . . . . . . . . . . . . . . . . . . . . . . . . . . . . . . . . . . . . . . . . . 107 Nm (77 ft-lbs)*
  1982 and 1983 XV920 . . . . . . . . . . . . . . . . . . . . . . . . . . . . . . . 110 Nm (80 ft-lbs)*
  1981 and 1982 XV920R . . . . . . . . . . . . . . . . . . . . . . . . . . . . . . 107 Nm (77 ft-lbs)*
Front axle pinch bolt . . . . . . . . . . . . . . . . . . . . . . . . . . . . . . . . . . 20 Nm (14 ft-lbs)
Rear axle nut . . . . . . . . . . . . . . . . . . . . . . . . . . . . . . . . . . . . . . . . 107 Nm (77 ft-lbs)*
Rear brake torque link nuts . . . . . . . . . . . . . . . . . . . . . . . . . . . . 20 Nm (14 ft-lbs)*
Brake disc mounting bolts . . . . . . . . . . . . . . . . . . . . . . . . . . . . . 20 Nm (14 ft-lbs)**
Caliper mounting bolts
  1982 XV920 . . . . . . . . . . . . . . . . . . . . . . . . . . . . . . . . . . . . . . . 35 Nm (25 ft-lbs)
  All other 1981 through 1983 models . . . . . . . . . . . . . . . . . . . . 26 Nm (19 ft-lbs)
Fluid hose union bolts . . . . . . . . . . . . . . . . . . . . . . . . . . . . . . . . 26 Nm (19 ft-lbs)
Caliper bleed valve . . . . . . . . . . . . . . . . . . . . . . . . . . . . . . . . . . . 6 Nm (4.3 ft-lbs)
Master cylinder clamp bolts . . . . . . . . . . . . . . . . . . . . . . . . . . . . 9 Nm (6.5 ft-lbs)
Rear brake cam lever bolt . . . . . . . . . . . . . . . . . . . . . . . . . . . . . 9 Nm (6.5 ft-lbs)

### 1984-on models

Front axle or axle nut
  XV700, XV1000 and XV1100 . . . . . . . . . . . . . . . . . . . . . . . . . . 105 Nm (75 ft-lbs)*
  XV750
    US . . . . . . . . . . . . . . . . . . . . . . . . . . . . . . . . . . . . . . . . . . . . . 110 Nm (80 ft-lbs)
    UK . . . . . . . . . . . . . . . . . . . . . . . . . . . . . . . . . . . . . . . . . . . . . 107 Nm (77 ft-lbs)
Front axle pinch bolt . . . . . . . . . . . . . . . . . . . . . . . . . . . . . . . . . . 20 Nm (14 ft-lbs)
Rear axle nut . . . . . . . . . . . . . . . . . . . . . . . . . . . . . . . . . . . . . . . . 105 Nm (75 ft-lbs)*
Rear brake torque link nuts . . . . . . . . . . . . . . . . . . . . . . . . . . . . 20 Nm (14 ft-lbs)*
Brake disc mounting bolts . . . . . . . . . . . . . . . . . . . . . . . . . . . . . 20 Nm (14 ft-lbs)
Caliper mounting bolts
  All except 1994 UK models . . . . . . . . . . . . . . . . . . . . . . . . . . . 35 Nm (25 ft-lbs)
  1994 UK models . . . . . . . . . . . . . . . . . . . . . . . . . . . . . . . . . . . Not specified
Fluid hose union bolts . . . . . . . . . . . . . . . . . . . . . . . . . . . . . . . . 26 Nm (19 ft-lbs)
Caliper bleed valve . . . . . . . . . . . . . . . . . . . . . . . . . . . . . . . . . . . 6 Nm (4.3 ft-lbs)
Master cylinder clamp bolts . . . . . . . . . . . . . . . . . . . . . . . . . . . . 9 Nm (6.5 ft-lbs)
Rear brake cam lever bolt . . . . . . . . . . . . . . . . . . . . . . . . . . . . . 9 Nm (6.5 ft-lbs)
*Use new cotter pins.*
**Use new lockwashers.*

## 1 General information

The models covered in this Chapter are equipped with a hydraulic disc brake at the front and a mechanical drum brake at the rear. Several different front brake designs are used, varying according to model. They may be equipped with wire spoke wheels and tubed tires or alloy wheels and tubeless tires.
*Caution: Disc brake components rarely require disassembly. Do not disassemble components unless absolutely necessary. If any hydraulic brake line connection in the system is loosened, the entire system should be disassembled, drained, cleaned and then properly filled and bled upon reassembly. Do not use solvents on internal brake components. Solvents will cause seals to swell and distort. Use only clean brake fluid, brake cleaner or alcohol for cleaning. Use care when working with brake fluid as it can injure your eyes and it will damage painted surfaces and plastic parts.*

2.2 On '81 - '83 XV750 and '83 XV920 models, remove the coil spring, pull out the pad pin . . .

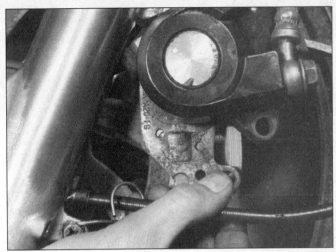

2.3a . . . and lower the pads out of the caliper

## 2  Brake pads - replacement

**Warning: The dust created by the brake system may contain asbestos, which is harmful to your health. Never blow it out with compressed air and don't inhale any of it. An approved filtering mask should be worn when working on the brakes.**

### 1981 through 1983 XV750; 1983 XV920

1 Support the bike securely so it can't be knocked over during this procedure.
2 Remove the coil spring from the pad retaining pin at the bottom of the caliper, then pull out the pin (see illustration).
3 Lower the pads out of the caliper (see illustrations).

### XV920R chain drive models and TR1

4 Remove the single bolt that secures the caliper body to its bracket (see illustration).

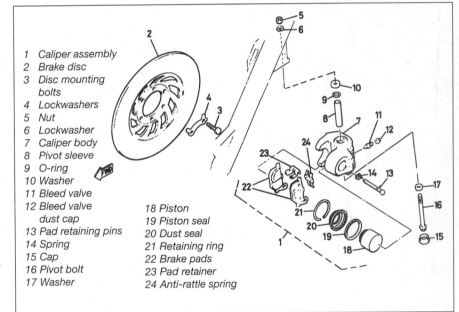

1  Caliper assembly
2  Brake disc
3  Disc mounting bolts
4  Lockwashers
5  Nut
6  Lockwasher
7  Caliper body
8  Pivot sleeve
9  O-ring
10  Washer
11  Bleed valve
12  Bleed valve dust cap
13  Pad retaining pins
14  Spring
15  Cap
16  Pivot bolt
17  Washer
18  Piston
19  Piston seal
20  Dust seal
21  Retaining ring
22  Brake pads
23  Pad retainer
24  Anti-rattle spring

2.3b  Front brake caliper (1981 through 1983 XV750, 1983 XV920 models) - exploded view

2.4a  On chain drive XV920R and TR1 models, remove the bolt and detach the caliper from the bracket . . .

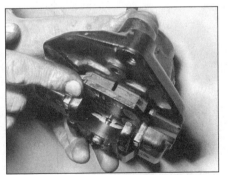

2.4b  . . . remove the brake pad retaining screw and the pads

2.5a  Remove the anti-rattle spring

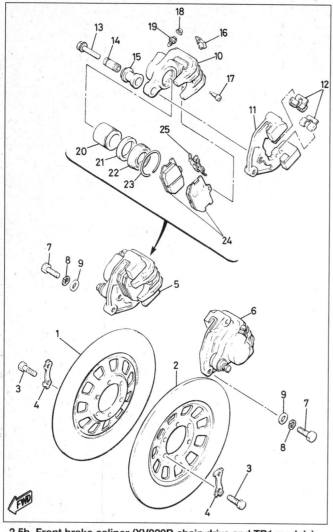

**2.5b Front brake caliper (XV920R chain drive and TR1 models) - exploded view**

1 Right brake disc
2 Left brake disc
3 Disc mounting bolts
4 Lockwashers
5 Right caliper assembly
6 Left caliper assembly
7 Caliper mounting bolts
8 Lockwashers
9 Washers
10 Caliper body
11 Caliper bracket
12 Anti-rattle shim
13 Caliper-to-bracket bolt

14 Sleeve
15 Boot
16 Inspection window
17 Pad retaining screw
18 Bleed valve cap
19 Bleed valve
20 Piston
21 Piston seal
22 Dust seal
23 Retaining ring
24 Brake pads
25 Anti-rattle spring

**2.7 Front brake caliper (1982 XV920) - exploded view**

1 Right caliper assembly
2 Left caliper assembly
3 Caliper body
4 Mounting bracket
5 Shim
6 Retaining plate
7 Screw
8 Bleed valve and cap
9 Pad retaining pin
10 Pad retaining pin
11 Cotter pin
12 Spring clip

13 Anti-rattle spring
14 Brake pads
15 Piston seals
16 Piston
17 Caliper mounting bolts
18 Lockwashers
19 Washers
20 Brake disc mounting bolts
21 Lockwashers
22 Right brake disc
23 Left brake disc

Remove the single screw that secures the pads, then lift the caliper off the bracket to expose the pads **(see illustration)**.
5 Note carefully which pad is on which side of the disc, then remove the anti-rattle spring and the pads **(see illustrations)**.

### 1982 XV920

6 Remove the front wheel (see Section 11).

7 Remove the pad pin clips, then pull out the pad pins **(see illustration)**.
8 Remove the anti-rattle spring, pads and shim.

### 1984 and later models (except 1994-on UK)

9 Remove the pad cover **(see illustration)**.

Remove the pad pin clips, then pull out the pad pins and remove the anti-rattle spring **(see illustration)**.
10 Pull out the pads.

### 1994 and later UK models

11 Remove the lower caliper bolt and pivot the caliper upward **(see illustration)**.

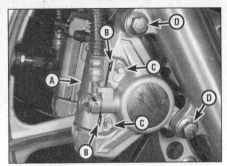

**2.9a Caliper mounting details (1984 and later models except 1994-on UK)**

A  Pad cover
B  Pad pin clips
C  Pad pins
D  Caliper mounting bolts

**12**  Remove the pad spring and pull out the pads.

## All models

**13**  Measure the amount of friction material left on the pads and replace them as a pair if worn, fouled with oil or damaged in any way. If you're working on a 1994-on UK model, replace the pads if the grooves in the friction material are worn away.

**14**  Check the condition of the brake discs (see Section 4). If they are in need of machining or replacement, follow the procedure in that Section to remove them.

**15**  Connect a length of rubber or plastic tubing to the caliper bleed valve and place the other end in a container. Open the bleed valve and push the pistons into the caliper as far as possible; displaced brake fluid will flow through the tubing into the container. If you can't depress the pistons with thumb pressure, try using a C-clamp (G-clamp). If the piston sticks, remove the caliper and overhaul it as described in Section 3. Once the pistons are pressed in, close the bleed valve, remove the tubing and install the bleed valve cap.

> ⚠️ **Warning: Step 16 is necessary to ensure that the pads move freely in the calipers.**

**16**  Because a large amount of salt is used on roads in the UK, special lubrication of the pads and calipers is required. Before installing the pads on UK models, apply a thin film of Duckhams Copper 10 or equivalent to the following areas (see illustrations 2.6a and 2.6b in Part A of this Chapter):
a)  To the edges of the metal backing on the brake pads
b)  To the areas of the caliper where the pads rub
c)  To the threads of the caliper mounting bolts.
Apply a thin film of Shin-Etsu G-40M or equivalent silicone grease to the following:
d)  Exposed areas of the caliper pistons
e)  The areas of the pad backing plates that contact the pistons.
**Caution: Don't use too much Copper 10. Make sure no Copper 10 contacts the brake discs or the pad friction surfaces.**

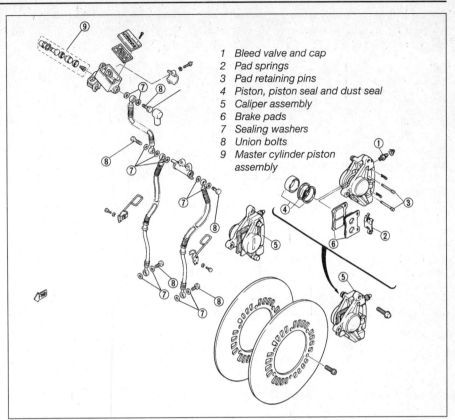

1  Bleed valve and cap
2  Pad springs
3  Pad retaining pins
4  Piston, piston seal and dust seal
5  Caliper assembly
6  Brake pads
7  Sealing washers
8  Union bolts
9  Master cylinder piston assembly

**2.9b Front brake caliper (1984 and later models except 1994-on UK) - exploded view**

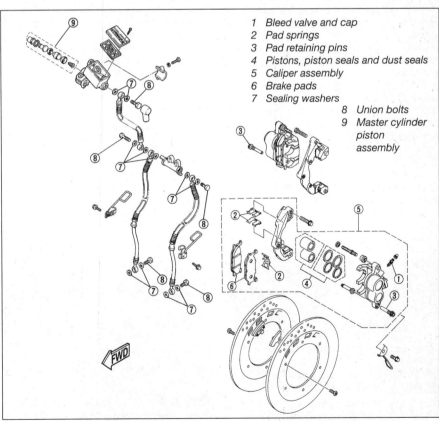

1  Bleed valve and cap
2  Pad springs
3  Pad retaining pins
4  Pistons, piston seals and dust seals
5  Caliper assembly
6  Brake pads
7  Sealing washers
8  Union bolts
9  Master cylinder piston assembly

**2.11  Front brake caliper (1994 and later UK models) - exploded view**

**3.2a Remove the union bolt (arrow); this type of caliper is used on '81 - '83 shaft drive models . . .**

**17** Install the pads and springs in the caliper. The rounded edge of the pad faces the rear of the motorcycle **(see illustration 2.3a)**.
**18** Check fluid level in the master cylinder reservoir (see Chapter 1) and add fluid if necessary.
**19** Operate the brake lever several times to bring the pads into contact with the disc. Check the operation of the brakes carefully before riding the motorcycle.

---

### 3  Brake caliper - removal, overhaul and installation

> **Warning: If a caliper indicates the need for an overhaul (usually due to leaking fluid or sticky operation), all old brake fluid should be flushed from the system. Also, the dust created by the brake system may contain asbestos, which is harmful to your health. Never blow it out with compressed air and don't inhale any of it. An approved filtering mask should be worn when working on the brakes. Do not, under any circumstances, use petroleum-based solvents to clean brake parts. Use brake cleaner or denatured alcohol only!**

#### Removal

**1** Support the bike securely so it can't be knocked over during this procedure.
**2** Remove the union bolt from the brake hose banjo fitting and separate the hose from the caliper **(see illustrations)**. Discard the sealing

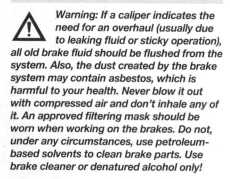

**3.3a If you're working on a '81 - '83 XV750, or an '83 XV920, remove the nut and washer . . .**

---

**3.2b . . . and this type is used on 1984 and later models (except 1994-on UK)**

washers. Place the end of the hose in a container and operate the brake lever to pump out the fluid. Once this is done, wrap a clean shop rag tightly around the hose fitting to soak up any drips and prevent contamination.
**3** If you're working on a 1981 through 1983 XV750, or a 1983 XV920, remove the nut and lockwasher from the top of the caliper, then slide the caliper down out of the bracket in the fork leg **(see illustrations)**.
**4** On all other models, unscrew the caliper mounting bolts and separate the caliper from the front fork **(see illustration)**.

#### Overhaul

**5** Clean the exterior of the caliper with denatured alcohol or brake system cleaner.
**6** Place a few rags between the piston and the caliper frame to act as a cushion, then use compressed air, directed into the fluid inlet, to remove the piston(s) **(see illustration 2.3c in Part A of this Chapter and illustrations 2.3b, 2.5b, 2.7, 2.9b and 2.11)**. Use only enough air pressure to ease the piston out of the bore. If a piston is blown out, even with the cushion in place, it may be damaged. On calipers with opposed pistons **(see illustration 2.9b)** insert a piece of flat wood into the caliper to hold one piston in place while the other is being removed, then pack the empty bore with clean rag and remove the second piston. On opposed piston and two-piston calipers, mark each piston and the caliper body to ensure that the pistons can be matched to their original bores on reassembly.

**3.3b . . . and slide the caliper off the pivot post**

---

> **Warning: Never place your fingers in front of the piston in an attempt to catch or protect it when applying compressed air, as serious injury could occur.**

**7** If compressed air isn't available, reconnect the caliper to the brake hose and pump the brake lever until the piston is free.
**8** Using a wood or plastic tool, remove the dust seal. Metal tools may damage the bore.
**9** Using a wood or plastic tool, remove the piston seal from the groove in the caliper bore.
**10** Clean the piston and the bore with denatured alcohol, clean brake fluid or brake system cleaner and blow dry them with filtered, unlubricated compressed air. Inspect the surfaces of the piston for nicks and burrs and loss of plating. Check the caliper bore, too. If surface defects are present, the caliper must be replaced. If the caliper is in bad shape, the master cylinder should also be checked.
**11** Lubricate the piston seal with clean brake fluid and install it in its groove in the caliper bore. Make sure it isn't twisted and seats completely. Note that on 1994-on UK models fitted with a two-piston caliper, the seals are of different sizes corresponding with the different sizes of caliper bore. Take care to ensure that the correct size seals are fitted to the correct bores.
**12** Lubricate the dust seal with clean brake fluid and install it in its groove, making sure it seats correctly.
**13** Lubricate the piston with clean brake fluid and install it into the caliper bore. Using your thumbs, push the piston all the way in, making sure it doesn't get cocked in the bore.
**14** On bracket-mounted calipers, the caliper body should be able to slide in relation to its mounting bracket. If it's seized or stiff in operation, lubricate the friction points or slide pins with high-temperature disc brake grease. If the dust boots are split or cracked, replace them with new ones.

#### Installation

**15** Install the caliper, tightening the mounting bolts or nut to the torque listed in this Chapter's Specifications.
**16** Connect the brake hose to the caliper, using new sealing washers on each side of the fitting. The neck of the hose union should

**3.4 Remove the caliper mounting bolts and detach the caliper from the fork**

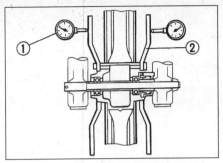

**4.3 Set up a dial indicator (1) to measure runout of the brake disc(s) (2)**

fit between the two cast lugs on the caliper body. Tighten the banjo fitting bolt to the torque listed in this Chapter's Specifications.

**17** Fill the master cylinder with the recommended brake fluid (see Chapter 1) and bleed the system (see Section 8). Check for leaks.

**18** Check the operation of the brakes carefully before riding the motorcycle.

---

## 4 Brake disc - inspection, removal and installation

### Inspection

**1** Support the bike securely so it can't be knocked over during this procedure.

**2** Visually inspect the surface of the disc for score marks and other damage. Light scratches are normal after use and won't affect brake operation, but deep grooves and heavy score marks will reduce braking efficiency and accelerate pad wear. If the disc is badly grooved it must be machined or replaced.

**3** To check disc runout, mount a dial indicator to the fork leg with the plunger on the indicator touching the surface of the disc about 1/2-inch from the outer edge **(see illustration)**. Slowly turn the wheel and watch the indicator needle, comparing your reading with the limit listed in this Chapter's Specifications or stamped on the disc itself. If the runout is greater than allowed, check the hub bearings for play (see Chapter 1). If the bearings are worn, replace them and repeat this check. If the disc runout is still excessive, it will have to be replaced.

**4** The disc must not be machined or allowed to wear down to a thickness less than the minimum allowable thickness, listed in this Chapter's Specifications. The thickness of the disc can be checked with a micrometer. If the thickness of the disc is less than the minimum allowable, it must be replaced.

### Removal

**5** Remove the wheel (see Section 11 for front wheel removal or Section 12 for rear wheel removal).

*Caution: Don't lay the wheel down and allow it to rest on the disc - the disc could become warped. Set the wheel on wood*

blocks so the disc doesn't support the weight of the wheel.

**6** Mark the relationship of the disc to the wheel, so it can be installed in the same position. Bend back the lockwasher tabs (1981 through 1983 models) and remove the bolts that retain the disc to the wheel **(see illustration 2.3b, 2.5b, 2.7, 2.9b or 2.11)**. Loosen the bolts a little at a time, in a criss-cross pattern, to avoid distorting the disc. Once all the bolts are loose, take the disc off.

**7** Take note of any paper shims that may be present where the disc mates to the wheel. If there are any, mark their position and be sure to include them when installing the disc.

### Installation

**8** Position the disc on the wheel, aligning the previously applied matchmarks (if you're reinstalling the original disc). Make sure the arrow (stamped on the disc) marking the direction of rotation is pointing in the proper direction.

**9** Apply a non-hardening thread locking compound to the threads of the bolts. Install the bolts with (use new lockwashers on 1981 through 1983 models), tightening them a little at a time, in a criss-cross pattern, until the torque listed in this Chapter's Specifications is reached. Clean off all grease from the brake disc using acetone or brake system cleaner.

**10** Install the wheel.

**11** Operate the brake lever several times to bring the pads into contact with the disc. Check the operation of the brakes carefully before riding the motorcycle.

---

## 5 Front brake master cylinder - removal, overhaul and installation

**1** If the master cylinder is leaking fluid, or if the lever does not produce a firm feel when the brake is applied, and bleeding the brakes does not help, master cylinder overhaul is recommended.

**2** Before disassembling the master cylinder, read through the entire procedure and make sure that you have the correct rebuild kit. Also, you will need some new, clean brake fluid of the recommended type, some clean rags and internal snap-ring pliers. **Note:** *To prevent damage to the paint from spilled brake fluid, always cover the fuel tank when working on the master cylinder.*

*Caution: Disassembly, overhaul and reassembly of the brake master cylinder must be done in a spotlessly clean work area to avoid contamination and possible failure of the brake hydraulic system components.*

### Removal

**3** Loosen but do not remove the screws holding the reservoir cover in place **(see the**

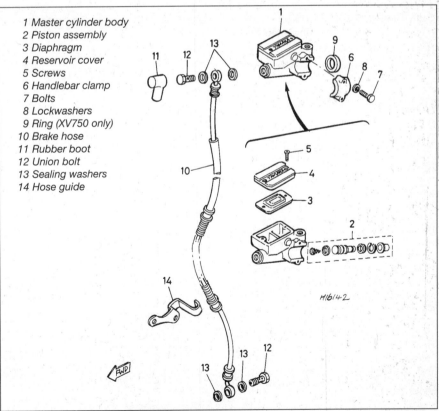

1 Master cylinder body
2 Piston assembly
3 Diaphragm
4 Reservoir cover
5 Screws
6 Handlebar clamp
7 Bolts
8 Lockwashers
9 Ring (XV750 only)
10 Brake hose
11 Rubber boot
12 Union bolt
13 Sealing washers
14 Hose guide

**5.3a Master cylinder (1981 through 1983 XV750, 1983 XV920 models) - exploded view**

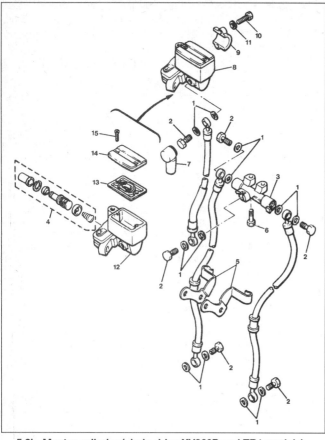

**5.3b  Master cylinder (chain drive XV920R and TR1 models) - exploded view**

| | |
|---|---|
| 1 Sealing washers | 9 Handlebar clamp |
| 2 Union bolts | 10 Bolts |
| 3 Hose joint | 11 Lockwashers |
| 4 Piston assembly | 12 Master cylinder body |
| 5 Hose guides | 13 Diaphragm |
| 6 Bolt | 14 Reservoir cover |
| 7 Rubber boot | 15 Screws |
| 8 Master cylinder assembly | |

**5.3c  Master cylinder (1982 XV920 models) - exploded view**

| | |
|---|---|
| 1 Master cylinder body | 9 Bolts |
| 2 Piston assembly | 10 Rubber boot |
| 3 Sensor unit | 11 Union bolts |
| 4 Diaphragm | 12 Sealing washers |
| 5 Reservoir cover | 13 Hose joint |
| 6 Screws | 14 Bolt |
| 7 Handlebar clamp | 15 Hose guides |
| 8 Lockwashers | |

accompanying illustrations, illustration 2.9b or illustration 2.11).

**4** Disconnect the electrical connectors from the brake light switch (see Chapter 8).

**5** Pull back the rubber boot (if equipped), loosen the banjo fitting bolt and separate the brake hose from the master cylinder. Wrap the end of the hose in a clean rag and suspend the hose in an upright position or bend it down carefully and place the open end in a clean container. The objective is to prevent excessive loss of brake fluid, fluid spills and system contamination.

**6** Remove the master cylinder mounting bolts and separate the master cylinder from the handlebar.

*Caution: Do not tip the master cylinder upside down or brake fluid will run out.*

## Overhaul

**7** This is the same as for XV535 models. Refer to Part A of this Chapter and illustration 2.9b, 2.11, 5.3a, 5.3b or 5.3c.

## Installation

**8** Attach the master cylinder to the handlebar, making sure the UP mark is upright, and tighten the bolts to the torque listed in this Chapter's Specifications.

**9** Connect the brake hose to the master cylinder, using new sealing washers. Tighten the banjo fitting bolt to the torque listed in this Chapter's Specifications. Fill the master cylinder with the recommended brake fluid (see Chapter 1), then refer to Section 8 and bleed the air from the system.

## 6  Rear drum brakes - removal, overhaul and installation

### Shoe removal

**1** Before you start, inspect the rear brake wear indicator (see Chapter 1).

**2** Support the bike securely so it can't be knocked over during this procedure.

**3** Remove the rear wheel (see Section 12). Lift the brake panel out of the wheel **(see illustration)**.

**4** Fold the shoes toward each other to release

**6.3  Lift the rear brake panel out of the wheel**

**6.5a Fold the shoes together to detach them from the brake panel**

the spring tension (see illustration). Remove the shoes and springs from the brake panel (see illustrations).

## Shoe inspection

**5** Check the linings for wear, damage and signs of contamination from road dirt and water. If the linings are visibly defective, replace them.

**6** Measure the thickness of the lining material (just the lining material, not the metal backing) and compare with the value listed in this Chapter's Specifications. Replace the shoes if the lining material is worn to less than the minimum.

**7** Check the ends of the shoes where they

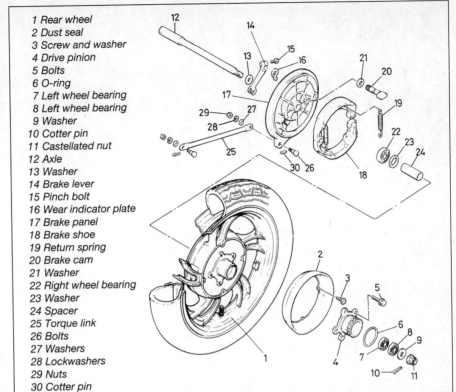

1 Rear wheel
2 Dust seal
3 Screw and washer
4 Drive pinion
5 Bolts
6 O-ring
7 Left wheel bearing
8 Left wheel bearing
9 Washer
10 Cotter pin
11 Castellated nut
12 Axle
13 Washer
14 Brake lever
15 Pinch bolt
16 Wear indicator plate
17 Brake panel
18 Brake shoe
19 Return spring
20 Brake cam
21 Washer
22 Right wheel bearing
23 Washer
24 Spacer
25 Torque link
26 Bolts
27 Washers
28 Lockwashers
29 Nuts
30 Cotter pin

**6.5b Rear wheel and brake details (shaft drive models)**

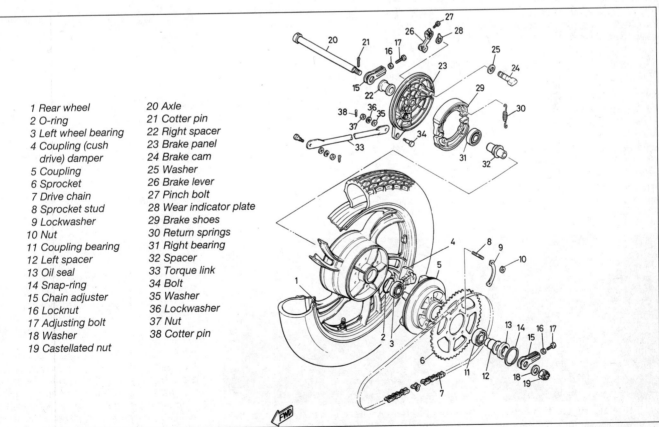

1 Rear wheel
2 O-ring
3 Left wheel bearing
4 Coupling (cush drive) damper
5 Coupling
6 Sprocket
7 Drive chain
8 Sprocket stud
9 Lockwasher
10 Nut
11 Coupling bearing
12 Left spacer
13 Oil seal
14 Snap-ring
15 Chain adjuster
16 Locknut
17 Adjusting bolt
18 Washer
19 Castellated nut

20 Axle
21 Cotter pin
22 Right spacer
23 Brake panel
24 Brake cam
25 Washer
26 Brake lever
27 Pinch bolt
28 Wear indicator plate
29 Brake shoes
30 Return springs
31 Right bearing
32 Spacer
33 Torque link
34 Bolt
35 Washer
36 Lockwasher
37 Nut
38 Cotter pin

**6.5c Rear wheel and brake details (chain drive models)**

**6.8a Loosen the pinch bolt and remove the brake lever . . .**

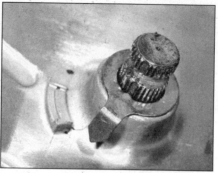

**6.8b . . . remove the wear indicator pointer . . .**

**6.8c . . . and withdraw the cam from the brake panel**

contact the brake cam and pivot post. Replace the shoes if there's visible wear.

**8** Check the brake cam and pivot post for wear and damage. If necessary, make match marks on the cam and cam lever, then remove the pinch bolt, lever, wear indicator pointer, seal and cam **(see illustrations)**.

**9** Check the brake drum (inside the wheel) for wear or damage. Measure the diameter at several points with a brake drum micrometer (or have this done by a Yamaha dealer). If the measurements are uneven (indicating the brake drum is out of round) or if there are scratches deep enough to snag a fingernail, have the drum turned (skimmed) by a dealer to correct the surface. If the drum has to be turned (skimmed) beyond the wear limit to remove the defects, replace it.

**10** Check the brake cam for looseness in the brake panel hole. If it feels loose, replace the brake cam or panel, whichever is worn.

**11** Reverse Step 8 to install the brake lever and cam.

### Shoe installation

**12** Apply high-temperature brake grease to the ends of the springs, the cam and the pivot post.

**13** Hook the springs to the shoes. Position the shoes in a V on the panel, then fold them down into position **(see illustration 6.5a)**. Make sure the ends of the shoes fit correctly against the cam and on the pivot post **(see illustration 6.4)**.

**6.16 Note the position of the match marks (A), unhook the spring (B) and loosen the pinch bolt (C)**

### Rear brake pedal removal and installation

**14** Remove the cotter pin and clevis pin and detach the brake rod from the pedal arm. Unhook the pedal return spring.

**15** Look for match marks on the pedal and shaft. If they aren't there, make your own.

**16** Unhook the brake light switch spring from the pedal **(see illustration)**. Loosen the pedal pinch bolt and slide the pedal off the shaft.

**17** Installation is the reverse of the removal steps. Adjust the rear brake (see Chapter 1).

### 7 Brake hoses - inspection and replacement

### Inspection

**1** Once a week, or if the motorcycle is used less frequently, before every ride, check the condition of the brake hose.

**2** Twist and flex the rubber hose(s) **(see illustration 2.9b, 2.11, 5.3a, 5.3b or 5.3c)** while looking for cracks, bulges and seeping fluid. Check extra carefully around the areas where the hoses connect with the banjo fittings, as these are common areas for hose failure **(see illustration)**.

**3** Inspect the metal banjo fittings connected to brake hoses. If the fittings are rusted, scratched or cracked, replace them.

**7.2 Remove the union bolts (A); note the position of the banjo fitting neck next to the cast lug (B)**

### Replacement

**4** Brake hoses have a banjo fitting on each end. Cover the surrounding area with plenty of rags and unscrew the union bolt on either end of the hose. Detach the hose from any clips that may be present and remove the hose.

**5** Position the new hose, making sure it isn't twisted or otherwise strained, between the two components. Make sure the neck of the hose union fits between the two cast lugs on the caliper body or on the clockwise side of the cast lug in the hose joint **(see illustration 7.2)**. Install the union bolts, using new sealing washers on both sides of the fittings, and tighten them to the torque listed in this Chapter's Specifications.

**6** Flush the old brake fluid from the system, refill the system with the recommended fluid (see Chapter 1) and bleed the air from the system (see Section 8). Check the operation of the front brake carefully before riding the motorcycle.

### 8 Brake system bleeding

This is the same as for XV535 models. Refer to Part A of this Chapter.

### 9 Wheels - inspection and repair

**1** For models equipped with wire spoke wheels, this is the same as for XV535 models. Refer to Part A of this Chapter.

**2** Wheel runout for alloy wheels is measured in the same way as for wire spoke wheels (refer to Part A of this Chapter). Alloy wheels with excessive runout must be replaced with new ones.

**3** Since models equipped with alloy wheels use tubeless tires, look very closely for dents in the area where the tire bead contacts the rim. Dents in this area may prevent complete sealing of the tire against the rim, which leads to deflation of the tire over a period of time. If damage is evident, the wheel will have to be replaced with a new one.

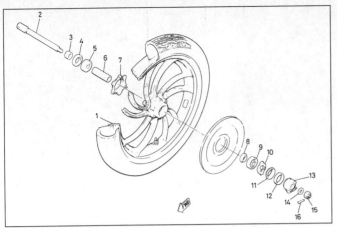

**11.3a  Front wheel (1981 through 1983 shaft drive models)**

| | | |
|---|---|---|
| 1 Front wheel | 7 Hub trim (except | 12 Grease seal |
| 2 Axle | 1982 XV920) | 13 Speedometer drive |
| 3 Collar | 8 Flanged spacer | unit |
| 4 Grease seal | 9 Left bearing | 14 Washer |
| 5 Right bearing | 10 Speedometer | 15 Castellated nut |
| 6 Spacer | clutch | 16 Cotter pin |
| | 11 Retaining ring | |

**11.3b  Front wheel details (1981 through 1983 chain drive models, including TR1)**

| | | |
|---|---|---|
| 1 Front wheel | 7 Castellated nut | 12 Retaining ring |
| 2 Center spacer | 8 Cotter pin | 13 Grease seal |
| 3 Right bearing | 9 Flanged spacer | 14 Washer (TR1 only) |
| 4 Grease seal | 10 Right bearing | 15 Speedometer drive |
| 5 Collar | 11 Speedometer | unit |
| 6 Washer | clutch | 16 Axle |

## 10  Wheels - alignment check

This is the same as for XV535 models. Refer to Part A of this Chapter.

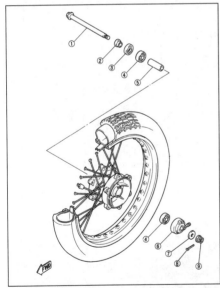

**11.3c  Front wheel details (1984 and later models) - wire wheel shown**

| | |
|---|---|
| 1 Axle | 7 Washer (early |
| 2 Collar | models) |
| 3 Grease seal | 8 Cotter pin (early |
| 4 Wheel bearing | models) |
| 5 Spacer | 9 Castellated nut |
| 6 Speedometer drive | (early models) |
| unit | |

## 11  Front wheel - removal and installation

### Removal

**1** Support the bike securely so it can't be knocked over during this procedure. Raise the front wheel off the ground by placing a floor jack, with a wood block on the jack head, under the engine.

**2** Disconnect the speedometer cable from the drive unit (see Chapter 8).

**3** The axle on early models is secured by a nut. Remove the cotter pin and unscrew the nut **(see illustrations)**. The axle on later models threads directly into the left fork leg.

**4** Support the wheel. Loosen the axle pinch bolt. If the axle has a round head **(see illustration)**, slip a bar through the removal hole and twist and pull the axle to remove it. If the axle has a hex head, unscrew the axle **(see illustration)**.

**11.4b  . . . if the axle has a hex head like this one, unscrew it**

**5** Carefully lower the wheel away from the forks. Remove the collar from the right side and the speedometer drive unit from the left side **(see illustrations)**. Set the wheel aside. *Caution: Don't lay the wheel down and allow it to rest on the brake disc - the disc could become warped. Set the wheel on*

**11.4a  Remove the pinch bolt; if the axle has a round head, pull it out with a bar through the hole . . .**

**11.5a  Remove the collar . . .**

11.5b . . . and the speedometer drive unit

11.8a  Make sure the dogs on the speedometer clutch . . .

11.8b . . . engage the slots in the drive unit

wood blocks so the disc doesn't support the weight of the wheel. **Note:** *Don't operate the front brake lever with the wheel removed.*

### Inspection

**6** Roll the axle on a flat surface such as a piece of plate glass. If it's bent at all, replace it. If the axle is corroded, remove the corrosion with fine emery cloth.
**7** Check the condition of the wheel bearings (see Section 13).

### Installation

**8** Installation is the reverse of removal. Apply a thin coat of grease to the seal lip, then slide the axle into the hub. Slide the wheel into

place. Make sure the lugs in the speedometer drive clutch line up with the notches in the speedometer drive unit **(see illustrations)**. Make sure the protrusion on the inner side of the left fork fits into the notch in the speedometer drive unit **(see illustration 11.5b)**.
**9** Slip the axle into place, then tighten the axle or axle nut to the torque listed in this Chapter's Specifications. If the axle is secured by a nut, install a new cotter pin. Tighten the axle pinch bolt to the torque listed in this Chapter's Specifications.
**10** Apply the front brake, pump the forks up and down several times and check for binding and proper brake operation.

### 12 Rear wheel -
removal and installation

### Removal

**1** Support the bike securely so it can't be knocked over during this procedure.
**2** Detach the torque link from the brake panel and the brake rod from the brake lever **(see illustration 6.5b or 6.5c and the accompanying illustrations)**.
**3** Remove the cotter pin from the axle nut, then remove the nut and washer **(see illustration)**.

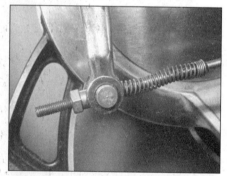

12.2a  Unscrew the nut and disconnect the brake rod

12.2b  Remove the cotter pin, washer and nut and disconnect the torque link

12.3  Remove the cotter pin and nut

12.4  Loosen the axle pinch bolt (if equipped)

12.5  Pull out the axle

12.6  On chain drive models, remove the spacer that fits between the brake panel and the swingarm

**12.10 On chain drive models, replace the dampers with new ones if they're deteriorated, worn or brittle**

**12.11a On shaft drive models, be sure the long spacer is in position before installing the wheel**

**12.11b On chain drive models, align the vanes in the coupling with the gaps between the dampers**

**4** Loosen the axle pinch bolt **(see illustration)**.

**5** Support the wheel, slide the axle out and remove the washer **(see illustration)**.

**6** On chain drive models, remove the spacer that fits between the brake panel and the swingarm **(see illustration)**.

**7** Pull the wheel to the right and remove it from the final drive assembly.

**8** Before installing the wheel, check the axle for straightness by rolling it on a flat surface such as a piece of plate glass (if the axle is corroded, first remove the corrosion with fine emery cloth). If the axle is bent at all, replace it.

**9** Check the condition of the wheel bearings (see Section 13).

**10** If you're working on a chain drive model, inspect the rubber coupling dampers **(see illustration)**. If they're deteriorated, brittle or worn, pull them out of the wheel and install new ones.

### Installation

**11** Installation is the reverse of the removal steps, with the following additions:

a) *Apply a light coat of multi-purpose lithium-based grease to the lips of the oil seals and to the splines on the final drive and wheel hub.*

b) *If you're working on a shaft drive model, be sure the long spacer is in place before*

*installing the wheel* **(see illustration)**.

c) *If you're working on a chain drive model, align the vanes on the coupling with the gaps between the rubber coupling dampers* **(see illustration)**.

d) *Tighten the axle nut to the torque listed in this Chapter's Specifications. Install a new cotter pin, tightening the axle nut an additional amount, if necessary, to align the hole in the axle with the castellations on the nut.*

e) *Tighten the axle pinch bolt to the torque listed in this Chapter's Specifications.*

f) *Make sure the tire clears the swingarm* **(see illustration)**.

**12** Adjust the rear brake (see Chapter 1) and check its operation carefully before riding the motorcycle.

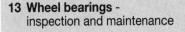
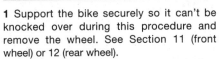

**13 Wheel bearings -**
inspection and maintenance

**1** Support the bike securely so it can't be knocked over during this procedure and remove the wheel. See Section 11 (front wheel) or 12 (rear wheel).

**2** Set the wheel on blocks so as not to allow the weight of the wheel to rest on the brake disc or hub.

**12.11c Make sure the tire clears the swingarm**

### Front wheel bearings

**3** Removal, inspection and installation of the front wheel bearings is the same as for XV535 models (see Part A of this Chapter). Refer to **illustration 11.3a, 11.3b or 11.3c** and the Part B Specifications.

### Rear wheel bearings

**4** If necessary for inspection, the dust seal and clutch hub can be detached from the wheel **(see illustration 12.3 and the accompanying illustration)**. The rear wheel bearings can be removed and installed with these parts in place.

**5** Rear wheel bearing removal, inspection and installation are generally the same as for front

**13.4 If necessary, unbolt the clutch hub and remove it**

**13.5a Use non-permanent thread locking agent on the threads of the clutch hub bolts**

**13.5b Drive the two bearings out of the left side of the hub with a long bar . . .**

**13.5c . . . and use the same tool to remove the single bearing from the right side**

**13.5d Remove the spacer and collar from the hub**

**13.5e Drive in new bearings with a bearing driver or a socket the same diameter as the outer race**

wheel bearings (see part A of this Chapter and the accompanying illustrations). On installation, be sure to install the spacer and its collar between the bearings. Apply non-permanent thread locking agent to the threads of the clutch hub bolts **(see illustration)** and tighten them securely.

## 14 Tires - general information

### General information

1 Models with spoked wheels are fitted with tubed tires and inner tubes. Do not fit tubeless

tires to these wheel rims.
2 Models with cast wheels are fitted with tubeless tires. Yamaha advise that tubed type tires and inner tubes can be fitted if desired - refer to the owners manual for details.
3 Refer to *Daily (pre-ride) checks* at the beginning of this manual, and to the scheduled checks in Chapter 1 for tire and wheel maintenance.

### Fitting new tubeless tires

4 When selecting new tires, refer to the tire information label on the motorcycle and the tire options listed in the owners manual. Ensure that front and rear tire types are compatible, the correct size and correct speed rating; if necessary seek advice from a

Yamaha dealer or tire fitting specialist **(see illustration)**.
5 It is recommended that tires are fitted by a motorcycle tire specialist rather than attempted in the home workshop. The force required to break the seal between the wheel rim and tire bead is substantial, and is usually beyond the capabilities of an individual working with normal tire levers. Additionally, the specialist will be able to balance the wheels after tire fitting.
6 Only certain types of puncture repair are suitable for tubeless motorcycle tires. Refer to a tire fitting specialist for advice.

### Fitting new tubed tires

7 Refer to Chapter 6A, Section 14 for details.

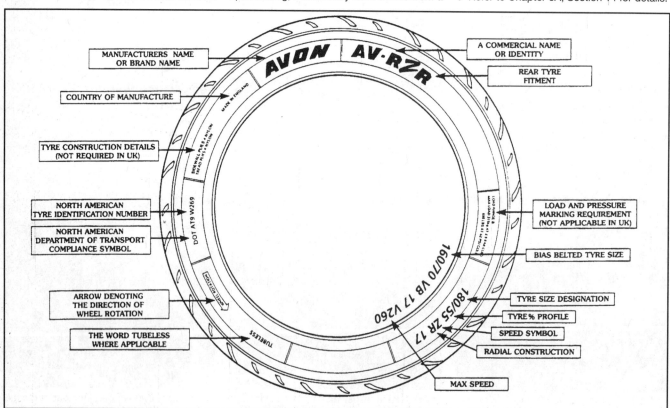

**14.4 Common tyre sidewall markings**

MANUFACTURERS NAME OR BRAND NAME

COUNTRY OF MANUFACTURE

TYRE CONSTRUCTION DETAILS (NOT REQUIRED IN UK)

NORTH AMERICAN TYRE IDENTIFICATION NUMBER

NORTH AMERICAN DEPARTMENT OF TRANSPORT COMPLIANCE SYMBOL

ARROW DENOTING THE DIRECTION OF WHEEL ROTATION

THE WORD TUBELESS WHERE APPLICABLE

A COMMERCIAL NAME OR IDENTITY

REAR TYRE FITMENT

LOAD AND PRESSURE MARKING REQUIREMENT (NOT APPLICABLE IN UK)

BIAS BELTED TYRE SIZE

TYRE SIZE DESIGNATION

TYRE % PROFILE

SPEED SYMBOL

RADIAL CONSTRUCTION

MAX SPEED

# Chapter 7 Part A
# Frame and bodywork (XV535 models)

## Contents

## Degrees of difficulty

| Easy, suitable for novice with little experience  | Fairly easy, suitable for beginner with some experience  | Fairly difficult, suitable for competent DIY mechanic 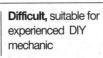 | Difficult, suitable for experienced DIY mechanic  | Very difficult, suitable for expert DIY or professional |

### 1 General information

The XV535 models use a steel frame composed of round-section tubing and a pressed steel backbone which incorporates the air cleaner housing.

Fenders and covers are steel, either painted or chrome plated.

### 2 Frame - inspection and repair

1 The frame should not require attention unless accident damage has occurred. In most cases, frame replacement is the only satisfactory remedy for such damage. A few frame specialists have the jigs and other equipment necessary for straightening the frame to the required standard of accuracy, but even then there is no simple way of assessing to what extent the frame may have been overstressed.

2 After the machine has accumulated a lot of miles, the frame should be examined closely for signs of cracking or splitting at the welded joints. Corrosion can also cause weakness at these joints. Loose engine mount bolts can cause ovaling or fracturing of the mounting tabs. Minor damage can often be repaired by welding, depending on the extent and nature of the damage.

3 Remember that a frame which is out of alignment will cause handling problems. If misalignment is suspected as the result of an accident, it will be necessary to strip the machine completely so the frame can be thoroughly checked.

### 3 Footpegs and pads - removal and installation

1 The front footpegs are mounted on a bracket that also serves to protect the engine. The rear footpegs are mounted on brackets bolted to the frame.

2 To remove a front or rear footpeg pad on early models, work the rubber pad off the end of the footpeg. The pad is a tight fit, so this may be difficult. Cutting off the old pad, then heating the new pad in hot water and lubricating it with soap, will make the job easier.

3 To replace a front footpeg pad on later models, remove the pad securing nuts from the underside of the footpeg and lift the pad off. Install the new pad and tighten the nuts securely.

4 To replace a rear footpeg pad on later models, remove the pad securing screws and lift it off. Install the new pad and tighten the screws securely.

5 To remove a front footpeg assembly (footpeg and pivot bracket), remove the bolts that secure the pivot bracket to the main bracket (see illustration).

6 To remove a front footpeg, remove the cotter pin, collar and clevis pin and separate the footpeg from the pivot bracket (see illustration).

7 To remove a left rear footpeg assembly, unbolt the pivot bracket from the main bracket (see illustration). To remove a right rear

3.5 Remove the footpeg mounting bolts (early models)

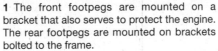

3.6 Remove the clip, washer and clevis pin (arrow)

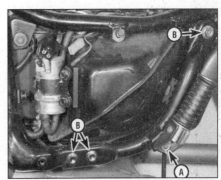
3.7 The rear footpegs are bolted to the brackets; the brackets are bolted to the frame

A Footpeg mounting bolt
B Bracket bolts

3.8a Make match marks on the shift shaft and lever, remove the pinch bolt (arrow), the mounting nut . . .

3.8b . . . and front mounting bolt . . .

3.8c . . . and detach the bracket from the motorcycle

footpeg assembly, support the exhaust system and unbolt the footpeg from the frame (the same bolt also secures an exhaust bracket).

8 To remove the left front footpeg bracket, check for match marks on the shift shaft and lever. Make your own marks if there aren't any, so the shift lever can be reinstalled in the correct orientation to the shaft. Loosen the shift lever pinch bolt **(see illustration)** and remove the bracket mounting bolt and nut **(see illustrations)**. Take the bracket off, turn it over and remove the snap-ring to separate the shift pedal from the bracket **(see illustrations)**.

9 To remove the right front footpeg bracket, disconnect the electrical connector for the brake light switch (see Chapter 8). Detach the brake cable from the slots on the assembly

(see Chapter 6). If you're going to remove the brake pedal, disconnect its return spring and remove the pedal snap-ring **(see illustration)**. Remove the nut at the rear of the bracket and the bolt at the front and take the assembly off **(see illustrations)**.

10 Installation is the reverse of removal. Lubricate the footpeg pivots (early models) (see Chapter 1).

## 4 Lower left frame cover - removal and installation

1 The lower left frame cover is secured by a nut at the bottom and a bolt at the top.

2 To remove the cover, remove the nut and the bolt and lift it off **(see illustrations)**.

3 Installation is the reverse of the removal steps.

## 5 Sidestand - maintenance

1 The sidestand is attached to a bracket on the frame. An extension spring(s) anchored to the bracket ensures that the stand is held in the extended or retracted position **(see illustration)**.

2 Make sure the pivot bolt is tight and the extension spring is in good condition and not

3.8d Remove the snap-ring to separate the shift pedal from the bracket

3.9a Detach the return spring, disconnect the cable and remove the snap-ring to detach the pedal

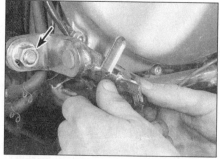

3.9b Follow the wiring from the brake switch and disconnect it; remove the mounting nut (arrow) . . .

3.9c . . . and the mounting bolt at the front

4.2a Remove the nut at the bottom . . .

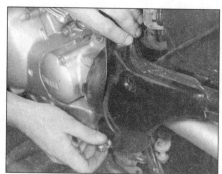

4.2b . . . and the bolt at the top to detach the lower left frame cover from the frame

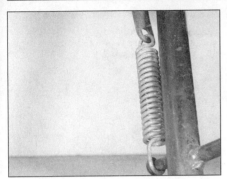

5.1  Make sure the sidestand spring is in good condition and correctly installed

6.2  Remove the sidestand pivot nut and slide it off the post

7.1  Remove one of the mounting bolts . . .

overstretched. An accident is almost certain to occur if the stand extends while the machine is in motion.

## 6  Sidestand - removal and installation

1  Support the bike securely so it can't be knocked over during this procedure.
2  Unhook the sidestand spring **(see illustration 5.1)**. Remove the pivot nut and take the sidestand off the pivot shaft **(see illustration)**.
3  Installation is the reverse of the removal steps.

## 7  Seat - removal and installation

### Single seat

1  Unlock and lift the seat and remove one of the mounting bolts **(see illustration)**.
2  Remove the clip, washer and clevis pin, then remove the remaining mounting bolt **(see illustrations)**.
3  Installation is the reverse of the removal steps.

### Dual seat

4  Unlock the passenger seat and lift it off the motorcycle **(see illustration)**.
5  Unbolt the rider's seat (there's one bolt on each side at the rear) **(see illustration)**. Disengage it from the hole in the frame and lift it off.
6  Installation is the reverse of the removal steps. Engage the tab front of the rider's seat with the hole in the frame.

## 8  Top cover - removal and installation

1  A top cover is used on models that don't have an upper fuel tank.
2  To remove the cover, lift the seat. Undo one mounting bolt on each side at the front **(see illustration)**. Slide the cover backwards to unhook it from the frame and lift it off.
3  Installation is the reverse of the removal steps. Be sure the mounting collars and grommets are in place on the front mountings and that the rear mounting peg engages the grommet.

7.2a  . . . pull out the clip, remove the washer and separate the support from its bracket . . .

7.2b  . . . then remove the other mounting bolt to detach the seat

7.4  Lift the passenger seat off . . .

7.5  . . . and remove the mounting bolts to detach the rider's seat

8.2  Remove the front mounting bolt on each side and detach the rear of the top cover from the bike

9.1 Remove the bolt from the mounting tab (arrow); disengage the cover tabs from the slot and grommet

9.2a Remove the mounting bolts (arrows) . . .

9.2b . . . and pull the hoses (if equipped) off the fittings on the back side of the bracket

## 9 Side covers - removal and installation

1 To remove a rear side cover, lift or remove the seat and undo the mounting bolt at the top (see illustration). Disengage the tab at the rear from the slot and the tab at the front from the grommet.

2 To remove either of the front side covers, remove the screws around the edge of the cover and lift it off. To remove the left

mounting bracket, undo its bolts (see illustration). Disconnect the carburetor hoses from the back side of the bracket (if equipped). Take the bracket off, complete with the air induction system components (if equipped) (see illustration).

3 To remove the right bracket, disconnect the electrical connectors from the components mounted on it. Undo the mounting bolts and take the bracket off (see illustrations).

4 Installation is the reverse of the removal steps.

## 10 Backrest and shock absorber cover - removal and installation

1 If you're working on a model with a backrest, lift the seat and remove the forward mounting screw on each side, then remove the washer and spacers (see illustrations).

2 Remove the Allen bolt and special nut at the rear of the backrest on each side and detach it from the motorcycle (see illustrations).

3 The shock absorber covers are retained by

9.3a Remove the mounting bolt at the upper rear . . .

9.3b . . . and at the lower front

10.1a Remove the backrest mounting bolts on each side . . .

10.1b . . . don't lose the washer and spacers

10.2a Remove the mounting bolt at the rear on each side . . .

10.2b . . . these thread into special nuts that fit inside the frame tubes

10.3  Remove the screw and washer to detach the shock absorber cover

11.2a  The fender mounting bolts are accessible from inside the fender

11.2b  Lift the fender off toward the front of the motorcycle

two screws and washers on each side. On models with a backrest, the rear screw forms the backrest front mounting **(see illustration)**.
**4** Installation is the reverse of the removal steps.

## 11  Front fender/mudguard - removal and installation

**1** If the upper fender/mudguard bolts will come all the way out without striking the wheel rim, it won't be necessary to remove the front wheel. If they won't, remove the front wheel (see Chapter 6).
**2** Unbolt the fender/mudguard from the forks and take it off **(see illustrations)**. Note that one left fender/mudguard bolt secures the speedometer cable retainer and one right fender/mudguard bolt secures the brake hose retainer.
**3** Installation is the reverse of the removal steps. Tighten the bolts securely.

## 12  Rear fender/mudguard - removal and installation

**1** Lift the seat (single seat models) or remove it (dual seat models) (see Section 7).
**2** Remove the screw at the bottom of the toolbox and disengage the rear end of the toolbox from the tab on top of the fender.
**3** Unbolt the inner rear fender/mudguard panel from the frame **(see illustration)**.

Disengage the tabs at the top of the panel from the rear fender and take the panel out **(see illustration)**.
**4** Follow the wiring harnesses for the brake/taillights and rear turn signals forward to their connectors. These are all single connectors, so labeling them will speed re-connection.
**5** Remove the fender/mudguard mounting bolts and take it off the motorcycle.
**6** Installation is the reverse of the removal steps.

12.3a  Unbolt the inner rear fender panel at the bottom . . .

12.3b  . . . and disengage the tabs at the top

**Notes**

# Chapter 7 Part B
# Frame and bodywork (XV700-1100 models)

## Contents

## Degrees of difficulty

| Easy, suitable for novice with little experience |  | Fairly easy, suitable for beginner with some experience |  | Fairly difficult, suitable for competent DIY mechanic |  | Difficult, suitable for experienced DIY mechanic |  | Very difficult, suitable for expert DIY or professional | 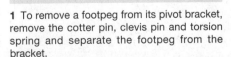 |

## 1 General information

1981 through 1983 XV750/920 models and the TR1 use a pressed steel backbone frame with a bolt-on rear section made of round-section steel tubing. The frame on later models is similar, but the rear section is welded to the backbone.

Fender/mudguards are steel, either painted or chrome plated.

## 2 Frame - inspection and repair

This is the same as for XV535 models. Refer to Part A of this Chapter.

## 3 Footpegs and pads - removal and installation

1 To remove a footpeg from its pivot bracket, remove the cotter pin, clevis pin and torsion spring and separate the footpeg from the bracket.
2 To remove a footpeg assembly on shaft drive models, unbolt the pivot bracket from the main bracket (see illustrations). If you're

3.2a On early shaft drive models, the front footpeg brackets are secured by two nuts

3.2b The rear footpeg bolt on early shaft drive models (arrow) also secures the muffler/silencer bracket

3.2c The front footpeg pivot brackets on later shaft drive models are secured by two bolts

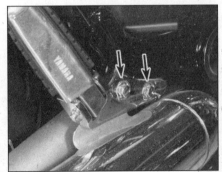
3.2d The rear footpeg pivot brackets on later shaft drive models are secured by two bolts (arrows)

**4.1 Remove one mounting nut, detach the prop rod and remove the other mounting nut**

**5.1a The sidestand spring must be properly connected and in good condition**

**5.1b ... the centerstand spring must also be properly connected and in good condition**

removing the right rear footpeg assembly on an early shaft drive model, support the exhaust system and unbolt the footpeg from the frame (the same bolt also secures an exhaust bracket).

**3** To remove a footpeg assembly on chain drive models, remove the pivot bracket nut and washer from the inside of the alloy bracket.

**4** Installation is the reverse of removal. Lubricate the footpeg pivots (see Chapter 1).

## 4 Seat - removal and installation

**1** If you're working on a hinged seat, unlock and lift the seat and remove one of the mounting nuts **(see illustration)**. Detach the prop rod, then remove the remaining mounting nut.

**2** If the seat is secured by clips, unlock it, then detach it from the clips.

**3** If you're working on a bolted seat (1984 and later models), remove the bolts (one on each side at the front of the seat). Detach the rear of the seat from its bracket and lift it off.

**4** Installation is the reverse of the removal steps.

## 5 Sidestand and centerstand - maintenance

**1** The sidestand (and centerstand on models so equipped) is attached to the frame. An extension spring(s) anchored to the bracket ensures that the stand is held in the extended or retracted position **(see illustrations)**.

**2** Make sure the pivot bolt or nuts are tight and the extension spring is in good condition and not overstretched. An accident is almost certain to occur if the stand extends while the machine is in motion.

## 6 Sidestand and centerstand - removal and installation

**1** Support the bike securely so it can't be knocked over during this procedure.

**2** Unhook the spring **(see illustration 5.1a or 5.1b)**. Remove the pivot bolt or nuts and take the stand off the pivot shaft(s).

**3** Installation is the reverse of the removal steps.

## 7 Side covers - removal and installation

**1** Side covers on all models are secured by rubber grommets. In some cases, posts fit into the grommets; in other cases, a slot in the edge of the cover fits into a slot in the grommet.

**2** To remove a side cover, pull it gently to disengage the cover from the grommets.

*Caution: Don't force the cover loose. If it won't come easily, make sure you're pulling in the right direction.*

**3** Installation is the reverse of the removal steps.

## 8 Front fender/mudguard - removal and installation

### Early models

**1** The front fender/mudguard on early models is bolted to the forks **(see illustration)**. If the upper fender/mudguard bolts will come all the way out without striking the wheel rim, it won't be necessary to remove the front wheel. If they won't, remove the front wheel (see Chapter 6).

**8.1 Remove the fender/mudguard mounting bolts**

**8.2 Slip the speedometer cable out of the guide**

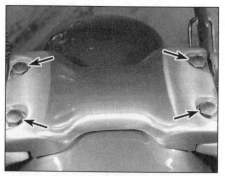

**8.4 On later models, remove the fork brace bolts (arrows)**

**2** Disconnect the lower end of the speedometer cable from the drive unit and slip the cable out of the guide **(see illustration)**.

**3** Unbolt the fender/mudguard from the forks and take it off.

### Later models

**4** Remove the fork brace bolts and lift off the fork brace **(see illustration)**. Unbolt the fender/mudguard and remove it from the motorcycle.

**5** Installation is the reverse of the removal steps. Tighten the bolts securely.

---

**9  Rear fender/mudguard -** removal and installation

---

**1** Remove the seat (see Section 4) and the rear wheel (see Chapter 6).

**2** If you're working on a fender/mudguard that's bolted to the swingarm, remove the bolts and take the fender/mudguard out.

**3** Unbolt the fender/mudguard (and lower front fender/mudguard panel, if equipped) from the frame **(see illustration)**. On models with backrests, the backrest is secured by some of the fender/mudguard bolts.

**4** Follow the wiring harnesses for the brake/taillights and rear turn signals to their connectors and disconnect them.

**5** Installation is the reverse of the removal steps.

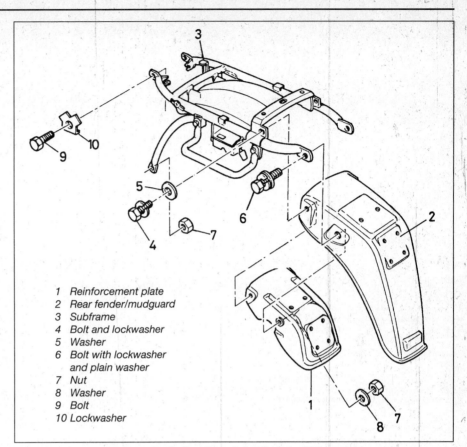

1  Reinforcement plate
2  Rear fender/mudguard
3  Subframe
4  Bolt and lockwasher
5  Washer
6  Bolt with lockwasher and plain washer
7  Nut
8  Washer
9  Bolt
10 Lockwasher

**9.2  Rear fender/mudguard details (later TR1 models)**

**Notes**

# Chapter 8  Part A
# Electrical system (XV535 models)

## Contents

## Degrees of difficulty

| Easy, suitable for novice with little experience 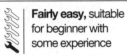 | Fairly easy, suitable for beginner with some experience 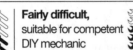 | Fairly difficult, suitable for competent DIY mechanic | Difficult, suitable for experienced DIY mechanic | Very difficult, suitable for expert DIY or professional |
|---|---|---|---|---|

## Specifications

**Battery type** ........................................ 12 V, 12 Ah

### Fuse specifications
Main fuse
  1987 through 1990 models ............................... 20 amps
  1991-on models ...................................... 30 amps
All other fuses
  1987 through 1990 models ............................... 10 amps
  1991-on models ...................................... 15 amps

### Charging system
Stator coil resistance ................................... 0.34 to 0.42 ohms
Charging system output .................................. 14 to 15 volts at 5,000 rpm

### Starter
Starter commutator diameter
  Standard ........................................... 28 mm (1.1 inch)
  Minimum ........................................... 27 mm (1.06 inch)
  Mica undercut ...................................... 1.6 mm (0.063 inch)
Starter brush length
  Standard ........................................... 12.0 mm (0.47 inch)
  Minimum ........................................... 5.0 mm (0.20 inch)

## Bulb specifications (US models)

| | |
|---|---|
| Headlight | 65/60W |
| Tail/brake lights | 8/27W |
| Rear turn signals | 27W |
| Front turn signals | 8W |
| Speedometer light | |
|   1987 through 1993 | 3W |
|   1994-on | 3.4W |
| Turn signal indicator | 3W |
| Neutral indicator | 3W |
| High beam indicator | 1.7W |

## Bulb specifications (UK models)

| | |
|---|---|
| Headlight | 60/55W |
| Tail/brake lights | 5/21 |
| Turn signals | 21W |
| Speedometer light | 3W |
| Turn signal indicator | 3W |
| Neutral indicator | 3W |
| High beam indicator | 1.7W |
| Parking light | 3.4W |

## Carburetor heater resistance

| | |
|---|---|
| Carburetor heater resistance | 5 to 6 ohms at 20-degrees C (68-degrees F) |

## Torque specifications

| | |
|---|---|
| Alternator rotor bolt | 80 Nm (58 ft-lbs) |
| Stator coil screws | 7 Nm (5.1 ft-lbs)* |
| Alternator cover bolts | 10 Nm (7.2 ft-lbs) |
| Starter mounting bolts | 10 Nm (7.2 ft-lbs) |
| Starter clutch body bolts | 20 Nm (14 ft-lbs)** |

*Apply non-permanent thread locking agent to the threads.
**Apply non-permanent thread locking agent to the threads and stake the bolts.

---

## 1 General information

The machines covered by this manual are equipped with a 12-volt electrical system.

The charging system on XV535 models uses a rotor with permanent magnets that rotates around a stator coil of copper wire. This produces alternating current, which is converted to direct current by the regulator/rectifier. The regulator/rectifier also controls the charging system output.

An electric starter mounted to the front of the engine is standard equipment. The starter on early models has four brushes; the starter on later models has two brushes. The starting system includes the motor, the battery, the relay and the various wires and switches. If the engine kill switch and the ignition (main key) switch are both in the On position, the circuit relay allows the starter motor to operate only if the transmission is in Neutral (Neutral switch on) or the clutch lever is pulled to the handlebar (clutch switch on) and the sidestand is up (sidestand switch on).

**Note:** *Keep in mind that electrical parts, once purchased, can't be returned. To avoid unnecessary expense, make very sure the faulty component has been positively identified before buying a replacement part.*

## 2 Electrical troubleshooting

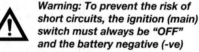

*Warning: To prevent the risk of short circuits, the ignition (main) switch must always be "OFF" and the battery negative (-ve) terminal should be disconnected before any of the bike's other electrical components are disturbed. Don't forget to reconnect the terminal securely once work is finished or if battery power is needed for circuit testing.*

**1** A typical electrical circuit consists of an electrical component, the switches, relays, etc. related to that component and the wiring and connectors that hook the component to both the battery and the frame. To aid in locating a problem in any electrical circuit, refer to the wiring diagrams at the end of this Chapter.

**2** Before tackling any troublesome electrical circuit, first study the wiring diagram (see Chapter 9) thoroughly to get a complete picture of what makes up that individual circuit. Trouble spots, for instance, can often be narrowed down by noting if other components related to that circuit are operating properly or not. If several components or circuits fail at one time, chances are the fault lies in the fuse or earth connection, as several circuits often are routed through the same fuse and earth connections.

**3** Electrical problems often stem from simple causes, such as loose or corroded connections or a blown fuse. Prior to any electrical troubleshooting, always visually check the condition of the fuse, wires and connections in the problem circuit. Intermittent failures can be especially frustrating, since you can't always duplicate the failure when it's convenient to test. In such situations, a good practice is to clean all connections in the affected circuit, whether or not they appear to be good. All of the connections and wires should also be wiggled to check for looseness which can cause intermittent failure.

**4** If testing instruments are going to be utilised, use the wiring diagram to plan where you will make the necessary connections in order to accurately pinpoint the trouble spot.

**5** The basic tools needed for electrical fault finding include a battery and bulb test circuit, a continuity tester, test light and a jumper wire. For more extensive checks, a multimeter capable of measuring ohms, volts and amps will be required. Full details on the use of this test equipment are given in *Fault Finding Equipment* at the end of this manual.

## 3  Battery - inspection and maintenance
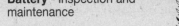

1 Most battery damage is caused by heat, vibration, and/or low electrolyte levels, so make sure the battery is securely mounted, check the electrolyte level frequently and make sure the charging system is functioning properly.
2 Refer to Chapter 1 for electrolyte level and specific gravity checking procedures.
3 Check around the base inside of the battery for sediment, which is the result of sulfation caused by low electrolyte levels. These deposits will cause internal short circuits, which can quickly discharge the battery. Look for cracks in the case and replace the battery if either of these conditions is found.
4 Check the battery terminals and cable ends for tightness and corrosion. If corrosion is evident, remove the cables from the battery (see illustration) and clean the terminals and cable ends with a wire brush or knife and emery paper.

**HAYNES HiNT** *Apply a thin coat of petroleum jelly to the battery connections to slow corrosion.*

5 The battery case should be kept clean to prevent current leakage, which can discharge the battery over a period of time (especially when it sits unused). Wash the outside of the case with a solution of baking soda and water. Do not get any baking soda solution in the battery cells. Rinse the battery thoroughly, then dry it.
6 If acid has been spilled on the frame or battery box, neutralize it with the baking soda and water solution, dry it thoroughly, then touch up any damaged paint. Make sure the battery vent tube is directed away from the frame and is not kinked or pinched.
7 If the motorcycle sits unused for long periods of time, disconnect the cables from the battery terminals. Refer to Section 4 and charge the battery approximately once every month.

## 4  Battery - charging
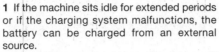

1 If the machine sits idle for extended periods or if the charging system malfunctions, the battery can be charged from an external source.
2 To properly charge the battery, you will need a charger of the correct rating, a hydrometer, a clean rag and a syringe for adding distilled water to the battery cells.
3 The maximum charging rate for any battery is 1/10 of the rated amp/hour capacity. As an example, the maximum charging rate for a 12 amp/hour battery would be 1.2 amps and the maximum charging rate for a 14 amp/hour battery would be 1.4 amps. If the battery is charged at a higher rate, it could be damaged.
4 Do not allow the battery to be subjected to a so-called quick charge (high rate of charge over a short period of time) unless you are prepared to buy a new battery.
5 When charging the battery, always remove it from the machine and be sure to check the electrolyte level before hooking up the charger. Add distilled water to any cells that are low.
6 Loosen the cell caps, hook up the battery charger leads (red to positive, black to negative), cover the top of the battery with a clean rag, then, and only then, plug in the battery charger.

⚠ *Warning: Remember, the gas escaping from a charging battery is explosive, so keep open flames and sparks well away from the area. Also, the electrolyte is extremely corrosive and will damage anything it comes in contact with.*

7 Allow the battery to charge until the specific gravity is as specified (refer to Chapter 1 for specific gravity checking procedures). The charger must be unplugged and disconnected from the battery when making specific gravity checks. If the battery overheats or gases excessively, the charging rate is too high. Either disconnect the charger or lower the charging rate to prevent damage to the battery.

**3.4 Disconnect the negative cable first and reconnect it last; sparks could cause the battery to explode.**

*A  Negative cable    B  Positive cable*

8 It's time for a new battery if:
a) *One or more of the cells is significantly lower in specific gravity than the others after a long slow charge.*
b) *The battery as a whole doesn't seem to want to take a charge.*
c) *Battery voltage won't increase.*
d) *The electrolyte doesn't bubble.*
e) *The plates are white (indicating sulfation) or debris has accumulated in the bottom of a cell.*
f) *The plates or insulators are warped or buckled.*
9 When the battery is fully charged, unplug the charger first, then disconnect the leads from the battery. Install the cell caps and wipe any electrolyte off the outside of the battery case.

## 5  Fuses - check and replacement

1 The fuse block is located beneath the top cover (early models) or the seat (later models) (see illustrations). It contains a 20-amp or 30-amp main fuse, spare fuses and accessory fuses (see illustration). Fuse functions and

**5.1a  The main and accessory fuses are located in a fuse block under the seat (early model shown) . . .**

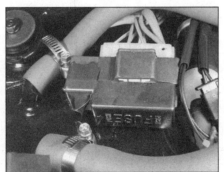
**5.1b  . . . and this is a later model**

**5.1c  Lift the cover for access to the fuses (early model shown)**

ratings are listed in this Chapter's Specifications. Fuse ratings are marked on the fuses.

2 If you have a test light, all of the fuses can be checked without removing them. Turn the ignition key to the On position, connect one end of the test light to a good ground, then probe each terminal on top of the fuse. If the fuse is good, there will be voltage available at both terminals. If the fuse is blown, there will only be voltage present at one of the terminals.

3 The fuses can also be tested with an ohmmeter or self-powered test light. Remove the fuse and connect the tester to the ends of the fuse. If the ohmmeter shows continuity or the test lamp lights, the fuse is good. If the ohmmeter shows infinite resistance or the test lamp stays out, the fuse is blown.

4 The fuses can be removed and checked visually. If you can't pull the fuse out with your fingertips, use a pair of needle-nose pliers. A blown fuse is easily identified by a break in the element.

5 If a fuse blows, be sure to check the wiring harnesses very carefully for evidence of a short circuit. Look for bare wires and chafed, melted or burned insulation. If a fuse is replaced before the cause is located, the new fuse will blow immediately.

6 Never, under any circumstances, use a higher rated fuse or bridge the fuse block terminals, as damage to the electrical system could result.

7 Occasionally a fuse will blow or cause an open circuit for no obvious reason. Corrosion of the fuse ends and fuse block terminals may occur and cause poor fuse contact. If this happens, remove the corrosion with a wire brush or emery paper, then spray the fuse end and terminals with electrical contact cleaner.

## 6 Lighting system - check

1 The battery provides power for operation of the headlight, taillight, brake light, license plate light, instrument and warning lights. If none of the lights operate, always check battery voltage before proceeding. Low battery voltage indicates either a faulty battery, low battery electrolyte level or a defective charging system. Refer to Chapter 1 for battery checks and Sections 26 and 27 for charging system tests. Also, check the condition of the fuses and replace any blown fuses with new ones.

### Headlight

2 If the headlight is out when the engine is running (US models) or it won't switch on (UK models), check the fuse first with the key or switch On (see Section 5), then unplug the electrical connector for the headlight and use jumper wires to connect the bulb directly to

the battery terminals (see Section 7). If the light comes on, the problem lies in the wiring or one of the switches in the circuit. Refer to Section 16 for the switch testing procedures, and also the wiring diagrams at the end of this Chapter.

### Taillight/license plate light

3 If the taillight fails to work, check the bulbs and the bulb terminals first, then check for battery voltage at the taillight electrical connector. If voltage is present, check the ground/earth circuit for an open or poor connection.

4 If no voltage is indicated, check the wiring between the taillight and the ignition switch, then check the switch. On UK models, check the lighting switch as well.

### Brake light

5 See Section 12 for the brake light switch checking procedure.

### Neutral indicator light

6 If the neutral light fails to operate when the transmission is in Neutral and the key switch is On, check the fuses and the bulb (see Section 14 for bulb removal procedures). If the bulb and fuses are in good condition, check for battery voltage at the connector attached to the neutral switch on the left side of the engine. If battery voltage is present, refer to Section 18 for the neutral switch check and replacement procedures.

**7.1a Remove the headlight cover screws . . .**

**7.2a Unscrew the retainer . . .**

7 If no voltage is indicated, check the wiring between the switch and the bulb for open circuits and poor connections.

## 7 Headlight bulb - replacement

 **Warning: If the bulb has just burned out, allow it to cool. It will be hot enough to burn your fingers.**

1 Remove the headlight cover screws **(see illustration)**. Tilt the cover forward out of the headlight assembly and disconnect the electrical connector **(see illustration)**.

2 Turn the bulb retainer counterclockwise (anti-clockwise) **(see illustration)**. Remove the bulb **(see illustration)**.

3 When installing the new bulb, reverse the removal procedure. Be sure not to touch the bulb glass with your fingers - oil from your skin will cause the bulb to overheat and fail prematurely. If you do touch the bulb, wipe it off with a clean rag dampened with rubbing alcohol.

4 The parking light bulb holder (auxiliary light) on UK models is a push fit in the grommet set in the rear of the reflector. Access may be possible via the cutout in the headlight housing, but if not remove the headlight as described in Step 1. Twist the bulb counterclockwise (anti-clockwise) to release it from its bulb holder.

**7.1b . . . tilt the cover out of the headlight assembly and disconnect the wiring connector**

**7.2b . . . and lift the bulb out; don't touch the glass on the new bulb**

**8.3 The vertical adjusting screw is at the lower right (arrow); the horizontal screw is at the upper left**

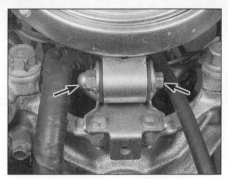

**9.2 Remove the pivot at the bottom (arrows), and the mounting bolt inside the headlight assembly**

**10.2 Press the bulb into the socket and turn it counterclockwise (anti-clockwise) to remove**

## 8 Headlight aim - check and adjustment

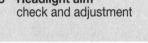

1 An improperly adjusted headlight may cause problems for oncoming traffic or provide poor, unsafe illumination of the road ahead. Before adjusting the headlight, be sure to consult with local traffic laws and regulations.
2 The headlight beam can be adjusted both vertically and horizontally. Before performing the adjustment, make sure the fuel tank is at least half full and have an assistant sit on the seat.
3 The horizontal adjusting screw is at the upper left of the headlight cover **(see illustration)**. The vertical adjusting screw is located at the lower right.

## 9 Headlight assembly - removal and installation

1 Remove the headlight cover (see Section 7). If you're planning to take the headlight assembly completely off the motorcycle, disconnect the electrical connectors inside the headlight assembly. If you're just removing the assembly for access to the speedometer, the connectors can be left attached.

 **HAYNES HiNT** *When disconnecting wiring, label the connectors to avoid confusion on reconnection.*

2 Remove the mounting bolt inside the headlight cover and the pivot bolt at the bottom **(see illustration)**. Slide the assembly down and forward so the mounting grommet can clear the post, then take the assembly off the motorcycle.
3 Installation is the reverse of the removal steps.

## 10 Turn signals and tail/brake light bulbs - replacement

### *Turn signal bulbs*

1 To replace a turn signal bulb, remove the screws that hold the lens to the turn signal housing and take off the lens.
2 Push the bulb in and turn it counterclockwise (anti-clockwise) to remove it **(see illustration)**.

 **HAYNES HiNT** *Check the socket terminals for corrosion and clean them if necessary. Spray them with electrical contact cleaner before a new bulb is installed.*

3 Line up the pins on the new bulb with the slots in the socket, push in and turn the bulb clockwise until it locks in place. **Note:** *The pins on US model front turn signal bulbs are offset so they can only be installed one way. It is a good idea to use a paper towel or dry cloth when handling the new bulb to prevent injury if the bulb should break and to increase bulb life.*
4 Position the lens on the housing and install

**10.5 Remove the lens screws (arrows) and take off the lens**

the screws. Be careful not to overtighten them or the lens will crack.

### *Tail/brake light bulbs*

5 Remove the lens screws and take the lens off **(see illustration)**.
6 Push the bulb in and turn it counterclockwise (anti-clockwise) to remove it **(see illustration)**.
7 Perform Steps 3 and 4 above to install the bulb, noting that the pins are offset.

## 11 Turn signal circuit - check

1 The battery provides power for operation of the signal lights, so if they do not operate, always check the battery voltage and specific gravity first. Low battery voltage indicates either a faulty battery, low electrolyte level or a defective charging system. Refer to Chapter 1 for battery checks and Sections 26 and 27 for charging system tests. Also, check the fuses (see Section 5).
2 Most turn signal problems are the result of a burned out bulb or corroded socket. This is especially true when the turn signals function properly in one direction, but fail to flash in the other direction. Check the bulbs and the sockets (see Section 10).

**10.6 Press the bulbs into their sockets and turn counterclockwise (anti-clockwise) to remove**

11.3 The turn signal relay/cancel unit is behind the right front side cover; it is identified by wire colors

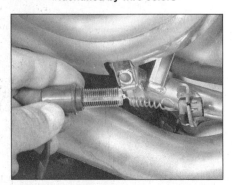

12.8 Disconnect the switch spring, loosen the locknut and compress the prongs to detach the switch

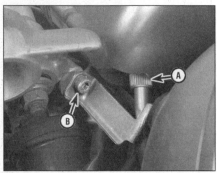

13.1 Unscrew the cable from the speedometer (A); note the mounting bracket attachment (B) . . .

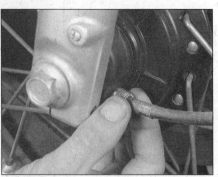

13.2 . . . and from the drive unit on the left fork leg

12.5 Remove the brake switch by pressing the retainer with a tool inserted into the hole under the bracket

3 If the bulbs and sockets check out okay, remove the right front side cover and check for power at the turn signal relay in the relay assembly (see illustration) with the ignition On. Refer to the Wiring diagrams at the end of the book to identify the power source terminal.
4 If the relay is okay, check the wiring between the turn signal relay and the turn signal lights (see the wiring diagrams at the end of the book).
5 If the wiring checks out okay, replace the turn signal relay.

## 12 Brake light switches - check and replacement

### Circuit check

1 Before checking any electrical circuit, check the fuses (see Section 5).
2 Using a test light connected to a good ground, check for voltage at the brake light switch. If there's no voltage present, check the wire between the switch and the fuse box (see the wiring diagrams at the end of this Chapter).
3 If voltage is available, touch the probe of the test light to the other terminal of the switch, then pull the brake lever or depress the brake pedal - if the test light doesn't light up, replace the switch.

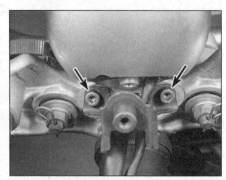

13.4 Remove the speedometer mounting nuts . . .

4 If the test light does light, check the wiring between the switch and the brake lights (see the wiring diagrams at the end of this Chapter).

### Switch replacement
#### Front brake lever switch
5 The switch slides into the handle pivot and is secured by a prong (see illustration). Disconnect the electrical connector. Insert a small screwdriver or probe into the release hole on the underside of the lever bracket, press up on the retaining prong and pull out the switch.
6 Installation is the reverse of the removal procedure. The brake lever switch isn't adjustable.

#### Rear brake pedal switch
7 Unplug the electrical connector in the switch harness.
8 Unhook the switch spring (see illustration).
9 Compress the retainer prongs and slide the switch out of the bracket (see illustration 12.8).
10 Install the switch by reversing the removal procedure, then adjust the switch by following the procedure described in Chapter 1.

## 13 Speedometer and cable - removal and installation

### Speedometer cable removal

1 Unscrew the speedometer cable end and pull the cable from the speedometer (see illustration). If necessary for access, lower the headlight assembly (see Section 9).
2 Note how it's routed, then unscrew the speedometer cable from the drive gear at the left front fork (see illustration).

### Speedometer removal

3 Disconnect the cable from the speedometer (see illustration 13.1).
4 Remove the Allen bolts and washers and detach the speedometer housing bracket (see illustration).
5 Lift the speedometer away from the bracket and turn it over. Remove the self-tapping screw and detach the speedometer from the housing (see illustration). Follow the

13.5 . . . and the mounting screws, then detach the speedometer from the housing

**14.1  The warning lights are contained in this housing**

**14.3  With the handlebar removed, remove the screws (arrows), lift off the cover and pull out the bulb**

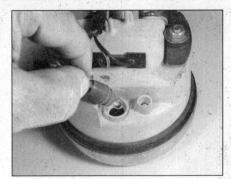

**14.6a  Pull the bulb socket out of the speedometer . . .**

speedometer wiring harness to its connector (inside a rubber cover below the speedometer) and disconnect it.

### Speedometer installation

6  Installation is the reverse of the removal procedure. Be sure the speedometer cable and wiring harness are routed so it doesn't cause the steering to bind or interfere with other components. The squared-off ends of the cable must fit into their spindles in the speedometer and drive gear.

---

**14  Instrument and warning light bulbs** - replacement

---

### Warning light bulbs

1  The warning light bulbs are beneath a cover located behind and beneath the handlebar **(see illustration)**.
2  For access to the bulbs, remove the handlebar (see Chapter 5). The cables, wiring and brake hoses can be left attached; just support the handlebar so no components are strained.
3  Remove the screws and lift off the cover **(see illustration)**. Pull the bulb out and install a new one.
4  Install the cover and the handlebar. Tighten the handlebar fasteners to the torque listed in the Chapter 5 Specifications.

### Speedometer light bulb

5  Remove the speedometer from the housing (see Section 13).
6  Pull the rubber socket out of the back of the speedometer **(see illustration)**, then pull the bulb out of the socket **(see illustration)**. If the socket contacts are dirty or corroded, they should be scraped clean and sprayed with electrical contact cleaner before new bulbs are installed.
7  Carefully push the new bulb into position, then push the socket into the speedometer.

---

**15  Ignition main (key) switch -** check and replacement

---

### Check

1  Lift the seat (single seat models) or remove the seat (dual seat models) (see Chapter 7).
2  Follow the wiring harness from the ignition switch to the connector and disconnect it.
3  Using an ohmmeter, check the continuity of the terminal pairs indicated in the accompanying table **(see illustrations)**. Continuity should exist between the terminals connected by a solid line when the switch is in the indicated position. **Note:** *Connect the ohmmeter to the switch side of the connector, not the wiring harness side.*

**14.6b  . . . and pull the bulb out of the socket**

4  If the switch fails any of the tests, replace it.

### Replacement

5  Disconnect the electrical connector, if you haven't already done so. Free the wiring harness from any clips or retainers.
6  Remove the screws and separate the switch from the bracket **(see illustration)**. These are accessible from the right side of the motorcycle with a ratchet handle, long extension, swivel and Phillips screwdriver bit. If you don't have these tools, remove the battery and battery case for access.
7  Attach the new switch to the bracket and tighten the screws securely.
8  The remainder of installation is the reverse of the removal procedure.

| Switch | Lead Color | | |
|---|---|---|---|
| Position | R | Br | L |
| ON | ○—○—○ | | |
| OFF | | | |
| P | ○—○ | | |

**15.3a  Continuity table for the ignition switch (US models)**

| Switch | Lead Color | | | |
|---|---|---|---|---|
| Position | R | Br | L | L/R |
| ON | ○—○ | | ○—○ | |
| OFF | | | | |
| P | ○ | | | ○ |

**15.3b  Continuity table for the ignition switch (UK models)**

**15.6  Remove the ignition main (key) switch mounting screws (arrows)**

**"LIGHTS" Switch (UK)**

|  | R/Y | L • | L/B |
|---|---|---|---|
| OFF |  |  |  |
| PO | ○—————○ |  |  |
| ON | ○—————○—————○ |  |  |

**"HORN" Switch**

| Switch Position | Lead Color | |
|---|---|---|
|  | P | B |
| OFF |  |  |
| ON | ○————————○ | |

**"ENGINE STOP" Switch**

| Switch Position | Lead Color | |
|---|---|---|
|  | R/W | R/B |
| OFF |  |  |
| RUN | ○————————○ | |

**"FUEL" (Reserve) Switch**

| Switch Position | Lead Color | |
|---|---|---|
|  | R/W | R/G |
| ON |  |  |
| RES | ○————————○ | |

**"START" Switch**

| Switch Position | Lead Color | | | |
|---|---|---|---|---|
|  | R/Y | L/B | L/W | B |
| OFF | ○————○ |  |  |  |
| ON |  |  | ○————○ |  |

*US models only*

**"LIGHTS" (Dimmer) switch**

| Switch Position | Lead Color | | |
|---|---|---|---|
|  | Y | L/B | G |
| HI | ○————○ |  |  |
| LO |  | ○————○ |  |

**"TURN" Switch**

| Switch Position | | Lead Color | | | | |
|---|---|---|---|---|---|---|
|  |  | Ch | Br/W | Dg | Y/R | B |
|  | L | ○——○ |  |  | ○——○ |  |
|  | L | ○——○ |  |  |  |  |
| N | OFF |  |  |  |  |  |
|  | R |  | ○——○ |  |  |  |
|  | R |  | ○——○ |  | ○——○ |  |

**"PASS" Switch (UK)**

|  | Y | R/Y |
|---|---|---|
| OFF |  |  |
| ON | ○————————○ | |

**16.4 Continuity table for the handlebar switches**

## 16 Handlebar switches - check

1 Generally speaking, the switches are reliable and trouble-free. Most troubles, when they do occur, are caused by dirty or corroded contacts, but wear and breakage of internal parts is a possibility that should not be overlooked. If breakage does occur, the entire switch and related wiring harness will have to be replaced with a new one, since individual parts are not usually available.

2 The switches can be checked for continuity with an ohmmeter or a continuity test light. Always disconnect the battery negative cable, which will prevent the possibility of a short circuit, before making the checks.

3 Trace the wiring harness of the switch in question and unplug the electrical connectors.

4 Using the ohmmeter or test light, check for continuity between the terminals of the switch harness with the switch in the various positions (see illustration). Continuity should exist between the terminals connected by a solid line when the switch is in the indicated position.

5 If the continuity check indicates a problem exists, refer to Section 17, remove the switch and spray the switch contacts with electrical contact cleaner. If they are accessible, the contacts can be scraped clean with a knife or polished with crocus cloth. If switch components are damaged or broken, it will be obvious when the switch is disassembled.

## 17 Handlebar switches - removal and installation

1 The handlebar switches are composed of two halves that clamp around the bars. They are easily removed for cleaning or inspection by taking out the clamp screws and pulling the switch halves away from the handlebars (see illustrations).

2 To completely remove the switches, the electrical connectors in the wiring harness should be unplugged.

3 When installing the switches, make sure the wiring harnesses are properly routed to avoid pinching or stretching the wires.

## 18 Neutral switch - check and replacement

### Check

1 Make sure the transmission is in neutral.

2 Remove the lower left frame cover (see Chapter 7). Locate the switch harness (it has a single connector with sky blue wires), then unplug the connector.

3 Connect the terminal in the harness side of the connector to ground/earth (bare metal on the motorcycle frame) with a short length of wire.

a) If the light stays out, check the bulb and

**17.1a The handlebar switches are held together by screws (arrows); this is the throttle side . . .**

**17.1b . . . the clutch side switches are also held together by screws (arrows)**

**17.1c Separate the switch halves for access to the individual switches**

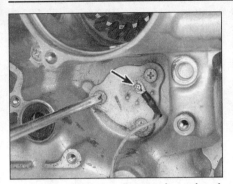

**18.5a Loosen the small screw (arrow) and disconnect the wire; remove the three mounting screws . . .**

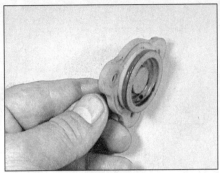

**18.5b . . . and take the switch out of the engine; replace the O-ring with a new one**

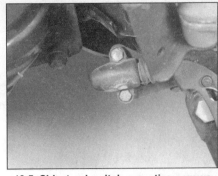

**19.5 Sidestand switch mounting screws**

*the wiring between the ignition switch and neutral switch.*

b) *If the neutral indicator light comes on, the neutral switch may be bad. Connect an ohmmeter between the terminal in the switch side of the connector and ground. Shift through the gears. The ohmmeter should indicate continuity (low resistance) in neutral and no continuity (infinite resistance) in all other gears. If not, replace the neutral switch.*

### Replacement

4 Remove the alternator cover (see Section 28).
5 Loosen the small screw on the switch and detach the wire **(see illustration)**. Remove the switch mounting screws and detach the switch from the crankcase **(see illustration)**. Remove the O-ring and install a new one.
6 Installation is the reverse of the removal steps.

## 19 Sidestand switch - check and replacement

### Check

1 Support the bike securely so it can't be knocked over during this procedure.
2 Follow the wiring harness from the switch to the connector, then unplug the connector. Connect the leads of an ohmmeter to the wire terminals. With the sidestand in the up position, there should be continuity through the switch (little or no resistance).
3 With the sidestand in the down position, the meter should indicate infinite resistance.
4 If the switch fails either of these tests, replace it.

### Replacement

5 With the sidestand in the up position, unscrew the two screws and remove the switch **(see illustration)**. Disconnect the switch electrical connector.
6 Installation is the reverse of the removal procedure.

## 20 Clutch switch - check and replacement

### Check

1 Disconnect the electrical connector from the clutch switch.
2 Connect an ohmmeter between the terminals in the clutch switch. With the clutch lever pulled in, the ohmmeter should show continuity (little or no resistance). With the lever out, the ohmmeter should show infinite resistance.
3 If the switch doesn't check out as described, replace it.

### Replacement

4 If you haven't already done so, disconnect the wiring connector. Insert a pointed tool into the mounting hole, compress the prong and pull the switch out **(see illustration)**.
5 Installation is the reverse of removal.

## 21 Horn - check and replacement

### Check

1 Disconnect the electrical connectors from

**20.4 Insert a pointed tool into the hole (arrow), compress the prong and pull out the clutch switch**

the horn **(see illustration)**. Using two jumper wires, apply battery voltage directly to the terminals on the horn. If the horn sounds, check the switch (see Section 17) and the wiring between the switch and the horn (see the wiring diagrams at the end of this Chapter).
2 If the horn doesn't sound, replace it.

### Replacement

3 Unbolt the horn bracket from the frame **(see illustration 21.1)** and detach the electrical connectors.
4 Unbolt the horn from the bracket and transfer the bracket to the new horn.
5 Installation is the reverse of removal.

## 22 Starter relay - check and replacement

### Check

1 Remove the seat (see Chapter 7). Disconnect the battery negative cable.
2 Make sure the battery is fully charged and the relay wiring connections are clean and tight. Corrosion can build up enough to prevent current flow and still not be readily visible, so it's best to disconnect the cables from the terminals and give the cable ends and terminal studs a thorough cleaning. Also

**21.1 Disconnect the horn wires (A) and remove the bracket bolt (B)**

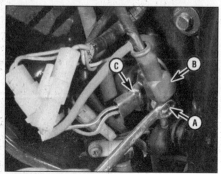

**22.4 Disconnect the cable that runs to the starter**

A  Cable to starter
B  Cable from battery positive terminal
C  Two-wire connector

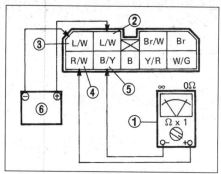

**23.2 Starting circuit cut-off relay test**

1  Ohmmeter
2  Blue/white terminal
3  Blue/white terminal
4  Red/white terminal (red/black on 1994 models)
5  Black/yellow terminal
6  12-volt battery

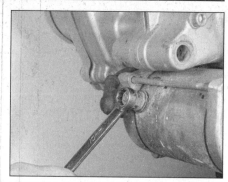

**24.2 Remove the nut and disconnect the cable**

disconnect the two-wire connectors and clean the terminals.

**3** Reconnect the wires to the starter relay.

 *Warning: Make sure the transmission is in neutral for step 4.*

**4** Pull back the protective cover and disconnect the cable that runs from the relay to the starter motor (see illustration). Connect a heavy-gauge jumper wire (the same gauge or heavier than the starter relay cables) directly from the battery positive terminal to the disconnected end of the cable.

 *Warning: Make the connection at the battery first and at the cable last; sparks are likely to occur, and if they occur near the battery they could cause it to explode.*

a)  If the starter motor cranks, the problem is somewhere in the starting circuit, possibly in the starter relay. Go to Step 5.
b)  If the starter doesn't crank, remove and inspect it (see Sections 24 and 25).

**5** If the starter cranks when the relay is bypassed, disconnect the two-wire connector from the relay (see illustration 22.4). Connect a jumper wire from the relay side of the red/white wire to the battery positive terminal. Connect another jumper wire from the blue/white wire to ground/earth (bare metal on the motorcycle frame).

a)  If the relay clicks and the starter motor cranks, the relay is good. Test the cut-off relay (see Section 23) and check the starter circuit wiring for breaks or bad connections (see the Wiring diagrams at the end of the book).
b)  If the relay doesn't click, it's probably bad. Replace it.

## Replacement

**6** Disconnect the cable from the negative terminal of the battery.
**7** Detach the battery positive cable, the starter cable and electrical connector from the relay (see illustration 22.4).

**8** Slide the relay off its mounting tabs.
**9** Installation is the reverse of removal. Reconnect the negative battery cable after all the other electrical connections are made.

### 23 Starting circuit cut-off relay - check and replacement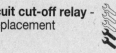

## Check

**1** Remove the right front side cover and locate the relay assembly (see illustration 11.3).
**2** Connect an ohmmeter between the terminals in the relay that connect to the red/white (red/black 1994-on) and black/yellow wires in the wiring harness (see illustration). The ohmmeter should show infinite resistance. **Note:** *The terminals in the relay are very close together – use thin probes to make the meter connections.*
**3** Set the ohmmeter aside and connect a 12-volt battery between the terminals for the two blue/white wires in the relay (see illustration 23.2). The motorcycle's battery can be used if fully charged. **Note:** *The terminals inside the relay are very close together – use two wires with small insulated alligator clips at each end to connect the relay terminals to the battery. Make the last connection to the battery negative terminal.*
**4** Reconnect the ohmmeter probes to the terminals for the red/white (red/black 1994-on) and black/yellow wires. The ohmmeter should show continuity (little or no resistance).
**5** Disconnect and reconnect the battery (detach and reattach the alligator clip at the battery negative terminal). The ohmmeter should show continuity whenever the battery is connected and no continuity whenever it's disconnected. If not, replace the relay.

## Replacement

**6** Remove the right front side cover if you haven't already done so (see Chapter 7).
**7** Disconnect the relay assembly's wiring connector (see illustration 11.3). Slip the relay assembly off its mounting tabs.
**8** Installation is the reverse of the removal steps.

### 24 Starter motor - removal and installation

## Removal

**1** Disconnect the cable from the negative terminal of the battery.
**2** Pull back the rubber cover, remove the nut retaining the starter cable to the starter and disconnect the cable (see illustration).
**3** Remove the starter mounting bolts.
**4** Lift the end of the starter up a little bit and slide the starter out of the engine case.
**5** Check the condition of the O-ring on the end of the starter and replace it if necessary. Also check the starter pinion gear and the driven gear inside the engine for chipped or worn teeth.

## Installation

**6** Apply a little engine oil to the O-ring and install the starter by reversing the removal procedure. Tighten the starter mounting bolts to the torque listed in this Chapter's Specifications.

### 25 Starter motor - disassembly, inspection and reassembly

**1** Remove the starter motor (see Section 24).

## Disassembly

### Four-brush starter

**2** Mark the position of the housing to each end cover. Remove the two through-bolts and their lockwashers and detach both end covers (see illustration).

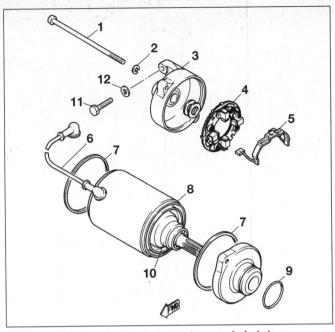

**25.2 Four-brush starter motor - exploded view**

| | | |
|---|---|---|
| 1 Through-bolt | 5 Plastic brush | 8 Starter housing |
| 2 Lockwasher | housing | 9 O-ring |
| 3 Brush end cover | 6 Cable | 10 Armature |
| 4 Brush plate | 7 O-rings | |

**25.5 Two-brush starter - exploded view**

| | | |
|---|---|---|
| 1 Cable | 4 Brush plate | 8 O-ring |
| 2 Terminal nuts and | 5 O-ring | 9 Through-bolt |
| washers | 6 Mounting bolt | 10 Armature |
| 3 Brush end cover | 7 Washer | 11 Starter housing |

**3** Remove the nut and push the terminal bolt through the starter housing, then reinstall the washers and nut on the bolt so you don't forget how they go. Pull the armature out of the housing and remove the brush plate.

**4** Remove the two brushes with the plastic holder from the housing.

### Two-brush starter

**5** Mark the position of the housing to each end cover. Remove the two through-bolts and detach both end covers **(see illustration)**.

**6** Remove the shims and brush plate from the brush housing after the terminal bolt nut and washers have been removed - note he exact order of the washers.

**7** Pull the armature out of the housing (toward the pinion gear side).

### Inspection

**8** The parts of the starter motor that most likely will require attention are the brushes. Measure the length of the brushes and compare the results to the brush length listed in this Chapter's Specifications **(see illustration)**. If any of the brushes are worn beyond the specified limits, replace the brush holder assembly with a new one. If the brushes are not worn excessively, cracked, chipped, or otherwise damaged, they may be re-used.

**9** Inspect the commutator **(see illustration)** for scoring, scratches and discoloration. The commutator can be cleaned and polished with crocus cloth, but do not use sandpaper or emery paper. After cleaning, wipe away any

residue with a cloth soaked in an electrical system cleaner or denatured alcohol. Measure the commutator diameter and compare it to the diameter listed in this Chapter's Specifications. If it is less than the service limit, the motor must be replaced with a new one.

**10** Using an ohmmeter or a continuity test light, check for continuity between the commutator bars **(see illustration)**. Continuity should exist between each bar and all of the others. Also, check for continuity between the commutator bars and the armature shaft **(see illustration)**. There should be no continuity between the commutator and the shaft. If the checks indicate otherwise, the armature is defective.

**11** Check for continuity between the brush

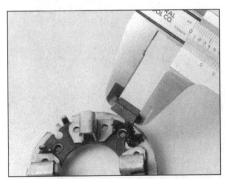

**25.8 Measure the brushes and compare the shortest brush with the length listed in the Specifications**

**25.9 Check for cracks and discoloring. Compare the diameter with the figure in the Specifications**

**25.10a Continuity should exist between the commutator bars**

25.10b There should be no continuity between the commutator bars and the armature shaft

25.11 There should be almost no resistance (0 ohms) between the brushes and the brush plate

25.12 There should be no continuity between the brush plate and the brush holders (infinite resistance)

plate and the brushes **(see illustration)**. The meter should read close to 0 ohms. If it doesn't, the brush plate has an open and must be replaced.

**12** Using the highest range on the ohmmeter, measure the resistance between the brush holders and the brush plate **(see illustration)**. The reading should be infinite. If there is any reading at all, replace the brush plate.

**13** Check the starter pinion gear for worn, cracked, chipped and broken teeth. If the gear is damaged or worn, replace the starter motor.

### Reassembly

#### Four-brush starter

**14** Install the plastic brush holder into the housing. Make sure the terminal bolt and washers are assembled in their original order. Tighten the terminal nut securely.

**15** Detach the brush springs from the brush plate (this will make armature installation much easier). Install the brush plate into the housing, routing the brush leads into the notches in the plate. Make sure the tongue on the brush plate fits into the notch in the housing.

**16** Install the brushes into their holders and slide the armature into place. Install the brush springs.

#### Two-brush starter

**17** Reinstall the brush plate in the end housing **(see illustration 25.5)**.

25.18 Be sure the shims and washers are in place on both ends of the armature shaft

### All models

**18** Install any washers that were present on the end of the armature shaft **(see illustration)**.
**19** Install the end covers, aligning the previously applied match marks (be sure to install the large O-rings between the starter housing and end covers). Install the O-rings and washers (if equipped) on the two through-bolts, then install the through-bolts and tighten them securely.

## 26 Charging system testing - general information and precautions

> **HAYNES HiNT** *Clues to a faulty regulator are constantly blowing bulbs, with brightness varying considerably with engine speed, and battery overheating.*

**1** If the performance of the charging system is suspect, the system as a whole should be checked first, followed by testing of the individual components (the alternator and the voltage regulator/rectifier). **Note:** *Before beginning the checks, make sure the battery is fully charged and that all system connections are clean and tight.*
**2** Checking the output of the charging system

27.7 Measure stator coil resistance at the electrical connector from the alternator

and the performance of the various components within the charging system requires the use of special electrical test equipment. A voltmeter or a multimeter are the absolute minimum tools required. In addition, an ohmmeter is generally required for checking the remainder of the system.
**3** When making the checks, follow the procedures carefully to prevent incorrect connections or short circuits, as irreparable damage to electrical system components may result if short circuits occur. Due to the special tools and expertise required, it is recommended that the job of checking the charging system be left to a dealer service department or a reputable motorcycle repair shop.

## 27 Charging system - output test

*Caution: Never disconnect the battery cables from the battery while the engine is running. If the battery is disconnected, the alternator and regulator/rectifier will be damaged.*
**1** To check the charging system output, you will need a voltmeter or a multimeter with a voltmeter function.
**2** The battery must be fully charged (charge it from an external source if necessary) and the engine must be at normal operating temperature to obtain an accurate reading.
**3** Attach the positive (red) voltmeter lead to the positive (+) battery terminal and the negative (black) lead to the battery negative (-) terminal. The voltmeter selector switch (if equipped) must be in a DC volt range greater than 15 volts.
**4** Start the engine.
**5** The charging system output should be within the range listed in this Chapter's Specifications. Stop the engine.
**6** Follow the wiring harness from the upper side of the alternator cover (on the left side of the engine) to the electrical connector and disconnect the connector.
**7** Connect an ohmmeter between each pair of terminals in the connector (the side that runs back to the alternator, not the wiring harness side) **(see illustration)**. Note the reading.

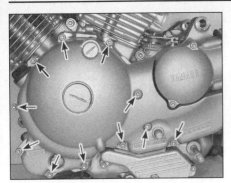

**28.1a  Remove the cover bolts (arrows) . . .**

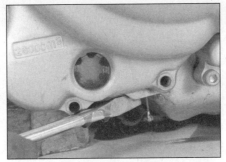

**28.1b  . . . and pry gently at the pry points (not between the gasket surfaces); there's one at the bottom . . .**

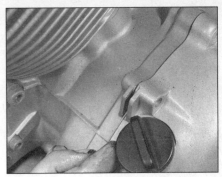

**28.1c  . . . and another at the top**

**8** If the reading is not within the range listed in this Chapter's Specifications, replace the stator (see Section 28).

**9** If the reading is within the Specifications, refer to the wiring diagrams at the end of the book and check the charging circuit for breaks or poor connections. If the wiring is good, replace the regulator/rectifier (see Section 28).

## 28 Alternator cover, stator, rotor and regulator/rectifier - removal and installation

### Cover

**1** Loosen the alternator cover mounting bolts

evenly in a criss-cross pattern and remove the cover **(see illustrations)**.

**2** Clean all traces of old gasket sealer from the cover and its mating surface on the engine.

**3** Make sure there are no metal particles stuck to the rotor magnets **(see illustration)**.

**4** Position a new gasket over the dowels **(see illustration)**.

**5** Guide the wiring harnesses through the opening at the back of the cover **(see illustration)**. Install the cover and tighten the Allen bolts evenly, in a criss-cross pattern, to the torque listed in this Chapter's Specifications.

### Stator

**6** Remove the alternator cover as described above.

**7** Remove the stator screws and take the stator out **(see illustration)**.

**8** Installation is the reverse of the removal steps. Tighten the stator screws securely.

### Rotor

**9** Remove the alternator cover as described above.

**10** Shift the transmission into gear and have an assistant apply the rear brake. Remove the rotor bolt and washer **(see illustration)**.

**11** Thread a rotor puller (either the Yamaha tool or an aftermarket version) into the rotor **(see illustration)**. Remove the rotor from the end of the crankshaft and take the Woodruff key out of its slot **(see illustration)**. If necessary, slide the starter driven gear off

**28.3  Be sure there are no metal fragments stuck to the rotor magnets (arrow)**

**28.4  Slip a new gasket over the dowels (arrows)**

**28.5  Guide the wiring harness out through the back of the cover**

**28.7  Remove screws (A) to detach the stator; screws (B) secure the ignition pick-up coil and its wiring**

**28.10  Loosen the rotor bolt with a socket, then unscrew the bolt and remove the washer**

**28.11a  Use a tool like this one to separate the rotor from the crankshaft . . .**

28.11b . . . then take the rotor off and lift the Woodruff key (arrow) out of its slot

28.11c If you remove the starter driven gear, be sure to reinstall the thrust washer behind it

28.13 The regulator/rectifier on early models is mounted on the lower rear portion of the frame

the crankshaft and remove its thrust washer **(see illustration)**.

**12** Installation is the reverse of the removal steps. Be sure to reinstall the Woodruff key. *Caution: Make sure no metal objects have stuck to the magnets inside the rotor. Tighten the rotor bolt to the torque listed in this Chapter's Specifications.*

### Regulator/rectifier

**13** On 1987 and 1988 models, the regulator/rectifier unit is mounted on the rear underside of the frame **(see illustration)**. On 1989 and later models, it is retained to the inside of the finned cover, just to the rear of the lower left frame cover.

**14** Follow the wiring harness from the

29.3a Compress the pin and spring (A) and remove the roller (B) . . .

regulator/rectifier to the connector. Disconnect the electrical connector and remove the regulator/rectifier mounting screws.

**15** Installation is the reverse of the removal steps. On later models, one of the mounting screws secures a ground/earth wire.

## 29 Starter clutch - removal, inspection and installation

**1** Remove the alternator rotor (see Section 28) and turn it over. Pull the starter idler gear and its shaft out of the engine case, then take the large starter driven gear and its washer off the end of the crankshaft.

**2** Place the large starter driven gear in the starter clutch and try to turn it. It should turn freely in one direction and not at all in the other. If it turns both ways or neither way, remove the idler gear and disassemble the starter clutch for inspection.

**3** Compress the pin against its internal spring with a pointed tool and take out the roller **(see illustration)**. Remove the pin and spring **(see illustration)**.

**4** Remove the remaining two pins, rollers and springs in the same way.

**5** Check all parts for wear and damage and replace parts with these conditions. If the starter clutch needs to be replaced, unstake

the ends of the retaining bolts inside the alternator rotor and unscrew them to separate the starter clutch body from the rotor. Position the new starter clutch on the rotor and apply non-permanent thread locking agent to the threads of the bolts. Install the bolts, tighten them to the torque listed in this Chapter's Specifications and stake their ends on the inside of the rotor.

**6** Position the spring inside one of the pins. Place the spring and pin in their bore, compress the pin against the spring with a pointed tool **(see illustration)** and install the roller.

**7** Install the remaining springs, pins and rollers in the same way.

**8** The remainder of installation is the reverse of the removal steps. When installing the starter driven gear, don't forget to install the thrust washer first **(see illustration 28.11c)**.

## 30 Fuel tap solenoid (1989 and later models) - removal, testing and installation

**1** Remove the main fuel tank (see Chapter 3). Pour the fuel into an approved container.

**2** Free the wiring harness and hose from their clips, remove the screws and detach the fuel tap from the tank **(see illustration)**.

**3** Disconnect the hose from the fuel nozzle

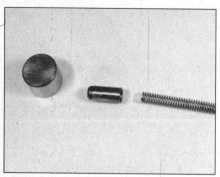

29.3b . . . then remove the pin and spring from their bore

29.6 Press the pin and spring into their bore with a pointed tool and install the roller

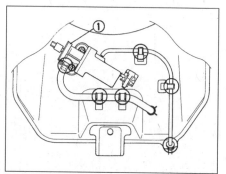

30.2 Free the wiring harness and hose, remove the screws and remove the fuel tap (1) from the tank

and connect a length of clean rubber hose in its place.

**4** Turn the fuel tap lever to On and try to blow air into the hose. It should go through. If it doesn't, replace the fuel tap.

**5** Connect a 12-volt battery (the motorcycle's battery will work) to the solenoid wire terminals (positive to black/yellow; negative to black). Try to blow air into the hose again. It shouldn't be possible with the battery connected to the solenoid. If air will go through, replace the solenoid.

## 31 Carburetor heater (1994-on UK models) - testing

**1** Follow the wiring harness from the heater unit at the carburetor assembly to the thermoswitch (it can be identified by its wire colors). Remove the thermoswitch from the wiring harness.

**2** Immerse the thermoswitch in a container of water (suspend it so it doesn't touch the sides or bottom of the container).

**3** Connect an ohmmeter to the thermoswitch wires and heat the water. Note the ohmmeter readings as the water heats, then cools down.

a) *Zero to 17 +/- 5-degrees C (32 to 63 +/- 9-degrees F) - continuity (little or no resistance)*

b) *17 +/- 5 to 70-degrees C (63 +/- 9 to 158-degrees F) - no continuity (infinite resistance)*

c) *70 to 11 +/- 3-degrees C (158 to 52 +/- 5-degrees F) - no continuity*

d) *Less than 11 +/- 3-degrees C (52 +/- 5-degrees F) - continuity*

**4** If the thermoswitch doesn't give the readings described, replace it.

**5** Disconnect the wiring from the heater unit at the carburetor assembly. Connect an ohmmeter to the terminal on the heater unit, note the reading and compare it to the value listed in this Chapter's Specifications. If the resistance reading is not with the specified range, replace the heater unit.

## 32 Wiring diagrams

Prior to troubleshooting a circuit, check the fuses to make sure they're in good condition. Make sure the battery is fully charged and check the cable connections.

When checking a circuit, make sure all connectors are clean, with no broken or loose terminals or wires. When unplugging a connector, don't pull on the wires - pull only on the connector housings themselves.

**Notes**

# Chapter 8  Part B
# Electrical system (XV700-1100 models)

## Contents

## Degrees of difficulty

| Easy, suitable for novice with little experience |  | Fairly easy, suitable for beginner with some experience | | Fairly difficult, suitable for competent DIY mechanic |  | Difficult, suitable for experienced DIY mechanic | | Very difficult, suitable for expert DIY or professional | 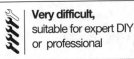 |

## Specifications

### Battery type

| | |
|---|---|
| XV700, XV750 .................................................. | 12 V, 16 Ah |
| XV920, XV1000 (TR1), XV1100 ................................ | 12 V, 20 Ah |

### Fuse specifications

**1981 through 1983 models and TR1**

| | |
|---|---|
| Main | |
|   XV920 (shaft) and TR1 .......................................... | 30 amps |
|   All others .................................................... | 20 amps |
| Headlamp ................................................... | 15 amps |
| Tail/brake lights ............................................ | 10 amps |
| Turn signals ................................................ | 15 amps |
| Ignition .................................................... | 10 amps |

**1984 and 1985, XV700 and 1000 models (except TR1)**

| | |
|---|---|
| Main ....................................................... | 20 amps |
| Headlight .................................................. | 15 amps |
| Turn signals ................................................ | 15 amps |
| Ignition .................................................... | 10 amps |
| Tail/brake lights ............................................ | 10 amps |

**1986 and later models**

| | |
|---|---|
| Main ....................................................... | 30 amps |
| Headlight .................................................. | 15 amps |
| Turn signals ................................................ | 15 amps |
| Ignition .................................................... | 10 amps |
| Tail/brake lights ............................................ | 10 amps |

## Charging system

| | |
|---|---|
| Stator coil resistance . . . . . . . . . . . . . . . . . . . . . . . . . . . . . | 0.5 ohms +/ 10 per cent at 20-degrees C (68-degrees F) |
| Charging system output . . . . . . . . . . . . . . . . . . . . . . . . . . . . | 14.3 to 15.3 volts at 2,000 rpm |

## Starter

| | |
|---|---|
| Starter commutator diameter | |
|   Standard . . . . . . . . . . . . . . . . . . . . . . . . . . . . . . . . . . . . | 28 mm (1.1 inch) |
|   Minimum . . . . . . . . . . . . . . . . . . . . . . . . . . . . . . . . . . . . | 27 mm (1.06 inch) |
|   Mica undercut . . . . . . . . . . . . . . . . . . . . . . . . . . . . . . . . | 0.5 mm (0.02 inch) |
| Starter brush length | |
|   Standard . . . . . . . . . . . . . . . . . . . . . . . . . . . . . . . . . . . . | 12.5 +/- 5 mm (0.492 +/- 0.02 inch) |
|   Minimum . . . . . . . . . . . . . . . . . . . . . . . . . . . . . . . . . . . . | 5.5 mm (0.217 inch) |
| Starter clutch spring clip turning force | |
|   Idle gear . . . . . . . . . . . . . . . . . . . . . . . . . . . . . . . . . . . . | 2.2 to 2.5 kg (4.9 to 5.5 lbs) |
|   Starter gear . . . . . . . . . . . . . . . . . . . . . . . . . . . . . . . . . | 2.0 to 2.3 kg (4.4 to 5.1 lbs) |

## Bulb specifications (1981 through 1983 models, including TR1)

| | |
|---|---|
| Headlight . . . . . . . . . . . . . . . . . . . . . . . . . . . . . . . . . . . . . | 60/55W |
| Tail/brake lights | |
|   TR1 . . . . . . . . . . . . . . . . . . . . . . . . . . . . . . . . . . . . . . . | 5/21W |
|   All others . . . . . . . . . . . . . . . . . . . . . . . . . . . . . . . . . . . | 8/27W |
| Turn signals | |
|   TR1 . . . . . . . . . . . . . . . . . . . . . . . . . . . . . . . . . . . . . . . | 21W |
|   All others . . . . . . . . . . . . . . . . . . . . . . . . . . . . . . . . . . . | 27W |
| Running light (1982 XV920 only) . . . . . . . . . . . . . . . . . . . . | 8W |
| License plate light | |
|   XV750, 1983 XV920 . . . . . . . . . . . . . . . . . . . . . . . . . . . . | 8W |
|   1982 XV920 . . . . . . . . . . . . . . . . . . . . . . . . . . . . . . . . . | 3.8W |
| Warning lights . . . . . . . . . . . . . . . . . . . . . . . . . . . . . . . . . | 3.4W |
| Parking light (UK only) . . . . . . . . . . . . . . . . . . . . . . . . . . . | 3.4W |

## Bulb specifications (1984 and later US models)

| | |
|---|---|
| Headlight . . . . . . . . . . . . . . . . . . . . . . . . . . . . . . . . . . . . . | 60/55W |
| Tail/brake lights . . . . . . . . . . . . . . . . . . . . . . . . . . . . . . . . | 8/27W |
| Turn signals/running lights . . . . . . . . . . . . . . . . . . . . . . . . | 27W |
| Instrument and warning lights . . . . . . . . . . . . . . . . . . . . . . | 4W |

## Bulb specifications (1984 and later UK models)

| | |
|---|---|
| Headlight . . . . . . . . . . . . . . . . . . . . . . . . . . . . . . . . . . . . . | 60/55W |
| Tail/brake lights . . . . . . . . . . . . . . . . . . . . . . . . . . . . . . . . | 5/21W |
| Parking light . . . . . . . . . . . . . . . . . . . . . . . . . . . . . . . . . . | 4W |
| Turn signals . . . . . . . . . . . . . . . . . . . . . . . . . . . . . . . . . . | 21W |
| Instrument and warning lights . . . . . . . . . . . . . . . . . . . . . . | 3W |

## Torque specifications

| | |
|---|---|
| Alternator rotor nut | |
|   1981 through 1983 models . . . . . . . . . . . . . . . . . . . . . . . | 155 Nm (112 ft-lbs) |
|   1984 and later models . . . . . . . . . . . . . . . . . . . . . . . . . . | 175 Nm (125 ft-lbs) |
| Alternator cover bolts . . . . . . . . . . . . . . . . . . . . . . . . . . . . | 7 Nm (5.1 ft-lbs) |
| Starter mounting bolts . . . . . . . . . . . . . . . . . . . . . . . . . . . | 10 Nm (7.2 ft-lbs) |
| Starter solenoid nuts . . . . . . . . . . . . . . . . . . . . . . . . . . . . | 8 Nm (5.8 ft-lbs)* |
| Drive lever cover bolts . . . . . . . . . . . . . . . . . . . . . . . . . . . | 10 Nm (7.2 ft-lbs) |
| Drive lever collar screw . . . . . . . . . . . . . . . . . . . . . . . . . . | 10 Nm (7.2 ft-lbs)* |

*Apply non-permanent thread locking agent to the threads.*

## 1  General information

The machines covered by this manual are equipped with a 12-volt electrical system.

The charging system models uses a rotor with permanent magnets that rotates around a stator coil of copper wire. This produces alternating current, which is converted to direct current by the regulator/rectifier. The regulator/rectifier also controls the charging system output.

An electric starter mounted to the front of the engine is standard equipment. The starter on all models has two brushes and uses reduction gears. The starting system includes the motor, the battery, the relay and the various wires and switches. If the engine kill switch and the ignition (main key) switch are both in the On position, the circuit relay allows the starter motor to operate only if the transmission is in Neutral (Neutral switch on) or the clutch lever is pulled to the handlebar (clutch switch on) and, on all US models and later UK models, the sidestand is up (sidestand switch on).

**Note:** *Keep in mind that electrical parts, once purchased, can't be returned. To avoid unnecessary expense, make very sure the faulty component has been positively identified before buying a replacement part.*

## 2  Electrical troubleshooting

This is the same as for XV535 models. Refer to Part A of this Chapter.

## 3  Battery - inspection and maintenance

These procedures are the same as for XV535 models, except that the 1982 XV920 (shaft) has a long-life battery. This battery has a single filler hole for the electrolyte and a sensor that indicates electrolyte level and activates a warning light on the instrument panel when it drops too low.

If the sensor isn't working properly, put on eye protection and rubber gloves and remove it from the battery. Clean the sensor thoroughly with water, then sand any corrosion from its surface and reinstall it.

 **Warning: Battery electrolyte is diluted sulfuric acid. It can cause burns and eye injury. Don't let it touch your skin.**

## 4  Battery - charging

This is the same as for XV535 models. Refer to Part A of this Chapter.

## 5  Fuses - check and replacement

1  The main fuse on all XV700 through 1100 models is located beneath the seat **(see illustration)**.
2  The fuse block on 1981 through 1983 models is behind a cover on the lower triple clamp **(see illustration)**.
3  The fuse block on 1984 and later models is located under the warning light panel **(see illustration)**.
4  The fuse block contains spare fuses and accessory fuses. Fuse functions and ratings are listed in this Chapter's Specifications. Fuse ratings are marked on the fuses.
5  If you have a test light, the accessory fuses can be checked without removing them. Turn the ignition key to the On position, connect one end of the test light to a good ground, then probe each terminal on top of the fuse. If the fuse is good, there will be voltage available at both terminals. If the fuse is blown, there will only be voltage present at one of the terminals.
6  The fuses can also be tested with an ohmmeter or self-powered test light. Remove the fuse and connect the tester to the ends of the fuse. If the ohmmeter shows continuity or the test lamp lights, the fuse is good. If the ohmmeter shows infinite resistance or the test lamp stays out, the fuse is blown.
7  The fuses can be removed and checked visually. If you can't pull the fuse out with your fingertips, use a pair of needle-nose pliers. A blown fuse is easily identified by a break in the element.
8  If a fuse blows, be sure to check the wiring harnesses very carefully for evidence of a short circuit. Look for bare wires and chafed, melted or burned insulation. If a fuse is replaced before the cause is located, the new fuse will blow immediately.
9  Never, under any circumstances, use a higher rated fuse or bridge the fuse block terminals, as damage to the electrical system could result.
10  Occasionally a fuse will blow or cause an open circuit for no obvious reason. Corrosion of the fuse ends and fuse block terminals may occur and cause poor fuse contact. If this happens, remove the corrosion with a wire brush or emery paper, then spray the fuse end and terminals with electrical contact cleaner.

## 6  Lighting system - check

1  The battery provides power for operation of the headlight, taillight, brake light, license plate light, instrument and warning lights. If none of the lights operate, always check battery voltage before proceeding. Low battery voltage indicates either a faulty battery, low battery electrolyte level or a defective charging system. Refer to Chapter 1 for battery checks and Sections 26 and 27 for charging system tests. Also, check the condition of the fuses and replace any blown fuses with new ones.

### Headlight

2  If the headlight is out when the engine is running (US models) or it won't switch on (UK models), check the fuse first with the key or switch On (see Section 5), then unplug the electrical connector for the headlight and use jumper wires to connect the bulb directly to the battery terminals (see Section 7). If the light comes on, the problem lies in the wiring or one of the switches in the circuit. Refer to Section 17 for the switch testing procedures, and also the wiring diagrams at the end of this Chapter.

### Taillight/license plate light

3  If the taillight fails to work, check the bulbs and the bulb terminals first, then check for battery voltage at the taillight electrical connector. If voltage is present, check the ground/earth circuit for an open or poor connection.
4  If no voltage is indicated, check the wiring between the taillight and the ignition switch, then check the switch. On UK models, check the lighting switch as well.

### Brake light

5  See Section 12 for the brake light switch checking procedure.

### Neutral indicator light

6  If the neutral light fails to operate when the

5.1  The main fuse is located beneath the seat; separate the halves of the fuse holder to expose the fuse

5.2  The accessory fuse block on '81 - '83 models is behind a cover on the front of the lower triple clamp

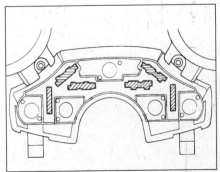

5.3  The accessory fuse block on 1984 and later models is beneath the warning light panel

7.1a Remove the headlight cover screws . . .

7.1c Tilt the headlight cover forward, remove the rubber dust cover and unplug the connector

7.2a If the bulb is secured by a retainer ring, turn it counterclockwise (anti-clockwise) and remove it . . .

7.2b . . . then lift out the bulb (but make sure it has cooled first)

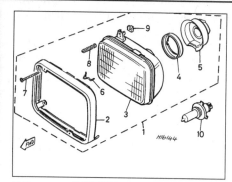

7.1b . . . on 1982 XV920 (shaft) models, don't confuse them with the adjuster screws

1 Headlamp assembly
2 Rim
3 Reflector
4 Bulb retaining ring
5 Cover
6 Spring clip
7 Adjusting screw
8 Spring
9 Nut
10 Headlamp bulb

transmission is in Neutral and the key switch is On, check the fuses and the bulb (see Section 14 for bulb removal procedures). If the bulb and fuses are in good condition, check for battery voltage at the connector attached to the neutral switch on the left side of the engine. If battery voltage is present, refer to Section 18 for the neutral switch check and replacement procedures.

7 If no voltage is indicated, check the wiring between the switch and the bulb for open circuits and poor connections.

## 7 Headlight bulb - replacement

⚠️ **Warning: If the bulb has just burned out, allow it to cool. It will be hot enough to burn your fingers.**

1 Remove the headlight cover screws (see illustrations). Tilt the cover forward out of the headlight assembly and disconnect the electrical connector (see illustration).
2 On models so equipped, turn the bulb

7.5 UK models have a parking light bulb in the headlight reflector

retainer counterclockwise (anti-clockwise) (see illustration). Remove the bulb (see illustration).
3 On models with a wire bulb retainer, unclip the retainer and remove the bulb.
4 When installing the new bulb, reverse the removal procedure. Be sure not to touch the bulb glass with your fingers - oil from your skin will cause the bulb to overheat and fail prematurely. If you do touch the bulb, wipe it off with a clean rag dampened with rubbing alcohol.
5 The parking light bulb holder (auxiliary light) on UK models is either a push fit in the grommet set in the rear of the reflector or has a bayonet-type socket (see illustration). Access may be possible via the cutout in the headlight housing, but if not remove the headlight as described in Step 1. Twist the bulb counterclockwise (anti-clockwise) to release it from its bulb holder.

## 8 Headlight aim - check and adjustment

1 An improperly adjusted headlight may cause problems for oncoming traffic or provide poor, unsafe illumination of the road ahead. Before adjusting the headlight, be sure to consult with local traffic laws and regulations.
2 The headlight beam can be adjusted both vertically and horizontally. Before performing the adjustment, make sure the fuel tank is at least half full and have an assistant sit on the seat.

### 1981 through 1983 models (inc. TR1)

3 Turn the Phillips screw to change horizontal adjustment (see illustration 7.1b or the accompanying illustration).
4 If you're working on an a 1982 XV920 model, turn the adjusting screw in the lower edgeof the retaining ring to change vertical adjustment.
5 If you're working on an XV920R or a TR1, loosen the mounting bolts and securing screw,

8.3 Horizontal adjustment is controlled by a screw

**8.5a  To make vertical adjustments on chain drive models, loosen the mounting bolts . . .**

then pivot the headlight assembly to change vertical adjustment **(see illustrations)**.

6 If you're working on an XV750 or 1983 XV920, loosen the securing screw at the bottom of the headlight assembly and use the pivot at the top of the assembly to change headlight adjustment.

### 1984 and later models

7 The horizontal adjusting screw is at the upper left of the headlight cover. The vertical adjusting screw is located at the lower right. Turn the screws to change adjustment as needed.

### 9  Headlight assembly - removal and installation

#### 1981 through 1983 models (inc. TR1)

1 Remove the headlight cover (see Section 7). If you're planning to take the headlight assembly completely off the motorcycle, disconnect any electrical connectors inside the headlight assembly.

> **HAYNES HiNT**  *When disconnecting wiring, label the connectors to avoid confusion on reconnection.*

2 If you're working on an XV750 or 1983 XV920, remove the two mounting bolts, collars and grommets that secure the headlight assembly brackets. Remove the pivot bolt at the top of the headlight assembly and take the assembly off.

3 If you're working on an XV920R or TR1, remove the mounting bolts and securing screws and take the assembly off **(see illustrations 8.5a and 8.5b)**.

4 If you're working on a 1982 XV920, remove the mounting bolt and nut on each side and take the assembly off.

5 Installation is the reverse of the removal steps. Be sure to reinstall all washers, lockwashers, grommets and collars.

**8.5b  . . . and the securing screw, then tilt the headlight assembly as needed and retighten the fasteners**

### 1984 and later models

6 This is the same as for XV535 models, described in Part A of this Chapter. Note that the two lower mounting bolts also secure the brake hose union.

### 10  Turn signals and tail/brake light bulbs - replacement

Procedures are the same as for XV535 models, although the shapes of the taillight lenses differ slightly. Refer to Part A of this Chapter.

### 11  Turn signal circuit - check

1 The battery provides power for operation of the signal lights, so if they do not operate, always check the battery voltage and specific gravity first. Low battery voltage indicates either a faulty battery, low electrolyte level or a defective charging system. Refer to Chapter 1 for battery checks and Sections 26 and 27 for charging system tests. Also, check the fuses (see Section 5).

2 Most turn signal problems are the result of a burned out bulb or corroded socket. This is especially true when the turn signals function

**11.3  The turn signal relay on 1981 through 1983 models is a separate unit**

properly in one direction, but fail to flash in the other direction. Check the bulbs and the sockets (see Section 10).

3 If the bulbs and sockets check out okay, check for power at the turn signal relay with the ignition On. On 1981 through 1983 models (inc. TR1), this is a separate unit **(see illustration)**. On 1984 and later models, it's incorporated into the relay assembly. Refer to the Wiring diagrams at the end of the book to identify the correct relay and its power source terminal.

4 If the relay is okay, check the wiring between the turn signal relay and the turn signal lights (see the Wiring diagrams at the end of the book).

5 If the wiring checks out okay, replace the turn signal relay.

### 12  Brake light switches - check and replacement

### Circuit check

1 Before checking any electrical circuit, check the fuses (see Section 5).

2 Using a test light connected to a good ground, check for voltage at the brake light switch. If there's no voltage present, check the wire between the switch and the fuse box (see the Wiring diagrams at the end of the book).

3 If voltage is available, touch the probe of the test light to the other terminal of the switch, then pull the brake lever or depress the brake pedal - if the test light doesn't light up, replace the switch.

4 If the test light does light, check the wiring between the switch and the brake lights (see the wiring diagrams at the end of this Chapter).

### Switch replacement

#### Front brake lever switch

5 This is the same as for XV535 models. Refer to Part A of this Chapter.

#### Rear brake pedal switch

6 Unplug the electrical connector in the switch harness.

7 Unhook the switch spring **(see illustration)**.

**12.7  Disconnect the connector and the spring. On later types, depress prongs (arrow) to remove switch**

**13.1 Unscrew the cable nut from the base of the speedometer**

**13.2a On models so equipped, remove the speedometer cable retainer bolt**

**13.2b Detach the speedometer cable from the guide (remove the guide if necessary)**

8 Either compress the retainer prongs and slide the switch and its adjusting nut out of the bracket or unscrew the switch completely from the adjusting nut **(see illustration 12.7)**.

9 Install the switch by reversing the removal procedure, then adjust the switch by following the procedure described in Chapter 1.

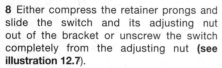

## 13 Speedometer and cable -
### removal and installation

### *Speedometer cable removal*

1 Unscrew the speedometer cable end and pull the cable from the speedometer **(see illustration)**. If necessary for access, lower the headlight assembly (see Section 9).

2 Note how it's routed, then detach the speedometer cable from the drive gear at the left front fork. On early XV750 models, remove the cable retaining bolt and detach the cable from the guide **(see illustration)**. On all others, unscrew the knurled nut from the speedometer drive unit **(see illustration)**.

### *Speedometer removal*

3 Disconnect the cable from the speedometer **(see illustration 13.1)**.

4 Remove the mounting fasteners and detach

**13.2c On models without a retaining bolt, unscrew the cable from the drive unit**

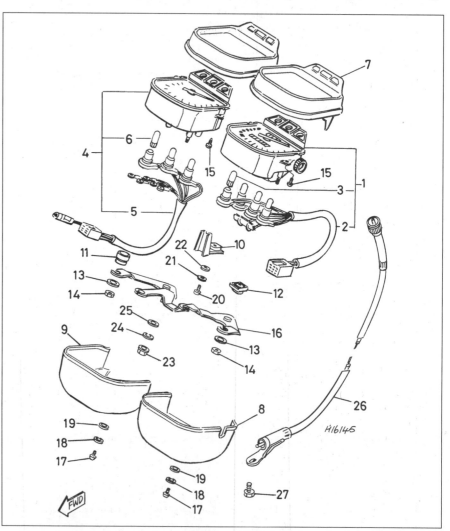

**13.4a Instrument cluster (XV750 and 1983 XV920) - exploded view**

| | | |
|---|---|---|
| 1 Speedometer | 10 Bracket | 19 Washer |
| 2 Wiring harness | 11 Grommet | 20 Screw |
| 3 Bulb | 12 Rubber damper | 21 Lockwasher |
| 4 Tachometer | 13 Washer | 22 Washer |
| 5 Wiring harness | 14 Nut | 23 Nut |
| 6 Bulb | 15 Screw | 24 Lockwasher |
| 7 Instrument top cover | 16 Mounting bracket | 25 Washer |
| 8 Speedometer lower cover | 17 Screw | 26 Speedometer cable |
| 9 Tachometer lower cover | 18 Lockwasher | 27 Bolt |

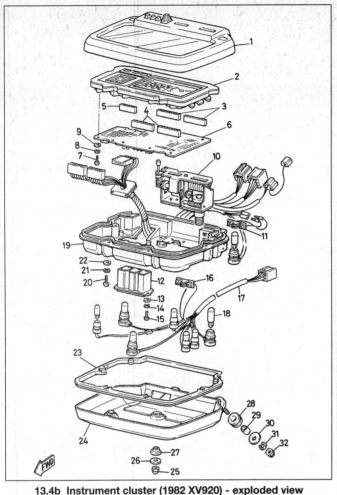

**13.4b  Instrument cluster (1982 XV920) - exploded view**

| | | |
|---|---|---|
| 1 Top cover | 12 Pilot box | 23 Rubber seal |
| 2 Display panel | 13 Washer | 24 Mounting bracket |
| 3 LCD unit | 14 Lockwasher | 25 Nut |
| 4 LCD unit | 15 Screw | 26 Washer |
| 5 LCD unit | 16 Sender unit | 27 Grommet |
| 6 Circuit board | 17 Wiring harness | 28 Grommet |
| 7 Screw | 18 Bulb | 29 Collar |
| 8 Lockwasher | 19 Lower cover | 30 Washer |
| 9 Washer | 20 Screw | 31 Lockwasher |
| 10 Odometer | 21 Lockwasher | 32 Nut |
| 11 Sender unit | 22 Washer | |

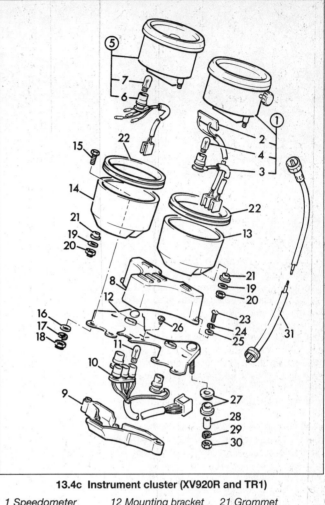

**13.4c  Instrument cluster (XV920R and TR1)**

| | | |
|---|---|---|
| 1 Speedometer | 12 Mounting bracket | 21 Grommet |
| 2 Distance sensor | 13 Speedometer | 22 Sealing ring |
| 3 Wiring harness | housing | 23 Screw |
| 4 Bulb | 14 Tachometer | 24 Lockwasher |
| 5 Tachometer | housing | 25 Washer |
| 6 Wiring harness | 15 Bolt | 26 Screw |
| 7 Bulb | 16 Washer | 27 Rubber damper |
| 8 Warning light cover | 17 Lockwasher | 28 Collar |
| 9 Lower cover | 18 Nut | 29 Lockwasher |
| 10 Wiring | 19 Washer | 30 Nut |
| 11 Bulb | 20 Nut | 31 Speedo cable |

the speedometer housing or instrument cluster **(see illustrations)**.

**5** If you're working on a 1981 through 1983 XV750 or XV920 (shaft), disassemble the cluster as necessary for access to speedometer.

**6** If you're working on an XV920R or TR1, remove the nut, washer and grommet from the back of the speedometer housing and remove the speedometer **(see illustration)**.

**7** If you're working on a 1984 or later model, lift the speedometer away from the bracket and turn it over. Remove the self-tapping screw and detach the speedometer from the

housing **(see illustration 13.5 in Part A of this Chapter)**. Follow the speedometer wiring harness to its connector (inside a rubber cover below the speedometer) and disconnect it.

### Installation

**8** Installation is the reverse of the removal procedure. Be sure the speedometer cable and wiring harness are routed so it doesn't cause the steering to bind or interfere with other components. The squared-off ends of the cable must fit into their spindles in the speedometer and drive gear.

**13.6  Remove the speedometer securing nut and lift the speedometer out**

14.1a Remove the warning light cover screws and lift off the cover . . .

14.1b . . . and pull the bulb from the socket

14.3 On chain drive models, remove the instrument, withdraw the bulb socket, and pull out the bulb

## 14 Instrument and warning light bulbs - replacement

1 To replace a warning light bulb on an XV920R or TR1, remove the warning light cover screws **(see illustration)**. Pull the bulb out of its socket **(see illustration)**, push in a new one and install the cover.
2 To replace an instrument light bulb on an XV920R or TR1, remove the speedometer or tachometer (see Section 13). Pull the bulb socket from the back of the instrument, pull the bulb out of the socket and push in a new one. Reinstall the instrument.
3 To replace bulbs on a 1982 XV920, remove the instrument cluster from its mounting bracket (see Section 13). Pull the bulb socket from the bottom of the instrument cluster **(see illustration)**, pull the bulb out of the socket and push in a new one. Reinstall the instrument cluster.
4 To replace bulbs on an XV750, or 1983 XV920, remove the cluster partway and remove the lower cover (see Section 13). Pull the bulb socket from the bottom of the instrument, pull the bulb out of the socket and push in a new one. Reinstall the instrument cluster.
5 To replace an instrument bulb on the 1984-on models, remove the two screws to free the chromed cover from the base of the instrument. Pull the bulb socket from the back of the instrument and gently pull the bulb out of its holder. Push the new bulb into the holder and press the socket

back into the instrument. Install the chromed cover.
6 To replace a warning light bulb on the 1984-on models, remove the screws on the base of the warning light housing and lower the housing cover. Pull the bulb socket from the underside of the housing and gently pull the bulb out of its holder. Push the new bulb into the holder and press the socket back into the housing. Install the cover.

## 15 Ignition main (key) switch - check and replacement

### Check

1 Follow the wiring harness from the ignition switch (on the upper triple clamp) to the connector and disconnect it.
2 Using an ohmmeter, check the continuity of the terminal pairs indicated in the accompanying table **(see illustration)**. Continuity should exist between the terminals connected by a solid line when the switch is in the indicated position. **Note:** *Connect the ohmmeter to the switch side of the connector, not the wiring harness side.*
3 If the switch fails any of the tests, replace it.

### Replacement

4 Disconnect the electrical connector, if you haven't already done so. Free the wiring harness from any clips or retainers.
5 Place the key in the unlocked position and remove the mounting bolts from the underside of the switch.
6 Attach the new switch to the bracket and tighten the bolts securely.
7 The remainder of installation is the reverse of the removal procedure.

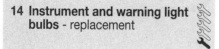

|  | R/Y (1) | R | Br | Bl | W/R (2) | W/R (2) |
|---|---|---|---|---|---|---|
| ON | O—O—O—O | | | | O—O | |
| OFF | O—O | | | | | |
| LOCK | | | | | | |
| P | O—O—O | | | O | | |

802-8B-15.2 HAYNES

15.2 Ignition (main key) switch continuity diagram

1  *1982 XV920 (shaft), 1984-on 1000 and XV1100 only*
2  *1982 XV920 (shaft) only*

| Switch position | Wire color | | | | | | | |
|---|---|---|---|---|---|---|---|---|
| | R | Br/Y | Br | Dg | Br/W | Ch | Y/R | B |
| ON | O—O | | | O—O | O—O | O—O | | |
| OFF | | O—O—O | | | | | | |

16.2 Hazard switch terminals (1984-on XV1000 and XV1100)

## 16 Handlebar switches - check

1 Switch testing procedures are the same as for XV535 models (see Part A of this Chapter).
2 Continuity diagrams are the same as for XV535 models **(see illustration 16.4 in Part A of this Chapter)**, except for the engine kill switch (both terminals have red/white wires) and the hazard switch used on XV1000 and XV1100 models **(see illustration)**.

## 17 Handlebar switches - removal and installation

This is the same as for XV535 models. Refer to Part A of this Chapter.

## 18 Neutral switch - check and replacement

### Check

1 Make sure the transmission is in neutral.
2 Locate the switch harness **(see illustration)**, then unplug the connector.
3 Connect the terminal in the harness side of the connector to ground/earth (bare metal on the motorcycle frame) with a short length of wire.
a)  *If the light stays out, check the bulb and the wiring between the ignition switch and neutral switch.*

18.2 The neutral switch is screwed into the left crankcase; the wire terminal is under a rubber cover

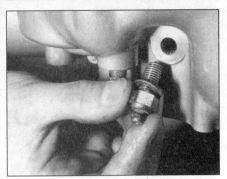

**18.4  Unscrew the switch; use a new sealing washer on installation**

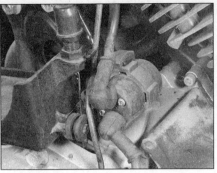

**22.2  The relay is on the right side of the motorcycle; pull back the covers to expose the terminal nuts**

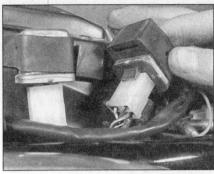

**23.1  The cut-off relay is under the seat (early XV750 shown); it can be identified by its wire colors**

*b)  If the neutral indicator light comes on, the neutral switch may be bad. Connect an ohmmeter between the terminal in the switch side of the connector and ground. Shift through the gears. The ohmmeter should indicate continuity (low resistance) in neutral and no continuity (infinite resistance) in all other gears. If not, replace the neutral switch.*

## Replacement

**4** Loosen the small screw on the switch and detach the wire **(see illustration 18.2)**. Unscrew the switch from the crankcase **(see illustration)**. Remove the sealing washer and install a new one.

**5** Installation is the reverse of the removal steps.

## 19 Sidestand switch -
### check and replacement

Testing and replacement procedures are the same as for XV535 models. Refer to Part A of this Chapter.

## 20 Clutch switch -
### check and replacement

Testing and replacement procedures are the same as for XV535 models. Refer to Part A of this Chapter.

## 21 Horn -
### check and replacement

These models use two horns, mounted at the front of the motorcycle. Testing and replacement procedures are the same as for XV535 models. Refer to Part A of this Chapter.

## 22 Starter relay -
### check and replacement

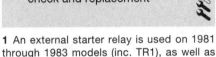

**1** An external starter relay is used on 1981 through 1983 models (inc. TR1), as well as 1984 and 1985 XV700 models.

**2** Testing and replacement procedures are the same as for XV535 models (see Part A of this Chapter). The relay is mounted on the right side of the motorcycle **(see illustration)**.

## 23 Starting circuit cut-off relay -
### check and replacement

**1** Lift or remove the seat (see Chapter 7) and remove the relay **(see illustration)**.

### 1981 through 1983 models (inc. TR1)

**2** Connect an ohmmeter and 12-volt battery to the relay terminals **(see illustration)**. The ohmmeter should indicate continuity (little or no resistance) while the battery is connected,

and infinite resistance (no continuity) when the battery is disconnected.

**3** Disconnect the battery and connect the ohmmeter between the coil winding terminals **(see illustration)**. Note the ohmmeter reading, then switch the ohmmeter leads. The ohmmeter should indicate very high resistance in one direction and very low resistance in the other direction.

**4** If the relay doesn't perform as described, replace it.

### 1984 and later models

**5** Connect an ohmmeter and 12-volt battery to the relay terminals **(see illustration)**. The ohmmeter should indicate continuity (little or no resistance) while the battery is connected, and infinite resistance (no continuity) when the battery is disconnected.

**6** If the relay doesn't perform as described, replace it.

## 24 Starter motor -
### removal and installation

## Removal

**Note:** *Disconnect the cable from the negative terminal of the battery.*

**1** On XV920 and 1981 through 1985 XV700 and XV750 models, the drive pinion end of the starter motor must be disconnected from inside the left outer crankcase cover before the starter motor can be removed. Remove

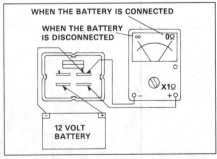

**23.2  Cutoff relay test connections (1981 through 1983 models)**

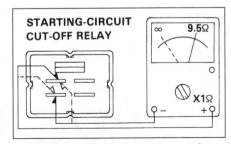

**23.3  Cutoff relay diode test connections (1981 through 1983 models)**

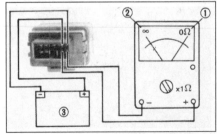

**23.5  Cutoff relay test connections (1984 and later models)**

*1 Continuity   2 No continuity*

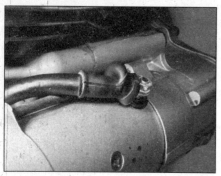

**24.2 Pull back the cover, remove the nut and disconnect the starter cable**

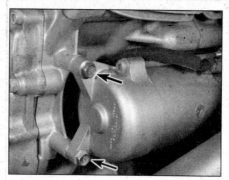

**24.3 Remove the mounting bolts (arrows)**

**24.4 Pull the starter motor out of the crankcase**

the cover as described in Section 28. Free the snap-ring from the end of the starter motor shaft and withdraw the drive pinion complete with spring clip **(see illustration 30.2).**

**2** Pull back the rubber cover, remove the nut retaining the starter cable to the starter and disconnect the cable **(see illustration)**.

**3** Remove the starter mounting bolts **(see illustration)**.

**4** Lift the end of the starter up a little bit and slide the starter out of the engine case **(see illustration)**.

**5** Check the condition of the O-ring on the end of the starter and replace it if necessary. Also check the starter pinion gear and the driven gear inside the engine for chipped or worn teeth.

## Installation

**6** Apply a little engine oil to the O-ring and install the starter by reversing the removal procedure. Tighten the starter mounting bolts to the torque listed in this Chapter's Specifications.

**7** On XV920 and 1981 through 1985 XV700 and XV750 models, make sure the spring clip is in place around the drive pinion and engage the spring clip's end in the crankcase slot. Secure the drive pinion with the snap-ring. Install the outer crankcase cover as described in Section 28.

## 25 Starter motor - disassembly, inspection and reassembly

**1** Remove the starter motor (see Section 24).
**2** All XV700 through 1100 models use a two-brush, reduction gear starter **(see illustration)**.
**3** Disassembly, inspection and assembly procedures are generally the same as for XV535 models (refer to Part A of this Chapter). In addition, check the reduction gears and bushings for wear and damage **(see illustrations)**. The gears aren't available separately, so the starter will have to be replaced if they're worn or damaged.

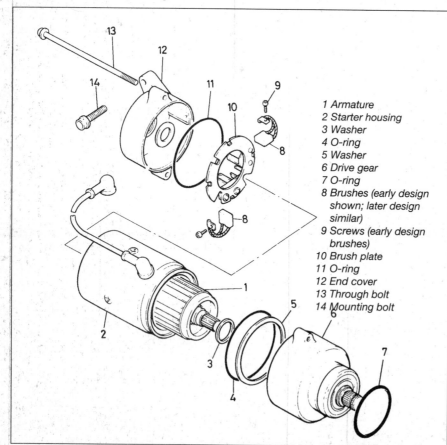

1 Armature
2 Starter housing
3 Washer
4 O-ring
5 Washer
6 Drive gear
7 O-ring
8 Brushes (early design shown; later design similar)
9 Screws (early design brushes)
10 Brush plate
11 O-ring
12 End cover
13 Through bolt
14 Mounting bolt

**25.2 Starter motor - exploded view**

**25.3a Check the reduction gears for wear or damage . . .**

**25.3b . . . and check the bushing inside the gear end plate**

## 26 Charging system testing - general information and precautions

**HAYNES HiNT** *Clues to a faulty regulator are constantly blowing bulbs, with brightness varying considerably with engine speed, and battery overheating.*

1 If the performance of the charging system is suspect, the system as a whole should be checked first, followed by testing of the individual components (the alternator and the voltage regulator/rectifier). **Note:** *Before beginning the checks, make sure the battery is fully charged and that all system connections are clean and tight.*

2 Checking the output of the charging system and the performance of the various components within the charging system requires the use of special electrical test equipment. A voltmeter or a multimeter are the absolute minimum tools required. In addition, an ohmmeter is generally required for checking the remainder of the system.

3 When making the checks, follow the procedures carefully to prevent incorrect connections or short circuits, as irreparable damage to electrical system components may result if short circuits occur. Due to the special tools and expertise required, it is recommended that the job of checking the charging system be left to a dealer service department or a reputable motorcycle repair shop.

## 27 Charging system - output test

*Caution: Never disconnect the battery cables from the battery while the engine is running. If the battery is disconnected, the alternator and regulator/rectifier will be damaged.*

1 To check the charging system output, you will need a voltmeter or a multimeter with a voltmeter function.

2 The battery must be fully charged (charge it from an external source if necessary) and the engine must be at normal operating temperature to obtain an accurate reading.

3 Attach the positive (red) voltmeter lead to the positive (+) battery terminal and the negative (black) lead to the battery negative (-) terminal. The voltmeter selector switch (if equipped) must be in 0-to-20 DC volt range.

4 Start the engine.

5 The charging system output should be within the range listed in this Chapter's Specifications. Stop the engine as soon as the voltage reading has been obtained, and turn the ignition key switch Off.

6 Follow the wiring harness from the

**28.2 Note the locations of the locating dowels as you remove the cover**

alternator cover (on the left side of the engine) to the electrical connector and disconnect the connector containing the three white wires.

7 Connect the probes of an ohmmeter set to the R x 1 range between each pair of white wires in the connector (the side that runs back to the alternator, not the wiring harness side). Note the reading of all three tests.

8 If each reading is not within the range listed in this Chapter's Specifications, replace the stator (see Section 28).

9 If the reading is within the Specifications, refer to the Wiring diagrams at the end of the book and check the charging circuit for breaks or poor connections. If the wiring is good, replace the regulator/rectifier (see Section 28). **Note:** *No test details are provided by the manufacturer for the regulator/rectifier unit. If the stator coils and wiring check out OK, the regulator/rectifier is probably defective.*

## 28 Alternator cover, stator, rotor and regulator/rectifier - removal and installation

### Cover

1 Remove the outer crankcase cover from the left side of the engine. Refer to Chapter 2 and disconnect the clutch cable at the engine. Remove the left footpeg assembly if necessary for access.

2 Loosen the alternator cover mounting bolts evenly in a criss-cross pattern and remove the cover **(see illustration)**.

3 Clean all traces of old gasket sealer from the cover and its mating surface on the engine.

4 Make sure there are no metal particles stuck to the rotor magnets.

5 Position a new gasket over the dowels.

6 On XV1000 models, XV1100 models and 1986 and later XV700 and XV750 models, hold the starter clutch thrust collar in with a flat steel ruler or similar tool **(see illustration)**.

7 Install the cover and tighten the Allen bolts evenly, in a criss-cross pattern, to the torque listed in this Chapter's Specifications.

### Stator

8 Remove the alternator cover as described above. Remove the stator screws and take the stator out **(see illustration)**.

**28.6 Hold the thrust collar in with a flat steel ruler or similar tool while installing the cover**

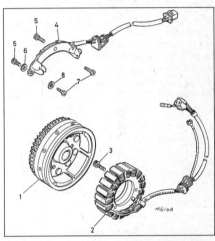

**28.8 Alternator rotor and stator details**

| | |
|---|---|
| 1 Rotor | 5 Pickup coil screws |
| 2 Stator | 6 Washers |
| 3 Bolt | 7 Pickup coil screws |
| 4 Pickup coils (dual pickup model shown) | (alternate locations) |
| | 8 Washers |

9 Installation is the reverse of the removal steps. Tighten the stator screws securely.

### Rotor

10 Remove the alternator cover as described above.

11 Shift the transmission into gear and have an assistant apply the rear brake. Remove the rotor nut and washer **(see illustration)**.

**28.11 Remove the rotor retaining nut and washer**

28.12a Take off the rotor together with the intermediate gear

28.12b Remove the Woodruff key from the crankshaft

28.13a The legs on the intermediate gear fit into the gaps between the rotor springs

**12** Thread a rotor puller (either the Yamaha tool or an aftermarket version) into the rotor. Remove the rotor from the end of the crankshaft and take the Woodruff key out of its slot **(see illustrations)**. **Note:** *Don't take the intermediate gear off the back of the rotor unless the gear or rotor is to be replaced.*

**13** Installation is the reverse of the removal steps, with the following additions:

a) *If the intermediate gear was removed from the back of the rotor, position the three pairs of rotor springs with gaps between them and press the gear into position. Make sure its alignment mark is lined up with the sighting hole in the rotor* **(see illustrations)**.

b) *Be sure to reinstall the Woodruff key.*

28.13b Make sure the mark on the gear aligns with the hole in the rotor

**Caution:** *Make sure no metal objects have stuck to the magnets inside the rotor.*

c) *Aligning the rotor and intermediate gear must be done in a specific way. Refer to the timing gear installation procedures in Part B of Chapter 2.*

d) *Tighten the rotor nut to the torque listed in this Chapter's Specifications* **(see illustration)**.

### Regulator/rectifier

**14** On 1981 through 1983 models (inc TR1), the regulator/rectifier unit is mounted on the rear subframe **(see illustration)**. On 1984 and later models, it is mounted inboard of the luggage box behind the left side cover.

**15** Follow the wiring harness from the regulator/rectifier to the connector. Disconnect

28.13c Tighten the rotor nut to the specified torque

the electrical connector and remove the regulator/rectifier mounting fasteners.

**16** Installation is the reverse of the removal steps.

## 29 Oil level switch - removal, check and installation

### Removal

**1** Drain the engine oil (see Chapter 1).

**2** The oil level switch is mounted in the bottom of the crankcase. Note how its wiring harness is routed, then unplug the electrical connector.

**3** Remove the cover, then unscrew the switch **(see illustrations)**.

### Check

**4** Connect an ohmmeter between the terminals of the switch harness. With the switch in its normal installed position, the ohmmeter should indicate infinite resistance.

**5** Turn the switch upside down. The ohmmeter should now read zero ohms.

**6** If the ohmmeter doesn't give the correct indication in Step 4 or 5, replace the switch.

### Installation

**7** Installation is the reverse of the removal steps. Use a new sealing washer and tighten the switch to the torque listed in this Chapter's Specifications.

28.14 The voltage regulator/rectifier on 1981 through 1983 models is mounted on the rear subframe

29.3a Remove the oil level switch cover . . .

29.3b . . . and unscrew the switch from the crankcase

**30.2  The spring clips must fit into the notches in the crankcase**

## 30  Starter clutch - removal, inspection and installation

1  Two different starter clutch designs are used, one on 1981 through 1985 XV750, XV700 and XV920 models, the other on XV1000, XV1100, and 1986 and later XV700 and XV750 models.

### *Removal*

#### XV920 and 1981 through 1985 XV700 and XV750 models

2  Remove the alternator cover (see Section 28). Free the snap-ring from the end of the starter motor shaft and withdraw the drive pinion complete with spring clip **(see illustration)**. Remove the starter motor if desired (see Section 24).
3  Extract the shaft from the centre of the idler

**30.5  Remove the drive lever cover and gasket**

**30.6  Loosen the collar screw**

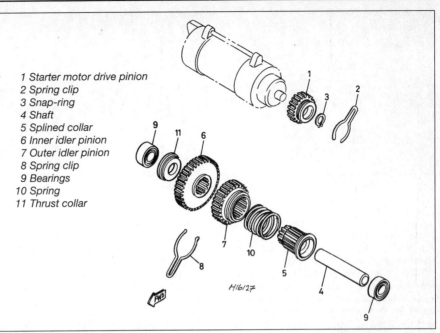

1 Starter motor drive pinion
2 Spring clip
3 Snap-ring
4 Shaft
5 Splined collar
6 Inner idler pinion
7 Outer idler pinion
8 Spring clip
9 Bearings
10 Spring
11 Thrust collar

*H16127*

**30.3  Starter clutch details (1981 through 1985 XV700 and XV750; XV920)**

pinions and then remove the splined collar with its spring. Remove the outer idler pinion with its spring clip, followed by the inner idler pinion and the thrust collar. Reassemble the components on the shaft as a guide to installation **(see illustration)**.

#### XV1000, XV1100, and 1986 and later XV700 and XV750 models

4  Remove the starter motor (see Section 24)

and the alternator cover (see Section 28).
5  Remove the drive lever cover and gasket **(see illustration)**.
6  Loosen the drive lever collar screw **(see illustration)**.
7  Remove the thrust collar **(see illustration)**. Remove the O-ring, shaft, starter wheel, spring (where fitted), outer idler gear, inner idler gear and remaining thrust collar.

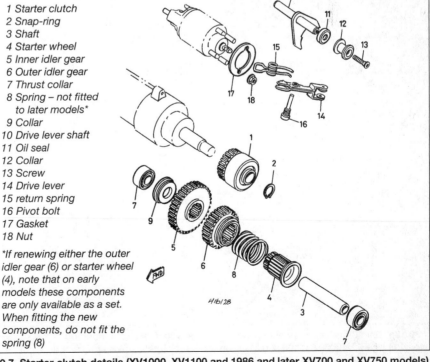

1 Starter clutch
2 Snap-ring
3 Shaft
4 Starter wheel
5 Inner idler gear
6 Outer idler gear
7 Thrust collar
8 Spring – not fitted to later models*
9 Collar
10 Drive lever shaft
11 Oil seal
12 Collar
13 Screw
14 Drive lever
15 return spring
16 Pivot bolt
17 Gasket
18 Nut

*If renewing either the outer idler gear (6) or starter wheel (4), note that on early models these components are only available as a set. When fitting the new components, do not fit the spring (8)

*H16128*

**30.7  Starter clutch details (XV1000, XV1100 and 1986 and later XV700 and XV750 models)**

30.10a Remove the solenoid screws and nuts . . .

30.10b . . . then remove the cover and remove the solenoid

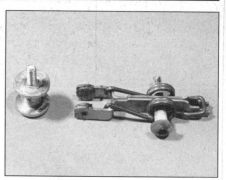

30.11 Remove the pivot and starter drive lever

**8** Remove the snap-ring, starter clutch and remaining snap-ring.
**9** Remove the drive lever collar screw **(see illustration 30.6)**.
**10** Remove the two solenoid securing nuts. Remove the solenoid screws, pull the solenoid out and remove the gasket **(see illustrations)**.
**11** Remove the drive lever pivot bolt, then remove the drive lever, collar and spring **(see illustration)**.

### Inspection

**12** If you're working on a 1981 through 1985 XV700, XV750 or XV920 model, clean the starter clutch components and check them for wear and damage **(see illustration)**. Replace any worn or damaged parts. Place the spring clips in

position and try to rotate them. If the turn easily, replace them. If you're in doubt about their condition, pull on them with a spring scale and measure the force required to rotate them **(see illustration)**. If it's less than the value listed in this Chapter's Specifications, replace them.
**13** If you're working on a 1986 or later XV700 or XV750, an XV1000 or an XV1100 model, clean the drive assembly components and check them for wear or damage **(see illustration)**. Replace worn or damaged parts. Check the starter clutch splines and bushing for wear or damage and replace the starter clutch if problems are found **(see illustrations)**. If replacing either the starter wheel or the outer idler gear, note that these components are only available as a set and that the large spring must not be fitted when using

the new parts – later models are fitted with the new parts as standard.

### Installation

#### 1981 through 1985 XV700, XV750 and XV920 models

**14** Centre the thrust collar, inner idler pinion and outer idler pinion (complete with spring clip) over the shaft bearing in the crankcase. Position the end of the spring clip in its channel in the crankcase.
**15** Insert the shaft through the pinions and into the bearing.
**16** Install the spring on the splined collar, then slip the splined collar over the shaft and through the idler pinions.
**17** Install the starter motor if this was previously removed (see Section 24).
**18** Make sure the spring clip is in place around the starter motor drive pinion, then slip the pinion over the end of the starter motor shaft and engage the spring clip's end in the crankcase slot **(see illustration 30.2)**. Secure the drive pinion with the snap-ring.
**19** Install the outer crankcase cover as described in Section 28.

#### XV1000, XV1100, and 1986 and later XV700 and XV750 models

**20** Install the gasket and starter solenoid. Install the solenoid screws and nuts.
**21** Position the drive lever collar and spring on the alternator cover. Apply non-permanent

30.12a Check the components for wear and damage (XV920 and 1981 through 1985 XV700 and XV750)

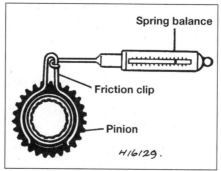

30.12b Assess spring clip tightness with a spring scale; replace them if they turn too easily

30.13a Check the components for wear and damage (XV1000, XV1100 and 1986-on XV700 and XV750)

30.13b Check the bushing in the starter clutch for wear or damage . . .

30.13c . . . also inspect the clutch splines

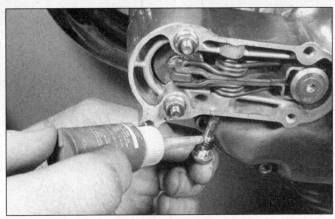

**30.21  Apply non-permanent thread locking agent to the threads of the pivot bolt**

**30.23  Install the starter drive assembly**

**30.24  Install the snap-ring, starter clutch and second snap-ring**

thread locking agent to the pivot bolt, then install it and tighten it securely **(see illustration)**.

**22**  Install the starter motor (see Section 24).

**23**  Install the thrust collar, idler gear, drive lever shaft, idler gear, spring (where fitted), starter wheel, shaft and thrust collar **(see illustration)**.

**24**  Install the snap-ring, starter clutch and second snap-ring **(see illustration)**.

**25**  Install the alternator cover (see Section 28).

### All models

**26**  The remainder of installation is the reverse of the removal steps.

**27**  Fill the engine with oil (see Chapter 1).

## 31  Wiring diagrams

Prior to troubleshooting a circuit, check the fuses to make sure they're in good condition. Make sure the battery is fully charged and check the cable connections.

When checking a circuit, make sure all connectors are clean, with no broken or loose terminals or wires. When unplugging a connector, don't pull on the wires - pull only on the connector housings themselves.

**Notes**

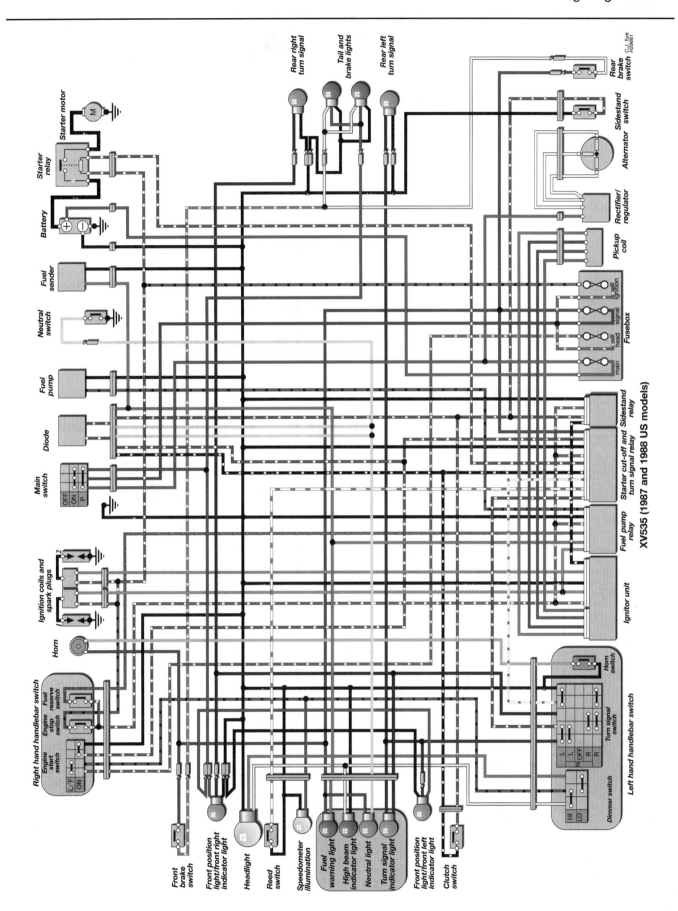

XV535 (1987 and 1988 US models)

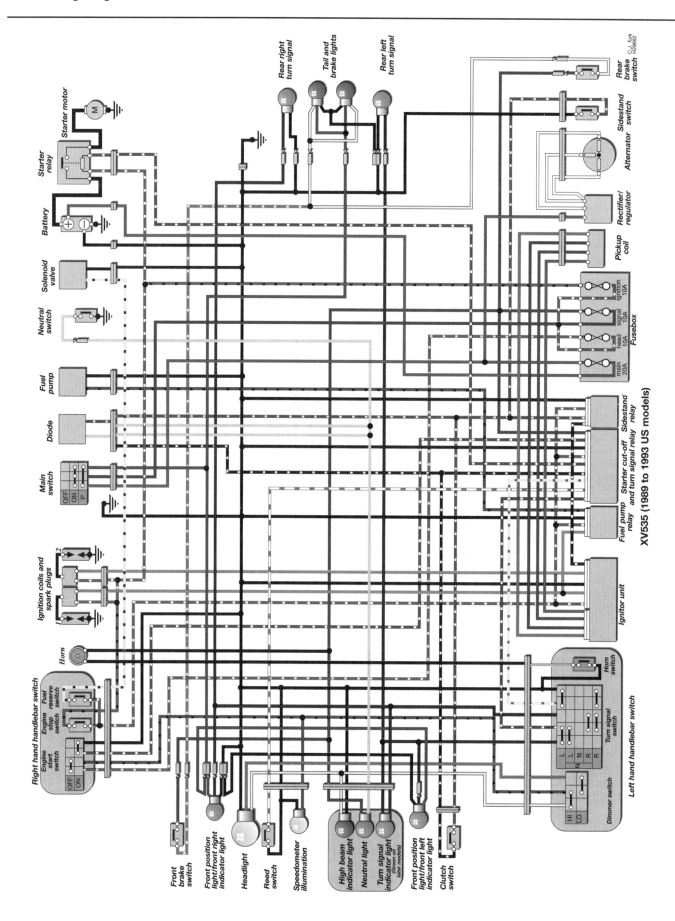

XV535 (1989 to 1993 US models)

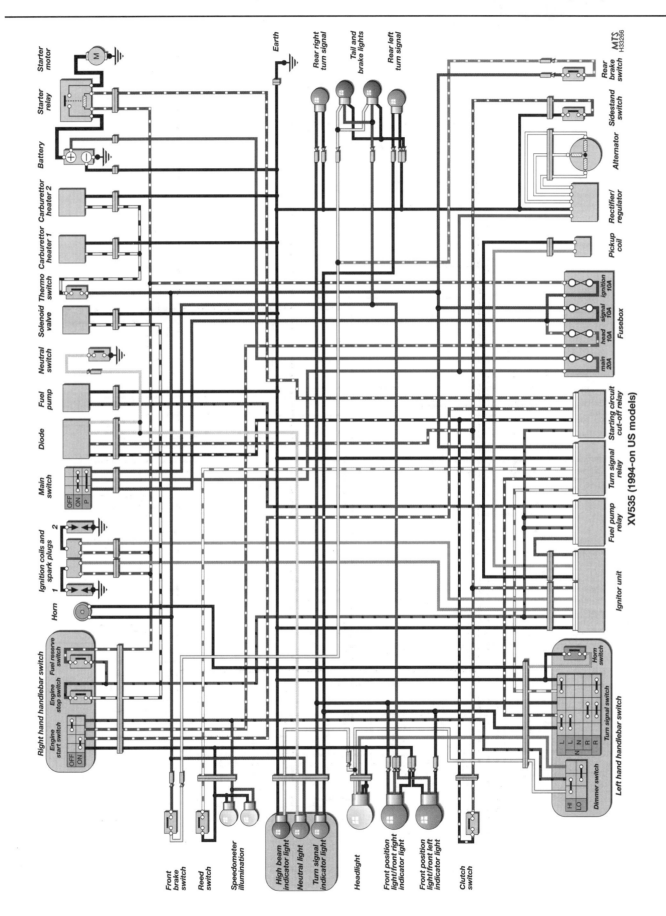

XV535 (1994-on US models)

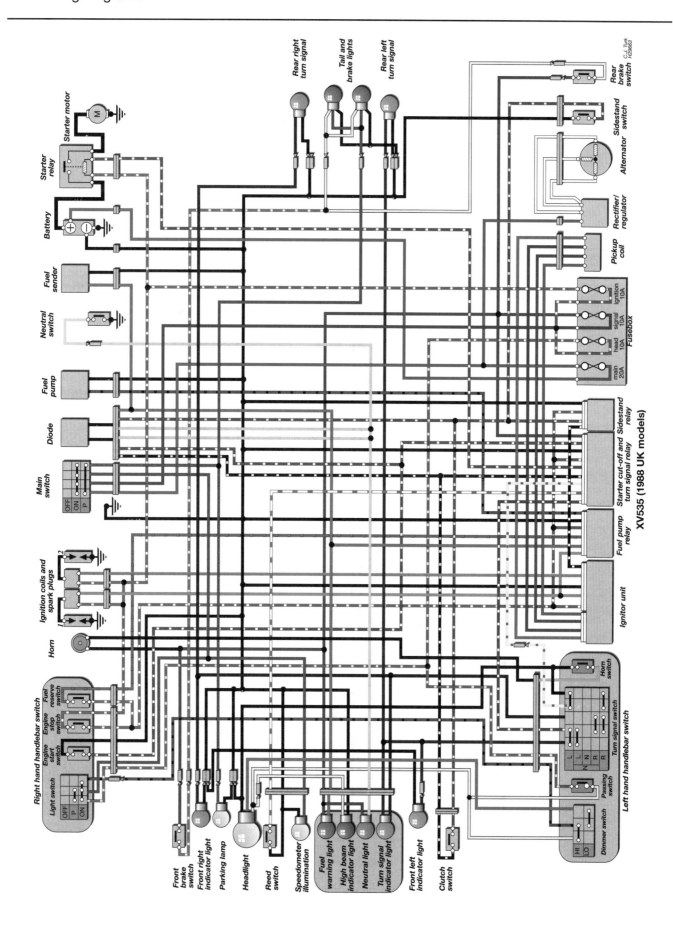

XV535 (1988 UK models)

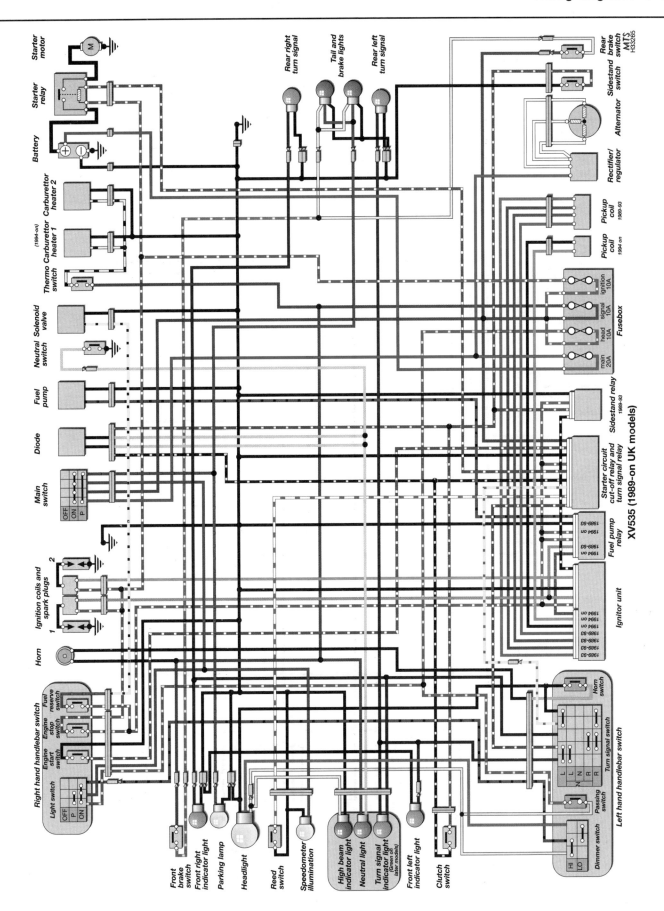

Starter motor

Starter relay

Battery

Carburettor heater 2

Carburettor heater 1 (1994-on)

Thermo switch

Solenoid valve

Neutral switch

Fuel pump

Diode

Main switch

Ignition coils and spark plugs

Horn

Right hand handlebar switch

Fuel reserve switch

Engine stop switch

Engine start switch

Light switch

Front brake switch

Front right indicator light

Parking lamp

Headlight

Reed switch

Speedometer illumination

High beam indicator light

Neutral light

Turn signal indicator light (Green on later models)

Front left indicator light

Clutch switch

Rear right turn signal

Tail and brake lights

Rear left turn signal

Rear brake switch

Sidestand switch

Alternator

Rectifier/ regulator

Pickup coil 1989-93

Pickup coil 1994 on

Ignition 10A

signal 10A

head 10A

main 20A

Fusebox

Sidestand relay 1989-93

Starter circuit cut-off relay and turn signal relay

Fuel pump relay 1994 on / 1989-93

Ignitor unit 1994 on / 1989-93

Horn switch

Turn signal switch

Passing switch

Left hand handlebar switch

Dimmer switch

XV535 (1989-on UK models)

MTS H33265

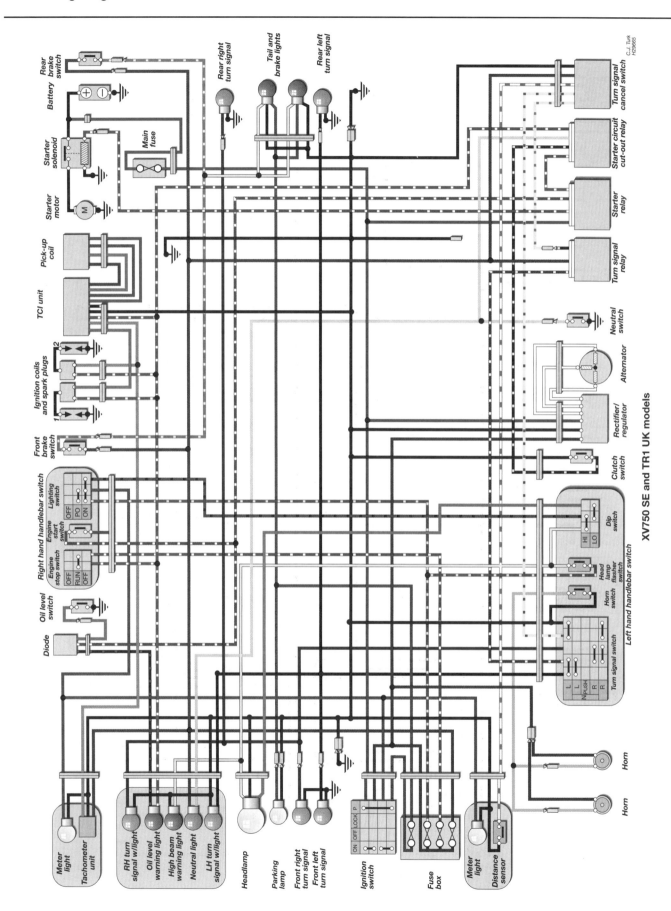

XV750 SE and TR1 UK models

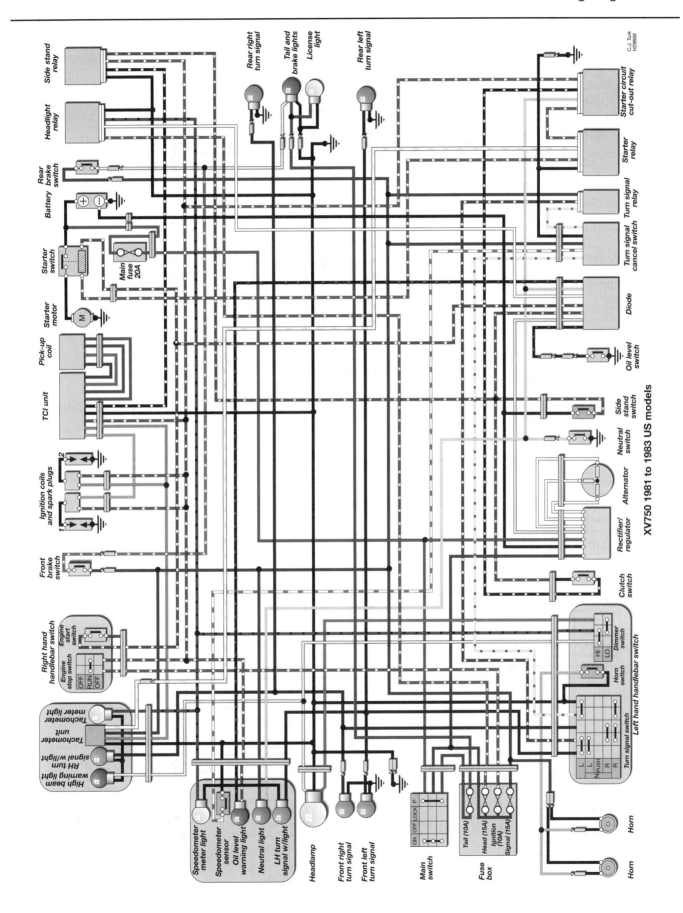

XV750 1981 to 1983 US models

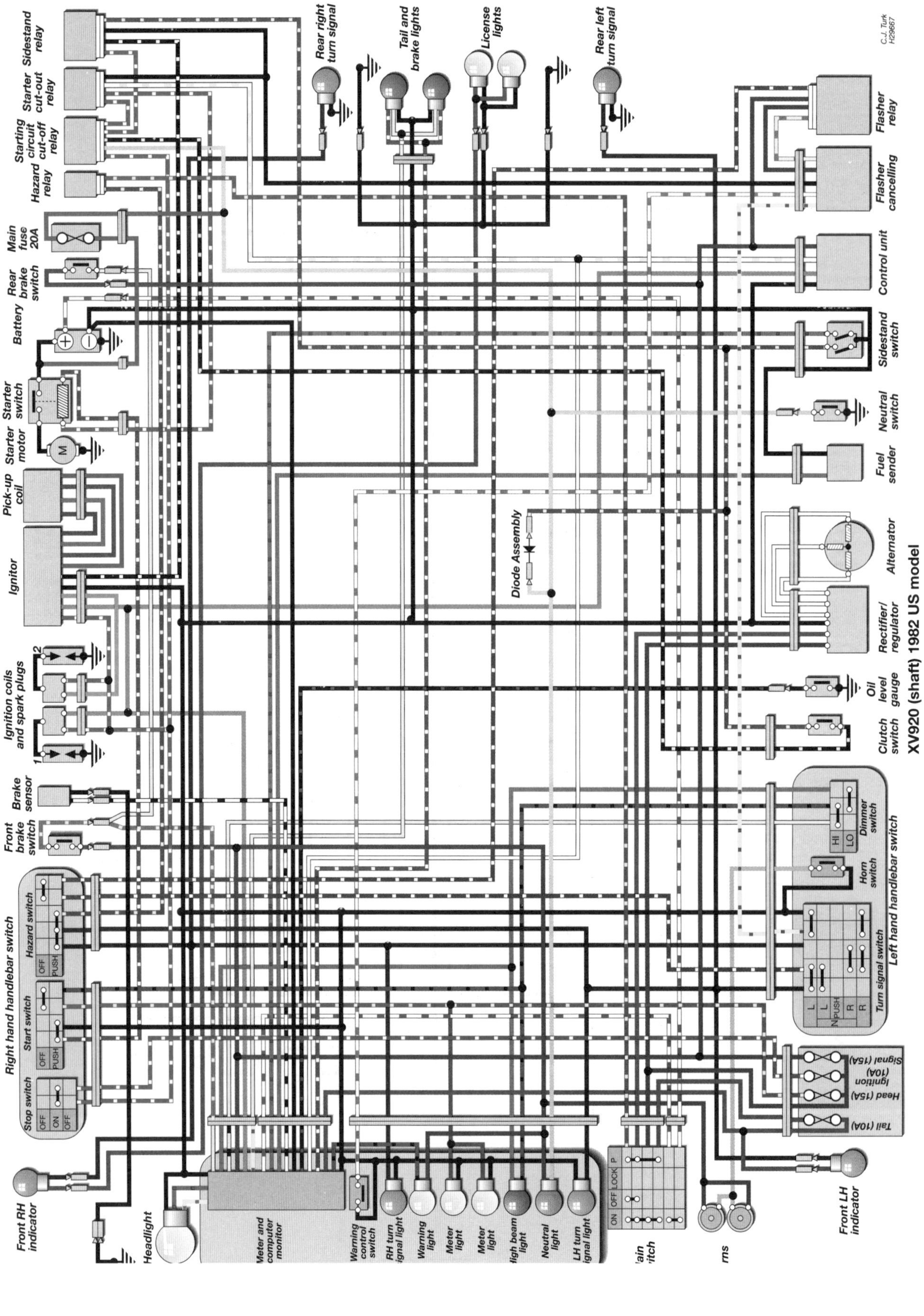
XV920 (shaft) 1982 US model
Hazard relay
Starting circuit cut-off relay
Starter cut-out relay
Sidestand relay
Main fuse 20A
Rear brake switch
Battery
Starter switch
Starter motor
Pick-up coil
Ignitor
Ignition coils and spark plugs
Brake sensor
Front brake switch
Right hand handlebar switch
Hazard switch
Start switch
Stop switch
Front RH indicator
Headlight
Meter and computer monitor
Warning control switch
Warning light
Meter light
Meter light
Neutral light
LH turn signal light
Rear right turn signal
Tail and brake lights
License lights
Rear left turn signal
Diode Assembly
Flasher relay
Flasher cancelling
Control unit
Sidestand switch
Neutral switch
Fuel sender
Alternator
Rectifier/ regulator
Oil level gauge
Clutch switch
Dimmer switch
Horn switch
Left hand handlebar switch
Turn signal switch
Tail (10A)
Head (15A)
Ignition (10A)
Signal (15A)
Front LH indicator
C.J. Turk H29667

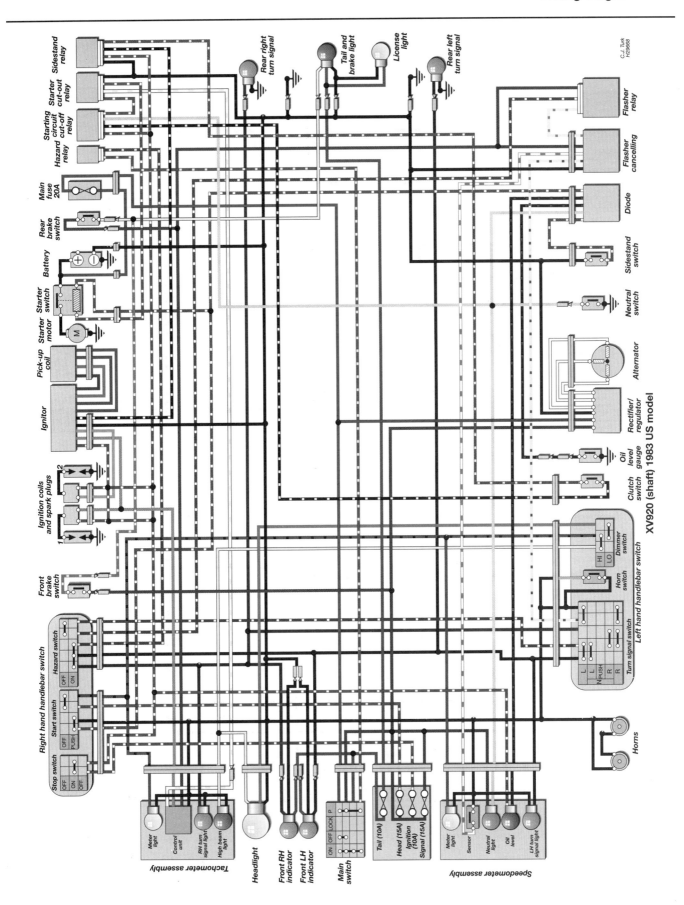

XV920 (shaft) 1983 US model

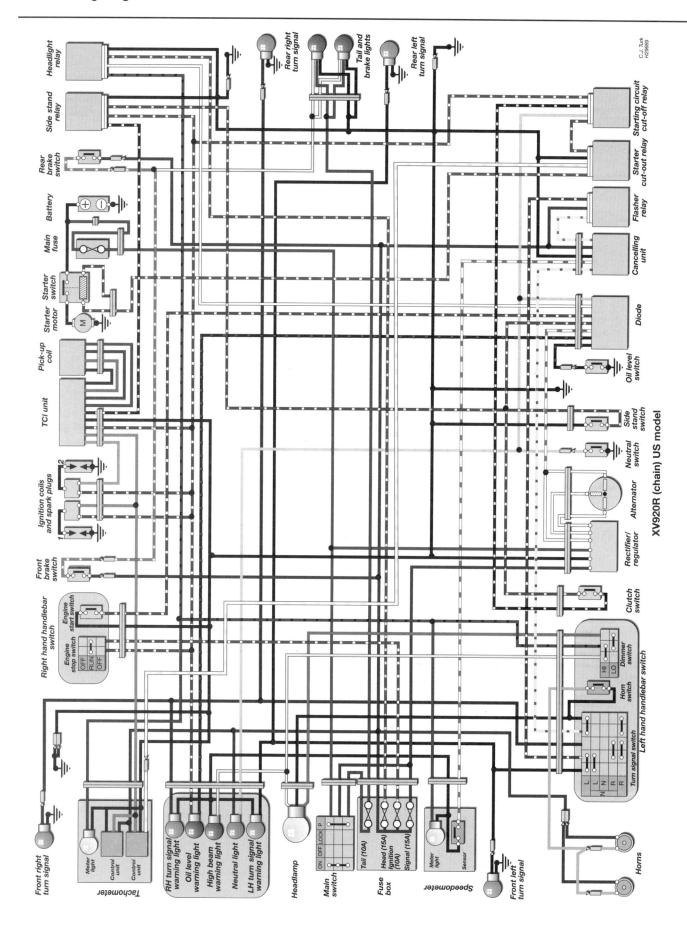

**XV920R (chain) US model**

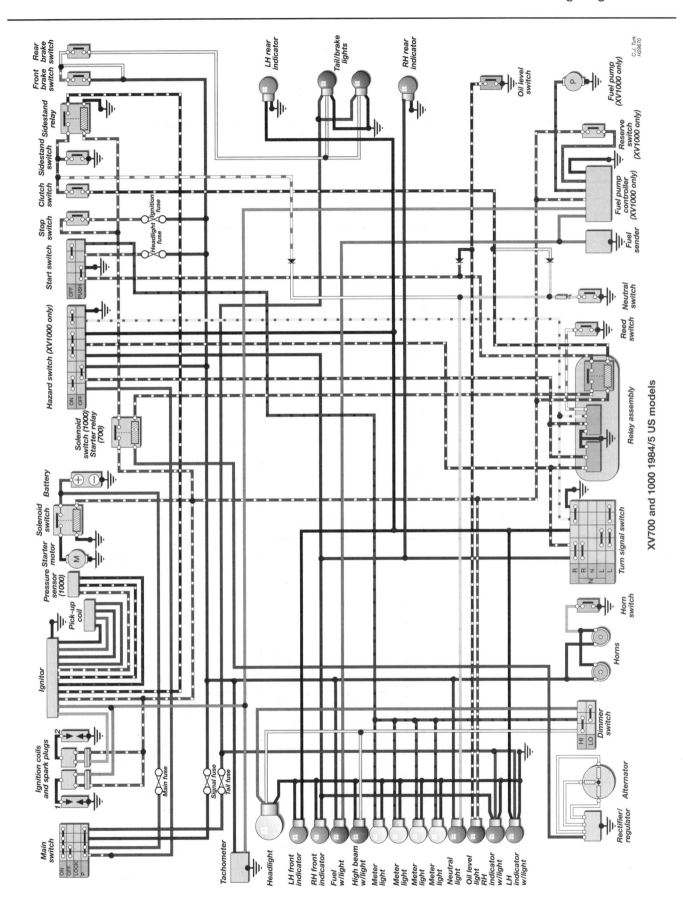

XV700 and 1000 1984/5 US models

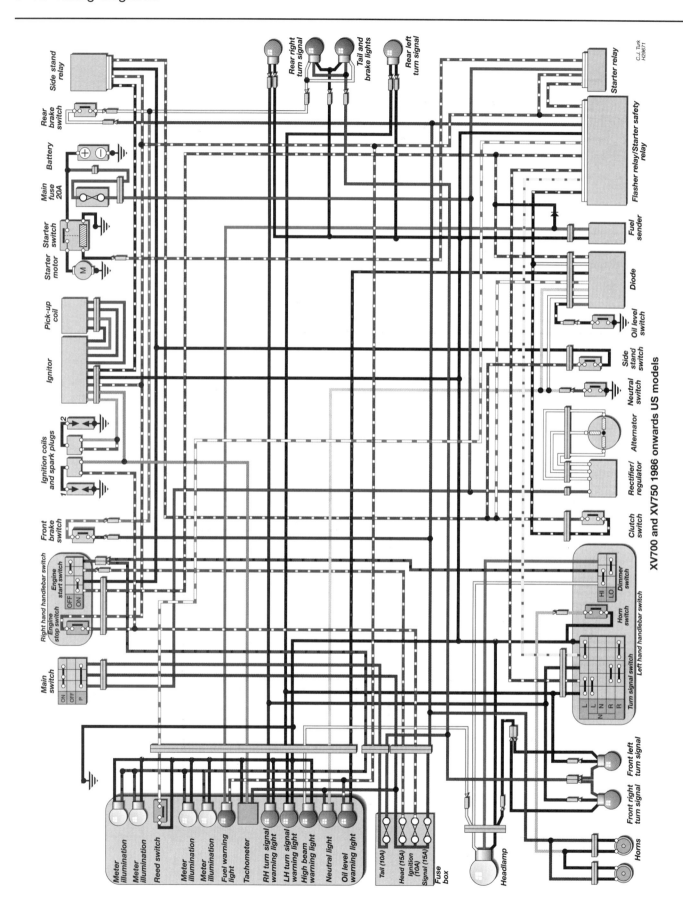

XV700 and XV750 1986 onwards US models

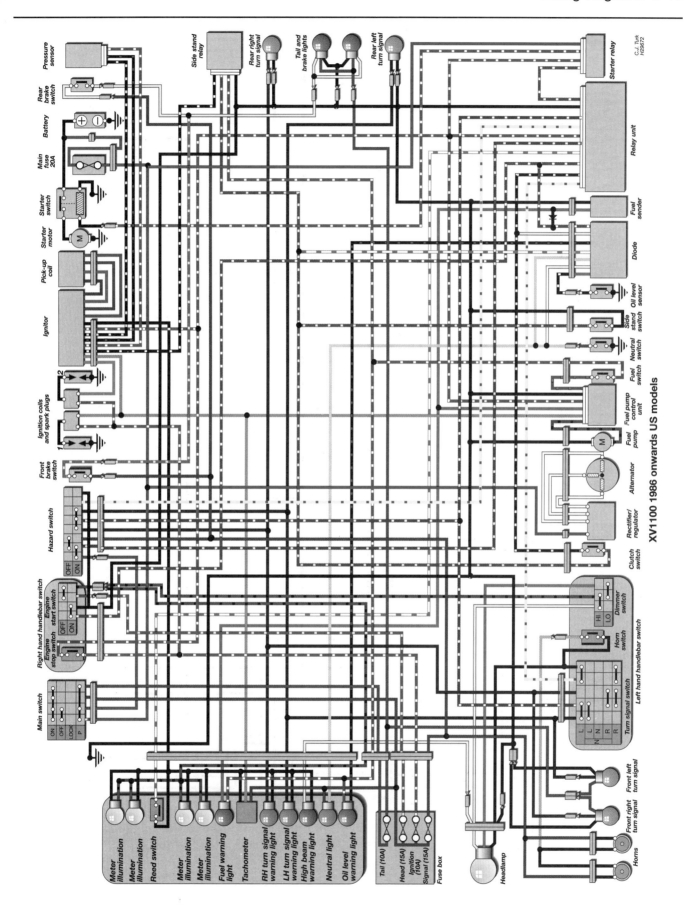

Pressure sensor

Rear brake switch

Battery

Main fuse 20A

Starter switch

Starter motor

Pick-up coil

Ignitor

Ignition coils and spark plugs

Front brake switch

Hazard switch

Right hand handlebar switch

Engine stop switch

Engine start switch

Main switch

ON
OFF
LOCK
P

Side stand relay

Rear right turn signal

Tail and brake lights

Rear left turn signal

Starter relay

Relay unit

Fuel sender

Diode

Oil level sensor

Side stand switch

Neutral switch

Fuel switch

Fuel pump control unit

Fuel pump

Alternator

Rectifier/ regulator

Clutch switch

Dimmer switch

HI
LO

Horn switch

Left hand handlebar switch

Turn signal switch

L  L  N  R  R

C.J. Turk
H29672

XV1100 1986 onwards US models

Front left turn signal

Front right turn signal

Horns

Meter illumination
Meter illumination
Reed switch
Meter illumination
Meter illumination
Fuel warning light
Tachometer
RH turn signal warning light
LH turn signal warning light
High beam warning light
Neutral light
Oil level warning light

Tail (10A)
Head (15A)
Ignition (10A)
Signal (15A)

Fuse box

Headlamp

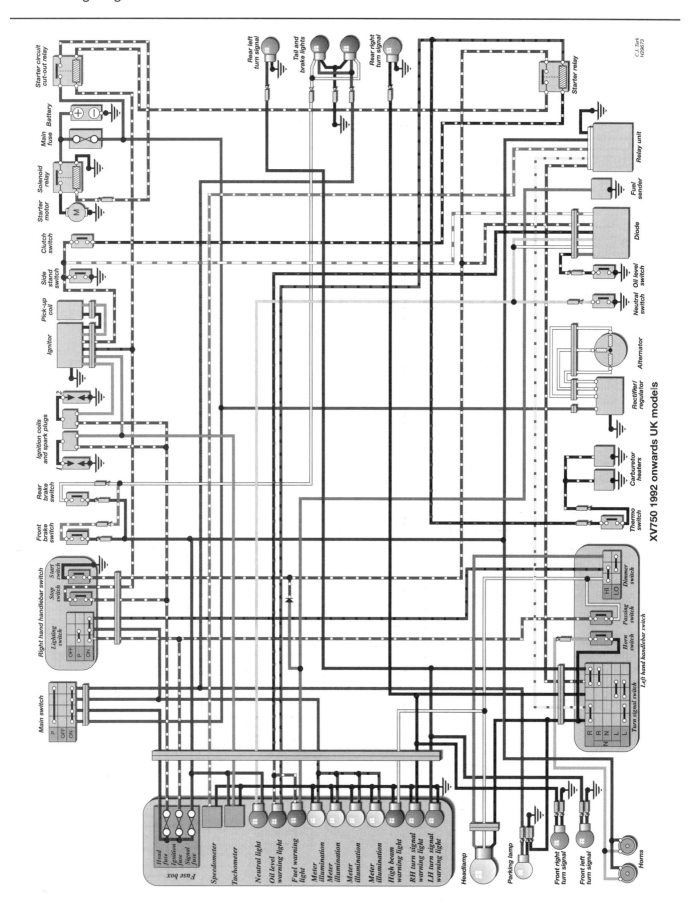

XV750 1992 onwards UK models

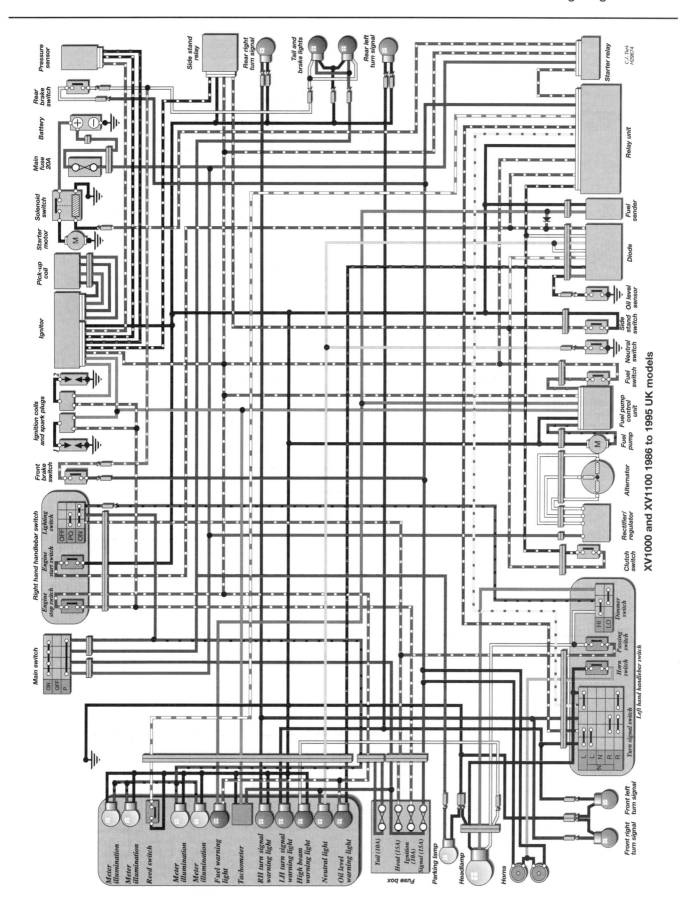

XV1000 and XV1100 1986 to 1995 UK models

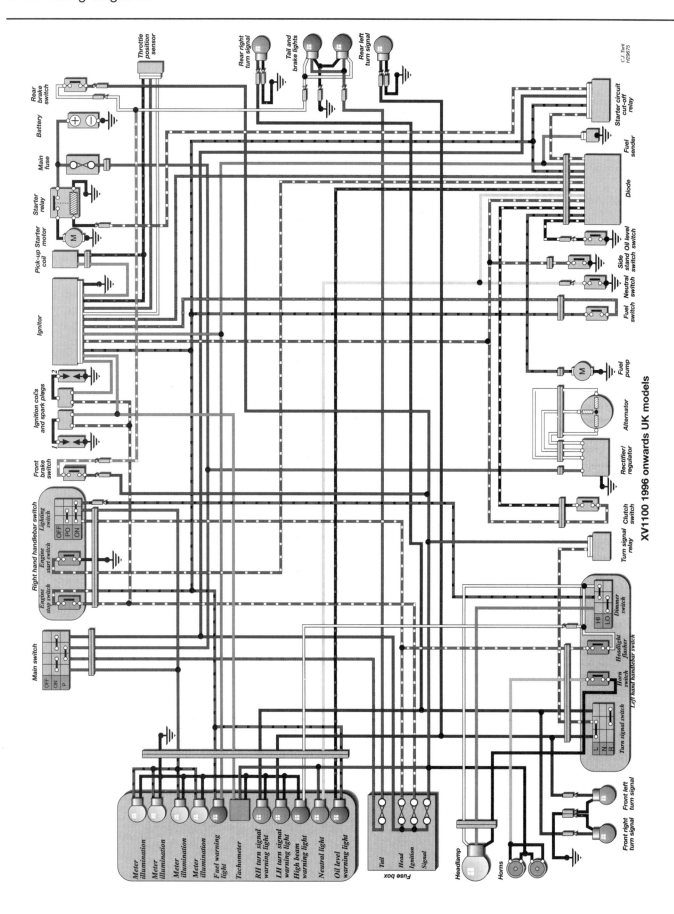

XV1100 1996 onwards UK models

# Reference

## Tools and Workshop Tips

- Building up a tool kit and equipping your workshop ● Using tools ● Understanding bearing, seal, fastener and chain sizes and markings ● Repair techniques

## Security

- Locks and chains ● U-locks ● Disc locks ● Alarms and immobilisers ● Security marking systems ● Tips on how to prevent bike theft

## Lubricants and fluids

- Engine oils ● Transmission (gear) oils ● Coolant/anti-freeze ● Fork oils and suspension fluids ● Brake/clutch fluids ● Spray lubes, degreasers and solvents

## Conversion Factors

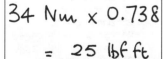

- Formulae for conversion of the metric (SI) units used throughout the manual into Imperial measures

## MOT Test Checks

- A guide to the UK MOT test ● Which items are tested ● How to prepare your motorcycle for the test and perform a pre-test check

## Storage

- How to prepare your motorcycle for going into storage and protect essential systems ● How to get the motorcycle back on the road

## Fault Finding

- Common faults and their likely causes ● How to check engine cylinder compression ● How to make electrical tests and use test meters

## Technical Terms Explained

- Component names, technical terms and common abbreviations explained

## Index

## Buying tools

A toolkit is a fundamental requirement for servicing and repairing a motorcycle. Although there will be an initial expense in building up enough tools for servicing, this will soon be offset by the savings made by doing the job yourself. As experience and confidence grow, additional tools can be added to enable the repair and overhaul of the motorcycle. Many of the specialist tools are expensive and not often used so it may be preferable to hire them, or for a group of friends or motorcycle club to join in the purchase.

As a rule, it is better to buy more expensive, good quality tools. Cheaper tools are likely to wear out faster and need to be renewed more often, nullifying the original saving.

> **Warning: To avoid the risk of a poor quality tool breaking in use, causing injury or damage to the component being worked on, always aim to purchase tools which meet the relevant national safety standards.**

The following lists of tools do not represent the manufacturer's service tools, but serve as a guide to help the owner decide which tools are needed for this level of work. In addition, items such as an electric drill, hacksaw, files, soldering iron and a workbench equipped with a vice, may be needed. Although not classed as tools, a selection of bolts, screws, nuts, washers and pieces of tubing always come in useful.

For more information about tools, refer to the Haynes *Motorcycle Workshop Practice TechBook* (Bk. No. 3470).

## Manufacturer's service tools

Inevitably certain tasks require the use of a service tool. Where possible an alternative tool or method of approach is recommended, but sometimes there is no option if personal injury or damage to the component is to be avoided. Where required, service tools are referred to in the relevant procedure.

Service tools can usually only be purchased from a motorcycle dealer and are identified by a part number. Some of the commonly-used tools, such as rotor pullers, are available in aftermarket form from mail-order motorcycle tool and accessory suppliers.

# Maintenance and minor repair tools

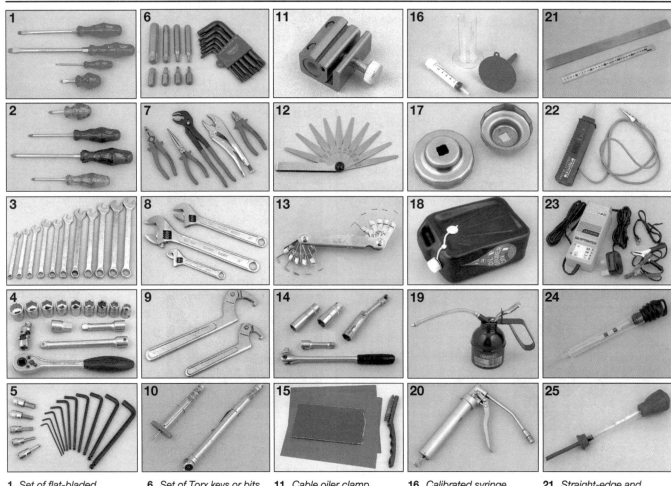

1 Set of flat-bladed screwdrivers
2 Set of Phillips head screwdrivers
3 Combination open-end and ring spanners
4 Socket set (3/8 inch or 1/2 inch drive)
5 Set of Allen keys or bits

6 Set of Torx keys or bits
7 Pliers, cutters and self-locking grips (Mole grips)
8 Adjustable spanners
9 C-spanners
10 Tread depth gauge and tyre pressure gauge

11 Cable oiler clamp
12 Feeler gauges
13 Spark plug gap measuring tool
14 Spark plug spanner or deep plug sockets
15 Wire brush and emery paper

16 Calibrated syringe, measuring vessel and funnel
17 Oil filter adapters
18 Oil drainer can or tray
19 Pump type oil can
20 Grease gun

21 Straight-edge and steel rule
22 Continuity tester
23 Battery charger
24 Hydrometer (for battery specific gravity check)
25 Anti-freeze tester (for liquid-cooled engines)

# Repair and overhaul tools

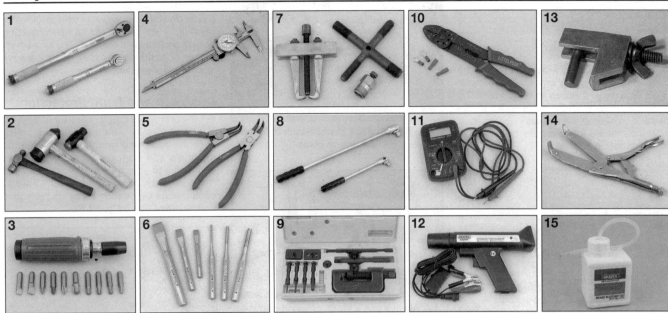

1 Torque wrench
   (small and mid-ranges)
2 Conventional, plastic or
   soft-faced hammers
3 Impact driver set

4 Vernier gauge
5 Circlip pliers (internal and
   external, or combination)
6 Set of cold chisels
   and punches

7 Selection of pullers
8 Breaker bars
9 Chain breaking/
   riveting tool set

10 Wire stripper and
   crimper tool
11 Multimeter (measures
   amps, volts and ohms)
12 Stroboscope (for
   dynamic timing checks)

13 Hose clamp
   (wingnut type shown)
14 Clutch holding tool
15 One-man brake/clutch
   bleeder kit

# Specialist tools

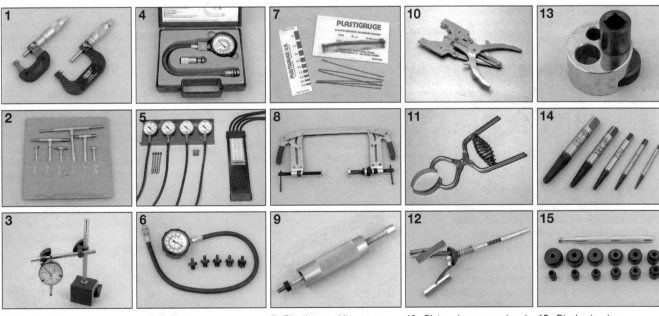

1 Micrometers
   (external type)
2 Telescoping gauges
3 Dial gauge

4 Cylinder
   compression gauge
5 Vacuum gauges (left) or
   manometer (right)
6 Oil pressure gauge

7 Plastigauge kit
8 Valve spring compressor
   (4-stroke engines)
9 Piston pin drawbolt tool

10 Piston ring removal and
   installation tool
11 Piston ring clamp
12 Cylinder bore hone
   (stone type shown)

13 Stud extractor
14 Screw extractor set
15 Bearing driver set

## 1 Workshop equipment and facilities

### The workbench

● Work is made much easier by raising the bike up on a ramp - components are much more accessible if raised to waist level. The hydraulic or pneumatic types seen in the dealer's workshop are a sound investment if you undertake a lot of repairs or overhauls (see illustration 1.1).

1.1 Hydraulic motorcycle ramp

● If raised off ground level, the bike must be supported on the ramp to avoid it falling. Most ramps incorporate a front wheel locating clamp which can be adjusted to suit different diameter wheels. When tightening the clamp, take care not to mark the wheel rim or damage the tyre - use wood blocks on each side to prevent this.

● Secure the bike to the ramp using tie-downs (see illustration 1.2). If the bike has only a sidestand, and hence leans at a dangerous angle when raised, support the bike on an auxiliary stand.

1.2 Tie-downs are used around the passenger footrests to secure the bike

● Auxiliary (paddock) stands are widely available from mail order companies or motorcycle dealers and attach either to the wheel axle or swingarm pivot (see illustration 1.3). If the motorcycle has a centrestand, you can support it under the crankcase to prevent it toppling whilst either wheel is removed (see illustration 1.4).

1.3 This auxiliary stand attaches to the swingarm pivot

1.4 Always use a block of wood between the engine and jack head when supporting the engine in this way

### Fumes and fire

● Refer to the Safety first! page at the beginning of the manual for full details. Make sure your workshop is equipped with a fire extinguisher suitable for fuel-related fires (Class B fire - flammable liquids) - it is not sufficient to have a water-filled extinguisher.

● Always ensure adequate ventilation is available. Unless an exhaust gas extraction system is available for use, ensure that the engine is run outside of the workshop.

● If working on the fuel system, make sure the workshop is ventilated to avoid a build-up of fumes. This applies equally to fume build-up when charging a battery. Do not smoke or allow anyone else to smoke in the workshop.

### Fluids

● If you need to drain fuel from the tank, store it in an approved container marked as suitable for the storage of petrol (gasoline) (see illustration 1.5). Do not store fuel in glass jars or bottles.

1.5 Use an approved can only for storing petrol (gasoline)

● Use proprietary engine degreasers or solvents which have a high flash-point, such as paraffin (kerosene), for cleaning off oil, grease and dirt - never use petrol (gasoline) for cleaning. Wear rubber gloves when handling solvent and engine degreaser. The fumes from certain solvents can be dangerous - always work in a well-ventilated area.

### Dust, eye and hand protection

● Protect your lungs from inhalation of dust particles by wearing a filtering mask over the nose and mouth. Many frictional materials still contain asbestos which is dangerous to your health. Protect your eyes from spouts of liquid and sprung components by wearing a pair of protective goggles (see illustration 1.6).

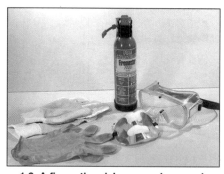

1.6 A fire extinguisher, goggles, mask and protective gloves should be at hand in the workshop

● Protect your hands from contact with solvents, fuel and oils by wearing rubber gloves. Alternatively apply a barrier cream to your hands before starting work. If handling hot components or fluids, wear suitable gloves to protect your hands from scalding and burns.

### What to do with old fluids

● Old cleaning solvent, fuel, coolant and oils should not be poured down domestic drains or onto the ground. Package the fluid up in old oil containers, label it accordingly, and take it to a garage or disposal facility. Contact your local authority for location of such sites or ring the oil care hotline.

OIL CARE
FOLLOW THE CODE
OIL BANK LINE
0800 66 33 66
www.oilbankline.org.uk

Note: It is antisocial and illegal to dump oil down the drain. To find the location of your local oil recycling bank, call this number free.

In the USA, note that any oil supplier must accept used oil for recycling.

## 2 Fasteners -
screws, bolts and nuts

### Fastener types and applications

#### Bolts and screws

● Fastener head types are either of hexagonal, Torx or splined design, with internal and external versions of each type (see illustrations 2.1 and 2.2); splined head fasteners are not in common use on motorcycles. The conventional slotted or Phillips head design is used for certain screws. Bolt or screw length is always measured from the underside of the head to the end of the item (see illustration 2.11).

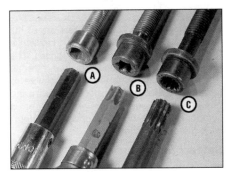

**2.1 Internal hexagon/Allen (A), Torx (B) and splined (C) fasteners, with corresponding bits**

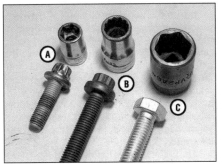

**2.2 External Torx (A), splined (B) and hexagon (C) fasteners, with corresponding sockets**

● Certain fasteners on the motorcycle have a tensile marking on their heads, the higher the marking the stronger the fastener. High tensile fasteners generally carry a 10 or higher marking. Never replace a high tensile fastener with one of a lower tensile strength.

#### Washers (see illustration 2.3)

● Plain washers are used between a fastener head and a component to prevent damage to the component or to spread the load when torque is applied. Plain washers can also be used as spacers or shims in certain assemblies. Copper or aluminium plain washers are often used as sealing washers on drain plugs.

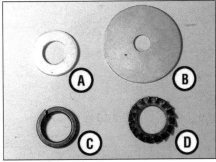

**2.3 Plain washer (A), penny washer (B), spring washer (C) and serrated washer (D)**

● The split-ring spring washer works by applying axial tension between the fastener head and component. If flattened, it is fatigued and must be renewed. If a plain (flat) washer is used on the fastener, position the spring washer between the fastener and the plain washer.
● Serrated star type washers dig into the fastener and component faces, preventing loosening. They are often used on electrical earth (ground) connections to the frame.
● Cone type washers (sometimes called Belleville) are conical and when tightened apply axial tension between the fastener head and component. They must be installed with the dished side against the component and often carry an OUTSIDE marking on their outer face. If flattened, they are fatigued and must be renewed.
● Tab washers are used to lock plain nuts or bolts on a shaft. A portion of the tab washer is bent up hard against one flat of the nut or bolt to prevent it loosening. Due to the tab washer being deformed in use, a new tab washer should be used every time it is disturbed.
● Wave washers are used to take up endfloat on a shaft. They provide light springing and prevent excessive side-to-side play of a component. Can be found on rocker arm shafts.

#### Nuts and split pins

● Conventional plain nuts are usually six-sided (see illustration 2.4). They are sized by thread diameter and pitch. High tensile nuts carry a number on one end to denote their tensile strength.

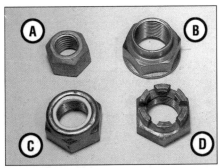

**2.4 Plain nut (A), shouldered locknut (B), nylon insert nut (C) and castellated nut (D)**

● Self-locking nuts either have a nylon insert, or two spring metal tabs, or a shoulder which is staked into a groove in the shaft - their advantage over conventional plain nuts is a resistance to loosening due to vibration. The nylon insert type can be used a number of times, but must be renewed when the friction of the nylon insert is reduced, ie when the nut spins freely on the shaft. The spring tab type can be reused unless the tabs are damaged. The shouldered type must be renewed every time it is disturbed.
● Split pins (cotter pins) are used to lock a castellated nut to a shaft or to prevent slackening of a plain nut. Common applications are wheel axles and brake torque arms. Because the split pin arms are deformed to lock around the nut a new split pin must always be used on installation - always fit the correct size split pin which will fit snugly in the shaft hole. Make sure the split pin arms are correctly located around the nut (see illustrations 2.5 and 2.6).

**2.5 Bend split pin (cotter pin) arms as shown (arrows) to secure a castellated nut**

**2.6 Bend split pin (cotter pin) arms as shown to secure a plain nut**

*Caution: If the castellated nut slots do not align with the shaft hole after tightening to the torque setting, tighten the nut until the next slot aligns with the hole - never slacken the nut to align its slot.*

● R-pins (shaped like the letter R), or slip pins as they are sometimes called, are sprung and can be reused if they are otherwise in good condition. Always install R-pins with their closed end facing forwards (see illustration 2.7).

**2.7 Correct fitting of R-pin. Arrow indicates forward direction**

## Circlips (see illustration 2.8)

● Circlips (sometimes called snap-rings) are used to retain components on a shaft or in a housing and have corresponding external or internal ears to permit removal. Parallel-sided (machined) circlips can be installed either way round in their groove, whereas stamped circlips (which have a chamfered edge on one face) must be installed with the chamfer facing away from the direction of thrust load **(see illustration 2.9)**.

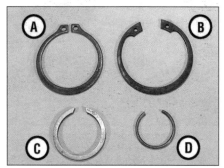

**2.8 External stamped circlip (A), internal stamped circlip (B), machined circlip (C) and wire circlip (D)**

● Always use circlip pliers to remove and install circlips; expand or compress them just enough to remove them. After installation, rotate the circlip in its groove to ensure it is securely seated. If installing a circlip on a splined shaft, always align its opening with a shaft channel to ensure the circlip ends are well supported and unlikely to catch **(see illustration 2.10)**.

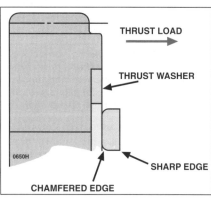

**2.9 Correct fitting of a stamped circlip**

THRUST LOAD
THRUST WASHER
SHARP EDGE
CHAMFERED EDGE
0650H

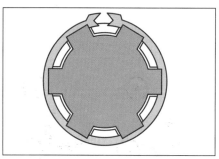

**2.10 Align circlip opening with shaft channel**

● Circlips can wear due to the thrust of components and become loose in their grooves, with the subsequent danger of becoming dislodged in operation. For this reason, renewal is advised every time a circlip is disturbed.

● Wire circlips are commonly used as piston pin retaining clips. If a removal tang is provided, long-nosed pliers can be used to dislodge them, otherwise careful use of a small flat-bladed screwdriver is necessary. Wire circlips should be renewed every time they are disturbed.

## Thread diameter and pitch

● Diameter of a male thread (screw, bolt or stud) is the outside diameter of the threaded portion **(see illustration 2.11)**. Most motorcycle manufacturers use the ISO (International Standards Organisation) metric system expressed in millimetres, eg M6 refers to a 6 mm diameter thread. Sizing is the same for nuts, except that the thread diameter is measured across the valleys of the nut.

● Pitch is the distance between the peaks of the thread **(see illustration 2.11)**. It is expressed in millimetres, thus a common bolt size may be expressed as 6.0 x 1.0 mm (6 mm thread diameter and 1 mm pitch). Generally pitch increases in proportion to thread diameter, although there are always exceptions.

● Thread diameter and pitch are related for conventional fastener applications and the accompanying table can be used as a guide. Additionally, the AF (Across Flats), spanner or socket size dimension of the bolt or nut **(see illustration 2.11)** is linked to thread and pitch specification. Thread pitch can be measured with a thread gauge **(see illustration 2.12)**.

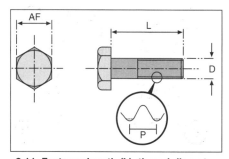

**2.11 Fastener length (L), thread diameter (D), thread pitch (P) and head size (AF)**

**2.12 Using a thread gauge to measure pitch**

| AF size | Thread diameter x pitch (mm) |
|---------|------------------------------|
| 8 mm | M5 x 0.8 |
| 8 mm | M6 x 1.0 |
| 10 mm | M6 x 1.0 |
| 12 mm | M8 x 1.25 |
| 14 mm | M10 x 1.25 |
| 17 mm | M12 x 1.25 |

● The threads of most fasteners are of the right-hand type, ie they are turned clockwise to tighten and anti-clockwise to loosen. The reverse situation applies to left-hand thread fasteners, which are turned anti-clockwise to tighten and clockwise to loosen. Left-hand threads are used where rotation of a component might loosen a conventional right-hand thread fastener.

## Seized fasteners

● Corrosion of external fasteners due to water or reaction between two dissimilar metals can occur over a period of time. It will build up sooner in wet conditions or in countries where salt is used on the roads during the winter. If a fastener is severely corroded it is likely that normal methods of removal will fail and result in its head being ruined. When you attempt removal, the fastener thread should be heard to crack free and unscrew easily - if it doesn't, stop there before damaging something.

● A smart tap on the head of the fastener will often succeed in breaking free corrosion which has occurred in the threads **(see illustration 2.13)**.

● An aerosol penetrating fluid (such as WD-40) applied the night beforehand may work its way down into the thread and ease removal. Depending on the location, you may be able to make up a Plasticine well around the fastener head and fill it with penetrating fluid.

**2.13 A sharp tap on the head of a fastener will often break free a corroded thread**

● If you are working on an engine internal component, corrosion will most likely not be a problem due to the well lubricated environment. However, components can be very tight and an impact driver is a useful tool in freeing them **(see illustration 2.14)**.

**2.14 Using an impact driver
to free a fastener**

● Where corrosion has occurred between dissimilar metals (eg steel and aluminium alloy), the application of heat to the fastener head will create a disproportionate expansion rate between the two metals and break the seizure caused by the corrosion. Whether heat can be applied depends on the location of the fastener - any surrounding components likely to be damaged must first be removed **(see illustration 2.15)**. Heat can be applied using a paint stripper heat gun or clothes iron, or by immersing the component in boiling water - wear protective gloves to prevent scalding or burns to the hands.

**2.15 Using heat to free a seized fastener**

● As a last resort, it is possible to use a hammer and cold chisel to work the fastener head unscrewed **(see illustration 2.16)**. This will damage the fastener, but more importantly extreme care must be taken not to damage the surrounding component.

*Caution: Remember that the component being secured is generally of more value than the bolt, nut or screw - when the fastener is freed, do not unscrew it with force, instead work the fastener back and forth when resistance is felt to prevent thread damage.*

**2.16 Using a hammer and chisel
to free a seized fastener**

## Broken fasteners and damaged heads

● If the shank of a broken bolt or screw is accessible you can grip it with self-locking grips. The knurled wheel type stud extractor tool or self-gripping stud puller tool is particularly useful for removing the long studs which screw into the cylinder mouth surface of the crankcase or bolts and screws from which the head has broken off **(see illustration 2.17)**. Studs can also be removed by locking two nuts together on the threaded end of the stud and using a spanner on the lower nut **(see illustration 2.18)**.

**2.17 Using a stud extractor tool to remove
a broken crankcase stud**

**2.18 Two nuts can be locked together to
unscrew a stud from a component**

● A bolt or screw which has broken off below or level with the casing must be extracted using a screw extractor set. Centre punch the fastener to centralise the drill bit, then drill a hole in the fastener **(see illustration 2.19)**. Select a drill bit which is approximately half to three-quarters the

**2.19 When using a screw extractor,
first drill a hole in the fastener . . .**

diameter of the fastener and drill to a depth which will accommodate the extractor. Use the largest size extractor possible, but avoid leaving too small a wall thickness otherwise the extractor will merely force the fastener walls outwards wedging it in the casing thread.

● If a spiral type extractor is used, thread it anti-clockwise into the fastener. As it is screwed in, it will grip the fastener and unscrew it from the casing **(see illustration 2.20)**.

**2.20 . . . then thread the extractor
anti-clockwise into the fastener**

● If a taper type extractor is used, tap it into the fastener so that it is firmly wedged in place. Unscrew the extractor (anti-clockwise) to draw the fastener out.

> ⚠ *Warning: Stud extractors are very hard and may break off in the fastener if care is not taken - ask an engineer about spark erosion if this happens.*

● Alternatively, the broken bolt/screw can be drilled out and the hole retapped for an oversize bolt/screw or a diamond-section thread insert. It is essential that the drilling is carried out squarely and to the correct depth, otherwise the casing may be ruined - if in doubt, entrust the work to an engineer.

● Bolts and nuts with rounded corners cause the correct size spanner or socket to slip when force is applied. Of the types of spanner/socket available always use a six-point type rather than an eight or twelve-point type - better grip

2.21 Comparison of surface drive ring spanner (left) with 12-point type (right)

is obtained. Surface drive spanners grip the middle of the hex flats, rather than the corners, and are thus good in cases of damaged heads (see illustration 2.21).

● Slotted-head or Phillips-head screws are often damaged by the use of the wrong size screwdriver. Allen-head and Torx-head screws are much less likely to sustain damage. If enough of the screw head is exposed you can use a hacksaw to cut a slot in its head and then use a conventional flat-bladed screwdriver to remove it. Alternatively use a hammer and cold chisel to tap the head of the fastener around to slacken it. Always replace damaged fasteners with new ones, preferably Torx or Allen-head type.

A dab of valve grinding compound between the screw head and screwdriver tip will often give a good grip.

## Thread repair

● Threads (particularly those in aluminium alloy components) can be damaged by overtightening, being assembled with dirt in the threads, or from a component working loose and vibrating. Eventually the thread will fail completely, and it will be impossible to tighten the fastener.

● If a thread is damaged or clogged with old locking compound it can be renovated with a thread repair tool (thread chaser) (see illustrations 2.22 and 2.23); special thread

2.22 A thread repair tool being used to correct an internal thread

2.23 A thread repair tool being used to correct an external thread

chasers are available for spark plug hole threads. The tool will not cut a new thread, but clean and true the original thread. Make sure that you use the correct diameter and pitch tool. Similarly, external threads can be cleaned up with a die or a thread restorer file (see illustration 2.24).

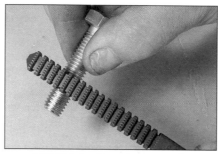

2.24 Using a thread restorer file

● It is possible to drill out the old thread and retap the component to the next thread size. This will work where there is enough surrounding material and a new bolt or screw can be obtained. Sometimes, however, this is not possible - such as where the bolt/screw passes through another component which must also be suitably modified, also in cases where a spark plug or oil drain plug cannot be obtained in a larger diameter thread size.

● The diamond-section thread insert (often known by its popular trade name of Heli-Coil) is a simple and effective method of renewing the thread and retaining the original size. A kit can be purchased which contains the tap, insert and installing tool (see illustration 2.25). Drill out the damaged thread with the size drill specified (see illustration 2.26). Carefully retap the thread (see illustration 2.27). Install the

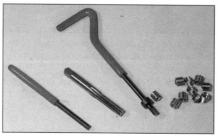

2.25 Obtain a thread insert kit to suit the thread diameter and pitch required

2.26 To install a thread insert, first drill out the original thread . . .

2.27 . . . tap a new thread . . .

2.28 . . . fit insert on the installing tool . . .

2.29 . . . and thread into the component . . .

2.30 . . . break off the tang when complete

insert on the installing tool and thread it slowly into place using a light downward pressure (see illustrations 2.28 and 2.29). When positioned between a 1/4 and 1/2 turn below the surface withdraw the installing tool and use the break-off tool to press down on the tang, breaking it off (see illustration 2.30).

● There are epoxy thread repair kits on the market which can rebuild stripped internal threads, although this repair should not be used on high load-bearing components.

## Thread locking and sealing compounds

● Locking compounds are used in locations where the fastener is prone to loosening due to vibration or on important safety-related items which might cause loss of control of the motorcycle if they fail. It is also used where important fasteners cannot be secured by other means such as lockwashers or split pins.

● Before applying locking compound, make sure that the threads (internal and external) are clean and dry with all old compound removed. Select a compound to suit the component being secured - a non-permanent general locking and sealing type is suitable for most applications, but a high strength type is needed for permanent fixing of studs in castings. Apply a drop or two of the compound to the first few threads of the fastener, then thread it into place and tighten to the specified torque. Do not apply excessive thread locking compound otherwise the thread may be damaged on subsequent removal.

● Certain fasteners are impregnated with a dry film type coating of locking compound on their threads. Always renew this type of fastener if disturbed.

● Anti-seize compounds, such as copper-based greases, can be applied to protect threads from seizure due to extreme heat and corrosion. A common instance is spark plug threads and exhaust system fasteners.

---

## 3 Measuring tools and gauges

---

## Feeler gauges

● Feeler gauges (or blades) are used for measuring small gaps and clearances (see illustration 3.1). They can also be used to measure endfloat (sideplay) of a component on a shaft where access is not possible with a dial gauge.

● Feeler gauge sets should be treated with care and not bent or damaged. They are etched with their size on one face. Keep them clean and very lightly oiled to prevent corrosion build-up.

**3.1 Feeler gauges are used for measuring small gaps and clearances - thickness is marked on one face of gauge**

---

● When measuring a clearance, select a gauge which is a light sliding fit between the two components. You may need to use two gauges together to measure the clearance accurately.

## Micrometers

● A micrometer is a precision tool capable of measuring to 0.01 or 0.001 of a millimetre. It should always be stored in its case and not in the general toolbox. It must be kept clean and never dropped, otherwise its frame or measuring anvils could be distorted resulting in inaccurate readings.

● External micrometers are used for measuring outside diameters of components and have many more applications than internal micrometers. Micrometers are available in different size ranges, eg 0 to 25 mm, 25 to 50 mm, and upwards in 25 mm steps; some large micrometers have interchangeable anvils to allow a range of measurements to be taken. Generally the largest precision measurement you are likely to take on a motorcycle is the piston diameter.

● Internal micrometers (or bore micrometers) are used for measuring inside diameters, such as valve guides and cylinder bores. Telescoping gauges and small hole gauges are used in conjunction with an external micro-meter, whereas the more expensive internal micrometers have their own measuring device.

### External micrometer

**Note:** *The conventional analogue type instrument is described. Although much easier to read, digital micrometers are considerably more expensive.*

● Always check the calibration of the micrometer before use. With the anvils closed (0 to 25 mm type) or set over a test gauge (for

---

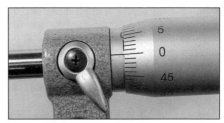

**3.2 Check micrometer calibration before use**

the larger types) the scale should read zero (see illustration 3.2); make sure that the anvils (and test piece) are clean first. Any discrepancy can be adjusted by referring to the instructions supplied with the tool. Remember that the micrometer is a precision measuring tool - don't force the anvils closed, use the ratchet (4) on the end of the micrometer to close it. In this way, a measured force is always applied.

● To use, first make sure that the item being measured is clean. Place the anvil of the micrometer (1) against the item and use the thimble (2) to bring the spindle (3) lightly into contact with the other side of the item (see illustration 3.3). Don't tighten the thimble down because this will damage the micrometer - instead use the ratchet (4) on the end of the micrometer. The ratchet mechanism applies a measured force preventing damage to the instrument.

● The micrometer is read by referring to the linear scale on the sleeve and the annular scale on the thimble. Read off the sleeve first to obtain the base measurement, then add the fine measurement from the thimble to obtain the overall reading. The linear scale on the sleeve represents the measuring range of the micrometer (eg 0 to 25 mm). The annular scale

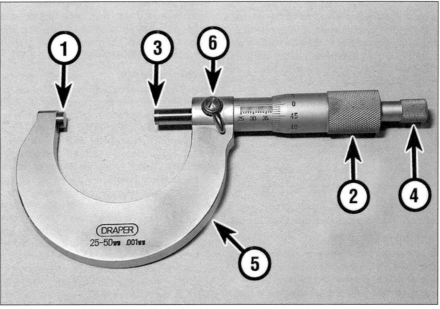

**3.3 Micrometer component parts**

| | | |
|---|---|---|
| 1 Anvil | 3 Spindle | 5 Frame |
| 2 Thimble | 4 Ratchet | 6 Locking lever |

on the thimble will be in graduations of 0.01 mm (or as marked on the frame) - one full revolution of the thimble will move 0.5 mm on the linear scale. Take the reading where the datum line on the sleeve intersects the thimble's scale. Always position the eye directly above the scale otherwise an inaccurate reading will result.

In the example shown the item measures 2.95 mm **(see illustration 3.4)**:

| | |
|---|---|
| Linear scale | 2.00 mm |
| Linear scale | 0.50 mm |
| Annular scale | 0.45 mm |
| **Total figure** | **2.95 mm** |

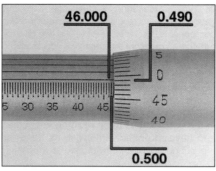

**3.5  Micrometer reading of 46.99 mm on linear and annular scales . . .**

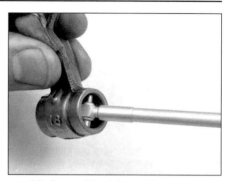

**3.7  Expand the telescoping gauge in the bore, lock its position . . .**

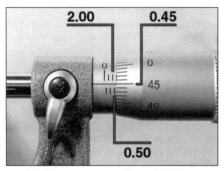

**3.4  Micrometer reading of 2.95 mm**

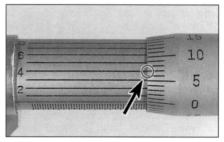

**3.6  . . . and 0.004 mm on vernier scale**

**3.8  . . . then measure the gauge with a micrometer**

Most micrometers have a locking lever (6) on the frame to hold the setting in place, allowing the item to be removed from the micrometer.
● Some micrometers have a vernier scale on their sleeve, providing an even finer measurement to be taken, in 0.001 increments of a millimetre. Take the sleeve and thimble measurement as described above, then check which graduation on the vernier scale aligns with that of the annular scale on the thimble **Note:** *The eye must be perpendicular to the scale when taking the vernier reading - if necessary rotate the body of the micrometer to ensure this.* Multiply the vernier scale figure by 0.001 and add it to the base and fine measurement figures.

In the example shown the item measures 46.994 mm **(see illustrations 3.5 and 3.6)**:

| | |
|---|---|
| Linear scale (base) | 46.000 mm |
| Linear scale (base) | 00.500 mm |
| Annular scale (fine) | 00.490 mm |
| Vernier scale | 00.004 mm |
| **Total figure** | **46.994 mm** |

### Internal micrometer

● Internal micrometers are available for measuring bore diameters, but are expensive and unlikely to be available for home use. It is suggested that a set of telescoping gauges and small hole gauges, both of which must be used with an external micrometer, will suffice for taking internal measurements on a motorcycle.
● Telescoping gauges can be used to

measure internal diameters of components. Select a gauge with the correct size range, make sure its ends are clean and insert it into the bore. Expand the gauge, then lock its position and withdraw it from the bore **(see illustration 3.7)**. Measure across the gauge ends with a micrometer **(see illustration 3.8)**.
● Very small diameter bores (such as valve guides) are measured with a small hole gauge. Once adjusted to a slip-fit inside the component, its position is locked and the gauge withdrawn for measurement with a micrometer **(see illustrations 3.9 and 3.10)**.

### Vernier caliper

**Note:** *The conventional linear and dial gauge type instruments are described. Digital types are easier to read, but are far more expensive.*
● The vernier caliper does not provide the precision of a micrometer, but is versatile in being able to measure internal and external diameters. Some types also incorporate a depth gauge. It is ideal for measuring clutch plate friction material and spring free lengths.
● To use the conventional linear scale vernier, slacken off the vernier clamp screws (1) and set its jaws over (2), or inside (3), the item to be measured **(see illustration 3.11)**. Slide the jaw into contact, using the thumbwheel (4) for fine movement of the sliding scale (5) then tighten the clamp screws (1). Read off the main scale (6) where the zero on the sliding scale (5) intersects it, taking the whole number to the left of the zero; this provides the base measurement. View along the sliding scale and select the division which

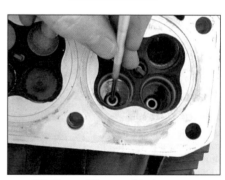

**3.9  Expand the small hole gauge in the bore, lock its position . . .**

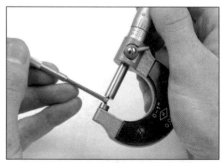

**3.10  . . . then measure the gauge with a micrometer**

lines up exactly with any of the divisions on the main scale, noting that the divisions usually represents 0.02 of a millimetre. Add this fine measurement to the base measurement to obtain the total reading.

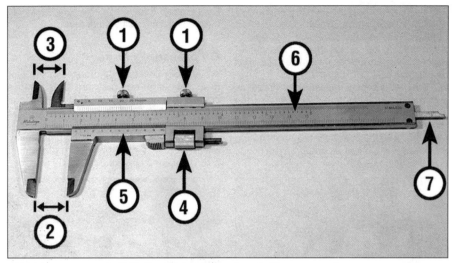

**3.11 Vernier component parts (linear gauge)**

| 1 | Clamp screws | 3 | Internal jaws | 5 | Sliding scale | 7 | Depth gauge |
| 2 | External jaws | 4 | Thumbwheel | 6 | Main scale | | |

In the example shown the item measures 55.92 mm **(see illustration 3.12)**:

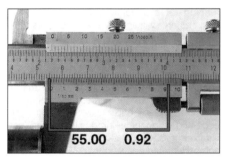

**3.12 Vernier gauge reading of 55.92 mm**

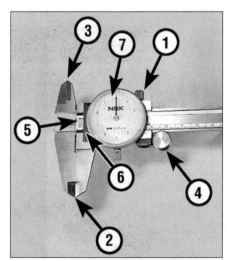

**3.13 Vernier component parts (dial gauge)**

| 1 | Clamp screw | 5 | Main scale |
| 2 | External jaws | 6 | Sliding scale |
| 3 | Internal jaws | 7 | Dial gauge |
| 4 | Thumbwheel | | |

| Base measurement | 55.00 mm |
| Fine measurement | 00.92 mm |
| Total figure | **55.92 mm** |

● Some vernier calipers are equipped with a dial gauge for fine measurement. Before use, check that the jaws are clean, then close them fully and check that the dial gauge reads zero. If necessary adjust the gauge ring accordingly. Slacken the vernier clamp screw (1) and set its jaws over (2), or inside (3), the item to be measured **(see illustration 3.13)**. Slide the jaws into contact, using the thumbwheel (4) for fine movement. Read off the main scale (5) where the edge of the sliding scale (6) intersects it, taking the whole number to the left of the zero; this provides the base measurement. Read off the needle position on the dial gauge (7) scale to provide the fine measurement; each division represents 0.05 of a millimetre. Add this fine measurement to the base measurement to obtain the total reading.

In the example shown the item measures 55.95 mm **(see illustration 3.14)**:

| Base measurement | 55.00 mm |
| Fine measurement | 00.95 mm |
| Total figure | **55.95 mm** |

**3.14 Vernier gauge reading of 55.95 mm**

## Plastigauge

● Plastigauge is a plastic material which can be compressed between two surfaces to measure the oil clearance between them. The width of the compressed Plastigauge is measured against a calibrated scale to determine the clearance.

● Common uses of Plastigauge are for measuring the clearance between crankshaft journal and main bearing inserts, between crankshaft journal and big-end bearing inserts, and between camshaft and bearing surfaces. The following example describes big-end oil clearance measurement.

● Handle the Plastigauge material carefully to prevent distortion. Using a sharp knife, cut a length which corresponds with the width of the bearing being measured and place it carefully across the journal so that it is parallel with the shaft **(see illustration 3.15)**. Carefully install both bearing shells and the connecting rod. Without rotating the rod on the journal tighten its bolts or nuts (as applicable) to the specified torque. The connecting rod and bearings are then disassembled and the crushed Plastigauge examined.

**3.15 Plastigauge placed across shaft journal**

● Using the scale provided in the Plastigauge kit, measure the width of the material to determine the oil clearance **(see illustration 3.16)**. Always remove all traces of Plastigauge after use using your fingernails.

*Caution: Arriving at the correct clearance demands that the assembly is torqued correctly, according to the settings and sequence (where applicable) provided by the motorcycle manufacturer.*

**3.16 Measuring the width of the crushed Plastigauge**

## Dial gauge or DTI (Dial Test Indicator)

● A dial gauge can be used to accurately measure small amounts of movement. Typical uses are measuring shaft runout or shaft endfloat (sideplay) and setting piston position for ignition timing on two-strokes. A dial gauge set usually comes with a range of different probes and adapters and mounting equipment.

● The gauge needle must point to zero when at rest. Rotate the ring around its periphery to zero the gauge.

● Check that the gauge is capable of reading the extent of movement in the work. Most gauges have a small dial set in the face which records whole millimetres of movement as well as the fine scale around the face periphery which is calibrated in 0.01 mm divisions. Read off the small dial first to obtain the base measurement, then add the measurement from the fine scale to obtain the total reading.

In the example shown the gauge reads 1.48 mm **(see illustration 3.17)**:

| | |
|---|---|
| Base measurement | 1.00 mm |
| Fine measurement | 0.48 mm |
| Total figure | **1.48 mm** |

**3.17 Dial gauge reading of 1.48 mm**

● If measuring shaft runout, the shaft must be supported in vee-blocks and the gauge mounted on a stand perpendicular to the shaft. Rest the tip of the gauge against the centre of the shaft and rotate the shaft slowly whilst watching the gauge reading **(see illustration 3.18)**. Take several measurements along the length of the shaft and record the

**3.18 Using a dial gauge to measure shaft runout**

maximum gauge reading as the amount of runout in the shaft. **Note:** *The reading obtained will be total runout at that point - some manufacturers specify that the runout figure is halved to compare with their specified runout limit.*

● Endfloat (sideplay) measurement requires that the gauge is mounted securely to the surrounding component with its probe touching the end of the shaft. Using hand pressure, push and pull on the shaft noting the maximum endfloat recorded on the gauge **(see illustration 3.19)**.

**3.19 Using a dial gauge to measure shaft endfloat**

● A dial gauge with suitable adapters can be used to determine piston position BTDC on two-stroke engines for the purposes of ignition timing. The gauge, adapter and suitable length probe are installed in the place of the spark plug and the gauge zeroed at TDC. If the piston position is specified as 1.14 mm BTDC, rotate the engine back to 2.00 mm BTDC, then slowly forwards to 1.14 mm BTDC.

## Cylinder compression gauges

● A compression gauge is used for measuring cylinder compression. Either the rubber-cone type or the threaded adapter type can be used. The latter is preferred to ensure a perfect seal against the cylinder head. A 0 to 300 psi (0 to 20 Bar) type gauge (for petrol/gasoline engines) will be suitable for motorcycles.

● The spark plug is removed and the gauge either held hard against the cylinder head (cone type) or the gauge adapter screwed into the cylinder head (threaded type) **(see illustration 3.20)**. Cylinder compression is measured with the engine turning over, but not running - carry out the compression test as described in

**3.20 Using a rubber-cone type cylinder compression gauge**

*Fault Finding Equipment.* The gauge will hold the reading until manually released.

## Oil pressure gauge

● An oil pressure gauge is used for measuring engine oil pressure. Most gauges come with a set of adapters to fit the thread of the take-off point **(see illustration 3.21)**. If the take-off point specified by the motorcycle manufacturer is an external oil pipe union, make sure that the specified replacement union is used to prevent oil starvation.

**3.21 Oil pressure gauge and take-off point adapter (arrow)**

● Oil pressure is measured with the engine running (at a specific rpm) and often the manufacturer will specify pressure limits for a cold and hot engine.

## Straight-edge and surface plate

● If checking the gasket face of a component for warpage, place a steel rule or precision straight-edge across the gasket face and measure any gap between the straight-edge and component with feeler gauges **(see illustration 3.22)**. Check diagonally across the component and between mounting holes **(see illustration 3.23)**.

**3.22 Use a straight-edge and feeler gauges to check for warpage**

**3.23 Check for warpage in these directions**

● Checking individual components for warpage, such as clutch plain (metal) plates, requires a perfectly flat plate or piece or plate glass and feeler gauges.

## 4 Torque and leverage

### What is torque?

● Torque describes the twisting force about a shaft. The amount of torque applied is determined by the distance from the centre of the shaft to the end of the lever and the amount of force being applied to the end of the lever; distance multiplied by force equals torque.

● The manufacturer applies a measured torque to a bolt or nut to ensure that it will not slacken in use and to hold two components securely together without movement in the joint. The actual torque setting depends on the thread size, bolt or nut material and the composition of the components being held.

● Too little torque may cause the fastener to loosen due to vibration, whereas too much torque will distort the joint faces of the component or cause the fastener to shear off. Always stick to the specified torque setting.

### Using a torque wrench

● Check the calibration of the torque wrench and make sure it has a suitable range for the job. Torque wrenches are available in Nm (Newton-metres), kgf m (kilograms-force metre), lbf ft (pounds-feet), lbf in (inch-pounds). Do not confuse lbf ft with lbf in.

● Adjust the tool to the desired torque on the scale (see illustration 4.1). If your torque wrench is not calibrated in the units specified, carefully convert the figure (see *Conversion Factors*). A manufacturer sometimes gives a torque setting as a range (8 to 10 Nm) rather than a single figure - in this case set the tool midway between the two settings. The same torque may be expressed as 9 Nm ± 1 Nm. Some torque wrenches have a method of locking the setting so that it isn't inadvertently altered during use.

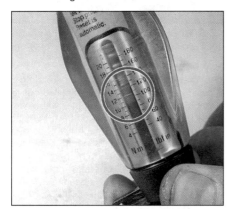

**4.1 Set the torque wrench index mark to the setting required, in this case 12 Nm**

● Install the bolts/nuts in their correct location and secure them lightly. Their threads must be clean and free of any old locking compound. Unless specified the threads and flange should be dry - oiled threads are necessary in certain circumstances and the manufacturer will take this into account in the specified torque figure. Similarly, the manufacturer may also specify the application of thread-locking compound.

● Tighten the fasteners in the specified sequence until the torque wrench clicks, indicating that the torque setting has been reached. Apply the torque again to double-check the setting. Where different thread diameter fasteners secure the component, as a rule tighten the larger diameter ones first.

● When the torque wrench has been finished with, release the lock (where applicable) and fully back off its setting to zero - do not leave the torque wrench tensioned. Also, do not use a torque wrench for slackening a fastener.

### Angle-tightening

● Manufacturers often specify a figure in degrees for final tightening of a fastener. This usually follows tightening to a specific torque setting.

● A degree disc can be set and attached to the socket (see illustration 4.2) or a protractor can be used to mark the angle of movement on the bolt/nut head and surrounding casting (see illustration 4.3).

**4.2 Angle tightening can be accomplished with a torque-angle gauge . . .**

**4.3 . . . or by marking the angle on the surrounding component**

### Loosening sequences

● Where more than one bolt/nut secures a component, loosen each fastener evenly a little at a time. In this way, not all the stress of the joint is held by one fastener and the components are not likely to distort.

● If a tightening sequence is provided, work in the REVERSE of this, but if not, work from the outside in, in a criss-cross sequence (see illustration 4.4).

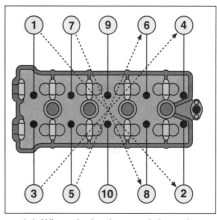

**4.4 When slackening, work from the outside inwards**

### Tightening sequences

● If a component is held by more than one fastener it is important that the retaining bolts/nuts are tightened evenly to prevent uneven stress build-up and distortion of sealing faces. This is especially important on high-compression joints such as the cylinder head.

● A sequence is usually provided by the manufacturer, either in a diagram or actually marked in the casting. If not, always start in the centre and work outwards in a criss-cross pattern (see illustration 4.5). Start off by securing all bolts/nuts finger-tight, then set the torque wrench and tighten each fastener by a small amount in sequence until the final torque is reached. By following this practice,

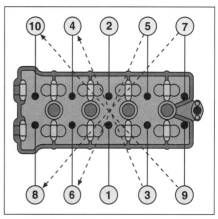

**4.5 When tightening, work from the inside outwards**

the joint will be held evenly and will not be distorted. Important joints, such as the cylinder head and big-end fasteners often have two- or three-stage torque settings.

## Applying leverage

● Use tools at the correct angle. Position a socket wrench or spanner on the bolt/nut so that you pull it towards you when loosening. If this can't be done, push the spanner without curling your fingers around it (see illustration 4.6) - the spanner may slip or the fastener loosen suddenly, resulting in your fingers being crushed against a component.

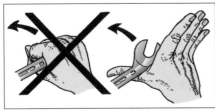

**4.6 If you can't pull on the spanner to loosen a fastener, push with your hand open**

● Additional leverage is gained by extending the length of the lever. The best way to do this is to use a breaker bar instead of the regular length tool, or to slip a length of tubing over the end of the spanner or socket wrench.
● If additional leverage will not work, the fastener head is either damaged or firmly corroded in place (see *Fasteners*).

## 5   Bearings

## Bearing removal and installation

### Drivers and sockets

● Before removing a bearing, always inspect the casing to see which way it must be driven out - some casings will have retaining plates or a cast step. Also check for any identifying markings on the bearing and if installed to a certain depth, measure this at this stage. Some roller bearings are sealed on one side - take note of the original fitted position.
● Bearings can be driven out of a casing using a bearing driver tool (with the correct size head) or a socket of the correct diameter. Select the driver head or socket so that it contacts the outer race of the bearing, not the balls/rollers or inner race. Always support the casing around the bearing housing with wood blocks, otherwise there is a risk of fracture. The bearing is driven out with a few blows on the driver or socket from a heavy mallet. Unless access is severely restricted (as with wheel bearings), a pin-punch is not recommended unless it is moved around the bearing to keep it square in its housing.

● The same equipment can be used to install bearings. Make sure the bearing housing is supported on wood blocks and line up the bearing in its housing. Fit the bearing as noted on removal - generally they are installed with their marked side facing outwards. Tap the bearing squarely into its housing using a driver or socket which bears only on the bearing's outer race - contact with the bearing balls/rollers or inner race will destroy it (see illustrations 5.1 and 5.2).
● Check that the bearing inner race and balls/rollers rotate freely.

**5.1  Using a bearing driver against the bearing's outer race**

**5.2  Using a large socket against the bearing's outer race**

### Pullers and slide-hammers

● Where a bearing is pressed on a shaft a puller will be required to extract it (see illustration 5.3). Make sure that the puller clamp or legs fit securely behind the bearing and are unlikely to slip out. If pulling a bearing

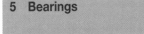

**5.3  This bearing puller clamps behind the bearing and pressure is applied to the shaft end to draw the bearing off**

off a gear shaft for example, you may have to locate the puller behind a gear pinion if there is no access to the race and draw the gear pinion off the shaft as well (see illustration 5.4).

*Caution: Ensure that the puller's centre bolt locates securely against the end of the shaft and will not slip when pressure is applied. Also ensure that puller does not damage the shaft end.*

**5.4  Where no access is available to the rear of the bearing, it is sometimes possible to draw off the adjacent component**

● Operate the puller so that its centre bolt exerts pressure on the shaft end and draws the bearing off the shaft.
● When installing the bearing on the shaft, tap only on the bearing's inner race - contact with the balls/rollers or outer race with destroy the bearing. Use a socket or length of tubing as a drift which fits over the shaft end (see illustration 5.5).

**5.5  When installing a bearing on a shaft use a piece of tubing which bears only on the bearing's inner race**

● Where a bearing locates in a blind hole in a casing, it cannot be driven or pulled out as described above. A slide-hammer with knife-edged bearing puller attachment will be required. The puller attachment passes through the bearing and when tightened expands to fit firmly behind the bearing (see illustration 5.6). By operating the slide-hammer part of the tool the bearing is jarred out of its housing (see illustration 5.7).
● It is possible, if the bearing is of reasonable weight, for it to drop out of its housing if the casing is heated as described opposite. If this

**5.6 Expand the bearing puller so that it locks behind the bearing . . .**

**5.7 . . . attach the slide hammer to the bearing puller**

method is attempted, first prepare a work surface which will enable the casing to be tapped face down to help dislodge the bearing - a wood surface is ideal since it will not damage the casing's gasket surface. Wearing protective gloves, tap the heated casing several times against the work surface to dislodge the bearing under its own weight **(see illustration 5.8)**.

**5.8 Tapping a casing face down on wood blocks can often dislodge a bearing**

● Bearings can be installed in blind holes using the driver or socket method described above.

## Drawbolts

● Where a bearing or bush is set in the eye of a component, such as a suspension linkage arm or connecting rod small-end, removal by drift may damage the component. Furthermore, a rubber bushing in a shock absorber eye cannot successfully be driven out of position. If access is available to a engineering press, the task is straightforward. If not, a drawbolt can be fabricated to extract the bearing or bush.

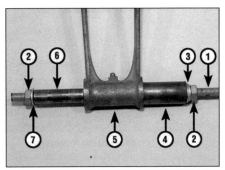

**5.9 Drawbolt component parts assembled on a suspension arm**

1 Bolt or length of threaded bar
2 Nuts
3 Washer (external diameter greater than tubing internal diameter)
4 Tubing (internal diameter sufficient to accommodate bearing)
5 Suspension arm with bearing
6 Tubing (external diameter slightly smaller than bearing)
7 Washer (external diameter slightly smaller than bearing)

**5.10 Drawing the bearing out of the suspension arm**

● To extract the bearing/bush you will need a long bolt with nut (or piece of threaded bar with two nuts), a piece of tubing which has an internal diameter larger than the bearing/bush, another piece of tubing which has an external diameter slightly smaller than the bearing/bush, and a selection of washers **(see illustrations 5.9 and 5.10)**. Note that the pieces of tubing must be of the same length, or longer, than the bearing/bush.
● The same kit (without the pieces of tubing) can be used to draw the new bearing/bush back into place **(see illustration 5.11)**.

**5.11 Installing a new bearing (1) in the suspension arm**

## Temperature change

● If the bearing's outer race is a tight fit in the casing, the aluminium casing can be heated to release its grip on the bearing. Aluminium will expand at a greater rate than the steel bearing outer race. There are several ways to do this, but avoid any localised extreme heat (such as a blow torch) - aluminium alloy has a low melting point.
● Approved methods of heating a casing are using a domestic oven (heated to 100°C) or immersing the casing in boiling water **(see illustration 5.12)**. Low temperature range localised heat sources such as a paint stripper heat gun or clothes iron can also be used **(see illustration 5.13)**. Alternatively, soak a rag in boiling water, wring it out and wrap it around the bearing housing.

> ⚠ **Warning: All of these methods require care in use to prevent scalding and burns to the hands. Wear protective gloves when handling hot components.**

**5.12 A casing can be immersed in a sink of boiling water to aid bearing removal**

**5.13 Using a localised heat source to aid bearing removal**

● If heating the whole casing note that plastic components, such as the neutral switch, may suffer - remove them beforehand.
● After heating, remove the bearing as described above. You may find that the expansion is sufficient for the bearing to fall out of the casing under its own weight or with a light tap on the driver or socket.
● If necessary, the casing can be heated to aid bearing installation, and this is sometimes the recommended procedure if the motorcycle manufacturer has designed the housing and bearing fit with this intention.

● Installation of bearings can be eased by placing them in a freezer the night before installation. The steel bearing will contract slightly, allowing easy insertion in its housing. This is often useful when installing steering head outer races in the frame.

### Bearing types and markings

● Plain shell bearings, ball bearings, needle roller bearings and tapered roller bearings will all be found on motorcycles (see illustrations 5.14 and 5.15). The ball and roller types are usually caged between an inner and outer race, but uncaged variations may be found.

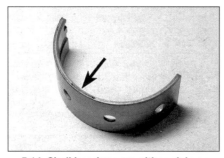

**5.14 Shell bearings are either plain or grooved. They are usually identified by colour code (arrow)**

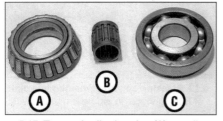

**5.15 Tapered roller bearing (A), needle roller bearing (B) and ball journal bearing (C)**

● Shell bearings (often called inserts) are usually found at the crankshaft main and connecting rod big-end where they are good at coping with high loads. They are made of a phosphor-bronze material and are impregnated with self-lubricating properties.
● Ball bearings and needle roller bearings consist of a steel inner and outer race with the balls or rollers between the races. They require constant lubrication by oil or grease and are good at coping with axial loads. Taper roller bearings consist of rollers set in a tapered cage set on the inner race; the outer race is separate. They are good at coping with axial loads and prevent movement along the shaft - a typical application is in the steering head.
● Bearing manufacturers produce bearings to ISO size standards and stamp one face of the bearing to indicate its internal and external diameter, load capacity and type (see illustration 5.16).
● Metal bushes are usually of phosphor-bronze material. Rubber bushes are used in suspension mounting eyes. Fibre bushes have also been used in suspension pivots.

**5.16 Typical bearing marking**

### Bearing fault finding

● If a bearing outer race has spun in its housing, the housing material will be damaged. You can use a bearing locking compound to bond the outer race in place if damage is not too severe.
● Shell bearings will fail due to damage of their working surface, as a result of lack of lubrication, corrosion or abrasive particles in the oil (see illustration 5.17). Small particles of dirt in the oil may embed in the bearing material whereas larger particles will score the bearing and shaft journal. If a number of short journeys are made, insufficient heat will be generated to drive off condensation which has built up on the bearings.

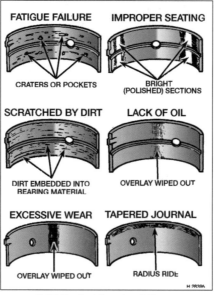

**5.17 Typical bearing failures**

● Ball and roller bearings will fail due to lack of lubrication or damage to the balls or rollers. Tapered-roller bearings can be damaged by overloading them. Unless the bearing is sealed on both sides, wash it in paraffin (kerosene) to remove all old grease then allow it to dry. Make a visual inspection looking to dented balls or rollers, damaged cages and worn or pitted races (see illustration 5.18).
● A ball bearing can be checked for wear by listening to it when spun. Apply a film of light oil to the bearing and hold it close to the ear - hold the outer race with one hand and spin the inner

**5.18 Example of ball journal bearing with damaged balls and cages**

**5.19 Hold outer race and listen to inner race when spun**

race with the other hand (see illustration 5.19). The bearing should be almost silent when spun; if it grates or rattles it is worn.

## 6 Oil seals

### Oil seal removal and installation

● Oil seals should be renewed every time a component is dismantled. This is because the seal lips will become set to the sealing surface and will not necessarily reseal.
● Oil seals can be prised out of position using a large flat-bladed screwdriver (see illustration 6.1). In the case of crankcase seals, check first that the seal is not lipped on the inside, preventing its removal with the crankcases joined.

**6.1 Prise out oil seals with a large flat-bladed screwdriver**

● New seals are usually installed with their marked face (containing the seal reference code) outwards and the spring side towards the fluid being retained. In certain cases, such as a two-stroke engine crankshaft seal, a double lipped seal may be used due to there being fluid or gas on each side of the joint.

● Use a bearing driver or socket which bears only on the outer hard edge of the seal to install it in the casing - tapping on the inner edge will damage the sealing lip.

## Oil seal types and markings

● Oil seals are usually of the single-lipped type. Double-lipped seals are found where a liquid or gas is on both sides of the joint.
● Oil seals can harden and lose their sealing ability if the motorcycle has been in storage for a long period - renewal is the only solution.
● Oil seal manufacturers also conform to the ISO markings for seal size - these are moulded into the outer face of the seal **(see illustration 6.2)**.

**6.2 These oil seal markings indicate inside diameter, outside diameter and seal thickness**

## 7 Gaskets and sealants

## Types of gasket and sealant

● Gaskets are used to seal the mating surfaces between components and keep lubricants, fluids, vacuum or pressure contained within the assembly. Aluminium gaskets are sometimes found at the cylinder joints, but most gaskets are paper-based. If the mating surfaces of the components being joined are undamaged the gasket can be installed dry, although a dab of sealant or grease will be useful to hold it in place during assembly.
● RTV (Room Temperature Vulcanising) silicone rubber sealants cure when exposed to moisture in the atmosphere. These sealants are good at filling pits or irregular gasket faces, but will tend to be forced out of the joint under very high torque. They can be used to replace a paper gasket, but first make sure that the width of the paper gasket is not essential to the shimming of internal components. RTV sealants should not be used on components containing petrol (gasoline).
● Non-hardening, semi-hardening and hard setting liquid gasket compounds can be used with a gasket or between a metal-to-metal joint. Select the sealant to suit the application: universal non-hardening sealant can be used on virtually all joints; semi-hardening on joint faces which are rough or damaged; hard setting sealant on joints which require a permanent bond and are subjected to high temperature and pressure. **Note:** *Check first if the paper gasket has a bead of sealant*

*impregnated in its surface before applying additional sealant.*
● When choosing a sealant, make sure it is suitable for the application, particularly if being applied in a high-temperature area or in the vicinity of fuel. Certain manufacturers produce sealants in either clear, silver or black colours to match the finish of the engine. This has a particular application on motorcycles where much of the engine is exposed.
● Do not over-apply sealant. That which is squeezed out on the outside of the joint can be wiped off, whereas an excess of sealant on the inside can break off and clog oilways.

## Breaking a sealed joint

● Age, heat, pressure and the use of hard setting sealant can cause two components to stick together so tightly that they are difficult to separate using finger pressure alone. Do not resort to using levers unless there is a pry point provided for this purpose **(see illustration 7.1)** or else the gasket surfaces will be damaged.
● Use a soft-faced hammer **(see illustration 7.2)** or a wood block and conventional hammer to strike the component near the mating surface. Avoid hammering against cast extremities since they may break off. If this method fails, try using a wood wedge between the two components.

**Caution: If the joint will not separate, double-check that you have removed all the fasteners.**

**7.1 If a pry point is provided, apply gently pressure with a flat-bladed screwdriver**

**7.2 Tap around the joint with a soft-faced mallet if necessary - don't strike cooling fins**

## Removal of old gasket and sealant

● Paper gaskets will most likely come away complete, leaving only a few traces stuck on

*Most components have one or two hollow locating dowels between the two gasket faces. If a dowel cannot be removed, do not resort to gripping it with pliers - it will almost certainly be distorted. Install a close-fitting socket or Phillips screwdriver into the dowel and then grip the outer edge of the dowel to free it.*

the sealing faces of the components. It is imperative that all traces are removed to ensure correct sealing of the new gasket.
● Very carefully scrape all traces of gasket away making sure that the sealing surfaces are not gouged or scored by the scraper **(see illustrations 7.3, 7.4 and 7.5)**. Stubborn deposits can be removed by spraying with an aerosol gasket remover. Final preparation of

**7.3 Paper gaskets can be scraped off with a gasket scraper tool . . .**

**7.4 . . . a knife blade . . .**

**7.5 . . . or a household scraper**

**7.6 Fine abrasive paper is wrapped around a flat file to clean up the gasket face**

**7.7 A kitchen scourer can be used on stubborn deposits**

the gasket surface can be made with very fine abrasive paper or a plastic kitchen scourer **(see illustrations 7.6 and 7.7)**.
● Old sealant can be scraped or peeled off components, depending on the type originally used. Note that gasket removal compounds are available to avoid scraping the components clean; make sure the gasket remover suits the type of sealant used.

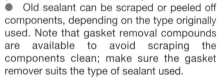

## 8 Chains

### *Breaking and joining final drive chains*

● Drive chains for all but small bikes are continuous and do not have a clip-type connecting link. The chain must be broken using a chain breaker tool and the new chain securely riveted together using a new soft rivet-type link. Never use a clip-type connecting link instead of a rivet-type link, except in an emergency. Various chain breaking and riveting tools are available, either as separate tools or combined as illustrated in the accompanying photographs - read the instructions supplied with the tool carefully.

> ⚠ **Warning: The need to rivet the new link pins correctly cannot be overstressed - loss of control of the motorcycle is very likely to result if the chain breaks in use.**

● Rotate the chain and look for the soft link. The soft link pins look like they have been

**8.1 Tighten the chain breaker to push the pin out of the link . . .**

**8.2 . . . withdraw the pin, remove the tool . . .**

**8.3 . . . and separate the chain link**

deeply centre-punched instead of peened over like all the other pins **(see illustration 8.9)** and its sideplate may be a different colour. Position the soft link midway between the sprockets and assemble the chain breaker tool over one of the soft link pins **(see illustration 8.1)**. Operate the tool to push the pin out through the chain **(see illustration 8.2)**. On an O-ring chain, remove the O-rings **(see illustration 8.3)**. Carry out the same procedure on the other soft link pin.

> **Caution: Certain soft link pins (particularly on the larger chains) may require their ends to be filed or ground off before they can be pressed out using the tool.**

● Check that you have the correct size and strength (standard or heavy duty) new soft link - do not reuse the old link. Look for the size marking on the chain sideplates **(see illustration 8.10)**.
● Position the chain ends so that they are engaged over the rear sprocket. On an O-ring

**8.4 Insert the new soft link, with O-rings, through the chain ends . . .**

**8.5 . . . install the O-rings over the pin ends . . .**

**8.6 . . . followed by the sideplate**

chain, install a new O-ring over each pin of the link and insert the link through the two chain ends **(see illustration 8.4)**. Install a new O-ring over the end of each pin, followed by the sideplate (with the chain manufacturer's marking facing outwards) **(see illustrations 8.5 and 8.6)**. On an unsealed chain, insert the link through the two chain ends, then install the sideplate with the chain manufacturer's marking facing outwards.
● Note that it may not be possible to install the sideplate using finger pressure alone. If using a joining tool, assemble it so that the plates of the tool clamp the link and press the sideplate over the pins **(see illustration 8.7)**. Otherwise, use two small sockets placed over

**8.7 Push the sideplate into position using a clamp**

**8.8 Assemble the chain riveting tool over one pin at a time and tighten it fully**

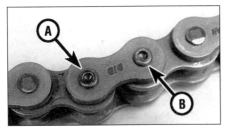

**8.9 Pin end correctly riveted (A), pin end unriveted (B)**

the rivet ends and two pieces of the wood between a G-clamp. Operate the clamp to press the sideplate over the pins.

● Assemble the joining tool over one pin (following the maker's instructions) and tighten the tool down to spread the pin end securely **(see illustrations 8.8 and 8.9)**. Do the same on the other pin.

 **Warning: Check that the pin ends are secure and that there is no danger of the sideplate coming loose. If the pin ends are cracked the soft link must be renewed.**

### Final drive chain sizing

● Chains are sized using a three digit number, followed by a suffix to denote the chain type **(see illustration 8.10)**. Chain type is either standard or heavy duty (thicker sideplates), and also unsealed or O-ring/X-ring type.

● The first digit of the number relates to the pitch of the chain, ie the distance from the centre of one pin to the centre of the next pin **(see illustration 8.11)**. Pitch is expressed in eighths of an inch, as follows:

**8.10 Typical chain size and type marking**

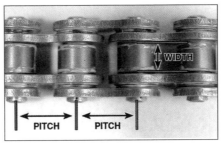

**8.11 Chain dimensions**

Sizes commencing with a 4 (eg 428) have a pitch of 1/2 inch (12.7 mm)

Sizes commencing with a 5 (eg 520) have a pitch of 5/8 inch (15.9 mm)

Sizes commencing with a 6 (eg 630) have a pitch of 3/4 inch (19.1 mm)

● The second and third digits of the chain size relate to the width of the rollers, again in imperial units, eg the 525 shown has 5/16 inch (7.94 mm) rollers **(see illustration 8.11)**.

## 9 Hoses

### Clamping to prevent flow

● Small-bore flexible hoses can be clamped to prevent fluid flow whilst a component is worked on. Whichever method is used, ensure that the hose material is not permanently distorted or damaged by the clamp.

a) A brake hose clamp available from auto accessory shops **(see illustration 9.1)**.
b) A wingnut type hose clamp **(see illustration 9.2)**.

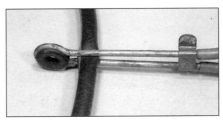

**9.1 Hoses can be clamped with an automotive brake hose clamp . . .**

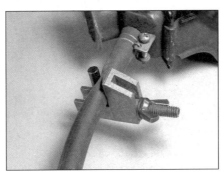

**9.2 . . . a wingnut type hose clamp . . .**

c) Two sockets placed each side of the hose and held with straight-jawed self-locking grips **(see illustration 9.3)**.
d) Thick card each side of the hose held between straight-jawed self-locking grips **(see illustration 9.4)**.

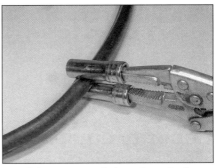

**9.3 . . . two sockets and a pair of self-locking grips . . .**

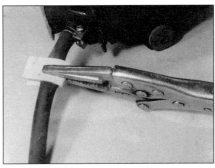

**9.4 . . . or thick card and self-locking grips**

### Freeing and fitting hoses

● Always make sure the hose clamp is moved well clear of the hose end. Grip the hose with your hand and rotate it whilst pulling it off the union. If the hose has hardened due to age and will not move, slit it with a sharp knife and peel its ends off the union **(see illustration 9.5)**.

● Resist the temptation to use grease or soap on the unions to aid installation; although it helps the hose slip over the union it will equally aid the escape of fluid from the joint. It is preferable to soften the hose ends in hot water and wet the inside surface of the hose with water or a fluid which will evaporate.

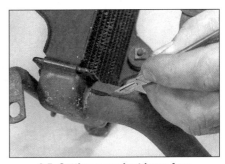

**9.5 Cutting a coolant hose free with a sharp knife**

## Introduction

In less time than it takes to read this introduction, a thief could steal your motorcycle. Returning only to find your bike has gone is one of the worst feelings in the world. Even if the motorcycle is insured against theft, once you've got over the initial shock, you will have the inconvenience of dealing with the police and your insurance company.

The motorcycle is an easy target for the professional thief and the joyrider alike and the official figures on motorcycle theft make for depressing reading; on average a motorcycle is stolen every 16 minutes in the UK!

Motorcycle thefts fall into two categories, those stolen 'to order' and those taken by opportunists. The thief stealing to order will be on the look out for a specific make and model and will go to extraordinary lengths to obtain that motorcycle. The opportunist thief on the other hand will look for easy targets which can be stolen with the minimum of effort and risk.

Whilst it is never going to be possible to make your machine 100% secure, it is estimated that around half of all stolen motorcycles are taken by opportunist thieves. Remember that the opportunist thief is always on the look out for the easy option: if there are two similar motorcycles parked side-by-side, they will target the one with the lowest level of security. By taking a few precautions, you can reduce the chances of your motorcycle being stolen.

# Security equipment

There are many specialised motorcycle security devices available and the following text summarises their applications and their good and bad points.

Once you have decided on the type of security equipment which best suits your needs, we recommended that you read one of the many equipment tests regularly carried out by the motorcycle press. These tests compare the products from all the major manufacturers and give impartial ratings on their effectiveness, value-for-money and ease of use.

No one item of security equipment can provide complete protection. It is highly recommended that two or more of the items described below are combined to increase the security of your motorcycle (a lock and chain plus an alarm system is just about ideal). The more security measures fitted to the bike, the less likely it is to be stolen.

### Lock and chain

**Pros:** *Very flexible to use; can be used to secure the motorcycle to almost any immovable object. On some locks and chains, the lock can be used on its own as a disc lock (see below).*

**Cons:** *Can be very heavy and awkward to carry on the motorcycle, although some types will be supplied with a carry bag which can be strapped to the pillion seat.*

● Heavy-duty chains and locks are an excellent security measure **(see illustration 1)**. Whenever the motorcycle is parked, use the lock and chain to secure the machine to a solid, immovable object such as a post or railings. This will prevent the machine from being ridden away or being lifted into the back of a van.

● When fitting the chain, always ensure the chain is routed around the motorcycle frame or swingarm **(see illustrations 2 and 3)**. Never merely pass the chain around one of the wheel rims; a thief may unbolt the wheel and lift the rest of the machine into a van, leaving you with just the wheel! Try to avoid having excess chain free, thus making it difficult to use cutting tools, and keep the chain and lock off the ground to prevent thieves attacking it with a cold chisel. Position the lock so that its lock barrel is facing downwards; this will make it harder for the thief to attack the lock mechanism.

Ensure the lock and chain you buy is of good quality and long enough to shackle your bike to a solid object

Pass the chain through the bike's frame, rather than just through a wheel . . .

. . . and loop it around a solid object

## U-locks

Pros: *Highly effective deterrent which can be used to secure the bike to a post or railings. Most U-locks come with a carrier which allows the lock to be easily carried on the bike.*

Cons: *Not as flexible to use as a lock and chain.*

● These are solid locks which are similar in use to a lock and chain. U-locks are lighter than a lock and chain but not so flexible to use. The length and shape of the lock shackle limit the objects to which the bike can be secured **(see illustration 4)**.

## Disc locks

Pros: *Small, light and very easy to carry; most can be stored underneath the seat.*

Cons: *Does not prevent the motorcycle being lifted into a van. Can be very embarrassing if you*

**U-locks can be used to secure the bike to a solid object – ensure you purchase one which is long enough**

forget to remove the lock before attempting to ride off!

● Disc locks are designed to be attached to the front brake disc. The lock passes through one of the holes in the disc and prevents the wheel rotating by jamming against the fork/brake caliper **(see illustration 5)**. Some are equipped with an alarm siren which sounds if the disc lock is moved; this not only acts as a theft deterrent but also as a handy reminder if you try to move the bike with the lock still fitted.

● Combining the disc lock with a length of cable which can be looped around a post or railings provides an additional measure of security **(see illustration 6)**.

## Alarms and immobilisers

Pros: *Once installed it is completely hassle-free to use. If the system is 'Thatcham' or 'Sold Secure-approved', insurance companies may give you a discount.*

Cons: *Can be expensive to buy and complex to install. No system will prevent the motorcycle from being lifted into a van and taken away.*

● Electronic alarms and immobilisers are available to suit a variety of budgets. There are three different types of system available: pure alarms, pure immobilisers, and the more expensive systems which are combined alarm/immobilisers **(see illustration 7)**.
● An alarm system is designed to emit an audible warning if the motorcycle is being tampered with.
● An immobiliser prevents the motorcycle being started and ridden away by disabling its electrical systems.
● When purchasing an alarm/immobiliser system, check the cost of installing the system unless you are able to do it yourself. If the motorcycle is not used regularly, another consideration is the current drain of the system. All alarm/immobiliser systems are powered by the motorcycle's battery; purchasing a system with a very low current drain could prevent the battery losing its charge whilst the motorcycle is not being used.

**A typical disc lock attached through one of the holes in the disc**

**A disc lock combined with a security cable provides additional protection**

**A typical alarm/immobiliser system**

**Indelible markings can be applied to most areas of the bike – always apply the manufacturer's sticker to warn off thieves**

## Security marking kits

**Pros:** *Very cheap and effective deterrent. Many insurance companies will give you a discount on your insurance premium if a recognised security marking kit is used on your motorcycle.*

**Cons:** *Does not prevent the motorcycle being stolen by joyriders.*

● There are many different types of security marking kits available. The idea is to mark as many parts of the motorcycle as possible with a unique security number **(see illustrations 8, 9 and 10)**. A form will be included with the kit to register your personal details and those of the motorcycle with the kit manufacturer. This register is made available to the police to help them trace the rightful owner of any motorcycle or components which they recover should all other forms of identification have been removed. Always apply the warning stickers provided with the kit to deter thieves.

**Chemically-etched code numbers can be applied to main body panels . . .**

## Ground anchors, wheel clamps and security posts

**Pros:** *An excellent form of security which will deter all but the most determined of thieves.*

**Cons:** *Awkward to install and can be expensive.*

**Permanent ground anchors provide an excellent level of security when the bike is at home**

**. . . again, always ensure that the kit manufacturer's sticker is applied in a prominent position**

● Whilst the motorcycle is at home, it is a good idea to attach it securely to the floor or a solid wall, even if it is kept in a securely locked garage. Various types of ground anchors, security posts and wheel clamps are available for this purpose **(see illustration 11)**. These security devices are either bolted to a solid concrete or brick structure or can be cemented into the ground.

# Security at home

A high percentage of motorcycle thefts are from the owner's home. Here are some things to consider whenever your motorcycle is at home:
✔ Where possible, always keep the motorcycle in a securely locked garage. Never rely solely on the standard lock on the garage door, these are usual hopelessly inadequate. Fit an additional locking mechanism to the door and consider having the garage alarmed. A security light, activated by a movement sensor, is also a good investment.

✔ Always secure the motorcycle to the ground or a wall, even if it is inside a securely locked garage.
✔ Do not regularly leave the motorcycle outside your home, try to keep it out of sight wherever possible. If a garage is not available, fit a motorcycle cover over the bike to disguise its true identity.
✔ It is not uncommon for thieves to follow a motorcyclist home to find out where the bike is kept. They will then return at a later date. Be aware of this whenever you are returning

home on your motorcycle. If you suspect you are being followed, do not return home, instead ride to a garage or shop and stop as a precaution.
✔ When selling a motorcycle, do not provide your home address or the location where the bike is normally kept. Arrange to meet the buyer at a location away from your home. Thieves have been known to pose as potential buyers to find out where motorcycles are kept and then return later to steal them.

# Security away from the home

As well as fitting security equipment to your motorcycle here are a few general rules to follow whenever you park your motorcycle.
✔ Park in a busy, public place.
✔ Use car parks which incorporate security features, such as CCTV.

✔ At night, park in a well-lit area, preferably directly underneath a street light.
✔ Engage the steering lock.
✔ Secure the motorcycle to a solid, immovable object such as a post or railings with an additional lock. If this is not possible,

secure the bike to a friend's motorcycle. Some public parking places provide security loops for motorcycles.
✔ Never leave your helmet or luggage attached to the motorcycle. Take them with you at all times.

# Lubricants and fluids

A wide range of lubricants, fluids and cleaning agents is available for motor-cycles. This is a guide as to what is available, its applications and properties.

## Four-stroke engine oil

● Engine oil is without doubt the most important component of any four-stroke engine. Modern motorcycle engines place a lot of demands on their oil and choosing the right type is essential. Using an unsuitable oil will lead to an increased rate of engine wear and could result in serious engine damage. Before purchasing oil, always check the recommended oil specification given by the manufacturer. The manufacturer will state a recommended 'type or classification' and also a specific 'viscosity' range for engine oil.

● The oil 'type or classification' is identified by its API (American Petroleum Institute) rating. The API rating will be in the form of two letters, e.g. SG. The S identifies the oil as being suitable for use in a petrol (gasoline) engine (S stands for spark ignition) and the second letter, ranging from A to J, identifies the oil's performance rating. The later this letter, the higher the specification of the oil; for example API SG oil exceeds the requirements of API SF oil. **Note:** *On some oils there may also be a second rating consisting of another two letters, the first letter being C, e.g. API SF/CD. This rating indicates the oil is also suitable for use in a diesel engines (the C stands for compression ignition) and is thus of no relevance for motorcycle use.*

● The 'viscosity' of the oil is identified by its SAE (Society of Automotive Engineers) rating. All modern engines require multigrade oils and the SAE rating will consist of two numbers, the first followed by a W, e.g.

10W/40. The first number indicates the viscosity rating of the oil at low temperatures (W stands for winter – tested at –20°C) and the second number represents the viscosity of the oil at high temperatures (tested at 100°C). The lower the number, the thinner the oil. For example an oil with an SAE 10W/40 rating will give better cold starting and running than an SAE 15W/40 oil.

● As well as ensuring the 'type' and 'viscosity' of the oil match the recommendations, another consideration to make when buying engine oil is whether to purchase a standard mineral-based oil, a semi-synthetic oil (also known as a synthetic blend or synthetic-based oil) or a fully-synthetic oil. Although all oils will have a similar rating and viscosity, their cost will vary considerably; mineral-based oils are the cheapest, the fully-synthetic oils the most expensive with the semi-synthetic oils falling somewhere in-between. This decision is very much up to the owner, but it should be noted that modern synthetic oils have far better lubricating and cleaning qualities than traditional mineral-based oils and tend to retain these properties for far longer. Bearing in mind the operating conditions inside a modern, high-revving motorcycle engine it is highly recommended that a fully synthetic oil is used. The extra expense at each service could save you money in the long term by preventing premature engine wear.

● As a final note always ensure that the oil is specifically designed for use in motorcycle engines. Engine oils designed primarily for use in car engines sometimes contain additives or friction modifiers which could cause clutch slip on a motorcycle fitted with a wet-clutch.

## Two-stroke engine oil

● Modern two-stroke engines, with their high power outputs, place high demands on their oil. If engine seizure is to be avoided it is essential that a high-quality oil is used. Two-stroke oils differ hugely from four-stroke oils. The oil lubricates only the crankshaft and piston(s) (the transmission has its own lubricating oil) and is used on a total-loss basis where it is burnt completely during the combustion process.

● The Japanese have recently introduced a classification system for two-stroke oils, the JASO rating. This rating is in the form of two letters, either FA, FB or FC – FA is the lowest classification and FC the highest. Ensure the oil being used meets or exceeds the recommended rating specified by the manufacturer.

● As well as ensuring the oil rating matches the recommendation, another consideration to make when buying engine oil is whether to purchase a standard mineral-based oil, a semi-synthetic oil (also known as a synthetic blend or synthetic-based oil) or a fully-synthetic oil. The cost of each type of oil varies considerably; mineral-based oils are the cheapest, the fully-synthetic oils the most expensive with the semi-synthetic oils falling somewhere in-between. This decision is very much up to the owner, but it should be noted that modern synthetic oils have far better lubricating properties and burn cleaner than traditional mineral-based oils. It is therefore recommended that a fully synthetic oil is used. The extra expense could save you money in the long term by preventing premature engine wear, engine performance will be improved, carbon deposits and exhaust smoke will be reduced.

● Always ensure that the oil is specifically designed for use in an injector system. Many high quality two-stroke oils are designed for competition use and need to be pre-mixed with fuel. These oils are of a much higher viscosity and are not designed to flow through the injector pumps used on road-going two-stroke motorcycles.

## Transmission (gear) oil

● On a two-stroke engine, the transmission and clutch are lubricated by their own separate oil bath which must be changed in accordance with the Maintenance Schedule.
● Although the engine and transmission units of most four-strokes use a common lubrication supply, there are some exceptions where the engine and gearbox have separate oil reservoirs and a dry clutch is used.
● Motorcycle manufacturers will either recommend a monograde transmission oil or a four-stroke multigrade engine oil to lubricate the transmission.
● Transmission oils, or gear oils as they are often called, are designed specifically for use in transmission systems. The viscosity of these oils is represented by an SAE number, but the scale of measurement applied is different to that used to grade engine oils. As a rough guide a SAE90 gear oil will be of the same viscosity as an SAE50 engine oil.

## Shaft drive oil

● On models equipped with shaft final drive, the shaft drive gears are will have their own oil supply. The manufacturer will state a recommended 'type or classification' and also a specific 'viscosity' range in the same manner as for four-stroke engine oil.
● Gear oil classification is given by the number which follows the API GL (GL standing for gear lubricant) rating, the higher the number, the higher the specification of the oil, e.g. API GL5 oil is a higher specification than API GL4 oil. Ensure the oil meets or

exceeds the classification specified and is of the correct viscosity. The viscosity of gear oils is also represented by an SAE number but the scale of measurement used is different to that used to grade engine oils. As a rough guide an SAE90 gear oil will be of the same viscosity as an SAE50 engine oil.
● If the use of an EP (Extreme Pressure) gear oil is specified, ensure the oil purchased is suitable.

## Fork oil and suspension fluid

● Conventional telescopic front forks are hydraulic and require fork oil to work. To ensure the forks function correctly, the fork oil must be changed in accordance with the Maintenance Schedule.
● Fork oil is available in a variety of viscosities, identified by their SAE rating; fork oil ratings vary from light (SAE 5) to heavy (SAE 30). When purchasing fork oil, ensure the viscosity rating matches that specified by the manufacturer.
● Some lubricant manufacturers also produce a range of high-quality suspension fluids which are very similar to fork oil but are designed mainly for competition use. These fluids may have a different viscosity rating system which is not to be confused with the SAE rating of normal fork oil. Refer to the manufacturer's instructions if in any doubt.

## Brake and clutch fluid

● All disc brake systems and some clutch systems are hydraulically operated. To ensure correct operation, the hydraulic fluid must be changed in accordance with the Maintenance Schedule.
● Brake and clutch fluid is classified by its DOT rating with most motorcycle manufacturers specifying DOT 3 or 4 fluid. Both fluid types are glycol-based and can be mixed together without adverse effect; DOT 4 fluid exceeds the requirements of DOT 3

fluid. Although it is safe to use DOT 4 fluid in a system designed for use with DOT 3 fluid, never use DOT 3 fluid in a system which specifies the use of DOT 4 as this will adversely affect the system's performance. The type required for the system will be marked on the fluid reservoir cap.
● Some manufacturers also produce a DOT 5 hydraulic fluid. DOT 5 hydraulic fluid is silicone-based and is not compatible with the glycol-based DOT 3 and 4 fluids. Never mix DOT 5 fluid with DOT 3 or 4 fluid as this will seriously affect the performance of the hydraulic system.

## Coolant/antifreeze

● When purchasing coolant/antifreeze, always ensure it is suitable for use in an aluminium engine and contains corrosion inhibitors to prevent possible blockages of the internal coolant passages of the system. As a general rule, most coolants are designed to be used neat and should not be diluted whereas antifreeze can be mixed with distilled water to provide a coolant solution of the required strength. Refer to the manufacturer's instructions on the bottle.
● Ensure the coolant is changed in accordance with the Maintenance Schedule.

## Chain lube

● Chain lube is an aerosol-type spray lubricant specifically designed for use on motorcycle final drive chains. Chain lube has two functions, to minimise friction between the final drive chain and sprockets and to prevent corrosion of the chain. Regular use of a good-quality chain lube will extend the life of the drive chain and sprockets and thus maximise the power being transmitted from the transmission to the rear wheel.
● When using chain lube, always allow some time for the solvents in the lube to evaporate before riding the motorcycle. This will minimise the amount of lube which will

'fling' off from the chain when the motorcycle is used. If the motorcycle is equipped with an 'O-ring' chain, ensure the chain lube is labelled as being suitable for use on 'O-ring' chains.

## Degreasers and solvents

● There are many different types of solvents and degreasers available to remove the grime and grease which accumulate around the motorcycle during normal use. Degreasers and solvents are usually available as an aerosol-type spray or as a liquid which you apply with a brush. Always closely follow the manufacturer's instructions and wear eye protection during use. Be aware that many solvents are flammable and may give off noxious fumes; take adequate precautions when using them (see Safety First!).

● For general cleaning, use one of the many solvents or degreasers available from most motorcycle accessory shops. These solvents are usually applied then left for a certain time before being washed off with water.

**Brake cleaner** is a solvent specifically designed to remove all traces of oil, grease and dust from braking system components. Brake cleaner is designed to evaporate quickly and leaves behind no residue.

**Carburettor cleaner** is an aerosol-type solvent specifically designed to clear carburettor blockages and break down the hard deposits and gum often found inside carburettors during overhaul.

**Contact cleaner** is an aerosol-type solvent designed for cleaning electrical components. The cleaner will remove all traces of oil and dirt from components such as switch contacts or fouled spark plugs and then dry, leaving behind no residue.

**Gasket remover** is an aerosol-type solvent designed for removing stubborn gaskets from engine components during overhaul. Gasket remover will minimise the amount of scraping required to remove the gasket and therefore reduce the risk of damage to the mating surface.

## Spray lubricants

● Aerosol-based spray lubricants are widely available and are excellent for lubricating lever pivots and exposed cables and switches. Try to use a lubricant which is of the dry-film type as the fluid evaporates, leaving behind a dry-film of lubricant. Lubricants which leave behind an oily residue will attract dust and dirt which will increase the rate of wear of the cable/lever.

● Most lubricants also act as a moisture dispersant and a penetrating fluid. This means they can also be used to 'dry out' electrical components such as wiring connectors or switches as well as helping to free seized fasteners.

## Greases

● Grease is used to lubricate many of the pivot-points. A good-quality multi-purpose grease is suitable for most applications but some manufacturers will specify the use of specialist greases for use on components such as swingarm and suspension linkage bushes. These specialist greases can be purchased from most motorcycle (or car) accessory shops; commonly specified types include molybdenum disulphide grease, lithium-based grease, graphite-based grease, silicone-based grease and high-temperature copper-based grease.

## Gasket sealing compounds

● Gasket sealing compounds can be used in conjunction with gaskets, to improve their sealing capabilities, or on their own to seal metal-to-metal joints. Depending on their type, sealing compounds either set hard or stay relatively soft and pliable.

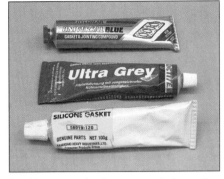

● When purchasing a gasket sealing compound, ensure that it is designed specifically for use on an internal combustion engine. General multi-purpose sealants available from DIY stores may appear visibly similar but they are not designed to withstand the extreme heat or contact with fuel and oil encountered when used on an engine (see 'Tools and Workshop Tips' for further information).

## Thread locking compound

● Thread locking compounds are used to secure certain threaded fasteners in position to prevent them from loosening due to vibration. Thread locking compounds can be purchased from most motorcycle (and car) accessory shops. Ensure the threads of the both components are completely clean and dry before sparingly applying the locking compound (see 'Tools and Workshop Tips' for further information).

## Fuel additives

● Fuel additives which protect and clean the fuel system components are widely available. These additives are designed to remove all traces of deposits that build up on the carburettors/injectors and prevent wear, helping the fuel system to operate more efficiently. If a fuel additive is being used, check that it is suitable for use with your motorcycle, especially if your motorcycle is equipped with a catalytic converter.

● Octane boosters are also available. These additives are designed to improve the performance of highly-tuned engines being run on normal pump-fuel and are of no real use on standard motorcycles.

Conversion Factors

## Length (distance)

| | | | | |
|---|---|---|---|---|
| Inches (in) | x 25.4 | = Millimetres (mm) | x 0.0394 | = Inches (in) |
| Feet (ft) | x 0.305 | = Metres (m) | x 3.281 | = Feet (ft) |
| Miles | x 1.609 | = Kilometres (km) | x 0.621 | = Miles |

## Volume (capacity)

| | | | | |
|---|---|---|---|---|
| Cubic inches (cu in; in³) | x 16.387 | = Cubic centimetres (cc; cm³) | x 0.061 | = Cubic inches (cu in; in³) |
| Imperial pints (Imp pt) | x 0.568 | = Litres (l) | x 1.76 | = Imperial pints (Imp pt) |
| Imperial quarts (Imp qt) | x 1.137 | = Litres (l) | x 0.88 | = Imperial quarts (Imp qt) |
| Imperial quarts (Imp qt) | x 1.201 | = US quarts (US qt) | x 0.833 | = Imperial quarts (Imp qt) |
| US quarts (US qt) | x 0.946 | = Litres (l) | x 1.057 | = US quarts (US qt) |
| Imperial gallons (Imp gal) | x 4.546 | = Litres (l) | x 0.22 | = Imperial gallons (Imp gal) |
| Imperial gallons (Imp gal) | x 1.201 | = US gallons (US gal) | x 0.833 | = Imperial gallons (Imp gal) |
| US gallons (US gal) | x 3.785 | = Litres (l) | x 0.264 | = US gallons (US gal) |

## Mass (weight)

| | | | | |
|---|---|---|---|---|
| Ounces (oz) | x 28.35 | = Grams (g) | x 0.035 | = Ounces (oz) |
| Pounds (lb) | x 0.454 | = Kilograms (kg) | x 2.205 | = Pounds (lb) |

## Force

| | | | | |
|---|---|---|---|---|
| Ounces-force (ozf; oz) | x 0.278 | = Newtons (N) | x 3.6 | = Ounces-force (ozf; oz) |
| Pounds-force (lbf; lb) | x 4.448 | = Newtons (N) | x 0.225 | = Pounds-force (lbf; lb) |
| Newtons (N) | x 0.1 | = Kilograms-force (kgf; kg) | x 9.81 | = Newtons (N) |

## Pressure

| | | | | |
|---|---|---|---|---|
| Pounds-force per square inch (psi; lbf/in²; lb/in²) | x 0.070 | = Kilograms-force per square centimetre (kgf/cm²; kg/cm²) | x 14.223 | = Pounds-force per square inch (psi; lbf/in²; lb/in²) |
| Pounds-force per square inch (psi; lbf/in²; lb/in²) | x 0.068 | = Atmospheres (atm) | x 14.696 | = Pounds-force per square inch (psi; lbf/in²; lb/in²) |
| Pounds-force per square inch (psi; lbf/in²; lb/in²) | x 0.069 | = Bars | x 14.5 | = Pounds-force per square inch (psi; lbf/in²; lb/in²) |
| Pounds-force per square inch (psi; lbf/in²; lb/in²) | x 6.895 | = Kilopascals (kPa) | x 0.145 | = Pounds-force per square inch (psi; lbf/in²; lb/in²) |
| Kilopascals (kPa) | x 0.01 | = Kilograms-force per square centimetre (kgf/cm²; kg/cm²) | x 98.1 | = Kilopascals (kPa) |
| Millibar (mbar) | x 100 | = Pascals (Pa) | x 0.01 | = Millibar (mbar) |
| Millibar (mbar) | x 0.0145 | = Pounds-force per square inch (psi; lbf/in²; lb/in²) | x 68.947 | = Millibar (mbar) |
| Millibar (mbar) | x 0.75 | = Millimetres of mercury (mmHg) | x 1.333 | = Millibar (mbar) |
| Millibar (mbar) | x 0.401 | = Inches of water (inH₂O) | x 2.491 | = Millibar (mbar) |
| Millimetres of mercury (mmHg) | x 0.535 | = Inches of water (inH₂O) | x 1.868 | = Millimetres of mercury (mmHg) |
| Inches of water (inH₂O) | x 0.036 | = Pounds-force per square inch (psi; lbf/in²; lb/in²) | x 27.68 | = Inches of water (inH₂O) |

## Torque (moment of force)

| | | | | |
|---|---|---|---|---|
| Pounds-force inches (lbf in; lb in) | x 1.152 | = Kilograms-force centimetre (kgf cm; kg cm) | x 0.868 | = Pounds-force inches (lbf in; lb in) |
| Pounds-force inches (lbf in; lb in) | x 0.113 | = Newton metres (Nm) | x 8.85 | = Pounds-force inches (lbf in; lb in) |
| Pounds-force inches (lbf in; lb in) | x 0.083 | = Pounds-force feet (lbf ft; lb ft) | x 12 | = Pounds-force inches (lbf in; lb in) |
| Pounds-force feet (lbf ft; lb ft) | x 0.138 | = Kilograms-force metres (kgf m; kg m) | x 7.233 | = Pounds-force feet (lbf ft; lb ft) |
| Pounds-force feet (lbf ft; lb ft) | x 1.356 | = Newton metres (Nm) | x 0.738 | = Pounds-force feet (lbf ft; lb ft) |
| Newton metres (Nm) | x 0.102 | = Kilograms-force metres (kgf m; kg m) | x 9.804 | = Newton metres (Nm) |

## Power

| | | | | |
|---|---|---|---|---|
| Horsepower (hp) | x 745.7 | = Watts (W) | x 0.0013 | = Horsepower (hp) |

## Velocity (speed)

| | | | | |
|---|---|---|---|---|
| Miles per hour (miles/hr; mph) | x 1.609 | = Kilometres per hour (km/hr; kph) | x 0.621 | = Miles per hour (miles/hr; mph) |

## Fuel consumption*

| | | | | |
|---|---|---|---|---|
| Miles per gallon (mpg) | x 0.354 | = Kilometres per litre (km/l) | x 2.825 | = Miles per gallon (mpg) |

## Temperature

Degrees Fahrenheit = (°C x 1.8) + 32          Degrees Celsius (Degrees Centigrade; °C) = (°F - 32) x 0.56

*It is common practice to convert from miles per gallon (mpg) to litres/100 kilometres (l/100km), where mpg x l/100 km = 282*

# Notes

## About the MOT Test

In the UK, all vehicles more than three years old are subject to an annual test to ensure that they meet minimum safety requirements. A current test certificate must be issued before a machine can be used on public roads, and is required before a road fund licence can be issued. Riding without a current test certificate will also invalidate your insurance.

For most owners, the MOT test is an annual cause for anxiety, and this is largely due to owners not being sure what needs to be checked prior to submitting the motorcycle for testing. The simple answer is that a fully roadworthy motorcycle will have no difficulty in passing the test.

This is a guide to getting your motorcycle through the MOT test. Obviously it will not be possible to examine the motorcycle to the same standard as the professional MOT tester, particularly in view of the equipment required for some of the checks. However, working through the following procedures will enable you to identify any problem areas before submitting the motorcycle for the test.

It has only been possible to summarise the test requirements here, based on the regulations in force at the time of printing. Test standards are becoming increasingly stringent, although there are some exemptions for older vehicles. More information about the MOT test can be obtained from the TSO publications, *How Safe is your Motorcycle* and *The MOT Inspection Manual for Motorcycle Testing*.

Many of the checks require that one of the wheels is raised off the ground. If the motorcycle doesn't have a centre stand, note that an auxiliary stand will be required. Additionally, the help of an assistant may prove useful.

Certain exceptions apply to machines under 50 cc, machines without a lighting system, and Classic bikes - if in doubt about any of the requirements listed below seek confirmation from an MOT tester prior to submitting the motorcycle for the test.

Check that the frame number is clearly visible.

**HAYNES HINT** *If a component is in borderline condition, the tester has discretion in deciding whether to pass or fail it. If the motorcycle presented is clean and evidently well cared for, the tester may be more inclined to pass a borderline component than if the motorcycle is scruffy and apparently neglected.*

# Electrical System

### Lights, turn signals, horn and reflector

✔ With the ignition on, check the operation of the following electrical components. **Note:** *The electrical components on certain small-capacity machines are powered by the generator, requiring that the engine is run for this check.*

a) *Headlight and tail light. Check that both illuminate in the low and high beam switch positions.*
b) *Position lights. Check that the front position (or sidelight) and tail light illuminate in this switch position.*
c) *Turn signals. Check that all flash at the correct rate, and that the warning light(s) function correctly. Check that the turn signal switch works correctly.*
d) *Hazard warning system (where fitted). Check that all four turn signals flash in this switch position.*
e) *Brake stop light. Check that the light comes on when the front and rear brakes are independently applied. Models first used on or after 1st April 1986 must have a brake light switch on each brake.*
f) *Horn. Check that the sound is continuous and of reasonable volume.*

✔ Check that there is a red reflector on the rear of the machine, either mounted separately or as part of the tail light lens.
✔ Check the condition of the headlight, tail light and turn signal lenses.

### Headlight beam height

✔ The MOT tester will perform a headlight beam height check using specialised beam setting equipment **(see illustration 1)**. This equipment will not be available to the home mechanic, but if you suspect that the headlight is incorrectly set or may have been maladjusted in the past, you can perform a rough test as follows.
✔ Position the bike in a straight line facing a brick wall. The bike must be off its stand, upright and with a rider seated. Measure the height from the ground to the centre of the headlight and mark a horizontal line on the wall at this height. Position the motorcycle 3.8 metres from the wall and draw a vertical

**Headlight beam height checking equipment**

line up the wall central to the centreline of the motorcycle. Switch to dipped beam and check that the beam pattern falls slightly lower than the horizontal line and to the left of the vertical line **(see illustration 2)**.

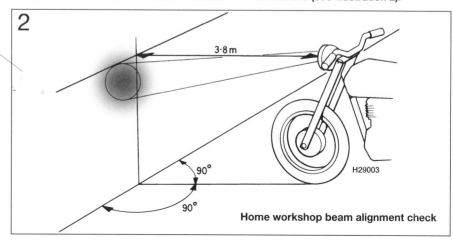

3·8 m

90°

90°

H29003

**Home workshop beam alignment check**

# Exhaust System and Final Drive

## Exhaust

✔ Check that the exhaust mountings are secure and that the system does not foul any of the rear suspension components.
✔ Start the motorcycle. When the revs are increased, check that the exhaust is neither holed nor leaking from any of its joints. On a linked system, check that the collector box is not leaking due to corrosion.

✔ Note that the exhaust decibel level ("loudness" of the exhaust) is assessed at the discretion of the tester. If the motorcycle was first used on or after 1st January 1985 the silencer must carry the BSAU 193 stamp, or a marking relating to its make and model, or be of OE (original equipment) manufacture. If the silencer is marked NOT FOR ROAD USE, RACING USE ONLY or similar, it will fail the MOT.

## Final drive

✔ On chain or belt drive machines, check that the chain/belt is in good condition and does not have excessive slack. Also check that the sprocket is securely mounted on the rear wheel hub. Check that the chain/belt guard is in place.
✔ On shaft drive bikes, check for oil leaking from the drive unit and fouling the rear tyre.

# Steering and Suspension

## Steering

✔ With the front wheel raised off the ground, rotate the steering from lock to lock. The handlebar or switches must not contact the fuel tank or be close enough to trap the rider's hand. Problems can be caused by damaged lock stops on the lower yoke and frame, or by the fitting of non-standard handlebars.
✔ When performing the lock to lock check, also ensure that the steering moves freely without drag or notchiness. Steering movement can be impaired by poorly routed cables, or by overtight head bearings or worn bearings. The tester will perform a check of the steering head bearing lower race by mounting the front wheel on a surface plate, then performing a lock to

lock check with the weight of the machine on the lower bearing **(see illustration 3)**.
✔ Grasp the fork sliders (lower legs) and attempt to push and pull on the forks **(see**

**Front wheel mounted on a surface plate for steering head bearing lower race check**

**illustration 4)**. Any play in the steering head bearings will be felt. Note that in extreme cases, wear of the front fork bushes can be misinterpreted for head bearing play.
✔ Check that the handlebars are securely mounted.
✔ Check that the handlebar grip rubbers are secure. They should by bonded to the bar left end and to the throttle cable pulley on the right end.

## Front suspension

✔ With the motorcycle off the stand, hold the front brake on and pump the front forks up and down **(see illustration 5)**. Check that they are adequately damped.

**Checking the steering head bearings for freeplay**

**Hold the front brake on and pump the front forks up and down to check operation**

Inspect the area around the fork dust seal for oil leakage (arrow)

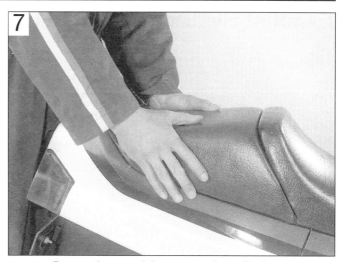

Bounce the rear of the motorcycle to check rear suspension operation

Checking for rear suspension linkage play

✔ Inspect the area above and around the front fork oil seals **(see illustration 6)**. There should be no sign of oil on the fork tube (stanchion) nor leaking down the slider (lower leg). On models so equipped, check that there is no oil leaking from the anti-dive units.
✔ On models with swingarm front suspension, check that there is no freeplay in the linkage when moved from side to side.

### Rear suspension

✔ With the motorcycle off the stand and an assistant supporting the motorcycle by its handlebars, bounce the rear suspension **(see illustration 7)**. Check that the suspension components do not foul on any of the cycle parts and check that the shock absorber(s) provide adequate damping.
✔ Visually inspect the shock absorber(s) and check that there is no sign of oil leakage from its damper. This is somewhat restricted on certain single shock models due to the location of the shock absorber.
✔ With the rear wheel raised off the ground, grasp the wheel at the highest point and attempt to pull it up **(see illustration 8)**. Any play in the swingarm pivot or suspension linkage bearings will be felt as movement. **Note:** *Do not confuse play with actual suspension movement.* Failure to lubricate suspension linkage bearings can lead to bearing failure **(see illustration 9)**.
✔ With the rear wheel raised off the ground, grasp the swingarm ends and attempt to move the swingarm from side to side and forwards and backwards - any play indicates wear of the swingarm pivot bearings **(see illustration 10)**.

Worn suspension linkage pivots (arrows) are usually the cause of play in the rear suspension

Grasp the swingarm at the ends to check for play in its pivot bearings

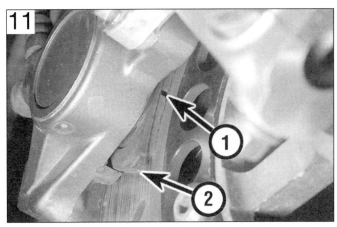

Brake pad wear can usually be viewed without removing the caliper. Most pads have wear indicator grooves (1) and some also have indicator tangs (2)

On drum brakes, check the angle of the operating lever with the brake fully applied. Most drum brakes have a wear indicator pointer and scale.

# Brakes, Wheels and Tyres

## Brakes

✔ With the wheel raised off the ground, apply the brake then free it off, and check that the wheel is about to revolve freely without brake drag.

✔ On disc brakes, examine the disc itself. Check that it is securely mounted and not cracked.

✔ On disc brakes, view the pad material through the caliper mouth and check that the pads are not worn down beyond the limit **(see illustration 11)**.

✔ On drum brakes, check that when the brake is applied the angle between the operating lever and cable or rod is not too great **(see illustration 12)**. Check also that the operating lever doesn't foul any other components.

✔ On disc brakes, examine the flexible hoses from top to bottom. Have an assistant hold the brake on so that the fluid in the hose is under pressure, and check that there is no sign of fluid leakage, bulges or cracking. If there are any metal brake pipes or unions, check that these are free from corrosion and damage. Where a brake-linked anti-dive system is fitted, check the hoses to the anti-dive in a similar manner.

✔ Check that the rear brake torque arm is secure and that its fasteners are secured by self-locking nuts or castellated nuts with split-pins or R-pins **(see illustration 13)**.

✔ On models with ABS, check that the self-check warning light in the instrument panel works.

✔ The MOT tester will perform a test of the motorcycle's braking efficiency based on a calculation of rider and motorcycle weight. Although this cannot be carried out at home, you can at least ensure that the braking systems are properly maintained. For hydraulic disc brakes, check the fluid level, lever/pedal feel (bleed of air if its spongy) and pad material. For drum brakes, check adjustment, cable or rod operation and shoe lining thickness.

## Wheels and tyres

✔ Check the wheel condition. Cast wheels should be free from cracks and if of the built-up design, all fasteners should be secure. Spoked wheels should be checked for broken, corroded, loose or bent spokes.

✔ With the wheel raised off the ground, spin the wheel and visually check that the tyre and wheel run true. Check that the tyre does not foul the suspension or mudguards.

✔ With the wheel raised off the ground, grasp the wheel and attempt to move it about the axle (spindle) **(see illustration 14)**. Any play felt here indicates wheel bearing failure.

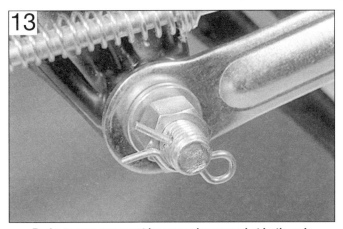

Brake torque arm must be properly secured at both ends

Check for wheel bearing play by trying to move the wheel about the axle (spindle)

Checking the tyre tread depth

Tyre direction of rotation arrow can be found on tyre sidewall

Castellated type wheel axle (spindle) nut must be secured by a split pin or R-pin

Two straightedges are used to check wheel alignment

✔ Check the tyre tread depth, tread condition and sidewall condition **(see illustration 15)**.
✔ Check the tyre type. Front and rear tyre types must be compatible and be suitable for road use. Tyres marked NOT FOR ROAD USE, COMPETITION USE ONLY or similar, will fail the MOT.

✔ If the tyre sidewall carries a direction of rotation arrow, this must be pointing in the direction of normal wheel rotation **(see illustration 16)**.
✔ Check that the wheel axle (spindle) nuts (where applicable) are properly secured. A self-locking nut or castellated nut with a split-pin or R-pin can be used **(see illustration 17)**.
✔ Wheel alignment is checked with the motorcycle off the stand and a rider seated. With the front wheel pointing straight ahead, two perfectly straight lengths of metal or wood and placed against the sidewalls of both tyres **(see illustration 18)**. The gap each side of the front tyre must be equidistant on both sides. Incorrect wheel alignment may be due to a cocked rear wheel (often as the result of poor chain adjustment) or in extreme cases, a bent frame.

# General checks and condition

✔ Check the security of all major fasteners, bodypanels, seat, fairings (where fitted) and mudguards.

✔ Check that the rider and pillion footrests, handlebar levers and brake pedal are securely mounted.

✔ Check for corrosion on the frame or any load-bearing components. If severe, this may affect the structure, particularly under stress.

# Sidecars

A motorcycle fitted with a sidecar requires additional checks relating to the stability of the machine and security of attachment and swivel joints, plus specific wheel alignment (toe-in) requirements. Additionally, tyre and lighting requirements differ from conventional motorcycle use. Owners are advised to check MOT test requirements with an official test centre.

# Preparing for storage

## Before you start

If repairs or an overhaul is needed, see that this is carried out now rather than left until you want to ride the bike again.

Give the bike a good wash and scrub all dirt from its underside. Make sure the bike dries completely before preparing for storage.

## Engine

● Remove the spark plug(s) and lubricate the cylinder bores with approximately a teaspoon of motor oil using a spout-type oil can **(see illustration 1)**. Reinstall the spark plug(s). Crank the engine over a couple of times to coat the piston rings and bores with oil. If the bike has a kickstart, use this to turn the engine over. If not, flick the kill switch to the OFF position and crank the engine over on the starter **(see illustration 2)**. If the nature on the ignition system prevents the starter operating with the kill switch in the OFF position,

remove the spark plugs and fit them back in their caps; ensure that the plugs are earthed (grounded) against the cylinder head when the starter is operated **(see illustration 3)**.

**⚠ Warning: It is important that the plugs are earthed (grounded) away from the spark plug holes otherwise there is a risk of atomised fuel from the cylinders igniting.**

**HAYNES HINT** *On a single cylinder four-stroke engine, you can seal the combustion chamber completely by positioning the piston at TDC on the compression stroke.*

● Drain the carburettor(s) otherwise there is a risk of jets becoming blocked by gum deposits from the fuel **(see illustration 4)**.

● If the bike is going into long-term storage, consider adding a fuel stabiliser to the fuel in the tank. If the tank is drained completely, corrosion of its internal surfaces may occur if left unprotected for a long period. The tank can be treated with a rust preventative especially for this purpose. Alternatively, remove the tank and pour half a litre of motor oil into it, install the filler cap and shake the tank to coat its internals with oil before draining off the excess. The same effect can also be achieved by spraying WD40 or a similar water-dispersant around the inside of the tank via its flexible nozzle.

● Make sure the cooling system contains the correct mix of antifreeze. Antifreeze also contains important corrosion inhibitors.

● The air intakes and exhaust can be sealed off by covering or plugging the openings. Ensure that you do not seal in any condensation; run the engine until it is hot,

Squirt a drop of motor oil into each cylinder

Flick the kill switch to OFF . . .

. . . and ensure that the metal bodies of the plugs (arrows) are earthed against the cylinder head

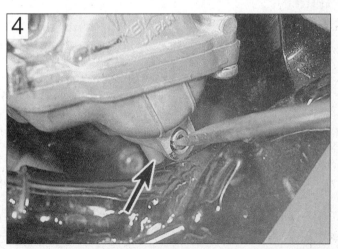

Connect a hose to the carburettor float chamber drain stub (arrow) and unscrew the drain screw

Exhausts can be sealed off with a plastic bag

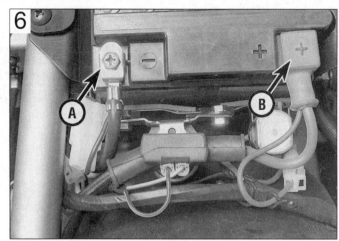

Disconnect the negative lead (A) first, followed by the positive lead (B)

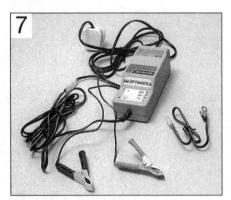

Use a suitable battery charger - this kit also assess battery condition

then switch off and allow to cool. Tape a piece of thick plastic over the silencer end(s) **(see illustration 5)**. Note that some advocate pouring a tablespoon of motor oil into the silencer(s) before sealing them off.

## Battery

● Remove it from the bike - in extreme cases of cold the battery may freeze and crack its case **(see illustration 6)**.

● Check the electrolyte level and top up if necessary (conventional refillable batteries). Clean the terminals.
● Store the battery off the motorcycle and away from any sources of fire. Position a wooden block under the battery if it is to sit on the ground.
● Give the battery a trickle charge for a few hours every month **(see illustration 7)**.

## Tyres

● Place the bike on its centrestand or an auxiliary stand which will support the motorcycle in an upright position. Position wood blocks under the tyres to keep them off the ground and to provide insulation from damp. If the bike is being put into long-term storage, ideally both tyres should be off the ground; not only will this protect the tyres, but will also ensure that no load is placed on the steering head or wheel bearings.
● Deflate each tyre by 5 to 10 psi, no more or the beads may unseat from the rim, making subsequent inflation difficult on tubeless tyres.

## Pivots and controls

● Lubricate all lever, pedal, stand and

footrest pivot points. If grease nipples are fitted to the rear suspension components, apply lubricant to the pivots.
● Lubricate all control cables.

## Cycle components

● Apply a wax protectant to all painted and plastic components. Wipe off any excess, but don't polish to a shine. Where fitted, clean the screen with soap and water.
● Coat metal parts with Vaseline (petroleum jelly). When applying this to the fork tubes, do not compress the forks otherwise the seals will rot from contact with the Vaseline.
● Apply a vinyl cleaner to the seat.

## Storage conditions

● Aim to store the bike in a shed or garage which does not leak and is free from damp.
● Drape an old blanket or bedspread over the bike to protect it from dust and direct contact with sunlight (which will fade paint). This also hides the bike from prying eyes. Beware of tight-fitting plastic covers which may allow condensation to form and settle on the bike.

# Getting back on the road

## Engine and transmission

● Change the oil and replace the oil filter. If this was done prior to storage, check that the oil hasn't emulsified - a thick whitish substance which occurs through condensation.
● Remove the spark plugs. Using a spout-type oil can, squirt a few drops of oil into the cylinder(s). This will provide initial lubrication as the piston rings and bores comes back into contact. Service the spark plugs, or fit new ones, and install them in the engine.

● Check that the clutch isn't stuck on. The plates can stick together if left standing for some time, preventing clutch operation. Engage a gear and try rocking the bike back and forth with the clutch lever held against the handlebar. If this doesn't work on cable-operated clutches, hold the clutch lever back against the handlebar with a strong elastic band or cable tie for a couple of hours **(see illustration 8)**.
● If the air intakes or silencer end(s) were blocked off, remove the bung or cover used.
● If the fuel tank was coated with a rust

Hold clutch lever back against the handlebar with elastic bands or a cable tie

preventative, oil or a stabiliser added to the fuel, drain and flush the tank and dispose of the fuel sensibly. If no action was taken with the fuel tank prior to storage, it is advised that the old fuel is disposed of since it will go off over a period of time. Refill the fuel tank with fresh fuel.

## Frame and running gear

● Oil all pivot points and cables.
● Check the tyre pressures. They will definitely need inflating if pressures were reduced for storage.
● Lubricate the final drive chain (where applicable).
● Remove any protective coating applied to the fork tubes (stanchions) since this may well destroy the fork seals. If the fork tubes weren't protected and have picked up rust spots, remove them with very fine abrasive paper and refinish with metal polish.
● Check that both brakes operate correctly. Apply each brake hard and check that it's not possible to move the motorcycle forwards, then check that the brake frees off again once released. Brake caliper pistons can stick due to corrosion around the piston head, or on the sliding caliper types, due to corrosion of the slider pins. If the brake doesn't free after repeated operation, take the caliper off for examination. Similarly drum brakes can stick

due to a seized operating cam, cable or rod linkage.
● If the motorcycle has been in long-term storage, renew the brake fluid and clutch fluid (where applicable).
● Depending on where the bike has been stored, the wiring, cables and hoses may have been nibbled by rodents. Make a visual check and investigate disturbed wiring loom tape.

## Battery

● If the battery has been previously removal and given top up charges it can simply be reconnected. Remember to connect the positive cable first and the negative cable last.
● On conventional refillable batteries, if the battery has not received any attention, remove it from the motorcycle and check its electrolyte level. Top up if necessary then charge the battery. If the battery fails to hold a charge and a visual checks show heavy white sulphation of the plates, the battery is probably defective and must be renewed. This is particularly likely if the battery is old. Confirm battery condition with a specific gravity check.
● On sealed (MF) batteries, if the battery has not received any attention, remove it from the motorcycle and charge it according to the information on the battery case - if the battery fails to hold a charge it must be renewed.

## Starting procedure

● If a kickstart is fitted, turn the engine over a couple of times with the ignition OFF to distribute oil around the engine. If no kickstart is fitted, flick the engine kill switch OFF and the ignition ON and crank the engine over a couple of times to work oil around the upper cylinder components. If the nature of the ignition system is such that the starter won't work with the kill switch OFF, remove the spark plugs, fit them back into their caps and earth (ground) their bodies on the cylinder head. Reinstall the spark plugs afterwards.
● Switch the kill switch to RUN, operate the choke and start the engine. If the engine won't start don't continue cranking the engine - not only will this flatten the battery, but the starter motor will overheat. Switch the ignition off and try again later. If the engine refuses to start, go through the fault finding procedures in this manual. **Note:** *If the bike has been in storage for a long time, old fuel or a carburettor blockage may be the problem. Gum deposits in carburettors can block jets - if a carburettor cleaner doesn't prove successful the carburettors must be dismantled for cleaning.*
● Once the engine has started, check that the lights, turn signals and horn work properly.
● Treat the bike gently for the first ride and check all fluid levels on completion. Settle the bike back into the maintenance schedule.

This Section provides an easy reference-guide to the more common faults that are likely to afflict your machine. Obviously, the opportunities are almost limitless for faults to occur as a result of obscure failures, and to try and cover all eventualities would require a book. Indeed, a number have been written on the subject.

Successful troubleshooting is not a mysterious 'black art' but the application of a bit of knowledge combined with a systematic and logical approach to the problem. Approach any troubleshooting by first accurately identifying the symptom and then checking through the list of possible causes, starting with the simplest or most obvious and progressing in stages to the most complex.

Take nothing for granted, but above all apply liberal quantities of common sense.

The main symptom of a fault is given in the text as a major heading below which are listed the various systems or areas which may contain the fault. Details of each possible cause for a fault and the remedial action to be taken are given, in brief, in the paragraphs below each heading. Further information should be sought in the relevant Chapter.

## 1 Engine doesn't start or is difficult to start

- ☐ Starter motor doesn't rotate
- ☐ Starter motor rotates but engine does not turn over
- ☐ Starter works but engine won't turn over (seized)
- ☐ No fuel flow
- ☐ Engine flooded
- ☐ No spark or weak spark
- ☐ Compression low
- ☐ Stalls after starting
- ☐ Rough idle

## 2 Poor running at low speed

- ☐ Spark weak
- ☐ Fuel/air mixture incorrect
- ☐ Compression low
- ☐ Poor acceleration

## 3 Poor running or no power at high speed

- ☐ Firing incorrect
- ☐ Fuel/air mixture incorrect
- ☐ Compression low
- ☐ Knocking or pinging
- ☐ Miscellaneous causes

## 4 Overheating

- ☐ Engine overheats
- ☐ Firing incorrect
- ☐ Fuel/air mixture incorrect
- ☐ Compression too high
- ☐ Engine load excessive
- ☐ Lubrication inadequate
- ☐ Miscellaneous causes

## 5 Clutch problems

- ☐ Clutch slipping
- ☐ Clutch not disengaging completely

## 6 Gear shifting problems

- ☐ Doesn't go into gear, or lever doesn't return
- ☐ Jumps out of gear
- ☐ Overshifts

## 7 Abnormal engine noise

- ☐ Knocking or pinging
- ☐ Piston slap or rattling
- ☐ Valve noise
- ☐ Other noise

## 8 Abnormal driveline noise

- ☐ Clutch noise
- ☐ Transmission noise
- ☐ Chain or final drive noise

## 9 Abnormal frame and suspension noise

- ☐ Front end noise
- ☐ Shock absorber noise
- ☐ Disc brake noise

## 10 Oil level indicator light comes on

- ☐ Engine lubrication system
- ☐ Electrical system
- ☐ Excessive exhaust smoke
- ☐ White smoke
- ☐ Black smoke
- ☐ Brown smoke

## 11 Poor handling or stability

- ☐ Handlebar hard to turn
- ☐ Handlebar shakes or vibrates excessively
- ☐ Handlebar pulls to one side
- ☐ Poor shock absorbing qualities

## 12 Braking problems

- ☐ Brakes are spongy, don't hold
- ☐ Brake lever pulsates
- ☐ Brakes drag
- ☐ Electrical problems
- ☐ Battery dead or weak
- ☐ Battery overcharged

# 1 Engine doesn't start or is difficult to start

## Starter motor does not rotate

☐ Engine kill switch Off.
☐ Fuse blown. Check fuse block (Chapter 8).
☐ Battery voltage low. Check and recharge battery (Chapter 8).
☐ Starter motor defective. Make sure the wiring to the starter is secure. Test starter relay (Chapter 8). If the relay is good, then the fault is in the wiring or motor.
☐ Starter relay faulty. Check it according to the procedure in Chapter 8.
☐ Starter switch not contacting. The contacts could be wet, corroded or dirty. Disassemble and clean the switch (Chapter 8).
☐ Wiring open or shorted. Check all wiring connections and harnesses to make sure that they are dry, tight and not corroded. Also check for broken or frayed wires that can cause a short to ground (see wiring diagram, Chapter 8).
☐ Ignition switch defective. Check the switch according to the procedure in Chapter 8. Replace the switch with a new one if it is defective.
☐ Engine kill switch defective. Check for wet, dirty or corroded contacts. Clean or replace the switch as necessary (Chapter 8).

## Starter motor rotates but engine does not turn over

☐ Starter motor clutch defective. Inspect and repair or replace (Chapter 8).
☐ Damaged idler or starter gears. Inspect and replace the damaged parts (Chapter 2).

## Starter works but engine won't turn over (seized)

☐ Seized engine caused by one or more internally damaged components. Failure due to wear, abuse or lack of lubrication. Damage can include seized valves, valve lifters, camshaft, pistons, crankshaft, connecting rod bearings, or transmission gears or bearings. Refer to Chapter 2 for engine disassembly.

## No fuel flow

☐ No fuel in tank.
☐ Fuel tap vacuum hose (if equipped) broken or disconnected.
☐ Tank cap air vent obstructed. Usually caused by dirt or water. Remove it and clean the cap vent hole.
☐ Inline fuel filter clogged. Replace the filter (Chapter 1).
☐ Electric fuel pump not working (if equipped). Test it according to the procedures in Chapter 8.
☐ Fuel line clogged. Pull the fuel line loose and carefully blow through it.
☐ Inlet needle valve clogged. For both of the valves to be clogged, either a very bad batch of fuel with an unusual additive has been used, or some other foreign material has entered the tank. Many times after a machine has been stored for many months without running, the fuel turns to a varnish-like liquid and forms deposits on the inlet needle valves and jets. The carburetors should be removed and overhauled if draining the float chambers doesn't solve the problem.

## Engine flooded

☐ Fuel level too high. Check and adjust as described in Chapter 3.
☐ Inlet needle valve worn or stuck open. A piece of dirt, rust or other debris can cause the inlet needle to seat improperly, causing excess fuel to be admitted to the float bowl. In this case, the float chamber should be cleaned and the needle and seat inspected. If the needle and seat are worn, then the leaking will persist and the parts should be replaced with new ones (Chapter 3).
☐ Starting technique incorrect. Under normal circumstances (i.e., if all the carburetor functions are sound) the machine should start with little or no throttle. When the engine is cold, the choke should be operated and the engine started without opening the throttle. When the engine is at operating temperature, only a very slight amount of throttle should be necessary. If the engine is flooded, turn the fuel tap off and hold the throttle open while cranking the engine. This will allow additional air to reach the cylinders. Remember to turn the fuel tap back on after the engine starts.

## No spark or weak spark

☐ Ignition switch Off.
☐ Engine kill switch turned to the Off position.
☐ Battery voltage low. Check and recharge battery as necessary (Chapter 8).
☐ Spark plug dirty, defective or worn out. Locate reason for fouled plug(s) using spark plug condition chart and follow the plug maintenance procedures in Chapter 1.
☐ Spark plug cap or secondary (HT) wiring faulty. Check condition. Replace either or both components if cracks or deterioration are evident (Chapter 4).
☐ Spark plug cap not making good contact. Make sure that the plug cap fits snugly over the plug end.
☐ Igniter defective. Check the unit, referring to Chapter 4 for details.
☐ Pickup coil(s) defective. Check the unit(s), referring to Chapter 4 for details.
☐ Ignition coil(s) defective. Check the coils, referring to Chapter 4.
☐ Ignition or kill switch shorted. This is usually caused by water, corrosion, damage or excessive wear. The switches can be disassembled and cleaned with electrical contact cleaner. If cleaning does not help, replace the switches (Chapter 8).
☐ Wiring shorted or broken between:
*Ignition switch and engine kill switch (or blown fuse)*
*Igniter and engine kill switch*
*Igniter and ignition coil*
*Ignition coil and plug*
*Igniter and pickup coil(s)*
☐ Make sure that all wiring connections are clean, dry and tight. Look for chafed and broken wires (Chapters 4 and 8).

# 1 Engine doesn't start or is difficult to start (continued)

## Compression low

☐ Spark plug loose. Remove the plug and inspect the threads. Reinstall and tighten to the specified torque (Chapter 1).

☐ Cylinder head not sufficiently tightened down. If a cylinder head is suspected of being loose, then there's a chance that the gasket or head is damaged if the problem has persisted for any length of time. The head nuts and bolts should be tightened to the proper torque in the correct sequence (Chapter 2).

☐ Improper valve clearance. This means that the valve is not closing completely and compression pressure is leaking past the valve. Check and adjust the valve clearances (Chapter 1).

☐ Cylinder and/or piston worn. Excessive wear will cause compression pressure to leak past the rings. This is usually accompanied by worn rings as well. A top end overhaul is necessary (Chapter 2).

☐ Piston rings worn, weak, broken, or sticking. Broken or sticking piston rings usually indicate a lubrication or carburetion problem that causes excess carbon deposits or seizures to form on the pistons and rings. Top end overhaul is necessary (Chapter 2).

☐ Piston ring-to-groove clearance excessive. This is caused by excessive wear of the piston ring lands. Piston replacement is necessary (Chapter 2).

☐ Cylinder head gasket damaged. If one of the heads is allowed to become loose, or if excessive carbon build-up on a piston crown and combustion chamber causes extremely high compression, the head gasket may leak. Retorquing the head is not always sufficient to restore the seal, so gasket replacement is necessary (Chapter 2).

☐ Cylinder head warped. This is caused by overheating or improperly tightened head nuts and bolts. Machine shop resurfacing or head replacement is necessary (Chapter 2).

☐ Valve spring broken or weak. Caused by component failure or wear; the spring(s) must be replaced (Chapter 2).

☐ Valve not seating properly. This is caused by a bent valve (from over-revving or improper valve adjustment), burned valve or seat (improper carburetion) or an accumulation of carbon deposits on the seat (from carburetion or lubrication problems). The valves must be cleaned and/or replaced and the seats serviced if possible (Chapter 2).

## Stalls after starting

☐ Improper choke action. Make sure the choke lever (XV535) or choke cable (all others) is getting a full stroke and staying in the out position.

☐ Ignition malfunction. See Chapter 4.

☐ Carburetor malfunction. See Chapter 3.

☐ Fuel contaminated. The fuel can be contaminated with either dirt or water, or can change chemically if the machine is allowed to sit for several months or more. Drain the tank and float bowls (Chapter 3).

☐ Intake air leak. Check for loose carburetor-to-intake joint connections, loose or missing vacuum gauge access port cap or hose, or loose carburetor top (Chapter 3).

☐ Engine idle speed incorrect. Turn throttle stop screw until the engine idles at the specified rpm (Chapter 1).

## Rough idle

☐ Ignition malfunction. See Chapter 4.

☐ Idle speed incorrect. See Chapter 1.

☐ Carburetors not synchronized. Adjust carburetors with vacuum gauge or manometer set as described in Chapter 1.

☐ Carburetor malfunction. See Chapter 3.

☐ Fuel contaminated. The fuel can be contaminated with either dirt or water, or can change chemically if the machine is allowed to sit for several months or more. Drain the tank and float bowls (Chapter 3).

☐ Intake air leak. Check for loose carburetor-to-intake joint connections, loose or missing vacuum gauge access port cap or hose, or loose carburetor top (Chapter 3).

☐ Air cleaner clogged. Service or replace air filter element (Chapter 1).

# 2 Poor running at low speed

## Spark weak

☐ Battery voltage low. Check and recharge battery (Chapter 8).
☐ Spark plug fouled, defective or worn out. Refer to Chapter 1 for spark plug maintenance.
☐ Spark plug cap or high tension wiring defective. Refer to Chapters 1 and 4 for details on the ignition system.
☐ Spark plug cap not making contact.
☐ Incorrect spark plug. Wrong type, heat range or cap configuration. Check and install correct plugs listed in Chapter 1. A cold plug or one with a recessed firing electrode will not operate at low speeds without fouling.
☐ Igniter defective. See Chapter 4.
☐ Pickup coil(s) defective. See Chapter 4.
☐ Ignition coil(s) defective. See Chapter 4.

## Fuel/air mixture incorrect

☐ Pilot screw(s) out of adjustment (Chapters 1 and 3).
☐ Pilot jet or air passage clogged. Remove and overhaul the carburetors (Chapter 3).
☐ Air bleed holes clogged. Remove carburetor and blow out all passages (Chapter 3).
☐ Air cleaner clogged, poorly sealed or missing.
☐ Air cleaner-to-carburetor boot poorly sealed. Look for cracks, holes or loose clamps and replace or repair defective parts.
☐ Fuel level too high or too low. Adjust the floats (Chapter 3).
☐ Fuel tank air vent obstructed. Make sure that the air vent passage in the filler cap is open.
☐ Carburetor intake joints loose. Check for cracks, breaks, tears or loose clamps or bolts. Repair or replace the rubber boots.

## Compression low

☐ Spark plug loose. Remove the plug and inspect the threads. Reinstall and tighten to the specified torque (Chapter 1).
☐ Cylinder head not sufficiently tightened down. If the cylinder head is suspected of being loose, then there's a chance that the gasket and head are damaged if the problem has persisted for any length of time. The head nuts and bolts should be tightened to the proper torque in the correct sequence (Chapter 2).
☐ Improper valve clearance. This means that the valve is not closing completely and compression pressure is leaking past the valve. Check and adjust the valve clearances (Chapter 1).

☐ Cylinder and/or piston worn. Excessive wear will cause compression pressure to leak past the rings. This is usually accompanied by worn rings as well. A top end overhaul is necessary (Chapter 2).
☐ Piston rings worn, weak, broken, or sticking. Broken or sticking piston rings usually indicate a lubrication or carburetion problem that causes excess carbon deposits or seizures to form on the pistons and rings. Top end overhaul is necessary (Chapter 2).
☐ Piston ring-to-groove clearance excessive. This is caused by excessive wear of the piston ring lands. Piston replacement is necessary (Chapter 2).
☐ Cylinder head gasket damaged. If a head is allowed to become loose, or if excessive carbon build-up on the piston crown and combustion chamber causes extremely high compression, the head gasket may leak. Retorquing the head is not always sufficient to restore the seal, so gasket replacement is necessary (Chapter 2).
☐ Cylinder head warped. This is caused by overheating or improperly tightened head nuts and bolts. Machine shop resurfacing or head replacement is necessary (Chapter 2).
☐ Valve spring broken or weak. Caused by component failure or wear; the spring(s) must be replaced (Chapter 2).
☐ Valve not seating properly. This is caused by a bent valve (from over-revving or improper valve adjustment), burned valve or seat (improper carburetion) or an accumulation of carbon deposits on the seat (from carburetion, lubrication problems). The valves must be cleaned and/or replaced and the seats serviced if possible (Chapter 2).

## Poor acceleration

☐ Carburetors leaking or dirty. Overhaul the carburetors (Chapter 3).
☐ Timing not advancing. The pickup coil(s) or the igniter may be defective. If so, they must be replaced with new ones, as they can't be repaired.
☐ Carburetors not synchronized. Adjust them with a vacuum gauge set or manometer (Chapter 1).
☐ Engine oil viscosity too high. Using a heavier oil than that recommended in Chapter 1 can damage the oil pump or lubrication system and cause drag on the engine.
☐ Brakes dragging. Usually caused by debris which has entered the brake piston sealing boot, or from a warped disc or bent axle. Repair as necessary (Chapter 6).

# 3 Poor running or no power at high speed

### Firing incorrect

☐ Air filter restricted. Clean or replace filter (Chapter 1).
☐ Spark plug fouled, defective or worn out. See Chapter 1 for spark plug maintenance.
☐ Spark plug cap or secondary (HT) wiring defective. See Chapters 1 and 4 for details of the ignition system.
☐ Spark plug cap not in good contact. See Chapter 4.
☐ Incorrect spark plug. Wrong type, heat range or cap configuration. Check and install correct plugs listed in Chapter 1. A cold plug or one with a recessed firing electrode will not operate at low speeds without fouling.
☐ Igniter defective. See Chapter 4.
☐ Ignition coil(s) defective. See Chapter 4.

### Fuel/air mixture incorrect

☐ Main jet clogged. Dirt, water or other contaminants can clog the main jets. Clean the fuel tap filter, the float bowl area, and the jets and carburetor orifices (Chapter 3).
☐ Main jet wrong size. The standard jetting is for sea level atmospheric pressure and oxygen content.
☐ Throttle shaft-to-carburetor body clearance excessive. Refer to Chapter 3 for inspection and part replacement procedures.
☐ Air bleed holes clogged. Remove and overhaul carburetors (Chapter 3).
☐ Air cleaner clogged, poorly sealed, or missing.
☐ Air cleaner-to-carburetor boot poorly sealed. Look for cracks, holes or loose clamps, and replace or repair defective parts.
☐ Fuel level too high or too low. Adjust the float(s) (Chapter 3).
☐ Fuel tank air vent obstructed. Make sure the air vent passage in the filler cap is open.
☐ Carburetor intake joints loose. Check for cracks, breaks, tears or loose clamps or bolts. Repair or replace the rubber boots (Chapter 3).
☐ Fuel tap clogged. Remove the tap and clean it (Chapter 1).
☐ Fuel line clogged. Pull the fuel line loose and carefully blow through it.

### Compression low

☐ Spark plug loose. Remove the plug and inspect the threads. Reinstall and tighten to the specified torque (Chapter 1).
☐ Cylinder head not sufficiently tightened down. If a cylinder head is suspected of being loose, then there's a chance that the gasket and head are damaged if the problem has persisted for any length of time. The head nuts and bolts should be tightened to the proper torque in the correct sequence (Chapter 2).
☐ Improper valve clearance. This means that the valve is not closing completely and compression pressure is leaking past the valve. Check and adjust the valve clearances (Chapter 1).
☐ Cylinder and/or piston worn. Excessive wear will cause compression pressure to leak past the rings. This is usually accompanied by worn rings as well. A top end overhaul is necessary (Chapter 2).
☐ Piston rings worn, weak, broken, or sticking. Broken or sticking piston rings usually indicate a lubrication or carburetion problem that causes excess carbon deposits or seizures to form on the pistons and rings. Top end overhaul is necessary (Chapter 2).
☐ Piston ring-to-groove clearance excessive. This is caused by excessive wear of the piston ring lands. Piston replacement is necessary (Chapter 2).
☐ Cylinder head gasket damaged. If a head is allowed to become loose, or if excessive carbon build-up on the piston crown and combustion chamber causes extremely high compression, the head gasket may leak. Retorquing the head is not always sufficient to restore the seal, so gasket replacement is necessary (Chapter 2).
☐ Cylinder head warped. This is caused by overheating or improperly tightened head nuts and bolts. Machine shop resurfacing or head replacement is necessary (Chapter 2).
☐ Valve spring broken or weak. Caused by component failure or wear; the spring(s) must be replaced (Chapter 2).
☐ Valve not seating properly. This is caused by a bent valve (from over-revving or improper valve adjustment), burned valve or seat (improper carburetion) or an accumulation of carbon deposits on the seat (from carburetion or lubrication problems). The valves must be cleaned and/or replaced and the seats serviced if possible (Chapter 2).

### Knocking or pinging

☐ Carbon build-up in combustion chamber. Use of a fuel additive that will dissolve the adhesive bonding the carbon particles to the crown and chamber is the easiest way to remove the build-up. Otherwise, the cylinder head will have to be removed and decarbonized (Chapter 2).
☐ Incorrect or poor quality fuel. Old or improper grades of fuel can cause detonation. This causes the piston to rattle, thus the knocking or pinging sound. Drain old fuel and always use the recommended fuel grade.
☐ Spark plug heat range incorrect. Uncontrolled detonation indicates the plug heat range is too hot. The plug in effect becomes a glow plug, raising cylinder temperatures. Install the proper heat range plug (Chapter 1).
☐ Improper air/fuel mixture. This will cause the cylinder to run hot, which leads to detonation. Clogged jets or an air leak can cause this imbalance. See Chapter 3.

### Miscellaneous causes

☐ Throttle valve doesn't open fully. Adjust the cable slack (Chapter 1).
☐ Clutch slipping. May be caused by a cable that is improperly adjusted or loose or worn clutch components. Refer to Chapter 2 for cable replacement and clutch overhaul procedures.
☐ Timing not advancing.
☐ Engine oil viscosity too high. Using a heavier oil than the one recommended in Chapter 1 can damage the oil pump or lubrication system and cause drag on the engine.
☐ Brakes dragging. Usually caused by debris which has entered the brake piston sealing boot, or from a warped disc or bent axle. Repair as necessary.

# 4 Overheating

## Engine overheats

- ☐ Engine oil level low. Check and add oil (Chapter 1).
- ☐ Wrong type of oil. If you're not sure what type of oil is in the engine, drain it and fill with the correct type (Chapter 1).
- ☐ Air leak at carburetor intake joints. Check and tighten or replace as necessary (Chapter 3).
- ☐ Fuel level low. Check and adjust if necessary (Chapter 3).
- ☐ Worn oil pump or clogged oil passages. Replace pump or clean passages as necessary.
- ☐ Clogged external oil lines (if equipped). Remove and check for foreign material (see Chapter 2).
- ☐ Carbon build-up in combustion chambers. Use of a fuel additive that will dissolve the adhesive bonding the carbon particles to the piston crowns and chambers is the easiest way to remove the build-up. Otherwise, the cylinder heads will have to be removed and decarbonized (Chapter 2).

## Firing incorrect

- ☐ Spark plug fouled, defective or worn out. See Chapter 1 for spark plug maintenance.
- ☐ Incorrect spark plug (see Chapter 1).
- ☐ Faulty ignition coil(s) (Chapter 4).

## Fuel/air mixture incorrect

- ☐ Main jet clogged. Dirt, water and other contaminants can clog the main jets. Clean the fuel tap filter, the float bowl area and the jets and carburetor orifices (Chapter 3).
- ☐ Main jet wrong size. The standard jetting is for sea level atmospheric pressure and oxygen content.
- ☐ Air cleaner poorly sealed or missing.
- ☐ Air cleaner-to-carburetor boot poorly sealed. Look for cracks, holes or loose clamps and replace or repair.
- ☐ Fuel level too low. Adjust the float(s) (Chapter 3).
- ☐ Fuel tank air vent obstructed. Make sure that the air vent passage in the filler cap is open.
- ☐ Carburetor intake joints loose. Check for cracks, breaks, tears or loose clamps or bolts. Repair or replace the rubber boots (Chapter 3).

## Compression too high

- ☐ Carbon build-up in combustion chamber. Use of a fuel additive that will dissolve the adhesive bonding the carbon particles to the piston crown and chamber is the easiest way to remove the build-up. Otherwise, the cylinder head will have to be removed and decarbonized (Chapter 2).
- ☐ Improperly machined head surface or installation of incorrect gasket during engine assembly.

## Engine load excessive

- ☐ Clutch slipping. Can be caused by damaged, loose or worn clutch components. Refer to Chapter 2 for overhaul procedures.
- ☐ Engine oil level too high. The addition of too much oil will cause pressurization of the crankcase and inefficient engine operation. Check Specifications and drain to proper level (Chapter 1).
- ☐ Engine oil viscosity too high. Using a heavier oil than the one recommended in Chapter 1 can damage the oil pump or lubrication system as well as cause drag on the engine.
- ☐ Brakes dragging. Usually caused by debris which has entered the brake piston sealing boot, or from a warped disc or bent axle. Repair as necessary.

## Lubrication inadequate

- ☐ Engine oil level too low. Friction caused by intermittent lack of lubrication or from oil that is overworked can cause overheating. The oil provides a definite cooling function in the engine. Check the oil level (Chapter 1).
- ☐ Poor quality engine oil or incorrect viscosity or type. Oil is rated not only according to viscosity but also according to type. Some oils are not rated high enough for use in this engine. Check the Specifications section and change to the correct oil (Chapter 1).
- ☐ Camshaft or journals worn. Excessive wear causing drop in oil pressure. Replace cam, bushing or cylinder head. Abnormal wear could be caused by oil starvation at high rpm from low oil level or improper viscosity or type of oil (Chapter 1).
- ☐ Crankshaft and/or bearings worn. Same problems as paragraph 3. Check and replace crankshaft and/or bearings (Chapter 2).

## Miscellaneous causes

- ☐ Modification to exhaust system. Most aftermarket exhaust systems cause the engine to run leaner, which make them run hotter. When installing an accessory exhaust system, always rejet the carburetors.

# 5 Clutch problems

### Clutch slipping

- [ ] Friction plates worn or warped. Overhaul the clutch assembly (Chapter 2).
- [ ] Steel plates worn or warped (Chapter 2).
- [ ] Clutch spring(s) broken or weak. Old or heat-damaged spring(s) (from slipping clutch) should be replaced with new ones (Chapter 2).
- [ ] Clutch release mechanism defective. Replace any defective parts (Chapter 2).
- [ ] Clutch boss or housing unevenly worn. This causes improper engagement of the plates. Replace the damaged or worn parts (Chapter 2).

### Clutch not disengaging completely

- [ ] Clutch lever play excessive (see Chapter 1). Clutch cable improperly adjusted (see Chapter 1).
- [ ] Clutch plates warped or damaged. This will cause clutch drag, which in turn will cause the machine to creep. Overhaul the clutch assembly (Chapter 2).

- [ ] Usually caused by a sagged or broken spring(s). Check and replace the spring(s) (Chapter 2).
- [ ] Engine oil deteriorated. Old, thin, worn out oil will not provide proper lubrication for the discs, causing the clutch to drag. Replace the oil and filter (Chapter 1).
- [ ] Engine oil viscosity too high. Using a thicker oil than recommended in Chapter 1 can cause the plates to stick together, putting a drag on the engine. Change to the correct viscosity oil (Chapter 1).
- [ ] Clutch housing seized on shaft. Lack of lubrication, severe wear or damage can cause the housing to seize on the shaft. Overhaul of the clutch, and perhaps transmission, may be necessary to repair the damage (Chapter 2).
- [ ] Clutch release mechanism defective. Worn or damaged release mechanism parts can stick and fail to apply force to the pressure plate. Overhaul the release mechanism (Chapter 2).
- [ ] Loose clutch boss nut. Causes housing and boss misalignment putting a drag on the engine. Engagement adjustment continually varies. Overhaul the clutch assembly (Chapter 2).

# 6 Gear shifting problems

### Doesn't go into gear or lever doesn't return

- [ ] Clutch not disengaging. See Section 5.
- [ ] Shift fork(s) bent or seized. Often caused by dropping the machine or from lack of lubrication. Overhaul the transmission (Chapter 2).
- [ ] Gear(s) stuck on shaft. Most often caused by a lack of lubrication or excessive wear in transmission bearings and bushings. Overhaul the transmission (Chapter 2).
- [ ] Shift cam binding. Caused by lubrication failure or excessive wear. Replace the cam and bearing (Chapter 2).
- [ ] Shift lever return spring weak or broken (Chapter 2).
- [ ] Shift lever broken. Splines stripped out of lever or shaft, caused by allowing the lever to get loose or from dropping the machine. Replace necessary parts (Chapter 2).

- [ ] Shift mechanism pawl broken or worn. Full engagement and rotary movement of shift drum results. Replace shaft assembly (Chapter 2).
- [ ] Pawl spring broken. Allows pawl to float, causing sporadic shift operation. Replace spring (Chapter 2).

### Jumps out of gear

- [ ] Shift fork(s) worn. Overhaul the transmission (Chapter 2).
- [ ] Gear groove(s) worn. Overhaul the transmission (Chapter 2).
- [ ] Gear dogs or dog slots worn or damaged. The gears should be inspected and replaced. No attempt should be made to service the worn parts.

### Overshifts

- [ ] Pawl spring weak or broken (Chapter 2).
- [ ] Shift drum stopper lever not functioning (Chapter 2).

# 7 Abnormal engine noise

## Knocking or pinging

☐ Carbon build-up in combustion chamber. Use of a fuel additive that will dissolve the adhesive bonding the carbon particles to the piston crown and chamber is the easiest way to remove the build-up. Otherwise, the cylinder head will have to be removed and decarbonized (Chapter 2).

☐ Incorrect or poor quality fuel. Old or improper fuel can cause detonation. This causes the pistons to rattle, thus the knocking or pinging sound. Drain the old fuel and always use the recommended grade fuel (Chapter 1).

☐ Spark plug heat range incorrect. Uncontrolled detonation indicates that the plug heat range is too hot. The plug in effect becomes a glow plug, raising cylinder temperatures. Install the proper heat range plug (Chapter 1).

☐ Improper air/fuel mixture. This will cause the cylinders to run hot and lead to detonation. Clogged jets or an air leak can cause this imbalance. See Chapter 3.

## Piston slap or rattling

☐ Cylinder-to-piston clearance excessive. Caused by improper assembly. Inspect and overhaul top end parts (Chapter 2).

☐ Connecting rod bent. Caused by over-revving, trying to start a badly flooded engine or from ingesting a foreign object into the combustion chamber. Replace the damaged parts (Chapter 2).

☐ Piston pin or piston pin bore worn or seized from wear or lack of lubrication. Replace damaged parts (Chapter 2).

☐ Piston ring(s) worn, broken or sticking. Overhaul the top end (Chapter 2).

☐ Piston seizure damage. Usually from lack of lubrication or overheating. Replace the pistons and bore the cylinders, as necessary (Chapter 2).

☐ Connecting rod upper or lower end clearance excessive. Caused by excessive wear or lack of lubrication. Replace worn parts.

## Valve noise

☐ Incorrect valve clearances. Adjust the clearances by referring to Chapter 1.

☐ Valve spring broken or weak. Check and replace weak valve springs (Chapter 2).

☐ Camshaft, bushing or cylinder head worn or damaged. Lack of lubrication at high rpm is usually the cause of damage. Insufficient oil or failure to change the oil at the recommended intervals are the chief causes.

## Other noise

☐ Cylinder head gasket leaking.

☐ Exhaust pipe leaking at cylinder head connection. Caused by improper fit of pipe(s) or loose exhaust flange. All exhaust fasteners should be tightened evenly and carefully. Failure to do this will lead to a leak.

☐ Crankshaft runout excessive. Caused by a bent crankshaft (from over-revving) or damage from an upper cylinder component failure. Can also be attributed to dropping the machine on either of the crankshaft ends.

☐ Engine mounting bolts or nuts loose. Tighten all engine mounting bolts and nuts to the specified torque (Chapter 2).

☐ Crankshaft bearings worn (Chapter 2).

☐ Camshaft chain tensioner(s) defective. Replace according to the procedure in Chapter 2.

☐ Camshaft chain, sprockets or guides worn (Chapter 2).

# 8 Abnormal driveline noise

## Clutch noise

☐ Clutch housing/friction plate clearance excessive (Chapter 2).
☐ Loose or damaged clutch pressure plate and/or bolts (Chapter 2).

## Transmission noise

☐ Bearings worn. Also includes the possibility that the shafts are worn. Overhaul the transmission (Chapter 2).
☐ Gears worn or chipped (Chapter 2).
☐ Metal chips jammed in gear teeth. Probably pieces from a broken clutch, gear or shift mechanism that were picked up by the gears. This will cause early bearing failure (Chapter 2).
☐ Engine oil level too low. Causes a howl from transmission. Also affects engine power and clutch operation (Chapter 1).

## Final drive noise

☐ Chain not adjusted properly (if equipped) (Chapter 1).
☐ Engine sprocket or rear sprocket loose (chain drive models). Tighten fasteners (Chapter 5).
☐ Sprocket(s) worn (chain drive models). Replace sprocket(s). (Chapter 5).
☐ Rear sprocket warped (chain drive models). Replace (Chapter 5).
☐ Wheel coupling (cush drive) worn (chain drive models). Replace coupling (Chapter 5).
☐ Final drive oil level low (shaft drive models).
☐ Final drive gear lash out of adjustment (shaft drive models).
☐ Final drive gears damaged or worn (shaft drive models).

# 9 Abnormal frame and suspension noise

## Front end noise

☐ Low fluid level or improper viscosity oil in forks. This can sound like spurting and is usually accompanied by irregular fork action (Chapter 5).
☐ Spring weak or broken. Makes a clicking or scraping sound. Fork oil, when drained, will have a lot of metal particles in it (Chapter 5).
☐ Steering head bearings loose or damaged. Clicks when braking. Check and adjust or replace as necessary (Chapter 5).
☐ Fork triple clamps loose. Make sure all triple clamp pinch bolts are tight (Chapter 5).
☐ Fork tube bent. Good possibility if machine has been dropped. Replace tube with a new one (Chapter 5).
☐ Front axle or axle clamp bolt loose. Tighten them to the specified torque (Chapter 6).

## Shock absorber noise

☐ Fluid level incorrect. Indicates a leak caused by defective seal. Shock will be covered with oil. Replace shock (Chapter 5).
☐ Defective shock absorber with internal damage. This is in the body of the shock and can't be remedied. The shock must be replaced with a new one (Chapter 5).
☐ Bent or damaged shock body. Replace the shock with a new one (Chapter 5).

## Brake noise

☐ Squeal caused by pad shim not installed or positioned correctly (Chapter 6).
☐ Squeal caused by dust on brake pads. Usually found in combination with glazed pads. Clean using brake cleaning solvent (Chapter 6).
☐ Contamination of brake pads. Oil, brake fluid or dirt causing brake to chatter or squeal. Clean or replace pads (Chapter 6).
☐ Pads glazed. Caused by excessive heat from prolonged use or from contamination. Do not use sandpaper, emery cloth, carborundum cloth or any other abrasive to roughen the pad surfaces as abrasives will stay in the pad material and damage the disc. A very fine flat file can be used, but pad replacement is suggested as a cure (Chapter 6).
☐ Disc warped. Can cause a chattering, clicking or intermittent squeal. Usually accompanied by a pulsating lever and uneven braking. Replace the disc (Chapter 6).
☐ Drum brake linings worn or contaminated. Can cause scraping or squealing. Replace the shoes (Chapter 6).
☐ Drum brake linings warped or worn unevenly. Can cause chattering. Replace the linings (Chapter 6).
☐ Brake drum out of round. Can cause chattering. Replace brake drum (Chapter 6).
☐ Loose or worn wheel bearings. Check/replace as needed (Chapter 6).

# 10 Oil level indicator light comes on

## Engine lubrication system

☐ Yamaha XV700 through 1100 models use an oil level light rather than an oil pressure light.

☐ Engine oil level low. Inspect for leak or other problem causing low oil level and add recommended oil (Chapters 1 and 2).

## Electrical system

☐ Oil level switch defective. Check the switch according to the procedure in Chapter 8. Replace it if it's defective.

☐ Oil level indicator light circuit defective. Check for pinched, shorted, disconnected or damaged wiring (Chapter 8).

# 11 Excessive exhaust smoke

## White smoke

☐ Piston oil ring worn. The ring may be broken or damaged, causing oil from the crankcase to be pulled past the piston into the combustion chamber. Replace the rings with new ones (Chapter 2).

☐ Cylinders worn, cracked, or scored. Caused by overheating or oil starvation. If worn or scored, the cylinders will have to be rebored and new pistons installed. If cracked, the cylinder block will have to be replaced (see Chapter 2).

☐ Valve oil seal damaged or worn. Replace oil seals with new ones (Chapter 2).

☐ Valve guide worn. Perform a complete valve job (Chapter 2).

☐ Engine oil level too high, which causes the oil to be forced past the rings. Drain oil to the proper level (Chapter 1).

☐ Head gasket broken between oil return and cylinder. Causes oil to be pulled into the combustion chamber. Replace the head gasket and check the head for warpage (Chapter 2).

☐ Abnormal crankcase pressurization, which forces oil past the rings. Clogged breather or hoses usually the cause (Chapter 2).

## Black smoke

☐ Air cleaner clogged. Clean or replace the element (Chapter 1).

☐ Main jet too large or loose. Compare the jet size to the Specifications (Chapter 3).

☐ Choke stuck, causing fuel to be pulled through choke circuit (Chapter 3).

☐ Fuel level too high. Check and adjust the float level as necessary (Chapter 3).

☐ Inlet needle held off needle seat. Clean the float bowls and fuel line and replace the needles and seats if necessary (Chapter 3).

## Brown smoke

☐ Main jet too small or clogged. Lean condition caused by wrong size main jet or by a restricted orifice. Clean float bowl and jets and compare jet size to Specifications (Chapter 3).

☐ Fuel flow insufficient. Fuel inlet needle valve stuck closed due to chemical reaction with old fuel. Float level incorrect. Restricted fuel line. Clean line and float bowl and adjust floats if necessary.

☐ Carburetor intake manifolds loose (Chapter 3).

☐ Air cleaner poorly sealed or not installed (Chapter 1).

# 12 Poor handling or stability

## Handlebar hard to turn

☐ Steering stem locknut too tight (Chapter 5).
☐ Bearings damaged. Roughness can be felt as the bars are turned from side-to-side. Replace bearings and races (Chapter 5).
☐ Races dented or worn. Denting results from wear in only one position (e.g., straight ahead), from a collision or hitting a pothole or from dropping the machine. Replace races and bearings (Chapter 5).
☐ Steering stem lubrication inadequate. Causes are grease getting hard from age or being washed out by high pressure car washes. Disassemble steering head and repack bearings (Chapter 5).
☐ Steering stem bent. Caused by a collision, hitting a pothole or by dropping the machine. Replace damaged part. Don't try to straighten the steering stem (Chapter 5).
☐ Front tire air pressure too low (Chapter 1).

## Handlebar shakes or vibrates excessively

☐ Tires worn or out of balance (Chapter 1 or 6).
☐ Swingarm bearings worn. Replace worn bearings by referring to Chapter 6.
☐ Rim(s) warped or damaged. Inspect wheels for runout (Chapter 6).
☐ Wheel bearings worn. Worn front or rear wheel bearings can cause poor tracking. Worn front bearings will cause wobble (Chapter 6).
☐ Handlebar clamp bolts or bracket nuts loose (Chapter 5).
☐ Steering stem or fork clamps loose. Tighten them to the specified torque (Chapter 5).
☐ Motor mount bolts loose. Will cause excessive vibration with increased engine rpm (Chapter 2).

## Handlebar pulls to one side

☐ Frame bent. Definitely suspect this if the machine has been dropped. May or may not be accompanied by cracking near the bend. Replace the frame (Chapter 5).
☐ Wheel out of alignment. Caused by improper location of axle spacers or from bent steering stem or frame (Chapter 5).
☐ Swingarm bent or twisted. Caused by age (metal fatigue) or impact damage. Replace the swingarm (Chapter 5).
☐ Steering stem bent. Caused by impact damage or by dropping the motorcycle. Replace the steering stem (Chapter 5).
☐ Fork leg bent. Disassemble the forks and replace the damaged parts (Chapter 5).
☐ Fork oil level uneven. Check and add or drain as necessary (Chapter 5).

## Poor shock absorbing qualities

☐ Too hard:
*Fork oil level excessive (Chapter 5).*
*Fork oil viscosity too high. Use a lighter oil (see the Specifications in Chapter 1).*
*Fork tube bent. Causes a harsh, sticking feeling (Chapter 5).*
*Shock shaft or body bent or damaged (Chapter 5).*
*Fork internal damage (Chapter 5).*
*Shock internal damage.*
*Tire pressure too high (Chapters 1 and 6).*
☐ Too soft:
*Fork or shock oil insufficient and/or leaking (Chapter 5).*
*Fork oil level too low (Chapter 5).*
*Fork oil viscosity too light (Chapter 5).*
*Fork springs weak or broken (Chapter 5).*

# 13 Braking problems

### Front brakes are spongy, don't hold

☐ Air in brake line. Caused by inattention to master cylinder fluid level or by leakage. Locate problem and bleed brakes (Chapter 6).
☐ Pad or disc worn (Chapters 1 and 6).
☐ Brake fluid leak. See paragraph 1.
☐ Contaminated pads. Caused by contamination with oil, grease, brake fluid, etc. Clean or replace pads. Clean disc thoroughly with brake cleaner (Chapter 6).
☐ Brake fluid deteriorated. Fluid is old or contaminated. Drain system, replenish with new fluid and bleed the system (Chapter 6).
☐ Master cylinder internal parts worn or damaged causing fluid to bypass (Chapter 6).
☐ Master cylinder bore scratched by foreign material or broken spring. Repair or replace master cylinder (Chapter 6).
☐ Disc warped. Replace disc (Chapter 6).

### Brake lever or pedal pulsates

☐ Disc warped. Replace disc (Chapter 6).
☐ Axle bent. Replace axle (Chapter 5).
☐ Brake caliper bolts loose (Chapter 6).

☐ Brake caliper shafts damaged or sticking, causing caliper to bind. Lube the shafts or replace them if they are corroded or bent (Chapter 6).
☐ Wheel warped or otherwise damaged (Chapter 6).
☐ Wheel bearings damaged or worn (Chapter 6).
☐ Brake drum out of round. Replace brake drum (Chapter 6).

### Brakes drag

☐ Master cylinder piston seized. Caused by wear or damage to piston or cylinder bore (Chapter 6).
☐ Lever balky or stuck. Check pivot and lubricate (Chapter 6).
☐ Brake caliper binds. Caused by inadequate lubrication or damage to caliper shafts (Chapter 6).
☐ Brake caliper piston seized in bore. Caused by wear or ingestion of dirt past deteriorated seal (Chapter 6).
☐ Brake pad damaged. Pad material separated from backing plate. Usually caused by faulty manufacturing process or from contact with chemicals. Replace pads (Chapter 6).
☐ Pads improperly installed (Chapter 6).
☐ Rear brake pedal free play insufficient (Chapter 1).
☐ Rear brake springs weak. Replace brake springs (Chapter 6).

# 14 Electrical problems

## Battery dead or weak

☐ Battery faulty. Caused by sulfated plates which are shorted through sedimentation or low electrolyte level. Also, broken battery terminal making only occasional contact (Chapter 8).
☐ Battery cables making poor contact (Chapter 8).
☐ Load excessive. Caused by addition of high wattage lights or other electrical accessories.
☐ Ignition switch defective. Switch either grounds/earths internally or fails to shut off system. Replace the switch (Chapter 8).
☐ Regulator/rectifier defective (Chapter 8).
☐ Stator coil open or shorted (Chapter 8).
☐ Wiring faulty. Wiring grounded or connections loose in ignition, charging or lighting circuits (Chapter 8).

## Battery overcharged

☐ Regulator/rectifier defective. Overcharging is noticed when battery gets excessively warm or boils over (Chapter 8).
☐ Battery defective. Replace battery with a new one (Chapter 8).
☐ Battery amperage too low, wrong type or size. Install manufacturer's specified amp-hour battery to handle charging load (Chapter 8)

## Checking engine compression

● Low compression will result in exhaust smoke, heavy oil consumption, poor starting and poor performance. A compression test will provide useful information about an engine's condition and if performed regularly, can give warning of trouble before any other symptoms become apparent.

● A compression gauge will be required, along with an adapter to suit the spark plug hole thread size. Note that the screw-in type gauge/adapter set up is preferable to the rubber cone type.

● Before carrying out the test, first check the valve clearances as described in Chapter 1.

1 Run the engine until it reaches normal operating temperature, then stop it and remove the spark plug(s), taking care not to scald your hands on the hot components.

2 Install the gauge adapter and compression gauge in No. 1 cylinder spark plug hole (see illustration 1).

Screw the compression gauge adapter into the spark plug hole, then screw the gauge into the adapter

3 On kickstart-equipped motorcycles, make sure the ignition switch is OFF, then open the throttle fully and kick the engine over a couple of times until the gauge reading stabilises.

4 On motorcycles with electric start only, the procedure will differ depending on the nature of the ignition system. Flick the engine kill switch (engine stop switch) to OFF and turn the ignition switch ON; open the throttle fully and crank the engine over on the starter motor for a couple of revolutions until the gauge reading stabilises. If the starter will not operate with the kill switch OFF, turn the ignition switch OFF and refer to the next paragraph.

5 Install the spark plugs back into their suppressor caps and arrange the plug electrodes so that their metal bodies are earthed (grounded) against the cylinder head; this is essential to prevent damage to the ignition system as the engine is spun over (see illustration 2). Position the plugs well

All spark plugs must be earthed (grounded) against the cylinder head

away from the plug holes otherwise there is a risk of atomised fuel escaping from the combustion chambers and igniting. As a safety precaution, cover the top of the valve cover with rag. Now turn the ignition switch ON and kill switch ON, open the throttle fully and crank the engine over on the starter motor for a couple of revolutions until the gauge reading stabilises.

6 After one or two revolutions the pressure should build up to a maximum figure and then stabilise. Take a note of this reading and on multi-cylinder engines repeat the test on the remaining cylinders.

7 The correct pressures are given in Chapter 1 Specifications. If the results fall within the specified range and on multi-cylinder engines all are relatively equal, the engine is in good condition. If there is a marked difference between the readings, or if the readings are lower than specified, inspection of the top-end components will be required.

8 Low compression pressure may be due to worn cylinder bores, pistons or rings, failure of the cylinder head gasket, worn valve seals, or poor valve seating.

9 To distinguish between cylinder/piston wear and valve leakage, pour a small quantity of oil into the bore to temporarily seal the piston rings, then repeat the compression tests (see illustration 3). If the readings show

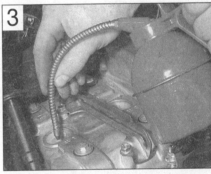

Bores can be temporarily sealed with a squirt of motor oil

a noticeable increase in pressure this confirms that the cylinder bore, piston, or rings are worn. If, however, no change is indicated, the cylinder head gasket or valves should be examined.

10 High compression pressure indicates excessive carbon build-up in the combustion chamber and on the piston crown. If this is the case the cylinder head should be removed and the deposits removed. Note that excessive carbon build-up is less likely with the used on modern fuels.

## Checking battery open-circuit voltage

 *Warning: The gases produced by the battery are explosive - never smoke or create any sparks in the vicinity of the battery. Never allow the electrolyte to contact your skin or clothing - if it does, wash it off and seek immediate medical attention.*

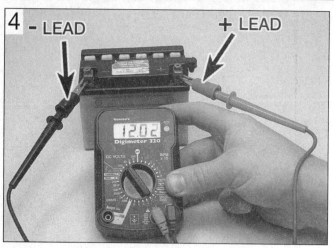

Measuring open-circuit battery voltage

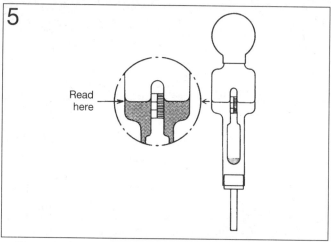

Read here

Float-type hydrometer for measuring battery specific gravity

● Before any electrical fault is investigated the battery should be checked.

● You'll need a dc voltmeter or multimeter to check battery voltage. Check that the leads are inserted in the correct terminals on the meter, red lead to positive (+ve), black lead to negative (-ve). Incorrect connections can damage the meter.

● A sound fully-charged 12 volt battery should produce between 12.3 and 12.6 volts across its terminals (12.8 volts for a maintenance-free battery). On machines with a 6 volt battery, voltage should be between 6.1 and 6.3 volts.

1 Set a multimeter to the 0 to 20 volts dc range and connect its probes across the battery terminals. Connect the meter's positive (+ve) probe, usually red, to the battery positive (+ve) terminal, followed by the meter's negative (-ve) probe, usually black, to the battery negative terminal (-ve) **(see illustration 4)**.

2 If battery voltage is low (below 10 volts on a 12 volt battery or below 4 volts on a six volt battery), charge the battery and test the voltage again. If the battery repeatedly goes flat, investigate the motorcycle's charging system.

## Checking battery specific gravity (SG)

⚠️ **Warning: The gases produced by the battery are explosive - never smoke or create any sparks in the vicinity of the battery. Never allow the electrolyte to contact your skin or clothing - if it does, wash it off and seek immediate medical attention.**

● The specific gravity check gives an indication of a battery's state of charge.

● A hydrometer is used for measuring specific gravity. Make sure you purchase one

which has a small enough hose to insert in the aperture of a motorcycle battery.

● Specific gravity is simply a measure of the electrolyte's density compared with that of water. Water has an SG of 1.000 and fully-charged battery electrolyte is about 26% heavier, at 1.260.

● Specific gravity checks are not possible on maintenance-free batteries. Testing the open-circuit voltage is the only means of determining their state of charge.

1 To measure SG, remove the battery from the motorcycle and remove the first cell cap. Draw

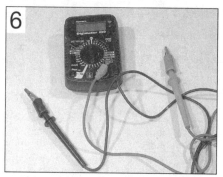

Digital multimeter can be used for all electrical tests

some electrolyte into the hydrometer and note the reading **(see illustration 5)**. Return the electrolyte to the cell and install the cap.

2 The reading should be in the region of 1.260 to 1.280. If SG is below 1.200 the battery needs charging. Note that SG will vary with temperature; it should be measured at 20°C (68°F). Add 0.007 to the reading for every 10°C above 20°C, and subtract 0.007 from the reading for every 10°C below 20°C. Add 0.004 to the reading for every 10°F above 68°F, and subtract 0.004 from the reading for every 10°F below 68°F.

3 When the check is complete, rinse the hydrometer thoroughly with clean water.

## Checking for continuity

● The term continuity describes the uninterrupted flow of electricity through an electrical circuit. A continuity check will determine whether an **open-circuit** situation exists.

● Continuity can be checked with an ohmmeter, multimeter, continuity tester or battery and bulb test circuit **(see illustrations 6, 7 and 8)**.

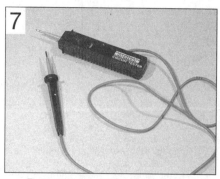

Battery-powered continuity tester

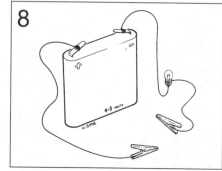

Battery and bulb test circuit

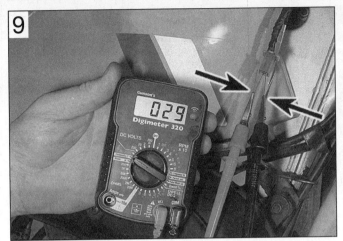

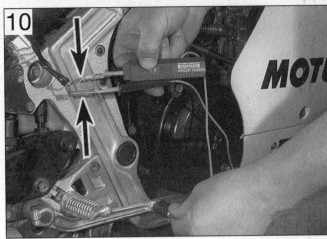

**Continuity check of front brake light switch using a meter - note split pins used to access connector terminals**

**Continuity check of rear brake light switch using a continuity tester**

● All of these instruments are self-powered by a battery, therefore the checks are made with the ignition OFF.

● As a safety precaution, always disconnect the battery negative (-ve) lead before making checks, particularly if ignition switch checks are being made.

● If using a meter, select the appropriate ohms scale and check that the meter reads infinity (∞). Touch the meter probes together and check that meter reads zero; where necessary adjust the meter so that it reads zero.

● After using a meter, always switch it OFF to conserve its battery.

## Switch checks

1 If a switch is at fault, trace its wiring up to the wiring connectors. Separate the wire connectors and inspect them for security and condition. A build-up of dirt or corrosion here will most likely be the cause of the problem - clean up and apply a water dispersant such as WD40.

2 If using a test meter, set the meter to the ohms x 10 scale and connect its probes across the wires from the switch **(see illustration 9)**. Simple ON/OFF type switches, such as brake light switches, only have two

wires whereas combination switches, like the ignition switch, have many internal links. Study the wiring diagram to ensure that you are connecting across the correct pair of wires. Continuity (low or no measurable resistance - 0 ohms) should be indicated with the switch ON and no continuity (high resistance) with it OFF.

3 Note that the polarity of the test probes doesn't matter for continuity checks, although care should be taken to follow specific test procedures if a diode or solid-state component is being checked.

4 A continuity tester or battery and bulb circuit can be used in the same way. Connect its probes as described above **(see illustration 10)**. The light should come on to indicate continuity in the ON switch position, but should extinguish in the OFF position.

## Wiring checks

● Many electrical faults are caused by damaged wiring, often due to incorrect routing or chaffing on frame components.

● Loose, wet or corroded wire connectors can also be the cause of electrical problems, especially in exposed locations.

1 A continuity check can be made on a single length of wire by disconnecting it at each end

and connecting a meter or continuity tester across both ends of the wire **(see illustration 11)**.

2 Continuity (low or no resistance - 0 ohms) should be indicated if the wire is good. If no continuity (high resistance) is shown, suspect a broken wire.

## Checking for voltage

● A voltage check can determine whether current is reaching a component.

● Voltage can be checked with a dc voltmeter, multimeter set on the dc volts scale, test light or buzzer **(see illustrations 12 and 13)**. A meter has the advantage of being able to measure actual voltage.

● When using a meter, check that its leads are inserted in the correct terminals on the meter, red to positive (+ve), black to negative (-ve). Incorrect connections can damage the meter.

● A voltmeter (or multimeter set to the dc volts scale) should always be connected in parallel (across the load). Connecting it in series will destroy the meter.

● Voltage checks are made with the ignition ON.

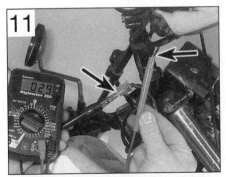

**Continuity check of front brake light switch sub-harness**

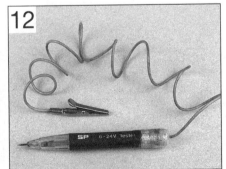

**A simple test light can be used for voltage checks**

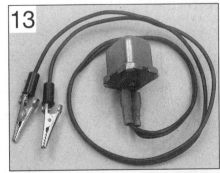

**A buzzer is useful for voltage checks**

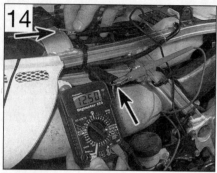

**Checking for voltage at the rear brake light power supply wire using a meter . . .**

**1** First identify the relevant wiring circuit by referring to the wiring diagram at the end of this manual. If other electrical components share the same power supply (ie are fed from the same fuse), take note whether they are working correctly - this is useful information in deciding where to start checking the circuit.

**2** If using a meter, check first that the meter leads are plugged into the correct terminals on the meter (see above). Set the meter to the dc volts function, at a range suitable for the battery voltage. Connect the meter red probe (+ve) to the power supply wire and the black probe to a good metal earth (ground) on the motorcycle's frame or directly to the battery negative (-ve) terminal **(see illustration 14)**. Battery voltage should be shown on the meter

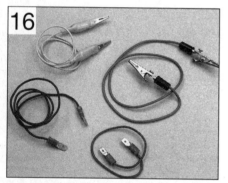

**A selection of jumper wires for making earth (ground) checks**

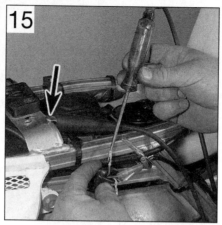

**. . . or a test light - note the earth connection to the frame (arrow)**

with the ignition switched ON.

**3** If using a test light or buzzer, connect its positive (+ve) probe to the power supply terminal and its negative (-ve) probe to a good earth (ground) on the motorcycle's frame or directly to the battery negative (-ve) terminal **(see illustration 15)**. With the ignition ON, the test light should illuminate or the buzzer sound.

**4** If no voltage is indicated, work back towards the fuse continuing to check for voltage. When you reach a point where there is voltage, you know the problem lies between that point and your last check point.

## Checking the earth (ground)

● Earth connections are made either directly to the engine or frame (such as sensors, neutral switch etc. which only have a positive feed) or by a separate wire into the earth circuit of the wiring harness. Alternatively a short earth wire is sometimes run directly from the component to the motorcycle's frame.
● Corrosion is often the cause of a poor earth connection.
● If total failure is experienced, check the security of the main earth lead from the

negative (-ve) terminal of the battery and also the main earth (ground) point on the wiring harness. If corroded, dismantle the connection and clean all surfaces back to bare metal.

**1** To check the earth on a component, use an insulated jumper wire to temporarily bypass its earth connection **(see illustration 16)**. Connect one end of the jumper wire between the earth terminal or metal body of the component and the other end to the motorcycle's frame.

**2** If the circuit works with the jumper wire installed, the original earth circuit is faulty. Check the wiring for open-circuits or poor connections. Clean up direct earth connections, removing all traces of corrosion and remake the joint. Apply petroleum jelly to the joint to prevent future corrosion.

## Tracing a short-circuit

● A short-circuit occurs where current shorts to earth (ground) bypassing the circuit components. This usually results in a blown fuse.

● A short-circuit is most likely to occur where the insulation has worn through due to wiring chafing on a component, allowing a direct path to earth (ground) on the frame.

**1** Remove any bodypanels necessary to access the circuit wiring.

**2** Check that all electrical switches in the circuit are OFF, then remove the circuit fuse and connect a test light, buzzer or voltmeter (set to the dc scale) across the fuse terminals. No voltage should be shown.

**3** Move the wiring from side to side whilst observing the test light or meter. When the test light comes on, buzzer sounds or meter shows voltage, you have found the cause of the short. It will usually shown up as damaged or burned insulation.

**4** Note that the same test can be performed on each component in the circuit, even the switch.

## A

**ABS (Anti-lock braking system)** A system, usually electronically controlled, that senses incipient wheel lockup during braking and relieves hydraulic pressure at wheel which is about to skid.

**Aftermarket** Components suitable for the motorcycle, but not produced by the motorcycle manufacturer.

**Allen key** A hexagonal wrench which fits into a recessed hexagonal hole.

**Alternating current (ac)** Current produced by an alternator. Requires converting to direct current by a rectifier for charging purposes.

**Alternator** Converts mechanical energy from the engine into electrical energy to charge the battery and power the electrical system.

**Ampere (amp)** A unit of measurement for the flow of electrical current. Current = Volts ÷ Ohms.

**Ampere-hour (Ah)** Measure of battery capacity.

**Angle-tightening** A torque expressed in degrees. Often follows a conventional tightening torque for cylinder head or main bearing fasteners **(see illustration)**.

**Angle-tightening cylinder head bolts**

**Antifreeze** A substance (usually ethylene glycol) mixed with water, and added to the cooling system, to prevent freezing of the coolant in winter. Antifreeze also contains chemicals to inhibit corrosion and the formation of rust and other deposits that would tend to clog the radiator and coolant passages and reduce cooling efficiency.

**Anti-dive** System attached to the fork lower leg (slider) to prevent fork dive when braking hard.

**Anti-seize compound** A coating that reduces the risk of seizing on fasteners that are subjected to high temperatures, such as exhaust clamp bolts and nuts.

**API** American Petroleum Institute. A quality standard for 4-stroke motor oils.

**Asbestos** A natural fibrous mineral with great heat resistance, commonly used in the composition of brake friction materials. Asbestos is a health hazard and the dust created by brake systems should never be inhaled or ingested.

**ATF** Automatic Transmission Fluid. Often used in front forks.

**ATU** Automatic Timing Unit. Mechanical device for advancing the ignition timing on early engines.

**ATV** All Terrain Vehicle. Often called a Quad.

**Axial play** Side-to-side movement.

**Axle** A shaft on which a wheel revolves. Also known as a spindle.

## B

**Backlash** The amount of movement between meshed components when one component is held still. Usually applies to gear teeth.

**Ball bearing** A bearing consisting of a hardened inner and outer race with hardened steel balls between the two races.

**Bearings** Used between two working surfaces to prevent wear of the components and a build-up of heat. Four types of bearing are commonly used on motorcycles: plain shell bearings, ball bearings, tapered roller bearings and needle roller bearings.

**Bevel gears** Used to turn the drive through 90°. Typical applications are shaft final drive and camshaft drive **(see illustration)**.

**Bevel gears are used to turn the drive through 90°**

**BHP** Brake Horsepower. The British measurement for engine power output. Power output is now usually expressed in kilowatts (kW).

**Bias-belted tyre** Similar construction to radial tyre, but with outer belt running at an angle to the wheel rim.

**Big-end bearing** The bearing in the end of the connecting rod that's attached to the crankshaft.

**Bleeding** The process of removing air from an hydraulic system via a bleed nipple or bleed screw.

**Bottom-end** A description of an engine's crankcase components and all components contained there-in.

**BTDC** Before Top Dead Centre in terms of piston position. Ignition timing is often expressed in terms of degrees or millimetres BTDC.

**Bush** A cylindrical metal or rubber component used between two moving parts.

**Burr** Rough edge left on a component after machining or as a result of excessive wear.

## C

**Cam chain** The chain which takes drive from the crankshaft to the camshaft(s).

**Canister** The main component in an evaporative emission control system (California market only); contains activated charcoal granules to trap vapours from the fuel system rather than allowing them to vent to the atmosphere.

**Castellated** Resembling the parapets along the top of a castle wall. For example, a castellated wheel axle or spindle nut.

**Catalytic converter** A device in the exhaust system of some machines which converts certain pollutants in the exhaust gases into less harmful substances.

**Charging system** Description of the components which charge the battery, ie the alternator, rectifier and regulator.

**Circlip** A ring-shaped clip used to prevent endwise movement of cylindrical parts and shafts. An internal circlip is installed in a groove in a housing; an external circlip fits into a groove on the outside of a cylindrical piece such as a shaft. Also known as a snap-ring.

**Clearance** The amount of space between two parts. For example, between a piston and a cylinder, between a bearing and a journal, etc.

**Coil spring** A spiral of elastic steel found in various sizes throughout a vehicle, for example as a springing medium in the suspension and in the valve train.

**Compression** Reduction in volume, and increase in pressure and temperature, of a gas, caused by squeezing it into a smaller space.

**Compression damping** Controls the speed the suspension compresses when hitting a bump.

**Compression ratio** The relationship between cylinder volume when the piston is at top dead centre and cylinder volume when the piston is at bottom dead centre.

**Continuity** The uninterrupted path in the flow of electricity. Little or no measurable resistance.

**Continuity tester** Self-powered bleeper or test light which indicates continuity.

**Cp** Candlepower. Bulb rating commonly found on US motorcycles.

**Crossply tyre** Tyre plies arranged in a criss-cross pattern. Usually four or six plies used, hence 4PR or 6PR in tyre size codes.

**Cush drive** Rubber damper segments fitted between the rear wheel and final drive sprocket to absorb transmission shocks **(see illustration)**.

**Cush drive rubbers dampen out transmission shocks**

## D

**Degree disc** Calibrated disc for measuring piston position. Expressed in degrees.

**Dial gauge** Clock-type gauge with adapters for measuring runout and piston position. Expressed in mm or inches.

**Diaphragm** The rubber membrane in a master cylinder or carburettor which seals the upper chamber.

**Diaphragm spring** A single sprung plate often used in clutches.

**Direct current (dc)** Current produced by a dc generator.

**Decarbonisation** The process of removing carbon deposits - typically from the combustion chamber, valves and exhaust port/system.

**Detonation** Destructive and damaging explosion of fuel/air mixture in combustion chamber instead of controlled burning.

**Diode** An electrical valve which only allows current to flow in one direction. Commonly used in rectifiers and starter interlock systems.

**Disc valve (or rotary valve)** A induction system used on some two-stroke engines.

**Double-overhead camshaft (DOHC)** An engine that uses two overhead camshafts, one for the intake valves and one for the exhaust valves.

**Drivebelt** A toothed belt used to transmit drive to the rear wheel on some motorcycles. A drivebelt has also been used to drive the camshafts. Drivebelts are usually made of Kevlar.

**Driveshaft** Any shaft used to transmit motion. Commonly used when referring to the final driveshaft on shaft drive motorcycles.

# E

**Earth return** The return path of an electrical circuit, utilising the motorcycle's frame.

**ECU (Electronic Control Unit)** A computer which controls (for instance) an ignition system, or an anti-lock braking system.

**EGO** Exhaust Gas Oxygen sensor. Sometimes called a Lambda sensor.

**Electrolyte** The fluid in a lead-acid battery.

**EMS (Engine Management System)** A computer controlled system which manages the fuel injection and the ignition systems in an integrated fashion.

**Endfloat** The amount of lengthways movement between two parts. As applied to a crankshaft, the distance that the crankshaft can move side-to-side in the crankcase.

**Endless chain** A chain having no joining link. Common use for cam chains and final drive chains.

**EP (Extreme Pressure)** Oil type used in locations where high loads are applied, such as between gear teeth.

**Evaporative emission control system** Describes a charcoal filled canister which stores fuel vapours from the tank rather than allowing them to vent to the atmosphere. Usually only fitted to California models and referred to as an EVAP system.

**Expansion chamber** Section of two-stroke engine exhaust system so designed to improve engine efficiency and boost power.

# F

**Feeler blade or gauge** A thin strip or blade of hardened steel, ground to an exact thickness, used to check or measure clearances between parts.

**Final drive** Description of the drive from the transmission to the rear wheel. Usually by chain or shaft, but sometimes by belt.

**Firing order** The order in which the engine cylinders fire, or deliver their power strokes, beginning with the number one cylinder.

**Flooding** Term used to describe a high fuel level in the carburettor float chambers, leading to fuel overflow. Also refers to excess fuel in the combustion chamber due to incorrect starting technique.

**Free length** The no-load state of a component when measured. Clutch, valve and fork spring lengths are measured at rest, without any preload.

**Freeplay** The amount of travel before any action takes place. The looseness in a linkage, or an assembly of parts, between the initial application of force and actual movement. For example, the distance the rear brake pedal moves before the rear brake is actuated.

**Fuel injection** The fuel/air mixture is metered electronically and directed into the engine intake ports (indirect injection) or into the cylinders (direct injection). Sensors supply information on engine speed and conditions.

**Fuel/air mixture** The charge of fuel and air going into the engine. See **Stoichiometric ratio**.

**Fuse** An electrical device which protects a circuit against accidental overload. The typical fuse contains a soft piece of metal which is calibrated to melt at a predetermined current flow (expressed as amps) and break the circuit.

# G

**Gap** The distance the spark must travel in jumping from the centre electrode to the side electrode in a spark plug. Also refers to the distance between the ignition rotor and the pickup coil in an electronic ignition system.

**Gasket** Any thin, soft material - usually cork, cardboard, asbestos or soft metal - installed between two metal surfaces to ensure a good seal. For instance, the cylinder head gasket seals the joint between the block and the cylinder head.

**Gauge** An instrument panel display used to monitor engine conditions. A gauge with a movable pointer on a dial or a fixed scale is an analogue gauge. A gauge with a numerical readout is called a digital gauge.

**Gear ratios** The drive ratio of a pair of gears in a gearbox, calculated on their number of teeth.

**Glaze-busting** see **Honing**

**Grinding** Process for renovating the valve face and valve seat contact area in the cylinder head.

**Gudgeon pin** The shaft which connects the connecting rod small-end with the piston. Often called a piston pin or wrist pin.

# H

**Helical gears** Gear teeth are slightly curved and produce less gear noise that straight-cut gears. Often used for primary drives.

**Installing a Helicoil thread insert in a cylinder head**

**Helicoil** A thread insert repair system. Commonly used as a repair for stripped spark plug threads **(see illustration)**.

**Honing** A process used to break down the glaze on a cylinder bore (also called glaze-busting). Can also be carried out to roughen a rebored cylinder to aid ring bedding-in.

**HT (High Tension)** Description of the electrical circuit from the secondary winding of the ignition coil to the spark plug.

**Hydraulic** A liquid filled system used to transmit pressure from one component to another. Common uses on motorcycles are brakes and clutches.

**Hydrometer** An instrument for measuring the specific gravity of a lead-acid battery.

**Hygroscopic** Water absorbing. In motorcycle applications, braking efficiency will be reduced if DOT 3 or 4 hydraulic fluid absorbs water from the air - care must be taken to keep new brake fluid in tightly sealed containers.

# I

**lbf ft** Pounds-force feet. An imperial unit of torque. Sometimes written as ft-lbs.

**lbf in** Pound-force inch. An imperial unit of torque, applied to components where a very low torque is required. Sometimes written as in-lbs.

**IC** Abbreviation for Integrated Circuit.

**Ignition advance** Means of increasing the timing of the spark at higher engine speeds. Done by mechanical means (ATU) on early engines or electronically by the ignition control unit on later engines.

**Ignition timing** The moment at which the spark plug fires, expressed in the number of crankshaft degrees before the piston reaches the top of its stroke, or in the number of millimetres before the piston reaches the top of its stroke.

**Infinity (∞)** Description of an open-circuit electrical state, where no continuity exists.

**Inverted forks (upside down forks)** The sliders or lower legs are held in the yokes and the fork tubes or stanchions are connected to the wheel axle (spindle). Less unsprung weight and stiffer construction than conventional forks.

# J

**JASO** Quality standard for 2-stroke oils.

**Joule** The unit of electrical energy.

**Journal** The bearing surface of a shaft.

# K

**Kickstart** Mechanical means of turning the engine over for starting purposes. Only usually fitted to mopeds, small capacity motorcycles and off-road motorcycles.

**Kill switch** Handebar-mounted switch for emergency ignition cut-out. Cuts the ignition circuit on all models, and additionally prevent starter motor operation on others.

**km** Symbol for kilometre.

**kmh** Abbreviation for kilometres per hour.

# L

**Lambda (λ) sensor** A sensor fitted in the exhaust system to measure the exhaust gas oxygen content (excess air factor).

**Lapping** see **Grinding**.
**LCD** Abbreviation for Liquid Crystal Display.
**LED** Abbreviation for Light Emitting Diode.
**Liner** A steel cylinder liner inserted in a aluminium alloy cylinder block.
**Locknut** A nut used to lock an adjustment nut, or other threaded component, in place.
**Lockstops** The lugs on the lower triple clamp (yoke) which abut those on the frame, preventing handlebar-to-fuel tank contact.
**Lockwasher** A form of washer designed to prevent an attaching nut from working loose.
**LT Low Tension** Description of the electrical circuit from the power supply to the primary winding of the ignition coil.

# M

**Main bearings** The bearings between the crankshaft and crankcase.
**Maintenance-free (MF) battery** A sealed battery which cannot be topped up.
**Manometer** Mercury-filled calibrated tubes used to measure intake tract vacuum. Used to synchronise carburettors on multi-cylinder engines.
**Micrometer** A precision measuring instrument that measures component outside diameters **(see illustration)**.

**Tappet shims are measured with a micrometer**

**MON (Motor Octane Number)** A measure of a fuel's resistance to knock.
**Monograde oil** An oil with a single viscosity, eg SAE80W.
**Monoshock** A single suspension unit linking the swingarm or suspension linkage to the frame.
**mph** Abbreviation for miles per hour.
**Multigrade oil** Having a wide viscosity range (eg 10W40). The W stands for Winter, thus the viscosity ranges from SAE10 when cold to SAE40 when hot.
**Multimeter** An electrical test instrument with the capability to measure voltage, current and resistance. Some meters also incorporate a continuity tester and buzzer.

# N

**Needle roller bearing** Inner race of caged needle rollers and hardened outer race. Examples of uncaged needle rollers can be found on some engines. Commonly used in rear suspension applications and in two-stroke engines.
**Nm** Newton metres.
**NOx** Oxides of Nitrogen. A common toxic pollutant emitted by petrol engines at higher temperatures.

# O

**Octane** The measure of a fuel's resistance to knock.
**OE (Original Equipment)** Relates to components fitted to a motorcycle as standard or replacement parts supplied by the motorcycle manufacturer.
**Ohm** The unit of electrical resistance. Ohms = Volts ÷ Current.
**Ohmmeter** An instrument for measuring electrical resistance.
**Oil cooler** System for diverting engine oil outside of the engine to a radiator for cooling purposes.
**Oil injection** A system of two-stroke engine lubrication where oil is pump-fed to the engine in accordance with throttle position.
**Open-circuit** An electrical condition where there is a break in the flow of electricity - no continuity (high resistance).
**O-ring** A type of sealing ring made of a special rubber-like material; in use, the O-ring is compressed into a groove to provide the sealing action.
**Oversize (OS)** Term used for piston and ring size options fitted to a rebored cylinder.
**Overhead cam (sohc) engine** An engine with single camshaft located on top of the cylinder head.
**Overhead valve (ohv) engine** An engine with the valves located in the cylinder head, but with the camshaft located in the engine block or crankcase.
**Oxygen sensor** A device installed in the exhaust system which senses the oxygen content in the exhaust and converts this information into an electric current. Also called a Lambda sensor.

# P

**Plastigauge** A thin strip of plastic thread, available in different sizes, used for measuring clearances. For example, a strip of Plastigauge is laid across a bearing journal. The parts are assembled and dismantled; the width of the crushed strip indicates the clearance between journal and bearing.
**Polarity** Either negative or positive earth (ground), determined by which battery lead is connected to the frame (earth return). Modern motorcycles are usually negative earth.
**Pre-ignition** A situation where the fuel/air mixture ignites before the spark plug fires. Often due to a hot spot in the combustion chamber caused by carbon build-up. Engine has a tendency to 'run-on'.
**Pre-load (suspension)** The amount a spring is compressed when in the unloaded state. Preload can be applied by gas, spacer or mechanical adjuster.
**Premix** The method of engine lubrication on older two-stroke engines. Engine oil is mixed with the petrol in the fuel tank in a specific ratio. The fuel/oil mix is sometimes referred to as "petroil".
**Primary drive** Description of the drive from the crankshaft to the clutch. Usually by gear or chain.
**PS** Pfedestärke - a German interpretation of BHP.
**PSI** Pounds-force per square inch. Imperial measurement of tyre pressure and cylinder pressure measurement.
**PTFE** Polytetrafluroethylene. A low friction substance.

**Pulse secondary air injection system** A process of promoting the burning of excess fuel present in the exhaust gases by routing fresh air into the exhaust ports.

# Q

**Quartz halogen bulb** Tungsten filament surrounded by a halogen gas. Typically used for the headlight **(see illustration)**.

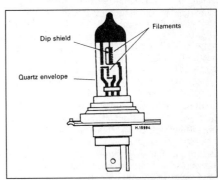

**Quartz halogen headlight bulb construction**

# R

**Rack-and-pinion** A pinion gear on the end of a shaft that mates with a rack (think of a geared wheel opened up and laid flat). Sometimes used in clutch operating systems.
**Radial play** Up and down movement about a shaft.
**Radial ply tyres** Tyre plies run across the tyre (from bead to bead) and around the circumference of the tyre. Less resistant to tread distortion than other tyre types.
**Radiator** A liquid-to-air heat transfer device designed to reduce the temperature of the coolant in a liquid cooled engine.
**Rake** A feature of steering geometry - the angle of the steering head in relation to the vertical **(see illustration)**.

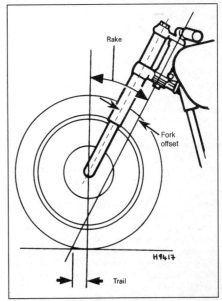

**Steering geometry**

**Rebore** Providing a new working surface to the cylinder bore by boring out the old surface. Necessitates the use of oversize piston and rings.

**Rebound damping** A means of controlling the oscillation of a suspension unit spring after it has been compressed. Resists the spring's natural tendency to bounce back after being compressed.

**Rectifier** Device for converting the ac output of an alternator into dc for battery charging.

**Reed valve** An induction system commonly used on two-stroke engines.

**Regulator** Device for maintaining the charging voltage from the generator or alternator within a specified range.

**Relay** A electrical device used to switch heavy current on and off by using a low current auxiliary circuit.

**Resistance** Measured in ohms. An electrical component's ability to pass electrical current.

**RON (Research Octane Number)** A measure of a fuel's resistance to knock.

**rpm** revolutions per minute.

**Runout** The amount of wobble (in-and-out movement) of a wheel or shaft as it's rotated. The amount a shaft rotates 'out-of-true'. The out-of-round condition of a rotating part.

# S

**SAE (Society of Automotive Engineers)** A standard for the viscosity of a fluid.

**Sealant** A liquid or paste used to prevent leakage at a joint. Sometimes used in conjunction with a gasket.

**Service limit** Term for the point where a component is no longer useable and must be renewed.

**Shaft drive** A method of transmitting drive from the transmission to the rear wheel.

**Shell bearings** Plain bearings consisting of two shell halves. Most often used as big-end and main bearings in a four-stroke engine. Often called bearing inserts.

**Shim** Thin spacer, commonly used to adjust the clearance or relative positions between two parts. For example, shims inserted into or under tappets or followers to control valve clearances. Clearance is adjusted by changing the thickness of the shim.

**Short-circuit** An electrical condition where current shorts to earth (ground) bypassing the circuit components.

**Skimming** Process to correct warpage or repair a damaged surface, eg on brake discs or drums.

**Slide-hammer** A special puller that screws into or hooks onto a component such as a shaft or bearing; a heavy sliding handle on the shaft bottoms against the end of the shaft to knock the component free.

**Small-end bearing** The bearing in the upper end of the connecting rod at its joint with the gudgeon pin.

**Spalling** Damage to camshaft lobes or bearing journals shown as pitting of the working surface.

**Specific gravity (SG)** The state of charge of the electrolyte in a lead-acid battery. A measure of the electrolyte's density compared with water.

**Straight-cut gears** Common type gear used on gearbox shafts and for oil pump and water pump drives.

**Stanchion** The inner sliding part of the front forks, held by the yokes. Often called a fork tube.

**Stoichiometric ratio** The optimum chemical air/fuel ratio for a petrol engine, said to be 14.7 parts of air to 1 part of fuel.

**Sulphuric acid** The liquid (electrolyte) used in a lead-acid battery. Poisonous and extremely corrosive.

**Surface grinding (lapping)** Process to correct a warped gasket face, commonly used on cylinder heads.

# T

**Tapered-roller bearing** Tapered inner race of caged needle rollers and separate tapered outer race. Examples of taper roller bearings can be found on steering heads.

**Tappet** A cylindrical component which transmits motion from the cam to the valve stem, either directly or via a pushrod and rocker arm. Also called a cam follower.

**TCS** Traction Control System. An electronically-controlled system which senses wheel spin and reduces engine speed accordingly.

**TDC** Top Dead Centre denotes that the piston is at its highest point in the cylinder.

**Thread-locking compound** Solution applied to fastener threads to prevent slackening. Select type to suit application.

**Thrust washer** A washer positioned between two moving components on a shaft. For example, between gear pinions on gearshaft.

**Timing chain** See **Cam Chain.**

**Timing light** Stroboscopic lamp for carrying out ignition timing checks with the engine running.

**Top-end** A description of an engine's cylinder block, head and valve gear components.

**Torque** Turning or twisting force about a shaft.

**Torque setting** A prescribed tightness specified by the motorcycle manufacturer to ensure that the bolt or nut is secured correctly. Undertightening can result in the bolt or nut coming loose or a surface not being sealed. Overtightening can result in stripped threads, distortion or damage to the component being retained.

**Torx key** A six-point wrench.

**Tracer** A stripe of a second colour applied to a wire insulator to distinguish that wire from another one with the same colour insulator. For example, Br/W is often used to denote a brown insulator with a white tracer.

**Trail** A feature of steering geometry. Distance from the steering head axis to the tyre's central contact point.

**Triple clamps** The cast components which extend from the steering head and support the fork stanchions or tubes. Often called fork yokes.

**Turbocharger** A centrifugal device, driven by exhaust gases, that pressurises the intake air. Normally used to increase the power output from a given engine displacement.

**TWI** Abbreviation for Tyre Wear Indicator. Indicates the location of the tread depth indicator bars on tyres.

# U

**Universal joint or U-joint (UJ)** A double-pivoted connection for transmitting power from a driving to a driven shaft through an angle. Typically found in shaft drive assemblies.

**Unsprung weight** Anything not supported by the bike's suspension (ie the wheel, tyres, brakes, final drive and bottom (moving) part of the suspension).

# V

**Vacuum gauges** Clock-type gauges for measuring intake tract vacuum. Used for carburettor synchronisation on multi-cylinder engines.

**Valve** A device through which the flow of liquid, gas or vacuum may be stopped, started or regulated by a moveable part that opens, shuts or partially obstructs one or more ports or passageways. The intake and exhaust valves in the cylinder head are of the poppet type.

**Valve clearance** The clearance between the valve tip (the end of the valve stem) and the rocker arm or tappet/follower. The valve clearance is measured when the valve is closed. The correct clearance is important - if too small the valve won't close fully and will burn out, whereas if too large noisy operation will result.

**Valve lift** The amount a valve is lifted off its seat by the camshaft lobe.

**Valve timing** The exact setting for the opening and closing of the valves in relation to piston position.

**Vernier caliper** A precision measuring instrument that measures inside and outside dimensions. Not quite as accurate as a micrometer, but more convenient.

**VIN** Vehicle Identification Number. Term for the bike's engine and frame numbers.

**Viscosity** The thickness of a liquid or its resistance to flow.

**Volt** A unit for expressing electrical "pressure" in a circuit. Volts = current x ohms.

# W

**Water pump** A mechanically-driven device for moving coolant around the engine.

**Watt** A unit for expressing electrical power. Watts = volts x current.

**Wear limit** see **Service limit**

**Wet liner** A liquid-cooled engine design where the pistons run in liners which are directly surrounded by coolant (see illustration).

**Wet liner arrangement**

**Wheelbase** Distance from the centre of the front wheel to the centre of the rear wheel.

**Wiring harness or loom** Describes the electrical wires running the length of the motorcycle and enclosed in tape or plastic sheathing. Wiring coming off the main harness is usually referred to as a sub harness.

**Woodruff key** A key of semi-circular or square section used to locate a gear to a shaft. Often used to locate the alternator rotor on the crankshaft.

**Wrist pin** Another name for gudgeon or piston pin.

**Note**: *References throughout this index are in the form "Chapter number" • "page number"*

# Haynes Motorcycle Manuals – The Complete List

| Title | Book No |
|---|---|
| **APRILIA** RS50 (99 - 06) & RS125 (93 - 06) | 4298 |
| Aprilia RSV1000 Mille (98 - 03) ♦ | 4255 |
| **BMW** 2-valve Twins (70 - 96) ♦ | 0249 |
| BMW K100 & 75 2-valve Models (83 - 96) ♦ | 1373 |
| BMW R850, 1100 & 1150 4-valve Twins (93 - 04) ♦ | 3466 |
| BMW R1200 (04 - 06) ♦ | 4598 |
| **BSA** Bantam (48 - 71) | 0117 |
| BSA Unit Singles (58 - 72) | 0127 |
| BSA Pre-unit Singles (54 - 61) | 0326 |
| BSA A7 & A10 Twins (47 - 62) | 0121 |
| BSA A50 & A65 Twins (62 - 73) | 0155 |
| **DUCATI** 600, 620, 750 and 900 2-valve V-Twins (91 - 05) ♦ | 3290 |
| Ducati MK III & Desmo Singles (69 - 76) ◊ | 0445 |
| Ducati 748, 916 & 996 4-valve V-Twins (94 - 01) ♦ | 3756 |
| **GILERA** Runner, DNA, Ice & SKP/Stalker (97 - 07) | 4163 |
| **HARLEY-DAVIDSON** Sportsters (70 - 03) ♦ | 2534 |
| Harley-Davidson Shovelhead and Evolution Big Twins (70 - 99) ♦ | 2536 |
| Harley-Davidson Twin Cam 88 (99 - 03) ♦ | 2478 |
| **HONDA** NB, ND, NP & NS50 Melody (81 - 85) ◊ | 0622 |
| Honda NE/NB50 Vision & SA50 Vision Met-in (85 - 95) ◊ | 1278 |
| Honda MB, MBX, MT & MTX50 (80 - 93) | 0731 |
| Honda C50, C70 & C90 (67 - 03) | 0324 |
| Honda XR80/100R & CRF80/100F (85 - 04) | 2218 |
| Honda XR 80, 100, 125, 185 & 200 2-valve Models (78 - 87) | 0566 |
| Honda H100 & H100S Singles (80 - 92) | 0734 |
| Honda CB/CD125T & CM125C Twins (77 - 88) ◊ | 0571 |
| Honda CG125 (76 - 07) ◊ | 0433 |
| Honda NS125 (86 - 93) ◊ | 3056 |
| Honda CBR125R (04 - 07) | 4620 |
| Honda MBX/MTX125 & MTX200 (83 - 93) ◊ | 1132 |
| Honda CD/CM185 200T & CM250C 2-valve Twins (77 - 85) | 0572 |
| Honda XL/XR 250 & 500 (78 - 84) | 0567 |
| Honda XR250L, XR250R & XR400R (86 - 03) | 2219 |
| Honda CB250 & CB400N Super Dreams (78 - 84) ◊ | 0540 |
| Honda CR Motocross Bikes (86 - 01) | 2222 |
| Honda CRF250 & CRF450 (02 - 06) | 2630 |
| Honda CBR400RR Fours (88 - 99) ◊ ♦ | 3552 |
| Honda VFR400 (NC30) & RVF400 (NC35) V-Fours (89 - 98) ◊ ♦ | 3496 |
| Honda CB500 (93 - 01) ◊ | 3753 |
| Honda CB400 & CB550 Fours (73 - 77) | 0262 |
| Honda CX/GL500 & 650 V-Twins (78 - 86) | 0442 |
| Honda CBX550 Four (82 - 86) ◊ | 0940 |
| Honda XL600R & XR600R (83 - 00) | 2183 |
| Honda XL600/650V Transalp & XRV750 Africa Twin (87 to 07) ♦ | 3919 |
| Honda CBR600F1 & 1000F Fours (87 - 96) ♦ | 1730 |
| Honda CBR600F2 & F3 Fours (91 - 98) ♦ | 2070 |
| Honda CBR600F4 (99 - 06) ♦ | 3911 |
| Honda CB600F Hornet & CBF600 (98 - 06) ◊ ♦ | 3915 |
| Honda CBR600RR (03 - 06) ♦ | 4590 |
| Honda CB650 sohc Fours (78 - 84) | 0665 |
| Honda NTV600 Revere, NTV650 and NT650V Deauville (88 - 05) ◊ ♦ | 3243 |
| Honda Shadow VT600 & 750 (USA) (88 - 03) | 2312 |
| Honda CB750 sohc Four (69 - 79) | 0131 |
| Honda V45/65 Sabre & Magna (82 - 88) | 0820 |
| Honda VFR750 & 700 V-Fours (86 - 97) ♦ | 2101 |
| Honda VFR800 V-Fours (97 - 01) ♦ | 3703 |
| Honda VFR800 V-Tec V-Fours (02 - 05) ♦ | 4196 |
| Honda CB750 & CB900 dohc Fours (78 - 84) | 0535 |
| Honda VTR1000 (FireStorm, Super Hawk) & XL1000V (Varadero) (97 - 00) ♦ | 3744 |
| Honda CBR900RR FireBlade (92 - 99) ♦ | 2161 |
| Honda CBR900RR FireBlade (00 - 03) ♦ | 4060 |
| Honda CBR1000RR Fireblade (04 - 07) ♦ | 4604 |
| Honda CBR1100XX Super Blackbird (97 - 07) ♦ | 3901 |
| Honda ST1100 Pan European V-Fours (90 - 02) ♦ | 3384 |
| Honda Shadow VT1100 (USA) (85 - 98) | 2313 |
| Honda GL1000 Gold Wing (75 - 79) | 0309 |
| Honda GL1100 Gold Wing (79 - 81) | 0669 |

| Title | Book No |
|---|---|
| Honda Gold Wing 1200 (USA) (84 - 87) | 2199 |
| Honda Gold Wing 1500 (USA) (88 - 00) | 2225 |
| **KAWASAKI** AE/AR 50 & 80 (81 - 95) | 1007 |
| Kawasaki KC, KE & KH100 (75 - 99) | 1371 |
| Kawasaki KMX125 & 200 (86 - 02) ◊ | 3046 |
| Kawasaki 250, 350 & 400 Triples (72 - 79) | 0134 |
| Kawasaki 400 & 440 Twins (74 - 81) | 0281 |
| Kawasaki 400, 500 & 550 Fours (79 - 91) | 0910 |
| Kawasaki EN450 & 500 Twins (Ltd/Vulcan) (85 - 04) | 2053 |
| Kawasaki EX500 (GPZ500S) & ER500 (ER-5) (87 - 05) ♦ | 2052 |
| Kawasaki ZX600 (ZZ-R600 & Ninja ZX-6) (90 - 06) ♦ | 2146 |
| Kawasaki ZX-6R Ninja Fours (95 - 02) ♦ | 3541 |
| Kawasaki ZX-6R (03 - 06) ♦ | 4742 |
| Kawasaki ZX600 (GPZ600R, GPX600R, Ninja 600R & RX) & ZX750 (GPX750R, Ninja 750R) ♦ | 1780 |
| Kawasaki 650 Four (76 - 78) | 0373 |
| Kawasaki Vulcan 700/750 & 800 (85 - 04) ♦ | 2457 |
| Kawasaki 750 Air-cooled Fours (80 - 91) | 0574 |
| Kawasaki ZR550 & 750 Zephyr Fours (90 - 97) ♦ | 3382 |
| Kawasaki Z750 & Z1000 (03 - 08) ♦ | 4762 |
| Kawasaki ZX750 (Ninja ZX-7 & ZXR750) Fours (89 - 96) ♦ | 2054 |
| Kawasaki Ninja ZX-7R & ZX-9R (94 - 04) ♦ | 3721 |
| Kawasaki 900 & 1000 Fours (73 - 77) | 0222 |
| Kawasaki ZX900, 1000 & 1100 Liquid-cooled Fours (83 - 97) ♦ | 1681 |
| **KTM** EXC Enduro & SX Motocross (00 - 07) ♦ | 4629 |
| **MOTO GUZZI** 750, 850 & 1000 V-Twins (74 - 78) | 0339 |
| **MZ** ETZ Models (81 - 95) ◊ | 1680 |
| **NORTON** 500, 600, 650 & 750 Twins (57 - 70) | 0187 |
| Norton Commando (68 - 77) | 0125 |
| **PEUGEOT** Speedfight, Trekker & Vivacity Scooters (96 - 05) ◊ | 3920 |
| **PIAGGIO** (Vespa) Scooters (91 - 06) ◊ | 3492 |
| **SUZUKI** GT, ZR & TS50 (77 - 90) ◊ | 0799 |
| Suzuki TS50X (84 - 00) ◊ | 1599 |
| Suzuki 100, 125, 185 & 250 Air-cooled Trail bikes (79 - 89) | 0797 |
| Suzuki GP100 & 125 Singles (78 - 93) ◊ | 0576 |
| Suzuki GS, GN, GZ & DR125 Singles (82 - 05) ◊ | 0888 |
| Suzuki 250 & 350 Twins (68 - 78) | 0120 |
| Suzuki GT250X7, GT200X5 & SB200 Twins (78 - 83) ◊ | 0469 |
| Suzuki GS/GSX250, 400 & 450 Twins (79 - 85) | 0736 |
| Suzuki GS500 Twin (89 - 06) ♦ | 3238 |
| Suzuki GS550 (77 - 82) & GS750 Fours (76 - 79) | 0363 |
| Suzuki GS/GSX550 4-valve Fours (83 - 88) | 1133 |
| Suzuki SV650 & SV650S (99 - 05) ♦ | 3912 |
| Suzuki GSX-R600 & 750 (96 - 00) ♦ | 3553 |
| Suzuki GSX-R600 (01 - 03), GSX-R750 (00 - 03) & GSX-R1000 (01 - 02) ♦ | 3986 |
| Suzuki GSX-R600/750 (04 - 05) & GSX-R1000 (03 - 06) ♦ | 4382 |
| Suzuki GSF600, 650 & 1200 Bandit Fours (95 - 06) ♦ | 3367 |
| Suzuki Intruder, Marauder, Volusia & Boulevard (85 - 06) ♦ | 2618 |
| Suzuki GS850 Fours (78 - 88) | 0536 |
| Suzuki GS1000 Four (77 - 79) | 0484 |
| Suzuki GSX-R750, GSX-R1100 (85 - 92), GSX600F, GSX750F, GSX1100F (Katana) Fours ♦ | 2055 |
| Suzuki GSX600/750F & GSX750 (98 - 02) ♦ | 3987 |
| Suzuki GS/GSX1000, 1100 & 1150 4-valve Fours (79 - 88) | 0737 |
| Suzuki TL1000S/R & DL1000 V-Strom (97 - 04) ♦ | 4083 |
| Suzuki GSX1300R Hayabusa (99 - 04) ♦ | 4184 |
| Suzuki GSX1400 (02 - 07) ♦ | 4758 |
| **TRIUMPH** Tiger Cub & Terrier (52 - 68) | 0414 |
| Triumph 350 & 500 Unit Twins (58 - 73) | 0137 |
| Triumph Pre-Unit Twins (47 - 62) | 0251 |
| Triumph 650 & 750 2-valve Unit Twins (63 - 83) | 0122 |
| Triumph Trident & BSA Rocket 3 (69 - 75) | 0136 |
| Triumph Bonneville (01 - 07) ♦ | 4364 |
| Triumph Daytona, Speed Triple, Sprint & Tiger (97 - 05) ♦ | 3755 |
| Triumph Triples and Fours (carburettor engines) (91 - 04) ♦ | 2162 |
| **VESPA** P/PX125, 150 & 200 Scooters (78 - 06) | 0707 |
| Vespa Scooters (59 - 78) | 0126 |
| **YAMAHA** DT50 & 80 Trail Bikes (78 - 95) ◊ | 0800 |
| Yamaha T50 & 80 Townmate (83 - 95) ◊ | 1247 |
| Yamaha YB100 Singles (73 - 91) ◊ | 0474 |

| Title | Book No |
|---|---|
| **Yamaha** RS/RXS100 & 125 Singles (74 - 95) | 0331 |
| Yamaha RD & DT125LC (82 - 87) ◊ | 0887 |
| Yamaha TZR125 (87 - 93) & DT125R (88 - 02) ◊ | 1655 |
| Yamaha TY50, 80, 125 & 175 (74 - 84) ◊ | 0464 |
| Yamaha XT & SR125 (82 - 03) ◊ | 1021 |
| Yamaha Trail Bikes (81 - 00) | 2350 |
| Yamaha 2-stroke Motocross Bikes 1986 - 2006 | 2662 |
| Yamaha YZ & WR 4-stroke Motocross Bikes (98 - 07) | 2689 |
| Yamaha 250 & 350 Twins (70 - 79) | 0040 |
| Yamaha XS250, 360 & 400 sohc Twins (75 - 84) | 0378 |
| Yamaha RD250 & 350LC Twins (80 - 82) | 0803 |
| Yamaha RD350 YPVS Twins (83 - 95) | 1158 |
| Yamaha RD400 Twin (75 - 79) | 0333 |
| Yamaha XT, TT & SR500 Singles (75 - 83) | 0342 |
| Yamaha XZ550 Vision V-Twins (82 - 85) | 0821 |
| Yamaha FJ, FZ, XJ & YX600 Radian (84 - 92) | 2100 |
| Yamaha XJ600S (Diversion, Seca II) & XJ600N Fours (92 - 03) ♦ | 2145 |
| Yamaha YZF600R Thundercat & FZS600 Fazer (96 - 03) ♦ | 3702 |
| Yamaha FZ-6 Fazer (04 - 07) ♦ | 4751 |
| Yamaha YZF-R6 (99 - 02) ♦ | 3900 |
| Yamaha YZF-R6 (03 - 05) ♦ | 4601 |
| Yamaha 650 Twins (70 - 83) | 0341 |
| Yamaha XJ650 & 750 Fours (80 - 84) | 0738 |
| Yamaha XS750 & 850 Triples (76 - 85) | 0340 |
| Yamaha TDM850, TRX850 & XTZ750 (89 - 99) ◊ ♦ | 3540 |
| Yamaha YZF750R & YZF1000R Thunderace (93 - 00) ♦ | 3720 |
| Yamaha FZR600, 750 & 1000 Fours (87 - 96) ♦ | 2056 |
| Yamaha XV (Virago) V-Twins (81 - 03) ♦ | 0802 |
| Yamaha XVS650 & 1100 Drag Star/V-Star (97 - 05) ♦ | 4195 |
| Yamaha XJ900F Fours (83 - 94) ♦ | 3239 |
| Yamaha XJ900S Diversion (94 - 01) ♦ | 3739 |
| Yamaha YZF-R1 (98 - 03) ♦ | 3754 |
| Yamaha YZF-R1 (04 - 06) ♦ | 4605 |
| Yamaha FZS1000 Fazer (01 - 05) ♦ | 4287 |
| Yamaha FJ1100 & 1200 Fours (84 - 96) ♦ | 2057 |
| Yamaha XJR1200 & 1300 (95 - 06) ♦ | 3981 |
| Yamaha V-Max (85 - 03) ♦ | 4072 |

**ATVs**

| Title | Book No |
|---|---|
| Honda ATC70, 90, 110, 185 & 200 (71 - 85) | 0565 |
| Honda Rancher, Recon & TRX250EX ATVs | 2553 |
| Honda TRX300 Shaft Drive ATVs (88 - 00) | 2125 |
| Honda TRX300EX, TRX400EX & TRX450R/ER ATVs (93 - 06) | 2318 |
| Kawasaki Bayou 220/250/300 & Prairie 300 ATVs (86 - 03) | 2351 |
| Polaris ATVs (85 - 97) | 2302 |
| Polaris ATVs (98 - 06) | 2508 |
| Yamaha YFS200 Blaster ATV (88 - 02) | 2317 |
| Yamaha YFB250 Timberwolf ATVs (92 - 00) | 2217 |
| Yamaha YFM350 & YFM400 (ER and Big Bear) ATVs (87 - 03) | 2126 |
| Yamaha Banshee and Warrior ATVs (87 - 03) | 2314 |
| Yamaha Kodiak and Grizzly ATVs (93 - 05) | 2567 |
| ATV Basics | 10450 |

**TECHBOOK SERIES**

| Title | Book No |
|---|---|
| Twist and Go (automatic transmission) Scooters Service and Repair Manual | 4082 |
| Motorcycle Basics TechBook (2nd Edition) | 3515 |
| Motorcycle Electrical TechBook (3rd Edition) | 3471 |
| Motorcycle Fuel Systems TechBook | 3514 |
| Motorcycle Maintenance TechBook | 4071 |
| Motorcycle Modifying | 4272 |
| Motorcycle Workshop Practice TechBook (2nd Edition) | 3470 |

◊ = not available in the USA   ♦ = Superbike

The manuals on this page are available through good motorcycle dealers and accessory shops.
In case of difficulty, contact: **Haynes Publishing**
(UK) **+44 1963 442030**   (USA) **+1 805 498 6703**
(SV) **+46 18 124016**
(Australia/New Zealand) **+61 3 9763 8100**

MCL23.12/07

# Preserving Our Motoring Heritage

< The Model J Duesenberg Derham Tourster. Only eight of these magnificent cars were ever built – this is the only example to be found outside the United States of America

Almost every car you've ever loved, loathed or desired is gathered under one roof at the Haynes Motor Museum. Over 300 immaculately presented cars and motorbikes represent every aspect of our motoring heritage, from elegant reminders of bygone days, such as the superb Model J Duesenberg to curiosities like the bug-eyed BMW Isetta. There are also many old friends and flames. Perhaps you remember the 1959 Ford Popular that you did your courting in? The magnificent 'Red Collection' is a spectacle of classic sports cars including AC, Alfa Romeo, Austin Healey, Ferrari, Lamborghini, Maserati, MG, Riley, Porsche and Triumph.

## A Perfect Day Out

Each and every vehicle at the Haynes Motor Museum has played its part in the history and culture of Motoring. Today, they make a wonderful spectacle and a great day out for all the family. Bring the kids, bring Mum and Dad, but above all bring your camera to capture those golden memories for ever. You will also find an impressive array of motoring memorabilia, a comfortable 70 seat video cinema and one of the most extensive transport book shops in Britain. The Pit Stop Cafe serves everything from a cup of tea to wholesome, home-made meals or, if you prefer, you can enjoy the large picnic area nestled in the beautiful rural surroundings of Somerset.

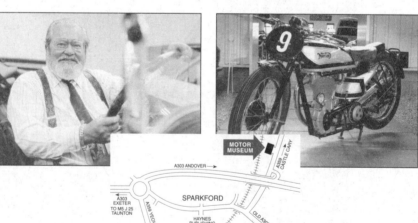

> John Haynes O.B.E., Founder and Chairman of the museum at the wheel of a Haynes Light 12.

< The 1936 490cc sohc-engined International Norton – well known for its racing success

The Museum is situated on the A359 Yeovil to Frome road at Sparkford, just off the A303 in Somerset. It is about 40 miles south of Bristol, and 25 minutes drive from the M5 intersection at Taunton.
Open 9.30am - 5.30pm (10.00am - 4.00pm Winter) 7 days a week, *except Christmas Day, Boxing Day and New Years Day*
Special rates available for schools, coach parties and outings  Charitable Trust No. 292048